HRAC

THE
USA &
THE
WORLD

DAVID M. KEITHLY

THE
WORLD
TODAY
SERIES®

2016–2017

12TH EDITION

Adapted, rewritten and revised annually
from a book entitled *The USA and the World*,
published in 2005 and succeeding years by

Rowman & Littlefield
A wholly owned subsidiary of The Rowman & Littlefield
Publishing Group, Inc.
4501 Forbes Blvd., Suite 200, Lanham, Maryland 20706
www.rowman.com

International Standard Book Number: 978-1-4758-2908-2

International Standard Serial Number: 1554-7809

Library of Congress Catalog Number 2005-213354

Cover design by nvision graphic design

Cartographer: William L. Nelson

Typography by Barton Matheson Willse & Worthington
Baltimore, MD 21244

David M. Keithly . . .

Dr. David M. Keithly combines professional writing with a wide range of business interests. He has published five books and over eighty articles in journals and magazines. He taught for over thirty years in colleges and universities, and served as editor of *The Defense Intelligence Journal* and *Civil Wars*. He was a Fulbright fellow in Europe twice, a fellow of the Institute on Global Conflict and Cooperation at the University of California, a scholar-in-residence at the Friedrich Naumann Foundation in Bonn, Germany, and a legislative fellow in the parliament of the German State of Thüringen. He is president of the Fulbright Association's Southeast Virginia Chapter. He has a Ph.D. from Claremont Graduate University and an M.A. from the University of Freiburg in Germany. He did additional graduate work at the French University of Rennes. Selected to "Outstanding Young Men of America," he was designated a Navy National Reserve Officer of the Year in 1993. In his younger years, he was on the Navy physical fitness team and is now an avid senior athlete. He was named the IMA (Individual Mobilization Augmentee) Officer of the Year at the Defense Intelligence Agency in 2000, and received the annual faculty research award at the Joint Military Intelligence College in 2001. A retired reserve officer, he held field-grade rank in two services.

The World Today Series has thousands of subscribers across the U.S. and Canada. A sample list of users who annually rely on this most up-to-date material includes:

Public library systems
Universities and colleges
High schools
Federal and state agencies
All branches of the armed forces & war colleges
National Geographic Society
National Democratic Institute
Agricultural Education Foundation
Exxon Corporation
Chevron Corporation
CNN

Photographs used to illustrate *The World Today Series* come from many sources, a great number from friends who travel worldwide. If you have taken any which you believe would enhance the visual impact and attractiveness of our books, do let us hear from you.

CONTENTS

ACKNOWLEDGMENTS

The friendly reception accorded this book during the first year it was in print nonetheless seems to justify some revisions. The original approach and purposes remain the same. The study is, above all, an introductory survey with emphasis upon America's global role, and with de-emphasis upon encyclopedic detail. I have made an effort to produce not only a study book, but a reading book also. I have paid considerable attention to main currents; to broad interpretations; and to economic, political, and social developments intertwined with global affairs. Some contemporary ambiance is recreated by brief quotations from original sources. The general framework is chronological, so that the reader may better follow salient events as these unfolded in U.S. history. I hope the book will shed light on some of the broader problems of international relations, such as the difficulties of diplomacy involving states with differing social systems and ideological foundations.

I would like to express my thanks to Sylvia Zareva and Michael Nix, whose critical commentary and eagle eyes resulted in a significantly better product. I am grateful to the Special Collections section of the University of Virginia Library and the George C. Marshall Research Library for providing many fine photographs. A deep sense of obligation is felt toward my friends and colleagues at the National Defense Intelligence College. Despite the encouragement and assistance from others, any errors of judgment or misinterpretation are solely the responsibility of the author.

Virginia Beach, Virginia
May, 2016

DEDICATION

To Wayne and Wes, submitting myself to all my teachers, masters, and spiritual pastors

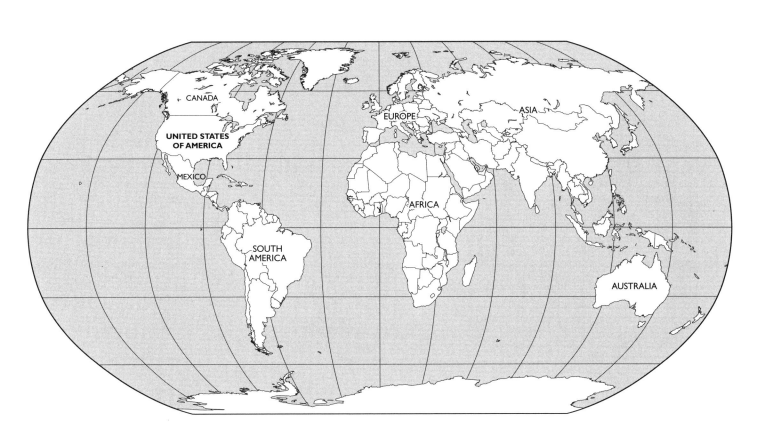

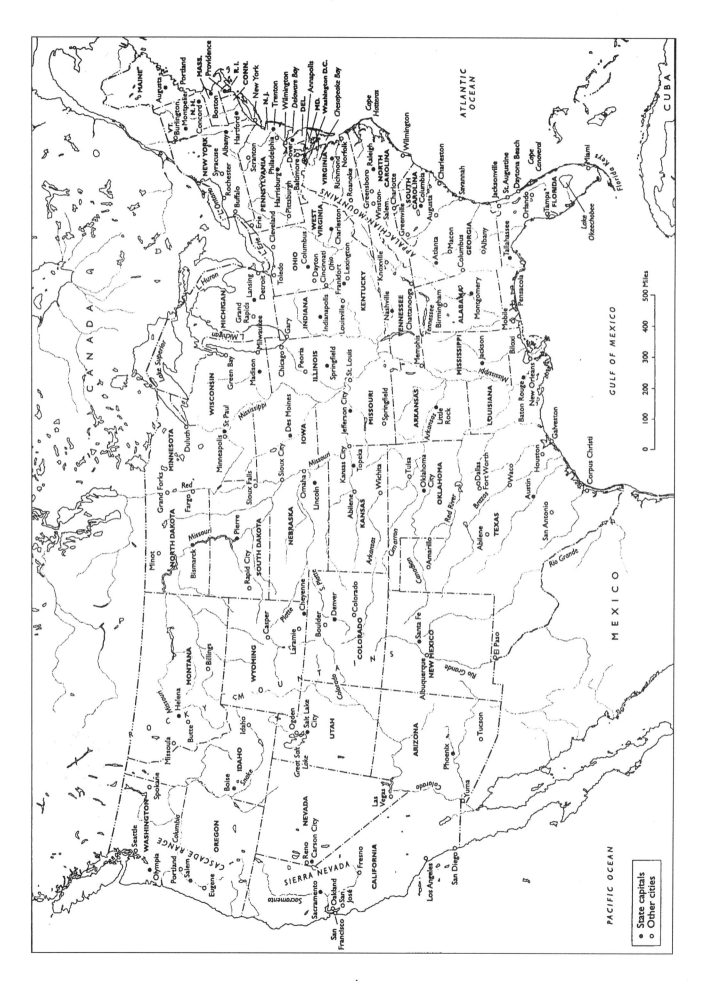

Introduction

The ascent of the United States to a position of world power focuses attention on the factors that contributed to the dramatic rise. When the future Founding Fathers met in 1776 to declare independence, they voiced the hope that they would "assume among the powers of the earth the separate and equal station to which the laws of Nature and of Nature's God entitle them." They could scarcely have imagined that these struggling colonies with a population of less than four million, huddled along a strip of ocean coast, weak and disunited, with survival their most pressing problem, would become perhaps the most powerful nation in history, whose influence on the world now rivals that of Rome two millennia ago.

How is one to clarify this extraordinary rise to power? The explanation is to be found less in the country's diplomacy or the record of the country's wars than in the vigor of U.S. institutions and in the features of the American character, hugely assisted by a cluster of favorable circumstances.

First among these is the geography that equipped the nation with resources on which power often rests. It provided the timber that made Americans a shipbuilding people and the sea lanes that made them a trading people while severing it by the span of oceans from the centers of world production. Natural resources provided America with the impetus to develop its own industries and furnished the sinews for technological advancement. Geography made available a great land mass ready to be settled and purchased, giving form to the ever-present sense of continental unity and providing a combination of safety and access. True, great land and great maritime empires have existed before. One finds few earlier land empires with their own sea lanes or earlier maritime empires with so vast an expanse as its land core, however. The availability of land and access by sea, and later, jobs and wealth, living standards, freedom, and the legendry of America, made the country the magnet that drew people from all over the world. Hence, people power was added to resources and technology as America's instruments of command over nature.

This command made possible high industrial productivity, which in turn gave weight to America's voice in peace and arms in war. It led to an inflow of foreign investments, and later turned America into an investing nation that exported capital to the world's underdeveloped regions. It was primarily investment that enabled America to become an engine of world finance, gleaning power from mature firms and establishing new enterprises supported by American capital. International finance shifted the economic center of the world westward across the Atlantic in the 20th century, making America the axis of power on which much of the world would turn.

HOPE SPRINGS ETERNAL

The necessity for American leadership in the 21st century is hardly in question. The United States is engaged on a global scale, and it is difficult to imagine how a major retrenchment of international commitments would be feasible. No other country is equipped to lead the management of worldwide prosperity and security, and both require careful and effective handling. Leadership will have to be pursued on a different basis from that of past decades, though. Economic wealth and military capacity have diffused to a considerable extent. Unilateral action is in sufficient for the most demanding problems, and international collaboration is frequently indispensable.

Dependence on the resources and services produced by other countries is a salient aspect of the globalization process. With interdependence comes the vulnerability of countries to the activities of others. Many products and raw materials critical to the developed countries come from the less-developed parts of the world. Hence, in an era of globalization, international economics is becoming a top priority on governments' policy agendas.

Economic policies of the United States are characterized by considerable pluralism, with U.S. firms and government agencies often pursuing different objectives internationally and domestically. In an effort to maximize profits and reduce operating costs, large corporations move plant and equipment to other countries where labor is less expensive and taxes are lower. Tariffs and other barriers to trade, which raise the price of imported goods, are still imposed on occasion to keep American products "competitive" with those of other countries. Organized labor tries to preserve jobs for workers in America. Such protectionism often boomerangs as other nations respond, sheltering their economies against competition from products imported from the United States.

Energy issues continue to play a prominent role on the global policy agenda, with countries roughly divided into energy producers and energy consumers. The issues associated with oil production are an example of how interdependency has come to dominate the politics of globalization. Higher oil prices affect balance of payments as consuming countries face larger import bills. Global environmental policies have emerged as major concerns recently and many countries have serious pollution problems that affect others.

The broadest measure of U.S. economic growth is Gross Domestic Product (GDP), which measures the total amount of goods and services produced by people, businesses, governments and property located in the country. Calculated quarterly by the Department of Commerce, GDP encompasses personal consumption, business investment in structures and equipment, residential investment, business inventory investment, net exports, and government purchases. Although personal consumption is by far the largest component of GDP (over 50% of the total), other sectors can be more volatile and have a greater influence on quarterly growth patterns. Gross National Product (GNP) differs slightly from GDP because it adds imports and overseas production to the equation. In recent years, GDP has been considered a more comprehensive measure of economic activity.

The United States had a GDP of $17.97 trillion (using purchasing power parity measurement) in 2015, with annual GDP growth of 2.5%. The economy officially slipped into recession in December 2007, and returned to growth in July 2009. Average GDP in 2002–2007 was 2.9%. Public debt reached 74% of GDP in 2014, with a budget deficit of 4% of GDP. Origins of GDP are: agriculture, 1.2%; industry, 22%; services, 76.8%. The breakdown of GDP generation by occupation is: farming, forestry, and fishing, 2.4%; manufacturing, extraction, transportation, and crafts, 24.1%; managerial, professional, and technical, 31%; sales and office, 28.9%; other services, 13.6%. These 2015 figures exclude the unemployed, which currently amount to approximately 5.1% of the labor force. Approximately 15% of the population lives below the official poverty line. The United States has the largest and most technologically advanced economy in the world, with a per capita GDP of around $50,000. In this market-oriented economy, private individuals and business firms make most of the decisions. Federal and state governments purchase goods and services mostly in the private sector. Business enterprises have considerably more flexibility than their counterparts in Western Europe and Japan about decisions concerning expansion of capital plant, workforce reduction, and new product development. Components of GDP are: private consumption, 71%; public consumption, 17%; non-government investment, 15.4%; exports, 13%; imports, –16%.

United States

Oil refining in Saudi Arabia

Courtesy: Royal Embassy of Saudi Arabia

America's principal trading partners in terms of exports are: Canada 19%, Mexico 14%, China 7.2%, Japan 5%, United Kingdom 4.3%, and Germany 4.3%. In terms of imports, these are: China 19%, Canada 14%, Mexico 12%, Japan 7.6%, and Germany 4.9%. Anchorage, Baltimore, Boston, Charleston, Chicago, Duluth, Hampton Roads, Honolulu, Houston, Jacksonville, Los Angeles, New Orleans, New York, Philadelphia, Port Canaveral, Portland (Oregon), Prudhoe Bay, San Francisco, Savannah, Seattle, Tampa, and Toledo are the main ports of the United States.

North America has around 6% of the world's people and is blessed by favorable geographic location. With a population of nearly 319 million, the United States, like Canada, has large sparsely inhabited land and small concentrations of densely populated areas. Geographically, the United States has a vast central plain, mountains in the west, hills and low mountains in the east, rugged mountains and broad river valleys in Alaska, and rugged, volcanic topography in Hawaii. The climate of the United States is mostly temperate, but tropical in Hawaii and Florida, arctic in Alaska, semiarid in the great plains west of the Mississippi River, and arid in the Great Basin of the southwest; low winter temperatures in the northwest are ameliorated occasionally in

January and February by warm chinook winds from the eastern slopes of the Rocky Mountains. The United States is the world's third-largest country by size (after Russia and Canada) and by population (after China and India). In contrast to Europe, the American birthrate has remained relatively high, sustaining levels of natural population growth greater than in other developed societies. The population is relatively young, with the median age being 36.7 years. Broken down by gender, the median age is 35.4 years for males and 38 years for females.

Like all developed countries, the United States has a high level of personal income, a high literacy rate, substantial (many say shameful) energy consumption, a low death rate, and a long life expectancy. The conditions that fostered industrial growth in North America are similar to those in developed areas elsewhere, yet they are distinct in terms of scale and profusion. Largely because the achievement of affluence has satisfied basic human needs, Americans have been able to address many different social questions. For example, the United States has considerable religious diversity and devotion: Protestant 52%, Roman Catholic 24%, Mormon 2%, Jewish 1%, Moslem 1%, other 10%, none 10% (2013 estimate). The size and variety of the resource base and the expanse of the country have provided room for

the restless, new lands for settlers, and opportunities for most. Despite a heavy reliance upon agriculture through the first half of the 19th century, the United States industrialized rapidly thereafter. The U.S. population was more urban than rural by 1920, and agricultural workers as a percentage of the workforce declined steadily in the 20th century. America's leading natural resources are: coal, copper, lead, molybdenum, phosphates, uranium, bauxite, gold, iron, mercury, nickel, potash, silver, tungsten, zinc, petroleum, natural gas, timber. Chief agricultural products are: wheat, corn, other grains, fruits, vegetables, cotton, beef, pork, poultry, dairy products, forest products, and fish.

GOVERNING THE ECONOMY

The American economy is based fundamentally on the system of competition, on the operation of private enterprise in the open market. If the competitive processes are crippled, if the functioning of the market is distorted, then the entire basis of the system evaporates. In the American constitutional design, capitalism exists not for the benefit of capitalists, but for the economic and political advantages accruing from the competitive process.

Many forces exist in an economy of private capitalism which can, if allowed to operate unchecked, produce undesirable results. The broad risk is that of any kind of restrictive business practices. People may well believe in a competitive system in principle, but they are naturally not too keen on much competition with their own trade or business. Business firms, understandably eager to escape the rigors of free competition, are often tempted to devise with each other various kinds of agreements or customs not to compete. Leading theorists of capitalism are aware of the tendency toward restrictive practices. "People of the same trade seldom meet together, even for merriment and diversion, but the conversation ends in a conspiracy against the public or in some contrivance to raise prices," one observer pointed out.

Price-fixing arrangements are obviously incompatible with the idea of a market economy. Other arrangements, smaller in scope or more in the public interest, are not detrimental, and in fact may even be desirable. The difficulty is that dense networks of restrictions can develop, so that the competitive system remains in appearance only, with the reality quietly strangled by understandings and accommodations among the supposed competitors. The ultimate danger is unregulated monopoly, where a single firm or a close-knit combination of firms achieves such dominance that it can exclude its competitors and can charge what it sees fit, thus rendering the market mechanism nugatory.

The problem first became publicly recognized in the 1870s and 1880s with the appearance of "trusts." One of the most famous was the vast Standard Oil combine, which by 1879 controlled about 95% of the oil-refining industry and much else besides. Another was the "sugar trust," which in the early 1890s controlled nearly 98% of its industry. Both, and many others, made enormous profits and engaged in some remarkably unscrupulous practices. The trusts and other forms of combination and restrictive agreements over a period of several decades in many instances interfered seriously with the effective operation of the competitive system.

It has long been agreed that the government, as the umpire of a free market economy, should take some measures to preserve competition. A good many have been taken, with varying degrees of effectiveness, using most of the familiar tools of government. Government regulation began with attempts at control by the classic tool of prohibitory statutes, to be enforced in the courts. The first and still most basic of these was the Sherman Act of 1890. It forbade, as to interstate commerce, agreements "in restraint of trade." Further, it forbade "monopolizing" whether by agreement or otherwise. It is enforced by lawsuits in the courts, either by government prosecuting attorneys or by private persons injured by violations of it. The Antitrust Division of the Department of Justice conducts a vigorous program of investigation and litigation.

The Act and litigation under it proved only partially adequate to the problem, however, and public policy had gone on to establish extensive programs of control by means of another tool, the administrative agency clothed with broad investigative and regulatory powers. The principal agency in this field, the Federal Trade Commission, was created in 1914. Today many statutes contain provisions forbidding restrictive practices in various specific lines of commerce, and most of the regulatory agencies and programs have responsibilities for acting against such practices.

MEMBERS AND PARTNERS

"The most common and durable source of factions," James Madison observed, "has been the various and unequal distribution of property." This circumstance has certainly been true in America. From that source, Madison continued, greatly varied interests "grow up of necessity in civilized societies." By that measure, America stands at the apex of civilization. Perhaps the most distinguishing characteristic of American economic relationship is the proliferation of specialized economic interests and their intense and varied political activity. Property—constitutionally protected, democratized, and specialized—generates factions. A free political order allows them access to politics to pursue their interests. According to the Federalist Papers, "the regulation of these various and interfering interests forms the principal task of modern legislation and involves the spirit of party and faction in the necessary and ordinary operations of government." These factions or, in neutral terms, these economic interest groups, are intensely affected by public policy. In turn, the number and variety of demands concerning the economy that are urged upon government, and of the groups that urge them, are both extraordinary.

Despite this variety of groups and demands, it is customary to emphasize three major groupings—business, labor, and agriculture. This categorization tends to understate the importance of many other important groups, such as the various professions, consumers, high-level

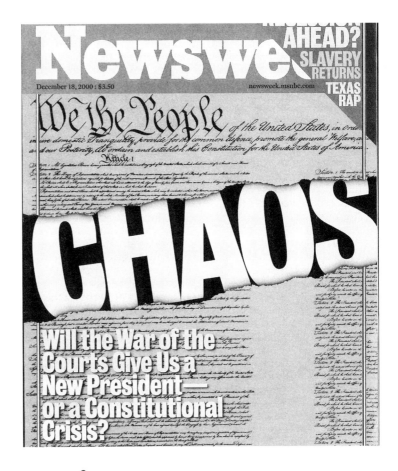

United States

government employees, as well as state and local entities. Above all, it understates the sharp differences within each of the three major categories themselves.

Business and businesspeople have always been concerned with the government. Hamiltonianism forged enduring links between the two. The importance of private business in American society has given them a special place. For seven or eight decades after the Civil War, the outlook and activities of business, especially of successful large-scale business, nearly dominated American life. Even now, in the continuous daily work of governing, business stands first in importance among economic interest groups.

Does business really form a political entity? Is there really a business community such as to produce cohesion and unity in business interest group activities? Many argue that, if the answer is negative, it is at least true that business is the most cohesive of the three major groups. There are intra-business conflicts of interests and many specific interests not widely shared, but there has long been a significant central core of shared interests and opinion.

Business is extensively organized in state and national trade associations on industry lines and into local associations on locality lines (the local Chambers of Commerce, but also groups like the Rotary or Kiwanis, where businesspeople usually predominate). These associations form the basis of two comprehensive nationwide organizations that are the principal spokesmen for business as a whole, the National Association of Manufacturers and the Chamber of Commerce of the United States. Contributing to business's relative political solidarity is the fact that American business, especially in industry and finance, has some elements of centralization and is influenced by a rather small number of large firms and by hierarchical corporation structures.

Modern labor organization dates from the success of the American Federation of Labor in the late 19th century. The cautious, conservative, but tough, craft unionism of the A.F. of L. won out over groups like the radical Knights of Labor, and thoroughly subdued socialist forces within the trade unions. Labor's efforts to organize workers and its political activity are shaped by deep divisions and rivalries within its ranks. These rivalries often result from conflicting interests among the specialized crafts and industries of the complex American economy. Craft union rivalries are an example of the fragmentation of faction envisaged by Madison. Each individual union tends to have a deep sense of particularity and of

the primacy of its narrow and immediate interests. Such entities will consent to join only a loose federal association—hence, the American Federation of Labor.

Organized labor's greatest handicap in the United States has always been the lack of any real belief among American working people that they belong to a "working class" with strong interests separate from the rest of society. Never more than a quarter of them have joined unions. They do not "vote labor" in a solid bloc on election day. They do not uniformly support union-sponsored candidates, causes, and activities. For example, in the 1968 presidential election, many American working people defected from Hubert Humphrey, the union-endorsed candidate, to George Wallace, who seemed to speak for some of their visceral needs, and to Richard Nixon, the conservative Republican candidate, who appeared attractive to many on broad grounds of public policy. Ronald Reagan enjoyed considerable support among working people in the 1980s, and among his leading backers were the so-called "Reagan Democrats." There are labor political devotees and diligent volunteer political workers, but there are also many labor Republicans as well as many political apathetics.

In light of these handicaps, however, labor has a remarkable record of political effectiveness. In alliance with various left-leaning organizations it has offered vigorous and frequently successful competition to politically organized business and other groups whose demands on government it opposes or competes with, or wants to modify. Much welfare legislation that unions support has been enacted in recent years. Labor is fully entitled to the status customarily given it as second among the great configurations of American political interest groups, even though its power and effect are often overstated.

Agriculture is in many respects the most obscure and puzzling of the big three. Farmers and farming as an industry are today distinctly a minority activity. Scientific agricultural productivity has increased astoundingly, enabling a constantly decreasing fraction of the labor force to supply the agricultural wants of the nation. Fewer than 5% of the country's population lives on farms, and only a small portion of the national income now comes from farming. Yet agriculture is still exceedingly powerful in politics. It annually commands tens of billions of dollars in unearned subsidies from the national government in the form of price support payments and other more or less dubious subventions. History and tradition largely explain this set of

circumstances. Agriculture has always been highly respected in American life, hallowed in the Jeffersonian tradition, and, despite their devotion to economic progress, Americans are a politically nostalgic people. Another reason is constitutional: farm states have two senators apiece just like the vast industrial states, and rural areas have traditionally been over-represented in the House and in state legislatures. Two others are political. Farm leaders tend to be adroit political actors. Some of the farm organizations, notably the Farm Bureau, tend to represent large-scale industrialized agriculture and effectively make common cause with the large business interest groups with which they thus share many values.

The convenient classification into the three main categories of business, labor, and agriculture can obscure the actual fragmentation of American economic interests into thousands of organized groups. That classification, which oversimplifies the actual economic diversity, also suggests a misleadingly simple picture of the American political process. If government really were dealing mainly with three large coherent interests, then the political process would likewise tend to be simple and coherent. Presumably, a clear-cut, unified political authority would deal directly with the three great economic interests, but that is precisely what does not happen.

Governmental multiplicity, the framework within which interest groups function and political relationships are conducted, results from the entire constitutional system—from the operation of the leading constitutional principles such as federalism, enumeration of powers, separation of powers, and bicameralism. Federalism, with its concomitant division of powers and responsibilities between nation and states, means there are differences in the economic affairs and situations that fall within the two purviews. Economic matters have historically provided major problems for the constitutional doctrine of enumerated powers. The question of how far the enumerated national powers reach has been the cause for substantial public controversy, politicking and lobbying, debate, and action in Congress and the executive, and, of course, for litigation in the courts and the exercise of judicial review.

By virtue of the separation of powers, national authority over the economy is neither vested in a single governmental authority, nor is it the exclusive province of any of the three branches. The economy is governed—as is the country in all important matters—by the conflict and cooperation of the three separated branches of government. Thus, when one examines any regulatory program, one needs to know not only what the statutes say and what Congress thinks, but also what the policies of the White House are, how the administrative system functions, and what the courts think.

SO NEAR, YET SO FAR

Governments conduct foreign affairs so as to secure the well-being or advantage of their respective countries. The most fundamental fact is that national interests clash—and in practically limitless ways. Burgeoning population, economic rivalry, desire to dominate a strategic territory or waterway, the need for economic resources, or sheer imperialistic greed, are only some familiar examples. Historically, it has been the irresistible impulse of countries to expand their trade, their religion, their belief, or simply to extend their might over land. The successful conduct of foreign affairs amid such complexity, intensity, and fatefulness of conflict places immense strains upon any political system.

Consideration of power and interest enter the foreign policy of all nations. Indeed, nations often pursue their interests to the limit of their power with little attempt to justify what they are doing. More often, nations believe or pretend to believe that their national interest coincides with some transcendent purpose, with the justifiable cause of a civilization or a political system. Of few nations has this been more true than the United States. The unusual persistence, emphasis upon, and specific content of the American version of transcendent purpose make the "American mission" a distinguishing feature of American conduct of foreign affairs.

The Framers' general sense of the originality and universal significance of the regime they were founding carried over into the realm of foreign affairs. The entire founding generation probably shared the view expressed by George Washington in his First Inaugural Address: "The preservation of the sacred fire of liberty and the destiny of the republican model of government are justly considered as deeply, perhaps as finally staked, on the experiment entrusted to the hands of the American people."

Republican government was not, he suggested, exclusively for the benefit of Americans; they were responsible for it to all mankind. This notion that American government was uniquely significant for the entire world deeply influenced the American posture in foreign affairs. From the very outset, American foreign policy was rationalized, discussed, formulated,

and administered, not alone with regard to what would profit and secure the nation, but also with an eye to the "American mission"—the responsibility somehow to uphold the cause of republicanism everywhere.

Arguably, foreign policy is becoming ever more important to the American people. U.S. foreign policy is a complex blend of traditional idealism and clear-eyed realism. Since the beginning of its history as a republic more than two centuries ago, the United States has been involved in world affairs, both to advance its ideals and democratic values and to promote its security and other interests.

Through its efforts, the United States has made substantial gains in advancing its interests. Prosperity, technological dynamism, and the vitality of alliances combine to make the United States the world's leading force for progress and human dignity. Of course, the world today is different from what it was six decades ago when the United States reluctantly assumed the mantle of world leadership. Economic and military power has become much more diffused. With U.S. help, the war-weakened countries of Europe reemerged as strong, prosperous, and vital democracies. In Asia, Japan has become an economic giant. South Korea, Taiwan, and Singapore have joined the ranks of developed countries. China and India have made huge economic progress. Elsewhere, Mexico and Brazil have made great economic and political strides.

Promoting economic growth in developing countries contributes directly to U.S. economic prosperity as well as theirs. Helping to raise per capita incomes of other countries enables them to increase their purchases of American products. Increases in U.S. exports lead to increases in U.S. jobs. It has been estimated that every billion dollars worth of goods the United States exports creates about 26,000 jobs at home. Promoting social and economic development abroad requires a sustained effort and the commitment of resources on a long-term basis. International problems are complex and cannot be easily resolved by quick fixes. Americans have to be prepared to address those problems on a steady, long-term basis.

According to the U.S. Advisory Commission on Public Diplomacy, the U.S. government's system for communicating with the world "has become outmoded, lacking both strategic direction and resources." The Commission has called for dramatic increases in international education and outreach programs. It is clear that the need for area studies in the United States has never been greater. Americans must improve their understanding of and sensitivity for the views of others in the

world, exactly because of U.S. global reach. At the dawn of the 21st century, Americans are deeply divided and to a considerable degree dissatisfied with the state of their country both at home and abroad. Many are frustrated by the complexity of modern conflict and, above all, by the thanklessness of having to deal with it. Disappointment with allies and disillusionment with the United Nations are widespread. Americans have come to enjoy their leadership role in the world, but they tend to suffer from sticker shock when the bills roll in. Moreover, a sizeable gap exists between the political elite and the general public concerning the need for and scope of foreign engagements. "The president's burden is to close that gap," remarked Lee Hamilton, former chairman of the foreign affairs committee in the House of Representatives and now chairman of the Woodrow Wilson International Center for Scholars. President George W. Bush appears to have widened it.

The decline in global political support for the United States during the past several years is difficult to overstate. Polls indicate that the number of people holding a favorable view of America has fallen from a majority to single digits in countries ranging from Indonesia to Spain. The damage is worst in the Arab Middle East, the very region where the United States wishes to propagate the values of liberal democracy and capitalism. True, some of this harm was unavoidable in the aftermath of the September 2001 terrorist attacks, when the United States had no choice but to act against its enemies. Some is due to a renewal of violence in the past several years between Israelis and Palestinians. The United States is hardly without fault for the deplorable situation, though, and there is plenty of blame to go around. Many at home and abroad complain that the United States increasingly exercises great power without much responsibility.

Some observers fear that the reaction to public frustration will take the form of greater isolationism and a determination to act for the short-term good of the United States alone. America's great temptation is unilateralism, international engagement strictly on American terms, or no international engagement at all. The hard reality is that neither course is good for the rest of the world, nor for the United States itself. In the 21st century, Americans face complex social and economic issues that must be addressed within North America and abroad.

The structure of this book is governed by the basic theme that the United States is interconnected with the world. Indeed, global connections imply that U.S. interests and policies are linked to those

United States

of other nations in a broader sense than simply through diplomatic relations. The chapters should be informative for readers seeking an overview of U.S. diplomatic history, the basic principles of the U.S. political system, the fundamentals of the U.S. economy, and the demographics of America. These subjects underscore the influence the world has upon the United States and vice versa.

The author designed the book to help one appreciate that America, though complicated, is ultimately comprehensible. The book encourages readers to expand their knowledge of the development of the United States. It offers an introduction to the nongovernmental structures—political parties, public opinion, and interest groups—that are crucial to the operation of the U.S. system and it explores the intricate organization and workings of the institutions of government in America. It examines the formal and informal institutions in action in certain areas of policy-making, including foreign policy, economic policy, and domestic policy.

Many people assume that policy is made in a definite way, with leaders choosing courses of action based on clear alternatives and decisions being implemented by various governmental bureaucracies. The reality of policy-making, however, is far more complex in America. Often a decision will result not from a careful, rational choice, but from political competition among diverse governmental organizations and groups within them.

Domestic politics have continuously been influenced by a number of key factors, such as the goals of the president, the political composition of the Congress, the relative power of various interest groups, and the continuing involvement of the bureaucracy. The topsy-turvy nature of American politics often produces messy processes in which numerous organized groups demand a piece of the action.

Isolation and avoidance of foreign commitments have been tenets of the American domestic and diplomatic heritage since the early days of the Republic. Yet, national expansionism in the Western Hemisphere was a consistent theme throughout much of U.S. history. In studying U.S. foreign policy, one should consider the changing status of the United States in the global community and the effects of this change on policy. Observers and policy makers frequently refer to historic changes and watershed events. Sometimes they also debate whether such tipping points have occurred, indicating that one international system has ended and a new one begun. What criteria are useful in determining meaningful transformations in world politics? Where have the most significant changes in diplomacy taken place? What factors have influenced new policy directions? What themes are evident throughout an historical epoch?

America was the stepchild of Europe's troubles in the 18th century. As a colonizing and imperial continent, Europe gave substantially of its strength and legacy to the nation that was destined ultimately to replace it in power and vitality. Perhaps the most important facet of America is the life force carried along from its cultural origins and crossed, blended, and transmuted with others in the development of a civilization. The shrewd French observer of American life in the 19th century, Alexis de Tocqueville, wrote that a democracy cannot function without a religion and a philosophy. Every civilization needs certain principles to hold it together, and democracies can encounter particular and disturbing problems with cohesion. American culture is a mosaic, diverse in ethnic tradition and geography, largely free of recognized social hierarchies, and preoccupied with personal rights and the individual. One of the paradoxes in a national story laden with them is that so varied a civilization has maintained cohesion so effectively and against the odds.

FIRST LINE OF DEFENSE

The conduct of foreign affairs is ultimately America's first line of defense. It represents the constant search for peace—through patient and arduous negotiation, the retention of strong allies, the pursuit of international cooperation, the effort to resolve local conflicts that otherwise might become broader, and the implementation of imaginative programs to stimulate economic growth and development. Spending to support U.S. interests abroad is an essential investment in America's strength and prosperity. Foreign affairs activities bring many benefits to the lives of American citizens whether at home or abroad in that these

- support a more stable and secure world by encouraging negotiated settlement of disputes and agreements to lessen the danger of war, helping to strengthen alliances, building cooperative defense relations with nations providing vital bases and facilities, and offering allies the means to meet their own legitimate security needs;
- stimulate the U.S. economy by creating markets abroad for U.S. goods and services, creating American jobs and paving the way for private investment overseas;
- advance democracy, human rights, and economic growth around the world;
- further humanitarian objectives by aiding the victims of natural disasters and promoting world health, education, and housing through technical and financial assistance programs and contributions to international institutions such as the World Health Organization;
- enable the United States to deal with nearly 200 other countries on many issues such as terrorism and narcotics control.

Chapter One
National Interest Priorities

NATIONAL SECURITY

This chapter examines particular regions and issues of major concern to the United States. It identifies important trends, U.S. regional interests, and key policy matters relating the two. The chief purpose is to explain the challenges and opportunities facing the United States. The world today is one that is constantly evolving with new security challenges. The proliferation of weapons of mass destruction threatens U.S. interests, those of U.S. allies, and even the American homeland. Hostile regimes, instability, and ethnic tensions jeopardize U.S. interests in key regions. Terrorism, international organized crime, and drug trafficking remain challenges to U.S. national interests and to peace and stability. As recent history reminds us, new dangers can arise suddenly and unpredictably.

How does one arrive at a generally acceptable definition of national interest? Who decides what the priorities of national action are going to be, and when and how they are to be implemented? The national interest might best be regarded as a synthesis of the subjective and the objective. Difficult, indeed agonizing, security decisions have always faced Americans, even prior to the establishment of the United States. The issues of the early 1770s spring to mind. Leaders have had to carry out policies they believe to be beneficial to the country, while leaving a good deal to chance and letting history be the ultimate judge. President Abraham Lincoln captured the essence of this approach during the Civil War: "I do the very best I know how, the very best I can, and I mean to keep doing so until the end. If the end brings me out all right, what is said against me won't amount to anything. If the end brings me out wrong, ten angels swearing I was right would make no difference."

In order to determine how national interests are pursued, one must consider various aspects of the exercise of national authority, including the qualities, personalities, and ideals of decision-makers; the types of government structures and processes; the customs and cultural styles of different societies; the geographic location and the capabilities of countries; and the sort of pressures and challenges countries face from neighboring countries, great powers, and international organizations. One must also distinguish between the national interest and the public interest. In the American context, the public interest entails the well-being of the people,

Abraham Lincoln, taken by Alexander Hesler in Springfield, Il, June 3, 1860

organizations and businesses within the United States itself. The national interest, on the other hand, involves the safety and prosperity of American citizens and enterprises worldwide and hence not within U.S. jurisdiction. Security and protection are salient foreign policy issues, especially when American rights are jeopardized by the policies of countries that are hostile to the United States.

The public interest and the national interest correspond with one another on many points. The public interest is at least in part shaped by the characteristics of the international situation the United States faces at a particular moment in time, especially when external antagonisms are

substantial or conflict occurs. In much the same way, the pursuit of national interests is affected by the amount of social stability and political unity that exist within the country at a given time. For our purposes here, one should consider the safeguarding of the public interest as the business of federal, state, and local government—with the President sharing authority with Congress, the judiciary, and the states—and the national interest as within the purview of the federal government, with the executive branch holding the prerogative for the nation's international well-being. International private interests derive from the overseas activities and operations of U.S. organizations and enterprises whose

United States

Queen Elizabeth II signs the Canadian Constitution, 1982. Prime Minister Trudeau is seated at left.
Public Archives Canada/PA/140705   Photo by Bob Cooper

world's sole superpower with a population and economy ten times larger but in a land area 10% smaller than Canada's. The relationship between the two countries is therefore lopsided and inherently difficult for the smaller of the two. Former Prime Minister Pierre Elliott Trudeau once remarked that sharing a border with the United States is like "sleeping with an elephant. No matter how friendly or even-tempered is the beast, if I may call it that, one is affected by every twitch and grunt!"

Canadians are at times offended that Americans are often unaware or unconcerned about their country's impact on Canada. Canadians have trouble getting their powerful neighbor to pay much attention to their concerns. Some Canadians assert that the United States takes advantage of its greater power and influence. The allegation is not unfounded. Nevertheless, Canada is that country in the world with which the United States is most successful at settling disagreements. Frictions between them are manageable. The chief reason for this collaboration is mutual respect; Americans and Canadians are well practiced at "splitting the difference."

In North America, proximity encourages cooperation. Canada is the upper half of the North American continent and shares a 5,335-mile border (including Alaska) with the United States. Shared values, economic progress and nearness to the United States require Canada to focus much of its foreign policy attention on its southern neighbor. Canada and the United States are allies in the North Atlantic Treaty Organization (NATO) and in the North American Aerospace Defense Command (NORAD). Polls indicate that Americans are more willing to defend Canada in case of attack than they are to shield any other foreign country. In 2004, 84% supported U.S. troops being sent to help Canada if attacked, and 75% of Canadians said the same about deploying their troops to defend the United States.

Washington has a reservoir of good will toward Canada, even though American leaders frequently need to be reminded of what Canadians want. Although the term is no longer frequently used, a sort of "special relationship" still exists between the two neighbors. In the absence of such a relationship, former British Prime Minister Winston S. Churchill would not have been able to speak of "that long frontier from the Atlantic to the Pacific Oceans, guarded only by neighbourly respect and honourable obligations."

True, differences and difficulties occur in the relationship. Trudeau observed that 70% of Canada's foreign policy involves its dealings with the United States. Far less of America's attention is focused on Canada. Some observers have called the relationship "asymmetrical," since Canada is more dependent upon the United States than vice versa. The Canadian government is acutely aware of the traditional ambivalence many Canadians display toward extensive cooperation with the United States. Former Foreign Minister John Manley once noted: "There are two rules in Canadian politics. The first is don't be too close to the United States. The second is don't be too far from the United States."

In November 2008 Americans elected a president whom many Canadians greeted as the near-ideal political leader: Barack Obama. They celebrated his inauguration on January 20, 2009, with an outpouring of enthusiasm not even shown to a Canadian prime minister for decades. Busloads of admirers made the nine-hour trip from Toronto and Ottawa to witness his swearing in, and some Canadian schools interrupted their classes to enable pupils to watch the ceremony. For the eight years of the Bush presidency, Canadians felt a kind of moral superiority to Americans, but that almost completely changed with his successor. By February 2009, when he made his first foreign trip as president—to Ottawa—Obama enjoyed an approval rating in Canada of 82%, higher than in the U.S. (64%) and much higher than that of former Prime Minister Stephen Harper (38%) and former opposition leader Mi-

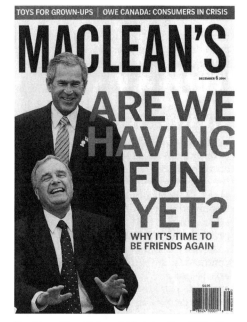

Ex-Canadian Prime Minister Paul Martin and U.S. President George W. Bush reconcile their differences.

chael Ignatieff (42%). He is more popular in Canada than most local politicians will ever be.

From the time he stepped off Air Force One in Ottawa, he commanded nonstop TV coverage during his six and a half hours in the country. Canadians clustered on overpasses and along the road to get a glimpse of him, and he greeted 2,500 of them who had gathered outside the Parliament in freezing weather. His welcome by Canada's first black governor general, Michaëlle Jean, was a historic moment for both nations.

Obama's charm never faltered, and he revealed a special attachment to Canada: that he has a brother-in-law who is Canadian and that two of his key staff people are from Canada. "And I love this country and think that we could not have a better friend and ally." It remains to be seen whether this affection will last and bear diplomatic fruit. An opinion survey at the time revealed that 41% of Canadian respondents desired greater ties with U.S., while 45% thought Canada should maintain the same level of relations. Only 9% wanted the country to distance itself from its southern neighbor.

Canadians have developed a certain boldness in social matters that sets them off somewhat from Americans. For example, more of them supported court-mandated same-sex marriage. In the 2006 *Maclean's* Canada Day Poll, 70% of women and 61% of men said they approved of homosexuality, and 56% and 39% indicated that they approved of gay marriage. Overall, 61% accepted or approved the idea of gay couples adopting children. The House of Commons voted gay marriage into law in July 2005.

Such social liberalism points to an increasingly self-confident country. These social issues may join gun control and health care in solidifying a Canadian sense of separateness from the U.S. Regarding health care, Canadians will continue to move progressively toward a dual public and private system.

Dramatic changes have taken place in Quebec in the last decades. The first was a Conservative prime minister from the western Canada, Stephen Harper, who speaks French confidently and often, and who showed a genuine interest in the needs and concerns of Quebec. At one point, he was opposed by a Liberal

leader, Michael Ignatieff, who grew up in Montreal and speaks decent French. He traveled to Quebec saying things like: "Quebec is my nation and Canada is my country" and "We offer you the freedom of belonging to Canada and to Quebec, in the order you prefer."

The second is that *Québécois* seem to accept Canada more than they used to. Only 2% of them now consider national unity a major issue. As the most socially liberal Canadians, *Québécois* like the social experimentalism they see in Canada, such as gay marriage, abortion and legalization of marijuana: 69% endorsed the statement that they are proud of what Canada is becoming "because it shows what a socially progressive and diverse country we live in." The figure in the rest of Canada is around 54%. They also now share anglophone Canadians' views on Canada's place in the world. *Québécois* were more critical of the 2003 war in Iraq; 90% opposed it, and some of the world's largest anti-war rallies were held in Montreal.

Thus, from being the most pro-American Canadians, *Québécois* have become perhaps the most skeptical of the foreign and social policies pursued by the United

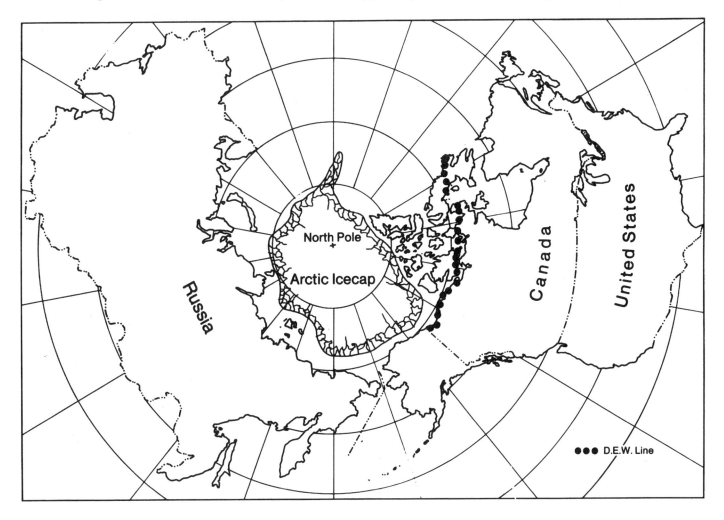

United States

States—60% indicate their attitude toward the U.S. had become more negative in recent years, compared with just under half of Canadians as a whole. A broad dislike for President George W. Bush and the war in Iraq had much to do with this, but the popularity of the current American president is bound to diminish this animosity.

A final reason for this unprecedented *Québécois* embrace of common Canadian values is the confidence *Québécois* now have that their language and culture are more firmly entrenched than ever before. In the October 2008 federal elections, the *Bloc Québécois* won the largest number of seats in the province by never mentioning separatism. The *Parti Québécois* also improved its standing in the December 2008 provincial elections because its new leader, Pauline Marois, put the independence issue into the deep freeze. Quebec separatism is in deep slumber.

Harper changed the tone in dealings with the United States, whom he called "our best friend" even before President Obama's election and triumphant six-hour visit to Ottawa in February 2009. He pleased many Canadians and Americans alike by moving his government back toward a muscular foreign policy designed to reflect "Canadian values." Among other things, this involved a serious combat commitment to neutralize the insurgency in Afghanistan. At the same time, his largest risks derived from this activist foreign policy. In a February 2009 poll, 65% of Canadians opposed continued engagement in Afghanistan even if Obama requested it. Only 20% were in favor. Well briefed on Canadian opinion, Obama did not ask.

Harper cuts a statesman-like figure at summits, and he gained visibility and respect in the United States and Europe. One of his chief challenges was to continue to heal the damaged relationship with the United States. Reconciliation was made easier by the popular American president. After proroguing Parliament for two months until the throne speech on March 3, 2010, the prime minister's popularity suffered. In a sense Harper was saved politically by the Winter Olympics in Vancouver. He was the chief fan for the victorious Canadian men's and women's hockey teams and basked in the glow of the thrilling sudden-death 3-2 victory of the Canadian men over their American rivals in the last event. Canada stunned the sporting world by winning more gold medals than any nation had ever won in the Winter Games. The world was treated to a rare glimpse of boisterous, flag-waving Canadian patriotism. Polls showed that Harper had widened his personal approval ratings over Michael Ignatieff during the Games. Shortly before the hockey

final, 37% of voters said they favored the Conservatives compared with 29% for the Liberals. Only in Canada could this happen.

Against a backdrop of a weakened economy, falling oil and resource prices, controversy over Muslim religious headwear, declining popularity of a Conservative prime minister who had been in office for a decade, and the appearance of a charismatic young Liberal leader with a magic name, Canadians went to the polls on October 19, 2015, to elect a new federal parliament. Excitement was demonstrated by a turnout of over 68%, the highest since 1993. The campaign lasted a record 78 days making it the longest race in modern Canadian history. These months were plenty of time for 43-year-old Justin Trudeau to disprove that he was "just not ready," as Tory politicians proclaimed, and to move his Liberal party from third place to the top of opinion polls. Although he is not the towering intellect his father was, he was boosted by an outstanding TV debate performance, both in English and French. He was the clear winner, becoming Canada's 23rd prime minister.

The Liberals staged a sweeping victory, their best showing since 1949. The party won 39.5% (up from 19%) of the votes enabling it to advance from only 36 seats to an absolute majority of 184 out of 338 seats, the largest seat gain in Canadian history. It captured every riding in Atlantic and Northern Canada. It more than doubled its seats in Quebec to 45, winning a majority of seats there and in Ontario. It even captured four seats in the Tory stronghold of Alberta, taking two in Calgary. Trudeau conducted an optimistic and positive campaign and succeeded in helping bring about a generational shift to young voters. Although the result was dramatic, one perplexed British Columbia voter quipped: "I see little real change with this election: another PM from Quebec, with central Canada politically controlling the country."

Many voters saw the election as a referendum on Tory leader Stephen Harper, whose 10-year rule many Canadians viewed as stern and divisive. Two-thirds of them rejected him at the polls and denied him a rare fourth consecutive victory, something that had not happened since 1908. He was not helped by the weak economy. He also came off as anti-Muslim by opposing so strongly a woman's insistence that she remain veiled during a ceremony in which she was to be sworn in as a new citizen. The Federal Court of Appeal dismissed his ban on the niqab in the ceremony.

The election was a calamity for the Conservatives, who lost 60 seats, falling to 99. They fell from 39.6% of the popular vote

down to 31.9%. By the time the votes had been counted, only one province, Saskatchewan, was still governed by a party associated with the federal Conservatives. Harper resigned as leader and was replaced by interim leader Rona Ambrose, an MP from Alberta. She is forbidden from running for permanent leadership in the race that followed.

In *Maclean's* 2003–04 year-end poll, 61% of Canadians approved of the idea of a North American "perimeter," which refers to measures the United States and Canada took in the wake of the attacks of September 11, 2001 to guard against acts of terror. Rather than establishing separate lines of demarcation around each, the two countries cooperate on immigration and asylum procedures. Such bilateral cooperation provides for a common boundary around both countries. In formulating new policies, Canadians tend to emphasize that Canada's number one challenge is keeping the American border open. Given that a truck crosses the Canada-U.S. border every 2.5 seconds and that every minute US$1 million in trade passes across it, trade must be kept unimpeded.

Before September 2001 half the 126 official crossings were unguarded at night, but they are all staffed around the clock now. The U.S. Coast Guard stops all boats that cross the maritime border in the Great Lakes and escorts all oil and gas tankers. When U.S. Coast Guard vessels in American waters installed machine guns and conducted periodic live-fire exercises in 2006, an outcry was heard all around the lakes. An 1817 treaty strictly limits armaments in the Great Lakes region. Eighty American and Canadian mayors demanded that the shooting stop.

The number of Americans who cross the border dropped by 22% between 1999 and 2005. This decline hits Ontario the hardest, where tourist trade is 95% dependent upon Americans. British Columbia and Alberta depend more on Asian visitors, and Quebec on Europeans. The stronger Canadian dollar and high Canadian gasoline prices account for part of this development. In the other direction, the opening in Canada of large American retail outlets like Wal-Mart and Best Buy, as well as growing internet purchasing, have contributed to the reduction of Canadian day trippers into the U.S.

The main factor for slower border crossings is the fear of terrorist attacks; 44 government agencies on both sides have some jurisdiction over border matters, which invariably means delays. Eight Canadian ministries alone have responsibility for some part of the border. In 2004 the United States began demanding fingerprints and photos at its borders for non-Canadian citizens between the ages of 14 and 80. In 2005 it adopted a new policy requiring all its citizens who are reentering the U.S. to show a passport. From January 2007 all airline passengers arriving in the U.S. need to show a valid passport, and that will be extended to land passengers in June 2009. However, relying on passports is a problem since only an estimated 34% of Americans over age 18 have one, compared to 41% of Canadians.

The two countries agreed in 2006 to work together to implement a kind of passport or document system for crossing the border. Canadian authorities fear that special ID cards would be unmanageable. President Bush asked his Canadian counterparts to "envision a card that can be swiped across a reading device that facilitates the movement of people." The future will determine the nature of such a document. Many advocate the creation of a passport card, or PASS card, that would fit in a wallet, cost around US$50 to acquire, and have some kind of toll-booth technology to make border crossings faster.

Bilateral cooperation has been stepped up, with a growing exchange of intelligence information and criminal records (allowing U.S. law enforcement agents to retrieve records from the Canadian Police Information Centre), consultation on visas (Canada requires no visa for 52 countries, while the U.S. exempts only 32), and collaboration at foreign embassies to stop people smuggling from overseas. At the time of the September 2001 attacks, only Canadians worked at the Royal Canadian Mounted Police (RCMP) headquarters in Ottawa. Now Americans from four agencies are based there. Cooperation is reported to be "pervasive." The two countries have acted in concert to plug a hole at St-Bernard-de-Lacolle along the Quebec border with New York. It is now more difficult to arrive in New York with a fraudulent passport and then to slip across the border to claim refugee status.

The Mexican and Canadian borders still differ in substantial ways. Whereas the Mexican border is normally divided by walls, the Canadian frontier is in most places no more than a ditch or a cleared area in a forest. By 2007 the U.S. stationed only 950 border patrol agents along the Canadian border, compared with 10,200 along the shorter boundary with Mexico. Yet, the U.S. is creating border security bases similar to those it has along its border with Mexico. Each equipped with two helicopters, an airplane, a high-speed boat, and a staff of about 70, the first will be located at Bellingham (Washington) and Plattsburgh (New York), followed by bases near Detroit, Grand Forks (North Dakota) and Great Falls (Montana). Both countries are targeting potential terror-

ists and smuggling. The latter includes marijuana from Canada and cocaine and weapons from the U.S., as well as large amounts of cash in both directions. To deal with the dangers of such crossborder criminality, the 4,400 officers of the Canada Border Services Agency will all carry firearms. The ultimate aim of such cooperation is an even more open and safe U.S.-Canada border.

The alliance with the United States, which involves many forms of military cooperation, is instrumental to Canadian defense. The Permanent Joint Board on Defense of the two countries coordinates the security relationship. The Defense Production Sharing Agreement exempts Canada from duties and "Buy American" policies. Cooperation in antisubmarine warfare (ASW) is extensive. Since Canada is economically dependent upon trade, freedom of navigation is vital, especially in times of crisis. Canada has several ASW destroyers and some long-distance coastal aircraft, but needs American air cover and nuclear attack submarines to deal with enemy submarine threats, especially in the Arctic Ocean.

Perhaps the closest form of military collaboration is in NORAD, created in 1957 and renewed by treaty every five years, with new and special emphasis on global surveillance from space. NORAD has a joint staff of American and Canadian officers and one of the world's most secure headquarters in Colorado. Both the United States and Canada were blessed with oceans that insulated them from European and Asian conflicts. They share a border that has remained undefended for more than a century and a half. Military concerns were never paramount in either country until well into the 20th century, when two world wars forced different roles upon them. With Europe in shambles and impoverished, and the Soviet Union emerging as a major security menace in Europe and Asia, the United States was compelled to assume a role as financial, military and political leader of the free world. This role required substantial increases in the military responsibility of the United States, and security concerns consequently became central to its body politic.

By contrast, Canada's military role remained relatively minor, and thus security issues have been much less important in Canadian politics. Canadian commitment to maintaining sovereignty and independence in global affairs, though, has fostered political sensitivities that are difficult for Americans to understand. Despite all their similarities, Canadians are *not* Americans and do not think like Americans in all matters of foreign and security policy. The two peoples' activi-

ties in world affairs are compatible, yet distinct.

It is doubtful that an enemy would ever consider Canada and the United States as separate entities, though, one neutral and one belligerent, in time of war. The two countries are linked so closely economically that no enemy could attack the United States without also adversely affecting Canada's vital interests. Also, Canada's location is so strategically important to the United States that no country could assault Canada without triggering a U.S. response. Consequently, Canadian governments have preferred to cooperate in North American defense arrangements largely to influence or shape defense policies. Such a calculation has been facetiously and gruesomely called, "no incineration without representation." One of Canada's most distinguished diplomats, J.H. Taylor, noted that although many Canadians find it hard to accept, they are "one of the most secure countries in the world . . . defended by the United States in the act of defending itself, whether we choose to defend ourselves or not."

The outgoing Liberal government decided in 2005 to deploy 2,500 troops to Afghanistan to strengthen the anti-insurgency effort in the province of Kandahar, south of Kabul. Canadian forces fight shoulder-to-shoulder there with NATO allies. In March 2006 Canada took command of the 6,000-strong multinational brigade that operates under robust NATO rules of engagement. This force includes 100 elusive commandos from the elite Joint Task Force 2 unit. Canadian officials customarily refer to the engagement as a "three-block war": humanitarian assistance, peace support operations, and high-intensity conflict, all within a relatively small area. Canada is paying for this deployment in lives because its soldiers are regularly sent into harm's way.

As early as 2007, polls indicated that half of all Canadians wanted the mission abandoned and the troops brought home. Many are appalled by the rising casualties and the sheer brutality of the fighting. One Army officer was badly wounded in the head by a young man wielding an ax while attending a meeting of village elders. One of the first political crises Prime Minister Harper faced in office was the reversion to the tradition of banning news media coverage of returning coffins from war and the flying of flags at half-staff to denote battlefield deaths. Harper argued that the families should be able to grieve out of the limelight, but critics accused him of not honoring the dead. He was forced to back down. The ensuing emotional debate merely underscored Canadians' uneasiness about the continuing combat in Afghanistan and the attendant

United States

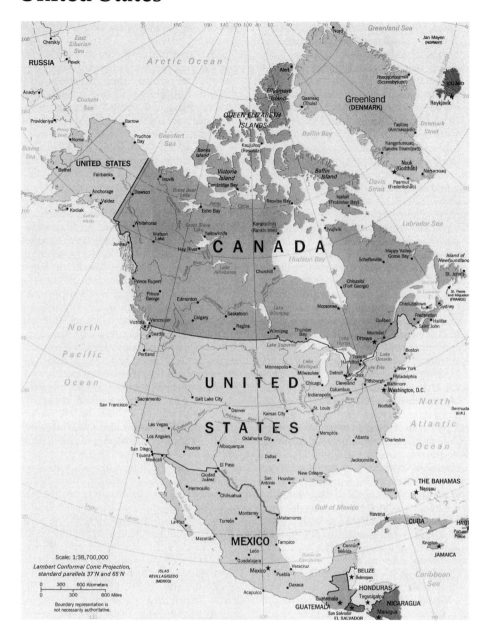

Scale: 1:38,700,000
Lambert Conformal Conic Projection,
standard parallels 37 'N and 65 'N

0   300   600 Kilometers
0   300   600 Miles

Boundary representation is
not necessarily authoritative.

Canada. While 51% of Americans believed that self-interest should guide a country's decision making, 61% of Canadians held that view.

An earlier POLLARA poll published in February 2004 found that two-thirds (67%) of Canadians had a generally positive attitude toward the U.S., but 58% said they disapproved of President Bush. Even though they accept the need for greater security along the border, increased police cooperation with U.S. authorities, common policies on immigration and refugees, and even restrictions on some of their personal freedoms in order to meet the terrorist threat, Canadians are as determined as ever to preserve their sovereignty and their independence of action.

Geography so closely links the two countries' economies that cooperation, not conflict, is in their mutual interest. Moreover, Canada is too open a country, with too vulnerable an economy, to pursue policies of economic nationalism. The United States and Canada are each other's most important trading partners and sources of foreign investment, and they have developed the world's largest bilateral trade relationship. Every day US$1.3 billion of goods and services cross the border. The United States conducts more trade with the single province of Ontario than with either Japan or the entire European Union (EU); Canada trades more with California than with Japan. In fact, more international trade passes over the Ambassador Bridge that connects Detroit and Windsor than either the United States or Canada conducts with any other country in the world. Canada sells more to a single American company, Home Depot, than it does to all of France.

The volume of U.S.–Canadian merchandise trade quintupled from $39 billion in 1974 to $200 billion in 1994, measured in constant dollars, rising by 19% in 1993 alone. By 1999 two-way trade had doubled since the Free Trade Agreement (FTA) went into effect in 1989. In the process, the FTA has reoriented Canada's economic axis from east-west to north-south. Every province, except two in the Eastern Maritimes, has more trade with the United States than with other Canadian provinces.

Trade with Canada is of increasing importance for the United States, with over a fifth of its exports and imports flowing to and from Canada. U.S. trade with Canada is, in dollar value, almost twice its trade with Japan, which was the second largest trading partner for *both* the United States and Canada until 1998, when their North American Free Trade Agreement (NAFTA) associate, Mexico, edged ahead of Japan as the number two trading partner of the United States. Canada's third

official nervousness about wavering public support for the war. Some Canadians feared the emergence of an Iraq-like quagmire, the wrong cause in the wrong place.

Canadians withheld support when the U.S.-led coalition attacked Iraq in March 2003, although they offered substantial humanitarian and training assistance after the fighting stopped. Three-fourths of Canadians and 90% of Québécois opposed the war, facts that still affect the two countries' relations with each other. Popular sentiment persists in some circles that the U.S. acts like a bully in the world. Almost a majority (48%) in the 2004–5 *Maclean's* annual poll feared "we are losing our independence to the United States," but those who believed Canadians are "mainly" or "essentially" different from Americans decreased to 52%. According

to the poll, 52% of Canadians said their attitude toward the U.S. has worsened since September 2001. Of these, half blame the war in Iraq or dislike of President Bush. Two-thirds think America's global reputation has worsened over the past decade. In 2005, 57% thought Americans have too much power (down from 73% in 1975).

An SES survey in October 2005 revealed that the two peoples think a lot more alike about important things and are, in fact, closer than one might think in the post-Iraq era. Most want to work closely with each other on such matters as counter-terrorism and still define their two nations more by their similarities than by their differences. Asked which country is most like their own in terms of human rights, Canadians picked the U.S. more than any other (43%), and 51% of Americans chose

14

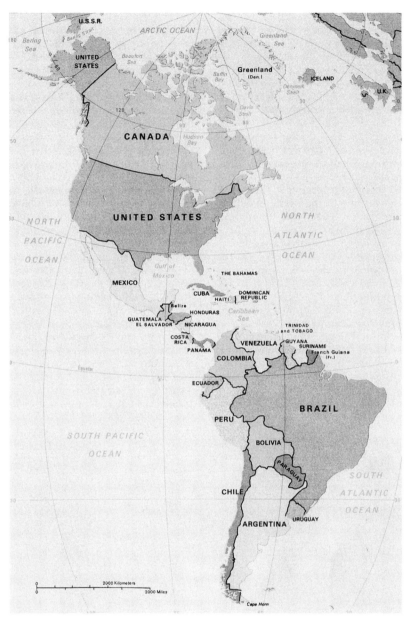

North and South America

the region, circumstances vary widely. Economic interests range from trade integration, involving primarily Brazil, Argentina, Chile, and Mexico; to reform of the structure of the economy, involving primarily Brazil, Mexico, and Argentina; to outright disaster management in Haiti and Cuba. The extension of democratic core values does not feature uniformly in the region. The English-speaking Caribbean, for example, has a strong tradition of democratic values compatible with those of the West, and most of the region accepts these values, at least in principle. The Cuban government rejects liberal democracy and suppresses civil liberties, and Haiti is so impoverished and politically unstable that basic rights are not generally respected.

Security concerns also vary significantly in Latin America. Perhaps the chief difference is an inability even to agree on what constitutes security. The various subregions have different interests and preoccupations, which diverge considerably and include border security, domestic stability, counterinsurgency, economic stability, trade policy and ecosystem protection. Military reform is an important issue for nearly all Latin American countries, largely because of the unfortunate and prevalent legacy of military involvement in politics. Most Latin American countries were, at one time or another, military dictatorships. The region has a tradition of regarding the armed forces as a sort of savior of the nation, assuming responsibility for domestic stability and ensuring a semblance of political cohesion in the wake of failures of the political class.

The opening of markets and the expansion of trade have had a significant effect on policy throughout the region and have promoted U.S. interests there. Examples of policies resulting from economic issues include: the North American Free Trade Agreement (NAFTA) with Canada and Mexico; improved U.S. relations with Chile, with negotiations for NAFTA accession; the negative effect of expanding drug trade and money laundering; and the glaring inequalities in wealth and income that underscore basic human rights issues internationally. Most serious observers view trade and investment in a global context. Within the Western Hemisphere, trade figures have skyrocketed in the last 15 years, and the trend toward greater regional economic integration continues. The single largest U.S. trading partner remains Canada, and nearly half of Latin America's trade flows north, while some 40% of U.S. non-NAFTA exports stay in the hemisphere. A hemispheric free-trade zone is a subject of considerable discussion, though the achievement of such a goal is a long way off. Moreover, eco-

largest partner is China, with whom Canada runs a large trade deficit that is more than compensated by Canada's trade surplus with the rest of the world. By 2004, 400 Canadian companies had established a permanent presence in China. Motor vehicles and parts account for 28% of U.S. merchandise exports to Canada and 31% of imports. The second largest category of U.S. exports is electronics and telecommunications equipment. Canada is the United States' largest supplier of imported energy—oil, uranium, natural gas and electricity. It supplies 17% of U.S. imports of crude and refined oil products and 94% of its natural gas imports, all through pipelines. By 1997 Americans were responsible for 65% of all foreign direct investments flowing into Canada. In 2000, Americans

accounted for 75% of Canada's foreign ownership. Both countries also suffer from similar problems: high labor costs, a decline of traditional industries, outsourcing of manufacturing jobs to lower-wage countries, and unemployment that, while higher in Canada, is regionally serious in parts of both countries. [See the separate volume on Canada in the World Today Series.]

REGIONAL COOPERATION IN THE WESTERN HEMISPHERE

U.S. interests in Latin America might be placed into four categories: economics, security concerns, military reform, and focus on democratic values. Although these categories apply broadly to all states in

United States

nomic competition from Europe and Asia is growing in Central and South America as developed trading nations seek new markets. Latin America was recently the second-fastest growing economic region in the world, and U.S. exports to Latin America and Canada now exceed those to Europe and Japan combined.

The United States has a keen interest in strengthening democracy in countries to its south. Latin America is in large part undergoing a prolonged process of democratization although commitment to liberal core values is far from complete. The goal of democratic governance advanced by the United States and others has been achieved to a considerable extent in certain areas although not without tribulations and setbacks. The current political situation with popularly elected governments in most Latin American countries differs markedly from that of only a generation ago, when the majority were authoritarian, and a few were still brutal dictatorships. Civil-military relations are patchy and often difficult, while civil unrest is still widespread. With a long tradition of charismatic, authoritarian leaders, governance problems in Latin America linger on.

Lower defense budgets and reductions in armed forces have been part and parcel of the emergence of popular democracy in Latin America. Yet, such an otherwise positive development has had a downside. In many countries the military and the police are the principal, sometimes sole, element of official presence in rural areas. Drastic cutbacks have encouraged the expansion of criminal activity, ranging from street crime to racketeering connected to narcotics trafficking. Changes in economic policies toward market-based systems have also had difficult aftereffects, including a marked decline in the living standard of certain groups, and higher unemployment rates in some areas.

A key aspect of U.S. foreign policy toward Latin America has been the prominence of human rights. U.S. participation in counterinsurgency operations, past aid to, recognition of, and dealings with military dictators, along with allegations of involvement in human rights violations have prompted many nongovernmental organizations (NGOs) to monitor such behavior. Points of emphasis are the association generally of the U.S. military with its counterparts in the region and demands for accountability from either

the White House or Congress. Washington now stresses local political responsibility as part of its effort to expand liberal democratic values in transition states. Cuba remains the primary subject of human rights attention for many in the public and private sphere. Cuba still lacks a representative government and mistreats its people. Washington continues to try to isolate Cuba economically and politically.

True, there is considerable room for improvement regarding human rights, but most Latin American governments display a commitment to advancing the cause of freedom. Many instances of violence and maltreatment of people have not in fact been perpetrated by government authorities, but rather by such nonstate actors as terrorists, insurgents, paramilitary organizations, and organized crime groups. The reduction of the flow of illegal drugs throughout the hemisphere and across its own borders is a salient strategic consideration for the United States. Drug-trafficking and money-laundering procedures are performed with such sophistication and entail such large amounts of money that they influence, and even jeopardize, nearly every law enforcement institution, judicial system, and banking and financial

NATO allies

institution in Latin America. Although amounts of contact, sleaze, chicanery, and corruption vary, states of ongoing concern with substantial domestic problems include Mexico, Colombia, Peru, Venezuela, and Bolivia. Bilateral and multilateral collaboration is a crucial component of efforts to defeat such transnational threats.

Besides the injurious societal effects, the underground economy catalyzed by money-spinning narcotics trafficking gives impetus to dark forces that undercut civil governance. Illegal drugs put in motion a vicious spiral of malice, vice, political violence, and social instability in the Andean region, the Caribbean, and Central America. Coercion and mob law are the inevitable upshot of the narcotics trade, which endangers the stability and even the sovereignty of several states, including Colombia, Mexico, and several Caribbean island states. The operations of drug gangs even threaten the civil order of transit states such as Brazil, Argentina, and Chile, as well as consumer areas like the United States, Canada, and most of Europe.

In recent decades, regional trends and global developments have produced a redefinition and reordering of U.S. economic and political interests, including a shift away from a relatively narrow focus on military security. Regional stability in Latin America and the Caribbean has sweeping implications, cooperation a new texture. Stability is no longer primarily a matter of strategic denial, that is, excluding the great powers from the Western Hemisphere under the auspices of the Monroe Doctrine and later thwarting Soviet adventurism during the cold war.

Now, stability entails more international involvement in Latin America. Cooperation involves the pursuit of mutual interests and goals, reciprocity, and transparency. These new, broader definitions reflect common efforts to promote liberal democracy, expand access to markets, resist crime syndicates, and control migration. Western hemispheric policies have substantial effects upon the individual and collective welfare of U.S. citizens. Whether it be trade, immigration, counter-narcotics measures, or actions toward Cuba and Haiti, hemispheric issues directly affect North Americans. The ability to sustain progress in the Western Hemisphere depends in part on meeting the challenges posed by weak democratic institutions, rising crime rates, and major income disparities. In many Latin American countries, people will not fully realize the benefits of political liberalization and economic growth without regulatory, judicial, law enforcement and educational reforms.

Yet, democracy has taken hold in the Western Hemisphere, with the potential for transforming politics, societies, and

EU Members

economies for the better. There are considerable grounds for hope that Latin American countries may finally be able to escape past cycles of civilian governments lacking authority and military governments lacking legitimacy. As late as 1976, less than one-third of Latin Americans lived under democratic governments. Now, most live in countries whose governments foster democratic practices.

The democratic process reflects complex forces, including social change and economic development, the growth of stable institutions, and political and cultural shifts. Encouragement from outside the region has been important, including U.S. support and the influence of Spain and Portugal, which themselves have made successful transitions to democratic rule.

The United States has contributed significantly to the democratic process in the region through a variety of policies and programs including

- regional cooperation among democratic parties
- democratic leadership training
- economic and security assistance
- support for private-sector organizations
- liaison with trade unions
- Peace Corps volunteers
- anti-narcotics assistance to such countries as Colombia, Bolivia, and Peru and
- educational development and exchange.

These programs alone cannot assure the region success in economic and political development. Nor can they assure the region's ultimate security. The real work must be done by the Latin American and Caribbean peoples themselves. U.S. efforts constitute essential support for regional and national efforts, though.

Stability is necessary for the functioning of liberal democracy, and thus America's long-range vision must be of a hemisphere with democratic states that favor free markets and have an affinity with other like-minded states. The United States recog-

nizes that as national economies become more integrated with the global economy, no state can thrive in isolation from developments abroad. Working with other countries and international economic institutions, the United States has improved the capacity to prevent and mitigate international financial crises. These efforts include the creation of a more effective early warning and prevention system with an emphasis on improved disclosure of financial and economic data. Countries in the Western Hemisphere are confronting crime and corruption by promoting greater transparency in government procurement regimes. Recent World Trade Organization (WTO) initiatives to pursue an agreement on transparency in all WTO member procurement regimes should make an additional important contribution.

Encouraged by the United States, exports have become a major factor in the economies of Latin America. An increase in manufactured and agricultural exports by developing countries requires access to international markets for their most competitive products, to enable them to earn foreign exchange. Export policies will succeed only to the extent that economic policies in the industrial countries complement them.

Trade issues are politically and socially sensitive in the United States, especially when imports from low-wage countries compete head-on with American production. The U.S. government, under these circumstances, has the dual responsibility of protecting jobs and living standards of its citizens and of helping create economic conditions abroad that discourage unauthorized immigration to the United States, with its own negative effects on jobs and living standards. The balance between these two concerns is not always carefully drawn.

Although the markets of migrant-seeking countries are now more open than at any time in the post-war period,

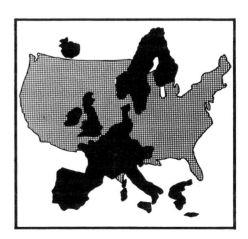

United States

U.S. exports to them have not increased substantially, often because their debt service burdens limit their ability to import. Notwithstanding certain American restrictions on trade, the North American market is significantly more open to developing-country exports than those of developed countries generally. Increasing free trade between Mexico and the United States is a platform on which to build for the future. Former Mexican president Carlos Salinas de Gortari once remarked that "We must export goods or we will continue indefinitely to export people." The most important remedy to undocumented immigration is the creation of more and better jobs in Latin American countries. The most effective way to accomplish this goal is through expanded trade between migrant-sending countries and the United States and other industrialized countries.

Changing demographics invariably affect how Washington views Latin America. The United States is already the fifth-largest Spanish-speaking country in the world, and the Hispanic population is America's largest and fastest growing minority. Voters of Hispanic and Caribbean origin have a crucial role in such key electoral states as Texas, Florida, and California, and politicians of Hispanic origin aspire to high office in America. In the parts of America with large Hispanic populations, such as Southern California and Eastern Texas, Latinos account for half of all children under 14. As the bulge of Latinos enters child-bearing age in a decade or two, the Hispanic share of America's population will soar. According to some estimates, a quarter of the U.S. population in 2050 will be Latino. Over time, America's cultural ties will intensify with the main sources of immigration, principally Latin America, but also East and South Asia.

Latin America entered the 21st century in the midst of impressive economic expansion that was giving rise at long last to a middle class. But it also was experiencing political growing pains as the young democracies sought to cope with perennial woes such as widespread poverty, drug trafficking and institutionalized corruption. Development of strong, viable democratic institutions for the future remains the challenge for the present.

The history of the relationship between the United States and Latin America can be divided into five relatively distinct periods: 1820-1880, the era of the Monroe Doctrine and U.S. paternalism; 1880-1934, the era of open U.S. imperialism, intervention, and the policies of gunboat diplomacy and the "big stick"; 1934-45, the "Good Neighbor Policy"; 1945-1990, the cold war, the Alliance for Progress, the Cuban and Nicaraguan revolutions and

U.S. support for anti-communist dictators; and 1990-present, the post-cold-war era, the emergence of democracy in Latin America and a growing U.S.-Latin American trade partnership. [See the separate volume on Latin America in the World Today Series.]

EUROPE'S POLITICAL AND ECONOMIC STABILITY

The United States maintains an abiding interest in the security of its European friends and partners, 26 of whom (not counting Canada) are now North Atlantic Treaty Organization (NATO) allies. Major wars in the last two centuries have underscored Europe's significance and consequence to the well-being of the United States, and bonds with Europe have become in some ways even firmer in an era of economic globalization. The promotion of democratic values globally is unthinkable without Europe, which is no longer divided by the iron curtain and whose newly democratizing countries have made huge political strides since 1989. Preservation of the political and social harmony that Europe has achieved is a crucial, even vital, U.S. interest.

Although Russia no longer poses a military threat to Europe, the United States and its allies must carefully monitor developments in Russia and in regions of the former Soviet Union. While the European Union (EU) becomes more prosperous and cohesive, many areas of Russia and the Commonwealth of Independent States (CIS), all former republics of the former Soviet Union except the three Baltic states, are impoverished and politically troubled. The Caucasus region in particular is in turmoil and could slide into chaos. Western countries share an interest in sustaining the independence and sovereignty of all former republics of the Soviet Union, although such political stability by itself is not enough. They must support the development of democratic institutions and processes, which is the only route to eventual prosperity.

Further deterioration of the situation in Russia would pose major challenges to the EU and the United States. Both have crucial interests in preventing the spread of crime, corruption, and terrorism. Weapons of mass destruction (WMD) proliferation poses a direct security challenge to Europe. Social upheaval in Russia or other parts of the CIS could result in an even greater influx of refugees to EU countries. The United States must continue to support across-the-board reform in the CIS countries, however uneven, however difficult. As the EU becomes politically more sure-footed, the United States should encourage the Europeans to assume more

responsibility for assisting reform efforts in the former Soviet Union.

Although the United States has at times been ambivalent toward European integration, it provided the initial and essential catalyst for the process in the 1940s, and now it must support a strong and united Europe. Politically, the EU is a beacon for other regions of the world, and the United States benefits economically from the efficiencies and affluence of larger markets. It should welcome developments that will eventually allow the EU to speak with one voice on economic and defense issues.

European efforts to forge what is generally known as the European Security and Defense Policy (ESDP) have received mixed U.S. reactions, at least until recently, and Washington has looked askance at attempts to create a European defense organization separate from NATO. According to some Americans, such an organization would represent an expensive and largely unnecessary duplication of certain NATO capabilities. Moreover, Washington has harbored concerns about exclusion from a decision process that could affect its security interests, suggesting that in an extreme case the United States might have to assist with Europe's defense under NATO obligations following actions taken outside the Alliance framework. The United States has thus insisted on maintaining NATO's primacy, while permitting European allies to conduct military operations with the concurrence of the Alliance. The principle of "separable, but not separate" forces and command structures allows U.S. European allies to engage militarily using NATO planning procedures and infrastructure. All-European forces can be supported although not led by the United States.

The decision to create combined joint task forces (CJTF) in 1994 provided the United States and NATO with more flexible military options for dealing with contingencies in and beyond Europe. The term "combined joint task force" is composed of a string of specific, but relatively straightforward, concepts of military organization. A task force is a military grouping that has been organized to achieve a specific mission or task. The addition of the term "joint" indicates that two or more services (army, navy, air force or marines) are part of the task force. The term "combined" means that the forces of two or more nations are involved. At present, the CJTF is the primary way for the United States to develop more effective sharing of global military burdens with its European allies. The CJFT concept accommodates joint U.S.-European missions as well as operations mounted by the Europeans with little or no direct U.S. involvement.

National Interest Priorities

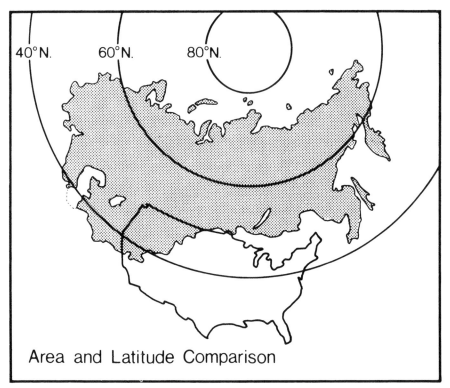

40°N.   60°N.   80°N.

Area and Latitude Comparison

Russia and U.S. in comparison

NATO has reached consensus about the way forward. European defense establishments have developed the NATO Response Force (NRF), essentially a small army of some 21,000 European troops focusing on demanding expeditionary operations. Within the next years, the EU plans to organize a European Rapid Reaction Force (ERRF) that could number up to 100,000 personnel to address peacekeeping and peace enforcement operations, primarily around the periphery of Europe.

With certainty, Europe has the wherewithal to contribute to global security. With 27 member states, the EU has a larger population and gross domestic product (GDP) than does the United States. NATO-Europe and Canada have even greater resources, but what has been lacking is sufficient political will, above all, to spend more money on defense. NATO-Europe alone has well over two million people under arms.

The United States is committed to safeguarding Europe's postwar harmony and preventing European countries from becoming rivals again. The great conflicts of the 20th century convinced Europeans of the need to overcome age-old rivalries. U.S. interests include not only maintaining peace in Europe, but also in strengthening the transatlantic partnership and encouraging European unification. A more united Europe would be a more critically constructive element in the world, and a

more influential EU would in turn ensure the solid incorporation and integration of the new democracies of East-Central Europe. On the other hand, a fractious EU would be ineffective in promoting political and economic development in parts of the former outer and inner empire of the Soviet Union. It would be less capable of responding to security threats or managing international financial crises. From America's point of view, what happens in Europe makes a huge difference in world affairs, and the United States can have a key role in influencing European movement toward unity.

It follows that America has a substantial stake in the expansion and enlargement of Europe's democratic core eastward. Widening the group of democratic countries promotes stronger partnerships to assume international responsibilities. The United States assisted substantially in eventually overcoming the artificial division of Europe and thereafter began developing cooperative relationships with former adversaries, above all, with Russia.

With the Soviet threat gone, does Europe still need the protective presence of the United States? Does the latter still need its close security involvement in Europe? Fresh security concerns make some European allies keen to maintain their American protection. New members of NATO regard the Alliance as the realization of a crucial foreign policy goal: an enduring security arrangement with the

United States. Uncertainties to the east and the worrisome threats emanating from Islamic extremism make U.S. security guarantees reassuring and gratifying. The United States and Europe share common interests in a stable world order that must be protected in a variety of ways. America should therefore welcome greater European willingness to accept political responsibilities for global stability. These include preventing the proliferation of WMD; maintaining peace in the Persian Gulf; assuring the international free flow of oil and access to the Suez Canal; and encouraging order in Asia, which presupposes cooperative relationships between China, Japan, and India.

The disaster in Yugoslavia in the 1990s was first and foremost a reminder to the world that post-communist Europe is still a fragile place. Europeans were unable to halt the ferocious fighting without American assistance, and the wars of Yugoslav succession made abundantly clear the humanitarian consequences of ignoring regional conflict. Europe still has a host of potential problems, and an important security challenge for the EU will be to stabilize states facing social upheaval or civil conflict. Maintaining long-term stability in the Balkans will thwart potential spillover of conflict into adjacent areas, while enhancing international confidence in European security institutions and perhaps setting important precedents for global peacekeeping efforts. Failed states anywhere directly affect the vital interests of the democratic core states, and by extension those of the United States.

For both idealistic and practical reasons, the EU is committed to the spread of democracy. To a large degree, the globalization process represents the attainment of Western ideals of free flows of trade, persons, and ideas. The EU boasts a large and affluent domestic market, political stability, and well-enforced laws governing financial and corporate activity. Hence, EU members are less threatened by the negative aspects of globalization than most other countries. On the other hand, troubled states run the risk of turning into failed states if they are wracked by ethnic or religious radicalism.

As a friendly but distant power, the United States is often in a position to alleviate regional disputes and to organize stabilization efforts. America has calmed Greek-Turkish tensions over the years, assisted with negotiations in Northern Ireland, and was instrumental in stopping the bloodshed and "ethnic cleansing" in the Balkans. The Caucasus region poses yet another challenge, and any conceivable solution to conflict there requires American involvement. The greatest potential for calming troubled international

United States

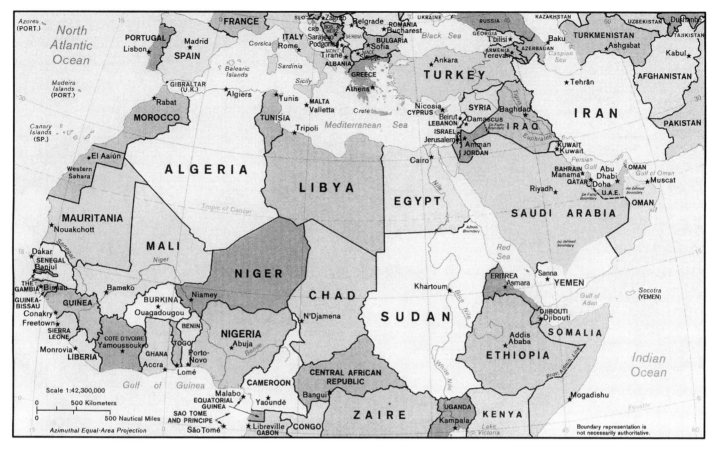

Northern Africa and the Middle East

Europeans must deal with America's large, highly decentralized institutions, which wield power of their own and often seem to be hostile to each other. Separation of powers is particularly troublesome for foreign policy: it is often impossible for a president to produce what he promises to foreign leaders. A U.S. president occupies a central position in the making of effective foreign policy. If he is not personally involved or committed to achieving certain foreign policy goals, little gets done. The political system enables persons who are largely unknown in Europe to rise to the highest national political office through a painfully long and complicated electoral system. The unique American selection procedure permits a person to arrive in the White House who has pursued a non-political career as a soldier (Eisenhower), farmer (Carter) actor (Reagan), or governor of a state (Carter, Reagan, Clinton, George W. Bush). The system often brings to the White House a neophyte in foreign policy; Eisenhower, Richard Nixon, and George H.W. Bush were exceptions. Most presidents learn diplomacy as on-the-job training, learning by doing.

When that president seems to overlook the multilateral dimension of U.S. dealings with the outside world and the need to engage former adversaries, Europeans tend to react negatively. Although many of the red-letter issues—such as the Comprehensive Test Ban Treaty, the Kyoto Protocol, and the International Criminal Court—had gained prominence during the Clinton administration, Bush's predecessor was able to give the appearance in public that he supported these international initiatives and to put the blame on the Republican Congress for not ratifying them.

A newly elected president may have little or no experience in foreign affairs and yet have the authority to select a multitude of foreign policy advisers, secretaries and agency chiefs, many with little or no foreign or defense policy background themselves. Such a presidential team appears often to operate in an uncoordinated way, frequently dispatching widely different signals. Such disparity inevitably creates and fuels doubts about U.S. leadership capabilities and the continuity of U.S. foreign policy. The complicated and extensive interagency bargaining in Washington confuses many people, European and American alike.

The powerful U.S. Congress can also be frustrating. In the last two decades of the 20th century, Congress underwent significant changes: the seniority system in committees had weakened, and the number of committees and subcommittees proliferated. Also, the legislative workload has become so demanding that congressmen and senators are retiring earlier. Therefore, an increasingly high percentage of legislators are new in Congress. For example, by the mid-1990s half the members of the House of Representatives had entered the chamber after the opening of the Berlin Wall. What these changes did, above all, was to take much of the power that heretofore was concentrated in a relatively few key figures and disperse it within Congress. In this more decentralized Congress, legislative work has become more complicated. More than 40 congressional committees and subcommittees, for example, deal with the defense budget alone.

[See the separate volumes on Europe in the World Today Series.]

RUSSIAN STABILITY AND ECONOMIC DEVELOPMENT

Political and economic reforms throughout the former Soviet Union are of critical interest to the United States. Economic dislocations and political turmoil, especially in Southern Russia, are cause for concern,

22

principally because of the spillover effects that could plunge entire regions into conflict and chaos. The implosion of the Soviet Union should be recognized for what it was. No recent historical precedent exists for as massive a sociopolitical collapse as the one experienced by the Soviet Union. The breakdown of the institutions of empire was accompanied by a complete disintegration of ideology, will, and perspective. The debacle of the Soviet empire requires Western responses and engagement. The United States and its allies must do what they can to prevent the failure of communism from becoming the failure of the USSR's successor states. Where some form of popular government does not emerge, a new political order rooted in intense nationalism and/or based on despotism is likely to be the result. The prospects of disorder and misrule loom large in regions of the former Soviet Union. Certain areas, particularly in the Caucasus, are already immersed in desperation, despair, and resignation.

During the cold war, the United States and its allies sought to limit or reduce the number of nuclear weapons targeted at them. To this end, the United States pursued arms reduction accords with the Soviet Union—SALT I, SALT II, and START II being important examples. Since the Soviet Union's collapse in 1991, Russia's difficulties ensuring control over its nuclear weapons, fissile material, and weapons scientists have posed a new nuclear threat. In recent years, the United States and Russia have tried to address the problem, but the possibilities for nuclear weapons proliferation remain substantial. It is very much in America's interest to prevent Russia's weapons, fissile material, and scientific expertise from falling into the wrong hands.

More broadly, it is in the U.S. interest for Russia to assume a responsible role in international affairs, and in this regard Washington must encourage Moscow. Specific international security issues include the handling of rogue states, halting the spread of weapons of mass destruction, battling terrorism, and combating organized crime. For its part, Russia desires international respect, while acknowledging that it will never have the influence the Soviet Union exercised during the cold war. In international affairs, more unites Russia and the United States than divides them.

Russia's frequent assertion of its right to be involved in the affairs of neighboring countries remains a source of friction. This stance toward the "near abroad" is prevalent not only among Russia's elite but the general public as well. Terrorist threats from adjacent areas have increased popular calls for assertiveness. Growing political and economic instability in the Caucasus and other areas will prompt demands for unifying parts of the former Soviet Union. Such overt displays of chauvinism worry many of Russia's neighbors, causing them to seek outside protection, which in turn could engender new problems.

Development and stability in Ukraine are of particular significance to the United States and its allies. In some ways, Ukraine remains a house divided, with the Russian majority in Eastern Ukraine favoring reunification with Russia, and the non-Russian majority in Western Ukraine intent on remaining independent. Quarreling between these two ethnic groups could have broad and very negative consequences for Europe and by extension for the United States. Beyond Ukraine, stability in the non-Slavic regions of the former Soviet Union is needed if economic progress is to occur. Many countries, including the United States, are interested in developing Caspian Sea oil. Turmoil in the Caucasus region already threatens the flow of oil, and widening political instability in Central Asia would disrupt oil production and distribution. Parts of the Caucasus are also spawning and harboring radical Islamic terrorists, a matter of substantial concern to Russia as the immediate target, but to the United States also.

The republics of former Soviet Central Asia have undergone sweeping transformations since 1991, and their people have experienced considerable adversity and hardship. Yet, these new countries have maintained their independence and have achieved a modicum of stability. Although the Central Asian republics are hardly liberal democracies, the elites and the general public appear to share common concerns about order, economic dislocations, and basic development. The region is rich in mineral resources and hydrocarbon deposits although extraction and transport represent significant challenges.

The United States now endeavors to support stability and eventually to promote democracy in Central Asia. It is evident that the United States has profited from the hard lessons of Afghanistan where a failed state became a haven and training ground for international terrorists. Few people in Central Asia long for the political system of the Soviet "stagnation period," but the future is clouded by uncertainty. The countries of Central Asia are weak. The regimes lack legitimacy and the countries have feeble national identities. Several, especially Kazakhstan, have large Russian minorities. In addition, their economies are closely tied to Russia. Yet, radical Islam has not taken root in the region in a way that could genuinely threaten stability. Even in this part of the former Soviet Union, people are becoming accustomed to voicing their concerns, and the United States should welcome openness and liberalization in the region, however limited, difficult and slow.

The world-wide economic crisis began affecting most of the area of the CIS by the autumn of 2008. Russia was particularly affected by the crisis, partly because financial difficulties were accompanied by a sharp decline in world energy prices, with crude oil dropping to less than $40 a barrel. Foreign investors sold off most of their Russian stocks and bonds at this time, contributing to a 60% decline in the overall value of stocks on Russian stock exchanges. In addition, Russian companies owed an estimated $437 billion to foreign banks and other companies when the crisis hit. As the ruble dropped in value and company revenues plummeted, Russian companies were hard-pressed to meet their repayment schedules.

Other republics were also adversely affected by the economic crisis, but in different ways. Those with significant oil and natural gas resources were, in general, affected the least. Domestic firms were affected to some extent, but the individuals most troubled were the emigrant workers who were the first to lose their jobs and many were forced to return to their home republics. Kyrgyzstan and Tajikistan, poor countries with large immigrant populations, were particularly hard hit by the crisis for the same reason.

The Russian economy began growing again in early 2010, though the recovery remains weak largely because the economic crisis in the European Union has cut demand for Russian energy exports. Russia is marking time, and so the economies of most of the "near abroad" are marking time as well. [See the separate volume on Russia in the World Today Series.]

THE GREATER MIDDLE EAST

Industrial and industrializing countries have common interests in maintaining access to world energy supplies at stable and reasonable prices. U.S. goals for energy security include availability from a variety of types and sources, and the operation of market forces rather than political factors for accessibility and the determination of price. Diversification contributes to market stability by minimizing the effect of disruption of any one supplier, and by creating alternative sources and permitting markets to make price adjustments. U.S. energy security interests include the participation of other developed countries in sharing the burdens associated with ensuring the availability of energy supplies.

In the Middle East, the United States has a time-honored commitment to upholding Israel's right to exist. Over the years,

United States

it has been actively involved in regional diplomacy. The United States has continuously insisted that a sustainable Arab-Israeli peace accord must be based upon the concurrence of all parties. The United States maintains close relations with several Arab states, including Egypt, Jordan, Saudi Arabia, and the smaller Gulf Cooperation Council (GCC) countries. Over time, it wishes to see these politically underdeveloped countries progress democratically with an aim to eventual integration into the core democratic world. In this regard, the United States has expressed a keen interest in the political development of moderate Middle East regimes. Reform includes such objectives as guaranteeing civil liberties, ensuring the rule of law, advancing civil society, and making government accountable and responsive to the citizenry. Yet, parliamentary rule in Middle Eastern countries still seems a long way off, although the monarchies in Morocco, Jordan, and Kuwait are presently carrying out modest reforms.

The economic well-being of the world is partly tied to the continued availability of Middle Eastern oil. The Middle East contains over half of the world's oil reserves and produces nearly a quarter of its crude oil. Important shipping and trade routes through the region must be kept open to ensure the unimpeded flow of oil. The United States faces many challenges in the Middle East and North Africa including

- the growth of anti-Western political movements that threaten the security of traditional friends and allies in the region and
- state-sponsored terrorism that endangers the lives of civilians and government officials, threatens those willing to make peace, complicates the ability to negotiate by souring the atmosphere, and weakens the economy of friendly states by discouraging tourism.

Prevention of state failure, such as occurred in Afghanistan, is a crucial U.S. interest, not least because political collapse, say, in North Africa would have far-flung effects upon European countries. The salient threat to domestic stability in the region comes from radical Islam, which seeks to justify rampant violence with firm religious convictions. The United States seeks to demonstrate its ability to work with devout Moslems, as it does for example with Saudi Arabia, while thwarting the spread of radical, aggressive Islam. American officials have repeatedly emphasized that the problem with radical Islamists is their violent political agenda, not their religion. Accordingly, a partnership with the United States is compatible with devout Islamic belief and practice.

The Late Chairman Yasser Arafat of the
Palestine Liberation Organization

The fragile liberalization process is periodically jeopardized by extremism and domestic disturbances. The United States strives to isolate and weaken regimes it considers radical, and to undermine fundamentalist popular elements. Moreover, few Middle Eastern regimes have anything approaching satisfactory human rights records. Many exercise oppression and intimidation of political opponents, to say nothing of the denial of civil liberties. Reform is still often regarded as inimical to the interests of established ruling families and power cliques.

The Palestinian-Israeli peace process is a major component of a U.S. vision for the Middle East, which includes the replacement of confrontational relationships with negotiations and the reduction of pan-Arabist sentiment. It would be in America's interest if the idea of Arab unity and integration would be replaced with regional integration, allowing Israel and Turkey, and perhaps eventually Iran, to enter the regional grouping. The ultimate responsibility for achieving peace in Palestine rests squarely on the participants—the Israelis and the Palestinians. Yet, if any outside mediators can assist in bringing the parties to a settlement, these remain the United States and the EU.

For many years, the United States has pursued an enduring peace settlement between Israel and its Arab neighbors and a just solution to the Palestinian problem.

Four major Arab-Israeli wars and frequent civil unrest have inflicted tremendous destruction on the people of the Middle East. The Arab-Israeli conflict continues to be a cause of political tension, violence, and extremism, all of which represent threats to U.S. interests in the region.

Democracy and liberty spread across the world in the 1980s and 1990s, a few remaining communist countries proving the rule. One notable exception was the Middle East, and for nearly two decades observers sought to explain why authoritarian regimes continued to dominate that region. Their analyses often concluded that Arab societies and politics were similar to one another, but somehow different from the rest of the world. For this uniqueness, often conflicting theories blamed the stable authoritarianism on the past, favorites being Islamic culture and the legacies of colonialism. Other theories emphasized the present—U.S. and European support for rulers pursuing certain foreign policies. Whatever the causes, though, consensus persisted that Arab countries missed the forces creating an increasingly democratic world.

Suddenly, almost without warning, in early 2011 the Arab world convulsed as demonstrators in their thousands and then hundreds of thousands defied their governments and filled public squares to demand "Irhal!" ("Go!"). What had so inflamed public opinion and created citizens brave enough to risk arrest, torture, and possibly death by publicly demanding their rulers' ouster?

Multiple explanations for what caused the previously sullen Arab population suddenly to demand change rapidly flooded the media. One false claim merits quick rebuttal. The "Arab Spring" did not begin as an Islamic revolution, though some commentators, Libya's Muammar Gaddafi, and Syria's Bashar al-Asad alleged that al-Qaeda and other radical Islamists ignited the protests. Those in the streets obviously represented a much wider segment of the region's population, from the wealthy to the urban poor, from the well-educated and more westernized to the more traditional.

On the other hand, cognizant that Islamic revolts would worry the influential West, demonstrators in Cairo's Tahir Square and elsewhere went out of their way to reinforce a more secular nationalist tone rather than a more public Islamic aspect. Most understood that the world was watching. Muslim groups seldom planted the seeds of revolution or cultivated its early growth—indeed, in Egypt, the Muslim Brotherhood leadership initially opposed the protests. Nonetheless, the Muslim groups were the best organized to reap their harvest.

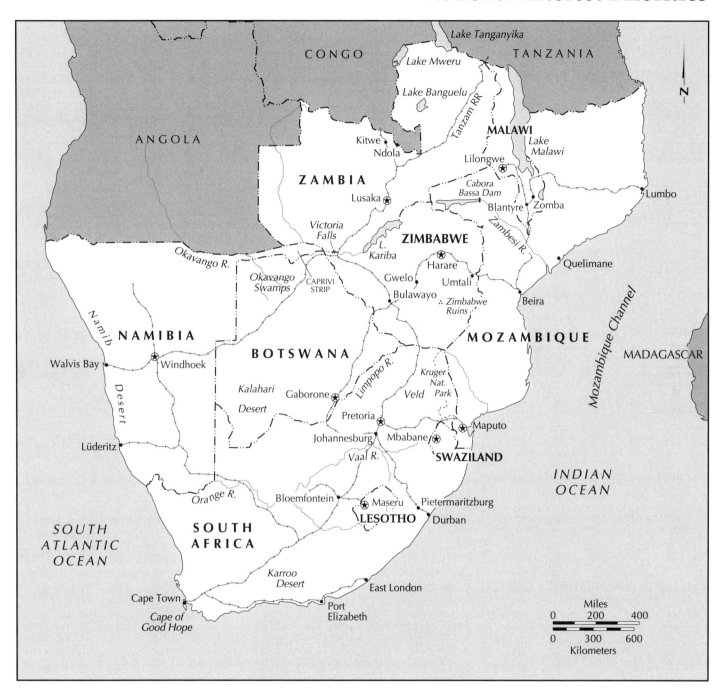

Economic distress played an undeniable role. Arab societies suffered high poverty and unemployment rates. On the personal level, male university graduates in their twenties were often unable to obtain jobs paying well enough to start a home and family. This was even more true for women. Though the culture traditionally depicted a woman's place in the home, the Egyptian TV program "I Want to Get Married" portrayed the resulting anguish and humor from a woman's point of view. It became a hit. Its political significance, largely overlooked, was the existence of a large pool of university graduates either poorly employed or jobless, with time, the Internet, social media and dissatisfaction on their hands. Indeed, the very useful American radio broadcast *America Abroad* highlighted the problem in a series of reports on the growing distress among Arab youth in the months leading up to the explosion.

Moreover, economies that had adopted free-market doctrines and were widely open to international trade appeared defenseless when prices rose sharply worldwide. Popular opinion often blamed the International Monetary Fund (IMF) and leaders sympathetic to it. Social distress also manifested itself in other ways. Inadequate low-income housing, insufficient public transportation, and poor government services made daily life difficult for the lower classes. Oil money or not, the region was filled with obviously frustrated youth sleeping late and spending their afternoon hours sitting in the streets. Unemployment and continuing poverty were significant challenges, and labor protests had intensified in Egypt. More immediately, the recent hike in food prices

United States

around the world affected countries in the region. Given the large proportion of typical family spending on food, the price increases provoked simmering discontent in the months before the 2011 "Arab Spring" began.

Nevertheless, socio-economic distress fails fully to explain the protests. The revolution began in Tunisia, statistically one of the better-off countries. In Egypt, unemployment was a problem but not to the point where it might have induced the overthrow of President Hosni Mubarak. When the "Arab Spring" formally began, the slogans and signs in Tunisia and Egypt were not about the price of bread and sustenance.

Given the traditional fawning pro-government media so common to the region, it seems plausible to conclude that the protests began in part because electronic communication—Al Jazeera on television, and the social media quartet on Facebook, YouTube, texting and Twitter—told truths and provided images about societies that governments could no longer control. Repression, corruption and nepotism had become endemic; now the public could visualize them, sometimes with graphic pictures of a victim of police torture. Images from Iran during the summer of 2009 had already shown what influence the new media could have on community organizing and activism.

While new social media increasingly allow people around the world convenient ways to circumvent local domestic censors, the ability of Al-Jazeera, Twitter, Facebook and YouTube to highlight events in neighboring countries was probably even more significant than focusing attention domestically. The social media contributed yet another essential element. These enable a small number of young organizers who were inspired with passions for freedom and rights to call for demonstrations in ways the regimes could not easily repress. As it happened, youthful activists had already studied the tactics of non-violent civil disobedience. In the broader perspective, the "Arab Spring" represents another element in political globalization.

Principal American interests in the Middle East can be summarized as:

Limiting WMD Proliferation. Dissemination of biological, chemical, and nuclear weapons, above all, combined with the development of long-range ballistic missiles poses a direct threat to U.S. interests in the region and is thus a lodestar of U.S. policy. The United States does not officially acknowledge the Israeli nuclear program, and it encourages all states in the region to support nonproliferation. A continuing problem is that some states regard WMD as relatively inexpensive yet high-status "more bangs-for-the-buck" weapons, effective for projecting power, potentially useful for intimidation, and valuable for countering similarly armed neighbors. The greatest danger involves the transfer of WMD to terrorist groups. Although some soft-pedal their views and all intensely dislike the fact that U.S. troops were the change agents, most countries in the region are relieved that the Iraqi threat is gone. WMD transfer to nonstate actors remains a cause for general concern.

Ensuring sea passage and access to oil. Since the reflagging of cargo vessels in 1987, when foreign ships flew U.S. flags and were escorted by the U.S. Navy, protection of Persian Gulf shipping has been one of the main reasons for the U.S. presence in the region. Although a modest amount (less than 10%) of its energy originates in the Gulf, America assists in safeguarding the uninterrupted flow of oil at reasonably stable prices to regions more dependent on Persian Gulf oil, such as Europe and Asia.

The defense of Israel. The United States and Israel have maintained a deep relationship based on many shared values and interests. The U.S. commitment to the security and integrity of Israel has been constant. The United States has no illusions that its economic and security assistance by itself can resolve the local conflicts and fully protect key U.S. interests. The peace process begun in Oslo in 1993 has broken down; the establishment of a Palestinian state seems as far off as ever; and the so-called second *intifada*, or uprising, periodically flares up. Israel has made its willingness to conclude peace contingent on security guarantees and the maintenance of modern military forces. Arab governments accuse the United States of favoring Israel over the Palestinians and express doubts about its willingness to serve as an honest broker in the peace process. With the death of Palestinian President Yasser Arafat in November 2004 and the emergence of a new Palestinian Authority (PA) leadership, there has been a flurry of diplomatic activity to reinvigorate the stalled peace process. Many people in all parts of the world hope a credible Palestinian leadership will evolve. American economic and security assistance can provide important building blocks on which to pursue a better future for the region.

Sustaining regional balances. U.S. policy seeks to restrain and isolate rogue states. Underpinning this policy is robust diplomacy, attempts to deter aggressive states, as well as economic and military measures aimed at such states as Syria, Iran, and Sudan. The U.S. Congress supports most policies and initiatives, at times through legislation mandating sanctions. U.S. policies are often strongly disliked in the region and frequently generate public criticism of America. The region remains volatile and any foreign intervention is widely resented.

The promotion of political and economic liberalization. With some justification, the United States has been frequently criticized for supporting autocratic governments in the region, while failing to encourage democratic reform. No country in the Middle East has yet embraced Western-style democracy, and many countries remain politically repressive. The United States now actively encourages liberalization and wider political participation in elective national assemblies, local government institutions, and consultative councils. Oman, Kuwait, Jordan, Morocco, Egypt, Lebanon, and even Saudi Arabia have modestly broadened political participation in recent years. Yet, they still have a long way to go toward liberal democracy. [See the separate volume on the Middle East in the World Today Series.]

STABLE TRANSITIONS IN AFRICA

During the cold war, principal U.S. strategic interests in Africa were closely connected to rival forces from outside the continent, chiefly from the Soviet Bloc and the Middle East. The collapse of communism ended most outside interference in Africa and reduced the need for the West to undertake measures to protect sea lines of communication in the Atlantic and Indian Oceans. Challenges to stability in Africa currently emanate from within the continent. The absence of major external threats offers an opportunity to focus on pressing African issues: combating disease, especially HIV/AIDS; eliminating hunger; providing peacekeeping and enforcement; improving living standards; and fostering economic growth. American interests are historical, personal, economic, social, and humanitarian.

The chief current U.S. objective is to assist African countries to build stable, liberal democracies that will be major participants in global trade and investment. Achievement of this ambitious development goal would allow Western countries to further their own national and commercial objectives of greater trade and investment, including assured access to Africa's resources. To help African countries along their path to development, the United States and its partners must address security and stability issues, above all, by helping to terminate internal conflict and the deplorable activities of militias, criminal gangs and terrorist groups.

Although Africa has more than its share of such troublemakers, the actual threats these pose to U.S. security are matters of some controversy. Clearly, terrorist attacks on U.S. property and citizens are dire threats. Support of terrorist organizations and activities by the Sudanese regime are of considerable concern. International trafficking in narcotics with the collusion or through the sheer incompetence of Nigerian officials is a serious problem. Mass killings are cause for major humanitarian distress in the United States. Certainly, serious transnational security threats emanate from Africa, including state-sponsored terrorism; drug trafficking; international crime; environmental degradation and disease. Enduring U.S. interests lie in countering roguish groups and regimes thwarting the progress of African states attempting to liberalize their societies.

Transition states need international support to bolster their chances of sustained development. They often require cooperative international efforts to reduce internal violence and, above all, to prevent them from degenerating into new failed states that cause misery and destabilize their neighbors. Consistent international efforts to promote stability and security among African states are needed to end the unrelenting conflict that hinders development, produces conditions conducive to humanitarian disaster, and can result in new failed states. Persistent and widespread conflict, often resulting from tribal divisions, is the key impediment to political, social, and economic progress on the continent. Most Africans readily acknowledge the grief and despair conflict brings, and yet the strife continues. For some African states, the attainment of relative security and stability must remain a first priority, taking precedence over all other goals.

Addressing root causes of failed states and managing humanitarian crises in Africa are in the U.S. interest for several reasons. Human rights issues are of concern generally to Americans. Many in America view the people of Africa as unfortunate and oppressed, a perception that increases public pressure for intervention in some cases. Yet, forestalling crises is less expensive in monetary terms, lives, and political capital than intervention in a messy conflict. Considerable resources were squandered in the 1993 Somalia operation, a largely humanitarian operation in a failed state. Little was accomplished, and nothing was done to prevent the next conflict. The half-hearted intervention sent the wrong signal to America's enemies.

Sub-Saharan Africa's debt is small in relative financial terms, but it is nonethe-

less a burden for African economies. Most African countries have difficulty servicing their debt and become trapped in a vicious cycle of borrowing new money to service old debt. Between 1985 and 2000, Africa paid more than $110 billion in debt servicing alone. The fresh loans did not reduce the principal, and overall capital inflows barely exceeded capital outflows. In 1998, sub-Saharan African countries owed approximately $180 billion, and 83% was owed to such public institutions as the World Bank, the International Monetary Fund (IMF), the Organization for Economic Cooperation and Development (OECD), and Western governments. The remainder was owed to commercial lenders, primarily European banks.

Without at least some relief of the debt burden, the economies of many African countries will not grow and could become dysfunctional. Debt will limit the ability of African countries to initiate policies supporting private sector expansion and job creation. Problems associated with large amounts of debt could stimulate the underground (unofficial) economy and prevent the integration of Africa into the world economy.

Indeed, Africa's political, economic, and security realities are hard ones. U.S. policies support significant change in Africa, including the emergence of multiparty democracy, the promulgation of new constitutions, more frequent and open elections, a freer press, and adherence to budgetary discipline. While America cannot address every challenge, it seeks to identify those issues that most directly affect its interests. Critics suggest that the U.S. approach often overlooks political repression in numerous countries. True, ignoring human rights abuses in the name of economic reform can be fraught with difficulties. Good governance and substantial economic reform are ultimately closely linked, which is the principal reason the United States makes foreign aid dependent on efforts to govern fairly and effectively. Political order is a prerequisite for the rule of law, and the combination of these attracts the foreign investment necessary for long-term economic growth. Hence, one of the principal challenges facing transition states is to scale down the protectionist trade practices of authoritarian regimes, encouraging openness without causing rampant disorder.

The United States might spur economic growth and promote trade and investment by examining new means to improve the economic policies of African countries and by sustaining critical bilateral and multilateral development assistance. While further integration of Africa into the global economy has political and economic benefits, it will also serve U.S.

interests by continuing to expand an already important new market for U.S. exports. The more than 600 million people of sub-Saharan Africa (that part of the continent south of the Sahara Desert) represent one of the world's largest remaining untapped markets. The United States exports more to sub-Saharan Africa than to all of the former Soviet Union combined. Yet, America has only a 7% market share in Africa. Increasing both the U.S. market share and the size of the African market should result in substantial mutual benefits. Full integration requires mutually beneficial commerce that opens U.S. markets to African exports. It also means continued development assistance, including investment in education, technological transfer to bolster Africa's human resources, and elevating the level of its exports. Africa represents a huge, untapped market, and efforts must be made to cement U.S.-Africa commercial ties over the middle and long term. Sustainable growth and development will require transforming Africa from a provider of primary commodities to an exporter of diversified goods and services. Diversification will encourage foreign investment, leading to job creation and ultimately alleviating poverty.

By assisting African nations to break through the barrier of poverty and civil turmoil, the United States can help achieve political stability, self-reliance, and sustained growth. Self-reliance helps to thwart subversion and civil war. Sustained growth leads to increased trade and mounting wealth. By improving social and economic conditions in African countries, the United States does more than help people in need, which is an important end in itself. It creates and expands markets for American farm produce and manufactured products, and helps ensure a continued flow of primary resources.

Africa nonetheless represents major challenges for U.S. foreign policy. Two of the greatest are

- how to help the countries of sub-Saharan Africa initiate and sustain economic growth to enable them to attain food self-sufficiency and equitable long-term economic development and
- how to assist the countries of southern Africa to achieve regional stability and internal peace.

Sustained and equitable economic development is the key to combating the social and economic problems that go hand-in-hand in Africa. Achieving long-term growth will require most African countries to adopt significant structural reforms.

Virtually all nations of sub-Saharan Africa, with a combined population of over

United States

into regional security arrangements and encouraging it to become more integrated in the world economy. True, China is still an emerging power and will have nothing like the national strength of the United States any time soon. Yet it is the one country in the region that could shift the regional power balance and change the international order in a manner damaging to U.S. interests. Given the combination of enormous potential and looming problems in China, the possibilities for the country in the next decade vary. Whether China emerges as an aggressive great power, evolves into a powerful country following a moderate and prudent foreign policy, or fails to solve its problems and slips into decline will be one of the most important events of the next two decades. Hence, the United States must carefully manage its relations with China, and its policies toward China are of considerable international consequence.

China's growing maritime focus, both military and commercial, is bound to increase its interaction with the United States in the Asia Pacific region on several levels. How the United States manages the relationship with China will invariably affect other countries' views of the regional and global leadership role of the United States. In the coming years, U.S. stature and influence in the region will largely depend on the ability to handle Chinese issues successfully. It is imperative that the United States and its friends and allies convince Beijing that Chinese interests are served through cooperation rather than confrontation. Conflict is not the inevitable result of the increase in China's power. More unites China with its neighbors and even with America than divides them. Japan is America's third largest trading partner and over 15% of U.S. imports come from China.

The United States, Japan, the Republic of Korea (South Korea), ASEAN (the Association of Southeast Asian Nations) and China share common interests in the establishment of an enduring, stable regional order. ASEAN is a ten-member trade organization designed to foster regional cooperation. A more open transpacific regionalism is embodied in the Asia-Pacific Economic Cooperation (APEC) Forum of which Japan and the United States are leading members. Following the recovery from the severe economic crisis of the late 1990s, most East Asian countries are now able to develop respectable military capabilities and assume roles in maintaining regional stability. Local security cooperation is in America's interest, and the U.S. military presence in the Asia Pacific of some 100,000 personnel is scheduled to decline in the next several years. Modernization and developments

East Asia

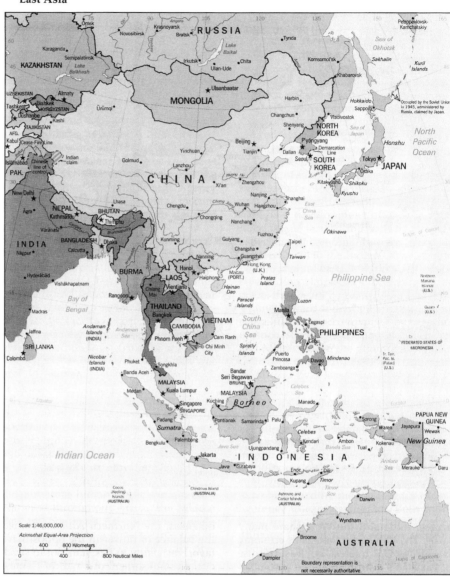

within the U.S. armed forces that are often described under the acronym RMA, that is, the Revolution in Military Affairs, will provide U.S. capabilities that compensate for lower deployment levels. America will continue to require the support of allies, including the use of bases in the area, above all in Japan and Korea, if it is to maintain its crucial security role. Should such assistance not be available, maintaining public and congressional backing for the continued stationing of the U.S. military in the Asia Pacific region would be a hard political sell.

Among the strategic dilemmas the United States faces in the region is that of burden sharing with allies and friendly countries. If the United States were perceived as attempting arbitrarily to foist increased responsibilities upon others, it would be rebuffed, and rejection could

have regrettable and unforeseen consequences. On the other hand, long-term security in the region is possible only with the active involvement of the major states. The next decade offers considerable grounds for concern, and conflict in the region could be either accidental or deliberate. North Korea in all likelihood has nuclear weapons and could threaten the South or even Japan with these. Another danger involves a miscalculation on the part of Beijing or Taipei (Taiwan's capital), precipitating a Chinese attack on Taiwan. Several countries assert rights on the Spratly Islands in the South China Sea, and any one could initiate a conflict should it perceive another to be determined to alter the status quo. In addition to the well-known Chinese claim to the Spratly Islands and to sovereignty over Taiwan, Beijing still has certain claims on parts of Kazakhstan, Tajikistan, Kyrgyzstan and Siberia. In the case of Taiwan, there can be no question that the island is an independent economic entity, but its official political status has not yet been settled. By the late 1990s the Chinese threat to Taiwan reached a dangerous level of a major cross-straits conflict that would involve the United States.

An added danger is that the United States would likely be drawn into a conflict in East Asia. At the very least such a conflict would set back the course of regional development for years. The potential perils underscore the need for the United States to cooperate with the countries of the region to encourage dialogue and, more importantly, to put in place measures for confidence building and conflict management. Present organizations and structures offer a utilizable framework within which to continue such efforts. For example, ASEAN has shown little ability to transform itself into a collective defense organization, largely because of the provincialism and nationalism of its individual members. If the organization could put aside its difficulties, it could contribute substantially to regional stability. Further development of organizations and structures would contribute to the consolidation of U.S. regional influence. [See the separate volume on East and Southeast Asia in the World Today Series.]

PROMOTING DEMOCRACY

The expansion of liberal democracy and market economies benefits the United States and most countries of the world. By encouraging the growth of democracy and free markets, the United States is promoting its enlightened self-interest. Coherent and astute foreign policies on the part of America and its allies are necessary if democratizing trends in the world are to continue. Democracy's expansion into troubled and unstable regions serves the cause of peace, but it requires assertive Western policies, often backed by the use of force. Once liberal democratic institutions are in place, a sort of virtuous circle develops, whereby popular participation helps alleviate domestic conflict and increases prospects for regional stability. Moreover, the emergence of new democracies extends Western influence into additional areas of the world. Western countries have a keen interest in protecting fragile new democracies and assisting transition states to stay on track.

The United States must therefore attend to more countries than ever before. East-Central Europe is the foremost example of active American and European involvement in support of the building of

Saddam Hussein on trial in Iraq

liberal institutions and the development of popular democracy. Similar prospects will present themselves in other regions as situations stabilize and democracy takes root. Although democracy usually has a calming effect in the longer term, transitions are invariably difficult and emerging democratic processes unruly. Political structures and institutions need to be functional and reasonably stable to manage the tension inherent in democratization. Democratic transition cannot be rushed.

The problems of new democracies are complex and serious setbacks will occur. Countries forced to manage sweeping social and economic transformations suffer reverses and often do not realize their full potential. Some transition states become democratic in name only, pursuing erratic and reactionary policies. America and its allies can expect to be entangled in a host of difficult situations and occasionally confronted with international political dilemmas at the dawn of the 21st century.

The efforts are usually worth the trouble, though. However imperfect, democracy ultimately brings greater stability and improves people's lives. Liberal democracies share common values that are the fundament of international cooperation. They also do not go to war with each other. Recent experience indicates that in the near term, newly democratizing states are not necessarily close American allies. Skepticism about U.S. intentions often reflects a combination of factors, including historical experiences and a new sense of independence. In areas of Latin America

where liberal democracy is spreading, for example, many people harbor suspicions of the United States and its alliance network, often voicing concerns openly. In another part of the world, America will have at best a cool relationship with most Arab countries for years to come.

In short, the price of being a world power is high. Internationally, America is often damned if it does something, but damned more vehemently if it does not do it. Because its influence is so great, regardless of what it does or how it acts, its policies are controversial. Often criticized as a hegemonic bully, the United States is sometimes chided when it shows constraint. Rightly or wrongly, moderation is sometimes viewed as a shirking of responsibility and a lack of leadership. Moreover, America's sheer wealth and power invariably breed resentment.

TRANSNATIONAL THREATS

Terrorism, transnational crime syndicates and international drug trafficking necessitate a wide-ranging reconsideration of international security. These scourges of the 21st century pose serious and mounting threats to Western interests. Military power alone is only one instrument in the contemporary security environment, and a blunt one at that. Evaluating transgressions with an aim to determining national security options can be perplexing. The nature of a threat to national security is not always easy to characterize. Activities of transnational groups are often furtive and can have weighty and unanticipated effects upon societies.

United States

Terrorists and criminal gangs were not generally regarded as major international problems until fairly recently, and their actions were usually handled at a local level. Some of these groups are now major actors on the world stage, and their operations can be determinants of global political patterns. Terrorists and gangsters can acutely undermine national authority, severely and adversely affecting a country's social and economic well-being.

The transnational threats of the 21st century, such as terrorism, the illegal drug trade, illicit arms trafficking, international organized crime, and uncontrolled refugee migrations, threaten U.S. interests and citizens. The threats themselves are not new, of course. What is new are the technological advancements that render these threats more potent. Most observers agree that the single greatest threat to U.S. security at present is the acquisition of WMD by terrorist groups.

It misses the mark to assert that international organized crime does not represent a direct threat to U.S. interests and national security. A reassessment of security threats and a careful identification of nontraditional threats indicate alarming developments. Criminal organizations can interrupt the effective functioning of society as never before. Moreover, terrorist groups and criminal gangs are increasingly mutually supportive and sometimes actually collude. The term narcoterrorism is frequently used to describe the symbiotic relationship that has emerged between international criminal narcotics trafficking organizations and terrorist associations intent on destabilizing the international system. Narcoterrorists have grown so forceful and organized that they are able to wield undue influence over governments in some countries, usually through a blend of bribery, blackmail, criminal activity and terrorist tactics. Their crimes frequently run the gamut of iniquities, but they will sometimes operate quasi-legal businesses on the side as well to launder their profits, among other reasons. Narcoterrorists are also involved in relatively sophisticated activities such as money laundering, computer manipulation, and financial fraud of every sort. Narcoterrorism is a 21st-century phenomenon and international security threat requiring transnational cooperation and innovative strategic approaches.

Hence, U.S. officials are called upon to respond to assorted transnational challenges that have moved to center stage with the cold war's end in 1989. Combating these dangers—which range from terrorism, international crime, narcoterrorism, trafficking in drugs and illegal arms, to environmental damage and intrusions into critical

A young officer in combat operations

information infrastructures—requires far-reaching cooperation among U.S. government agencies as well as coordination with other countries. U.S. counterterrorism approaches are intended to prevent, disrupt, and defeat terrorist operations, and, if terrorist acts do occur, to respond accordingly, with determined efforts to bring the perpetrators to justice. U.S. policy to counter international terrorists rests on several basic principles: to make no concessions to terrorists; to bring all pressure to bear on state sponsors of terrorism; to exploit all available legal mechanisms to punish international terrorists; and to help other governments to improve their capabilities to combat terrorism. Countering terrorism effectively requires day-to-day coordination with other governments and organizations. Substantial results have been achieved through the increasing integration of intelligence, diplomatic, investigative and prosecutorial activities among the Departments of State, Homeland Security, Justice, Defense, Treasury, Transportation, and the Central Intelligence Agency (CIA).

One of the most serious threats confronting the United States is the unconventional warfare challenge emanating from the Middle East. Terrorism and guerrilla hostilities have in many ways become the hallmark of future conflict. This development belies the notion that conflict in the 21st century will be waged largely with high-technology weaponry. Although the history of this century will probably record many bloody conflicts, few outcomes are likely to be determined by the extensive utilization of the most advanced weaponry. Indeed, one of the challenges facing the U.S. military in the 21st century will be to refute the myth that the United States can successfully wage swift wars that will render combat effective, clean, and bloodless, at least insofar as American forces are concerned. The cur-

rent U.S. battle against insurgency in Iraq is an instructive case in point.

The U.S. response to the global bane of drug abuse and drug trafficking is to integrate domestic and international efforts to reduce both the demand and the supply of drugs. Its ultimate success will depend on concerted efforts by the public, all levels of government, and the private sector together with other governments, private groups and international organizations. U.S. counter-drug strategy includes efforts to strengthen democratic institutions; root out corruption; destroy trafficking organizations; prevent money laundering; eradicate illegal drug crops in the Western Hemisphere, Asia, and the Middle East, and encourage alternative crop development. The United States engages international organizations, financial institutions, and nongovernmental organizations in counter-narcotics cooperation.

International organized crime undermines fragile new democracies as well as developing countries. In parts of the former Soviet Union, for instance, organized crime poses a grave threat to U.S. interests because of the potential for theft and smuggling of nuclear weapons materials remaining in those countries. To combat organized crime, the United States seeks to mount an international effort to counter the major international criminal cartels, notably those based in the former Soviet Union, Colombia, Southeast Asia, and Nigeria. The United States is working to thwart money laundering and other criminal activities in the major offshore financial centers, create indigenous criminal investigation and prosecution capabilities in key countries and implement measures to address several other financial crimes, including counterfeiting, large-scale international fraud and embezzlement, computer intrusion of banks, and alien smuggling.

THE ENVIRONMENTAL DIMENSION

Environmental threats do not heed national borders and can pose long-term dangers to U.S. security and prosperity. Natural resource scarcities often trigger and exacerbate conflict. Environmental threats such as climate change, ozone depletion and transnational movement of dangerous chemicals directly threaten the health of U.S. citizens. Decisions regarding the environment and natural resources can affect U.S. security for decades.

The daily lives of all people on earth are substantially affected by the environment—the changing climate, the quality of air and water, the purity of rivers, lakes, and seas. Pollution of the air, water, and soil from the products of industrial civilization is a growing global problem. The world's heritage of natural resources—its tropical forests, its reserves of biological diversity, its wild plants and animals—is seriously threatened by human activities. The advances of science and technology have a significant impact on living standards and lifestyles because of new products, work practices, and communications. The benefits of technology should be made more available to the citizens of all countries. The United States must work with other nations in dealing with global and regional environmental and scientific problems to permit the sustainable use of the world's resources so that future generations will also benefit from them.

Economic development and population growth have had dramatic effects on the global environment. At the same time, the reach of technology has been extended to the seafloor and outer space. These two developments have opened new frontiers of international responsibility and cooperation. Since the landmark U.N. Conference on the Human Environment in Stockholm in 1972, assessment and response to environmental problems have become a priority international activity. Subsequent economic summits have identified as key problems "stratospheric ozone depletion, climate change, acid rain, endangered species, hazardous substances, air and water pollution, and destruction of tropi-

cal forests." Environmental cooperation is an area where political will and scientific wisdom have worked together to make a difference, though much more remains to be done.

The United States was one of the first countries to address domestic environmental concerns, and it has supported the development of international law and practice on environmental matters. America's international role, in cooperation with other countries and key multinational organizations, has been to focus effort and attention on the most urgent issues and to assure that control strategies are based on the best available science and on a realistic assessment of costs and benefits.

With its long coastline, the United States is vulnerable to marine pollution. This pollution, especially from spills and dumping, has been assigned high priority by the international community. The United States is party to several global agreements including: The Convention for the Prevention of Pollution from Ships, which regulates discharges of harmful substances from ships; and The London

United States

Dumping Convention, which attempts to prevent marine pollution by banning sea disposal of some wastes and listing others which may be disposed of only with special care.

The United States is also party to the Cartagena Convention, which protects the marine environment of the Caribbean region. The United States also signed the Convention for the Protection of the Natural Resources and Environment of the South Pacific Region. Both agreements have important protocols on cooperation in combating oil spills. The conventions were sponsored by the U.N. Environmental Program (UNEP).

Acidification of water bodies, the growing evidence of harm to the protective stratospheric ozone layer, and climate change resulting from greenhouse gases make atmospheric pollution a priority international issue. Joint studies by the United States and Canada have shown that the causes of acid rain are more complex than originally supposed, and the two countries are continuing to search for an effective joint strategy. Scientific consensus has been reached that depletion of stratospheric ozone—which protects human health, crops, and marine life by filtering the sun's rays—is a serious and growing problem.

Consequently, the U.N. Environmental Program, with the support of the U.S. government, developed a global legal framework to protect stratospheric ozone. International negotiations led to the adoption of the 1985 Vienna Convention for the Protection of the Ozone Layer, which called for monitoring, data exchange, and further research.

Carbon dioxide, the product of the use of fossil fuels, and other greenhouse gases allow short-wave energy from the sun to reach the earth's surface but do not allow long-term radiant energy to escape. As a result, temperature increases are anticipated in this century with unknown consequences to human life and agriculture. Higher temperatures would mean rising sea levels that would affect costal regions of the United States and other countries. A changing climate could result in major shift in food-producing regions throughout the world, including adverse effects on the U.S. grain belt.

In many areas of the earth, entire species of plants and animals are becoming extinct or seriously endangered at alarming rates. Since so much of the world's agriculture, medicine, and science depend on a constantly refreshed base of genetic diversity, the destruction of this base can have serious consequences for the human race.

The United States participates actively in a wide range of international efforts to protect vital ecosystems across the globe.

It is a founding member of and the largest contributor to the Convention on International Trade in Endangered Species of Wild Fauna and Flora. The United States also protects wildlife resources through an extensive variety of bilateral relationships.

Current trends indicate that this century could see nearly a doubling of the global population. Most of this growth will take place in developing countries. Some projections indicate that economic activity must expand five- to tenfold to meet the basic needs of this population. The impact of an expansion of this magnitude on an already-stressed environment could be catastrophic, if not handled properly. Paradoxically, development is essential to avoid further damage to the environment. For example, many developing nations have growing rural populations that are pushing agriculture into areas not suitable for farming. The landscape is being altered and forests lost for only marginal gain, in terms of agriculture. Solutions must be found to foster environmentally suitable development. Ways must be determined to increase economic activity without mortgaging the future. The problem is all the more difficult because most economic growth must take place in areas that are, perhaps, ill-equipped to manage development.

Environmental degradation must be placed on the national security agenda for at least two reasons. First, scarcity exacerbated by environmental mismanagement increasingly will become a source of conflict. Streams of refugees are pushed by environmental considerations; problems caused by deforestation are an example. Second, the scale of human activity around the globe has reached the point that national solutions to environmental problems will not suffice. Events or economic activities in one nation can have profound effects on others. Global warming, the greenhouse effect, and industrial accidents that cause significant environmental damage are examples of potential sources of conflict. The Paris Climate Accord, signed by more than 130 nations in 2016, represents the most ambitious international effort to date to head off disastrous warming. Even if all countries hold to their promises to curb emissions of greenhouse gases, the pledges might not be sufficient to meet the target of keeping the planet below three degrees of warming. In order to avoid or manage conflict in the future, it will be essential to address environmental issues in the context of security, stability, and sustainability.

REALISM AND DEMOCRACY

While a professor at the University of Chicago in the late 1940s, Hans Morgen-

thau published the first edition of his pathbreaking book, *Politics Among Nations*. Its impact was immediate, and its message alarming to many. It focused on the reality of power politics and the balance of power, as well as the evils of the "Old World conflicts" that immigrants had come to America to escape.

Morgenthau supported the premise that diplomatic strategy should be motivated by national interest rather than by utopian and moralistic, legalistic, and ideological criteria. Morgenthau equated national interest with the pursuit of state power, where power stands for anything that establishes and maintains control by one state over another. This power-control relationship can be achieved by coercive as well as cooperative techniques. Morgenthau has been criticized for constructing two abstract and imprecise concepts—power and interest—which he uses as the ends and the means of international political action. His critics, mostly from the scientific school of thought, have demanded more precise operational definitions of these basic units of analysis in the field of international affairs. Morgenthau remained firmly in support of his position that great abstractions such as power and interest cannot and should not be quantified.

Morgenthau believed that political action is not finite and precise. Therefore, if political concepts are to reflect accurately the hazy reality of politics, they must also be somewhat vague and imprecise. "The concept of national interest," argued Morgenthau, "is similar in two respects to the 'great generalities' of the American Constitution, such as the general welfare and due process. It contains residual meaning which is inherent in the concept itself, but beyond these minimum requirements its content can run the whole gamut of meanings that are logically compatible with it. That content is determined by the political traditions and the total cultural context within which a nation formulates its foreign policy."

The residual meaning inherent in the concept of national interest is survival. In Morgenthau's view, the minimum requirement of nation-states is to protect their physical, political, and cultural identity against encroachments by other nation-states. The preservation of physical identity is equated with the maintenance of the territorial integrity of a nation-state. Preservation of political identity is equated with preservation of existing political-economic regimes, such as democratic-competitive, communist, socialist, and authoritarian. Preservation of cultural identity is equated with ethnic, religious, linguistic, and historical norms in a nation-state. From these general objectives, argued Morgenthau, leaders can derive specific cooperative and conflictive policies, such as competitive armaments, balance of power, foreign-aid alliances, subversion, and economic and propaganda warfare.

Over the years, a number of challenging questions have been raised that emphasize the elusiveness of national interest as a political concept. First, how do we differentiate national interest from group, class, elite-establishment, or foreign-inspired interest? How, by whom, and on what basis are the national interests of the United States, Japan, China or Italy defined? Morgenthau's answer is simple, but not straightforward. The national interest is a compromise of conflicting political interests. It is not an ideal that is arrived at abstractly and scientifically, but a product of constant internal political competition. The government, through its various agencies, is ultimately responsible for defining and implementing national interest-oriented policies.

Second, what should be the scope and range of a country's national interests? Morgenthau responded categorically that a country's national interest should be proportionate to its capabilities. He would argue, for example, that it would be a mistake for countries such as France and Britain to aspire to superpower status. Further, Morgenthau would argue that nationalist universalism—aspiring to turn the world into the image of a single country—would be beyond the capabilities of any single state. So, the legitimate exercise of state power should not be equated with the arrogance of power.

Third, how should a country's national interests be related to the interests of other countries? A good diplomat, according to Morgenthau, is a rational diplomat, and a rational diplomat is a prudent diplomat. Prudence is the ability to assess one's needs and aspirations while carefully balancing them against the needs and aspirations of others: "The national interest of a nation that is conscious not only of its own interest, but also of that of other nations must be defined in terms compatible with the latter. In a multinational world this is a requirement of political morality; in an age of total war it is also a condition for survival." This observation coincides with Morgenthau's assumption that the international system is neither naturally harmonious nor condemned to inevitable wars. Morgenthau assumes varying levels of continual conflict and threats of war, which can be minimized by the piecemeal and prudent adjustment of conflicting interest by diplomatic action.

Finally, how should national interest be related to the requirements of collective security or regional security? Morgenthau opposed state action founded on abstract and universal principles other than that of national interest. If the security of every nation-state of the world is equated with the security of every other nation-state (a prerequisite of the theory of collective security), then conflict cannot be localized and disputes will quickly escalate and have dangerous consequences in the nuclear era. Morgenthau was thus skeptical toward leaders who justify their policies on the basis of collective security rather than plain national interest. He would, for example, have been systematically opposed to American intervention anywhere in the world in the name of principles such as democracy or collective security.

In regard to the relationship between national interests and regional or alliance interests, Morgenthau emphasized the precedence of national interests over regional interests. For Morgenthau, useful alliances are best supported by foundations of reciprocal advantage and mutual security of participating nation-states rather than by ideological or moralistic frameworks. A regional alliance that does not genuinely serve the interests of the participating nation-states is not likely to survive or be effective in the long run.

Viewing the realist school of thought as exemplified by Morgenthau, we are left with one central question: In the struggle between realist and idealist motivations of the human conscience, how does one pursue national interests prudently? The answer for the realist is that decisions concerning national interest should always be made on the basis of concrete and demonstrable national advantage rather than on the basis of abstract and impersonal criteria of morality, law, and ideology. A salient example of a statesman acting on the basis of concrete national advantage rather than moralistic principles was provided by President Abraham Lincoln. In August 1862, he wrote:

If there be those who would not save the Union unless they could at the same time save slavery, I do not agree with them. If there be those who would not save the Union unless they could at the same time destroy slavery, I do not agree with them. My paramount objective in this struggle is to save the Union and is not either to save or to destroy slavery. If I could save the Union without freeing any slave, I would do it, and if I could save it by freeing all the slaves, I would do it; and if I could save it by freeing some and leaving others alone I would also do that. What I do about slavery, and the colored race, I do because I believe it helps to save the Union; and what I forbear, I forbear because I do not believe it would help to save the Union. I shall do less whenever I shall believe what I am doing hurts the cause, and I shall do more whenever I shall believe doing more will help the cause. I shall try to correct errors when shown to be errors; and I shall adopt new views so fast as they shall appear to be true views. I have here stated my purpose according to my view of official duty; and I intend no modification of my oft-expressed personal wish that all men everywhere could be free.

This powerful passage contains the essence of the great debate between idealism and realism. The personal ideals of Lincoln clearly oppose slavery and favor freedom for all people everywhere. But his official duty is to safeguard the Union. When his personal ideals conflict with his official objectives, he is convinced that the ideals must give way to the duty—the perpetuation of the Union.

Morgenthau concluded that the debate between idealists and realists is not one of morality versus cynicism, but one of alternative conceptions of collective morality:

The contest between idealism and realism is not tantamount to a contest between principle and expediency, morality and immorality, although some spokesmen for utopianism would like to have it that way. The contest is rather between one type of political morality and another type of political morality, one taking as its standard universal moral principles abstractly formulated, the other weighing those principles against the moral requirements of concrete political action, their relative merits to be decided by a prudent evaluation of the political consequences to which they are likely to lead.

The challenge the United States has always faced has been to forge policies that could combine morality and realism that would be in keeping with the country's ideals without doing damage to its national interests. Morgenthau's work shaped the national debate about this challenge with an unprecedented intensity and clarity. The present reality is that America's moral principles and national interests are converging to a considerable extent. Events in one part of the world have a more far-reaching impact than ever before on the international environment and the country's national security. Even individual acts of violence by terrorists can affect the world in ways not possible before the advent of international electronic media.

United States

will achieve its national security goals only through a better integration of its multi-agency capabilities and the application of a systems approach. Observers are given to referring to this *modus operandi* as "smart power." America must blend economic, political, military, and sustainment components, while taking a long-term perspective. Emphasis should be on transfer of skills, self-reliance, and market forces.

In developing an integrated strategy, capabilities of the armed services to contribute should not be overlooked. The military services, in both uniformed and civilian members, have substantial support capabilities that are often what is needed in developing countries. The services can assist in planning, construction, and provision of health care, for example. They can provide training to engineers, health care specialists, and officials from host nations in public and private institution development and, in the process, provide an example of the role of the military in a democratic society, a role that is subordinate to civil authority.

GERALD R. FORD, 1913 - 2006

38th President Leaves A Legacy of Healing

Ford to Lie in State at Capitol Before Funeral At Cathedral

By PETER BAKER
Washington Post Staff Writer

A nation deeply polarized by war and partisanship came together yesterday to mourn Gerald Rudolph Ford as a healer during a previous era of division, while Washington began preparing an elaborate, pageantry-filled farewell for the most modest of presidents.

Ford, who died at his California home Tuesday night at age 93, will lie in state at the U.S. Capitol for two days starting Saturday. He is to be memorialized at a service at Washington National Cathedral on Tuesday, following the pattern set by Ronald Reagan's death two years ago.

With presidents and lawmakers of both parties assembling in the nation's capital for the occasion, the ceremonies marking Ford's passage promise to set a bipartisan tone to begin a week in which power will change hands in Washington. Two days after the funeral, Democrats will assume control of Congress for the first time in a dozen years, opening a period of divided government for the remainder of President Bush's time in office.

Ford's legacy as a bridge builder before, during and after his short presidency dominated the discus-

38

Chapter Two
National Expansion

ENDURING INTERESTS

Since the founding of the Republic, the United States has had at least six fundamental and long-term foreign policy objectives: freedom of the seas; pan-Americanism; protecting the security of North America; preserving the country's unity in the face of secessionist movements; securing control over national frontiers; and gaining access to global markets. In addition, a number of secondary interests have been identified throughout the country's history, for the most part to deal with specific situations. These have included disarmament, containment, nonrecognition of rogue states, commercial reciprocity, and good neighborism. National interests underpinning broader goals in the 20th century were couched in somewhat vague terminology as foreign policy objectives were defined in terms of specific enemies—above all, Nazi Germany, Imperial Japan, and the Soviet empire. The cardinal interests of the United States are largely constant, though. Whether or not discernible and prevailing threats are identified, these form the basis of relatively consistent policies.

Efforts to secure a political identity actually preceded the establishment of an independent republic by decades, as did the need to protect the physical safety of North America. Beginning in the late 17th century, the Americas faced threats of all sorts from the European powers. In 1716, for example, the governor of New France in what is now Canada remarked that "The English, on the first rupture between France and England, would employ all their efforts to seize the entirety of North America, whence might follow the loss of Mexico, from which they would expel the Spaniards in a few years without any resistance." To thwart Anglo-American expansion, the French sought alliances with the Indian nations and Spain. France lost its North American empire in the French and Indian War (1754–63), the counterpart of the Seven Years War in Europe, only to assist the American colonies in achieving their independence two decades later. Following the French Revolution, new threats from France against the young United States led to an undeclared war in the 1790s. Even the final eradication of a French presence in North America through the Louisiana Purchase in 1803 did not end French dreams of empire in the Americas.

Try as they might, people residing in North America have never succeeded in keeping out of Europe's great conflicts. American blood began to be shed in European wars toward the end of the 17th century. By most accounts, Europe was involved in nine major wars, defined as substantial combat on more than one continent, between 1688 and 1945, beginning with the War of the League of Augsburg. Americans fought and died in every one of these.

As early as the 1720s, the American colonists began to call for "all the Colonies appertaining to the Crown of Great Britain on the Northern Continent of America to be united under a Legal, Regular and firm Establishment; over which, it's proposed a Lieutenant, or Supreme Governour, may be constituted, and appointed to preside on the spot, to whom the Governours of each Colony shall be subordinate." Perhaps Great Britain's greatest error in judgment with respect to North America in the 18th century lay in its efforts to keep its American colonies divided and subjugated. It was reluctant even to entertain the possibility of permitting the formation of a North American assembly federated with the London Parliament. Colonial cooperation and unification were matters of security broadly defined, and mistrust of Britain extended to uncertainties about adequate defense provisions. Britain's refusal to transform its North American possessions into something like a commonwealth prompted Americans to rebel. Britain was fortunate not to have lost Canada in the bargain.

Following the achievement of American independence in 1783, efforts to realize closer national union, such as through the Articles of Confederation, failed because of the absence of strong central government. Under the Articles the weakness of the federal government gave rise to so many problems that historians refer to the political arrangement as "the critical period" of American history. Congress found itself virtually bankrupt because the states provided only a small part of the funds that it requested. Without effective control from above, the states acted like 13 separate little countries. They quarreled amongst themselves and engaged in disputes over their boundaries.

The Constitution of 1787 changed that, and thereafter the principal threat to American political cohesion took the form of regional secessionist movements. In the late 18th and early 19th centuries, federalists in America, those favoring a strong central government, were troubled by fears that disaffected Western settlers would secede or establish their own republics in French or Indian or Spanish-Mexican territory. President Thomas Jefferson, for example, accused his vice president, Aaron Burr, of committing treasonous acts by his involvement in efforts to establish a new Western republic. Jefferson's charges were probably justified. Although Burr's schemes remain mysterious, he apparently planned to separate the western part of the United States and unite it with territories west of the Louisiana Purchase. During the War of 1812, while the United States attempted to seize what is now Canada, pro-British New Englanders contemplated seceding from the Union and placing themselves once again under British rule. The greatest secession crisis was the American Civil War that lasted over four years from 1861–65 and resulted in over one million casualties, including dead, wounded and missing.

Threats to the control of frontiers were posed initially by incursions of hostile Indians from the trans-Appalachian regions and later by the political unrest in Mexico. A close historical parallel is to be found in European Russia, which bordered on Asian tribal groups in the northeast, and the Central Asian potentates and the wobbly Ottoman empire in the south. In drawing a distinction between frontiers and boundaries, observers as a rule define the latter as simply a territorial limit, whereas a frontier is often an unsettled area between different civilizations. European powers often armed and supported American native peoples hostile to settlers who themselves contributed to hostility by moving steadily westward. The conquest of native people eventually resolved the difficulties, but at tremendous human cost.

The Mexican War in the 1840s resulted in new frontier problems when the United States acquired a 2,000-mile border with a much poorer and often anarchic country. To this day, the United States has only partial control of this border and grudgingly tolerates a certain amount of smuggling and illegal migration. During the decade-long Mexican Revolution beginning around 1910, the U.S. military repeatedly launched strikes into Mexico in response to banditry and freebooting, at a time when the United States harbored concerns not only about social turmoil but also about great power interference of the sort Germany engaged in during the First World War.

To this day, instability in Mexico, which might result in many more millions of immigrants streaming into the United States, is a worrisome prospect for many Americans. Although such a dire scenario is unlikely, it is still in the back of American

United States

minds. Lingering apprehensions about the situation south of the border now reinforce U.S. policies to promote economic development and political liberalization in Mexico. Expanded trade with Mexico is a priority item on the national agenda not only because of the economic benefits accruing to America, but also because lucrative commerce helps make Mexico stable and prosperous. Once a relatively affluent Mexico joins in a more-or-less-equal partnership with its two North American neighbors, the U.S. southern border will cease to be a frontier and become a boundary similar to the one between the United States and Canada.

U.S. efforts to exclude French influence from Mexico in the 19th century illustrate the persevering commitment to continental security. In a blatant power grab, France took advantage of America's travails during the U.S. Civil War in the 1860s by developing a lucid scheme to establish permanent control of Mexico. Following French intervention in 1862 to overthrow Mexican President Benito Juarez, Napoleon III installed his relative, Maximilian of Austria, as emperor in Mexico in 1864. Preoccupied with the fighting raging in North America, the United States was in no position to expel the French from Central America. In 1866, though, with the Confederacy conquered, Secretary of State William Seward clarified to Napoleon III in no uncertain terms what a dim view Americans took of the Mexican adventure and respectfully requested that the French leave. The United States then dispatched a large, battle-hardened army to the Texas frontier, and France, already under pres-

William H. Seward
Courtesy of Special Collections,
University of Virginia Library

sure from indigenous insurgents, decided that prudence was the better part of valor and withdrew its forces. Maximilian and members of his entourage were summarily executed by the Mexicans who heartily supported this particular application of the Monroe Doctrine.

Great Britain also periodically meddled in the Americas in the 19th century and on several occasions actually endeavored to contain the growth of the United States, which in British eyes threatened Canada and British control of the Oregon territory. During the Napoleonic Wars after 1803, Britain so interfered with and hindered U.S. shipping and commerce that the United States declared war in 1812. In the 1840s, Britain, alarmed by U.S. continental ambitions, approached France and Mexico about an anti-U.S. alliance to preserve the status quo of the Republic of Texas, Mexico and California. Astute U.S. diplomacy prevented this encirclement by inducing the British to compromise in the partition of the Oregon territory. America then proceeded to annex California and other territories in the wake of the Mexican War of 1846–48.

In the late 19th century the rise of Russia, Japan and Germany eclipsed the potential British threat to the United States. Concern about a German naval challenge in the Western Hemisphere began around the turn of the century after German naval forces stood poised to attack the Philippines had the United States not struck first. Japanese aggression in Asia became a focus of U.S. attention beginning in the 1930s and culminated in the titanic conflict over vast stretches of sea and land in the 1940s. After the defeat of Japan and Germany in World War II, the Soviet Union became the chief Eurasian challenge to American continental security.

U.S. responses to episodic threats of great power interference reflect several basic foreign policy tenets. Any meddling in North America was and still is regarded as an unfriendly act. As the hemispheric hegemon, the United States allows no outside powers to play off any group against another, such as in the support provided to the Confederacy and other "causes." The Louisiana Purchase in 1803, the annexation of Texas in 1845, and the defeat of succession in 1865 represented in large part efforts to exclude the great powers from North America.

Beginning in the 20th century, the United States began to assert exclusive control over the sea, air, and space approaches to the hemisphere. What logically follows is that continental security also requires that the North Atlantic, the North Pacific, the Gulf of Mexico, the Caribbean, and the Arctic be essentially "American lakes." The United States en-

tered both great wars of the 20th century in part because of threats to its control of the continental sea approaches, by Germany's submarine warfare in both conflicts, and by the Japanese encroachments deep into the Pacific in the early 1940s. National missile defense initiatives during the cold war and thereafter sought to extend the principle of continental hegemony to the space approaches to the United States.

As articulated in the Monroe Doctrine of 1823, alliances of other American countries with hostile foreign powers are unacceptable in U.S. eyes. Enunciating the non-colonization principle, the Monroe Doctrine specified that the European powers should refrain from intervention in the Western Hemisphere. Like other aspects of U.S. foreign policy, the Monroe Doctrine had some precedent in colonial history, for example, in the Anglo-Spanish Treaty at the end of the War of Spanish Succession in 1713, which ensured that Spanish territories in the Americas not be ceded to another European power. Moreover, the Monroe Doctrine has been flexibly interpreted and applied since 1823. Theodore Roosevelt added his "Corollary" in the early 20th century, specifying that the United States reserved the exclusive right to safeguard stability and implement foreign claims against governments in the Western Hemisphere. The "Roosevelt Corollary" was used to justify several "gunboat diplomacy" operations and other interventions in Central America. It was officially disavowed by the administration of Franklin D. Roosevelt (1932–45) in connection with the "Good Neighbor" policy of the 1930s. Some regarded the "Corollary" as still constituting operational policy, though.

Access to overseas markets and resources has been a crucial facet of American policy since the colonial period, when the colonies opposed British imperial trade regulations. Throughout its history, the United States has advocated the non-preferential axiom regarding trade, especially for regions from which it feared its commercial enterprises would be excluded by rival powers. In the Oregon territory in the early 19th century, Britain and the United States agreed to an arrangement about trading rights with the indigenous peoples. Since the middle of the 19th century considerable American attention has been devoted to maintaining open markets in East Asia. One of the first significant U.S. efforts to secure commercial access to the Far East was Commodore Matthew Perry's visit to Japan with four warships in 1853 and with a substantially larger squadron the following year. Perry's display of force and assertive diplomacy paved the way for fu-

National Expansion

Commodore Matthew C. Perry

Courtesy of Library of Congress and Special Collections, University of Virginia Library

ture commercial agreements between the two countries.

The Open Door Policy of the early 20th century embodied American determination to preserve commercial access in East Asia. In September 1899, President William McKinley's secretary of state, John Hay, urged Britain, Germany, Russia, France, and Japan officially to accept the concept of equal commercial access to China. The McKinley administration wished to nip in the bud any effort by a great power to monopolize the Chinese markets. To this end, it developed a multilateral approach to maintaining trade relations. Following the outbreak of the nationalist Boxer Rebellion in 1900, which sought to rid China of its emperor as well as of foreigners, Hay made a follow-on recommendation, calling upon the great powers to uphold the principle of Chinese autonomy.

The U.S. appeal for Chinese independence was self-serving, of course, involving as it did the irresistible combination in diplomacy of principle and pragmatism. President Woodrow Wilson's administration continued to lend support to open door policies in East Asia. Secretary of State William Jennings Bryan offered to help China resist external interference and warned Japan not to abuse commercial arrangements with its neighbors or to challenge China's sovereignty when Japan entered World War I against Germany.

The same reasoning in this explains U.S. championing of decolonization in Africa and Asia, and the strong support for multilateral trade liberalization through institutions such as the General Agreement on Trade and Tariffs (GATT) after World War II. The goal of commercial access has also been achieved at times through bilateral deals, for example, the U.S.-Canadian free-trade agreement of 1990, later extended to Mexico, thereby establishing in 1994 the North American Free Trade Agreement (NAFTA).

INTERNATIONAL COMMERCE

National security concerns are seldom separable from economic motives, and these purposes have frequently gone hand-in-hand in U.S. history. Procuring New Orleans, San Francisco Bay, Hawaii, and the Panama Canal were at least as important for national defense as for commercial pursuits. Safeguarding the principle of freedom of the seas *vis-à-vis* Great Britain in the early 19th century and Germany a century later was critical to national security, and was essential for commercial access. Many 20th-century interventions in Latin America and the Caribbean—above all, those during the Wilson administration and the cold war—were motivated by widespread apprehensions about German or Soviet incursions into the Western Hemisphere.

At the same time, the United States has subordinated its pursuit of commercial access to broader national security concerns. Throughout the cold war, American policymakers tolerated East Asian and European discrimination against American products and services to avoid burdening the U.S.-led anti-Soviet partnership with trade disputes and to promote general alliance harmony. It should not be surprising that certain differences of opinion about trade and commerce have materialized since the end of the Soviet threat. Many Americans, both liberal and conservative, argue that the key to the American future lies far more in economic revitalization than in the pursuit of military power. They cite continuing economic tensions with Asian nations as symptomatic of America's growing economic plight. U.S. manufacturers, the automobile industry in particular, claim that, due to unfair trade practices, Asian producers have gained market share at their expense.

Nonetheless, historically, and largely because it so benefited from the squabbling of the great powers in the first decades of its existence, America's attitude has usually been one of deliberate distance from other countries. The United States should, recommended Thomas Jefferson, seek honest friendship with all nations, but "entangling alliances with none." Prior to the Second World War, every American entrance on the world stage was followed, sooner or later, by its withdrawal. For all the loose talk of American imperialism and covert action around the world, the United States has harbored no territorial ambitions since the end of the 19th century. Only Latin America had much cause to regard the United States as a menacing imperialist, meddling either

Commodore Perry's fleet in Tokyo Bay

United States

to protect property and commerce or to repulse communist insurgency.

At the dawn of the 21st century, achieving the basic and time-honored goals of U.S. foreign policy requires promoting an international environment in which

- critical regions are stable, at peace, and free from domination by hostile powers;
- international commerce and the global economy are growing;
- democratic norms and respect for human rights are widely accepted;
- the spread of nuclear, biological, and chemical (NBC) and other potentially destabilizing weapons technologies is minimized;
- the international community is willing and able to prevent and, if necessary, respond to calamitous events.

IN THE BEGINNING

Great Britain emerged from the Seven Years War (1756–1763), which ended the French empire in North America, as the world's most powerful nation. British fleets ruled the waves and the British empire extended over two hemispheres. Nonetheless, with the upsurge of British power came high and mighty arrogance, at least in the minds of many Europeans. Comparison between Britain and the empires of Greece and Rome were plentiful in an age of literary inspirations in the classical past. The writer Horace Walpole quipped that his contemporaries in England were "born with Roman insolence" and had "more haughtiness than an Asian monarch." Many Britons felt that the siege of Quebec deserved to be set alongside that of Troy as an epic of courage.

In the decade after the war's end, trouble brewed in Britain's American colonies. Outraged at what they considered callous and improper treatment, the colonials began to resist British suzerainty. Yet, even after the colonies were in open rebellion, most colonials hoped for reconciliation and reform. Rough handling of the Americans continued, though, and in July 1776, the Continental Congress declared the colonies independent. The official severance of relations with Britain was of major significance in world history. Foreign alliances became possible and the American declaration of independence offered the European powers an opportunity to wreak vengeance on Britain by assisting the American colonies. France, above all, was keen to weaken the British empire, and Catherine II of Russia remarked prophetically long before the colonies actually achieved independence that "they have told England goodbye forever."

What had begun as an intellectual and political revolt became an armed rebel-

Washington Taking Command of the Army
Courtesy of Special Collections, University of Virginia Library

Catherine the Great

lion, the consequences of which no one could foresee at the time. How had it come to this? It can be argued that the revolt began at Jamestown in 1607. For the most part, the people who migrated to the New World were rugged individualists who went their own ways and resented any interference or restraint. The nature of this New World—a wild, rough wilderness—encouraged, in fact, demanded, this characteristic if the settlements were to grown and prosper. Then, as the colonies developed and spread along the east coast, the English government tended to leave them to their own devices, its primary interest being in the passage of laws that protected the trade and industry of the mother country. The result was that the political relationship between England and the young colonies evolved too haphazardly. Bacon's rebellion against the Royal Governors' autocratic rule in Virginia in 1676 pointed up the inability of the English constitution to provide intelligent and satisfactory government for the ever-increasing number of Englishmen outside the realm. The great distance between the colonies and England, the mass influx of non-English peoples, the enormous extent of the American continent and the conditions existing in it, automatically created political, social, and economic ideas and values, divergent from those of the mother country. Thus, by the 1760s it seemed evident to many colonists that some dramatic events or startling occurrences which would emphasize these differences, some acts of provocation or unnecessary show of power and authority alone were needed to arouse a strong spirit of protest in the colonies. Once aroused, that spirit, if properly led and encouraged, would inevitably develop into a spirit of revolt should its demands not be met.

Then, in the 1760s Parliament passed the Stamp Act, which levied an internal tax on such things as legal documents and newspapers, and the Townshend Acts,

which put a duty or external tax on the importation of glass, paper, dyes, and tea. The strong, united opposition to these laws took the mother country by surprise, so both were repealed, with the exception of the tax on tea. But these taxes succeeded in keeping the spirit of revolt alive, and led to the formation of a secret organization known as the Sons of Liberty, begun by Sam Adams in Boston, which soon spread to the other colonies. Most of the members were extreme anti-British radicals, and they were not at all averse to rioting, looting, and other illegal activities. Under the leadership of Adams, the Massachusetts Assembly sent a circular letter to all the other colonies urging armed action. King George II then ordered the Royal Governors to dissolve any assembly that endorsed the letter. Wholesale dissolutions followed, as many of the colonies agreed with Massachusetts, including Virginia, whose action was most significant. Most of the taxes would have hurt the commercial colonies, but would have had relatively little effect on agricultural Virginia. Yet when the governor dissolved the Virginia Assembly, the delegates proceeded to Raleigh Tavern and adopted a nonimportation, nonconsumption agreement similar to those adopted by her sister colonies. Thus the landed gentry gave notice to the mother country that they would stand by the merchants and patriots of the commercial colonies when it came to the issue of right and freedom, regardless of the economic impact.

Even in the early stages of rebellion, France secretly permitted American warships ("privateers") to prey on British merchant shipping. In the autumn of 1776, Congress sent a commission to France to request military assistance. America's chief representative was Benjamin Franklin, the famous Philadelphian, who would succeed beyond all expectations in America's first diplomatic missions. In fact, the United States has seldom sent a person abroad better qualified for the task in hand. Franklin was known throughout Europe as the most distinguished person in America. His writings had been translated into several European languages and his thoughtful experiments captivated the science-loving French. In France, Franklin became the personification of the cause of freedom and he was often compared with Socrates, the Biblical prophets, and Jean-Jacques Rosseau's "noble savage," which he cultivated with his attire. He became the leading social figure of Paris and his portrait appeared on rings, medals, medallions, watches, bracelets and snuff boxes. French ladies even did him the honor of developing the *coiffure à la Franklin* in imitation of his fur cap. Following the American victory at Saratoga, New York, in 1778,

the French decided to come to the aid of "Franklin's troops" in a large way.

The signing of the Treaty of Comity and Commerce in 1778 constituted official recognition of the United States by France. When Britain responded with a declaration of war, the second and more important treaty came into force. The Franco-American Treaty of Alliance contained three crucial provisions. First, both nations pledged themselves to fight until American independence was "formally and tacitly assured." Second, neither France nor the United States would conclude a "truce or peace" with Britain without the "formal consent of the other obtained." Third, each of the two nations guaranteed the possessions of each other in America "mutually from the present time and forever against all other powers."

Spain joined France in the war against Britain in 1779. By this time, most of the major European trading nations had declared "armed neutrality" in an effort to avail themselves of the opportunities created by Britain's political woes. These included Russia, Prussia, Denmark, Norway, Sweden, the Holy Roman Empire and Portugal. Although none actually declared war, all took an unfriendly, even menacing attitude that complicated Britain's strategic situation. The enterprising Dutch, for their part, took advantage of Britain's misfortunes by snatching away trade and establishing profitable new markets in the Western Hemisphere, much of it in the contraband of war. Exasperated, the British finally found a pretext to declare war on the Netherlands in 1780 and dispatched a large fleet to seize Dutch possessions in the Caribbean. The operation tied down so many British ships, however, that a substantial French fleet was able to slip away from the West Indies to join a French-American army at Yorktown, Virginia, to force the surrender of the largest British army in the colonies in October 1781, in what would be one of the most decisive battles of the century.

Britain thus lost its American colonies and signed the Anglo-American Treaty, often known as the Peace of Paris, on September 3, 1783, with the full permission of the French. Britain recognized the independence of the United States and granted it extensive boundaries. The new Republic was to stretch westward to the Mississippi, with the northern border approximating the one existing now with Canada. The southern boundary was to be the frontier of Spanish Florida. The Treaty also secured for the Americans fishing privileges in the North Atlantic, chiefly on the Grand Banks of Newfoundland.

Portions of the treaty also dealt with loyalists in America. Tens of thousands of colonists had remained loyal to the Crown

The Mature Benjamin Franklin, 1777
Courtesy of Special Collections,
University of Virginia Library

United States

and had suffered confiscations, abuse, and exile. Over 80,000 had been driven from the United States. The parties to the treaty agreed that all persecutions should cease and that Congress would "earnestly recommend" that the states restore property taken from the loyalists. In light of the inflamed passions in America fueled by over seven years of warfare, the words were largely hollow. The recommendation was widely ignored and few loyalists had either property or rights restored.

THE NEW NATION AND ITS CONSTITUTION

The United States experienced six troubled years after independence in 1783. The country consisted of thirteen separate entities, each going its own way under a loose form of organization called "The Articles of Confederation." Apathy and bankruptcy threatened what passed for a central government and the new country enjoyed no respect abroad. Europeans did not bother with the United States and the very name of the country was a misnomer.

The Constitution of 1787, which replaced the Articles of Confederation, clothed the Federal government with sufficient power to deal vigorously with both domestic and foreign affairs. President George Washington selected as his Secretary of the Treasury the young Alexander Hamilton, who had almost miraculously reestablished American credit. The new Department of State was entrusted to Thomas Jefferson, then the U.S. minister to France. Hamilton and Jefferson were, in fact, politically quite different from one another and their rapport was not without frictions. Hamilton was a deeply conservative man who warmly admired British institutions. Jefferson was far more liberal and almost enamored of French civilization. He cared little for the English whom he once referred to in France as "rich, proud, hectoring, swearing, squibbling, carnivorous animals who live on the other side of the Channel."

Largely as a result of such differences, two principal political parties crystallized during the first Washington administration: the Federalists, led by Hamilton, and the Democratic-Republicans, led by Jefferson. The patriotism of neither could be doubted, but the Federalists believed that the interests of America would be better served by closer relations with England rather than with France. The Jefferson Republicans, for their part, favored closer relations with France rather than with England. Hamilton was so eager to preserve friendly interaction with Britain that he kept in close contact with British officials in America, even supplying them with confidential information.

In the early days of the nation, when the new Republic was still weak, its leaders knew that their political independence and their ideological democracy were threats to the existing great powers. Fearing these powers, Americans attempted to maintain neutrality amidst the European dynastic struggles. Yet this posture did not prevent them from playing off each of the great powers against the others. It is likely that the infant Republic was saved more than once from being snuffed out by the fact that the European powers were at one another's throats. No one of them could crush the United States and they could not agree to do it together. Europe's distress thus proved America's salvation. Early American leaders combined wisdom with good fortune, swallowing insults from the British and French and putting survival ahead of pride. The varying combinations of neutrality and balance-of-power politics were the basis for the strategies of Washington, of John Adams and John Jay, of Thomas Jefferson, James Monroe, and John Quincy Adams.

"I always consider the settlement of America with reverence and wonder," wrote John Adams in 1765, "as the opening of a grand scheme and design in Providence for the illumination and emancipation of the slavish part of mankind over all the earth." There is a literature of the "American mission" that stretches from the divines of the Colonial period to recent newspaper editorials proposing liberation of oppressed peoples. Nor is the global mission restricted to liberal internationalists. What affords this mission its strength has been the belief in the reality of American revolutionary idealism. Perhaps nothing better displays the intertwining of the tough-minded and the tender-hearted, the realist and the idealist, in American thinking than this notion of "liberation."

FIRST DIPLOMATIC STEPS

Cataclysmic events shook Europe to its core soon after the ratification of the

President Washington's First Cabinet. From left to right: Henry Knox, Thomas Jefferson, Edmund Randolph, Alexander Hamilton, George Washington.

Courtesy of Special Collections, University of Virginia Library

44

National Expansion

U.S. Constitution. In July 1789, less than three months after Washington's inauguration, the Parisian masses rose in revolt. Many Americans felt their own example had inspired the French uprising, which to a considerable extent it had, and they greeted the news with a wave of rejoicing known as "Bastille fever" and the "frenzy for France." The names of streets in the United States that suggested monarchical allegiance were altered. In Boston, for example, "Royal Exchange Alley" became "Equality Lane." Exclusive, and therefore supposedly undemocratic, societies fell into disrepute, including the scholarship fraternity, Phi Beta Kappa. Titles such as "Judge" and "Mister" that suggested social inequalities became simply "Citizen" in many republican circles, as in France. The worst fear of the European monarchs, it seemed, had come to pass. America's great experiment in democracy was succeeding and the rulers of France and Spain helped create a sort of Frankenstein monster that was to be their undoing.

The French Revolution entered upon a tyrannical phase in 1792, when the monarchs of Europe, assisted by many exiled nobles, invaded France to crush the Republican regime. When the French citizen army finally managed to hurl back the invaders, American enthusiasm appeared boundless. Crowds sang French songs and celebrated publicly.

Disillusionment with the French Revolution was not long in coming, though, at least in America. The miserable excesses of the revolution and the tyranny into which it sank alienated many Americans, especially the more conservative Federalists. For many, the French Revolution meant the end of private property, of religion, and even of freedom, those very things Americans held most dear. The international situation became perplexing for the United States when France declared war on Britain on February 1, 1793, the date that would actually mark the beginning of the crucible of fire, sword, and war that would last nearly a quarter of a century and into which the United States would be drawn several times. The Federalists soon came to regard Britain as civilization's hope, while the Jeffersonian Republicans continued to view Britain with disdain and considered the conflict another example of Britain's imperial scheming. Revolutionary France maintained its cadre of apologists and sympathizers in America, including Secretary of State Jefferson who quipped about the lingering revolutionary violence that a nation could not be transformed "from despotism to liberty in a featherbed."

The following year, 1794, the United States signed a commercial treaty with Britain, the widely criticized "Jay Treaty,"

which was the price of neutrality and stability in an increasingly turbulent world. Yet it also represented British acceptance of America on a more-or-less equal footing. Eleven years after independence, Britain displayed considerable generosity toward its former colonies by opening trade with the British Isles on a most-favored-nation (nondiscriminatory) basis and, moreover, by making available the East Indian trade. In the West Indies, though, direct American commerce was restricted to ships with a transport capacity of not more than 70 tons. The United States committed itself not to export certain tropical products, such as sugar and cotton, in American ships. This latter provision soon became crucial to America, since in 1793 Eli Whitney developed a serviceable cotton gin. The restriction on tropical products might have throttled the cotton industry in the Southern states of America had the treaty been strictly observed in the coming decades, which it was not. Even though it was unsatisfactory to America in some respects, the Jay Treaty went far in preventing war with Britain for nearly two decades.

The French, for their part, meddled repeatedly in American affairs. French agitators tried to arouse American public sentiment against Great Britain through the press and certain republican organizations. Attempts to bring about the defeat of George Washington for reelection in 1796 and the elevation of the pro-French Thomas Jefferson to the presidency caused considerable popular indignation. Against the backdrop of war in Europe and the intrigue of the belligerents at home, President Washington issued a sober warning to the American people in his Farewell Address in 1796. In particular, he expressed his disgruntlement with the increase in partisan feelings in America that encouraged people to harbor strong likes and dislikes of foreign countries. He remarked:

Nothing is more essential than that permanent, inveterate antipathies against particular nations and passionate attachments for others should be excluded, and that in place of them just and amicable feelings toward all should be cultivated. The nation which indulges toward another an habitual hatred or an habitual fondness is in some degree a slave . . . Against the insidious wiles of foreign influence (I conjure you to believe me, fellow-citizens) the jealousy of a free people ought to be constantly awake . . .

Washington also discussed "formal entanglements," for which the speech is best known. Regarding such disputes as caused by the "forever French alliance" concluded during the American War of Independence, Washington asserted, "It is

our true policy to steer clear of permanent alliances with any portion of the foreign world . . . but we may safely trust to temporary alliances for extraordinary emergencies." This position would be widely quoted thereafter as justification for America's isolation from the wider world.

That is too narrow an interpretation. Washington was offering specific advice to a struggling and squabbling nation in difficult times. To read his statements as a policy recommendation in perpetuity is probably to misconstrue the meaning. The policy of noninvolvement he advocated was not so much detachment from Europe as it was the barring of European intrigue from America. The American people might then have the blessings of liberty without being an appendage of European imperialism. The course Washington recommended, though, struck such a chord with those harboring isolationist instincts, extending far back into colonial times, that it was destined to become a shibboleth of policy.

Tensions with France mounted in the 1790s, and in June 1793, commerce with France was suspended by act of Congress. That same month, President John Adams declared to Congress: "I will never send another minister to France without assurances that he will be received, respected, and honored as the representative of a great, free, powerful, and independent nation." In July 1798, Congress finally acknowledged that the two treaties of 1778 with France were void on the ground that

they had been repeatedly violated by the French government.

An undeclared naval war with France ensued in 1798, lasting over two-and-a-half years. The small U.S. navy, supplemented by privately owned vessels, captured more than 80 armed French ships, most of them operating in Caribbean waters against American merchantmen. George Washington was called out of retirement to command an army of 10,000 men to fight the French on land should it become necessary. The former president was aged and in poor health, though, and actual command was held by Hamilton, battle-hardened at a tender age during the War of Independence. Hamilton and the Federalists spoiled for a fight, especially if an altercation might result in the seizure of New Orleans, Florida and Mexico from Spain, which had allied itself with France in 1796. Major conflict did not occur, however, and Hamilton never had the opportunity to fight on Britain's side.

The election of 1800 swept the Federalists from office and elevated Jefferson to the presidency. Still pro-French but opposed to European involvements of any sort, Jefferson also rebuked "entangling alliances" in his inaugural address and committed his administration to frugality and a reduction of the national debt. A vigorous opponent of war, he advocated mothballing the Navy's heavy warships. "Peace is our passion" was his ringing declaration. Advocating a strict (narrow) construction of the Constitution, he chided the Federalists for bolstering the federal government. Jefferson still displayed considerable revolutionary idealism, yet he was fearful of allowing its logic to carry America into foreign military adventures. He seemed somehow convinced that America could best perform its historic mission by cultivating its own continental garden.

The new president quickly confronted the hard realities of a complex world. Attacks by the Barbary pirates against American citizens and property in the Mediterranean area had for years represented a humiliating outrage. Presidents Washington and Adams had been forced to "purchase" treaties with three North African states, Algiers, Tripoli and Tunis, and by dispatching tens of thousands of dollars for "protection" (read: extortion). It was bitterly ironic that at the very time the slogan "Millions for defense but not one cent for tribute" gained wide currency, the United States was paying substantial sums in blackmail money to petty North African tyrants. National degradation reached its nadir, when in October 1800, the dey of Algiers forced a U.S. warship, mockingly named the "George Washington," to haul down the Stars and Stripes, replace it with the banner of Algiers and

sail to Istanbul with an ambassador and presents for the sultan.

The simmering confrontation came to blows in May 1801 when the pasha of Tripoli, apparently angered at the paucity of the shakedown payoffs, declared war on the United States and proceeded to chop down the flagstaff at the American consulate. Although scarcely enamored of the navy and no enthusiast for war under any circumstances, Jefferson was nonetheless determined to counter the insult to the flag and to chastise the Barbary pirates. Deeply concerned about the safety of U.S. seamen and keenly aware of past Barbary brutalities, Jefferson bit the bullet and took a hard line. He began dispatching U.S. warships to the Mediterranean. After a number of vicious sea fights over the next years, he was able to force Tripoli to sign a favorable treaty, which nonetheless required a payment of $60,000 in ransom for the return of U.S. prisoners. Jefferson's commitment to frugality and peace had gone out the window.

The War of 1812 delayed a thorough chastisement of the remaining North African pirates, but in 1816 the United States dictated at gunpoint an altogether satisfactory treaty from its perspective with Algiers. The pirate state, and later both Tunis and Tripoli, were finally forced to pay for losses over the years to American shipping. Jefferson's decisive action inaugurated operations that freed American commerce in the Mediterranean, strengthened patriotic feelings at home, and fostered a new respect for the United States in the world. By accepting the tough realities, the man of peace reaped a rich harvest by drawing the sword.

RECONSTRUCTING STRICT CONSTRUCTIONISM

Popular attention was drawn in the early 1800s to a more pressing problem in North America, the future of the Louisiana Territory. The French ceded this immense tract to Spain in 1762 as compensation for losses to Britain during the Seven Years' War. Yet few Frenchmen could forget the loss, and in the early 1790s, the French began concocting plans to regain the vast expanse of land. Napoleon Bonaparte and his cohorts developed a vision to regain a lost colonial empire in North America. In fact, the trans-Mississippi colony had become such a liability for Spain that the latter was eager to dispose of it. Administration and defense of the colony were expensive undertakings Spain could ill afford. Louisiana was a standing invitation to an invader and was likely to fall during hostilities with Britain or the United States. Spain regarded Louisiana chiefly as a buffer for its more valuable possessions to the

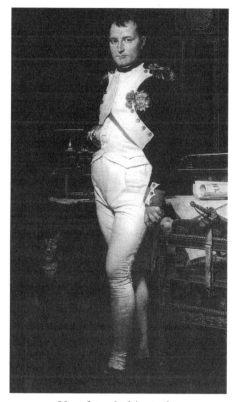

**Napoleon in his study,
by Jacques-Louis David, 1812**
National Gallery of Art, Washington, D.C.

south. If France could be persuaded to take over Louisiana, it would bear the cost of keeping aggressors in check with a minimal burden to Spain. In 1800, the terms of transfer from Spain to France were specified whereby Napoleon offered to give the son-in-law of the Spanish king the Italian kingdom of Tuscany in exchange for all of Louisiana. Two years would lapse before the Spanish king, displaying a growing mistrust of Napoleon, finally signed the fateful order in October 1802.

American Westerners, whose wartime prosperity was substantially reduced by the temporary 1802 Peace of Amiens between Britain and France, began expressing their well-founded worries. The loss of the "right of deposit," that is, the authorization to land cargoes while waiting for oceangoing ships, invited a showdown. The Spanish authorities in New Orleans, allegedly in response to American smuggling, suspended the right of deposit in violation of the Pinckney Treaty of 1795. Westerners assumed the decree had been dictated by Napoleon and that a complete closure of the river would ensue once the French officially took control of Louisiana.

President Jefferson soon shared the worries. The looming crisis in Louisiana, he wrote, was "the most important the United States have ever met since their independence." He was content to have weak Spain as a neighbor since the country could not threaten anyone. Moreover, he and many others were convinced the Americans could take what they wanted when they wanted it. Yet, French possession was an entirely different matter. French control might have distinctly adverse effects for the growing young country. Hence, pragmatism would triumph again. Faced with the hard realities of the situation, the pro-French Jefferson abandoned his principles of frugality, peace and, above all, strict constructionism. "We stand completely corrected of the error that either the Government or the nation of France has any remains of friendship for us." With the eventual acquisition of Louisiana in 1803, Jefferson would more than double the size of the United States, and would virtually ensure the opening of the entire continent to American settlement. So great were Jefferson's anxieties at the time of French acquisition that he would write to the American minister in Paris: "The day that France takes possession of New Orleans, fixes the sentence which is to restrain her forever within her low-water mark . . . from that day we must marry ourselves to the British fleet and nation."

Here was a politician, whose warnings against "entangling alliances" was still fresh in some minds, proposing an entanglement with his former enemy, Britain, possibly to fight his former friend, France, a country that had relinquished republicanism for tyranny. Jefferson matched his words with deeds, undertaking forceful military measures in the Mississippi Valley in anticipation of French acquisition of Louisiana. Congress, reflecting the popular mood, authorized the president to request 80,000 militiamen from the state governors for federal service.

The French never posed a threat from Louisiana, and fortune once again smiled on the young Republic. Napoleon became disillusioned with colonies in the Western Hemisphere following the loss of an entire army in an attempt to reconquer Santo Domingo in 1802. "Damn sugar, damn coffee, damn colonies," he roared as the extent of the French defeat in the Caribbean became clear. Louisiana's destiny was closely connected to the unfolding crisis in Europe. The Peace of Amiens was merely an interlude in the monumental struggle for the mastery of Europe. A few victorious campaigns would more than compensate for the Santo Domingo debacle, the French reasoned. Moreover, France could not hold Louisiana against British naval power, so it made sense to sell the entire territory to the Americans. French coffers were already depleted and the resumption of hostilities in Europe would be an expensive proposition. Napoleon was thus keen to sell the entire territory.

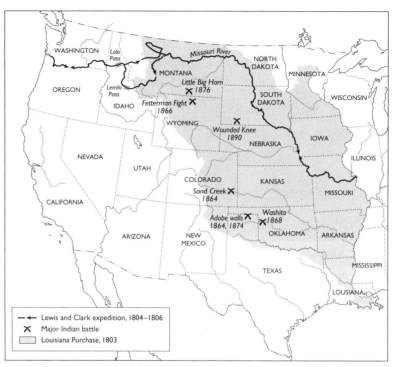

Map of Lewis and Clark Expedition

The U.S. envoys, Robert Livingston and James Monroe, exceeded their instructions to pay $10 million for New Orleans and as much land *east* of the city as they could negotiate. In April 1803, Livingston and Monroe concluded a deal for all of Louisiana for $15 million. They banked on the common sense of the president and the American people to uphold their decision. Jefferson recognized what was at stake. "On the globe," he wrote, "there is one single spot, the possessor of which is our natural and habitual enemy. It is New Orleans, through which the produce of three eighths of our territory must pass to market."

Moreover, Jefferson dreamed of extending the country to the Pacific Ocean and the acquisition of a large part of the continent moved him closer to realizing his vision of an empire of liberty. The Louisiana Territory was in fact so vast that there was considerable uncertainty about its actual boundaries. The only undisputed limits were the Mississippi River on the east and the Gulf of Mexico on the south. No one was quite sure whether it included western Florida or parts of Texas. The French had no answer, as reflected in the famous quip of their foreign minister, Charles Maurice Talleyrand, that "I can give no direction, but you have made a noble bargain for yourselves, and I suppose you will make the most of it." A noble bargain it was indeed: the Americans had purchased the western part of the world's most valuable river valley bordered somewhere by British North America. Paying

about $18 a square mile, the United States had made one of the sweetest real-estate deals in history. The French foreign minister, who negotiated the Louisiana treaties, later recalled that Livingston remarked at the signing: "We have lived long, but this is the noblest work of our whole lives . . . From this day the United States take their place among the powers of the first rank . . . The instruments which we have just signed will cause no tears to be shed: they prepare ages of happiness for innumerable generations of human creatures."

Shortly after clinching the deal, Jefferson dispatched an expedition to explore the new western territories of the United States and beyond. In their legendary two-year voyage, beginning in 1803, Meriwether Lewis and William Clark traveled some 8,000 miles, following the Missouri River upstream as it ascended the Rocky Mountains and crossed the Snake and Columbia rivers on the way to the Pacific. Although the party ran out of such luxuries as whiskey and tobacco, it was not wanting for writing materials and was able to contribute to America's rich literary legacy. Clark served as the artist and cartographer of the expedition.

The crippling of Spain, resulting from its unhappy alliance with France and the conflict with Britain, and its even more costly war with France and subsequent alliance with Britain, provided the Spanish-American colonies with the opportunity to slip the leash, paving the way for the cession of Florida to the United States in 1819. Also related to the events in Europe

United States

States, in their view, should have been fighting against the great despot, Napoleon, on the side of the surviving defender of constitutional government in Europe.

The United States was unprepared for war, and its military forces were inadequate and scattered. The poorly trained militia were often useless against disciplined, regular troops. An ill-conceived invasion of Canada failed although American forces achieved notable successes on the Great Lakes and in Michigan. America's wartime fortunes hit rock bottom in August 1814, when a powerful British force landed in the Chesapeake Bay area, put the defending militia to flight, and entered the capital. The British torched most of the public buildings, including the Capitol and the White House, while President Madison and his entourage helplessly watched the billowing smoke from the distant hills. It was not one of the finer moments of U.S. military history.

War weariness in Britain, fresh dangers emerging in chaotic Europe, and the tenacity of the American military helped produce a conciliatory British attitude at Ghent, where a peace treaty was signed in December 1814. In the Treaty of Ghent, both governments agreed to restored conditions as they had existed prior to war, or *status quo ante bellum*. Impressment and Orders in Council were both phased out prior to the signing of the treaty and European peace removed them as current hazards.

In the wake of the conflict, the people of the United States acquired a far stronger sense of national unity. Arguably it was under President Madison that the struggling young Republic won an equal position among the free nations of the world and began its long but steady climb to leadership. New industries sprang up to produce goods formerly imported from Great Britain. To save these "infant industries" from foreign competition, Congress enacted a protective tariff. A vigorous program of internal improvements—roads, canals, and railroads—strengthened the American economy and further helped unify the country.

A CAUTIONARY TALE

Following the Napoleonic Wars, the monarchs of Europe joined together to eliminate liberal and democratic movements that might once again threaten their autocratic rule. In crushing any challenge to their efforts to restore the idyllic world as they perceived it prior to 1789, they endeavored to make that world irretrievably safe from democracy. The forces of reaction in Europe became sources of considerable apprehension in America, the cradle of democratic ideals. Many in

America feared that the European powers would shift their attention to the Spanish-American republics in their efforts to turn back the political clock. And who was to say whether they would stop there? The opportunity beckoned to eliminate the all-too-visible and successful democracy in North America, it was feared, and few put it past the European monarchies to try just that. Even if the great powers did not attack the United States directly, they could seize territory dangerously close by and reestablish autocratic rule there.

Some U.S. administration officials, above all Secretary of State John Quincy Adams, shrewdly assessed the strategic situation from another perspective. Should the European powers decide to intervene in Latin America or the Caribbean, the British navy would surely thwart their operations. Britain was intent on keeping the Latin American markets open, so regardless of what policies the United States pursued, foreign intervention would be unlikely. Safeguarded by Britain's "wooden walls," America could sound a defiant republican trumpet blast toward the Continental monarchies. The lucky Republic would once again take advantage of Europe's distresses. President James Monroe resolved to anchor the U.S. position in doctrine and make the Western Hemisphere the special preserve of the United States.

Enunciating significant nonintervention and anti-imperial principles, the president specified in his annual address to Congress

in December 1823 that . . . "The occasion has been judged proper for asserting that the American continents, by the free and independent condition which they have assumed and maintain, are henceforth not to be considered as subjects for future colonization by any European powers." Monroe went on to state that "the political [monarchical] system of the allied powers is essentially different . . . from that of America . . . We owe it, therefore, to candor and to amicable relations existing between the United States and those powers to declare that we should consider any attempt on their part to extend their system to any portion of this hemisphere as dangerous to our peace and safety." This assertion became the "Monroe Doctrine."

Americans were shaking their fists collectively at potential oppressors. Sympathetic to democracy everywhere, Americans championed the freshly minted republics that had thrown off Spanish shackles. To be sure, Americans were only secondarily concerned about their neighbors and primarily interested in defending themselves from foreign adventurism. The administration proclaimed its determination to repel any European incursion in the Western Hemisphere.

Promulgation of the "Monroe Doctrine" elevated spirits countrywide, and nothing better illustrated the rising tide of nationalism in the United States than the confident defiance shown toward the reactionary autocrats. The brave new doctrine struck a popular chord. One newspaper editorialized that it "has been received throughout the country with a warm and universal burst of applause." Another captured its essence in stating: "If the Holy Alliance attempt to control the destinies of South America, they will find not only a British lion, but an American eagle in the way." More of the former than the latter: American military forces were small, but unchallengeable British sea power prevented the doctrine from becoming a scrap of paper.

MANIFEST DESTINY

From the outset, American statesmen realized the importance of the Western territories and therefore adopted policies designed to attract settlers. The first great step was taken even before the Constitution was ratified, when the Congress of the Confederation passed the Northwest Ordinance of 1787. This law dealt with the future of the rich territory northwest of the Ohio River, and the settlers to the area were promised a considerable measure of self-government. As soon as a district had 60,000 inhabitants, it could apply to Congress for admission into the Union as a state. The new states were to

National Expansion

of the country's history, from the War of 1812 through the era of Manifest Destiny to today's bitter conflicts, demonstrates that the American attitude toward the world has been far more nationalistic than that of non-frontier countries and that this attitude has been strongest in the newest regions. Similarly, the pioneering experience converted settlers into individualists. Gain was the magnet that attracted most migrants to the cheaper lands of the West, while once there they lived in units where cooperative enterprise—for protection against the Indians, for cabin-raising, law enforcement, and the like—was more essential than in the better established towns of the East. Yet the fact remains that the abundant resources and the greater social mobility of frontier areas did instill into frontiersmen a uniquely American form of individualism.

The resolve to expand had numerous unintended consequences. Above all, sectional differences arose over the "peculiar institution" of slavery. The federal government and the individual states both claimed authority in the territories. The southern slave states were keenly interested in the expansion of slavery into new areas. But who would exercise primary control of the rights and policies of Western settlers? This fundamental question of the nation's existence was ultimately settled on the ghastly battlefields of the Civil War.

One of the greatest misfortunes of American history was that the persistent urge to enlarge and develop collided fiercely with the resolve of native Americans to protect their tribal lands. The sad saga is now well known. In 1830 President Andrew Jackson pushed through Congress the Indian Removal Act that authorized white settlement in the vast territory still held by the Indians east of the Mississippi River. The act, he said, would allow those states "to advance rapidly in population, wealth, and power." The human cost was formidable. In 1838, for example, federal troops brutally forced the Cherokee Indians from their land in the dreadful episode known as the "Trail of Tears." Most of the Indians died.

ADVANCES IN DEMOCRACY

Political ideas changed to keep pace with new conditions. Democracy in America was further strengthened by the growing influence of the West. The spirit of equality flourished in the new states along the frontier. They granted universal male suffrage, abolished property qualifications for holding public office, and introduced other important reforms. Gradually, these democratic reforms were also adopted by the older states.

be equal in all respects to the 13 original states. Thus the Northwest Ordinance assured all Americans of equal status and avoided the creation of resentful colonies. The same judicious procedure was later followed for other territories and represented an important factor in the rapid settlement of the West.

People moved west for the abundant land and the seemingly inexhaustible resources. Westward expansion rolled on: nine frontier states had joined the original thirteen between 1791 and 1819. With an eye to preserving the North-South sectional balance, most of these commonwealths had been admitted alternatively, free or slaveholding. The expansion continued the generations-old westward movement, which had been going on since early colonial days. In addition, the siren call of cheap lands—the "Ohio fever"—had a special appeal to European immigrants. Land exhaustion in the older tobacco states, where the soil was "mined" rather than cultivated, likewise drove people westward.

The Western boom was stimulated by additional developments. Economic distress turned many saddened faces toward the setting sun. The crushing of the Indians in the Northwest and South soothed the frontier and opened up vast virgin tracts of land. The building of highways improved the land routes to the Ohio Valley. A noteworthy route was the Cumberland Road, begun in 1811, which ran ultimately from western Maryland to Illinois. The employment of the first steamboat on Western waters, also in 1811, heralded a new era of upstream navigation.

In 1810, only a seventh of white Americans lived west of the Appalachians. By 1840, more than a third did. Some critics argued that the continent was too large to exist as a single country, but technology—

steamboats, canals, railroads—proved them wrong and helped create a national market economy. With rising nationalism following the War of 1812, expansionism became not just an economic necessity but an ideological one also. John L. O'Sullivan wrote in 1845 of "the right of our manifest destiny to overspread and to possess the whole of the continent which Providence has given us for the development of the great experiment of liberty." According to the proposition of Manifest Destiny, it was God's will that the United States control the continent. The frontier accentuated the spirit of nationalism and individualism in the United States. Every page

Reenactment of Indian fighting in the South in the 1820s

Andrew Jackson

Courtesy of Special Collections,
University of Virginia Library

51

United States

Democratic influences made notable gains during the administration of Andrew Jackson (1829–1837). The first Westerner to occupy the White House, Jackson claimed to be a "people's president," or what would now be known as a populist. He refused to renew the charter of the Bank of the United States, which he perceived to be unduly controlled by Eastern banking interests. He successfully fought other groups demanding special privileges. The Jacksonian era also brought social changes, with humanitarian causes enjoying widespread support and public education spreading rapidly.

Throughout the Jacksonian era the movement westward continued. Thousands of Americans settled in Texas, then a province of Mexico. When friction developed with the Mexican government, the Texans revolted and won their independence in 1836. A few years later, Texas was annexed to the United States. A dispute over the Texas boundary then led to war between the United States and Mexico.

Mexico had long threatened war if the United States should attempt to annex Texas. By 1846, the will to maintain peace was no longer present on either side and aggressiveness was in fact rampant in the United States, where, according to some newspapers, the majority of Americans "would rather have a little fighting than not." The *New York Journal of Commerce* asserted simply "Let Us Go To War," while the *Richmond Enquirer* editorialized that the American people wanted "a full and thorough chastisement of Mexican arrogance and folly." Many Mexicans seemed even more eager to fight the Americans than vice versa. Moreover, Mexican military leaders were somehow convinced the United States would not fight, and there was even talk of invading Louisiana, arming the slaves and inciting the Indians to rebellion. Some Mexicans hoped for the outbreak of war between Britain and the United States over other boundary disputes, which might give Mexico a free hand in the Southwest.

When the United States won the Mexican War (1846–1848), it annexed a vast area in the Southwest, including some of the richest territory in North America. Mexico and the United States concluded a peace treaty at Guadalupe Hidalgo in February 1848. The accord ceded New Mexico and California to the United States, and acknowledged the U.S. claim to Texas to the Rio Grande River. This huge area was approximately one-half the size of Mexico. The United States agreed to pay an indemnity of $15 million and assume the claims of its citizens for around $3 million. Two years prior, in 1846, the United States and Britain arranged a peaceful settlement

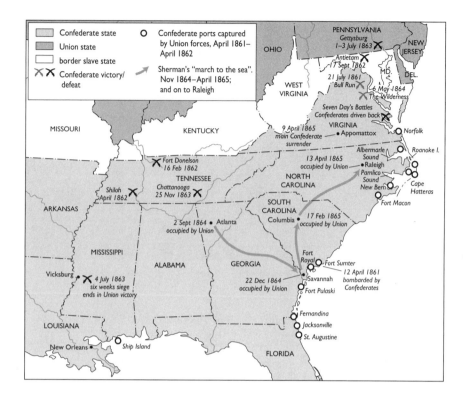

of their conflicting claims to the Oregon Territory in the northwest. Thus, by the middle of the 19th century, America's boundaries extended in an almost unbroken expanse from the Atlantic Ocean to the Pacific. In December 1853, a prominent Southern railway magnate serving as minister to Mexico, James Gadsden, succeeded in negotiating a treaty whereby Mexico agreed to sell a large area now comprising the southern portions of Arizona and New Mexico. In addition to expanding the United States even farther in the southwest, the Gadsden Purchase in 1853 secured a coveted railroad route, still utilized by the Southern Pacific line. Nonetheless, the Treaty of Guadalupe Hidalgo hardly ended tensions between Mexico and the United States, which would endure for decades, well into the next century.

The acquisition of new territory brought to a head America's most troublesome problem—Negro slavery. In the South, it had long been the custom to use black slaves on the large plantations. Most Southerners defended this practice, offering the self-serving argument that slaves were better off in the South than were people in many other areas of the world, including in factories in Northern American cities. Many Northerners, on the other hand, considered slavery contrary to democratic and Christian principles. A relatively small group, the abolitionists, angered the South enormously by demanding that slavery be abolished at once. If the slavery issue had not come

to the forefront of American politics in the 1850s, the United States would, in all likelihood, have expanded even more than it did. After all, the vast imperial expanse of Texas, the Mexican cession territories, and Oregon had fallen into U.S. hands in less than five years. Even European countries displayed a grudging admiration for Yankee military prowess and diplomatic acumen. Astute Europeans recognized the emergence of a potential great power. In the 1850s, U.S. officials were able to remark for the first time without wincing: "The Europeans do not love us, but they are compelled to respect us."

By the late 1700s, so much tobacco had been grown in the South that the soil was wearing out. Throughout the nation, many believed that the practice of slavery would fade away along with the tobacco industry. Except for the innovation of a clever Northerner named Eli Whitney, such would in all likelihood have been the case. In 1792, Whitney visited a Southern plantation, where he was told that agriculture in the Southern states could easily produce huge amounts of cotton, but that the process of separating cotton lint from seeds was too arduous and hence uneconomical.

When Whitney designed a machine, the cotton gin, to assist with the separation procedure, the South's cotton industry was born. By 1850, the South had become the world's largest producer, exporting more than a million tons of cotton a year. Along with the burgeoning industry, the number of slaves in the South rose to over

National Expansion

Also in 1854, antislavery Northerners formed the new Republican Party, which was pledged to bar any further expansion of slavery. When Northern and Southern Democrats split on this question, the Republican candidate, Abraham Lincoln, was elected president in 1860. Eleven Southern states thereafter seceded in fairly rapid succession, forming the Confederate States of America.

The American Civil War, or the War Between the States (as it was known in the South) lasted four years and cost the lives of over a half-million Americans. The federal government had the advantage of greater manpower and industrial production. Furthermore, it was eventually able to impose an effective naval blockade, which deprived the Confederacy of essential supplies from abroad. The war decided two major issues, with the Union being preserved and the slaves freed. Nonetheless, over a generation passed before the scars of defeat in the Southern states began to heal.

The Civil War was one of the most critical periods in U.S. diplomatic history. Many Americans at the time feared that the European powers, casting greedy eyes upon North American territory and resources, would conduct themselves in accordance with the time-honored "divide and rule" principle of international affairs. Britain, which was inclined to favor the separation of the Confederacy from the Union for geostrategic reasons, quickly recognized the belligerency status of the South under international law and

Federal troops take Vicksburg, 1863

four million, approximately a third of the population of the entire region. Most of these slaves worked the fields to produce what the planters called "King Cotton."

The slavery question was further complicated by disputes between the North and South over the tariff and other issues. The interests of the Southern plantation owners, who had to sell most of their cotton abroad, conflicted with those of the Northern industrialists and factory workers, who for the most part demanded protective duties. Since the North was growing far more rapidly in population than the South, it would inevitably gain control of Congress and pass the laws it wanted. Long champions of "states' rights," Southerners asserted vigorously that each state had the right to set aside Federal laws of which it disapproved and even to secede from the Union if it so wished.

Relations between the North and South reached a breaking point over the issue of slavery in the new territories. The position taken by the slaveholders was that they could take their human property wherever they settled. Those Northerners who did not advocate the abolition of slavery sought to restrict slavery to the states where it already existed. Attempts to achieve a compromise failed. In 1854, Congress passed the Kansas-Nebraska Act declaring that the people in these two territories should decide the slavery issue for themselves. They hardly settled the issue peacefully. To the contrary: both the proslavery and antislavery settlers organized and brought in weapons, setting the stage for civil war. So many settlers were wounded and killed that the territory soon became known as "Bleeding Kansas." Violence in fact spread throughout the states and territories, and even to the halls of Congress. After one Northern senator spoke out against slavery, a Southern senator brutally beat him with his cane. The nation slid into rapid social decline.

Portrait of General Robert E. Lee by Swiss painter Frank Buchser, 1869

United States

Napoleon III
Courtesy of Special Collections,
University of Virginia Library

proclaimed its own neutrality. The South relied on "King Cotton diplomacy" to win British and French support, but alternative sources and substitutes largely undermined Southern hopes. Furthermore, President Abraham Lincoln's Emancipation Proclamation of 1863 substantially improved the moral position of the United States to many Europeans. Depriving the Confederacy of any semblance of moral cause, while raising the epic struggle to a crusade in the eyes of many at home and abroad, the Proclamation represented one of the great masterstrokes in U.S. diplomatic history. Even the conservative elites of Britain were uneasy about thwarting the efforts of a government to end slavery where it was most widespread. The able and astute U.S. minister in London reported in the autumn of 1863: "The Emancipation Proclamation has done more for us here than all our former victories and our diplomacy. It is creating an almost convulsive reaction in our favor all over this country." British abolitionist senti-

ment proved stronger than the attraction of some members of the nobility to the genteel Southern aristocracy.

France under Emperor Napoleon III turned the civil conflict in North America to good account, intervening in Mexico and placing his relative the Austrian Hapsburg Prince Maximilian on the throne. Resentful of the growing power of the United States, Napoleon ardently hoped for a permanent division of the North American republic. An independent Confederacy, he reasoned, would ultimately support his satellite empire in Central America. A United States permanently sundered would be unable to invoke the Monroe Doctrine, allowing for the founding of French colonies in Latin America. Proudly trumpeting the rescue of the Catholic Church in Mexico from the anticlerics, he was in fact responding to pleas from Mexican monarchists to erect a Latin, Catholic kingdom as a bulwark against the "Anglo-Saxon" colossus to the north.

Yet, Napoleon III never officially recognized the Confederacy either. It is ironic that, despite the country's strong republican tradition, French public opinion seemed more favorably disposed toward a slave state than did popular British sentiment. Napoleon would not move until the British did, and British leaders were always apprehensive about the prospect of war with the United States. Neutrality offered certain advantages to both European powers—above all, profitable trade. Many in Britain were convinced that the South was going to win its independence in any event. Thus, war was an unnecessary risk, in the prevailing view of British officialdom, especially if the future of Canada were on the line. War with the United States might well have changed everything. In the end, the external threat that America posed to Canada contributed to a stable and more unified country. As usual, Canada was vulnerable to invasion.

By assuming a Confederate victory, Napoleon III had bet on the wrong horse, and in time, French plans went very awry. For starters, France had purchased large amounts of Confederate bonds that by the end of the conflict were not worth the paper on which they were written. In the spring of 1865, the United States began warning of dire consequences should Napoleon not terminate his Mexican adventure. Paris riposted that it "derived neither pleasure nor satisfaction" from the American position. The following year, Secretary of State William Seward finally threw down the gauntlet by declaring: "We shall be gratified when the Emperor shall give to us definitive information of the time when French military operations may be expected to cease in Mexico." The federal government had at its disposal the

largest and most battle-hardened army in the world at the time, and only the willfully blind could discount American determination. France's challenge to the Monroe Doctrine rapidly collapsed, and the hapless Maximilian was left to face a firing squad in June 1867.

The short-lived French puppet empire in Mexico displayed outright contempt for the Monroe Doctrine and represented Europe's most blatant challenge to it. Maximilian's rule involved the subjugation of a country in the Western Hemisphere by a foreign power and the supplanting of a republic by a satellite monarchy. Napoleon and Maximilian not only openly sympathized with the Confederate states in rebellion against the Federal government, but dreamed of expanding French fiefdom into South America once the United States was no longer in a position to check European ambitions.

French adventurism in Mexico thus threatened the security of the United States. With the firm action taken by Seward, the Monroe Doctrine was elevated to the level of operational policy and even national heritage. The Mexicans were pleased by the forceful U.S. stand that rid them of foreign shackles. U.S. policies somewhat lessened the lingering bitterness associated with the Mexican War, and Seward was warmly received in Mexico in 1869. *Harper's Weekly* editorialized:

> The United States Government has now furnished Europe with an argument which every government understands. It has proved itself, by the most tremendous test, to be practically invincible. We are not surprised, therefore, to hear of the sudden and

The young Lincoln
Courtesy of the National Archives

54

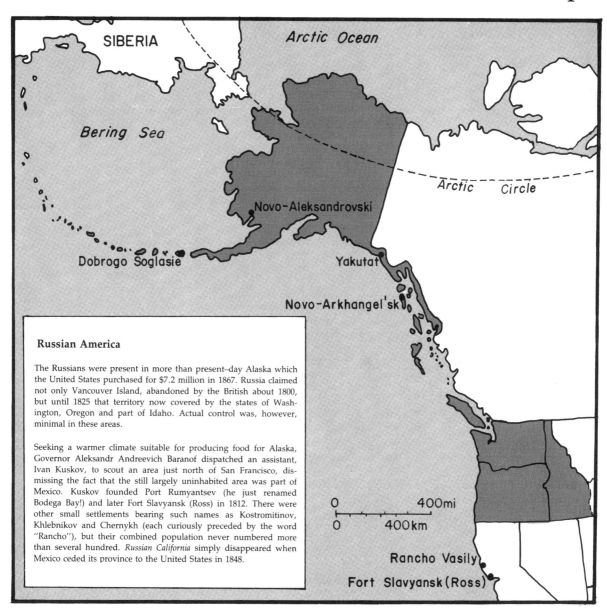

Russian America

The Russians were present in more than present–day Alaska which the United States purchased for $7.2 million in 1867. Russia claimed not only Vancouver Island, abandoned by the British about 1800, but until 1825 that territory now covered by the states of Washington, Oregon and part of Idaho. Actual control was, however, minimal in these areas.

Seeking a warmer climate suitable for producing food for Alaska, Governor Aleksandr Andreevich Baranof dispatched an assistant, Ivan Kuskov, to scout an area just north of San Francisco, dismissing the fact that the still largely uninhabited area was part of Mexico. Kuskov founded Port Rumyantsev (he just renamed Bodega Bay!) and later Fort Slavyansk (Ross) in 1812. There were other small settlements bearing such names as Kostromitinov, Khlebnikov and Chernykh (each curiously preceded by the word "Rancho"), but their combined population never numbered more than several hundred. *Russian California* simply disappeared when Mexico ceded its province to the United States in 1848.

amazed respect for us which has suddenly arisen in the most hostile foreign circles.

The Mexican imbroglio damaged French-American relations at an unfortunate time for Napoleon III. French leaders and the French press for the most part displayed considerable resentment about what they perceived to be bullying American policies. Not surprisingly, when Napoleon III blundered into war with Prussia in 1870, the French found precious little approval in the United States. Northerners remembered the widespread support the Union cause had enjoyed in the German-speaking states. The noted author Louisa May Alcott struck a popular chord in asserting that she sided with the Prussians, "for they sympathized with us in our war." Tens of thousands of Ger-

man immigrants who had served in the Union army exhibited a sense of *Schadenfreude* at the decisive French defeat. Many welcomed the conflict that finally brought about the unification of their homeland. The Franco-Prussia War resulted in the toppling of Napoleon III and the subsequent establishment of a new French republic. The great power to emerge in Central Europe began on a good footing with the United States.

The vanquishing of the Confederacy hardly brought swift relief at home, and the protracted war had been exorbitantly expensive in treasure and blood. In strictly monetary terms, the Civil War cost well over $3 billion dollars for the Union alone. The cost to the South is impossible to measure. Yet the North's economy was strong enough to survive, and some argue that the war effort, entailing the churning

out of masses of supplies and munitions, ultimately strengthened Northern industry. The Southern economy, however, was ruined.

President Lincoln was convinced that the Union needed to treat the defeated South with magnanimity and assist it in getting back on its feet economically, politically, and socially. He also wanted the federal and state governments to help the freed slaves to become full citizens of a reborn country. The assassination of Lincoln at the moment of victory by a Southern die-hard inflicted perhaps more permanent damage upon the South than legions of Federal troops could have. Lincoln's plans were never carried out and in 1866, after a bitter political struggle, the 14th Amendment to the Constitution was passed, giving full citizenship to all black Americans and allowing them to vote for

United States

the first time. Sadly for the nation, under subsequent presidents the federal government looked the other way as the Southern states blatantly violated the rights of black Americans. Southern state governments reverted to control by segregationist whites, and although blacks were technically free, the era of "Jim Crow" had emerged.

The last great expansion of the United States came with another of Seward's diplomatic triumphs in 1867. Russian friendliness toward the North during the Civil War helped pave the way for the eventual purchase of Alaska. The tsarist government had come to regard Alaska as a largely unprofitable colony. The Russian American Company, which administered the region had gone bankrupt, and the Russian government wished to avoid shouldering the burdens of administering the vast expanse of territory. Political reasons for the sale presented themselves as well. The Russians assumed that in the probable event of another conflict with the British colonial archrival, Alaska would fall into British hands. Transfer to the United States would prevent such a seizure, while improving relations with a country whose friendliness it needed. Moreover, Alaska was a source of potential trouble with the United States. The operations of the Russian American Company caused frictions from time to time with U.S. merchants, and Russia could ill afford jeopardizing good relations with America. Russia had difficulties aplenty in Europe and Asia and needed no more. Europe's rivalries benefited the United States once again. In March 1867, the United States purchased Alaska for $7.2 million.

Initially derided by many Americans as a fundamental error, the treaty ceding Alaska was labeled "an egregious blunder" and a "bad bargain palmed off on the silly administration by the shrewd Russians." The great unknown northern territory was to some a "barren, worthless, God-forsaken region of icebergs." It was "Walrussia," "Frigidia," and the "national icehouse." But Seward had fulfilled his dream of extending the United States to arctic regions, and by the purchase of Alaska, America had increased its territory by around 40%. In hindsight, "Seward's polar bear garden" was one of history's greatest real estate bargains.

AMERICA BECOMES A GREAT POWER

The Americans rode out their Civil War diplomatically, increased their strength and population, stretched their new territories westward and southward until the country reached its present continental limits. The United States achieved an imperial domain in the hemisphere under

John Hay
Courtesy of Special Collections,
University of Virginia Library

the protecting shadow of lingering great power conflicts.

Following the Civil War, however, Americans were so preoccupied with binding up the nation's wounds, settling Western lands, building the transcontinental railroad, and promoting commerce that foreign affairs were widely ignored.

It was characteristic of American isolationist tradition that secretaries of state were not expected to bring any diplomatic experience to their post, and from the Civil War onward none did before John Hay was elevated to cabinet rank at the close of the century. When America itself became a great power, its strategy shifted, becoming one of preventing any other power from overshadowing it. Such was the logic of Hay's "Open Door" policy that endeavored to keep the Far East from becoming the private preserve of any one European country. It was the point-of-departure for Theodore Roosevelt's policy of utilizing Russia as a counterweight to Japanese power when he made himself a conciliator between the two. It was also the logic of America's entry into both world wars when it joined to prevent German domination of Eurasia. During the British-Venezuelan boundary dispute in the early 1890s, President Grover Cleveland's secretary of state, Richard Olney, insinuated that the United States could force the arbitration of any dispute arising between a European power and a Western Hemisphere state. The U.S. position provoked a distinguished British diplomat,

Lord Salisbury, to lecture Olney on the correct meaning of the Monroe Doctrine.

U.S. industry was substantially stimulated by the demands of war in the 1860s, and thereafter the country entered upon industrial development of tremendous scope and speed. War profits enabled enterprising businessmen to construct railroads, to open new mines, and to build modern factories. Large-scale immigration provided an abundant supply of cheap labor. Republican Congresses assisted industry with relatively high tariffs and granted large tracts of land and other generous financial assistance to railroad builders. In a single generation, 1861–1890, the United States became one of the world's leading industrial nations, as well as a foremost producer of foodstuffs and raw materials. The country became increasingly outwardly focused as exports of industrial and agricultural products shot up.

The year 1890 marked a turning point in American history. The last fertile government-owned lands in the West had been given away. The frontier that served as an outlet for the dissatisfied and unemployed rapidly began to disappear. In America's fast-growing cities, large numbers of poor people were crowded together in crime-infested slums. Giant "trusts" or monopolies strangled their competitors, defrauded the public, and sought to corrupt the government. Farmers, who had expanded production too far, too fast, faced substantial losses as agricultural prices fell. In short, the United States was suffering from acute growing pains as a result of its rapid expansion and industrialization.

To meet these grave problems, a number of reform movements sprang into existence. They found most of their support among the Western farmers and the industrial workers of the East. Blaming the railroads and bankers for their sorry plight, the farmers formed strong organizations, such as the National Grange, to combat powerful interests. Entering politics, they won control of the legislatures in several Midwestern states and enacted laws to regulate railroad, storage and interest rates. The workers likewise sought to improve their conditions by forming nationwide organizations and by entering politics. A number of states responded by passing laws designed to eliminate the worst industrial abuses.

The farm and labor organizations also brought pressure on the federal government to enact a wide variety of reforms. They were especially eager to have the government adopt an "easy money" policy that would raise prices for the farmers and wages for labor. "Easy money" required the treasury to print more paper dollars and to mint silver coins freely. Following years of agitation, the reformers succeeded in securing a number of their demands. For example, Congress created a federal commission to regulate the railroads. It also passed the first federal antitrust law. The reformers' hopes soared during the presidential campaign of 1896, when the Democratic Party included in its platform a large part of the reformers' program and made easy money the main issue.

America's burgeoning interest in the world manifested itself in a variety of ways. A Republican secretary of state in the 1880s, James G. Blaine, advocated what he termed "spirited diplomacy," in general, and "big sister" policies toward Latin American countries in particular. In 1889, he organized the first Pan-American Conference in Washington, D.C. Though it brought about only modest first steps toward economic cooperation and tariff reduction, it nonetheless laid the groundwork for future inter-American assemblies.

The development of a new steel navy and pathbreaking doctrine for its use underscored the expansion of America's horizons. Alfred Thayer Mahan's book, *The Influence of Seapower upon History 1660–1783*, asserted that sea control was crucial for the achievement of world empire. According to Mahan, international influence was attained primarily by sea power, and the concept quickly gained considerable popular appeal. Many American luminaries expressed the conviction that a large blue-water fleet was essential to the country's national security.

THE PATH OF EMPIRE

A reawakening of manifest destiny in America revealed itself in impulses toward imperialism. Assertive international positions toward the great and the small suggested a rising spirit of outward-looking nationalism. Growing numbers of Americans believed that the future belonged to strong and assertive nations. Policies still lacked coherence and were frequently not on an even keel. Partly in consequence, a number of serious diplomatic crises marked the course of U.S. foreign policy in the late 1880s and early 1990s. U.S. and German warships nearly exchanged fire over a confrontation about the Somoan Islands in the South Pacific in 1889 although the United States acquired Somoa shortly thereafter. America and Italy experienced a crisis in 1891 in the wake of the murder of a number of Italians in New Orleans. Hostilities between the United States and Chile very nearly erupted in 1892. A lingering dispute with Canada over seal hunting off the coast of Alaska was finally settled in 1893. Anti-British feeling in the United States bub-

Capt. Alfred Thayer Mahan

bled to the surface once again in 1895–96 over a territorial dispute in Venezuela. By attempting to dominate Venezuela and interfering in a border dispute, Britain was in blatant violation of the Monroe Doctrine, according to the United States. The two powers came perilously close to blows. But the crisis was resolved peacefully and the standing of the Monroe Doctrine was again upheld. In fact, the row impressed upon many people on both sides of the Atlantic the need for peaceful settlement of disputes. If proper mechanisms were in place, it was reasoned, countries would not find themselves on the verge of war so quickly. As a result, the United States negotiated a general

William McKinley

arbitration treaty with Britain in 1897. Although the U.S. Senate ultimately rejected the agreement, the latter did much to popularize arbitration and improve relations with Britain. As a result, British leaders tended to cheer America on as it set off on the course of imperialism during the Spanish-American War.

In 1887, the United States concluded a treaty with the native government of Hawaii guaranteeing naval basing rights at Pearl Harbor. Over a period of years in the 1890s, Hawaii became Americanized in growing measure and was finally annexed in 1898. In 1900, residents of Hawaii were granted U.S. citizenship and received full territorial status. With the Hawaiian Islands a virtual extension of the U.S. coastline, the country's reach expanded far into the Pacific, permitting the subsequent domination of the Philippines.

The imperialist movement in the United States, led principally by Senators Albert J. Beveridge and Henry Cabot Lodge and by Theodore Roosevelt, assistant secretary of the navy, and later president—all disciples of Mahan—judged national power to be largely predicated upon the ability to conduct foreign commerce. Commerce in turn necessitated a merchant fleet supported by an oceangoing navy. The great maritime empires, they deduced from Mahan, had derived their sway and influence from powerful naval forces and overseas colonies to serve as bases. The United States, they concluded, was still hugely deficient in naval power and world vision. If the country was ultimately to attain its full potential and contribute to civilization, it would have to shun isolationism and look outward.

Cuba proved the true catalyst for a sweeping U.S. involvement in world affairs. In the late 1890s, Cuba, long restive under Spanish rule, finally exploded into popular rebellion. Both sides, the Spanish and the insurgents, demonstrated considerable ruthlessness and brutality in their tactics. Practicing a scorched earth policy with the aim of so devastating the island that the Spanish would withdraw, the insurgents frequently destroyed property indiscriminately. Americans, with substantial investments in the island, were invariably caught in the middle.

The grisly rebellion in Cuba coincided with the development of sensational "yellow" journalism in the United States. The country's largest competing newspaper publishers, William Randolph Hearst and Joseph Pulitzer, had a field day in Cuba and ultimately pushed the country into war. Both newspaper syndicates employed lurid style, took breathtaking liberties with the truth, and offered banner headlines and eye-catching illustrations. In the popular phraseology, Hearst and

United States

Theodore Roosevelt, 1898
Courtesy of Special Collections,
University of Virginia Library

Pulitzer "snooped, scooped and stooped to conquer." Hearst certainly whetted the popular taste for adventures abroad. And he was nothing if not obvious, having remarked to one of his on-site artists, "You furnish the pictures and I'll furnish the war."

Each of the rival "czars of sensation" specialized in Cuban atrocity stories and sold newspapers by the hundreds of thousands to a receptive American audience. In light of the danger to American lives and property, both publishers demanded in shrill tones a showdown with Spain. When the U.S. battleship Maine exploded and sank in Havana harbor in February 1898, the yellow press immediately blamed Spanish treachery and unleased a torrent of oratorical pyrotechnics.

"Remember the Maine! To hell with Spain!" became a popular slogan. Prodded by the relentless demands of the yellow press, a frenzied American public demanded war to liberate Cuba and finally to expel the colonial power from the Western Hemisphere. President William McKinley, a Civil War veteran who well knew the horrors of war, hesitated but yielded to public pressure in April 1898. Following the President's message to Congress urging armed intervention in Cuba, the legislators adopted the Teller Amendment proclaiming Cuban freedom once the yoke of Spanish misrule had been lifted.

In May 1898, Commodore George Dewey sailed the U.S. Asian Squadron into the fortified harbor of Manila and destroyed the entire Spanish fleet. U.S. ground troops arrived in the Philippines in August and in collaboration with Filipino insurgents captured Manila and overthrew Spanish colonial rule. In July, combined U.S. land and sea operations crushed what remained of the Spanish forces in Cuba. The Americans also seized Puerto Rico, the last vestige of Spain's empire in the Western Hemisphere and Guam fell easily into American hands since the Spanish garrison there was not even aware of the hostilities. Spain signed an armistice on August 12, 1898. In 1900, Congress accorded the Puerto Ricans limited self-government and in 1917 residents of the island were granted U.S. citizenship. In accordance with the Teller Amendment, the United States withdrew from Cuba in 1902. Through the conquest of the Philippines, the United States would become a full-fledged Pacific power, although an insurgency would smolder in the new U.S. colony for several years in the early 1900s.

Following the conclusion of a peace treaty with Spain, many policy makers turned their attention again to reform as a group of gifted young writers, the "muckrakers," exposed many evils of American life. The able young Republican President, Theodore Roosevelt (1901–1909), in fact, the youngest in history, responded by proclaiming a "Square Deal" for the common man. Though friendly toward business, President Roosevelt introduced a number of policies favorable to the farmers and labor. He tried to break up unfair business monopolies. He also started a large-scale program to conserve the nation's natural resources. "The great development of industrialism," said Roosevelt, "means that there must be an increase in the supervision by the Government over private enterprise."

A few years later, a liberal Democratic President, Woodrow Wilson (1913–1921), announced a new reform program called "New Freedom." At his request, Congress established the Federal Reserve System to supervise the nation's banks. It passed new antitrust laws, reduced tariffs, and levied an income tax on the well-to-do. Numerous laws were also passed to help workers and farmers. So much was achieved during these early years of the 20th century that this period is often called "the era of reform" or the "Progressive Era."

The Spanish-American War underscored in the minds of many the urgent need finally to construct a canal somewhere through Central America in order that merchant shipping and battle fleets would be spared the passage around South America. An earlier attempt to dig a canal had failed, having fallen victim to engineering difficulties and the ever-present yellow fever. Two possibilities for the Central American canal presented themselves: either through Nicaragua or the shorter route across Panama, which at the time was part of Colombia. When Panamanians rose in revolt against Colombia in November 1903, President Roosevelt justified U.S. intervention by a strained interpretation of an obscure earlier agree-

American, British, and Japanese troops storming Peking (Beijing), August 1900

ment. The interference was one example of many of what is generally known as the "Roosevelt Corollary" of the Monroe Doctrine. Moreover, the United States had fomented the Panamanian revolt. The newly recognized state of Panama eagerly offered to allow the construction of a canal. Claiming the United States had a "mandate from civilization," Roosevelt began to "make the dirt fly" in 1904. The main stumbling block to canal construction was, as before, sanitation. Colonel William C. Gorgas, the indomitable conqueror of yellow fever in Cuba, rapidly eliminated the dreadful disease in the designated Canal Zone. Ultimately, the Canal Zone became as "safe as a health resort" and the engineering feat was completed in the summer of 1914. It was, in the memorable words of the British author James Bryce, "the greatest liberty man has ever taken with nature."

After establishing predominance in the Caribbean and emerging as a contending power in east Asia, the United States found itself suddenly involved in the great power games of Asia. When China's

Manchu Dynasty crumbled in the early 1900s, the United States jostled for favorable economic and political position along with the other Western powers. Above all, the United States wished to ensure its own manufacturers access to the Chinese market, fueled by the "countless consumers" many producers in the West dreamed of for decades. Asian market access translated into the policy of the "Open Door," which involved rock-solid commercial opportunity for all nations. Britain, controlling the lion's share of China trade, advocated commercial openness, at least in theory, and objected to the compartmentalization of China as reflected in the policies pursued by Germany, Japan, Russia and France.

Following the outbreak of a nationalist uprising in China known widely as the "Boxer Rebellion," the United States contributed a contingent of soldiers to an international expeditionary rescue force. The State Department reiterated U.S. commitment to the principle of equal commercial access as well as to China's political independence and territorial integrity.

Yet, initially, the United States declared it would not undertake any military action to enforce the "Open Door." Many Americans supposed that foreign policy objectives could be achieved by asserting moralistic ideals, apparently forgetting, for example, that the Monroe Doctrine, however idealistic, was most effective when backed by force. Roosevelt pursued the Open Door with diplomatic means and sought to avoid the use of force in East Asia if possible. His mediation of the Russo-Japanese War of 1904–1905 demonstrated, though, that he grasped the essential features of the balance-of-power in Asia. Favoring an outcome that would maintain Russian influence in East Asia as a counterweight to waxing Japanese power, Roosevelt brokered a deal that many in Japan found abhorrent. The U.S. administration was made a scapegoat for an unfavorable peace treaty, and U.S.-Japanese relations deteriorated decade by decade thereafter. Great power competition with the inexplicable East Asian rules would eventually lead to the endgame in 1941.

Colonel Roosevelt with some of the "Rough Riders"

President Roosevelt "making the dirt fly" in Panama

United States

after, the Germans and the Austrians struck at the main Russian armies. They inflicted crippling losses on the Russians and drove them out of Austria-Hungary and Poland. With the aid of Bulgaria, which had entered the war on the side of the Central Powers, Austria-Hungary succeeded in crushing Serbia.

Meanwhile, the Western Allies launched an expedition in 1915 to force open the straits between the Black Sea and the Aegean, through which much-needed supplies could be sent to Russia. The operation, known as the Gallipoli Campaign, proved a disastrous failure. Three times the British and the Anzacs (Australians and New Zealanders) tried to capture the Turkish forts guarding the straits. They suffered heavy losses and finally had to abandon the plan. The southern supply route to Russia remained closed throughout the war. If it had been open, the Russian Revolution might never have happened.

The British and French also tried to ease the pressure on Russia by repeated attacks on the German trench lines on the Western Front in 1916, but the assaults were repulsed with heavy casualties. The greatest British operation was launched along the Somme River in northern France in the summer of 1916. The attack netted them only small gains at heavy cost. Eventually, this offensive too bogged down in the autumn mud. Offensives were also launched by Italy, which had been induced to join the Allies by secret promises of territory after the war. The Italian army was not sufficiently strong to break through Austria's defenses in the Alpine regions.

As the target of their 1916 offensive, the Germans chose the French fortresses around Verdun. By attacking this vital area, the German high command hoped to bleed the French white and finally to break the country's morale. At Verdun, the French army rallied to the famous battle cry "They shall not pass!" After four months of slaughter, the Germans had to give up the offensive. The Western Front remained intact.

"Humanity . . . must be mad to do what it is doing," a young French lieutenant wrote in his Verdun diary in May 1916. Although the fighting dragged on for another two years, nothing in the war ever equaled or surpassed the slaughter at Verdun and the Somme. The statistics for these two battles can only be given in round numbers: 900,000 Germans and French killed, wounded, or taken prisoner at Verdun; 1,250,000 for Britain, France, and Germany at the Somme. All British empire casualties during World War II barely match the toll of the three countries at the Somme, in which the maximum Allied gain was eight miles over a twelve-mile front. Generals spoke loftily of attri-

tion or wearing the enemy down. Winston Churchill knew better, describing the blood-letting as "merely exchanging lives upon a scale at once more frightful than anything witnessed before . . . and too modest to produce a decision."

The Russians, for their part, used the breathing space to reorganize their forces and then staged a sudden attack against Austria-Hungary and gained a good deal of territory before German reinforcements arrived to stall the drive. Romania, impressed by the Russian victories and by Allied promises of territory, then entered the war, only to be conquered rapidly by the Germans, who profited immensely from its grain and oil. By early 1917, Russia was nearing exhaustion both in manpower and equipment. Cannon shells were rationed and soldiers often had to attack only with bayonets because of the ammunition shortage. In Great Britain, the prime minister was forced to resign, and there was frequent talk of defeat in France and Italy. Yet, the Central Powers had also suffered heavy losses and were feeling the strains of war. Though they had won numerous battles, victory seemed a will-of-the-wisp, as impossible to grasp as ever.

Soon after the outbreak of the war, the Allies gained control of the seas, allowing them to cut off and conquer most of Germany's colonies in Africa and East Asia. Sea control also facilitated the opening of new fronts against the weaker points of the Central Powers. They launched attacks on Bulgaria through Greece and on Turkey through Mesopotamia and Palestine in 1914–15. Above all, they were able to impose a blockade against the Central Powers in Europe. Foodstuffs and other essential commodities gradually became scarce in both Germany and Austria-Hungary. Though the war effort of these countries was not seriously hampered, the people's morale began to decline. The longer the war continued, the more decisive Allied naval power proved to be.

The Germans desperately sought countermeasures to break the Allied blockade. Their battle fleet was kept bottled up in its home ports by the more powerful British Navy. Their fast cruisers, dispatched to prey on Allied shipping were hunted down and sunk. It soon became clear that the only weapon that offered them any real hope of success was the submarine or "U-boat." German submarines found it easy to slip through the Allied blockade and to attack Allied shipping. The submarine of the time was a frail craft, though. Even a freighter could sink it by shelling or ramming and many merchant ships were armed with six-inch guns. Submarines thus had little choice but to launch torpedoes without warning, a violation of international law, which required that

the safety of the passengers and crew be guaranteed. In February 1915, the German government announced its intention to engage in unrestricted submarine warfare. It asserted the policy was justified because the Allied blockade was also illegal.

President Wilson faced the unenviable task of keeping the United States out of war, but at the same time maintaining its rights, above all, its maritime freedom. The United States was not only the wealthiest neutral state, but also the most important neutral carrier. Its shipping would almost inevitably cruise into the turbulent shoals of belligerent restrictions, as it had during Europe's past wars.

The United States initially ran afoul of Great Britain, which, as the dominant sea power and as in wars past, interpreted and modified maritime rules. It has been well said that in peacetime Britain ruled the waves and in wartime Britain waived the rules. To be sure, Britain took considerable international legal liberties, justifying her "exceptional measures" by the time-honored arguments that the conflict created "new," "peculiar" or "unusual" conditions. It also invoked "reprisals," "retaliation," and "military necessity." Beginning with the "Orders in Council," of August 20, 1914, with ominous echoes of those of the past century, Britain arbitrarily defined contraband and began intercepting U.S. ships bound for enemy territory. As was its wont, the British Navy took a highly permissive view regarding the right of visit and search on the high seas.

U.S. relations with Germany also deteriorated rapidly after the first year of war, though. Americans were shipping large quantities of munitions to the Allies and providing enormous amounts of credits

THE
BRITISH NAVY
guards the freedom of us all

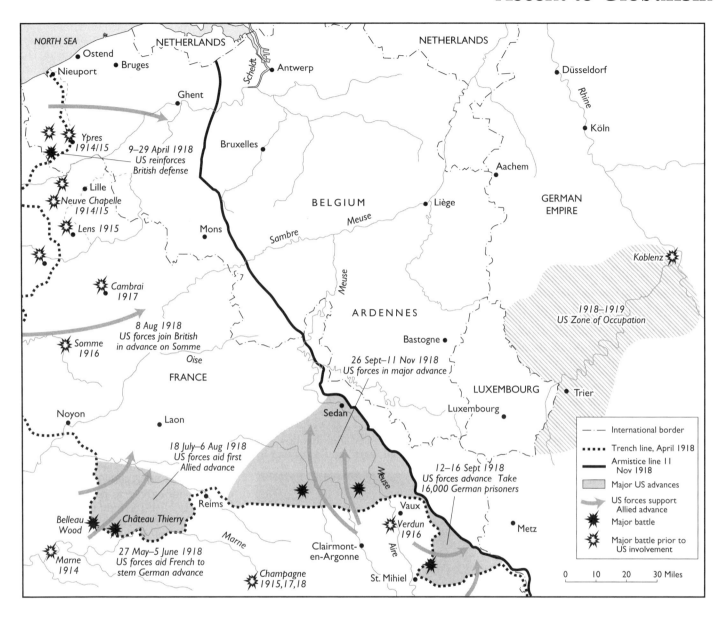

and loans for the Allied war effort. American actions led one of the chief German-American newspapers in the United States to editorialize in 1915: "We Americans prattle about humanity, while we manufacture poisoned shrapnel and picric acid for profit. Ten thousand German widows, ten thousand orphans, ten thousand graves bear the legend 'Made in America.'"

Unrestricted submarine warfare soon aroused popular hostility in the United States. Most Americans and especially the president and his cabinet were horrified when a German submarine sank the great British passenger liner *Lusitania* in May 1915. Twelve hundred people, including more than one hundred Americans drowned. The U.S. press rang with denunciations of what it termed "mass murder." The *New York Times* demanded that the Germans should "no longer make

wars like savages drunk with blood." The *New York Nation* stated that: "The torpedo that sank the *Lusitania* also sank Germany in the opinion of mankind . . . It is a crime and a monumental folly." Allied propagandists fanned this ill-feeling by spreading exaggerated stories of German atrocities in Belgium and other occupied countries. In the face of growing American anger, Berlin announced that its submarines in the future would abide by the rules of international law.

Yet, Germany was still determined to stop the flow of American supplies to the Allies. German secret agents abroad stirred up strikes, blew up armament plants, and started fires on ships laden with war materials. A German plot was discovered to get Mexico to attack the United States by promising to cede large parts of the American West to Mexico if

the United States entered the war against Germany.

American interest in the global conflict was partially eclipsed by the boisterous presidential election of 1916 in which the incumbent Wilson ran against Supreme Court Justice Charles Evans Hughes. Hughes criticized Wilson for his "leisurely discussions" of the nation's rights. But his own campaign slogans such as "America first and America efficient" invited the nickname Charles "Evasive" Hughes and prompted the remark that he had left the bench for the fence. The election involved a number of issues, such as Mexico, the tariff, domestic reform, and the railroads, but it is best known for the popular proclamation about President Wilson that "He Kept Us out of War."

Shortly after his reelection, Wilson redoubled his efforts to broker a negotiated

United States

made to pay for the misery they had inflicted on the world. He was primarily concerned with the future, not the past, however. Wilson's program rested on the belief that if the peoples of the world were free to choose their own governments, a union of these governments could maintain stability. A combination of self-determination, democracy, and a league of nations would make possible reduction of armaments, removal of economic barriers, open diplomacy, and, as the highest good, peace. Wilson believed that outside of Europe many people were not yet ready for self-government, but he insisted that the well-being of the indigenous peoples, as well as the interests of the colonizing powers, be considered in regard to colonial claims. In his program as originally formulated, there had been no place for indemnities. But to secure Allied acceptance of the program, he had agreed that the Germans must make reparations for the damage done to civilian populations of the Allied countries.

In total, the Paris Peace Conference developed five separate treaties. First, and most important, was the Treaty of Versailles imposed on Germany. That country lost about one-tenth of its territory and population in Europe. Alsace and Lorraine were returned to France. Several small border districts were transferred to Belgium and Denmark. A large area in the east was given to the new country of Poland, including the "Polish Corridor,"

which cut Germany into two parts in order to provide the Poles an outlet to the sea. The city of Danzig, the natural port for this region, was taken from Germany and placed under international control.

The central issue at Paris was the settlement with Germany, and it was here that the peacemakers deviated most conspicuously from their original intent. Even before the formal meetings, the delegates took up the matter of dismantling Germany's large colonial empire. Although it was understood that the territories in question would be administered as mandates under the soon-to-be-created League of Nations, and despite vocal pledges to end imperialism, the nations who were awarded mandates regarded them as colonies. These were divided among Great Britain, France, Belgium, and various other Allied countries. Officially they were granted a new status, that is, territories held in trust. The powers promised to govern the mandates in the interests of the native population and to prepare the more "advanced" peoples for early independence. A special international body, the Mandates Commission, was created to supervise their administration.

The Treaty of Versailles contained a number of other important provisions. Germany, along with the other Central Powers, had to admit responsibility for having caused the war. It was therefore obliged to pay reparations for all the damage it had done. It was permitted to have

only a small army and navy. It agreed to let the Allies place on trial those German officers, including the Kaiser himself, who had "committed acts in violation of the laws and customs of war." Finally, as a guarantee that the peace terms would be carried out, Allied troops were to occupy a large section of western Germany, the Rhineland, for a period of fifteen years.

As Wilson feared, the German people deeply resented the treaty. On the other hand, Clemenceau and the French were also displeased. Germany had not really been crushed, and it remained superior to France in manpower, resources, and industry. By striking a compromise between the two opposing views, the Treaty of Versailles left Germany angry and humiliated, but still strong enough to hope for a war of revenge. Far worse was the fate of the once mighty Dual Monarchy. In the final days of the war, Austria-Hungary fell apart as the subject nationalities proclaimed their independence. The Czechs and Slovaks created the new nation of Czechoslovakia. The South Slavs united with Serbia to form the new Kingdom of Yugoslavia. The Austrian Poles joined with the Poles formerly under Russian and German rule to restore an independent Poland.

The Paris Peace Conference formally recognized these changes in the peace treaties with Austria and Hungary. In accordance with the secret agreements, it also awarded large territories to Italy and Romania. Austria and Hungary were left as two small, separate, landlocked nations. Both were disarmed and required to pay reparations. Though many Austrians wanted to join Germany, union of the two countries was forbidden.

In distributing the territory of the former Dual Monarchy among the successor states, the peacemakers were bound only by the promises of self-determination they had made during the war. By the pre-armistice agreement, a formal pledge had been made that the settlement with Germany would conform to the Fourteen Points and Wilson's other wartime pronouncements. Where the promise of self-determination entailed the loss of territory that had been part of prewar Germany, the only clear violation of the promise was the few hundred square miles given to Belgium. The Saar Basin was temporarily placed under League administration, and ownership of the coal mines of the basin was given to France as compensation for German destruction of French mines. But after fifteen years the inhabitants of the Saar were to decide their own fate. German territory on the left bank of the Rhine was to be permanently demilitarized, but the Rhineland remained under German control. By treaties signed in June 1919,

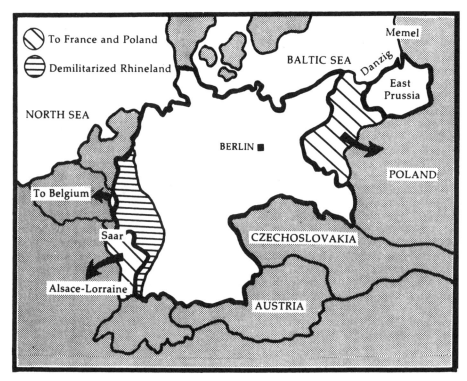

German territorial losses to the Allies following World War I

66

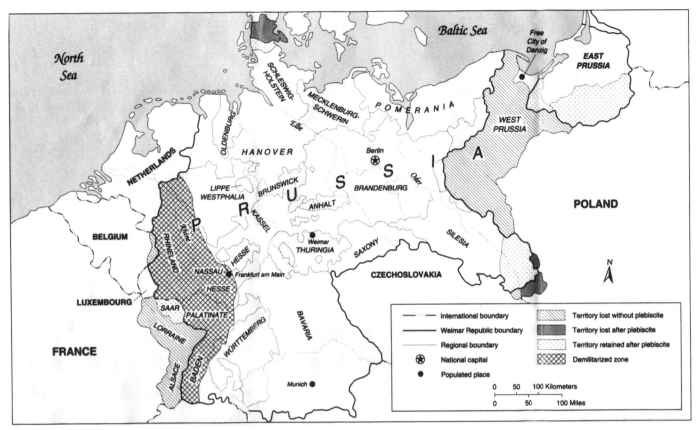

Effects of the Versailles Treaty
Source: *Germany, A Country Study*/Federal Research Division, Library of Congress

the United States and Great Britain guaranteed assistance to France in case of unprovoked aggression by Germany.

Bulgaria likewise lost some territory. It was also disarmed and had to pay reparations. A similar treaty was drawn up for Turkey, but a new nationalist government resisted it. It refused to accept the treaty and finally managed to obtain better terms. Even so, Turkey was shorn of all its former possessions and became just another country in Asia Minor.

One of the most difficult problems confronting the peace conference concerned Russia. Russia had been one of the Allied powers, but the Bolshevik government, led by Vladimir Lenin, which had seized control during the war, had signed a separate peace with Germany. It had also denounced the secret treaties and refused to honor the debts of the tsarist government. Perhaps most disconcerting, it was busily engaged in spreading communist propaganda across Central Europe.

As a result, the Allies were hostile to the Bolshevik government. They refused to admit its representatives to the peace conference. They also recognized the independence of five nations—Poland, Lithuania, Latvia, Estonia, and Finland—which had freed themselves from Russian rule. The new nations were strongly antiBolshevik

in character and the Allies viewed them as a sort of quarantine against the spread of communism.

Although the peace treaties contained many violations of President Wilson's principles, they also included a number of positive elements that were inserted at his insistence. The frontiers of the new Europe were drawn mainly on the basis of nationality. Plebiscites, or special elections, were arranged in some doubtful areas to enable the inhabitants to decide for themselves the exact boundary lines. As a result of these policies, the number of minority groups within European nations was supposed to be reduced. Moreover, the remaining minorities were protected by special treaties that guaranteed them equal rights with the majority. The peacemakers thereby hoped to eliminate the nationalistic conflicts that had long been a threat to peace. The dilemma was that only rarely did ethnic boundaries coincide with geographic and economic divisions, and in most cases a strict adherence to ethnic lines would have created a patchwork of territories with little chance of economic or political survival. Self-determination was sometimes ignored in the interest of practicality.

The most idealistic feature of the Paris peace settlement was the creation of a new

international organization, the League of Nations. Wilson agreed to many compromises in the peace treaties in order to secure its acceptance. The League was authorized to settle problems arising from the treaties and to revise them as circumstances required. It was also assigned many other functions in order to fulfill its long-term task, the building of a lasting peace.

The League Covenant did not set out to create a world government. Decisions, ex-

Lenin

United States

The Bolsheviks march into Moscow

cept on procedural matters and on the admission of members, required unanimous approval, which did not mean the unanimous vote of all members. The assembly of the League, in which every member was represented, had the right to consider any matter within the sphere of action of the League. Decisions, however, were reserved on most questions for the Council of the League. Permanent membership in the Council was given to the "Principal Allied and Associated Powers" (Britain, France, Italy, the United States and Japan). Four non-permanent members were to be selected by the assembly. At the outset, membership in the League was given to all signatories of the Treaty of Versailles, except Germany. Most neutral states were invited to join, but not Russia. These exceptions made it easy for Germans to describe the League as an organization of the victors to protect their victory, and for the Russians to say the League was a union of capitalist states against communism.

Observers frequently suggest that the League and Wilson failed because of inordinate idealism. The League lacked the

legal authority and political competence to make the international decisions necessary to manage a collective security system. Potential aggressors were not sufficiently discouraged by international law, and member states were not required to enforce the League's principle in the event of a violation. Article 16 of the League Covenant provided for economic boycotts against states flouting the agreements of the Covenant and allowed for the possibility of collective military sanctions. Because of the obstructive power of universal veto, the economic sanctions were never followed consistently enough to be effective, and military sanctions never came into being at all. Even though members of the League banded together long enough in 1935 to initiate economic boycotts against Italy because of the Italian attack on Ethiopia, national interest soon outweighed the need for unity. The boycott withered, and the Italian fascists triumphed in their contempt for the League.

Wilson's failure to get the United States to join the League left a yawning political gap in the organization that could never

be properly filled. Established to prevent another world conflagration, the League was ill-equipped to handle a calculated war by design. Without Wilsonian idealism, the noble principles of the League would never have been fleshed out into an organization. But just as perfection is the ultimate enemy of the good, so powerlessness undercuts idealism. The League was never equal to the political challenges of the 20th century.

Only 20 years after the peace treaties were signed, the world was plunged into a second and even more destructive conflict. It has therefore become customary to refer to the Paris peace settlement as "the peace that failed." To a considerable extent, this failure was the fault of the victors. Because of their opposing viewpoints, they drafted treaties that neither crushed nor won over the defeated nations. Victors can as a rule have peace or vengeance, but they cannot have both from the same treaty. In international affairs, there are two types of peace treaty: the retributive peace, which invariably causes resentment, and the peace of accommodation, which is conducive to forgiving and forgetting. The Treaty of Versailles actually fell somewhere in between, and Europe tragically ended up with the worst of both. Moreover, the Allies often quarreled among themselves and sometimes failed to enforce the peace terms they had imposed. By reason of their inability to work together, the nations that won the war eventually lost the peace. Much more could be said for the treaty if the Allies had proceeded to carry out its terms in good faith.

From the start, Germany was the most dangerous foe of the peace settlement. The German people widely referred to the Treaty of Versailles as a "dictated peace" because they had no part in drafting it and had been forced to sign it by Allied threats. They denied that Germany and the other Central Powers were solely responsible for causing the war. They objected to the payment of reparations, the restrictions on their armed forces, and the loss of their colonial empire. Above all, they resented the loss of the Polish Corridor and the other territories inhabited by Germans.

The other defeated nations had similar grievances. Austria, deprived of most of its former territory and natural resources, faced bankruptcy and starvation. Hungary loudly protested the transfer to Romania of a region inhabited by many Magyars. Bulgaria was livid because it had been deprived of access to the sea.

To make matters worse, two of the former Allied Powers were also dissatisfied with the peace settlement. Russia's new Bolshevik government was angered by its large territorial losses and by its treatment as a kind of international outlaw. Italy was hostile because it did not gain all the territory it had hoped to receive for entering the war. These two countries, like the former Central Powers, were determined to revise the peace terms.

The peace settlement also gave rise to various other types of problems. The creation of many new nations in Central Europe meant still more rivalries, still more boundary lines to quarrel over, and still more tariffs to interrupt the flow of trade. Moreover, most of the new nations aroused the hostility of their subject nationalities by violating the minorities' treaties. In Central Europe, at least, national self-determination failed to provide a durable basis for peace.

Arguably, to preserve the peace settlement, the remaining Allies had to maintain common policies. Instead, they soon began to drift apart. First to go its own way was the United States. Upon his return from Europe, Wilson met with a storm of criticism. Some of his detractors denounced the Paris peace settlement as an excessively harsh peace, while others deplored it as too soft. Still others, the isolationists, attacked the League of Nations on the ground that it was a "super government," entangling the United States in the world's troubles. Many Republican leaders also opposed the Democratic President's policies for reasons of party politics—in order to win votes in the coming presidential election.

The opposition was strong enough to keep the Senate from ratifying the Treaty of Versailles and joining the League of Nations. In the presidential election of 1920, the Republicans won a landslide victory. The United States then made a separate peace with Germany and refused to join the League of Nations or even to recognize it. The new Republican administration reverted to the prewar policies of isolation, that is, of taking no direct part in Europe's affairs. Throughout America, one encountered strong impulses to return to such old isolationist ways since disillusionment with America's squabbling and imperialistic allies ran deep. The great war, it seemed, was not going to make the world safe for democracy, nor was it going to end all wars.

The French, unable to count on American support, were more concerned than ever that Germany would rise again. The British, on the other hand, felt secure because Germany was no longer a naval or colonial rival. They failed to understand why the French continued to fear their neighbor even after it had been weakened and disarmed. Moreover, British companies, eager to increase trade, became more and more interested in Germany's economic recovery. The difference in attitude led to an open split between the two powers.

The dangers of Allied disunity soon became apparent. Germany profited by ignoring and violating the treaty terms. For example, the Allies were supposed to try a large number of war criminals. The German government refused to turn them over. Instead, it brought a few of the worst offenders to trial itself. When they pleaded that they had acted under orders in defense of the *Vaterland* (fatherland), the courtroom audience burst into cheers. Only a handful of the accused were found guilty and were given nominal sentences.

The Germans also quickly found ways to evade the military restrictions of the peace treaty. Despite the presence of Allied officials, they secretly maintained military strength. The German general staff, though outlawed by the treaty, continued to exist. The small German army was carefully selected, and the troops trained as future officers. Forbidden to build any large battleships, they designed warships of a new type, smaller, yet powerful, they became known as "pocket battleships." Most ominously, although Germany was forbidden to manufacture submarines or aircraft, it conducted secret experiments and training in Russia and other countries.

ISOLATION AND NORMALCY: THE 1920S

The decade of American life that became known as the Jazz Age, or the Roaring Twenties, ran its course from the election of President Warren G. Harding in 1920 to the catastrophic stock market crash of October 1929. These two events were symbolically appropriate. The first confirmed what the Senate had augured

Prohibition in the 1920s

United States

in 1919 when it refused to ratify the Versailles Treaty: an outright rejection of Woodrow Wilson's idealistic internationalism and a turning inward toward ease, prosperity, and the self-indulgent complacency of what Harding called "normalcy." The second demonstrated the folly of such a course.

Between the two was the seemingly limitless joyride of jazz, bootleg liquor, and a "fling in the market" for some easy earnings in boom times. The reckless gaiety of the period was only half the story, for in the aftermath of World War I, a split opened in the American national character between puritanical conservatism on the one hand and cynicism and radical self-expression on the other.

The hypocrisy engendered by Prohibition and the general disappointment in the failure of the Versailles peace agreement caused many intellectuals of the 1920s to become disenchanted with American society. Prior to the war, they had been in the vanguard of the Progressive movement, calling for reforms in favor of the working class. In the 1920s they became cynical.

A leading spokesman for these disillusioned writers, artists, and thinkers was H. L. Mencken. In his monthly magazine, *American Mercury*, Mencken applied his acid wit to democracy and idealism, organized religion, and what he regarded as prim smugness. In a similar vein were Sinclair Lewis's condemnations of middle-class mediocrity in *Main Street, Babbitt,* and *Elmer Gantry*.

Other writers, members of the so-called Lost Generation, also chronicled their postwar disillusionment. F. Scott Fitzgerald's *The Great Gatsby* summarized the glitter and pathos of the Jazz Age and in *A Farewell to Arms* Ernest Hemingway attacked what he saw as the phony idealism of the war. British novelist Aldous Huxley, widely read in America, captured the era's hectic atmosphere in *Chrome Yellow* and *Antic Hay*.

The 1920s still holds a powerful grip on the American imagination. The era was immortalized almost immediately after it ended by Frederick Lewis Allen, a journalist whose *Only Yesterday: An Informal History of the 1920s* was published in 1931 and has remained the standard work. Its closest sequel is to be found in William Manchester's *The Glory and the Dream*. The United States before the 1920s and the country after the 1920s were two very different places. The country entered the decade still rooted in the values of the farm and the small town. The 1930s brought a perplexing struggle with domestic and international hard times.

Presiding over the new prosperity was a man amply suited not to rock the boat. Harding was an easygoing man who appears not to have had much sense of what was happening around him. His ineptitude was seized upon by top aides who fashioned what was, until Watergate, the most famous betrayal of public trust in American history: the Teapot Dome scandal. The story of the outrage broke in October 1923, three months after Harding had died. Harding's cronies had benefited financially by leasing government oil reserves, one of which was Teapot Dome, near Casper, Wyoming. Former Secretary of the Interior Albert B. Fall was later found guilty of having accepted a bribe during the Harding Administration to lease lands.

In 1921 the United States issued invitations to a conference to be held in Washington to discuss reduction of armaments and problems in the Pacific. Germany was not invited, and the Germans interpreted the snub as new evidence of determination to keep their country in a permanently inferior position. Russia was not invited either, and the Soviet government protested vigorously but in vain about exclusion.

The Washington Conference met from November 1921 to February 1922 and seemed at the time almost a model of what a successful international meeting should be. The Anglo-Japanese alliance was widened into what was called the Four-Power Pact by the inclusion of France and the United States, and it changed from a military alliance into an agreement to consult in case of controversy over any Pacific question. Three documents dealt with mainland Asia: an agreement between China and Japan; a Japanese declaration promising evacuation of Russian territory; a Nine-Power Treaty giving assurances against new incursions on Chinese territory.

The Treaty for the Limitation of Armaments that emerged from the conference put limits only on capital ships, that is, the most powerful men-of-war. No limitation was placed on smaller vessels such as destroyers and submarines. The United States proposed specific reductions in capital ships, which would leave the British and American navies with about 500,000 tons each in this category and Japan with 300,000. The ratio of 5:5:3 was envisaged for use in determining allowable tonnage in other categories as well. Under considerable American pressure, all conferees agreed to accept the ratio for capital ships and thus permitted the completion of the naval treaty. Yet, the treaty set no limit on building smaller naval craft, and largely because of this gap, naval rivalry was to revive until the Japanese finally discarded arms control in the late 1930s.

The Washington treaties did not, as Secretary of State Charles Evans Hughes

President Calvin Coolidge

promised, end competition in naval armament. Neither did they prove "the greatest forward step in history to establish the reign of peace." To a considerable extent, the shortcomings reflected the unwillingness of the American people to take more than one step. After the repudiation of the League, some Americans had an uneasy conscience about their refusal to accept responsibility for the world order. The Washington conference for many ended the twinges of conscience. America, it was thought, had shown the way to peace in the field of disarmament and in settlement of problems in the Pacific. If Europe continued in turmoil, that was the upshot of Europeans not displaying the magnanimous view taken by the United States and instead pursuing the old secret diplomacy and balance-of-power politics that President Wilson had condemned.

Harding's successor, Calvin Coolidge, was a conscientious man who was in some respects out of step with the times, but whose honesty and integrity did much to repair the damage of Teapot Dome. He was succeeded by Herbert Hoover, who shared with him enthusiasm for an expanding, and largely unrestricted, economy. Under these two men, prosperity grew as would an expanding financial bubble. The late 1920s was a highly visible boom period, apparent in the giddily rising figures on the stock exchanges and the installment-plan mania for consumer goods. Despite a longstanding depression afflicting farmers, nearly everyone seemed to be achieving affluence. The three staid Republican administrations, with the big business affiliations, carried their political isolationism, rooted in tradition and disillusionment, to the economic sphere in many ways as well. Prosperity, it seemed, could be America-centered. By 1919, with the war over, America turned its attention to making money, and during the next decade it succeeded almost beyond its dreams. Mechanization, electrification, and the spread of assembly-line techniques led to a manufacturing output increase of 64% between 1919 and 1929. Wages and real earnings increased, and corporate profits rose even higher.

The business boom was based largely on two great industries, automobiles and construction. By 1929, a finished car rolled off the Ford production line in Detroit every 17 seconds, and there were 26 million automobiles and trucks on U.S. roads, or one for every five Americans. The automobile business led to a rise in a host of related industries; boosted consumption of oil, steel, and rubber; and helped spur a nationwide clamor for better roads. Increased mobility led to the growth of suburbia, which boosted still higher the already prosperous construction industry. American cities grew not only up but out as gleaming skyscrapers rose in the city centers and commuter suburbs spread around them.

America's inventive genius, its need to fill leisure time, and the spread of electrification all corresponded with the advertising industry's newly developed talent for making luxuries seem like necessities. Factories could hardly keep up with the demand for consumer goods and household appliances. Tourism and entertainment became multibillion-dollar industries. Sports became big business. Radio, movies, and phonograph records brought the smallest towns up to date. Americans seemed caught up in a new craze for possessions and the status quo these conferred.

Yet, beneath the glittering surface lurked hidden financial dangers, early and unheeded signs of great difficulties to come. Corporate profits soared 62% between 1923 and 1929. The average worker's real income rose only 11%, though. Since wages did not rise proportionally to industrial production and profits, workers could not afford the ever-increasing quantity of goods. More plant space had been created than could be profitably utilized, and production chronically outstripped demand. The widespread refusal of business to share profits with workers actually helped bring about a business downfall.

By 1929, the richest 5% of the population earned one-third of all personal income. The possibility of making large sums inevitably lured the unscrupulous, and the aftermath of the 1929 crash laid bare massive frauds by once respected financiers. Some 6,000 banks collapsed during the four-year period 1929–1932.

Furthermore, some elements of the economy had no share in the national prosperity. Several key industries, notably coal and textiles, never regained their prewar levels, unemployment was high, and wages were alarmingly low. Greater efficiency, improved farming techniques, and new fertilizers and machinery enabled farmers to greatly increase their yields, but a chronic glut resulted, and farm prices fell steadily. Between 1919 and 1929 agricultural income fell 22%.

ECONOMIC PROBLEMS OF THE PEACE 1919–1939

Trouble also developed because the war gave rise to a number of other serious problems. Above all, it upset the complex economic structure that had developed as a result of the Industrial Revolution. Most European nations suffered from unemployment and had a difficult time regaining their former prosperity. People naturally tended to place the blame on their governments. The latter tried hard to solve the chief problems, but proved unable to do so. To complicate matters, the war had hastened the rise of nationalism among colonial peoples. Revolts by native nationalists further weakened Europe's economy.

In the broader sweep of things, the First World War marked a turning point in Europe's history. For centuries, the Continent had been the economic, cultural, and political center of the world. Beginning in the 1920s, a period of decline set in. Europe's world position grew weaker and it was torn by internal problems. Moreover, World War I planted the seeds of a second, still more deadly, conflict. Allied disunity initially enabled Germany to escape the payment of reparations specified in the Versailles Treaty. The Peace Conference had not even been able to agree on the amount Germany should be forced to pay. When an amount finally was determined, Germany soon fell behind in the payments and requested they be reduced.

The British suggested a compromise. During and immediately after the war, the Allies borrowed large sums from the U.S. government. Britain proposed that the United States should cancel these war debts and that reparations should be reduced. The United States rejected this proposal, insisting that there was no connection between reparations and war debts that the Allies had to pay regardless of what Germany did. As technically sound as the position might have been, it was simply unrealistic. Debts and reparations were inseparable.

The French, supported by the Belgians and Italians, then took action to force Germany to pay in full. French troops occupied the Ruhr area, the industrial heart of Germany. The German government replied by stopping reparation payments completely. It also called on the people of the Ruhr to adopt a policy of passive resistance against the French. In answer to this appeal, Germans called a general strike. The dispute between the powers had disastrous results. Germany's economy collapsed completely and France too went through a severe financial crisis. All of Europe suffered as a result.

Britain stepped in to break the deadlock. A committee of bankers and economists, headed by the American financier, Charles G. Dawes, was appointed to restudy the reparations problem. The committee soon succeeded in working out a satisfactory compromise, whereby Germany agreed to resume reparations payments. Though its total obligation remained unchanged, its payments were cut in half and it received a large international loan to help restore the economy. France agreed to withdraw its troops from the Ruhr.

In the next few years, Germany floated numerous other loans abroad, mainly in the United States. With this foreign aid, it was able to make payments to the Allies. The latter, in turn, used this money to pay the installments on their war debts to the United States. Nonetheless, Germany continued to carp about its economic problems. In 1929, another committee—headed by another American, Owen D. Young—was appointed to reexamine the reparations question. On its recommendation, the powers agreed to a sizeable reduction in Germany's total obligation.

The war left in its wake serious economic problems. Governments staggered under a crushing burden of debt. Businesses had to shift from wartime to peacetime production. In many cases, these found it difficult or even impossible to regain their former markets. Millions of war workers and returning veterans had difficulty finding new jobs.

Inflation also resulted from the war. Unable to meet their expenses through taxation, governments borrowed heavily and printed large amounts of paper money, whose value dropped rapidly. Prices rose accordingly and in a few extreme cases, as in Germany and Hungary, inflation continued until the currency became completely worthless. Nonetheless, in many countries, governments succeeded in putting on the brakes. They cut expenses, balanced the budget, and stabilized the value of their currency. Prices dropped in some areas suddenly, and there was a period of hard times until businesses adjusted to the new conditions.

United States

The Great Depression: unemployed men board a train for Ottawa, June 1935
Public Archives Canada/C29461

ness, they spread the legend that German forces had not been defeated in the war, but had been "stabbed in the back" by the socialists and defeatists who had stirred up rebellion on the home front.

The rightists, like the communists, made several unsuccessful attempts to overthrow the republic. These were treated differently from communist insurgents and often enjoyed considerable popular support. Right-wing extremists assassinated several prominent officials who sought to cooperate with the Allies, and Germany's military leaders had scant respect for elected leaders.

The runaway inflation that resulted from the occupation of the Ruhr industrial areas in 1923 had disastrous effects upon the country. The savings of the once prosperous middle class were rapidly wiped out. Teachers, civil servants, and persons with fixed incomes were threatened with destitution. Industrial workers suffered because their wages did not keep pace with prices. The very classes whose support was crucial to the republic became disillusioned because they had lost so much. The extremist groups of the right- and left-wing varieties won many new followers.

The Dawes Plan eased the reparations burden and started a flow of foreign loans to Germany to prevent economic collapse.

After promising to live at peace with its neighbors, Germany was admitted to the League of Nations and a period of relative stability followed in Europe. The German government balanced the budget and issued new sound paper money. With the aid of foreign loans, the industrialists modernized and expanded their factories. Germany's export trade flourished, and its merchant marine was rebuilt. As the country prospered, the standard of living rose.

This period of relative prosperity was only temporary, though. It came to a halt after the Depression began in late 1929. Foreign investors refused to make new loans to Germany. German businesses were increasingly unable to sell their goods abroad. Factories and banks closed down, and the number of unemployed soared until one out of every three workers was idle. The country was once again laden with suffering and unrest. Hungry men wanted hard answers.

For the second time in a decade, the Republic seemed helpless to cope with these problems and people turned again to extremist parties. A large number of Communists won elected political office. Still greater were the gains made by the extremist parties of the right, above all, the National Socialists or Nazis. Although bitter political enemies and often involved

in violent clashes with one another, the Nazis and Communists found common ground in their hatred of Weimar Germany. Together, they brought about the destruction of the first German republic.

When Herbert Hoover entered the White House in 1929, he was among America's most admired men. He left it four years later in largely undeserved disgrace. An able engineer and self-made millionaire, he had given up private gain for public service during World War I. Known to his admirers as the "Great Engineer," he seemed ideally suited to guide the nation through any crisis. The crash that shook the country only seven months after his inauguration shattered America's confidence both in business and in Hoover, though. Suddenly thousands of holding companies and investment trusts were bankrupt. So were many of the people who relied on them.

On December 1, 1930, in New York City, the powerful Bank of the United States went belly up, destroying the savings of a half-million depositors. Some 2,300 banks collapsed in 1931 alone. Manufacturers with overstocked inventories cut losses by shutting down plants; between 1930 and 1933 an average of 64,000 workers joined the ranks of the unemployed each week. By 1933, some 13 million Americans were

74

out of work. Most of those with jobs had their wages slashed. Manufacturing output slid back to 1916 levels.

These grim statistics only hint at the human suffering caused by the Depression. Traditional American virtues—thrift, tenacity, and hard work—seemed no longer to make any difference. Many people were unsure whether they would be able to feed their families. Thousands were threatened with actual starvation. Hundreds of thousands of jobless men and boys roamed the countryside, stowing away on freight trains and haunting "hobo jungles."

The repercussions of the American Depression were worldwide. Japan lost its lucrative U.S. markets for exports, and in Latin America the withdrawal of U.S. loans left many governments in the middle of ambitious projects for which they no longer had funds. Australia and Canada, primarily agricultural countries, suffered from the sharp drop in farm prices. In Australia, the unemployment rate went from 10% in 1929 to over 30% in 1932. Around the world, more than 30 million people were unemployed. While hungry people in urban areas searched for food in refuse containers, thousands of acres of grain were allowed to rot in the fields because harvesting and shipping were unprofitable. In Brazil, millions of pounds of coffee were burned for the same reason. Early in the spring of 1931, just as the U.S. economy was beginning to show signs of a slight upturn, events abroad conspired to send it tumbling down again.

When the 1929 crash withdrew American loans from Europe, many economies went into a tailspin. Hardest hit were Germany and Austria, each saddled with heavy reparations payments to the Allies and wracked by unstable currencies and political strife. The two nations sought to merge their economies in a desperate effort to survive. In March 1931, France, partly for political reasons, demanded immediate payment of German short-term notes. A Viennese bank, the Creditanstalt, a traditional mainstay of Central European economies collapsed in May. The desperate German government, with nowhere else to turn, appealed to Washington for help, but in vain.

A decade of lofty U.S. tariffs on foreign imports had severely restricted foreign trade. Thus the United States made it difficult for European countries to earn the dollars with which the former allies could pay their war debts and the former enemies their reparations. By 1932, some six million Germans were unemployed; half the men between 16 and 30 were out of work. With over three million people without jobs in Great Britain, the government abandoned the convertibility of the

Benito Mussolini
Courtesy of Special Collections,
University of Virginia Library

pound sterling into gold, a move swiftly imitated by some 40 other countries. As nations retreated behind barriers of high tariffs, import quotas, competitive devaluations, and other attempts to protect their own industries, international trade collapsed, and national self-interest supplanted the international cooperation that would have speeded recovery.

THE DICTATORS TAKE OVER

Italy

In Italy, Benito Mussolini established the Fascist party, with a program designed to appeal to all classes. The fascists promised to provide jobs for the unemployed, land for the farm laborers, better conditions for the city workers, and protection for private property and private enterprise. Above all, fascism stressed the importance of jingoism and hard-edge nationalism. Mussolini promised to end political disunity in Italy and to provide the country with a strong and efficient government. Then it would be able to take its "rightful place" as one of the world's leading powers.

After Mussolini was named premier in 1922, he did not destroy Italian democracy all at once. First he persuaded the parliament to grant him emergency powers "for the purpose of restoring order." He slowly converted the government to fascism by filling important posts with his followers. He also redoubled his campaign of violence and terror against the opponents of fascism. When moderates in parliament protested, Mussolini dissolved it.

Once in control, Mussolini introduced many far-reaching political changes. He became head of government responsible only to the king. He served as commander-in-chief of the armed forces, appointed all significant officials throughout Italy, and issued decrees having the force of law. He proclaimed himself *Il Duce* (The Leader) of the Fascist party, which became the only legal political party in the country. His secret police sought to eliminate most vestiges of opposition. Rival political leaders were killed, imprisoned, or driven into exile. Only fascist or pro-fascist newspapers were allowed to appear.

In dealing with Italy's economic problems, the Italian dictator operated in accordance with the time-honored principle that the new broom sweeps clean. He dismissed thousands of unnecessary public officials and slashed government spending. To help check inflation, he also increased taxes. Italian businesses regained confidence and the country gradually went back to work. Mussolini took steps to solve the problem of Italy's lack of natural resources by developing hydroelectric power and making the nation less dependent on imports of coal. He also sought to make it self-sufficient in food by launching the "Battle of the Wheat." The government reclaimed wastelands, spread information about scientific farming, and gave prizes to farmers who introduced progressive methods. Very high tariffs and other restrictions on trade helped to reduce purchases from abroad.

Mussolini originally posed as a staunch defender of capitalism. Nonetheless, once in power, he gradually brought both labor and business under government control. Strikes and lockouts were strictly forbidden. All existing trade unions and employers associations were made part of a new system, "the corporate state." The nation's economy was divided into more than a score of different fields, such as building construction, mining industries, and textile products. Each was placed under a "corporation" or council, composed of representatives of the employers, the workers and the Fascist party.

The main duties of these corporations were to fix wages and hours, settle other industrial disputes, and regulate the price and quality of goods. Mussolini was the president of each corporation, and all its decisions had to be approved by him. Through the corporate system, the Italian dictator carried out his precept, "Everything in the state, nothing against the state, nothing outside the state."

An extreme nationalist, Mussolini was determined to restore Italian greatness. Even while he was cutting other government expenses, he steadily built up the army, navy and air force. He spoke con-

United States

Mussolini and his "Black Shirts"

stantly about the glories of war. "Fascism," he said, "rejects the pacifism which masks surrender and cowardice. War alone brings all human energies to their highest tension and sets a seal of nobility on the people who have the courage to face it." Military training became an important activity in the schools and especially in the fascist youth organizations. To increase Italy's manpower, Mussolini forbade emigration, taxed bachelors, and gave prizes to large families. "The Mediterranean is destined to return to us," he promised. "Rome is destined to become once more the city which directs the civilization of the whole western world."

Germany

In the weeks after being named Chancellor of Germany in January 1933, Adolf Hitler effected changes it had taken Mussolini years to bring about. He swiftly seized dictatorial powers. The old German states were abolished and the new districts were placed under Nazi officials. All political groups were dissolved. The Nazis became the only legal party in Germany. Opposition newspapers were suppressed or placed under Nazi control. A large secret police, the Gestapo, was organized. Persons suspected of opposing the "New Order" were arrested, beaten, killed, or sent off to concentration camps.

Adolf Hitler—Germany's Mussolini?

Courtesy of Special Collections,
University of Virginia Library

Like other dictators, Hitler was eager to control public opinion. A Ministry of Propaganda and Enlightenment was created to indoctrinate the German people with Nazi ideas. It controlled all publishing firms, instructed the newspapers what to print, and ran the radio stations. Art, music, and the theater were also used to spread Nazi propaganda. Books that displeased the Nazis were banned and often torched. Anti-Nazi intellectuals were imprisoned or driven into exile. To keep out "alien ideas," foreign newspapers and books were barred from Germany and foreign radio programs were jammed by special transmitters.

Hitler stressed the importance of "nazifying" the younger generation, and schools were rigidly controlled by the Nazi Ministry of Education. Military discipline, unquestioning obedience, and painful corporal punishment were introduced. The course of study and the textbooks were carefully revised. History, for example, was twisted to accord with Hitler's race theories, and a special study of "race science" was inaugurated. After school and on weekends, training was continued by special Nazi youth organizations.

As he had threatened earlier, Hitler also introduced a crude and cruel anti-Semitic program. Step by step, he deprived German Jews of their rights. First, he dis-

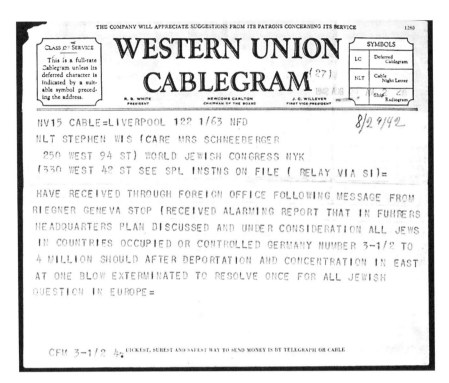

THE COMPANY WILL APPRECIATE SUGGESTIONS FROM ITS PATRONS CONCERNING ITS SERVICE

WESTERN UNION
CABLEGRAM (27)

Evidence of the Holocaust, 1942

the French frontier. He negotiated alliances with two other dissatisfied nations, Italy and Japan, and secretly authorized a full-scale buildup of Germany's armed forces, still theoretically restricted by the Versailles Treaty. In March 1935 the Nazis publicly disclosed plans to create a modern air force and a conscript army. In the first overt act of aggression a year later, German troops reoccupied the Rhineland, which had been demilitarized in the peace treaty. The Western Powers responded with little more than half-hearted protests.

In November 1937, Hitler met secretly with his top military and political aides to present his plans for the expansion into East-Central Europe to obtain more *Lebensraum* ("living space") and natural resources. The first step would be the consolidation of Austria and part of Czechoslovakia into the Nazi Third Reich. Then Germany could push eastward into Poland and the Ukraine.

Spain

In 1936, Spain became a testing ground for Europe's new aggressors. On the Iberian Peninsula, Germany rehearsed military operations; Britain, France and the United States practiced appeasement; and the Soviet Union engaged in a sideshow performance of mischief and foreign adventurism. Tens of thousands of troops from various countries would acquire a preview of the coming horrors of global war.

In July 1936, antigovernment risings occurred in numerous Spanish army garrisons. That same month, German aircraft began to transport General Francisco Franco's troops from Morocco to the mainland and by the end of the month the Nationalists controlled most of northern Spain. The

missed them from government service and the professions. Next, he took away their citizenship, forbade them to marry Aryans, and declared mixed marriages illegal. Later, he ordered employees to discharge their Jewish workers and forced Jewish businessmen to sell out their holdings. When a young Polish Jew killed a minor Nazi official in 1938, Hitler ordered even harsher measures. Throughout Germany, Jewish shops were smashed and looted. Synagogues were blown up and holy articles were defiled. A heavy fine was imposed on the entire Jewish community. Thousands of Jewish leaders were imprisoned in concentration camps.

Many Germans simply closed their eyes to Hitler's inhumane measures in part because he acted vigorously to address the country's economic problems. To deal with unemployment, he ordered employees to hire additional workers. He also organized the unemployed into labor battalions and set them to work building roads, airfields, fortifications, and other public works. Most important of all, he launched a huge program to rearm Germany. The economy boomed as hundreds of thousands of young men were drafted for the armed forces and large orders were placed for military supplies. Instead of unemployment, a labor shortage developed.

The workers gained economic security at the expense of their liberty. Trade unions were abolished and strikes were outlawed. A Nazi-controlled organization—the National Labor Front—fixed wages and hours and settled disputes with employers. Workers were forbidden to leave their jobs without permission and could be shifted from one job to another by the government. To increase efficiency, the government encouraged the growth of giant trusts and monopolies at the expense of small business. Hitler was even more eager than Mussolini to preserve the capitalist system, but German businessmen, like all other Germans, came under the heel of the authoritarian state.

The chief purpose of the Nazi economic controls was to strengthen the nation's economy and to make it self-sufficient in time of war. The government constructed huge plants to produce steel from low-grade iron ore. It built other plants to produce synthetic petroleum and rubber from coal and synthetic cloth from wool. Stockpiles were created of essential raw materials that could not be produced in Germany. To pay for this costly program, as well as for armaments, Hitler had to increase taxes and to mobilize the population.

The Nazis proved quite successful in winning popular support for their foreign policy. From the start, the Nazi dictator made it clear that he meant to tear up the Treaty of Versailles. When the powers refused to allow Germany equal armaments, Hitler withdrew from the League of Nations. He created a large citizen army, built powerful air and naval forces, and erected strong fortifications along

General Francisco Franco

United States

The horror of April 26, 1937, in Guernica . . .

. . . and Picasso's stark depiction—*Guernica*

A victim of the civil war amidst the ruins of her home

Republican government soon discovered it would encounter difficulties purchasing the arms needed for its defense. Traditionally, international law permits the sale of arms to a legitimate government and forbids their sale to rebels. But France, though sympathetic to the Spanish Republican cause, did not dare risk a domestic political split by selling weapons to Spain, nor was it willing to antagonize Hitler or Mussolini. Britain forcefully advocated an arms embargo to both Republicans and Nationalists. The United States, under the Neutrality Act of May 1937, was prohibited from selling arms to any belligerent nation. France, Britain and the United States together remained committed to their "non-intervention" policies. Germany and Italy provided substantial military assistance to Franco without scruple or hesitation.

From October 1936 to March 1937, the Nationalists, united under Franco, consolidated their gains against the fragmented Republican coalition of left-wing and liberal groups. By October 1937, backed by massive German and Italian aid, they overcame a stubborn pocket of resistance in the northern provinces. During the next nine months, Franco's troops pushed westward to the coast, and by July 1938, had driven a wide wedge between Catalonia and the rest of the republic. By February 1939, the Catalonian provinces had fallen, and in the last days of March, the Republican garrisons around Madrid surrendered. On April 1, 1939, the Nationalists took control of the Spanish capital.

For the Republican losers in the Spanish Civil War, the process of arrest and summary execution continued. Tens of thousands were imprisoned. Franco promised to restore the "traditional values" of Spain. His interpretation of those values resulted in a dictatorship as strict as anything in Spanish history.

The traditional policy of the United States had been to export arms to the legitimate government, in this case, the republicans. So strong was antiwar feeling in America, though, that Congress, taking its cue from President Roosevelt, extended the existing neutrality legislation to civil conflict in January 1937. The Western democracies, determined to stay out of the Spanish Civil War, condemned a fellow democracy to death. While standing on the sidelines, the United States tacitly encouraged a conflict that proved to be a dress rehearsal for the Second World War.

Japan

The Great Depression led to the emergence of a reactionary government in Japan. The island empire suffered a sharp drop in its exports, many businesses went bankrupt, and millions became unemployed. Peasants were paid ruinously low prices for their produce. In Japan, as in Germany and other countries, large numbers of people lost all confidence in democracy and capitalism. Japanese reactionary forces gained rapidly in influence as a result. Their nationalistic secret societies became increasingly active in politics. Mili-

tary leaders assumed a new role as champions of the peasants and workers. They announced that they could solve the country's economic problems through a course of aggression and conquest in China.

The first target of the military leaders was Manchuria where Japan had long kept an army, primarily to protect its investments. In 1931, the leaders of this army suddenly began military operations without consulting the government in Tokyo. Charging that Chinese "bandits" were attacking Japanese property and citizens, they launched a large-scale police action against them. Despite the protests of the League of Nations, they quickly overran the entire province. They gave it a new name, Manchukuo, and established a puppet government to rule there. The new Japanese protectorate was larger than France and Germany combined.

Japanese imperialism in Manchuria prompted a new wave of nationalism in China. Protests rang out and Chinese students demanded a boycott of Japanese goods. In response, the Japanese navy attacked the port city of Shanghai in 1932, where fierce fighting raged for several weeks. Casualties on both sides were heavy, especially among the city's civilian population. Despite strong pressure from the Western Powers, the Japanese ended their attack only after the Chinese government agreed to call off the boycott.

The aggressive policies of the military leaders aroused considerable criticism among the liberal elements in Japan. In an effort to silence them, right-wing extremists murdered the premier and other liberal leaders in 1932. The policy of violence proved effective in weakening the opposition. For the next few years, the militarists dominated the government and were free to proceed with their ambitious plans of conquest. Using Manchuria as their base, they soon began to penetrate northern China. Beginning in 1934, the Japanese began to proclaim what they called their own "Monroe Doctrine," whose basic concept was "Asia for the Asiatics," or rather China for the Japanese, to the exclusion of America's Open-Door privileges.

The costs of conquest soon became a tiresome burden for the Japanese people, who returned a liberal government to power in the election of 1936. Angered by this defeat, the military leaders resorted to terror for the second time. A group of young officers assassinated several liberal cabinet ministers and seized control of important public buildings. The emperor himself had to intervene to end their revolt.

The militarists achieved their purpose, though. The liberal cabinet fell from power and was replaced by a cabinet dominated by the army. Thereafter, the militarists were completely in control. The

United States

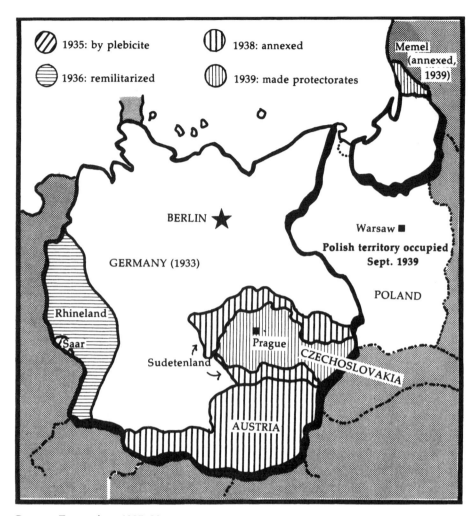

Map legend:
- 1935: by plebiscite
- 1936: remilitarized
- 1938: annexed
- 1939: made protectorates

Memel (annexed, 1939)

BERLIN ★

GERMANY (1933)

Rhineland

Saar

Sudetenland

Prague

CZECHOSLOVAKIA

AUSTRIA

Warsaw ■

Polish territory occupied Sept. 1939

POLAND

German Expansion, 1935–39

Soviet dictator, Joseph Stalin, was angered because he was not consulted about the fate of Czechoslovakia. He charged that the Western Powers were deliberately encouraging Hitler to advance eastward to attack the Soviet Union. He thereafter began to reconsider his limited cooperation with the democracies against fascism.

INTO THE ABYSS

In the spring of 1939, Hitler provoked a new crisis by demanding the return to Germany of the city of Danzig (now Gdansk), a largely German-speaking city on the Baltic Sea, but Poland's chief port. Supported by Britain and France, Poland refused to yield. The European democracies prepared for war and turned to the Soviet Union for help. The British government sent a mission to Moscow to arrange for a military alliance. The negotiations stalled, and then in August, a startled world learned that Stalin had concluded an accord with Nazi Germany. Hitler and Stalin had agreed to divide Poland as well as consign the Baltic states (Estonia, Lat-

via, and Lithuania) and Bessarabia to Soviet rule. The following week, on September 1, 1939, German armies smashed into Poland. Britain and France, fulfilling their pledges to their ally, declared war on Germany. Less than three weeks later, the Soviet Union also invaded Poland although the Allies did not declare war on it.

The policies of ruthless conquest pursued by Germany, Japan, and Italy made war almost inevitable. To the historian, though, the fundamental question is, "What made each of these nations act as it did?" The basic causes of World War II were not dissimilar from those of World War I. British Foreign Secretary Sir Edward Grey captured the spirit of an entire era the day his country went to war in 1914. Looking from a window across London, he remarked ruefully, "The lamps are going out all over Europe; we shall not see them lit again in our time." The observation was prophetic. The elation of the 1918 armistice was soon blemished by unemployment, hunger, and inflation. The promises of self-determination often were disregarded in fixing postwar

boundaries, leaving dissatisfied minorities as breeding places for future ethnic strife. Nations hardly abandoned war, as many hoped they would after the horrors of 1914–18. Turks fought Greeks; Russians fought Russians; Poles fought Russians. Hindsight shows that in the years following the First World War, people and nations had already proceeded down the path that would lead to another and greater world conflict. The lamps had indeed gone out. Future historians are likely to view the period 1914–1945 as a time of continuous world struggle, the 30-Years War of the 20th century. Hence, the two world wars were part of the same conflict, the years between only an armed truce. The principal causes were:

Nationalism. Nationalism reached new extremes in the years prior to the Second World War. The Nazis were determined to fight and prepared their people for a war of revenge and aggression. Hitler rewarded his followers with the illusion that they were part of a master race. The militaristic Japanese rulers told the public that it was their divine mission to dominate the other peoples of East Asia. Mussolini promised the Italian people that he would restore the glories of the Roman empire. By unleashing the spirit of belligerent nationalism, the Axis leaders mobilized their peoples for wars of conquest.

Imperialism. The desire to gain new territories was another basic cause of the war. The Axis Powers asserted they lacked sufficient raw materials, markets, and land for their fast-growing populations. They wanted to possess great empires, surpassing those of Britain and France.

Militarism. As usual, militarism went hand in hand with nationalism and imperialism. The dictators built up their armed forces and were full of sound and fury. The exorbitant cost of armaments increased financial difficulties. To solve their economic problems and make good their boasts, they had to deliver on their promised conquests, even when this meant war.

Absence of international order. Why did the other powers fail to stop the aggressors before they became so strong? The main reason was that they placed their own narrow interests above the common cause of international cooperation. As a result, the League of Nations failed and the world once again suffered from lack of international order. Democratic nations, especially Great Britain and France, were unwilling to make the sacrifices necessary to preserve peace. In the end, they were compelled to make far greater ones in the Second World War.

Hitler speaking to historical Reichstag session, September 1, 1939

Courtesy of Special Collections,
University of Virginia Library

During the early years of World War II, the Axis Powers gained the upper hand over the Allies. They had larger amounts of modern equipment, and above all, superior strategy and tactics. Since they were on the offensive, they could choose the places to strike with concentrated force. The defenders had to spread themselves thin to protect against many points of attack. The Axis Powers also enjoyed the advantages of a central location, whereas the Allies were often encumbered by long supply lines.

The situation gradually changed as a result of the great Axis victories early in the war. Germany, and particularly Japan, acquired long supply lines and needed large forces to protect them. The conquered people, affronted by foreign rule, formed underground resistance movements that organized sabotage.

When German armies invaded Poland in September 1939, they gave the world a fearful demonstration of the powerful new offensive weapons developed after World War I. Nazi heavy bombers smashed the small Polish air force on the ground. Dive bombers and tanks shattered the Polish infantry. Polish forces retreated eastward in confusion where Soviet forces, cooperating with the Nazis, struck them in the rear. In less than three weeks, the Polish army virtually ceased to exist. The capital city of Warsaw, battered by German aircraft and artillery, held out a few days longer.

Moscow reaped a rich reward from its alliance with Hitler. The Soviets annexed eastern Poland and took control of the three small Baltic republics. A short time later, they demanded that Finland cede territory adjacent to Leningrad. When Finland refused, the Soviet Union invaded. Although the Finns succeeded in holding out for a time and put up a fierce fight, they were eventually overwhelmed by Soviet superiority in troops and equipment. True, the Soviets obtained the territory they demanded, but lost heavily in prestige and were expelled from the League of Nations. Suffering fearful casualties, the Red Army appeared inept.

Through the autumn and winter of 1939–1940, the French and German armies in the west sat quietly in their fortified lines. Neither side demonstrated any inclination to open a full-scale offensive. Then, when spring came, German forces struck with startling suddenness. Without warning, Germany invaded Denmark and Norway. Denmark surrendered in a matter of hours. Southern Norway also quickly fell to the invaders. In an attempt to stiffen Norwegian resistance, the British and French rushed forces to central and northern Norway. German aircraft and armor inflicted such heavy losses that the Allies were soon compelled to withdraw. By taking Denmark and Norway, Germany acquired valuable submarine and air bases along the Atlantic.

Even before the battle of Norway was over, Germany launched attacks against France and its neutral neighbors, Belgium and the Netherlands. Thousands of German troops poured suddenly across the Dutch border and special forces seized the water gates to prevent the defenders from flooding the country. German bombers carried out paralyzing raids on Rotterdam and other important cities. The Netherlands, assaulted from within and without, surrendered in less than a week. A second German force quickly broke through the Belgian frontier defenses and advanced into that country. The Belgians, reinforced by sizeable British and French forces, managed to fight on for two weeks. Recognizing that further resistance served no purpose, the Belgian king surrendered to the Germans.

Meanwhile, the main German attack was directed against France. With dive bombers and armor leading the way, the German forces quickly broke through the weak points of the French defenses. Infantry then poured through the gaps, cutting French supply lines and communications. Looping northward to the English Channel, they cut off the Allied forces in Belgium and northern France. Hundreds of thousands of Allied troops were trapped with their backs to the sea near the French city of Dunkirk. The British government hastily mobilized all available craft and managed to evacuate nearly 300,000 British and French troops to Great Britain. Though most of the army's equipment was lost, the "miracle of Dunkirk" offered the Allies some consolation in the midst of disasters.

Signing the German–Soviet Pact (August 23, 1939) which divided Poland between them. L. to r.: Germany's Ribbentrop with Stalin, Molotov.

United States

Finnish soldiers—the "invisible wall"

Pockets of resistance broke quickly as the German forces resumed their advance southward into France. They smashed through a new defense line and moved rapidly on Paris. Mussolini, confident that the war was almost over, joined his Axis partner and attacked in the south. Thereafter, French resistance collapsed completely. Ignoring British pleas to carry on the war from North Africa, the French government sued for an armistice. A mere six weeks after the start of the offensive, Hitler became the master of Western Europe.

At relatively little cost, the Germans took two million prisoners and gained control of one of the richest countries in Europe. Axis forces proceeded to occupy the entire Atlantic coast and the important industrial areas, including Paris. The southern area of the country not occupied by German forces, commonly known as Vichy France, was ruled by an authoritarian regime that collaborated closely with the Nazi Reich.

Under a stubborn and determined leader, General Charles de Gaulle, a group of French patriots formed the "Free French" movement in Britain. With British help, the Free French organized an underground resistance movement within occupied France. The resistance secretly fought the Nazi occupation and kept alive the hopes of liberation.

In the summer of 1940, Britain stood alone. Like Napoleon before him, Hitler had to gain command of the English Channel in order to invade Britain. His first problem was the destruction of the Royal Air Force (RAF). Without an air umbrella, the British fleet would be at the mercy of German aircraft. For weeks, swarms of German planes flew daily over England to engage the RAF in air combat. The British, though heavily outnumbered, inflicted such heavy losses on the enemy that Hitler had to abandon his invasion plans. Britain's wartime prime minister, Winston Churchill, paid grateful tribute to the RAF pilots who had effectively saved their country. "Never in the field of human conflict," he declared, "was so much owed by so many to so few."

Nonetheless, the trials of the British people had only begun. The German air force continued the bombing offensive to break their spirit and compel the government to give up. Night after night, through the autumn and winter months, the mass raids continued. Thousands of British civilians were killed. Cities were damaged and normal life was disrupted. Yet, the British doggedly worked on, producing a flood of war materials for both defense and counterattack. By the spring of 1941, the RAF was able to conduct large-scale bombing attacks upon Germany, which brought the war home to the German people.

Envious of Hitler's triumphs, Mussolini set out to gain some successes of his own. In the autumn of 1940, Italian forces suddenly attacked Greece. The results were disastrous for the Italian dictator. In little more than a month, the Greeks drove the invaders out and pursued them into Albania. Mussolini also suffered serious setbacks on other fronts. In North Africa, a large Italian army advanced from Libya into western Egypt where a much smaller British force launched a surprise counteroffensive. They easily routed the Italians, chasing them back across Libya and taking many thousands of prisoners. British imperial forces also began the liberation of Ethiopia and the conquest of the neighboring Italian colonies.

When spring came, the Germans moved to rescue their Italian partner and

Norway's Quisling returning the salute of a German officer

Ascent to Globalism

power, coupled with the uncertainty, after the successes of the first weeks of the eastern campaign, as to whether it was more important to capture Moscow or to press on to occupy the Don industrial region and towards the oil of the Caucasus.

Although Germany and the Soviet Union cooperated in the invasion and partition of East-Central Europe from Finland to the Black Sea, as specified in the Hitler-Stalin Pact of 1939, neither the Germans nor the Soviets ever really trusted one another. Stalin became alarmed as Hitler gained one spectacular victory after another. Hitler, in turn, resented the easy gains of the Soviets in Poland and in the Baltic area as a result of stunning Nazi victory. Relations worsened when the two dictators disagreed over the division of the Balkans and other spoils. In July 1940, Hitler ordered his generals to prepare for an attack in the east.

In June 1941, the Nazi juggernaut fell upon Russia without warning, supported by Finnish, Hungarian, Italian, Romanian, and some Spanish troops. The Axis forces inflicted enormous casualties on the ill-

General de Gaulle inspecting Free French troops, London

Courtesy of Special Collections, University of Virginia Library

to extend Axis control over the Balkans. The German dictator had earlier occupied Romania and Bulgaria without a struggle. Using these countries as their bases, German forces advanced against Yugoslavia and Greece. German armored columns, aided by squadrons of aircraft, smashed through the defenders' positions. Yugoslavia was conquered in 12 days, and the Greeks, though reinforced by a British army hastily drawn from North Africa, were crushed only days later. The operations were certainly impressive: in the entire campaign, German forces suffered fewer than 700 casualties. They had overrun most of the Balkans. The British managed to evacuate most of their troops from Greece to the nearby island of Crete, but the Germans seized Crete also in the next weeks. Only about half of the original British expeditionary army succeeded in escaping back to Egypt.

The Germans also dispatched a specially trained desert force to stiffen the Italians in North Africa. The combined Axis armies quickly defeated the weakened British and launched a new invasion of Egypt. The Suez Canal and the entire oil-rich Middle East lay open to conquest. Instead of pressing the advantage, however, Hitler began his ill-fated invasion of Russia. There has been much speculation whether it was the delay caused by the Balkan campaign that prevented the achievement of final victory by the time of the onset of winter. Perhaps even more fundamental was the basic German underestimation of Russia's resources and

United States

prepared Red Army. Initial German successes were even more impressive than those in Western Europe and the Balkans. As great land masses were swallowed up, so were entire Soviet armies. In the first months of the campaign, the Soviet Union suffered over two and one-half million casualties and the Soviet air force in Western Russia was almost completely destroyed in the first week of operations. By November, the invading armies had conquered eastern Poland, the Baltic Republics, White Russia, most of the Ukraine, and had laid siege to Leningrad.

As the war ground on, the Axis forces confronted Russia's great ally, winter. The offensive froze before the gates of Moscow and it became evident that the Germans would win no quick or easy victory. Once again, as in the Battle of Britain, Hitler's plans had miscarried. Yet, Berlin still dominated most of Western Europe and European Russia.

THE ARSENAL OF DEMOCRACY

In September, 1939, the great majority of Americans had certain definite ideas regarding the war which had broken out in Europe. One was that there was little doubt as to where "war guilt" lay. They had watched Hitler's increasing disregard of Germany's treaty obligations and had seen him become ever more and more aggressive. At the same time they had witnessed the leaders of Great Britain and France make numerous efforts to appease the Führer in order to prevent the outbreak of another war, even when such appeasement had entailed the destruction or dismemberment of weaker states. Most Americans were convinced, therefore, that the war was the direct outcome of Nazi designs and technique, and, since they abhorred these, most Americans were openly sympathetic with the Allies and hoped they would win what was feared would be a long war. But the great majority of Americans fervently hoped that the United States would not be drawn into this conflict as it had been in 1917. President Roosevelt, in a radio address on September 3, 1939, to some extent expressed these two ideas when he stated that he could not "ask that every American remain neutral in thought," but at the same time stated his hope and belief that "the United States will keep out of this war."

These two fundamental ideas of the American people were further expressed in a new Neutrality Act which was passed on November 4, 1939. Under the Neutrality Act of 1937 the United States government was compelled to place an embargo on the shipment of implements of war to belligerent powers. Obviously, because of Britain's control of the seas,

this act operated not to the detriment of Germany but to that of the Allies. Most Americans were willing to supply the Allies with the sinews of war if it could be done without involving the United States directly in conflict. The new act was designed to accomplish these two ends. The Allies were free to purchase war materials in the United States, but such materials might not be carried to a belligerent country in American ships. Furthermore, the act empowered the President to forbid American citizens and ships to enter combat areas in war zones. Thus, it was hoped, there would be no occasion for the United States to be dragged into this war as in 1917 because of the sinking of American ships by German submarines. Most Americans, it appeared, were willing to sit on the sidelines and watch the Allies defeat the Nazi dictator.

From this somewhat placid state the United States was rudely shaken by the startling developments in Europe in 1940. After the fall of France the feeling grew among Americans that Great Britain was their first line of defense against the Nazi and Fascist dictators, and that the British must be assisted with all aid "short of war." After Dunkirk the United States government turned back to American manufacturers—who rushed them to Britain—rifles, machine guns, field guns, and airplanes, which were needed to re-equip the evacuated British troops. In September, 50 over-age U.S. destroyers were transferred to Great Britain in return for 99-year leases of naval and air bases in the islands of Newfoundland, Bermuda, the Bahamas, Jamaica, St. Lucia, Trinidad, and Antigua, and in British Guiana. By this transaction Great Britain was strengthened to defend her overseas lifeline and the United States secured advance bases for the defense of North America and the Caribbean.

While there was some difference of opinion among Americans regarding the policy of all aid to Great Britain "short of war," there were few who doubted that the United States should itself embark upon a sweeping program of national preparedness. In September, 1940, Congress passed and President Roosevelt approved the first American law to prescribe compulsory military service in time of peace. By the terms of the Selective Training and Service Act every male citizen who was between the ages of twenty-one and thirty-six was "liable for training and service in the land or naval forces of the United States." On November 18 the first groups of drafted men were inducted into the army. But men without weapons would, of course, be of little use in defending the country. During 1950 the government authorized the expenditure of more than $17

billion for a "two-ocean navy" and for all the latest and most efficient weapons for land and air warfare, and in the first six months of 1941 more billions of dollars were voted for similar purposes.

On December 29, 1940, President Roosevelt in a radio address pointed out that the American people faced the possibility of an Axis victory, which would mean " a new and terrible era in which the whole world, our hemisphere included, would be run by threats of brute force." In that address the President defined what many considered a doctrine worthy to rank alongside the Monroe Doctrine, namely, that the American people were determined not to permit control of the seaways leading to their coast to pass into the hands of a power hostile to their own democratic way of life and bent on its destruction. British sea power in the Atlantic was recognized as a bulwark friendly to democracy.

This bill, which was popularly called the Lend-Lease Bill, after long debate in both houses of Congress finally became law on March 11. It represented another long step away from neutrality and isolationism. The act authorized the President to manufacture for, exchange with, sell, lease, lend or in other ways make available any defense article to "the government of any country whose defense the President deems vital to the defense of the United States." Payment might be made by any means which the President deemed satisfactory, meaning that Great Britain and other nations at war with the Axis would be able to obtain large amounts of military aid which they otherwise could not have afforded. Roosevelt promised that United States would become the great "arsenal of democracy."

Even prior to the outbreak of the Second World War, the aggressive actions of the Axis Powers raised serious problems for the United States. For a considerable time, the American people engaged in a great debate over the proper course to follow. In his heart-of-hearts, President Roosevelt was convinced that the United States could not stand idly by while the Axis set out to dominate the world. Like-minded thinkers believed that the country could be safe only if it supported the Western democracies against the aggressors. Another large and influential group, with many champions in Congress, urged the government to follow a strict policy of neutrality. They sought to avoid the actions they thought had led the United States into the First World War.

In 1939 the United States was still emerging from the depths of economic depression. Although the worst was over, close to 10 million people remained unemployed. The mood of the country

Ascent to Globalism

Franklin D. Roosevelt
Courtesy of Special Collections,
University of Virginia Library

Airpower advocate William "Billy" Mitchell

Joseph Stalin receiving applause
Courtesy of Special Collections,
University of Virginia Library

mans, once Britain fell, would invade the Americas. A poll taken in March 1940 showed that 43% of Americans believed a German victory would menace their security. By July, the figure reached 69%.

The delivery of American supplies to Britain posed a difficult problem, though. German submarines and aircraft were taking a heavy toll of British shipping. The United States therefore established a "neutrality patrol system" in the western Atlantic to warn of the presence of German raiders. Hitler replied by ordering his U-boats to attack American vessels. Roosevelt then directed the U.S. Navy to shoot on sight any Axis submarine found anywhere in the Atlantic. By the autumn of 1941, an undeclared naval war between Germany and the United States was already underway. Yet, it was turmoil in the Pacific, rather than the Atlantic, which finally brought the United States into war.

Japan's militaristic rulers, although still unable to conquer China, sought to profit from the difficulties of the Western Powers. They sent strong forces into French Indo-China and sought to gain control of the rich Netherlands East Indies. As a warning to the United States not to interfere, Japan signed a full-fledged military assistance alliance with Germany and Italy.

The U.S. government, although seeking to avoid open conflict, took a series of steps to restrain Japan. First, it terminated the trade treaty between the two countries. Next, it forbade the export of scrap iron and aviation fuel. Finally, it froze Japan's assets in the United States, thereby making it almost impossible for that country to obtain goods on credit. The United States supported the Chinese by granting them several large loans and by sending them military supplies.

AMERICA'S ENTRY

The Japanese leaders had no intention of abandoning their programs of conquest, however. In preparation for a showdown, one of the foremost extremists, Hinsheki Tojo, became premier. Tojo called a special session of the parliament to vote a larger military budget. Secretly, he also ordered a powerful fleet, including several aircraft carriers, to sail eastward across the Pacific. At the same time, he sent a last peace mission to Washington.

The Japanese envoys presented several demands that were unacceptable to the United States. The counterproposals of the U.S. government were equally unacceptable to Japan. While the negotiations were still going on, the Japanese fleet was ordered to carry out a prearranged plan of action. The Japanese air strike hit the American Pacific fleet, lying peacefully at its base in Pearl Harbor on December 7,

1941. Japanese aircraft sank or damaged eight battleships, as well as many other vessels. The attack ended the long debate between the isolationists and those who favored helping Britain and its allies. The

for a decade had been turned inward, as government and private citizen alike struggled with economic problems. In the mid-1930s, the prevailing mood was isolationist. Yet several years later, President Roosevelt, supported by a coalition of eastern and southern Democrats, intellectuals, some businessmen, and many newspapers, was able to prevail against prominent isolationists like Republican Senator William E. Borah of Idaho and Colonel Charles A. Lindbergh. When Britain and France declared war on Germany after the invasion of Poland, the arms embargo section of the latest neutrality act was lifted, enabling Britain to purchase weapons.

The United States gradually shifted its position as the war continued. The "cash and carry" provision permitted purchase of war materials by future allies. When France surrendered in 1940, many Americans began to fear that Germany would crush Britain and then commence operations in the Western Hemisphere. The U.S. government then began to take measures to forestall this threat, and Congress continued to vote for large-scale armament programs. Despite isolationist opposition, President Roosevelt supplied Britain with large quantities of military equipment.

Ordinary Americans reacted to Hitler's conquest of Europe with substantial apprehension. Some even thought the Ger-

87

United States

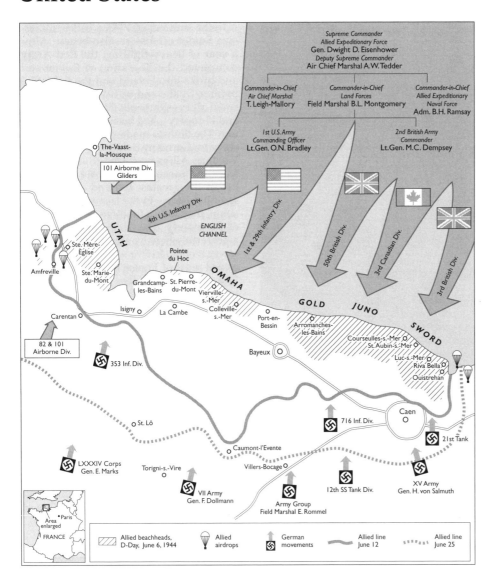

A few weeks later, the Japanese launched another offensive. The largest force they had yet assembled sailed out into the central Pacific, in the direction of Midway Island. The U.S. fleet, though still heavily outnumbered, advanced to meet the foe. Catching the Japanese by surprise, U.S. naval aircraft sank several aircraft carriers and a number of other capital ships. The Battle of Midway brought to an end Japan's westward advance in the Pacific.

In the summer of 1942, the United States finally went over to the offensive. The Japanese had earlier occupied the Solomon Islands, from which they could menace the American supply line to Australia. A strong force of Marines was sent to capture the little island of Guadalcanal, at the southern tip of the Solomons. The battle was long and bitterly fought. Four months passed before the Japanese defenders, protected by thick jungle, were finally crushed.

For the next two years, the Allied forces in the southwest Pacific followed the strategy of "island hopping." They would conquer an island, quickly build airfields, and fly in planes. With strong aerial protection, they would then attack another important island a few hundred miles nearer Japan. The Japanese forces in the southwest Pacific were gradually cut off from supplies and began to wither on the vine. Even so, the fierce resistance made the Allied advances relatively slow and costly.

Meanwhile, the Allies also gained successes against the Japanese on other fronts. In August 1943, a U.S. force retook the Aleutian Islands off the coast of Alaska, which had been captured by the Japanese early in 1942. A Japanese invasion of India was driven back by the British. The latter then began a slow reconquest of mountainous, jungle-clad Burma. To keep hard-pressed China in the war, American aircraft flew in vital supplies from India over the towering Himalaya Mountains. Later, a Chinese-American force succeeded in

The German capital, heavily assaulted by the Soviet forces, was transformed into an inferno of flame and destruction. Hitler committed suicide in his underground shelter. A few days later, the German military leaders agreed to unconditional surrender. On May 8, 1945, the conflict in Europe came to a close.

WAR IN THE PACIFIC

In the Pacific theater of the war, the tide of battle also turned. In 1942, the Allied forces in Australia had been placed under the command of General Douglas MacArthur, whose first task was to stop a dangerous two-pronged enemy offensive. The spring of that year denoted the high-water mark of empire when Japanese troops landed on Northern New Guinea and headed overland toward Australia. At the same time, a powerful Japanese troop convoy sailed across the Coral Sea toward the northern coast of the Australian continent.

The Japanese fleet came under heavy attack from American aircraft and was compelled to withdraw. The overland thrust was stopped by Allied troops, rushed to New Guinea.

D-Day Landing, June 1944

Courtesy of George C. Marshall Research Library, Lexington, Virginia. George M. Elsey Collection, Box 3.

An American landing craft evacuating wounded American and German soldiers from Normandy Coast, June 1944

Courtesy of George C. Marshall Research Library, Lexington, Virginia. George M. Elsey Collection, Box 3.

Russian soldiers shake hands in Germany with men of the 82d Airborne Division, 1945.

Courtesy of George C. Marshall Research Library, Lexington, Virginia. GCMRL #1636

hacking a road through the Burma jungle and reopened the overland supply route to China.

By the autumn of 1943, the United States had built up sufficient strength for a direct assault on Japan's heavily fortified island bases in the central Pacific. The new offensive began with an attack on the small island of Tarawa, in the Gilberts. Despite weeks of heavy bombardment by U.S. ships and aircraft, the Americans took several thousand casualties in capturing the outpost.

In February 1944, a strong U.S. naval force followed up by attacking several key islands in the Marshalls and by capturing them after bloody struggles. The next large target was the Mariana Islands, about 1,500 miles from Japan. A strong Japanese fleet, which sailed out to stop the invasion, was severely battered by American naval aircraft and forced to retreat. From the Marianas, long-range American bombers opened the attack on Japan itself.

The climax of the war in the Pacific came some two and one-half years after U.S. defeat in the Philippines. To counter the returning American forces, the Japanese sent out their remaining fleets in a desperate effort to halt the invasion. The ensuing Battle of Leyte Gulf was the greatest air-naval battle in history. Although the Americans suffered heavy losses, they succeeded in destroying most of the Japanese navy. The American army, with the help of strong Filipino guerrilla forces, freed the Philippines after several months of hard fighting.

Continuing the direct advance toward Japan, U.S. forces seized the small volcanic island of Iwo Jima and the war was carried to Japan's very doorstep. A large American force captured the key island of Okinawa after months of bitter fighting. The Americans were then poised to invade the main Japanese island only a few hundred miles away. By this time, the war in Europe had come to a close and the United States began the tremendous task of moving vast amounts of personnel

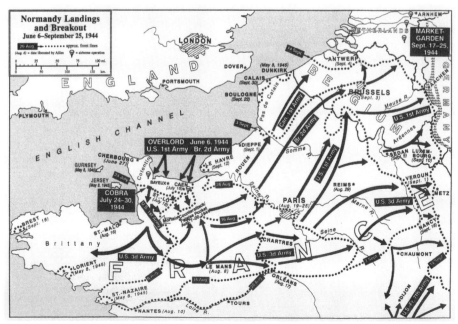

Courtesy of George C. Marshall Research Library, Lexington, Virginia. Marshall Papers, Vol. 4.

United States

In Germany . . . desolation

and equipment around the world for the final assault on Japan. Waiting for them were several million undefeated Japanese troops resolved to defend their homeland. The invasion of Japan doubtless would have been a bloodbath, with huge military and civilian casualties.

In the spring and summer of 1945, U.S. heavy bombers dropped many thousands of tons of bombs on Japan. American and British warships sailed up and down the coast, shelling targets. Submarines had already destroyed most of the Japanese merchant fleet. Carrier-based aircraft roamed inland to further the work of de-

struction. Japan's navy and air force had been virtually annihilated.

Nonetheless, the Japanese military leaders were resolved to fight to the end. They rejected Allied warnings that continued resistance would bring utter destruction to their nation. On August 6, 1945, a U.S. plane flew over the city of Hiroshima and dropped a single bomb, which exploded with a blinding flash that could be seen for 200 miles. Eighty thousand people, more than a quarter of the city's total population, were killed. An area two and a half miles in diameter was left a mass of twisted wreckage and damage was spread

over an additional ten square miles. The attack was mankind's introduction to its newest weapon, the atomic bomb.

Two days later, the Soviet Union declared war on Japan and its troops advanced rapidly into Manchuria. The next day, a second atomic bomb virtually destroyed the city of Nagasaki. The Japanese government then sued for peace. On September 2, 1945, the formal surrender documents were signed in a dramatic ceremony aboard the U.S. battleship Missouri in Tokyo Bay. Six years, almost to the day, after Hitler's invasion of Poland, World War II came to an end.

PANDORA'S BOX OF ATOMIC WEAPONRY

Responsibility for the decision to use the atomic bomb—described by Winston Churchill as the "Second Coming in Wrath"—has been substantially debated by historians. The final decision was made by President Harry Truman, who had taken office in April 1945 upon President Roosevelt's death. As vice president, Truman had not been told of the top-secret Manhattan Project, which had created the bomb. As president, he alone could authorize its use.

By the summer of 1945, with Germany defeated and Japan the sole threat to the Allies, Truman's advisors on the Interim Committee—a civilian council on atomic policy headed by Secretary of War Henry L. Stimson—issued a report urging that the bomb be used. They recommended that the target be both a military installation and a large population center susceptible to maximum blast effect. The committee believed, and Truman agreed, that the bomb might preclude a mass invasion of the Japanese home islands and thereby save millions of lives. Another factor influencing the president and his advisors was the growing fear of the Soviet Union. The Soviets had already seized control of Eastern Europe and had expressed their eagerness for a major role in any invasion and occupation of Japan. Many scientists and even some top military men urged alternatives—warning the Japanese, demonstrating the bomb on an unpopulated area before using it on a major city, or concluding the war by conventional means—but their suggestions were rejected as impractical. Japan's determination was well known, and conventional warfare would take too long, especially in view of the Soviet threat. Any warning might prove unpopular at home and would give the Japanese time to intercept an atomic mission. Whether the decision was morally justified is still a matter of bitter contention. But the question remains whether it was possible, by the summer of 1945, not

Courtesy of George C. Marshall Research Library, Lexington, Virginia. Marshall Papers, Vol. 4.

Ascent to Globalism

Lord Louis Mountbatten, supreme allied commander in Southeast Asia (1943–46), later *Earl Mountbatten of Burma*, talks with British troops near Mandalay in April 1945.

of the United States, with its relative invulnerability to attack, its enormous industrial capacity, and its faith in science and technology.

The top-priority, top-secret Manhattan Project, responsible for developing the atomic bomb drafted captains of industry and Nobel Prize-winning scientists and coaxed $2 billion dollars in secret funds from the U.S. Treasury. It imposed total secrecy on the thousands of workers employed in the project and selected the isolated sites where the actual work was done. A city sprouted at Hanford, Washington, where plutonium was produced; and rural Oak Ridge, Tennessee, where U-235 was separated, became the fifth-largest urban center in the state. Major theoretical work had already begun at several American universities. In the spring of 1943 at Los Alamos, New Mexico, where the work was most dangerous and the security tightest, a team led by Oppenheimer undertook the designing of a workable bomb that would fit inside the new B-29 long-range bomber.

WARTIME PLANNING FOR PEACE

to use the bomb. J. Robert Oppenheimer, the physicist who was in charge of the actual construction of the bomb, expressed the dimensions of the dilemma when he recalled: "The decision was implicit in the project. I don't know whether it could have been stopped."

The nuclear age might well have been born in Nazi Germany, had Hitler paid more heed to the works of his own scientists. In December 1938, two German scientists in Berlin succeeded, after six years of experimentation, in splitting the uranium atom. Their work implied the possibility of a controlled chain reaction and the subsequent release of enormous quantities of energy. Word of their accomplishment spread rapidly through the scientific world. The great Danish physicist Niels Bohr learned of it from two colleagues who had fled the Nazis. In early 1939, Bohr traveled to the United States and passed his knowledge along to American scientists. Most notable were two refugee physicists, the Italian Enrico Fermi and the Hungarian Leo Szilard. But subsequent efforts to convince the U.S. government of the atom's military possibilities bore little fruit until Szilard persuaded Albert Einstein, America's most famous scientist and himself a German-Jewish refugee, to sign a letter written to President Roosevelt in October 1939.

In late 1939, the question facing scientists was not whether to develop atomic weapons but how to do so before the Na-

zis did. On December 6, 1941—the day prior to the Japanese attack on Pearl Harbor—the U.S. Office of Scientific Research and Development received presidential approval for an all-out effort in atomic research. The scientific-military-industrial program that followed was characteristic

In an effort to avoid the difficulties associated with the peace treaties after the First World War, President Roosevelt and Prime Minister Churchill decided to plan the peace while the Allied nations were still united in their wartime struggle. They therefore arranged a series of meetings, established friendly personal rela-

Atomic test, 1946

Courtesy of George C. Marshall Research Library, Lexington, Virginia, GCMRL # 259370.

United States

U.S.S. *Missouri* in Japanese waters

In February 1945, when Germany had already been brought to the verge of defeat, Roosevelt and Churchill met with Stalin for a second time. This conference, held at Yalta, in the Crimea Peninsula, resulted in three important agreements. First, after laying plans for the final assault on Germany, the Allied leaders agreed to divide that country and its capital, Berlin, into occupation zones. To prevent disunity, the Allied military commanders would meet together regularly and issue joint directives for the zones.

The second agreement concerned the liberated nations and the former Axis satellites. The Big Three decided that the new governments should be democratic, chosen on the basis of free elections, and "responsive to the will of the people." In this connection, the Western statesmen immediately raised questions about the situation in newly liberated Poland. Stalin, ignoring the legal Polish government that had fled to London early in the war, set up a new communist-controlled government subservient to Moscow. The Soviet dictator defended his actions by asserting that the Soviet Union needed friendly nations along its frontiers.

The third of the Yalta agreements, which was kept secret until after the war, dealt with the Far East. Stalin promised to enter the war against Japan within three

tions, and reached an understanding on basic principles. Later, they succeeded in bringing Stalin into their partnership. Before the end of the war, the "Big Three" had negotiated a number of important agreements. Unfortunately, it soon became evident that these agreements provided very shaky foundations for the future peace.

Roosevelt and Churchill met for the first time off the coast of Newfoundland in the summer of 1941. Though the United States was still technically at peace with the Axis Powers, the two statesmen drafted a statement of war aims known as the Atlantic Charter. The lofty ideals of this declaration served as an inspiration to all of the nations opposed to the Axis Powers.

In the Atlantic Charter, the American and British leaders pledged their governments to seek no territorial gains and to make no territorial changes against the wishes of the peoples concerned. They promised to restore self-government to those people who had been forcibly de-

prived of it. They also announced their intention to improve economic conditions and to create a world in which all people might "live out their lives in freedom from fear and want." Finally, to preserve peace in the future, they agreed to bring about disarmament and to establish a new international organization to replace the League of Nations.

After the Japanese attack on Pearl Harbor, Roosevelt and Churchill held several other conferences, devoted mainly to military planning. The first meeting of the Big Three (including Stalin) took place at Teheran, the capital of Iran, in November 1943. At the Teheran Conference, the leaders of the Allied coalition mapped out plans for a coordinated attack on Germany "from the east, west, and south." They discussed Soviet intervention in the war against Japan, the territorial claims being made by Stalin, and a future world security system. They expressed the conviction that cooperation among their nations would guarantee a lasting peace.

Japan's Foreign Minister Shigimitsu signs the documents of surrender aboard the U.S.S. *Missouri*, while General MacArthur broadcasts the ceremonies.

94

Ascent to Globalism

Churchill, Roosevelt, Stalin at Yalta Conference, February 1945

Courtesy of George C. Marshall Research Library, Lexington, Virginia. GCMRL #349

That country was to be stripped of all its colonial conquests, most of which were to be returned to China and the Soviet Union. Like Germany, Japan was to be placed under Allied military occupation and was to be transformed into a democratic, peaceful nation. Then, it too would be given a formal peace treaty by the United States alone.

During the war, the Allied leaders also sought to provide economic assistance to the peoples being liberated from Axis rule. They created the United Nations Relief and Rehabilitation Administration, UNRRA for short. With funds contributed mainly by the United States, UNRRA fought a largely victorious battle against famine and disease in Europe. During its brief existence, from 1943 to 1948, it distributed millions of tons of essential supplies—including food, clothing, seeds, farm equipment, and industrial machinery. UNRRA's assistance saved millions of lives and hastened the world's economic recovery.

The most important foundation stone for the future peace was laid with the creation of the new United Nations organization. Agreement on the basic framework was first reached at a small conference of the great powers late in 1944. A few months later, in the spring of 1945, representatives of all the nations at war with the Axis met in San Francisco and completed the final draft of the United Nations Charter. The

months of Germany's surrender. In compensation, the Soviet Union was to obtain certain islands from Japan and the special rights in Manchuria that it had lost as a result of the Russo-Japanese War. When this secret provision of the Yalta agreements was published, it aroused widespread protests. Many people considered it a violation of the Atlantic Charter and objected to rewarding the Soviet Union at the expense of another ally, China.

The final conference of the three great powers took place at Potsdam, a suburb of Berlin, soon after Germany's surrender. There were, however, two important changes in membership. The sudden death of President Roosevelt in April 1945 brought Vice President Harry Truman into the White House. Three months later, a general election was held in Great Britain. Churchill's Conservative Party was defeated and the Labour Party, led by Clement Attlee, came to power. Thus, three strangers conferred at Potsdam, but they nonetheless quickly succeeded in drafting detailed plans for dealing with defeated Germany.

The purpose of the Allied occupation, according to the statesmen at Potsdam, was to transform Germany into a peaceful and democratic nation. Germany's armed forces were to be completely abolished. Its war industries were to be dismantled and the machinery was to be distributed as part of the reparations payments. The Nazi Party and other Nazi organizations were to be destroyed, and Nazi leaders were to be tried as war criminals. Democratic institutions were to be introduced gradually, beginning on a local basis.

Later, when democracy took root among the German people, a national government would be established. Then a formal peace treaty would be drafted and Germany would be readmitted into the family of nations.

The Potsdam Conference also made plans for the future treatment of Japan.

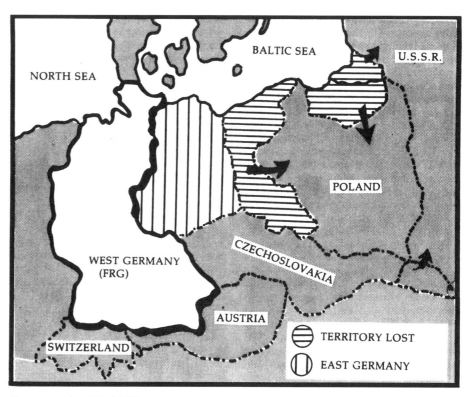

Germany after World War II

95

United States

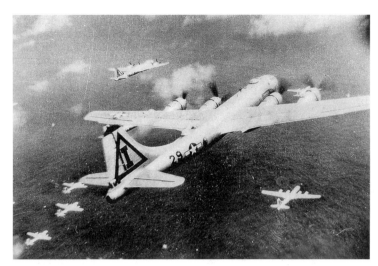

B-29s attack Japan

its permanent members, the great powers. The Soviet Union would wield its veto repeatedly to prevent "interference" in the pursuit of its own policies after the war. Deeply insecure through the centuries, invaded and ravaged time and again, the Russians were determined to create a security buffer around their borders to augment their security against the threat of attack. That said, all permanent members of the council have wielded and threatened to use the veto.

Both historical circumstance and misperceptions that arose between two dissimilar social systems generated out of this situation an ever-growing conflict between East and West. It was historical circumstance that only in Finland did popular attitudes and skillful leaders emerge to permit a mixture of Soviet hegemony and internal democracy. It was historical circumstance that a power vacuum developed after the war in Central and Western Europe, where victor and vanquished countries alike retained tiny armies and tottering economies. It was historical circumstance that these Europeans, watching American power ebb away over the seas, felt deeply insecure in the shadow of the mighty Red Army. Yet, the Soviets also felt insecure and overshadowed by the atomic bombs that only capitalist America possessed. And it was historical circumstance that the victorious Allies' arrangements for occupying Germany until 1949 would intensify conflicts once they split, and that the most urgent issues there were economic ones that East and West viewed in profoundly different ways.

It was Soviet misperception that the Marshall Plan for European recovery (discussed below) represented a sinister intervention by capitalist America to return Europe, now teetering on the brink of

revolution, to a reactionary social system. There was an element of misperception on both sides about the geopolitics and timing of events. The West did not understand that the Soviet hegemony looked to the Soviets like a defensive barrier only, or that their steps to complete that hegemony were triggered by Western actions. In their turn, the Soviets did not understand that, from the outside, all their actions looked like a steady and relentless push forward, or that outsiders would have to be alarmed when each step was more violent than the last.

By 1947, the West, led by the United States, was turning away from collective security as the principal instrument for securing the peace, at least as far as conflict involved in the cold war was concerned. Thereafter, collective security remained a phrase often employed to describe American intentions, but with a new and different meaning, namely, security for one collection of countries united against another. The United States, a leader of its group, arrived finally at a problem that it never before had to face—coping with a serious, continuing menace to its security.

THE EAST-WEST CONFLICT

After World War II, much of U.S. policy followed the strategic logic of the balance of power. Even before America had wholly defeated Germany and Japan, an American political geographer, Nicholaus Spykman, pointed out that America would have to rebuild German power in Europe and Japanese power in Asia. This appeared cynical at the time, but it was prophetic of the policy that was actually followed. In some of his letters, Spykman also backed American support of a U.N. organization not from idealist or internationalist motives, but on the grounds that

it would be useful as a counterweight to the Soviet network of satellites. Hence, despite the stigma attached to the power politics idea in the American mind, America has continued to practice balance-of-power politics.

The traditional policy had to be pursued under drastically new world conditions. These included the emergence of a great power axis stretching west from Moscow to Berlin, east from Moscow to Beijing, south from Moscow to Cairo. In meeting this challenge, the United States had to change its policies along three main lines of direction. One was the arms race and the testing of each aspect of U.S. policy by its impact on the country's military potential. The traditional American fear of standing armies faded and American soldiers and air bases could be found in every part of the world. The second change was the new economic diplomacy that sought to strengthen the shaky economies of the areas the Americans hoped to bring within their sphere of influence. Third, Americans accustomed themselves to think in terms of psychological warfare, that is, of a war of ideas. For all its traditional idealism, the pull in American policy was toward nuclear weapons, economic pressures, and political warfare. The aim was to prevent strategic areas from falling into the opposing camp, to consolidate their strength, and to employ them effectively in coordinated international action.

The term "bipolar world" or the theory of two international "camps" oversimplified the complex reality. Not only did a Western world and a communist bloc exist, but an entire array of peoples in the third world refused to commit themselves to either. Whenever one of the two "polar" powers strained too hard to hold its allies and dependents within tight discipline, there were inner tensions that showed there were forces of dynamic change in the world. A number of the newly emerged countries of Asia, Africa and the Middle East were determined to stay clear of the bipolar struggle as far as possible. The concept of America's national interest would have to be defined broadly enough to include America's stake in international action and in the formulation of collective sanctions. In a world largely characterized by anarchy, the pursuit of international order invariably involved substantial realism. As typified by the theoretical writings of Hans Morgenthau and George F. Kennan, what the national interest school of thought stresses is toughness of approach. It is in the tough-minded tradition of the international system, applied to America's situation, as against the supposedly tender-minded approach of Presidents Woodrow Wilson and Franklin D. Roosevelt.

Ascent to Globalism

Soviet armor in East Germany

Despite the creation of the United Nations, ambitious plans for organizing a world peace failed. The main reason for the failure was the emergence of fundamental differences between the Western Powers, notably the United States, and the Soviet Union and its satellites. During the war and for several years thereafter, America sought to follow a policy of cooperation with all of its former allies. After Japan's surrender, the United States hastily demobilized most of its armed forces. It contributed generously to UNRRA, thereby aiding the Soviet Union, as well as other nations, to rebuild its war-shattered economy. It even offered to share its atomic energy secrets with foreign governments, in the Baruch Plan for example, provided that they agreed to international controls. In its fundamentals, the Baruch Plan provided for a transition to peaceful atomic control by stages, with each stage dependent on the successful implementation of the preceding stage before further progress would be attempted. It called for the creation of an International Atomic Development Authority that would operate an elaborate inspection and control system under Security Council direction unhampered by the veto power.

Stalin, on the other hand, seized the opportunity to expand Soviet influence by filling the power vacuum created by the defeat of Germany and Japan. Moscow kept millions of men under arms and maintained large garrisons in the liberated and occupied countries. The Soviets conducted wholesale looting of machinery and other goods, especially in Germany and Manchuria. Arguing that they had to safeguard their country against future attack, they sought to establish per-

manent control over Eastern and Central Europe.

Events in Poland first made it evident that the Soviets had little intention of abiding by their wartime agreements. After the Yalta Conference, a number of Polish leaders returned from London to join the new government and were treated as virtual prisoners by the Communists. When elections were held, only a single list of candidates was permitted. Despite the protests of the Western Powers, Poland became a Soviet protectorate, a political satellite. Similar developments also occurred in the other countries "liberated" by the Soviet forces. In Hungary, Romania, Yugoslavia, Bulgaria, and Albania, the local communists gained control, usually with the aid of Soviet troops and secret police. Even democratic Czechoslova-

kia, which had regained its independence after the war, fell victim to a communist coup early in 1948.

Once securely in power, the satellite governments drove out Western observers and imposed rigid censorship. In effect, they placed their nations behind an "iron curtain," a term coined by Churchill, to thwart contacts with the outside world. They then proceeded to bolshevize their countries along the lines dictated by Moscow. The United States and Great Britain protested that these policies were violations of the wartime agreements, but their objections fell on deaf ears. Stalin had shifted from a policy of cooperation with the democratic powers to one of almost open hostility.

In this atmosphere of mounting tension, the Allies began the difficult task of drawing up the peace treaties for Italy and the smaller Axis nations—Hungary, Romania, Bulgaria, and Finland. Bitter controversies arose when the foreign ministers of the great powers met to draft the preliminary agreements. After months of bickering, they succeeded in settling most of their differences. A general peace conference, representing all of the nations at war with the Axis, then met in Paris. Once again, disputes between the Western Powers and the Soviet Union prevented agreement. The peace treaties were finally signed in Paris by the five former enemy states early in 1947.

The treaty with Italy was the most important of the Paris peace agreements. It was deprived of all its colonial possessions and had to cede several small border districts to France and Yugoslavia. The port city of Trieste, hotly disputed by both Italy and Yugoslavia, was established as a free territory under the U.N. Italy also agreed to pay reparations in goods over a period of years, with the bulk of the

Stalin: Ruler of the Soviet Union

99

United States

Entire families form a crew of builders working on a block of apartments funded by the Marshall Plan.

Courtesy of George C. Marshall Research Library, Lexington, Virginia. GCMRL #179

pan's surrender, he proclaimed Vietnam's independence. The French promptly sent large forces into Indochina and sought to restore their control. The communist-led nationalists withdrew into the jungle and resorted to guerrilla warfare. The "Dirty War," as the French called it, dragged on for almost ten years.

In 1954, thanks to large-scale military assistance from the People's Republic of China (PRC), the rebels were able to win a decisive victory at Dienbienphu. The French then agreed to grant Indochina its independence. The former colony was divided into four separate countries. North Vietnam came under communist control. South Vietnam set up a pro-Western government that was bolstered by economic and military aid from the United States. The other two countries, Laos and Cambodia, sought to maintain a neutral position in the cold war.

In 1949, the same year Stalin launched his offensive against the Marshall Plan in Europe, communist-led revolts also broke out in southern and eastern Asia—in India, Burma, Malaya, the East Indies, and the Philippine Islands. Although all of these revolts were eventually crushed, the communists for a time won considerable popular support. Early in 1949, Truman announced a plan to deal with Asia's problems. He called for "a bold new program . . . making the benefits of scientific progress available for the improvement and growth of underdeveloped areas."

The United States soon began to send engineers, farm experts, medical personnel, educators, and other advisors to Asia. It also built important public works, supplied food to famine-stricken areas, and

Soviet attack. The Alliance has arguably been history's most successful and long-lasting one.

Western plans for containing communism met with far less success in Asia than in Europe. World War II had left the Asian peoples even poorer than before and had intensified the spirit of colonial nationalism. The Soviet Union took advantage of the situation, constantly denouncing the Western Powers as imperialists and posing as the champions of all native independence movements. It sent communist agents into many Asian countries to fan the flames of revolt. The communists won widespread support by promising the common people land and other radical reforms.

The greatest communist triumph occurred in strife-torn China. Soon after the Japanese surrender, the old hostility between the Nationalists and the Communists flared up into renewed civil war. After trying vainly to arrange a peaceful settlement, the United States threw its support behind the Nationalists. The fighting in China raged for more than four years, from 1945–1949, and ended in victory for the Communists. Chiang Kai-shek was compelled to withdraw with his remaining forces to the island of Formosa, off the southern coast of China. The Communist leader, Mao Zedong, became head of the People's Republic of China (PRC).

The communists won a second substantial victory in the French colony of Indochina. During the Japanese occupation, a communist leader, Ho Chi Minh, had secretly formed a strong nationalist movement in Vietnam, which constituted approximately half of the colony that included Cambodia and Laos. Following Ja-

Berlin Airlift, 1948–49

A/P Wide World Photo

102

Ascent to Globalism

institutions in the nation's postwar national security establishment. Each new organization sought to improve on the institutional apparatus in place prior to and during World War II. And with the annual U.S. defense budget running into the tens of billions of dollars by the early 1950s, a huge interlocking network of government agencies, industrial corporations and military bureaucracies formed to supply America's ponderous military establishment. Critics have periodically charged that the military conspires with defense contractors and other strategic elites to maintain a vast network of bases and fleets around the world. Even former general Dwight Eisenhower remarked in his last speech as president in 1961, that the "military-industrial complex" had the potential for unwarranted power within the councils of government.

POWER AND PURPOSE

Before the vast aid programs could take effect, a new emergency arose in the mountainous peninsula of Korea. The latter had been liberated from Japanese rule by U.S. and Soviet occupation troops at the end of World War II, and the 38th Parallel had been fixed as the dividing line between the American and Soviet occupation zones. The Soviet Union promptly set up a communist regime in North Korea. In South Korea, a pro-Western government was established in 1948 under United Na-

tions supervision. A few months later, the Soviet Union and the United States both withdrew their occupation forces.

Border clashes soon broke out between the troops of the two rival Korean governments. A full-scale war began in June 1950, when the North Koreans sent a powerful Soviet-equipped force across the 38th Parallel. American troops were rushed in from nearby Japan to help the South Koreans slow down the Red advance. The United States also brought the North Korean aggression before the United Nations. With the Soviet Union boycotting the Security Council at the time, that body called on all members to help the Republic of Korea repel the invaders and restore peace.

The U.N. army, fighting under the command of MacArthur, soon inflicted a crushing defeat on the North Koreans. When it crossed the 38th Parallel, however, and approached the Manchurian frontier, the PRC entered the war. Several hundred thousand Chinese troops poured across the border and sent the U.N. forces reeling. With the aid of fresh reinforcements, the U.N. troops succeeded in checking the Chinese advance and resumed the offensive. Their movement forward was slow and at heavy cost. By the time they again crossed the 38th Parallel, both sides were prepared to discuss an armistice.

The truce talks dragged on for nearly two years, 1951–1953. When the fighting finally ended, the truce was an uneasy

The Air Bridge Monument in Berlin commemorates the blockade of 1948/49.

encouraged the U.N. to set up a technical assistance agency. With help from both the United States and the U.N., a number of Asian nations initiated projects to strengthen their economies and raise living standards.

The National Security Act of 1947 established the framework of American national security during the cold war. Authorizing the creation of the National Security Council (NSC) "to advise the President with respect to the integration of domestic, foreign and military policies relating to the national security," it spawned new government bureaucracies and private organizations to support the process. The Central Intelligence Agency (CIA), the Department of Defense, and the Joint Chiefs of Staff became central

General George C. Marshall and Mao Zedong during the former's mission to China, March 1946

Courtesy of George C. Marshall Research Library, Lexington, Virginia. GCMRL #2505.

103

United States

Nikita Khrushchev

committed communist, but first and foremost a nationalist. Unlike other satellite leaders, he won power largely by national efforts and he refused to be a Soviet puppet. Tito won acclaim during the war as a partisan leader, and Yugoslavia had freed itself from the Nazi yoke largely by its own efforts without Soviet forces. Tito's independent attitude led to an open clash with Stalin.

Determined to make an example of Tito, the Soviet ruler ordered all communist nations to impose an economic boycott against Yugoslavia. He also directed the neighboring satellites to launch attacks against Yugoslavia's lengthy frontiers. In desperation, Tito appealed to the West for assistance. The United States, after some hesitation, sent economic aid and military support to Yugoslavia. Tito then felt strong enough to openly defy Stalin. He accused the Soviet dictator of violating communist principles and called upon satellites to join in resisting Soviet imperialism. The idea of "Titoism" or national communism, that is, communism independent of Soviet control, began slowly to take hold in other satellite countries.

In the summer of 1956, in the wake of Khruschev's denunciation of Stalin, strikes and riots broke out in the Polish city of Poznan. Although these were suppressed, unrest in Poland surged. Wladislaw Gomulka, a Polish communist who

had been imprisoned for "Titoism," came to power. Openly defying Khrushchev, Gomulka announced that Poland was going to follow a policy of national communism. Like Tito, he sought and obtained aid from the United States. Gomulka later reached a reconciliation with Moscow, but retained considerable freedom of action.

Encouraged by Poland's success, the Hungarians rose in revolt in October 1956 against both their own hated communist regime and the Soviet occupation forces. Fighting with remarkable courage, the Hungarians won some surprising initial successes. Moscow then sent in a powerful army, spearheaded by hundreds of main battle tanks, to augment the Soviet occupation forces. Moscow crushed the rebellion without mercy and set up a puppet government that kept a tight lid on the entire country. The Western Powers, fearing escalation of the conflict and distracted by a serious crisis in the Middle East, limited themselves to strongly worded protests.

By the late 1950s, new difficulties arose in Moscow's relations with the PRC and the smallest of the satellites, Albania. The Chinese complained, among other reasons, that the amount of aid they were receiving was inadequate and that they were being charged excessive prices for Soviet products. Moreover, Mao Zedong rejected Khrushchev's frequently stated policy of "peaceful coexistence" between

East and West. He deemed it essential to conduct unrelenting war against the capitalist world. The communist ruler of Albania, seeking to assert his independence from Moscow, supported the Chinese doctrine of inevitable conflict.

At the 1961 Communist Party Congress, Khrushchev had Albania's delegates expelled as "Stalinists." The Chinese representatives responded by attacking Khrushchev's actions and abruptly leaving the congress. Thereafter, Chinese-Soviet relations continued to deteriorate, until an open breach between the two leading communist powers occurred. Albania left the Warsaw Pact and the East Bloc economic organization, the Council for Mutual Economic Assistance (CMEA or Comecon), in 1961.

NATIONALISM TRIUMPHS

Over a billion people, more than one-third of the world's population at the time, gained their independence after the Second World War. The sweeping triumph of colonial nationalism began in Asia, largely the result of World War II. The colonial peoples were aroused by Japanese wartime propaganda of "Asia for the Asians" and by Allied promises of self-government after the defeat of the Axis. Economic problems resulting from the war, such as food shortages and inflated prices, added greatly to the unrest. When the fighting ended, many people organized revolts to obtain their freedom. Weakened by the war, the colonial powers had little choice but to surrender control. The successes won by the Asians inspired the peoples

Marshal Josip Broz-Tito, leader of the *Partisans* in World War II

of Africa also to seek their freedom. Once again, most of the European powers deemed it wiser to yield than to attempt repression. Western imperialism, which had reached its pinnacle in the early 20th century, came to a virtual end.

Yet, the new nations that emerged in Asia and Africa were soon plunged into a sea of difficulties. Large numbers of their citizens were poverty-stricken and illiterate. Population continued to rise at an alarming rate. Clashes occurred between groups with different religions, languages, and political ideas. Experienced and competent leaders were in short supply. Many of the new nations were distrustful of their former rulers. Communists sometimes won support by playing on fears of Western colonialism and by offering to help with industrialization and other modernization projects. There was the danger that Asians and Africans would gain freedom from European control only to fall victim to a new and more ruthless imperialism.

One of the worst trouble spots was Palestine, where a three-sided conflict developed among the Arabs; Zionists, Jews striving to establish the state of Israel; and the British. Before World War II, the British tried to appease the Arabs by virtually barring further Jewish immigration into the country. After the war, the Zionists were determined to bring into their homeland those Jews who had managed to survive Hitler's concentration camps. British efforts to stop this illegal immigration led to violent clashes and acts of terrorism. Two terrorist organizations, the Irgun Zvai Leumi and the Stern Gang, conducted campaigns of violence against both Arabs and British forces.

Harassed on all sides—by Arabs who demanded no softening of policy, by Jews who insisted that Zion's gates be thrown open to all Jews, by U.S. President Truman, who supported the Zionists—Britain in 1947 turned the problem over to the U.N., giving up its mandate. The U.N., though, was unable to find a satisfactory solution. In November 1947, after weeks of intensive debate, the General Assembly voted to partition Palestine into two independent states. For the Jews, this was a moment of victory. The U.N. decision promised the beginning of a viable state, which would be a refuge for the survivors of Hitler's death camps.

Accordingly, the Jews proclaimed the establishment of a new independent Jewish state, Israel. The latter was attacked almost immediately by the armies of five nearby Arab countries—Egypt, Jordan, Iraq, Saudi Arabia and Syria. Though greatly outnumbered, the Israelis repelled the enemy forces and advanced beyond the frontiers. After more than a year of hard fighting, the U.N. finally succeeded

Soviet leader Nikita Khrushchev, 1962
Courtesy of Special Collections,
University of Virginia Library

in bringing about a cease-fire. Yet, the Arab countries refused to discuss peace terms. They organized an economic boycott of the Jewish state and made frequent guerrilla attacks on Israeli border settlements. The Israelis replied with sharp reprisal raids against their Arab neighbors.

The United States was the first country to recognize the new Jewish state in 1948. Within ten years after World War II, three main reasons for U.S. concern with the Middle East presented themselves: oil, Palestine, and Soviet encroachment. The first two are still pertinent today. In the Arab areas of the Middle East, circumstances became increasingly difficult because the establishment of Israel and its later territorial expansion were largely irreconcilable with the principle of national self-determination and invariably damaged American-Arab relations. Mounting disaffection of the Arabs for U.S. policies not only undermined earlier friendships but also resulted in at least three adverse consequences: leftist radicalization of a number of Arab political systems, invitations to Soviet penetration, and threats to the uninterrupted supply of Arab oil to the United States and some of its allies.

Following the Palestine war, Egypt became the storm center of Arab nationalism. In 1952, a group of nationalist army officers overthrew the monarchy, which they blamed for their country's humiliating defeat by Israel. One of these military leaders, Gamal Abdel Nasser, soon

emerged as dictator. Nasser promised to unite the Arab countries, to end Western influence in the Arab world, and to destroy Israel. In 1956, Nasser made an agreement with the Soviet Union for the purchase of large amounts of modern military equipment. He also nationalized the Suez Canal, whose stock was owned mainly by the British and French, and stepped up Egyptian raids into Israel.

The Israelis, pleading self-defense, suddenly launched a full-scale attack on Egypt. They quickly routed the Egyptian border forces and took over most of the Sinai Peninsula. Britain and France joined in the war, with the purpose of regaining control of the Suez Canal. This breach of the peace was promptly referred to the U.N. Many Americans were profoundly shocked at the British and French intervention, above all, because they had kept Washington in the dark to prevent interference. The timing of the attack indicated outright collusion with Israel, and the operation clearly weakened the West's moral stand against the concurrent Soviet aggression in Hungary in October 1956. In an unusual display of harmony, both the United States and the Soviet Union supported strong action by the international body. The U.N. brought about an end to the fighting and compelled the invaders to withdraw their troops from Egyptian soil. A small international police force was stationed along the Egyptian-Israeli frontier to prevent future incidents. Although

United States

Prime Minister David Ben-Gurion signs the independence declaration, May 14, 1948

reluctant to yield conquered territory, the Israelis finally gave in, following assurances from Washington of diplomatic support. The British and French displayed their basic weaknesses and the operation was one of their last imperial gasps. Their departure would inevitably result in a power vacuum in the Middle East that would prompt the United States to move in. Though unable to thwart the tragedy in Hungary, the U.N emerged from the Suez Crisis with new laurels. The effective deployment of a U.N. peacekeeping force into a troubled area awakened new hopes for international cooperation.

Despite his military defeat, Nasser's prestige in the Arab world reached a new high. The Egyptian dictator obtained large amounts of military hardware from the Soviet Union and intensified his campaign of Pan-Arab nationalism. He won two successes in 1958, when Syria joined with Egypt to form the United Arab Republic and anti-Western nationalists seized power in Iraq. Nonetheless, Nasser's soaring ambitions were soon deflated. The new rulers of Iraq insisted on maintaining their independence and Syria broke away from Egyptian control in 1961.

In India, the largest and most important of the new nations, nationalism was already well developed before World War II. By the end of the conflict, popular dissatisfaction was so intense that the British were prepared to grant India immediate

self-government. Indian leaders fell out among themselves, though. The emergence of the Indian nationalist movement in the late 19th century created a problem for the subcontinent's Muslims, who numbered only about a quarter of the population. They hated British rule but feared that in a free India, ruled by the mainly Hindu Indian National Congress, their fate might be even worse. A short-term answer was found in the All-India Muslim League, established in 1906. This rival organization agitated for separate electorates to safeguard Muslim rights, and the Indian National Congress and the British government acceded to some of its relatively modest demands. As independence became more feasible, certain visionaries within the League began to dream of an autonomous Muslim state.

After World War II, the Muslim League demanded that the five northern provinces, in which the Muslims were a majority, should be established as a separate country. After India was swept by bloody Muslim-Hindu clashes, the Congress leaders reluctantly agreed to a division of the country. Two new countries, India and Pakistan, were created in 1947. For more than a quarter of a century, both nations had to turn their efforts to fighting a host of internal problems, including poverty, disease, illiteracy, and overcrowding.

The final, tragic irony emerged in 1971 when Pakistan was itself torn in two. The

Bengali-speaking people of East Pakistan, rejecting the rule of the Punjabi government of West Pakistan, declared their independence as the new nation of Bangladesh. In the ensuing struggle, in which the Indian Army finally took part, perhaps as many as three million lives were lost. Once again, a new nation had been born amid bloodshed. Violence had bred violence.

In short, the transition from colonial rule to self-government was by no means a peaceful one. Fresh waves of religious outbreaks occurred in both countries, and millions of people were forced to flee from their homes. Sharp disagreements also arose between India and Pakistan over boundaries, water rights, and other matters formerly controlled by the British. Actual fighting broke out over possession of the large northern states of Kashmir, inhabited by both Muslims and Hindus, with Muslims in the majority. Although the United Nations arranged a cease-fire, it was unable to work out a permanent settlement. The Kashmir dispute continued to poison relations between the two countries. Such regional rivalries pose serious foreign policy dilemmas for the United States. During the cold war, the United States alienated India, one of the Third World's few democracies, and drove it into Moscow's arms for political support and weapons.

Independence for the rich colony of Malaya was delayed by two factors. One was a guerrilla war started by communist insurgents in 1948. It took British-led forces almost ten years to flush the guerrillas out of the jungles. The second problem was tension between the native Malays and the rapidly growing Chinese minority population. The British solved this problem by separating the island of Singapore, where most of the people of Chinese descent lived, from the rest of the country. The Federation of Malaya was granted dominion status in 1957. Singapore's residents were accorded full power over internal affairs two years later. In 1963, Malaya, Singapore, and two former British colonies on the island of Borneo united to form the new nation of Malaysia—only to encounter powerful opposition from their powerful neighbor, Indonesia. The short-lived union of Singapore with the Federation of Malaysia came to an end in 1965.

Burma, unlike the other British colonies in Southeast Asia, rejected membership in the Commonwealth of Nations. From the outset, the new republic had to overcome many difficulties. So many political parties arose that it was difficult to form a stable government. There were numerous revolts by communists and warlike border tribes, and the constant disorders left the country in desperate financial straits. Considerable aid from the Commonwealth, the United States, and the United Nations helped improve economic conditions. Communist influence nonetheless continued to grow. In 1958, the commander of the armed forces took power, and despite efforts to restore civil authority, military rule has continued until the present time.

In the Netherlands East Indies, the nationalists demanded freedom at the end of World War II. Bitter fighting followed. The Dutch, under pressure from the U.N., recognized the islands as independent in 1949. Though the new Republic of Indonesia was a potentially rich country, its progress was hindered by serious economic and political difficulties. The multiethnic population increased rapidly, but production of foodstuffs and other crops declined considerably because of attacks on Dutch subjects and their properties. The democratic government was weakened by clashes between conservative Muslims and communists. Revolts also broke out on several islands because their inhabitants resented control by the central administration in Java.

In 1959, after a tour of the communist countries, President Sukarno assumed dictatorial powers and announced that he would follow a policy of strict neutrality. Yet, he whipped up domestic nationalism by demanding that the Dutch "return" West New Guinea to Indonesia. Soon afterward, Sukarno began armed raids into Malaysia and withdrew Indonesia from the U.N.

Developments in the Philippines, despite some initial difficulties, were more encouraging to the West than those in Indonesia and Burma. The United States granted the Philippines full independence immediately after the war and helped the new country rebuild the devastated areas. Nevertheless, there arose a strong radical movement, which promised to take over the large landholdings and divide them among the poor peasants. Communists soon gained control of this movement and launched an open rebellion against the government. Efforts at suppression met with little success until a young defense minister, Ramon Magsaysay, assumed command of the campaign. He won the support of the villagers by his sincere concern with their problems. Their assistance enabled him to crush the rebellion. In 1953, he was elected president of the Philippine Republic by an overwhelming vote.

With American aid, Magsaysay made needed financial reforms and reclaimed large areas of wasteland for resettling poor peasants. He also helped the common people by discharging dishonest officials, reducing land rents, and providing government loans at low interest rates. Magsaysay was a staunch friend of the United States and often declared that its policy toward his country was the best proof that the former had no imperialist ambitions. In large part because of his efforts, the Philippine Republic became a center of pro-American influence in Asia. To a certain extent, it remains so.

Still another scene of nationalist disturbances was French North Africa. After vainly attempting to suppress popular disorders, the Paris government recognized the independence of both Tunisia and Morocco in 1956. Algeria, however, presented a much more complex problem. That territory had been ruled by the French for more than a century and legally was part of France. Its value was substantially increased by the discovery of rich petroleum deposits after World War II. Most important of all, one million inhabitants were of European origin and insisted that Algeria must remain French. This view was challenged by a rebel nationalist movement, which claimed to represent the nine million Muslim natives.

The nationalists started their struggle for independence in 1954. Using guerrilla tactics, they successfully resisted the powerful French forces sent out against them. President Charles de Gaulle, eager to end this futile conflict, decided to reopen negotiations. Despite the fierce opposition of the European settlers, led by many of the military leaders and rightists who had restored him to power in 1958, he finally agreed to self-determination for Algeria. A cease-fire agreement was signed in 1962, but the opponents of a Muslim Algeria formed an outlaw movement known as the Secret Army Organization. They resorted to a last-ditch campaign of terror to prevent the settlement from taking effect. Their efforts failed and Algeria became independent in 1962.

U.S. soldiers in war and peace

Chapter Four
The Anguish of Power

WORLD TENSIONS

Even during the years of lessened tension following Stalin's death in 1953, sharp rivalry for influence between East and West continued in the world's undeveloped areas. The United States was invariably drawn into the contention. One such area was the Middle East, extending from Egypt to Iran, which is strategically important primarily for its oil resources. To protect the Middle East from Soviet aggression, a new defensive alliance, the Baghdad Pact, was formed in 1955. Its members were Great Britain, Turkey, Iraq, Iran and Pakistan. Though not formally a member, the United States supported the arrangement. Early in 1957, President Eisenhower promised military assistance, even the direct intervention of American armed forces, to any Middle Eastern country threatened by communist aggression.

Despite the Baghdad Pact and the new "Eisenhower Doctrine," Moscow made some inroads into the Middle East. The Soviet leaders maintained the friendship of Nasser of Egypt, above all, by supplying him with modern arms and by supporting Egypt diplomatically. The Soviets also encouraged Nasser's propaganda campaign for a pan-Arab union. In 1958, revolts broke out against the pro-Western governments of Lebanon, Jordan, and Iraq. The dispatch of U.S. and British troops saved the governments of Lebanon and Jordan, but an anti-Western group gained control in Iraq. The new leaders withdrew their nation from the Baghdad Pact, which was then replaced by a new regional security alliance, the Central Treaty Organization (CENTO). In the years that followed, CENTO was weakened by dissensions among its members.

In eastern Asia, it was primarily the People's Republic of China (PRC), rather than the Soviet Union, that aggressively sparked communist expansion. After the French withdrawal from Indochina, the Chinese furnished substantial aid to communist guerrilla groups fighting to win control of the new nations of Laos and South Vietnam. They also demanded the return of Taiwan to China and were prevented from invading that island only by the presence of a powerful U.S. fleet. In 1959, the PRC conquered Tibet and seized sizeable frontier districts from both India and Burma.

The Soviet Union also stepped up its efforts to penetrate Latin America. Despite U.S. economic assistance and some economic progress, the living standards of the great majority of people throughout the region were low. One reason for this widespread poverty was the rapid increase in population; another was the failure of many governments to introduce needed economic and social reforms. As elsewhere, the people's misery, which agitators blamed on the capitalist democracies, provided fertile soil for the seeds of communism.

Events in Cuba, less than a hundred miles from the Florida coast, brought the problem home to the American people. Early in 1959, the island's right-wing dictator was overthrown by a popular revolt. The successful rebel leader, Fidel Castro, posed as a liberal and enjoyed the support of many Cubans. Once in power, Castro moved rapidly toward the left. He denounced the United States as an imperialist power and signed economic and military agreements with the Soviet Union. Plantations and other businesses, some American-owned, were seized and reorganized as workers' or peasants' cooperatives. A virtual reign of terror, especially after the Bay of Pigs fiasco in 1961, was launched against Cuba's religious, business, and intellectual leaders, thousands of whom fled to the United States. Castro also converted Cuba into a center for the spread of communist propaganda, agents, and weaponry throughout Latin America.

While the Western powers were combating communist intrigues in the underdeveloped countries, the Soviets provoked a new crisis over the German question. In the autumn of 1958, Nikita Khrushchev demanded that the Allies withdraw their occupation forces from West Berlin. Otherwise, he warned, he would sign a separate peace treaty with the East German government and would turn over to it control of all routes entering Berlin. He left no doubt that the East Germans, with Soviet support, would then restrict the Allies' access to that city.

A prolonged period of international tension followed. It was increased period-

Ernest Hemingway and Fidel Castro meet in Havana, 1959

110

ically by new Soviet threats and by the harassment of Allied traffic passing through Soviet-held German territory. The situation was temporarily eased in the autumn of 1959, when Khrushchev visited the United States and conferred with Eisenhower. The two chiefs of state agreed to another summit conference, to be held in Paris the next spring.

Shortly before the Paris summit met, however, Khrushchev announced that an American U-2 reconnaissance aircraft had been shot down inside the Soviet Union. He indignantly accused the U.S. government of spying on his country and broke up the conference only a few hours after it had convened. Khrushchev also asserted he would not carry on negotiations with the United States during the remainder of Eisenhower's term of office.

Castro's Cuba sounded a new alarm for the United States. U.S. aid began to flow to Latin America in the last years of the Eisenhower Administration, and President John Kennedy advocated a ten-year, ten-point $20 billion program of development named "The Alliance for Progress." Like the Marshall Plan for Europe, the Alliance Program involved primarily self-help, not charity. The chief idea was that if communist penetration (*fidelismo*) was to be thwarted in Latin America, the widespread poverty that bred discontent should be alleviated, especially in densely populated areas. The Kennedy administration specified such goals as improved housing, medical care, sanitation, and education. The United States also promoted land reform, since land ownership in many areas was concentrated in a small number of families and large holders maintained monopolies in some places. The detractors of the "Alliance for Progress" point out that it was neither an alliance nor did it progress. Development in Latin America remained uneven, and the rich tended to profit most from dollars flowing from America. American efforts to encourage reform or even to prevent the pervasive corruption invariably led to charges of Yankee intervention.

The Kennedy administration also took more drastic measures to deal with the perceived threat of *fidelismo* in Latin America when it attempted to engineer the overthrow of Castro in 1961. Having promised in his presidential campaign to "do something" about Cuba, Kennedy reluctantly accepted an earlier plan that authorized the training of bands of exiles for the invasion of Cuba. The organization of the stratagem was assigned to the CIA, which following a number of schemes in Latin America, became disparagingly known as the "Cuban Invasion Authority." The invaders were quickly forced to surrender at the Bay of Pigs in April 1961.

The CIA had made a complete mess of things and the nation's prestige suffered a staggering blow. The new President assumed full responsibility for the debacle and suffered considerable embarrassment. Castro redoubled his charges of Yankee imperialism at the U.N. and to his own people. The United States had violated the spirit, if not the letter, of the Charter of the Organization of American States (OAS) that forbids any aggression against a fellow member. Kennedy's Republican critics sarcastically quipped that the president had indeed "got the country moving again"—straight downhill.

ON THE BRINK

The Caribbean fiasco was followed by renewed difficulties in Europe. Khrushchev again put the heat on Berlin, a point of perennial vulnerability for the West, while apparently searching for a way to accommodate the satellite regime of the GDR. The latter had to stanch the refugee flow, for it was losing so many people by the summer of 1961 that its economy was faltering. A popular observation was that the GDR was "hemorrhaging to death." The answer came in August 1961 when Moscow authorized the sudden construction of a wall between East and West Berlin. The final closure of the Berlin escape route, through which thousands of East Germans had been pouring every week, caught the Allies unprepared. Resistance to the Communist move was limited to a

few verbal protests. Once again, the U.S. President came across as weak and indecisive. The Berlin Wall, though, was a conspicuous admission of Communist failure and a monument to tyranny. At length, the West could hardly have hoped for a better propaganda instrument.

Then, serious trouble began to brew in the Caribbean. Lavishly equipped with modern Soviet military hardware, Fidel Castro built one of the largest military forces in the Western Hemisphere. Official Washington in October 1962 was shocked when aerial reconnaissance revealed that Soviet technicians were assembling nuclear missiles in Cuba with a range up to 2,000 miles and thus capable of striking large sections of the United States. The deployment of such weapons systems threatened to shift the balance of power and represented a serious menace to the Monroe Doctrine. Although Soviet intentions may not have been immediately clear, the implications were profound. Moscow could heat up Berlin with impunity, bolstered by a credible threat to destroy American population centers. The United States would not dare to launch an attack against the nuclear-armed island, while Castro could export his revolution to other parts of Latin America.

Kennedy acted swiftly to counter the threat before Cuba became an operational missile-launching pad. The United States imposed a "quarantine" on all ships headed to Cuba, an embargo in all but name, which would not have been

Family separated by Berlin Wall, September 1961
Courtesy of Presse – und Informationsamt der Bundesregierung

United States

Berlin Wall and Brandenburg Gate seen from Reichstag Building, 1962

States was released from its pledge not to invade. Of course, it never did, but during the Cuban Missile Crisis, the world came appallingly close to nuclear war.

The following year, the Kremlin began to make friendly gestures toward the West. The thaw in the cold war confrontation was at least in part the result of the worsening of relations between the two largest communist powers. Khrushchev was stung by the growing criticism of the Chinese, above all, because of his "capitulationism" during the Cuban Missile Crisis. In July 1963, the Kremlin chief proposed a nuclear test-ban agreement, along with a non-aggression pact between the democratic West and the Soviet bloc. Having advocated such a test ban for years, the United States eagerly embraced the first part of the Soviet proposal. The non-aggression pact was a non-starter that rapidly faded from view. Such a superpower accord would have been largely meaningless. The following month, the Nuclear Test Ban Treaty was signed amid much fanfare. The treaty prohibited further nuclear tests in the atmosphere, in outer space, or under the water. Underground tests would continue, and the Soviets never consented to intrusive inspections. France refused to become party to the agreement, as did the Chinese, who denounced the "dirty fraud" perpetrated by the Kremlin "freaks and monsters." Soviet-Chinese relations were heading straight down.

permissible in peacetime. Vessels that refused to halt on the high seas for inspection were to be fired upon. The measures ran counter to the time-honored principle of freedom of the seas, to be sure, and the two fundamental U.S. principles, the Monroe Doctrine and freedom of the seas, clashed during the crisis. Such was the peril that the OAS, in an unusual display of unity, backed U.S. actions. Nuclear-tipped missiles that could strike the United States could easily reach other targets in the hemisphere. The Soviets insisted that the Americans had started the rocket-rattling game by placing nuclear missiles in places like Turkey. The charge was standard Soviet noise. Little strategic symmetry existed between U.S. missiles in Turkey and Soviet missiles in Cuba. The United States had deployed missiles to Turkey in the wake of an open debate within NATO, followed by the approval of elected officials. The Soviet Union, by contrast, sought to put missiles in Cuba suddenly and clandestinely.

Yet, the channels of communication remained open, and Kennedy left the Soviets with political options. The U.N. Secretary-General mediated as best he could, and Khrushchev was made to realize that if he did not remove the missiles, the United States would seize or destroy them. Faced with dire consequences, Moscow backed down and recalled Cuban-bound ships. Toward the end of the month, a compromise was reached, whereby the Krem-

lin would withdraw all its missiles from Cuba, and Washington agreed to lift the "quarantine" and not invade the island. Since Castro never permitted on-site inspections, it followed that the United

Willy Brandt as Mayor of West Berlin hosting President John F. Kennedy

The next major step in diplomatic efforts at nuclear arms limitation came in August 1967 with a treaty to halt the spread of nuclear weapons. The Nuclear Nonproliferation Treaty (NPT) bound the signatories with nuclear arsenals not to transfer such weaponry to countries not possessing nuclear arms. The non-nuclear powers party to the accord agreed not to produce nuclear devices. The treaty entered into force when ratified by the United States, the Soviet Union, Great Britain and 40 other signatories. Beijing vociferously condemned the accord as a "plot" concocted by Moscow and Washington.

THE ORDEAL OF VIETNAM

In a broader sense, the passage of the Gulf of Tonkin resolution in 1964, which authorized the use of force in Vietnam, was not so much the beginning of a war as it was the culmination of a policy originating more than ten years earlier. The United States had become involved in Southeast Asian affairs in the early 1950s, when France was struggling in vain to retain the colonial control it had held over Vietnam since the 19th century. The fight to expel the French was being carried out by the Vietminh, a nationalist guerrilla movement that had spearheaded Vietnamese resistance against Japanese invaders during World War II. Its leader, Ho Chi Minh, was acknowledged even by opponents as the country's most popular figure. What concerned the United States was that Ho was a Communist, determined not only to defeat the French but also to establish Vietnam as a unified and independent Marxist state.

Domestic political pressures prevented direct U.S. involvement in the Indochina war in the 1950s, but increasing economic aid was provided until, by 1954, the French war effort was being financed almost entirely by American money. The financial aid brought poor results. After seven years of effort, France was still unable to defeat the elusive, resilient Vietminh. When the French failed to lift a long and bloody siege of their key fortress at Dienbienphu in early 1954, they finally gave up.

In April of that year, a 14-nation peace conference was convened in Geneva to work out a political settlement for Vietnam. The negotiations produced an agreement that temporarily divided Vietnam into two sections, separated by a demilitarized zone (DMZ) along the 17th Parallel. The Vietminh agreed to withdraw to the north, where Ho's regime would be in control, while the southern half was to be administered by the French-backed emperor Bao Dai. Finally, internationally supervised elections were to be held in July 1956 to reunify the country—elections that, in the absence of organized opposition in the south, the communists expected to win easily.

Events did not follow as planned. In mid-1954, Bao Dai called upon Ngo Dinh Diem, a member of a prominent Catholic family, to form a government in Saigon. Bolstered by a pledge of U.S. support from President Eisenhower, Diem set about consolidating his authority in the south. In October 1955, having eliminated potential rivals in the army and elsewhere, Diem deposed Bao Dai and named himself president of the Republic of South Vietnam. The next year he canceled the scheduled elections, counting on American assistance to strengthen his regime.

Following the 1954 partition, some 90,000 Vietminh troops had been withdrawn north of the 17th parallel as required by the Geneva agreement. Others, however, had returned to their villages in the south—some to conduct propaganda activities, but most simply to wait for reunification. Diem continued to view them as a threat, and through 1956 and 1957, he conducted a campaign of censorship, imprisonment and terror that destroyed what remained of the Vietminh organization in the south. At the same time, a hard core of well-trained communist partisans evaded Diem's troops and secret police by fleeing into the same jungle areas they had used as sanctuaries during the war with the French. In the next three years, the rebels regrouped and laid the groundwork for resistance. They raided government outposts for weapons, recruited new members, and organized revolutionary committees in villages around the countryside. In December 1960, they formed the National Liberation Front (NLF) to serve as the political arm of the rebellion. The military arm of the movement came to be known as the Vietcong.

Ho Chi Minh leaves the French Foreign Ministry, July 1946

United States

President Lyndon B. Johnson delivering his 1965 State of Union address

Although the Saigon and U.S. governments accused the NLF of being controlled by North Vietnam, the insurgent group nonetheless remained a largely indigenous South Vietnamese force. As the guerrilla war intensified, Diem's forces proved less and less able to cope with the rebels, and urgent requests were made to Washington for more help. President Kennedy, fearful of the political effects of a communist victory, responded with a major increase in the U.S. commitment. By the end of 1961, 900 military advisors had been sent to Vietnam; a year later, the number was over 11,000, accompanied by an avalanche of military hardware.

The Vietcong nevertheless continued to outfight government troops and gained control over large areas of the countryside. In addition, Diem's increasingly repressive security measures were alienating large segments of the population. In the cities, hundreds of non-communist politicians and intellectuals were jailed for dissent of almost any kind. At length, mounting public pressure burst into the open, sparked by an uprising of Buddhists in May 1963. Within a month, demonstrations had spread across the country, focusing world attention on Diem's dictatorial policies. The uprising, and Diem's ruthless attempts to suppress it, proved the final blow to his already dwindling support in Washington. In the early autumn, it was quietly made known to South Vietnamese generals that America would not oppose a coup, and in November the regime was overthrown with almost no resistance.

For the next two years, a succession of inept regimes paraded in and out of power. It was in the midst of this turmoil that the Gulf of Tonkin resolution was passed by Congress. In early 1965, U.S. air strikes were conducted against enemy strongholds above and below the DMZ. President Lyndon Johnson then launched what was to become a heavy bombing campaign against North Vietnam. In May 1965, following a major Vietcong offensive, the United States responded with a major troop deployment. The upward spiral then began in earnest. In August, there were 90,000 U.S. troops in South Vietnam; by the end of the year, the number had jumped to 184,000. America was then committed to a large-scale war, and for the next three years the escalation continued, peaking at more than 540,000 troops in 1968.

But even this massive infusion of manpower, along with a protracted bombing campaign, proved inadequate. Like the Vietminh, the Vietcong were a skillful, stubborn, and resilient enemy. Supplied with arms from the Soviet Union and the PRC, they were willing to accept heavy casualties and were prepared to fight on until the Americans decided the war was no longer worth the price.

Upon assuming office, President Richard M. Nixon described his ultimate goal in Vietnam as "peace with honor" and announced a plan for the gradual withdrawal of U.S. combat troops and a simultaneous "Vietnamization" of the war. By the end of 1969, U.S. troop levels had been reduced from more than 540,000 to 479,000, and a year later the number was down to 339,000. The overall level of violence was scarcely decreasing. To compensate for the troop cutbacks, bombing raids were intensified. During Nixon's first three years in office, some 15,000 U.S. troops were killed and more than 100,000 wounded.

Richard M. Nixon (right) meets with Indonesia's leader Sukarno.

Courtesy of Special Collections, University of Virginia Library

114

By mid-1972, U.S. troop strength was down to below 50,000. Then began the final bloody chapter of American participation in the war. The Vietcong launched a major new offensive, and in response Nixon announced his decision to mine North Vietnam's harbors and begin an intensive bombing campaign. During the next months, Nixon's national security advisor, Henry Kissinger, began a series of negotiations with the North Vietnamese. Finally in January 1973, a cease-fire agreement was signed by representatives of the United States, North Vietnam, the Saigon government, and the NLF. The accord provided for the withdrawal of all U.S. service personnel within 60 days, concurrent with the release by the enemy of all U.S. prisoners of war. An international commission would supervise the truce while a national council of Saigon and NLF delegates worked out a political settlement for the country.

In effect, the cease-fire agreement was a face-saving device for the United States. Saigon had not been toppled by the Communists; the prisoners were coming home; no more Americans were dying in combat. Nixon could claim to have achieved "peace with honor." But in Vietnam, as in Laos and Cambodia, talk of peace was sadly premature. From the outset, the cease-fire was marred by frequent violations, and within months, the fighting in many areas had resumed the intensity of full-scale war. Through 1973 and 1974, the United States continued to pour aid into Saigon.

So the conflict started all over again, with the crucial difference that U.S. combat troops and aircraft were no longer there. Without them, the South Vietnamese army proved no match for its opponents. Month by month, Communist forces widened their control of the countryside, nourished by a steady influx of fresh troops and supplies from the north. In early 1975, the final chapter unfolded. A large-scale North Vietnamese offensive forced the South Vietnamese troops out of the Central Highlands, and the withdrawal soon turned into a rout. Within six weeks, almost every important city and town north of Saigon had been captured, often with no resistance, and the capital was virtually encircled. South Vietnam collapsed in April 1975. In the end, South Vietnam's leaders were unduly concerned with their own power and failed to develop a social strategy to mobilize the support of their people.

So ended the long agony, ten years and eight months after the passage of the Tonkin Gulf resolution. The United States had come and gone—at a cost of more than 55,000 American lives and well over a million Asian lives—but the war continued, propelled by its own logic and momentum. The long-term effects of the war on the United States—on its role in the world, the use of power, the relationship between Congress and the President—would be revealed only by history. The Vietnam War divided America deeply and undermined the domestic consensus that had been the basis of the cold war. U.S. involvement in Indochina began faintly, but in the end it ran through America like a plague. The awful truth about the Vietnam War is that combatants and civilians probably died in vain. Without U.S. assistance, Vietnam would have gone communist years earlier. Its form of communism would in all likelihood have been of the Titoist-nationalist variety, though. For years thereafter, America would be haunted by the "Vietnam syndrome"—the national anxiety about being entrapped in prolonged military campaigns.

THE MIDDLE EAST CONFLICT

In June 1967, war broke out again in the Middle East. Nasser provoked a showdown when he sent Egyptian forces into the Sinai desert and obtained the withdrawal of the U.N. peacekeeping forces there. Moreover, Egypt blockaded the Gulf of Aqaba, through which Israel received its oil and other goods. Israel struck preemptively at the neighboring Arab countries. In a textbook display of precision bombing and strafing, Israeli aircraft devastated the Egyptian air force on the ground. Israeli air units simultaneously attacked airfields in Jordan, Syria and Iraq. Within a day, Israel had secured complete control of the skies.

After six days of combat, a nation that had comprised 8,000 square miles had 26,500 square miles under its control. Israel captured or destroyed 430 enemy aircraft and 800 tanks while inflicting 15,000 casualties on Egypt, Jordan, and Syria. Yet, despite its overwhelming victory, Israel did not find peace. In the years that followed, the Arab nations, with Soviet aid, rebuilt their shattered forces. The U.N. became a stage for the mouthing of much anti-Zionist propaganda, and Israel was often condemned as a racist and imperialist power.

The Middle East was a major focus of the foreign policy of the Nixon administration. It faced a situation in the early 1970s whereby the belligerents did not officially communicate with one another. The Soviet Union was involved and supplying large amounts of weapons to several states, in particular, Egypt, Syria and Iraq. The United States engaged in diplomatic efforts that included four-power discussions with other permanent members of the Security Council, together with a series of bilateral talks with the Soviet Union. The ultimate goal was a political settlement based on Security Council Resolution 242 of November 1967, calling for Israel's withdrawal from territories taken during the Six-Day War of 1967 in "return for secure and recognized boundaries free from threats or acts of force."

In 1970, American diplomacy endeavored to halt the spiraling level of violence and drift toward broader conflict through an interim agreement that was intended as an important step toward a broader settlement. By 1970, a low-intensity "war of attrition" smoldered along the Suez Canal, which divided Israeli and Egyptian forces. Both sides exchanged artillery fire and Israeli aircraft launched strikes into neighboring countries. Palestinian guerrillas instigated frequent attacks into Israel from Jordan and Lebanon. The United States succeeded in brokering a cease-fire accord in August 1970 that represented not only an effort to halt the deteriorating political situation but was also intended as a basis for wider negotiations. Egypt unceremoniously expelled Soviet military personnel from the country in July 1972 and seized all military equipment installed by the Soviets.

War broke out again when Egypt and Syria attacked Israel on October 6, 1973. The Egyptian assault across the Suez Canal, coordinated with a Syrian strike on the Golan Heights, caught Israel off-guard on Yom Kippur, the holiest day of the Jewish calendar. Although the Israelis suffered initial setbacks and sizeable losses of equipment, the Israeli Defense Force (IDF) recovered the initiative. Egypt found itself in a precarious situation and would have faced ultimate defeat but for U.S. pressure for a cease-fire and the eventual separation of forces. The Soviet role in the conflict alarmed the United States and its allies. The Egyptians achieved initial success in crossing the Suez Canal and driving into the Sinai Desert largely because of the substantial amounts of Soviet arms and equipment they possessed. Although Moscow threatened to intervene and Washington placed its forces on worldwide alert, the conflict did not escalate and the opposing forces were gradually withdrawn. The United States demonstrated once again that it could produce a political settlement in the region. The diplomatic efforts coming in the wake of the Yom Kippur War set the stage for the Camp David Agreement of 1978 whereby Egypt and Israel would sign a peace treaty and exchange diplomatic recognition.

Yet, the immediate economic consequences of the conflict were severe. The Yom Kippur War triggered an oil embargo against the United States and its allies that resulted in a temporary five-fold

United States

Presidents Sadat, Carter and Prime Minister Begin, September 17, 1978, at the White House
Courtesy: Jimmy Carter Library

increase in crude oil prices. The oil price hike set in train an inflationary spiral that led to the worst recession in the industrialized countries since the Great Depression of the 1930s. In the early 1970s, the United States had become for the first time a net importer of oil. Western Europe and Japan enjoyed rapid economic growth in the 1950s and 1960s based in part upon readily available and relatively inexpensive energy. By the 1970s, Western Europe imported more than 70% of its oil from the Middle East and its economy was profoundly affected by events there. Japan was also heavily dependent on oil imports and less able to handle an energy crisis than the United States. The United States maintained close relations with major energy-producing states, especially Saudi Arabia and Iran, but the ambitious modernization programs financed by oil revenues did not always bring the results that the West or the indigenous regimes wished. Energy-generated wealth promoted not only the modernization the elites generally wanted but also a backlash in the form of Islamic extremism.

After the 1973 Arab-Israeli war, the United States assumed direct responsibility for a diplomatic process that involved negotiations between Israel and its neighbors. Since the 1967 war, that task had been left in the hands of the U.N. mediator while the United States was still preoccupied with Vietnam. In January and May 1974, the United States mediated disengagement agreements between Egypt and Israel and then between Israel and Syria. All parties stated that those partial agreements were intended as preludes to the negotiation of a larger peace. In August 1975, a second agreement, called Sinai II, was negotiated between Egypt and Israel.

Washington and Moscow joined as co-sponsors of the Middle East Peace Conference in Geneva in December 1973, and the agreements of 1974–1975 were worked out through the shuttle diplomacy of Secretary of State Henry Kissinger with the Soviets on the sidelines. While efforts to progress toward a comprehensive peace at the Geneva Conference were resumed under the administration of President Jimmy Carter in 1977, Egyptian President Anwar Sadat's visit to Jerusalem in November of that year returned diplomacy to the U.S.-Egyptian-Israeli track. The leaders of these three states met at Camp David in September 1978 and produced

Anwar Sadat

two agreements. One led to the signing of a peace treaty between Egypt and Israel the following March. The other a framework for negotiating a settlement of the Israel-Palestinian conflict and of the war between Israel and other neighboring states.

The Framework of Peace agreed at Camp David provided for two stages of negotiation on the Israeli-Palestinian conflict. The purpose of the first stage of negotiation was to bring into being a Palestinian self-governing authority in the West Bank and Gaza to replace the Israeli military government and its civilian administration through a five-year transition period. After the transition period, a second round of negotiations was planned in which representatives of the Palestinian self-governing authority would join in negotiating the final status of the West Bank and Gaza.

The United States intended the negotiations to be steps in a just settlement for the Palestinian people, both in the occupied territories and in the diaspora. Despite the intentions of the United States, the Camp David Accords were initially denounced by other Arabs for splitting Egypt from the Arab world and for ignoring the right of the Palestinian people to self-determination in Palestine.

To understand what might be required in efforts to move the Arab-Israeli conflict toward eventual resolution, it is necessary initially to isolate the chief problems to be addressed. The first problem has been to define whether and how Jews and Arabs will live together in peace and mutual respect in the former Palestinian Mandate west of the Jordan River. Another way to put this is to say that one purpose of the negotiating process is to achieve peace between Israel and the Palestinian people. The second problem, which hinges on the first, is to define whether and how Israel will live at peace with neighboring states as an accepted and recognized state in the Middle East. Many Arabs today are prepared to live at peace with a Jewish state. Most Israelis acknowledge that peace with the Palestinian Arabs is essential and that there will be no peace while the Palestinian Arabs remain under military occupation. Serious negotiation is unlikely to take place until there is agreement that the purpose is a *modus vivendi* between Israel and the Palestinian people. Nonetheless, the Middle East has become "balkanized," with political instability and regional rivalry causing periodic explosions. Even Arab states friendly to America argue that the increasing frustration and anger about Palestinian issues are the main danger to Western interests, and that all Arabs, not just Israel's neighbors, feel the same way.

Yassir Arafat leads Palestinians until November 2004.

SECURITY IN THE NUCLEAR AGE

During the postwar years of the Truman administration, particularly after the Soviet Union's first atomic test in 1949, U.S. leaders began to adapt their polices and programs to the realities of atomic weapons. But recognition of how profoundly these weapons had changed the traditional military characteristics and political dimensions of war took time to evolve, partly because people and institutions are naturally reluctant to modify established plans, procedure and thinking. On a practical level, in both the United States and the Soviet Union atomic destructive power and delivery potential increased slowly. Indeed, it took ten years for the two characteristics of the strategic nuclear age, sizeable nuclear arsenals and long-range delivery systems, to be reflected in the actual weapons capabilities of each nation.

In the early years of the Eisenhower administration, American leaders faced the problem of dealing with the unavoidable fact that the U.S. population had become vulnerable to Soviet intercontinental nuclear strikes. By the late 1950s, the concept of deterrence had taken hold, and the procurement of retaliatory forces capable of withstanding a Soviet nuclear strike became central to American strategic doctrine. The Eisenhower administration, however, attached overriding importance to the goal of keeping military spending in check. Even though nuclear arms were vital to America's basic defense posture under the "massive retaliation" policy, restraint was exercised in certain strategic weapons programs.

The period 1961–68 saw an institutionalization of the doctrine of "assured destruction," the completion of the Minuteman and Polaris missile deployments, and the development of the advanced technology of multiple independently targetable reentry vehicles (MIRVs). MIRVed missiles carry multiple warheads that can be targeted on different areas. The "flexible response" doctrine, which emphasized conventional defense and was designed to maximize defense options, reflected the Kennedy and Johnson administrations' awareness of the limited utility of nuclear weapons and the importance of casting a strategic posture designed to minimize arms buildups on both sides. The principal aim of flexible response was to deter aggression by the threat of escalation from conventional to tactical nuclear warfare.

After the Cuban missile crisis of October 1962, the systematic expansion of the Soviet Union's strategic offensive capacity led to the loss of overwhelming U.S. superiority of the 1950s. This same expansion resulted in plans to begin the strategic arms limitation talks (SALT), which were forestalled by the Soviet move into Czechoslovakia in the summer of 1968. SALT stemmed from the desire to dampen the cycle of U.S.-Soviet strategic arms actions and reactions that had represented a waste of resources for both countries, had become a source as well as a signal of tensions between Washington and Moscow, and had contributed to fears that "balance of terror" deterrence might fail to prevent nuclear war. Neither country pursued an all-out strategic arms buildup throughout the 1950s and 1960s. But the web of mis-

trust between East and West, combined with the constant advance in weapon technology, made unilateral restraint on either side strategically questionable and politically impossible and precluded the negotiation of measures designed to reduce the risks and costs of the nuclear arms race.

By the start of the 1970s, after nearly two decades of U.S. nuclear superiority, "strategic parity" or essential equality of arsenals had been accepted as a reality in the U.S.-Soviet nuclear relationship. The Nixon administration adopted the doctrine of "sufficiency" in response to the changes in the strategic environment and a reevaluation of U.S. commitments around the world after Vietnam. "Sufficiency" referred to the deployment of enough weapons to ensure defense.

In October 1972, the governments of the United States and the Soviet Union put into effect the strategic arms limitation accords reached during President Nixon's historic visit to Moscow in May of that year. The Moscow accords, establishing a temporary offensive arms balance between U.S. and Soviet forces but leaving room for unilateral arms decisions on both sides, sharpened public debate in the United States over the proper direction strategic policy should take.

Arms control arrangements during the cold war were generally evaluated according to their contribution to political stability. The first was deterrence stability—assuring that U.S. forces were capable and credible enough to deter the Soviet Union from political adventures that could lead to war through miscalculation. The sec-

Presidents Carter and Brezhnev exchange signed copies of the SALT II Treaty agreement, Vienna, June 1979

United States

Four-power negotiations on Berlin, 1970

ond was arms-race stability—controlling the weapons buildup in the two countries so that the military relationship was more predictable and resources could be used for purposes other than weaponry. The third was crisis stability—creating forces of a type providing little incentive for either side to launch a first strike in a time of crisis. In addition to these basic criteria, arms-control proposals and agreements were judged in terms of negotiability and verification.

The key to superpower deterrence was to prevent one country from becoming so far ahead of the other in technology and nuclear delivery capacity that the temptation to strike first was overwhelming. Yet, the deterrence principle led to a spiraling arms race between the superpowers, in effect making the world less secure for everybody. Each country was motivated to seek more advanced and devastating weapons. A critical aspect of U.S. policy was to dampen the technological arms race and effect arms control through the SALT negotiations. By agreeing with the Soviet Union to limit the development of certain kinds of weapons, U.S. policy makers saved billions of dollars and strengthened national security.

Yet, more extensive agreements depended upon a modicum of mutual trust and reliable international inspection, difficult prerequisites in light of the ideological differences on both sides. Moreover, the SALT I accord of 1972, complemented by U.S. defeat in Vietnam and the domestic Watergate scandal, led to a decrease in U.S. military power. The Soviet Union did not wind down but escalated its drive for

military predominance. Arms limitation treaties are effective only to the extent that they are based on rough parity between the forces and weapons involved. Détente policies helped to undermine the willingness of the United States to keep up with the Soviet Union militarily.

In 1974, U.S. strategic weapons policies were in a state of flux. True, new programs such as Trident and the B-1 bomber were underway, but the Soviet Union continued to improve the quality of its nuclear forces, and the outcome of further SALT negotiations was uncertain. By the time SALT II was to go into effect, it was questionable whether parity, or rough balance, existed between the Soviet Union and the United States. The strongest argument for American support of SALT II was to sign in order to slow down the Soviet buildup, lest the United States fall further behind. Most critics of the 1979 SALT agreement rejected this argument out-of-hand.

Nuclear realities underscored a series of policy questions that received more prominent attention than did earlier discussions. In the 1970s, some observers began to fear that the Soviet Union might attempt to gain some form of nuclear advantage, even within the framework of U.S.-Soviet agreements. They argued that further increases and improvements in Soviet weaponry could endanger the effectiveness of components of the U.S. retaliatory deterrent. In addition to taking appropriate measures to prevent substantial erosion of the deterrent capability, U.S. leaders also had to deal with the issue of whether a new strategic balance might alter the perception of U.S. power at home

and abroad and increase the temptation of Soviet leaders to risk aggressive actions. These questions were closely related to the problems associated with the need to balance the goal of seeking mutually stabilizing measures against the equally important objective of retaining America's flexibility to pursue a national strategic policy consistent with national objectives, alliance commitments, and worldwide political interests.

Beginning in 1954, the United States had a policy of extending its nuclear umbrella over its Western European NATO allies in order to deter an attack. The growth of Soviet strategic forces diminished the credibility of a threat to launch a nuclear attack against the Soviet Union unless the United States itself were attacked. Because the United States did not possess a disarming "first-strike" capability, an attack on the Soviet Union could prove suicidal and was thus unlikely.

When NATO was founded in 1949, it was basically a unilateral American nuclear guarantee of European security in the guise of an alliance. With the advent of at least strategic parity, the U.S. nuclear commitment to defend Europe was reduced to a pact of mutual suicide. True, the balance of nuclear terror kept the peace for over four decades, the longest period in modern European history. Had deterrence ever failed, whether due to Soviet design, miscalculation or unrest in its empire, NATO strategy may well have institutionalized a nuclear doomsday machine that could be triggered by the slightest East-West skirmish. As Henry Kissinger once pointed out, it was absurd for the alliance to base its defense on a strategy that only promises American devastation, if not "the destruction of civilization."

It is instructive to remember that NATO's founders never envisaged what amounts to a continuing U.S. military occupation of Europe. They believed that with time Europe would recover, eventually unify, and assume its own defense. More than three decades later, the conditions for this development existed. Western Europe combined had three times the gross national product of the Soviet Union, four times its population, and technological superiority. All that was lacking for the Europeans to develop a credible deterrent was the will and incentive.

In addition to the growth of its strategic forces, the Soviet Union continued to increase its conventional and tactical nuclear weapons forces to the point that they could threaten the security of Western Europe. Some defense analysts argued that the use of nuclear weapons would be necessary to halt an invasion by Warsaw Pact forces. Yet, the actual use of these weapons

The Anguish of Power

was always hotly debated. Deployment of the Enhanced Radiation Weapon (ERW) was an example. The ERW, or the "neutron bomb" as it was commonly called, was a small nuclear weapon designed to be used on the battlefield. It offered the possibility of countering a massive tank invasion of Western Europe while limiting damage to civilians and property. Its prospective deployment met with worldwide opposition, including from Western Europe itself. The reluctance to deploy this weapon raised interesting questions about the adequacy of NATO's defense doctrine. President Carter decided ultimately not to deploy the ERW.

The 1979 NATO "dual-track" decision resulted in another political row. That year, NATO decided to modernize NATO's longer-range intermediate nuclear forces (LRINF) and the intermediate-range nuclear forces (INF). Unlike earlier nuclear weapons programs, INF modernization was the product of a European initiative and was supported and adopted unanimously by the allies. It was implemented by five European stationing countries—Great Britain, Italy, the Netherlands, Belgium and West Germany.

The Pershing II and ground-launched cruise missiles (GLCM) programs were as political as military in nature. The deployment was political since it reflected resolve to defend Europe using European-based systems. The INF modernization remained controversial and generated substantial frictions within the Alliance. Chancellor Helmut Schmidt of West Germany was generally considered the father of INF, taking the occasion of a 1977 address in London to draw attention to the implications of SALT II and the deployment of new Soviet weapons systems for Europe. He stressed the growing imbalance in Euro-strategic missiles, which threatened to weaken the deterrence on which NATO's strategy was based.

Whether Schmidt's concerns were directed only at the Soviet Union's new intermediate-range ballistic missiles, mobile and with a 5,000-kilometer range, or also included shorter-range nuclear weapons was never entirely clear. In any case, NATO selected Pershing II and GLCMs to answer the Soviet threat and spent 1979–83 pursuing both arms control and development and deployment of the two missile systems. When by 1983 no agreement with Moscow proved possible, deployment began in Britain, Italy and West Germany. Belgium and the Netherlands subsequently agreed to station GLCMs, and by 1986, basing activities had begun in all five countries.

Irrefutable as the deployment decision's logic may have been, implementation was by no means certain. In 1981–83,

demonstrators took to German streets in the greatest numbers since the 1930s. The German peace movement found in the INF modernization an issue of considerable concern, and a number of groups quickly joined the opposition. Student groups and the Protestant churches contributed support and articulate leadership to the "peace movement." The Soviet Union did its best to deepen and exploit the NATO missile modernization crisis. Local communist groups were involved in such events as the Krefeld Appeal. Some claimed the Soviet hand was apparent in the nuclear disarmament movement and the anti-deployment demonstrations. Moscow doubtless tried to influence the movements, but its total contribution was relatively minor.

The question of how to deal with an attack on Western Europe was part of the larger problem of how the United States should respond to Soviet aggression that fell short of an attack on U.S. cities. In the age of nuclear parity, a policy of "assured destruction" that threatened an attack on Soviet urban areas could hardly be deemed adequate to cope with limited attacks. It was not for nothing that "mutual assured destruction" was commonly known as MAD. The problem led to a search for alternative doctrines that would allow the United States to prevent the Soviet Union from exploiting its considerable military strength. Other crucial questions raised during the great strategy debates were: What happens if, despite everything, deterrence fails? What policies would limit civilian casualties? And would such policies strengthen or weaken deterrence?

The Pentagon

THE SECOND COLD WAR

The Soviet Union's invasion of Afghanistan in December 1979 precipitated a full-blown crisis of the international system. Soviet-American relations plummeted to a new low. West-West relations were also affected, and the partners on the two sides of the Atlantic showed the strains of the differences between them. Fearful of the consequences of a renewed superpower confrontation that would render their position yet more precarious, the Europeans offered various interpretations and reached different policy conclusions from the United States. The imbroglio over Afghanistan had not yet subsided when a major upheaval in Poland against Communist rule began to unfold, threatening the stability of the communist system in that troubled country and thus the fragile balance of East-West relations in Europe.

In the summer of 1979, few Europeans expected that the stability of relations on their continent would be jolted by developments outside the European region. Although the Iranian revolution was in full progress by then, not many anticipated the showdown that was to ensue between the regime of the Ayatollah Khomeini and the U.S. administration by November 1979. Few had seen Afghanistan as a flash point that would threaten to set the international system aflame.

The Soviet invasion of Afghanistan represented a watershed in East-West relations. At the same time, it precipitated a crisis in the Western Alliance. Troubling problems that had been developing for some time suddenly became acute policy questions requiring hard answers. The most penetrating question posed by the Soviet strike into Central Asia was whether détente was "divisible." Could the Western Alliance pursue détente relations in Europe, while the Soviet Union violated these elsewhere in the world?

Moscow's action underscored the tough reality of growing Soviet military capabilities and reflected a corresponding confidence of the Soviet leadership in these capabilities. U.S. observers viewed with increasing dismay the expanding scope of Soviet military involvement in distant places—such as Angola and Ethiopia—through advisors, proxy (local substitute forces) and logistical support. Yet, the invasion of Afghanistan was the first time that Soviet troops had been used openly in an area the West regarded as lying outside the sphere of direct Soviet dominance. The invasion confirmed a trend that had long been apparent to many observers. It seemed to signal the drive of Soviet power southward toward the Gulf region, an area of crucial importance

United States

December 1980: Lech Walesa with supporters

to the West and about which the United States was understandably sensitive.

President Carter condemned the Soviet Union and invoked sanctions. He called on the European allies to join in criticizing the Soviet Union as an international outlaw and in punishing it through sanctions and boycotts. Most Europeans expressed grave concern about the military and political consequences the projection of Soviet armed forces into Afghanistan would entail. Yet, they tended to be critical of Carter's precipitous reaction as hysterical and incongruous on the part of a weak and indecisive leader. He had proved incapable of resolute action against revolutionaries in Iran who had occupied the U.S. embassy in 1979 and held a large number of American hostages.

In a parallel development, many Europeans became skeptical about America's leadership qualities. The crisis of leadership in the Western Alliance significantly affected the drift in American-European relations. The problems that arose could not be attributed completely to the personal traits of U.S. leaders, nor to the different character of East-West relations in Europe and between the United States and the Soviet Union. The relationship between America and Europe changed. While Western Europe remained dependent on the United States for military security, it had largely freed itself from American tutelage, politically and economically. Europeans saw no cause to be submissive to the United States. If any-

thing, they tended to be overly critical of American faults. Failure to take the altered West-West relationship into account was in large part responsible for many difficulties with which the alliance had to contend.

Signs of growing Soviet military might, while U.S. capability stagnated and even declined, led to preoccupation in the United States with these adverse trends, well before the Soviet invasion of Afghanistan. It became obvious that imbalances in the military relationship between the United States and the Soviet Union had to be redressed. Similar considerations applied to force relations between NATO and the Warsaw Pact. At Carter's initiative in 1978, NATO adopted a Long-Term Defense Program (LTDP) that called for a sustained real growth of 3% in defense spending. Soviet intervention in Afghanistan accentuated the urgency to shore up Western defenses globally and regionally. Afghanistan also introduced a new dimension into alliance security in the form of "out of area" contingencies, that is, handling conflicts outside Europe. The United States insisted that its European allies do more in terms of both assuming a greater share of the defense burden in Europe and providing direct assistance to the United States in the Gulf region.

The full dimensions of the Polish drama that began in the summer of 1980 took years to unfold. One of the most astute observers of European political developments, the Oxford scholar Timothy Gar-

ton Ash, pointed out that the popular revolutions throwing off the yoke of communism in East-Central Europe took ten years in Poland, ten months in Hungary, ten weeks in the GDR (East Germany), and ten days in Czechoslovakia. The 1980 crisis was the result of a unique combination of circumstances that brought Polish Communism to the brink of disaster and the Polish people to a state of hopelessness and despair. The economic and moral bankruptcy of the system was so evident by mid-1980 that one still wondered how the Soviet Union could have allowed things to so deteriorate. A specter began to haunt Moscow in the early 1980s: the specter of free trade unionism in a satellite. In demanding free trade unions, the Poles rejected the communist claim to embody the workers' aspirations. One of the great ironies of the 20th century was that in Poland, a "people's democracy" and communist state purporting to represent the interests of the working class, a spontaneous workers' revolution against the exploiters (the communists) took place. After the emergence of the Solidarity trade union, which rapidly recruited over ten million members and emerged as the symbol of Polish national reawakening, nothing in the Soviet empire was ever the same again.

Moscow faced an agonizing dilemma. To intervene for the fourth time in the affairs of a "fraternal" communist country brought to the verge of collapse by mismanagement and corruption would have had sweeping adverse consequences, not only affecting the Soviet Union's status in the world, but shaking it internally as well. The tangible costs of intervention were far greater than in 1953, 1956 or 1968. Both the local and international situations were different and far more complicated. For starters, Poland was the largest and most religious of the Eastern Bloc countries. Many Poles, including units of the armed forces, would have resisted a Warsaw Pact invasion.

Although the Polish events were not a direct outgrowth of the Afghanistan crisis, these were to a degree interconnected. Moscow was doubtless reluctant to become militarily involved in two countries at the same time. Under such circumstances, the Poles had somewhat more latitude than they would otherwise have had to press the Communist party to fulfill their demands. Moreover, in the autumn of 1980 a tough, conservative, and ideologically strongly anti-communist administration came to power in the United States—that of President Ronald Reagan.

Indeed, at historic junctures, the fate of Poland and the destiny of Europe have been intertwined. This was the case in 1939 and again in 1980–81. In 1939, listless

Western governments that had tolerated a series of aggressive ventures by Nazi Germany finally aroused themselves from their moral inertia and resisted the aggression against Poland. In 1980–81, the Polish crisis also had extensive international implications, despite Moscow and Warsaw's arguments that the matter was purely a domestic one in which others should not meddle. In hindsight, we can cast these events in a broader historical context. What would ultimately become the Polish revolution was in large measure a consequence of the unfinished legacy of the Second World War. The Nazi assault on Poland occurred in overt collusion with Stalin, and the Soviet Union became a direct beneficiary of the renewed partition of Poland. The territory seized in 1939 was reconquered by the westward thrust of the Red Army and was not again relinquished until the collapse of the Soviet Union in 1991.

The Second World War changed the face of Europe forever. New power arrangements emerged that were enshrined in the agreement concluded by Roosevelt, Stalin and Churchill at Yalta in February 1945. From then until 1989, marking the end of the cold war, "Yalta" was a convenient catchword for the division of Europe into two spheres of influence, with specific reference to the predominance of the Soviet Union in East-Central Europe.

The legacy of Yalta burdened international relations for over four decades. The Soviet Union considered its sphere of influence a privileged sanctuary and permitted no outside interference. The "captive nations" of East-Central Europe were confined behind an iron curtain. Beginning in the late 1960s, the West attempted to open clogged channels of interaction and overcome the worst effects of the division of Europe. The centerpiece of the new policies of détente was the Helsinki Agreement, signed in August 1975 by 33 European and two North American countries. A new proper noun entered the vocabulary of international relations: Helsinki. It did not consign Yalta to oblivion although that is what it was intended to accomplish in the Western view.

Moscow saw the Helsinki Agreement as a sort of surrogate peace treaty, ratifying the inviolability of the postwar frontiers in Europe and setting the stage for a gradual erosion of the Western powers' will to face up to the threat of armed conflict on the continent. The Western powers, in turn, expected that the Helsinki Agreement would promote processes of expanded political and trade relations and encourage the adoption of an acceptable international standard of human rights in the East. Altogether, these processes would lead to a reduction of tensions and mutual suspicions. Confidence building would be conducive to arms control, and that would diminish the threat of armed conflict. They hoped that gradual processes of multilateral interaction in the long run would tame the communist regimes, so that peaceful coexistence would become a permanent reality resting on solid foundations. In other words, the effects of Yalta would at last be mitigated without threatening the security of the Soviet Union.

STRATEGIC DEFENSE

Although the Reagan administration confronted perplexing foreign policy challenges, in hindsight it also had substantial opportunities to reshape world affairs to the advantage of the United States. The President's instinct was to be tough with the Soviet Union and to increase military capabilities. The approach did ultimately encourage the Soviet Union to be more amenable to engage in serious, meaningful negotiations to achieve a *modus vivendi*. Moscow was periodically awed by the enormous U.S. capacity to gear up for military production, and it was fully aware of the disadvantages that would ensue from greater competition in arms buildup with the United States. The Soviet Union was beset by formidable economic problems at home and considerable political and military adversity on its borders. Diversion of still greater resources to the military would strain the economy beyond endurance. The opportunity for the United States was to link the acquisition of more military clout with a prudent and balanced approach to the curtailment of Soviet expansionism and a mutually acceptable control of arms.

When the Reagan administration took office in 1981, it confronted a growing imbalance in U.S. and Soviet forces by any reasonable standard. The response was a modernization of U.S. strategic forces in order to restore what Washington perceived as basic offensive equality. In doing so, U.S. policy makers came to the realization that the present course left the United States with diminishing means to assure the survival of the retaliatory forces. They also saw that future leaders might have even fewer options to maintain secure deterrents to Soviet nuclear weapons forces.

Three motivating factors led Reagan in March 1983 to propose to develop the means to shift away from the reliance on offensive nuclear weapons to a gradually increasing reliance on defensive, non-nuclear systems. The first was what many perceived as the inherent unacceptability, or even immorality, of mutual assured destruction (MAD) as the guarantor of strategic stability. The second was the lack of options for future presidents to maintain a secure offensive deterrent. The third was the failure of mechanisms of arms control, as practiced over decades, to halt the buildup of enormous stockpiles of nuclear weapons.

The Strategic Defense Initiative (SDI) became a research and development program to investigate technologies that could evolve into parts of a defensive system that would be survivable and cost-effective. The objective was to explore options by which the United States might effectively defend against ballistic missiles. The Soviet intercontinental ballistic missile (ICBM) arsenal, the administration argued, was structured for a certain purpose—to launch or to threaten a preemptive strike against U.S. retaliatory forces. The ICBM would be an ideal weapon by which to wage intimidation, if not outright war. The threat of preemptive attack

Soviet leader Mikhail Gorbachev meets President Ronald Reagan in Reykjavik, Iceland, to discuss SDI and nuclear reductions, 1986. White House photo by Terry Arthur

United States

was the continuing single most destabilizing factor in the arms race. It prevented either side from backing down, and it caused each to proliferate its weapons in order to retain a survivable retaliatory force. The preemptive option dominated defense planning and public anxiety for good reason. In the absence of defenses against incoming missiles, it conferred the perception of an advantage on the side that struck first.

The administration hoped the Soviets would conclude that their margin in ICBMs would become meaningless and agree to serious negotiations to reduce ICBMs. SDI, therefore, would play a major role in arms reductions. The Reagan administration proposed a course that would drastically diminish the Soviet advantage by eliminating the utility of the ICBMs as a preemptive force. Moscow would then turn to other, less dangerous weapon systems.

In its first five years of the 1980s, the United States combined strategic force modernization with new arms control initiatives. In addition to cruise missiles, force modernization involved procurement of the B-1 bomber, limited deployment of the MX missile, research on the single-warhead missile, Midgetman, and an upgrading of the strategic command, control, communications, and intelligence (C3I) systems. Arms control proposals, however reluctantly and belatedly developed, involved deep reductions in the levels of both intercontinental and intermediate-range systems. These proposals were initially unacceptable to the Soviets.

The U.S. initiatives, however, entailed more than strategic force modernization, arms control, and SDI. Administration officials warned that the changing conventional military balance cast "a shadow over every significant geopolitical decision . . . It influences the management of international crises and the terms on which they

are resolved." In short, deterring future Soviet threats or aggression would be possible only if the United States possessed capable conventional land, sea, and air forces. As a consequence, the United States adopted four initiatives related to conventional forces: an increase in the Navy's fleet from around 450 warships to more than 600; an imprecise plan to pressure peripheral Soviet interests around the world in order to gain military leverage in other areas of critical interest to the United States; a move to accelerate development and procurement of "smart" battlefield weapons and to increase the stockpile of war materials needed for protracted conflict in Europe; and finally, steps to increase the level of training and combat readiness of existing conventional forces.

SOUTH OF THE BORDER

Foreign policy officials in the Reagan administration tended to view Central America in a strategic context to a far greater extent than previous administrations. Especially alarming was the worsening of prevalent social and economic problems caused in part by East Bloc arms shipments beginning in the 1970s. The strategic significance of Central America and the Caribbean extended beyond traditional hemispheric security and involved the fulfillment of security commitments elsewhere, above all, in Europe and East Asia if the United States were tied down by communist regimes in its own backyard. Moreover, the United States wanted moderate reformers in the region to be offered alternatives to the conservative authoritarianism of the past and the communist authoritarianism of Castro's Cuba.

The latter was identified as the chief security problem. For decades, the Soviet Union had been subsidizing the Cuban economy and bolstering its military establishment for power projection purposes in

troubled regions. By the late 1970s, Cuba had far and away the largest military force in Latin America and seemed increasingly bent on foreign adventures. When the Reagan administration came to office, Cuba had the largest number of military forces stationed abroad as a percentage of population of any country in the world. Cuba was in the business of fomenting insurrections and intervening directly in civil wars. In short, Cuba was a small country with a great-power foreign policy.

Nicaragua became the chief target for East Bloc intervention in the early 1980s. To bolster "revolutionary armed struggle," thousands of Cuban and East Bloc troops were deployed to Nicaragua, which served as a base of support for insurgents in neighboring countries. Nicaragua built a military establishment whose purpose was to assist communist expansion in the region.

The dilemma for the United States had become profound. Countries threatened by armed insurgencies, such as El Salvador, Guatemala and Honduras, were unlikely to reform and democratize. Efforts to combat the insurgencies not only resulted in domestic repression but prompted the curtailment of foreign aid. Instability borne of insurgency, repression, and lingering deprivation ratcheted upward. The Reagan administration subsequently shored up those indigenous forces, official and unofficial, which were resisting communist insurgency. In Nicaragua, opposition coalesced around disillusioned adherents of both the right and left to form a guerrilla organization commonly known as the "contras." The following quote from a June 1982 presidential address reflected administration thinking on Central America.

For months and months the world news media covered the fighting in El Salvador. Day after day, we were treated to stories and film slanted toward the brave freedom fighters battling oppressive government forces on behalf of the silent, suffering people of that tortured country. Then one day those silent suffering people were offered a chance to vote to choose the kind of government they wanted. Suddenly the freedom fighters were in the hills exposed for what they really are: Cuban-backed guerrillas who want power for themselves, not democracy for the people.

In general, the Reagan administration approach to Central America was based on the concept of political and military symmetry. When the United States encouraged reforms and free elections in El Salvador, it would do so in Nicaragua also. If the

British Marines on the Falkland Islands, 1982

Nicaraguan regime, backed by Havana and Moscow, fostered insurgency in El Salvador and Honduras, then the United States would support opposition groups. The administration quickly found itself at odds with Congress and some of America's allies over Central American policy, though. In 1982, the House of Representatives passed the Boland Amendment that prohibited U.S. funding of groups dedicated to the overthrow of the Nicaraguan regime. Support for the contras and other opposition groups in the face of congressional opposition later resulted in a political scandal that rocked the Reagan presidency to its very fundaments.

Mexico, Venezuela, Colombia and Panama formed the Contadora Group, which developed a framework for a negotiated Central American settlement and worked to prevent a U.S.-sponsored invasion of Nicaragua. The Contadora Group produced a peace plan that included the withdrawal of foreign forces and an agreement that no country would be used as a staging ground for attacks against neighboring countries. Verification and enforcement proved the stumbling blocks of the peace plan, and the low-intensity conflict ground on.

In March 1982, Argentina, then ruled by a military junta, invaded the Falkland Islands, British territory in the South Atlantic. Argentinian forces quickly overwhelmed the handful of British defenders. The Argentines assumed the British would not fight to reclaim the islands and that the United States, already confronted with problems aplenty in Latin America, would not stand by its European ally. The U.N. Security Council subsequently passed a resolution calling for the withdrawal of all forces, an end to hostilities and a negotiated settlement. The British government asserted the right of self-determination of the islanders whose preference for British administration was evident.

In a vicious war lasting less than two months, Britain retook the Falkland Islands. Although other Latin American countries voted for resolutions favoring Argentina in the OAS, the junta overestimated the support it would find within the hemisphere. Even though the United States abstained on the resolutions, it nonetheless faced a dilemma. British action was widely viewed as another colonial war and quite evidently involved major military operations in the Western Hemisphere. America nonetheless sided with Great Britain for geostrategic reasons and on international legal grounds involving several well-recognized principles, above all, that of self-determination. It chose to maintain the "special relationship" with a key ally and to thwart the severe political and psychological damage

British defeat might have had upon the transatlantic alliance. Forced to tread a fine line between transatlantic and hemispheric relations, the United States chose NATO solidarity.

In 1983, pressing difficulties on the Caribbean island of Grenada surfaced. The combination of Soviet weapons shipments and the construction of a huge airport apparently for military purposes by Cuban construction workers and soldiers set off alarm bells in Washington and neighboring Caribbean states. When the Marxist prime minister, Maurice Bishop, who headed the New Jewel Movement, was toppled and executed by government officials even more leftist than he, members of the Organization of Eastern Caribbean States requested outside intervention. Their fear, shared by the United States, was that a radical Grenadan regime would become a base for revolutionary armed struggle, dished up Moscow and Cuban style.

In October 1983, U.S. forces landed on Grenada, seized the airport and the Cubans, and freed 1,000 American students and the British governor-general who had been held as effective hostages. Soviet weapons caches on the island far exceeded intelligence estimates. The U.S. administration determined that Grenada was indeed designated for Soviet/Cuban use in political-military operations.

Despite the turmoil, genuine democratic change occurred in many parts of Latin America in the 1980s. Brazil, the

largest country in South America, began holding local elections for the first time in nearly two decades in the early 1980s. The military-backed government eased up on press censorship, released political prisoners, and held a national election in 1985. All five Andean countries—Ecuador, Venezuela, Peru, Columbia, and Bolivia—were being run by elected presidents by the mid-1980s. Mexico, Costa Rica, and the Dominican Republic all elected presidents, reinforcing existing albeit shaky democratic foundations. In Uruguay, citizens participated in their first elections since 1973, voting overwhelmingly to terminate military rule and placing the country on a course of full democracy. Even in the southern tip of the continent, where the military ruled with a mailed fist, popular pressure in Argentina and Chile prevailed upon the junta leaders to hold elections. Military rule in Argentina ended in late 1983, and Chile held free and fair national elections in 1988. The political dominance of the brass hats was over.

THE ARC OF CRISIS

Upon the assumption of office, the Reagan administration faced a new and bewildering problem in the Middle East, the Iran-Iraq war, which had broken out in late summer of 1980. With its large Shi'ite population, Iraq was a prime target for Iran's fundamentalist propaganda directed against allegedly illegitimate, secularist regimes such as that of Saddam Hus-

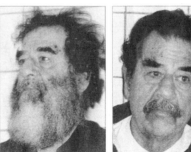

The Washington Post

127TH YEAR No. 10   R   DC MD VA   MONDAY, DECEMBER 15, 2003

NEWSSTAND 35¢
HOME DELIVERY 39¢

Hussein Captured

U.S. Forces Uncover Iraqi Ex-Leader Near Home Town

The Hunt

When Focus Shifted Beyond Inner Circle, U.S. Got a Vital Clue

By Barton Gellman and Dana Priest
Washington Post Staff Writers

BAGHDAD, Dec. 14—Thirty-eight weeks after the United States began stalking Saddam Hussein with an arsenal of lethal force, technology and coercion, it fell to a soldier with a spade to flush the fallen leader from a hole.

About a mile from his nearest palace, Hussein spent his final minutes of freedom in an underground chamber of hand-packed dirt, just wide enough to permit a man to recline. After decades as self-proclaimed heir to the iconic 12th-century warrior, Saladin, Hussein surrendered meekly without a shot from the pistol he clutched in his lap.

The clues that led to Hussein's capture emerged three weeks ago, officials said, when intelligence analysts and Special Operations forces shifted the focus of their hunt from Hussein's innermost circle to the more distant relatives and tribal allies who they suspected had been sheltering the deposed president. U.S. officials here and in Washington, speaking on condition of anonymity, said the new strategy led to the capture in Baghdad on Friday of a relative from Hussein's Tikriti clan. Under interrogation, the man contributed a vital, though still undisclosed, clue to

The Prisoner

A Select Few Confront Their Tormentor

Saddam Hussein is shown just after his capture, left. He was later examined by a military doctor and shaved.

U.S. ARMY VIA AGENCE FRANCE-PRESSE   U.S. ARMY VIA REUTERS

Detention Could Lead To Trial on Charges of War Crimes, Genocide

By Rajiv Chandrasekaran
Washington Post Foreign Service

BAGHDAD, Dec. 14—Former Iraqi president Saddam Hussein was captured without a shot Saturday night by American soldiers who discovered him hiding in the dark of a tiny, underground burrow near his home town, U.S. military officials said on Sunday.

Hussein was detained outside Dawr, a hamlet along the Tigris River about 10 miles southeast of Tikrit, by soldiers of the U.S. Army's 4th Infantry Division, military officials said. He was spirited to Baghdad, officials said, where he was subjected to a medical examination and questioning that could lead eventually to a trial for crimes against humanity and genocide.

Within hours of his capture, however, the man who exercised absolute power in Iraq for almost three decades was confronted by several politicians he had tormented. In a 30-minute meeting at a detention facility at Baghdad International Airport, four of the country's new leaders grilled Hussein about his rule.

"He had no regret or remorse," said Mowaffak Rubaie, a member of Iraq's U.S.-appointed Governing Council. "He remains the street thug that he always was."

"He was unrepentant and defiant," said Adel Abdel-Mehdi, a senior Shiite Muslim politician. "He was not at all apologetic. He just made excuses for

United States

sein of Iraq. Alarmed, and hoping to gain rapid victory over a country weakened by revolutionary upheaval, Iraq attacked Iran in September 1980 and achieved initial military successes. Hussein believed the regime of the Iranian ayatollahs could be relatively easily toppled, a view shared by other Arab regimes that supported him. The Iraqi onslaught soon ground to a halt, though, and by 1982, Iranian counteroffensives had driven Iraqi forces from all the territory that had been seized. The conflict became a stalemated slugfest. By 1984, Teheran was in a position to threaten Hussein's regime. Concerned at the prospect of a victory by an anti-Soviet, fundamentalist regime, the Soviet Union began again to deliver massive amounts of weaponry to Iraq. The casualty toll on both sides remained heavy, and Iraq used chemical weapons against entrenched Iranian troops and massed infantry assaults. Urban areas on both sides suffered substantial destruction, and Iraq escalated the conflict by launching airborne attacks against Iranian oil facilities. Iran responded with attacks against tankers and other surface vessels in the Persian Gulf, threatening to shut the Strait of Hormuz. The United States, Britain and France deployed warships to the area and made clear they would tolerate no closure of the strait.

The suffering and inherent tragedy in Iraq and Iran were great. As the fighting dragged on, with mounting casualties and drains on the economies of the two countries, so also grew the threat of the war spilling over to nearby states in the Gulf. The spread of conflict in geographic terms and the increasing impact on third parties created circumstances in which the Soviet Union might have found opportunities to get involved. A constant in U.S. policy for decades in the Gulf region was the prevention of greater Soviet influence and presence. As the war ground on, Western naval patrols were stepped up. Eventually Kuwaiti tankers were "reflagged" with the Stars and Stripes to provide naval protection. Although the United States was officially neutral in the conflict, unofficially it "tilted" toward Iraq to contain Iran. The ghastly conflict lasted more than eight years and resulted in hundreds of thousands of casualties on both sides. Both exhausted and nearly bankrupt, Iran and Iraq finally ceased the senseless fighting.

Following the sobering experience of having relied upon the weak Shah of Iran as a proxy for America in the Persian Gulf region, many in the United States came to realize that no real substitute existed for U.S. power that could be projected into the region in support of U.S. interests. Accordingly, the Reagan administration enlarged maritime forces and augmented the strength of the Rapid Deployment Force, slotted for use in Middle East contingencies. An early statement of the administration's strategic concept specified that U.S. conventional forces had to be capable of responding to a wide range of possible contingencies. The new strategic approach, particularly applied to operations outside Europe, had two dimensions. First, it called for a U.S. capacity rapidly to deploy enough force to hold important positions and to interdict and blunt a Soviet attack. Second, it recognized that the United States had options for fighting on other fronts and for building up allied strength that would lead to consequences unacceptable to the Soviet Union.

Shifts in the U.S. strategic concept in the 1980s originated to a significant extent in changed threat perception. True, containment of the Soviet Union guided actions taken by the Carter administration as much as it did other postwar administrations, but the choice between confrontation or cooperation during the Carter administration was left to Moscow. The Reagan administration leaned more toward a confrontational stance with the Soviets and emphasized the central role the USSR played in the formulation of American foreign and defense policy. The primary task the United States faced in the early 1980s was to revitalize containment by building and brandishing U.S. military power.

More than any other part of the world, the Middle East had the potential for escalation of local conflict, such as between Israel and its neighbors or between Iran and Iraq to a superpower military confrontation. The United States tried to temper unilateralist inclinations prompted by increased military clout with an effort to subordinate political differences in the Middle East to a broad strategic consensus about the perils of the Soviet threat. To be included in this consensus was the "northern tier," with echoes of the earlier Baghdad Pact of the 1950s, which had not survived the forces of revolutionary nationalism. "Northern tier" states were those sharing a border with or in close proximity to the Soviet Union and which could serve as a barrier against Soviet encroachments into the Gulf region. The decline of the overall strategic position of the United States in the Middle East was underscored by the fact that only two "northern tier" states, Turkey and Pakistan, were candidates for any sort of strategic consensus. The Arab states and Israel agreed on little. Some conservative Arabs regarded communism and Zionism as twin evils.

Saudi Arabia remained key to U.S. policy in the Middle East, especially after the fall of the Shah of Iran. In addition to being the world's leading producer of oil, Saudi Arabia maintained crucial relationships with smaller oil-producing states. Although the Saudi regime had been friendly toward the United States since the Second World War, it did not want a formal alliance nor would it allow the stationing of U.S. military forces on its territory. Such a close relationship would have

Israeli troops in combat operations Courtesy of the Department of Defense

124

been incompatible with Saudi notions of independence. The Saudis insisted on U.S. training and equipment for their own forces. It would take a genuine, tangible threat in the form of an Iraqi seizure of Kuwait in 1990 to induce the Saudis to allow U.S. forces in their country.

Meanwhile, the Palestinian question resurfaced with vengeance in the 1980s as profound differences emerged on the meaning of the concept of "full autonomy" for the Palestinians as specified in the 1979 Camp David Accords. Israel retained possession of the West Bank until an arrangement was in place, a circumstance that worked in Israel's favor by allowing it to continue building settlements and extend administrative authority. In the 1980s, despite objections voiced by the United States and others, Israel built hundreds of new settlements on the West Bank. A number of designs for Palestinian autonomy, such as the 1982 Saudi peace plan, went nowhere. The Palestinian problem continued to fester until it exploded into the *intifada* or uprising of the late 1980s.

Lebanon, torn by years of civil war, was closely connected to the Palestinian issue because of the Palestine Liberation Organization (PLO) stronghold there and the influence exercised by Syria. Lebanon never constituted a modern political system. It remained in fact the last remnant of the Ottoman Empire, a precarious republic that is really a feudal arrangement among Muslim, Christian and Druse leaders and their militias. Syria sought to extend its influence throughout the country, and the PLO used Lebanon as a base for the eventual establishment of a Palestinian state that would include the West Bank and other adjacent areas as well. Such a chaotic situation invites the intervention of outside powers, and Lebanon was certainly no exception. Regarding the Lebanese situation as a lingering security threat, Israel periodically launched air and ground strikes in that troubled country.

In the spring of 1982, Israel decided to take decisive military action in Lebanon apparently to eliminate the dual threats posed by the PLO and Syria. Israeli goals vacillated and were never made completely clear. Ariel Sharon, the defense minister who planned the campaign, had no intention of limiting the war to the quick-strike, 40-kilometer (25 miles) operation initially specified. Instead, Sharon pursued an Israeli imperial ambition in Lebanon and attempted to impose a new political order upon the country in collusion with Israel's Lebanese Christian allies. Although Israeli forces drove to Beirut, the operation nonetheless went awry and Israel got stuck in a political-military quagmire. Israel's supposed Lebanese al-

lies rendered no support. The Christian Phalange proceeded to pursue a Lebanese Arab policy, meaning that it would fight to the last Israeli soldier while cutting a deal with Saudi Arabia for the establishment of a Christian-Arab Lebanon. The Reagan administration was furious about the wanton destruction and the lack of consultation by Israel, but did play a crucial diplomatic role by arranging for the departure of the PLO from Beirut and an eventual cessation of hostilities. Israeli forces would fight periodically in the country for years thereafter.

LOOKING EAST

The Asian Pacific was a strategic focal point for global U.S. policies in the 1980s. It also became the site for a number of dynamic economies with which the United States was developing commercial relations that surpassed those with Western Europe. While European economies stagnated by comparison, it became fashionable to refer to the newly industrialized economies of East Asia in such terms as the "Asian Tigers," referring to South Korea, Hong Kong, Taiwan and Singapore. These countries achieved unprecedented economic growth largely as a result of economic development approaches based on laissez-faire, openness and direct investment from abroad. Despite a modicum of uncertainty about the future of Hong Kong after its scheduled reversion from Britain to China in 1997, East Asia remained for the most part economically dynamic, with growth rates in many countries exceeding 5%. In advanced technological sectors, the United States and some European countries regarded Japan with a combination of admiration, apprehension and even some envy as a global contender for financial and economic "high-tech" leadership.

The United States encountered substantial frictions with Japan. The row arose largely because of lingering "burden sharing" issues regarding defense and growing Japanese trade surpluses that suggested Japan focused on the economic instruments of statecraft conducive to export competition on terms unfavorable to trading partners. Japan thus became the chief target for the protectionist sentiment that emerged in the United States in the late 1970s. American compulsion brought "voluntary" restrictions on Japanese automobile exports to the United States. Pressure mounted from American manufacturers and labor unions for domestic-content legislation designed to certify that products marketed by Japan in the United States contained a suitable percentage of components manufactured domestically. Japan reduced its tariffs on numerous

imports, but a variety of other barriers remained on a number of products such as petrochemicals, fertilizers, pharmaceuticals, data-processing software, electronic equipment, citrus fruit, and beef. In its defense, Japan asserted that its economy was being penalized for its efficiency, innovation, and effective marketing techniques, while the United States and other exporting countries had not maintained a competitive edge in global markets. Japanese officials repeatedly pointed out that their country was one of the world's largest importers of goods and services. It followed that manufactured goods comprised a relatively small percentage of total Japanese imports because Japan, lacking natural resources, had to acquire most of its raw materials from abroad.

The United States substantially changed its policy toward China in the 1980s, given the fundamental and widely acknowledged need to sustain a cooperative, mutually beneficial relationship. In light of the tensions with the Soviet Union prior to 1985, the United States continued to attach considerable strategic importance to the PRC. More broadly, several factors tended to shape U.S. policy in East Asia. These included a determination that Asia had become more salient in U.S. foreign policy, but China was only one of several pivotal Asian-Pacific actors whose interests the United States had to scrutinize. The last years of the Carter administration brought a closer Sino-American relationship that foreshadowed outright strategic cooperation, especially in the wake of the Soviet invasion of Afghanistan.

The Reagan administration tended to view closer links between Beijing and Washington in a broader context. Despite the prominence given to human rights as a cardinal foreign policy principle, the Carter administration developed a rapport with the unrepresentative Beijing regime based exclusively on strategic interest. It is somewhat ironic that the Reagan administration, committed to the restoration of American military strength and prepared to utilize other capabilities to counterbalance the Soviet Union, was more inclined to assess the Sino-American relationship within the context of other interests, including U.S. assurances to Taiwan. During the 1980 presidential campaign, Reagan criticized the Carter administration for having normalized diplomatic relations with the PRC in a manner detrimental to Taiwan. Some Reagan administration officials would continue to criticize the Carter administration for agreeing to accord full recognition to the PRC while severing all official association with Taiwan. True, the Carter administration resumed arms sales to Taiwan in accordance with the Taiwan Relations Act of 1979, despite opposition

United States

Prime Minister Margaret Thatcher meets Soviet leader Mikhail Gorbachev in London, 1989

Leonid Brezhnev

from Beijing. Such weapons deliveries were stepped up in the 1980s.

The new defense consensus in the United States that was instrumental in bringing the Reagan administration into office ensured a substantial American military buildup and a more spirited foreign policy. These were all very satisfactory from Beijing's perspective, and the Reagan administration shared Chinese concerns about "hegemonism" (read Soviet imperialism). Fundamental agreement on many strategic issues in fact lessened the need in Beijing's view for a formal strategic relationship with the United States. A more powerful America, opposing Soviet foreign political adventures, allowed the Chinese to maintain a certain distance from both superpowers and thus to maximize Beijing's room for diplomatic maneuver. From the American perspective also, unilateralist impulses and an administration vehemently opposed to communism in any form worked against a friendly diplomatic relationship with China. Although considerable benefit accrued to the West from the stationing of huge Soviet military forces along the Sino-Soviet frontier, capabilities that were not available for use elsewhere, the deployment of such units was unaffected by U.S. strategy and long preceded Sino-American diplomatic normalization. It followed that the United States needed to make no major concessions, least of all regarding Taiwan, within the broader strategic framework. In short, the PRC, in its own self-interest, would maintain its geostrategic course and it needed America more than the latter needed it. The combi-

nation of the vast military disparity in the Soviet Union's favor and China's apparently enduring economic backwardness led many U.S. policy makers to conclude that in strategic terms China could offer little more to the United States than it was already providing.

THE WORLD TURNED RIGHTSIDE UP

Political instability in the Kremlin during the succession crisis in 1982–84 at least ensured that little would be done to provoke the West to further accelerate its military buildup. As soon as Mikhail Gorbachev became the new party general secretary in March 1985, the Soviet Union froze its missile deployments in Eastern Europe. It reversed itself by essentially accepting the U.S. position on INF and returning to the Geneva arms control talks despite NATO's failure to fulfill any of the preconditions Moscow had set for the resumption.

By then a reassessment of Soviet security policy was underway. The beginnings of it can be traced to the aftermath of Reagan's announcement of SDI. It revealed significant differences of outlook between civilian experts, better attuned to Western

President Reagan and General Secretary Gorbachev, Reykjavik, Iceland, October 11, 1986

thinking because of their frequent interaction with Western officials, and the more parochial military officers, who lacked the same educational experience. The emergence within the Soviet establishment of an influential group of people with a vested interest in continued dialogue with the West was as an important by-product of détente. Thus, even insiders began to harbor doubts about maintaining an authoritarian system.

The Gorbachev leadership soon embraced such concepts of the Western left as "non-provocative defense" and "structural inability" to attack. A 1986 meeting of the Warsaw Pact supported a restructuring that would "exclude not only the possibility of a surprise attack" but also the waging of large-scale offensive operations. Gorbachev came to realize that progress was possible only when the interests of all parties were taken into account. Following the inconclusive Gorbachev-Reagan summit at Reykjavik in 1986, the Warsaw Pact attempted to convince Western publics, not only by words but also by deeds, that it was no longer a threat. It began to issue statements describing its military doctrine as that of "defensive sufficiency."

Troubled by growing systemic weaknesses, Moscow found itself nonetheless on the defensive before an ascendant and confident United States. In response, the Gorbachev leadership attempted to shore up its alliance system by initiating reforms toward a real partnership along the Western model. In the longer term, the seachange in the Soviet empire came about because the West had remained stalwart and resolute. It was the direct consequence of Moscow's renunciation of the "Brezhnev Doctrine," that is, the alleged right of the Soviet Union to intervene to defend communist regimes, however unpopular. By convincing Moscow of the necessity of sweeping reform, which eventually caused it to tolerate the dissolution of its East-Central European empire and later of the Soviet Union itself, NATO significantly contributed to ensuring the peaceful outcome of the cold war. In summer 1989, the first signs appeared of the disintegration of communism in East-Central Europe. The first of the dominos to fall was Poland, when Solidarity won the elections in June and a noncommunist government assumed office. Moscow accepted the result, having substituted, in the famous words of Soviet foreign ministry officials, the "Sinatra Doctrine" (they do it their way) for the Brezhnev Doctrine.

With the communist satellite regimes collapsing in late 1989, the Soviet foreign minister called for the Warsaw Pact to be transformed from a military-political alliance to a largely political one, free from ideological content. By then Poland, no longer ruled by a communist government, opposed any alliance obligations that would affect the internal order of the member states. Other Warsaw Pact members insisted on their sovereign right to shape that order in accordance with the Helsinki principles. The Warsaw Pact's efforts to remodel itself in a Western image had by 1989 effectively neutralized the communist alliance as an instrument for bolstering the crumbling Soviet bloc. NATO's costly military buildup set this process into motion by helping to convince Moscow and its East-Central European clients that by adopting Western models they could modernize their system and somehow keep themselves in power. By the time they realized that the circle could not be squared, it was too late. The opening of the Berlin Wall in November 1989 symbolized the end of the Soviet "outer" empire.

As the brutal communist dictatorship in Romania toppled around Christmastime 1989, the United States launched a yule-tide invasion of Panama to overthrow the corrupt government of Panama strongman Manuel Noriega. The operation involved the largest commitment of American troops abroad since the Vietnam War and represented an effective execution of a "small war," a term recently reintroduced into the strategic vocabulary. U.S. casualties were relatively light, operations were concluded in a relatively short time, and all objectives were met. The operation received the overwhelming support not only of the American people but of Panamanians as well. Polls indicated that 80% of Americans approved of the invasion and the modicum of muted criticism was swept aside, as events in Romania pushed Panama out of the headlines. Although U.S. firepower was carefully utilized in an effort to keep casualties to a minimum, fighting was fierce at times. In the densely urbanized areas where much of the conflict was conducted, death and injury of many noncombatants was the result.

The Warsaw Pact's lingering existence after the collapse of Moscow's "outer" empire in East-Central Europe highlighted the difficulties both alliances encountered in grasping how much had changed how fast in Europe. What rendered impractical the maintenance of the alliance system in its existing form was the pending unification of Germany. Even though Soviet leaders were still making noises in late 1989 that they would not abandon their "East German ally," the relevant question was actually how a united Germany would be integrated into NATO. In the summer of 1990, Soviet leaders, strongly influenced by President George H.W. Bush, Secretary of State James Baker, and Chancellor Helmut Kohl of West Germany, announced that the decision

General Manuel Antonio Noriega

to join NATO should be left to the German people. Germany's neighbors would settle for nothing less than a united Germany tightly integrated into the Western alliance and the European Community. Having just thrown off Moscow's yoke, the East-Central European states above all wanted to preserve the time-honored security arrangements that would keep the Americans in, the Russians out, and the Germans down. As part of the unification accord, Germany agreed to abstain from introducing foreign troops and extending military infrastructure, especially installations with nuclear weapons, into the territory of the former GDR.

In July 1991, the Warsaw Pact ended its existence with the dissolution of its political remnants at its last meeting. Few Soviet leaders bemoaned its passing by then, but some publicly questioned NATO's suitability to meet Europe's security requirements. It is notable that Soviet foreign ministry officials were heard to quip that they could then tell the petulant Russian generals that they were wrong about the Western threat. In December 1991, the red flag was hauled down from Red Square in Moscow and the Soviet Union was cast into the dustbin of history.

THE MIDDLE EAST IN PEACE AND WAR

On August 2, 1990, Iraq conducted a full-scale military invasion of Kuwait, claiming it was an internal coup, and assumed complete control of the oil-rich country. Saddam Hussein had made the grave mistake of committing international

East and West German leaders, especially former premier Hans Modrow and Chancellor Helmut Kohl officially opening the border, December 22, 1989

United States

two important hemispheric trends: the rapid globalization of the U.S. economy and the rising fear among many Americans about their personal economic security. Political campaigns at various levels focused public attention on the alleged connection between the internationalization of the American economy and wage stagnation and employment anxiety in the United States.

Despite the righteous sentiments of the Good Neighbor Policy of the 1930s and the Alliance for Progress in the 1960s, economic integration was never a crucial aspect of U.S. policies toward Latin America. The principal aim, founded in the Monroe Doctrine, was often exclusion—using diplomacy and military power to thwart outside intervention in the U.S. backyard. Anxiety about unrest, especially in the Caribbean Basin, resulted in numerous U.S. diplomatic and military interventions. During the cold war, U.S. unease led to concerted efforts to restrict the influence of the Soviet Union and its Cuban surrogate in the region. Confrontation and mistrust have characterized relations between the United States and many of its neighbors in the Western Hemisphere, especially Mexico. The situation changed substantially for the better in the 1990s, however, when shared interests in economic development and democratic stability promoted mutual confidence and cooperation. Regional transformation was accelerated by the end of the cold war. The modernizing societies of Latin America and the Caribbean had little use for dictators and guerrillas. In growing mea-sure, they demonstrated their preference for representative governments over the abuses and shenanigans of leftist and rightist extremes.

Economic liberalization assisted mightily in the long-awaited political transformation of Mexico. In 2000, Vicente Fox Quesada, heading the "Alliance for Change" coalition, was elected president of Mexico, defeating the candidate of the Institutional Revolutionary Party (PRI), which had exercised authoritarian rule to maintain its 71-year grip on power. Fox was committed to greater openness between Mexico and its affluent northern neighbors to facilitate the flow of people and money. Advocating a new relationship between his country and the United States and Canada, Fox enthusiastically recommended that North America emulate the European Union (EU) by eventually permitting the free movement of capital and labor and embracing a common currency. The rub is that the post-cold war era has been characterized by a host of nontraditional security concerns affecting all three North American states, including the cross-border flow of illicit drugs, con-

traband weapons and illegal immigrants. Such security concerns are distinctive because the nonstate actors associated with them have tentacles reaching across national boundaries.

NAFTA is now more than an economic arrangement and represents an acknowledgment that the future prosperity of all three countries is interdependent. Recession, social decay, or political disorder anywhere in North America has repercussions throughout the continent. In a world increasingly defined by economic competitiveness and regional trading blocs, none of the partners can afford to become isolated from its neighbors. Perceptive observers point out that it makes no sense for Mexico to put all its eggs in one basket and then quarrel with the owner of the basket. National security elites in all three nations recognize that they share substantial interests in common, including economic prosperity and political tranquility.

U.S. assistance for regional transformation since the late 1980s has ranged from expressing public support for democratic movements and governments to sending election observers to furnish technical and organizational assistance for the democratic process. In a 1991 resolution approved by the General Assembly, the OAS declared that the interruption of legitimately elected governments in the region constituted grounds for collective action. Subsequently, the OAS member states, overcoming their historically rooted apprehensions about questions of independence and sovereignty, acted on this commitment on several occasions. OAS condemnation, for example, terminated attempted coups in Peru in 1992 and in Guatemala in 1993. Haiti's continuing troubles have proved beyond the ability of the OAS to handle and prompted the dispatching of U.S. and Canadian forces in 1995 and again in 2004.

Neighboring countries have become the fastest growing markets for U.S. trade and investment. These are essential for an open and expanding American economy. Several Latin American countries are now key providers of oil and other essential raw materials to the U.S. economy. Yet, political and economic liberalization have brought not only democratic elections and market-oriented economies, but fresh difficulties and anxieties as well. The inability of Latin American governments to alleviate enduring mass poverty and assuage long-standing social inequalities has encouraged urban and rural violence in a number of countries. According to U.N. estimates, around 40% of Latin America's people still live in poverty, and wealth disparities are the highest in the world. Massive and sustained migration, in large part the upshot of deprivation and de-

spondency, is reshaping the United States in employment and education. The political significance of immigrants, already substantial in Florida, Texas, and California, is increasing on the national level and creating new linkages with northern Latin America and the Caribbean.

HEIRS OF PERICLES: NATO AND OSCE

The Organization for Security and Co-operation in Europe (OSCE) derives its legitimacy largely from the universality of its membership in the Northern Hemisphere. From 1975 to 1990, the OSCE, previously known as the Conference for Security and Cooperation in Europe (CSCE), operated as an important channel of East-West communication and was instrumental in providing confidence-building measures, resolving humanitarian issues, monitoring human rights, and assessing compliance with international law. The CSCE was recognized as a regional organization under the U.N. Charter, affording every country in Europe and North America membership and the right of veto. The CSCE remained in session and discussions continued. Using moral pressure and striving for consensus even when the latter was infeasible, the CSCE is now best known for scrutinizing human rights in the Soviet bloc, which all communist countries committed themselves to respecting in the 1975 Helsinki Accords.

Beginning in the 1990s, the OSCE undertook a number of crucial steps to transform itself from a cold war consultative forum to a Europe-wide political organization pertinent to an entirely new set of circumstances. The OSCE restructured itself, establishing a revamped organization with an annual council meeting of foreign ministers, and standing committees of senior officials. It currently has three institutional centers reflecting its political and geographic focus: an Office for Democratic Institutions and Human Rights in Warsaw, a Conflict Prevention Center in Vienna, and a secretariat in Prague. It has assumed a mandate to undertake peacekeeping operations with the option to appeal to NATO, the EU or the U.N. Security Council for assistance if the need arises. The OSCE has been actively involved in confidence-building measures, arms control and the enforcement of sanctions. Yet, even though the OSCE affords a legitimizing function in fact-finding missions, international dialogue and conflict prevention, it cannot stop conflict or thwart aggression. Its modest response capabilities and continued operation on the basis of consensus limit its effectiveness, although the prestige it acquired during the cold war assure it of considerable moral stature.

The Anguish of Power

The collapse of the Soviet empire and the end of European division invariably raised questions about the future purpose of NATO. A decade later, after the U.S.-led intervention in Bosnia and Kosovo, and the first and second rounds of NATO expansion completed, existential issues seemed resolved. Nearly every non-NATO European country sought entry into or association with the Alliance. The widespread hope is that NATO will help promote democracy, market-based economies, and effective, defensively oriented militaries responsible to duly elected civilian governments.

NATO began its outreach program in East-Central Europe in November 1991 with the establishment of the North Atlantic Cooperation Council (NACC), now the Euro-Atlantic Partnership Council (EAPC). While the NACC specified the commendable objectives of establishing security contacts and providing technical assistance to former communist states, its shortcomings were apparent. The diversity among NACC members prompted a more differentiated approach and encouraged calls for membership in NATO of several NACC members, above all, of Poland. Disagreements among the allies about how, if at all, the NACC should accommodate the military operational requirements of the partner states further limited the scope of NACC actions.

NATO's response was to adopt the Partnership for Peace (PFP) program in January 1994, whose goals are to: (1) enhance operational cooperation between NATO and the partner states; (2) develop defense transparency among partner states; (3) advance the development of democratic means of control over the military in the newly emerging democracies; (4) provide a vehicle to help the partners realize that

Vaclav Havel, Czech President who oversaw "Velvet Divorce," 1992–3.
Courtesy of Oldrich Skácha

participation in NATO activities has obligations as well as benefits. The PFP program represented a workable solution to diffuse Central European demands for reassurance. It extended to them but also to Russia and other former Soviet republics a framework for cooperation short of NATO membership as extensive or limited as they themselves would wish. Twenty-seven countries became PFP partners, including the Central and Eastern European states, Sweden, Switzerland, Finland, Ireland, Slovenia, Russia, Ukraine and several ex-Soviet Eurasian republics. With NATO enlargement, the number of members declined to 20. Representation for PFP is maintained at the NATO headquarters and military exercises involving NATO members and PFP countries occur regularly. PFP was never intended as a substitute for NATO enlargement nor as a mere mechanism for rejuvenating the Alliance. Instead, it is an ambitious military cooperation effort involving former adversaries for the most part. PFP has fostered the establishment of new structures and the creation of new activities designed to enhance security and stability. It represents the logical extension of the first post-cold war heads of state meeting that directed NATO to begin cooperating with former Warsaw Pact members to engender trusting political relations. Yet, NATO must continue to balance its intention to control its own destiny and not be subject to a veto by outside powers, such as Russia. NATO is still considering how many countries it can embrace without completely diluting its mission, which is clearly changing.

Also in January 1994, NATO approved the Combined and Joint Task Force (CJTF) initiative that is intended to furnish the Alliance with a powerful new organizational concept for responding to crises by the rapid deployment of forces. The CJTF initiative is designed to: (1) satisfy the requirements of the NATO strategic concept for more flexible and mobile forces; (2) provide a vehicle for NATO participation in crisis management and peace support operations; (3) facilitate operations with non-NATO countries such as PFP partners; and (4) permit the use of NATO infrastructure and forces to support the evolution of the European Security and Defense Identity (ESDI, also called ESDP), the eventual common EU defense policy. In the future, rapid reaction forces under joint multinational commands will replace larger, territorial units.

Following the withdrawal of the last Russian troops from East-Central Europe, the continent became less troubled by outside threats than it had ever been in history. Poland, where World War II and the cold war began, in effect no longer shared a common border with Russia (al-

Slobodan Milosevic at The Hague

though Kaliningrad remains a problem), and was surrounded by friendly states, all of whom were preoccupied with domestic issues. Hungary, no longer anguished about existential threats identified its chief foreign policy goal as achievement of membership in European organizations. The peaceful breakup of Czechoslovakia in 1992, commonly known as the "Velvet Divorce," suggested that Europe's time-honored ethnic difficulties were not unmanageable.

Yugoslavia, however, rapidly degenerated into Europe's lasting shame. Although the recent explosion of the Balkan "powder keg" did not, as in the past, spill over in a large way into adjacent areas, what became the wars of Yugoslav succession involved the bloodiest fighting seen on the continent since 1945. The protracted conflict, which the European powers were embarrassingly unable to halt, fostered renewed uncertainty about NATO's usefulness. Paradoxically, and perhaps serendipitously, the inability of Europe's most successful alliance to handle the prolonged Balkan crisis provided substantial incentive for the Alliance later to welcome new members.

Apart from the serious and brutal fighting in parts of the former Soviet Union, primarily in the Caucasus region, Europe experienced two major conflicts in the 1990s involving outside intervention. U.S. engagement and leadership were instrumental in both. Many observers on both sides of the Atlantic chide the United States for not having taken decisive action in the Balkans in the early 1990s to halt the bloodshed. NATO military action against the Bosnian Serbs in 1995 finally ended the fighting in Bosnia-Herzegovina. It made possible the U.S.-sponsored Dayton Accords, a plan for peace and stability effected by a powerful Alliance Implementation Force (IFOR), whose success brought the subsequent shift to the Stabilization Force (SFOR). The lengthy

war, and in the face of asymmetric threats, involving conflict on disproportionate levels. Asymmetric threats include the prospect of an opponent designing a strategy that fundamentally alters the terrain in which a conflict is fought. Asymmetric conflict invariably entails surprise and the employment of shock tactics. America's great capability in high-technology power projection forces will encourage future opponents to devise a variety of asymmetric counters to frustrate U.S. military advantages.

In the last decade, a spate of terrorist attacks against U.S. targets, some domestic and some international, has occurred. The October 2000 bombing of the destroyer USS Cole in Yemen and the August 1998 destruction of the U.S. embassies in Nairobi and Dar Es Salaam by the al-Qaeda terror network followed the June 1996 bombing of the Khobar Towers near Dhahran, Saudi Arabia, and the 1994 bombing of the U.S. military Assistance Headquarters in Jiddah, Saudi Arabia. The terror network al-Qaeda has developed into a beacon for Islamic radicalism and the principal source of financing and coordinating Middle East terrorism. It has links to other dangerous terrorist organizations, including the Islamic Group and Islamic Jihad. The Middle East is of considerable importance to the United States, and terrorism in or flowing from the region is a major problem for America and its allies.

The terrorist threat has changed markedly in recent years due to a number of factors: changing terrorist motivations; the proliferation of technologies of mass destruction; increased access to information and information technologies; and the accelerated centralization of crucial components of the national infrastructure. As a result of constantly changing threats, the United States has been struggling to stay ahead of terrorists' expanding capabilities.

Some observers assert that the spate of terrorist attacks in recent years is symptomatic of deeper changes occurring in the world. Technology would seem to be diffusing power away from governments and empowering individuals and organizations to assume international roles, including the infliction of mass destruction, which were once reserved to governments. If privatization is on the rise, then terrorism is a sort of perverse privatization of conflict. Globalization is shrinking world dimensions in such a way that occurrences in far-off places, such as Afghanistan, can profoundly influence the American people.

"All the News That's Fit to Print"

The New York Times

Late Edition

New York: **Today**, sunny, a few afternoon clouds. High 77. **Tonight**, slightly more humid. Low 65. **Tomorrow**, sun then clouds. High 81. **Yesterday**, high 81, low 63. Weather map, Page C19.

VOL. CL . . . No. 51,874 — Copyright © 2001 The New York Times — NEW YORK, WEDNESDAY, SEPTEMBER 12, 2001 — $1 beyond the greater New York metropolitan area. — 75 CENTS

U.S. ATTACKED

HIJACKED JETS DESTROY TWIN TOWERS AND HIT PENTAGON IN DAY OF TERROR

A CREEPING HORROR

Buildings Burn and Fall as Onlookers Search for Elusive Safety

By N. R. KLEINFIELD

It kept getting worse.

The horror arrived in episodic bursts of chilling disbelief, signified first by trembling floors, sharp eruptions, cracked windows. There was the actual unfathomable realization of a gaping, flaming hole in first one of the tall towers, and then the same thing all over again in its twin. There was the merciless sight of bodies helplessly tumbling out, some of them in flames.

Finally, the mighty towers themselves were reduced to nothing. Dense plumes of smoke raced through the downtown avenues, coursing between the buildings, shaped like tornadoes on their sides.

Every sound was cause for alarm. A plane appeared overhead. Was another one coming? No, it was a fighter jet. But was it friend or enemy? People scrambled for their lives, but they didn't know where to go. Should they go north, south, east, west? Stay outside, go indoors? People hid beneath cars and each other. Some contemplated jumping into the river.

For those trying to flee the very epicenter of the collapsing World Trade Center towers, the most horrid thought of all finally dawned on them: nowhere was safe.

For several panic-stricken hours yesterday morning, people in Lower Manhattan witnessed the inexpressible, the incomprehensible, the unthinkable. "I don't know what the gates of hell look like, but it's got to be like this," said John Maloney, a security director for an Internet firm in the trade center. "I'm a combat veteran, Vietnam, and I never saw anything like this."

The first warnings were small ones. Blocks away, Jim Farmer, a film composer, was having breakfast at a small restaurant on West Broadway. He heard the sound of a jet. An odd sound — too loud, it seemed, to be

Continued on Page A7

A Somber Bush Says Terrorism Cannot Prevail

By ELISABETH BUMILLER with DAVID E. SANGER

WASHINGTON, Sept. 11 — President Bush vowed tonight to retaliate against those responsible for today's attacks on New York and Washington, declaring that he would "make no distinction between the terrorists who committed these acts and those who harbor them." "These acts of mass murder were intended to frighten our nation into chaos and retreat, but they have failed," the president said in his first speech to the nation from the Oval Office. "Our country is strong. Terrorist acts can shake the foundation of our biggest buildings, but they cannot touch the foundation of America."

His brief speech this evening came after a day of trauma that seems destined to define his presidency. Seeking to at once calm the nation and declare his determination to exact retribution, he told a country numbed by repeated scenes of carnage that "these acts shattered steel, but they cannot dent the steel of American resolve."

Mr. Bush spoke only hours after returning from a zigzag course across the country, as his Secret Service and military security teams moved him from Florida, where he woke up this morning expecting to press for his education bill, to command posts in Louisiana and Nebraska before it was determined the attacks had probably ended and he could safely return to the capital.

It was a sign of the catastrophic

Steve Ludlum

Justin Lane for The New York Times

Paul Hosefros/The New York Times

AMERICAN TARGETS A ball of fire exploded outward after the second of two jetliners slammed into the World Trade Center; less than two hours later, both of the 110-story towers were gone. Hijackers crashed a third airliner into the Pentagon, setting off a huge explosion and fire.

President Vows to Exact Punishment for 'Evil'

By SERGE SCHMEMANN

Hijackers rammed jetliners into each of New York's World Trade Center towers yesterday, toppling both in a hellish storm of ash, glass, smoke and leaping victims, while a third jetliner crashed into the Pentagon in Virginia. There was no official count, but President Bush said thousands had perished, and in the immediate aftermath the calamity was already being ranked the worst and most audacious terror attack in American history.

The attacks seemed carefully coordinated. The hijacked planes were all en route to California, and therefore gorged with fuel, and their departures were spaced within an hour and 40 minutes. The first, American Airlines Flight 11, a Boeing 767 out of Boston for Los Angeles, crashed into the north tower at 8:48 a.m. Eighteen minutes later, United Airlines Flight 175, also headed from Boston to Los Angeles, plowed into the south tower.

Then an American Airlines Boeing 757, Flight 77, left Washington's Dulles International Airport bound for Los Angeles, but instead hit the western part of the Pentagon, the military headquarters where 24,000 people work, at 9:40 a.m. Finally, United Airlines Flight 93, a Boeing 757 flying from Newark to San Francisco, crashed near Pittsburgh, raising the possibility that its hijackers had failed in whatever their mission was.

Kelly Guenther for The New York Times

SECOND PLANE United Airlines Flight 175 nearing the trade center's south tower.

There were indications that the hijackers on at least two of the planes were armed with knives. Attorney General John Ashcroft told reporters in the evening that the suspects on Flight 11 were armed that way. And Barbara Olson, a television commentator who was traveling on American Flight 77, managed to reach her husband, Solicitor General Theodore Olson, by cell phone and to tell him that the hijackers were armed with knives and a box cutter.

In all, 266 people perished in the four planes and several score more were known dead elsewhere. Numerous firefighters, police officers and other rescue workers who responded to the initial disaster in Lower Manhattan were killed or injured when the buildings collapsed. Hundreds were treated for cuts, broken bones, burns and smoke inhalation.

But the real carnage was concealed for now by the twisted, smoking, ash-choked carcasses of the twin towers, in which thousands of people used to work on a weekday. The collapse of the towers caused another World Trade Center building to fall 10 hours later, and several

Continued on Page A14

Awaiting the Aftershocks

Washington and Nation Plunge Into Fight With Enemy Hard to Identify and Punish

By R. W. APPLE Jr.

News Analysis

WASHINGTON, Sept. 11 — Today's devastating and astonishingly well-coordinated attacks on the World Trade Center towers in New York and on the Pentagon outside of Washington plunged the nation into a warlike struggle against an enemy that will be hard to identify with certainty and hard to punish with precision.

The whole nation — to a degree the whole world — shook as hijacked airliners plunged into buildings that symbolize the financial and military might of the United States. The sense of security and self-confidence that Americans take as their birthright suffered a grievous blow, from which recovery will be slow. The aftershocks will be nearly as bad, as hundreds and possibly thousands of people discover that friends or relatives died awful, fiery deaths.

Scenes of chaos and destruction evocative of the nightmare world of Hieronymus Bosch, with smoke and debris blotting out the sun, were carried by television into homes and workplaces across the nation. Echoing Franklin D. Roosevelt's description of the attack on Pearl Harbor as an event "which will live in infamy," Gov. George E. Pataki of New York, a Republican, spoke of "an incredible outrage" and Senator Charles E. Schumer of New York, a Democrat, spoke of "a dastardly attack."

But mere words were inadequate vessels to contain the sense of shock and horror that people felt.

a sense of equilibrium, with warplanes and heavily armed helicopters crossing overhead, past and present national security officials earnestly debated the possibility of a Congressional declaration of war — but against precisely whom, and in what exact circumstances? Warships were maneuvering to protect New York and Washington. The North American Air Defense Command, which had seemed to many a relic of the cold war, adopted a pos-

Continued on Page A24

MORE ON THE ATTACKS

RESCUERS BECOME VICTIMS Firefighters who rushed to the Trade Center were killed. PAGE A2

OFFICIALS SUSPECT BIN LADEN Eavesdropping intercepts after the attacks were cited. PAGE A21

TERRORISTS EXPLOITED WEAKNESS Investigators had criticized precautions against hijacking. PAGE A17

CASUALTIES IN WASHINGTON An unknown number of people were killed at the Pentagon. PAGE A3

SEARCH FOR SURVIVORS Some people trapped in the rubble were rescued. PAGE A2

FOR HOME DELIVERY CALL 1-800-NYTIMES

A NATION APART?

The suicidal terrorist attacks of September 11, 2001, on the World Trade Center and the Pentagon traumatized America. The loss of over 3,000 innocent lives in less than an hour was appalling enough, but such attacks upon the political and financial capitals of the country were a stunning blow for the world's superpower. For 50 years, America almost complacently assumed that no enemy would attack the country for fear of a devastating retaliatory strike. September 11 ended that sense of security, perhaps forever. Furthermore, the terrorist attacks constituted one of the greatest intelligence failures since the Second World War. Indeed, one of America's founding notions was that it was a nation apart, protected by the high seas and legit-

The Anguish of Power

imized through a set of principles. From warnings of the founders against "entangling alliances" to President Reagan's call to refurbish the "city on the hill," Americans have perceived their country as secure and separate. Until the dawn of the 21st century, no invaders had seriously struck America since 1812. "The myth of virtuous isolation," as some observers have called it, has been a crucial aspect of what makes America different. Reflecting a high level of planning and co-ordination, the attacks of 2001 certainly required months of planning to execute in what was a sophisticated, suicidal and utterly ruthless crime against humanity. Most Americans now realize that the future will be influenced by actions taken to control, deter and punish global terrorism.

The atrocities suggested a widely held perception among extremists that since America is the hegemonic power in the post-cold war world, it is largely responsible for an international order perpetrating severe injustices on certain groups and countries. A chief aim of the attacks in New York and Washington was to demonstrate the inherent vulnerability of the world's most powerful country, one regarded as militarily unassailable after the end of the cold war. Following the September attacks, the Bush administration declared an all-out war on what it called global terrorism. President George W. Bush characterized the conflict as a long

struggle and said that America found itself engaged in "a fight to save the civilized world, and values common to the West, to Asia, to Islam." Resolute before a cheering Congress in September 2001, the President vowed to lead an anxious nation and its allies in a decisive campaign against the forces of terror. "From this day forward," he declared, "any nation that continues to harbor or support terrorism will be regarded by the United States as a hostile regime."

In the aftermath of the terrorist attacks, the Bush administration seemed to distance itself from the unilateralism to which it seemed inclined. U.N. Security Council Resolution 1368, passed unanimously just 24 hours after the attacks on America, recognized that terrorism was a "threat to international peace and security" and in effect authorized the use of force to curb such threats. "We are all Americans now," pronounced the highbrow French newspaper *Le Monde*, while NATO invoked Article V of its charter for the first time, committing all its members to solidarity with a United States under attack. No country was quicker with tangible responses than Russia, America's cold-war adversary. President Vladimir Putin graciously accepted U.S. abrogation of the Anti-Ballistic Missile (ABM) treaty, consented to the deployment of U.S. forces in the former Soviet republics of Central Asia and Georgia, and shrugged off the likelihood of a large expansion of NATO.

Military operations began in October 2001 when the U.S.-led coalition launched a series of air strikes in Afghanistan

President Vladimir V. Putin

against the al-Qaeda terrorist training camps, troop concentrations and military installations sheltered by the extremist Taliban regime. The air strikes facilitated ground assaults by indigenous armed opponents of the Taliban, most notably the Northern Alliance. By mid-December, the Taliban had lost control of all the major cities in the country and was forced to retreat to its Pashtun heartland in the south. The Taliban's defeat was widely seen as a triumph of special forces: elite army units and intelligence operators, sometimes on horseback, pressing on to victory. The real operational key, though, was a fresh breakthrough in the use of air power. Virtually every trooper on the ground could

Former President Bush with former Secretary of State, Colin Powell, and former National Security Advisor, Condoleeza Rice

United States

Nonetheless, the coalition faced an uphill task maintaining order in Iraq thereafter, especially in the so-called "Sunni triangle" around Baghdad. The "regime change" that constituted the principal objective of the U.S.-led coalition entailed a good deal more than the mere toppling of an aged dictator and America's mission in Iraq will not be accomplished until a durable new civic order is in place there.

For Muslims throughout the world, the war in Iraq set off a wave of anger, sadness, frustration and despair. The televised daily scenes of triumphant U.S. warriors rolling through Mesopotamia left a bitter taste in the mouths of millions. Political Islam, a potent albeit divided force, expanded its suspicions of the West, while public skepticism remains very strong. For example, a poll released in the spring of 2004 by the Pew Global Attitudes project indicate that foreign approval of America plummeted since the war in Iraq, particularly in the Muslim world. It is there, the report says that "the bottom has fallen out of support for America." Many Muslim publics actually feel threatened by the United States. Fewer than a quarter of Indonesians, Turks, Pakistanis and Jordanians, and a tenth of Moroccans, even support the war on terror, much less large-scale Western intervention. By contrast, in seven of the Muslim countries surveyed, a majority of the population asserted that America might pose a military threat to their country.

America's dilemma in the Middle East is even more perplexing, though. In the autumn of 2001, the United States embarked on a vastly ambitious undertaking not only to combat terrorism directly but to effect sweeping change in the Arab world and Central Asia, the areas in which the worst forms of international terrorism originate. The continuation of intense violence between Israelis and Palestinians indicates that American efforts to push the various sides toward peace failed. The breathtaking demonstrations of U.S. military prowess in the years 2001–2003, combined with the general weariness of conflict in Israel and Palestine, seemed to offer a fresh opportunity to get a handle on festering problems in the Middle East. The U.S. administration initially seized on this with its "road map" toward peace, which had been endorsed by the U.N., the European Union, Russia, and most Arab countries. Among other things, the "road map" reflected the acknowledgement by the United States and Israel's neighbors of the need for a sovereign Palestinian state and Israel's right to exist. Yet, at the crucial moment, U.S. efforts were weak and unavailing, raising the instinctive question whether America's stunning military victories would ultimately prove hollow ones.

It is one of the great early ironies of the 21st century that a Republican administration coming to office determined to shrink the size of government, to reduce taxes and disentangle America from "unnecessary foreign involvements" ratcheted up spending on the military and undertook a risky invasion of Iraq over the objections of much of the world. The president who initially preached a modest foreign policy became the architect of the "Bush doctrine" that portends American activism internationally for years to come. The new war on terrorism needs to be waged on many fronts at once, through intelligence and diplomacy as much as through warfare.

America had little choice but to seek international assistance with the postwar costs in Iraq and Afghanistan. With tens of billions of dollars being spent annually in Iraq, the reconstruction effort there makes it the costliest since the Marshall Plan for

The Anguish of Power

U.S. troops in the Middle East

Europe. The military operation and the subsequent stabilization program alone increased America's 2003–2004 budget deficit from 4.2 % of GDP to 4.7%. Critics argue that the United States has begun biting off more than it can chew and question the wisdom of weakening alliances and international organizations through precipitate unilateral action. Many observers would agree that the country's activism reflects a natural stubbornness in the American people. The presidential election of 2000 manifested the rather lackadaisical view of world affairs Americans harbored during the 1990s. Then came the shock of September 2001. The new President and most Americans shared similar experiences in the days and weeks thereafter: profound anguish, followed by the sudden recognition that the world is a far more grim and dodgy place than they ever imagined. Nor is this all. The Bush administration substantially expanded the powers of the federal government, citing the "new war" against terrorism as the chief justification for an extension of governmental authority. The Patriot (Provide Appropriate Tools Required to Intercept and Obstruct Terrorism) Act, for example, voted into law in the wake of the attacks of September 11, defined terrorism to include direct action by protesters, widened the use of wiretapping on telephone calls and emails, and also in certain cases authorized the Justice Department to detain foreign nationals on mere suspicion with only minimal legal protection of the U.S. Constitution. The Patriot Act, which was renewed in 2005 enhances electronic surveillance authority for law enforcement, enabling greater access to communication by email, telephones, and other electronic devices. It permits the government to detain or deport individuals suspected of connections with terrorism. It allows law enforcement to survey records of political and religious organizations and monitors financial transactions. It expands the monitoring of foreign students makes posses-

sion of any biological agent or toxin (except for bona fide research or a peaceful project) a criminal act.

Proponents argue that the Patriot Act updates some laws to keep up with the evolving technologies that make tracking of terrorists difficult. With the increasing use of cell phones, satellite phones and computers to communicate, law enforcement officers need to track suspected terrorists without the previously required assistance from specified third parties. This "roving wiretap" authority allows law enforcement entities to target the communications of any facility in which or through which a suspect might be operating, and enhances the ability to hone in on terrorist suspects.

The Patriot Act not only updates laws, but also provides the authority to use them in counter-terror investigations. Some of the same tools available to prosecute drug, fraud, and crime cases are now also available to investigate and prosecute suspected terrorists. These tools have been in use for decades and they have been reviewed and approved by the courts.

Civil libertarians express misgivings about some of these expanded authorities, arguing, for example, that the inclusion of "domestic" terrorism gives way to possible harassment and prosecution of political groups that dissent with U.S. policies. Yet, the Patriot Act does not abrogate laws protecting civil liberties. The argument that the Patriot Act infringes on First Amendment rights is also used by critics who object to government scrutiny of business records, to include those of Internet service providers, libraries, or banks. But laws already in place prior to the Patriot Act are unaffected by it. Other critics decry the use of delayed notification search warrants. They deem this an authority to conduct secret searches. What the provisions of the act state is that notice of a warrant be given in "reasonable time" and can be extended by the courts for "good reason." In other words, it eliminates the prior requirement to provide

a contemporaneous notice of a search. The new authority is designed to allow law enforcement the ability to conduct a search without notice in cases where there is "reasonable cause" to believe that providing immediate notification may have adverse effects. While delayed notice searches had been authorized prior to the Patriot Act, they were limited to a small number of circumstances. The Patriot Act expanded the authority to all searches, not just those related to terrorism investigations.

In some ways, America began to reflect the traits of a country reorganizing itself for war at home, by tightening domestic security and establishing a new government department for homeland defense. In the largest reorganization of the federal government since 1947, the administration established an agency to oversee U.S. domestic security. The Department of Homeland Security (DHS) currently has an operating budget of over $40 billion and a staff of 170,000, second in size only to the Defense Department. It is set to become one of the most far-reaching of federal departments, with vast authority embracing huge swaths of private activity as well as areas of state and local jurisdiction.

The Department of Homeland Security is organized as follows:

- Office of the Secretary
- Directorate of Preparedness
- Directorate of Science and Technology
- Directorate of Management
- Office of Operations Coordination
- Office of Policy
- Office of Intelligence and Analysis
- U.S. Citizenship and Immigration Services
- Transportation Security Administration
- U.S. Customs and Border Protection
- U.S. Immigration and Customs Enforcement
- Law Enforcement Training Center
- Federal Emergency Management Agency
- U.S. Coast Guard
- U.S. Secret Service

In November 2002, the President and Congress established the National Commission on Terrorist Attacks Upon the United States, also known as the 9/11 Commission, which examined what happened, what went wrong, and what required change. It was tasked to offer specific recommendations. An authorized edition of the Commission's final report was published and released to the public in July 2004. The 9/11 Commission listed 41 recommendations in its report. Some focused on coalition strategies with friendly nations. Others dealt with border security,

United States

planned a new strategy for dealing with Central Asia, involving closer cooperation with Pakistan, Russia, the former Soviet states, and perhaps even Iran, to help stabilize Afghanistan. Boosting popular support for the NATO presence by curbing corruption and improving governance is deemed crucial to defeating the insurgents. At the same time, U.S. chances of convincing NATO allies to deploy substantial numbers of additional forces were slim, and the NATO mission is winding down in 2014. Continuing casualties rendered the war unpopular in member states, and few allies were willing or able to send additional troops.

The Obama administration faces several difficult choices in its dealings with Russia. The U.S. and its allies need to keep bases in Central Asia and to develop access routes through the Caucasus and Central Asia to sustain defense and reconstruction efforts in Afghanistan. These require Russian concurrence. The Kremlin is likely to extract concessions for cooperation, for example, by requiring final termination of U.S. plans for missile shield bases in East-Central Europe. U.S. acquiescence on certain high visibility issues causes considerable uneasiness among some new NATO allies, who are now requesting other security guarantees. These are likely to take the form of more advanced weapons systems and attendant training, along with the deployment of more NATO combat forces on their territory. Russia will look askance at such moves, labeling them a fresh security challenge. Since Russia's invasion of Crimea in February of 2014, the U.S. and Europe have issued denunciations and threats of sanctions while calling for a de-escalation of the crisis. A Russia that can invade Georgia and Ukraine with apparent impunity may not stop there, observers argue. For the second time in six years, Russian troops have crossed an internationally recognized border to occupy territory. Fear is growing in the West that Moscow's actions in Ukraine portend Russian efforts to seize more territory and to destabilize the broader region.

The Pentagon had withdrawn 100,000 troops from Iraq by August of 2010, while leaving some 30,000 in the country until the mission formally ended in December 2011. The remaining troops were tasked with advising Iraqi forces, targeting terrorists and protecting U.S. interests generally. The final column of U.S. vehicles crossed the Kuwaiti border eight years and nearly nine months after U.S. forces, over 150,000 strong, poured across the same border, confident of swift and stunning victory. Instead, Iraq and the United States found themselves locked in a long, brutal, and at times insolvable conflict that exacted an awful toll from both. The two coun-

tries still seem to have quite different understandings of what happened and what lies ahead. The war cost tens of thousands of coalition casualties, more than 100,000 Iraqi lives, and over $1 trillion from the U.S. Treasury. Whether the conflict was worth such a price is for history to judge.

By 2014, transformed threats were demanding fresh U.S. attention. Islamic State rebels seized control of parts of Syria and Iraq. Al Qaeda in the Arabian Peninsula continued to perpetrate terrorist campaigns, while al Shabab and Boko Haram launched fearsome assaults in Africa. In the spring of 2015, Yemen devolved into civil war, causing neighboring Saudi Arabia to feel the heat. The Yemeni Shia Houthi rebels would appear to detest the Saudis and the (Sunni) al Qaeda more than they do the United States.

COLD DAWN

Historically, commentators have pointed to democracy as no better than a mixed blessing for foreign policy purposes. There are at least two schools of thought on the question, the first associated with Federalists like James Madison and Alexander Hamilton. It views democratic government as a distinct disadvantage in foreign policy. This "inefficiency argument" was given its most eloquent expression by Alexis de Tocqueville:

For my part, I have no hesitation in saying that in control of society's foreign affairs democratic governments do appear decidedly inferior to others . . . Foreign policy does not require the use of any of the good qualities peculiar to democracy but does demand the cultivation of almost all that it lacks. A democracy finds it difficult to coordinate the details of a great undertaking and to fix on some plan and carry it through with determination in spite of obstacles. It has little capacity for combining measures in secret and waiting patiently for the result.

The second school of thought, clearly identified with President Woodrow Wilson is variously labeled "idealism" or "legal-moralism." It stresses the inherent goodness of democratic government, asserting that democracies naturally pursue peaceful foreign policies and enter into conflict only for self-defense. This "goodness argument" gained limited adherence even in Wilson's own time, and reaction against it formed a cornerstone of political realism's triumph as the dominant approach to American foreign policy following World War II. Walter Lippman, for example, argued that placing foreign policy in the "people's hands" was of dubious virtue:

Former House Speaker Nancy Pelosi
Courtesy of Judicial Watch

The people have imposed a veto upon the judgments of informed and responsible officials. They have compelled the governments which usually knew what would have been wiser, or was necessary, or was more expedient, to be too late with too little, or too long with too much, too pacifist in peace and too bellicose in war, too neutralist or appeasing in negotiation or too intransigent.

Political realism, which continues to dominate the rhetoric and execution, if not consistently the analysis of American foreign policy, appears sometimes at odds with the world it purports to explain. Like other national governments vying for position on a global chessboard, the United States is supposed to possess an identifiable national interest that can be defined in terms of power. Yet the issues in current global politics are not only military-security matters, irrespective of how broadly defined or aggregated. National interests and legalisms grounded in sovereignty only partially explain a world in which non-state actors abound. Hence, the analytic task has become enormously complicated for scholar and policy maker alike. One observer suggested recently that the single most striking feature of America's conduct in the world was fragmentation. Fragmentation results largely from the diversity of issues composing the global political agenda. Comprehending the effects of a complex world requires several theoretical perspectives.

The necessity for substantial power, especially with regard to diplomacy and defense, was stated in the *Federalist*.

It is impossible to foresee or to define the extent and variety of national exigencies, and the correspondent extent and variety of means which may be necessary to satisfy them. The circumstances that endanger the safety of nations are infinite, and for this reason no constitutional shackles can wisely be imposed on the power to which the care of it is committed.

But Publius' warning against "constitutional shackles" seems almost to point to an unrestrained power in the government. The constitutionally granted power necessary to cope with all "national exigencies" is inevitably power sufficient also to undermine the liberties the Constitution was established to preserve. On the other hand, fidelity to the restrictive side of the Constitution can enfeeble government. The problem is to find the mean, a prudent path of sound judgment without falling over into either extreme.

Since achieving independence, the United States has had to deal with four distinct world orders. These were characterized by sets of relationships among the great powers: the upheaval of the late 18th century and the Napoleonic period; the Congress of Vienna system until 1914, concurrent with the establishment of vast colonial empires in Africa and Asia; the "thirty years' war" of the 20th century; and the cold war era, concurrent with the end of colonization. The world has now entered a fifth period, one in which European issues do not govern the global agenda as they did for the past several centuries.

The transition has been lengthy, spanning the decade of the 1990s and into the 21st century, largely because there was no categorical, shattering end of the old order. The Soviet empire disintegrated on its own, rather than being defeated in war and occupied. The new "post-cold war" order has not yet become completely manifest and will not do so until after 2015. The fluid character of the new order is a principal cause of considerable uncertainty worldwide, including in the United States. What is certain is that the nature

of the emerging global order will depend substantially upon such factors as

- the extent of U.S. involvement in world affairs,
- the advancement of European integration, both within the European Union and through the expansion of Western institutions (the "widening and deepening"),
- developments within Russia and its relations with neighboring countries,
- the political cohesion of China and its commitment to peaceful progress,
- the control of nuclear proliferation,
- the expansion of international terrorism.

The comparison between Rome and America has absorbed many political thinkers. Some striking parallels suggest themselves here. One may, for example, stretch the features common to both civilizations somewhat as follows: a world power span, by land and sea; a pride in republican institutions, with the emphasis theoretically on limited powers even while in practice the executive is powerful; the reduction of politics to sloganeering and political recrimination.

One can add other parallels: a capitalist economy growing strong on worldwide resources and selling in far-flung markets, with cyclical swings of prosperity and recession; a distribution of wealth which arrays side by side affluence and poverty; vast outlays on public works and an arms economy; the piling up of a national debt, and a preoccupation with taxes and tax collection; the emergence of groups absorbed with "bread and circuses;" a succession of conflicts draining the country's resources, spreading over the world the clamor of its arms; the absorption with the strategy, logistics, and technology of war; the use of military reputation as a road to civilian office; the creation of a remarkable

system of administration and law, with forces and proconsuls enveloping a turbulent world; the prestige and pride of citizenship in the world's power structures.

To finish the portrait, one might add the cult of magnificence in public buildings and the growth of gladiatorial arts at which the vast majority of the people are passive spectators but emotional participants; the increasing violence within the culture; the desensitizing and depersonalization of life; the weakening of the sense of civic pride; the uprooting of people in a mobile culture; the concentration of urbanism. In the area of personal life, one might add the split between moral standards and operative codes; the greater looseness of family ties; the refinements of luxury; the turning toward new religious cults; the search for the sources of evil; and the feeling of general, widespread frustration.

GLOSSARY OF INTERNATIONAL TERMS

Abrogate Formally to annul, as of agreements.

Ad hoc Pertaining to one case alone, as an ad hoc committee.

Admiralty court Tribunal having jurisdiction over maritime questions.

Ambassador A diplomatic representative of the highest rank.

Appeasement Giving in to the demands of another power in an effort to effect particular actions.

Armistice A suspension of military operations by mutual agreement.

Asylum The granting of protection to political refugees by a foreign government or its representatives.

Autarky A state of economic self-sufficiency.

Balance of power A state of basic equilibrium in the influence and weight of neighboring states.

From the depths of depression to victory in World War II

United States

Belligerent A party to a particular conflict.

Benevolent neutrality Technical neutrality favoring one belligerent.

Bilateral Involving two parties, as a bilateral agreement.

Blockade The thwarting of communication by armed force, usually involving the patrolling of a belligerent's ports so closely by warships as to endanger ingress and egress.

Buffer state A small nonthreatening state between two or more larger states.

Capitulation Surrender on specified terms; also, an agreement granting extraterritorial jurisdiction.

Cartel A combination of trust to promote monopolistic practices.

Casus belli An alleged justification for war.

Cold war An international struggle waged by means short of armed conflict.

Collective security Maintenance of peace by a concerted action of the powers, or by an organization of the powers.

"Colossus of the North" Non-laudatory synonym for the USA in Latin America.

Condominium Joint administration by several powers.

Containment The restraint of state influence to a defined territorial limit.

Continuous voyage A maritime journey, which in view of its apparent purposes, is constant, even if interrupted.

Convention A treaty, often multipower and specific in nature, such as one relating to postage or air travel.

Convoy A group of ships assembled to provide merchantmen with armed escort.

Détente A lessening of international tensions.

Dollar diplomacy Public use of private investors to advance foreign policy goals; also, conducting foreign policy to assist private investors.

Entente An accord between two or more countries.

Executive agreement An international accord made by or on behalf of the President, not subject to Senate approval.

Expropriation Confiscation of property by a national government.

Extradition The delivering up of a person charged with a crime by one country to another.

Extraterritoriality Exemption from the jurisdiction of local laws.

Freedom of the seas The passage right of merchantmen on the high seas.

Genocide Mass extermination of an entire group of people.

Good Offices Services of a third party to assist in the mediation of a dispute.

Hegemony The preponderant authority of a state.

Imperialism The policy of attempting to extend influence and control over a foreign territory.

Insurgency Condition of revolt short of an organized revolutionary government.

International law or law of nations Assemblage of accords, treaties, and principles that countries consider binding on them in their relations with others.

Jingoist An advocate of a bellicose pursuit of foreign affairs.

Open Door Equal opportunity for commercial pursuits.

Pan-Americanism Policies fostering cooperation among the countries of the Western Hemisphere.

Plebiscite Polling in a particular region, often on sovereignty issues.

Plenipotentiary Diplomatic representative vested with complete authority to negotiate as instructed.

Protectorate A dependent territory over which another country assumes responsibility.

Rapprochement The establishment of more cordial relations between countries.

Reciprocity The granting of commercial privileges to a country in exchange for reciprocal concessions.

Recognition The formal acknowledgement of the full exercise of the powers of state.

Reparations Payment in money or products by a country for prior damages.

Reprisal Retaliatory action by one country against another.

Right of visit and search Asserted right of a belligerent to inspect merchant-men to determine the origin of the cargo.

Sanctions Penalties, often economic, imposed for a purported violation of an international obligation.

Self-determination Asserted right of a people in a certain area to govern themselves.

Sovereignty The autonomous exercise of authority.

Sphere of influence An area in which a country exercises substantial influence and authority.

Territorial waters The adjacent belt included within a state's sovereign boundaries.

Trusteeship The exercise of authority granted by an international organization.

Ultimate destination The final destination of goods in international shipment.

Courtesy of the National Archives

Chapter Five
Political Ideas and Political System

DELIBERATIVE BODIES

The Founding Fathers deliberately designed the federal government to be inefficient. They carefully divided powers among the executive, legislative, and judicial branches, rendering them coequal. By distributing power among the three branches, the authors of the Constitution intended each branch to guard against the other two becoming too powerful. The principle of separation of powers, propounded by 17th- and 18th-century political philosophers John Locke and Charles de Montesquieu, was a device for limiting governmental power by taking from the monarch his ancient lawmaking power and vesting it in a legislature elected by the people. The American development of this doctrine went much further. In place of a simple division into legislative and executive, the American colonies adopted a three-fold separation, elevating the judiciary to a coequal position and putting all three under the rule of law established by a written constitution.

That is why, for example, the President is commander-in-chief, but only Congress can declare war. Only the Congress can pass laws. The President can veto them, and the Supreme Court determines whether they are compatible with the Constitution. The Founding Fathers wanted the government to have enough power to operate effectively, but not so much as to threaten either the liberties of the people or the sovereignty of the state governments. Displaying profound understanding of human nature, they reasoned that while politicians would always seek more power, their first priority would be to maintain what they already had and would zealously guard against encroachment on it, thereby keeping the whole constitutional order in place in a sort of delicate balance. The result is often what is commonly known as "gridlock," but this is merely a by-product of the balance of political power.

Let us briefly compare the system of government devised by the Founding Fathers with the one they were most familiar with, the British system of parliamentary government. In Britain, the prime minister and the cabinet members, who form "the government," are parliamentarians in the House of Commons, the lower house of Parliament. This arrangement has been more or less the case for centuries, and Britain has divided government only in terms of the separation of Parliament and Crown. The legislature elects the executive, and the latter must maintain a working majority in the House of Commons. Largely in consequence, the British government has strict party discipline. Members of Parliament (MPs) almost always vote according to the instructions of the party whips, or else they can find themselves denied renomination at the next election. Hence, the British government is usually able to enact legislation rapidly.

U.S. members of Congress, for their part, are nominated by state parties, or by primary election if they have any opposition. Party discipline in both the House of Representatives and the Senate is lax. The President has certain powers of persuasion and can sometimes use his "bully pulpit." Of course, some presidents have been famously, or infamously, persuasive. Lyndon Baines Johnson, looking for support on an important bill, once invited a group of freshman congressmen to the Oval Office for a talk. As they filed in this storied place for the first time, Johnson quipped, "Take a look around, because if you aren't with me on this bill, this is the last time you'll ever see this room." Accordingly, most important legislation moves slowly. For example, it took 20 years after Harry Truman first put civil rights on the national agenda before the major civil rights bills were passed during the Johnson administration in the 1960s.

Neither single-party control nor divided government guarantees that good laws get passed. In 1928, for instance, President Herbert Hoover won a smashing victory over the Democrat Al Smith, and the Republicans enjoyed solid majorities in both houses of Congress, with 56 seats in the Senate and a thumping 100-seat edge in the House. Hoover's platform had a plank promising help to hard-pressed farmers by raising tariffs on agricultural commodities, and he submitted a bill to Congress to fulfill his promise. But the country began to go into recession in the spring of 1929, and after the stock market crash that October, the economy deteriorated further. Hoover's modest tariff bill to assist farmers turned into a classic Congressional feeding frenzy as every interest group in the nation, from shipbuilders to tombstone makers, sought similar tariff protection, and most received it. The unfortunate upshot was the Smoot-Hawley Act, one of the most damaging pieces of legislation in the nation's history, raising import surcharges to record levels. The end result was not the protection of the American economy from global competition, but rather the disastrous collapse in world trade as other nations imposed additional tariffs in retaliation. American exports in 1932 were only $1.6 billion, compared with $5.3 billion in 1929. The export sector of the American economy, as well as that of several overseas trading partners, was ruined as world production ratcheted downward in a descending spiral. The Smoot Hawley Tariff was one of the principal reasons that an ordinary recession in 1929–30 developed into the Great Depression in the United States, but

John Locke
Courtesy of Special Collections,
University of Virginia Library

Charles de Montesquieu

United States

House of Commons. View of the Chamber showing the Speaker's Chair, seating for Clerk of the House and assistants

above all, abroad. It is also one of America's chief motivating factors in presently striving to lower barriers to foreign trade.

Divided government can sometimes do just as badly. As the Depression deepened in 1930, voters turned the House over to the Democrats, and the Republicans held on to the Senate by their fingernails, with only 48 of the 96 seats. Then in 1932, in hopes of reducing a growing budget deficit, Hoover asked for, and Congress passed, a sharp increase in income tax rates. The result was the opposite of what was intended. With the economy already in free fall, the increased taxes caused it to weaken still further, and the budget deficit, instead of vanishing as was widely anticipated, sharply increased.

Of course, while usually slow, the federal government can move quickly to enact legislation in pressing circumstances. A good example is the *Corporate Responsibility Act*, passed in the summer of 2002. The Enron scandal broke in November 2001, to be quickly followed by the WorldCom outrage and other dire economic difficulties, including a plunging stock market. Reforms, such as separating consulting from auditing functions and giving corporate boards more independence, were clearly needed. The necessary legal modifications passed both the Republican House and the Democratic Senate and were signed into law by the President within a few months.

The New Deal of the 1930s is also instructive on this score. The election of 1932 was a landslide for Franklin D. Roos-

evelt and the Democrats, who afterwards held 60 out of 96 seats in the Senate and 310 out of 435 in the House. The economic circumstances of the country were desperate by this time. Indeed, the situation was so critical that Congress, in effect, gave Roosevelt sweeping special powers. Some even refer to Roosevelt as a sort of dictator in its original sense, harking back to the

constitution of the Roman Republic, when in times of crisis, one man was given full power for six months in order to save the republic.

Roosevelt called Congress into special session in March 1933, and both chambers remained in conference until June, a period known in American history as "The Hundred Days." During that time, Congress gave the President almost everything he asked for, and the people's representatives accomplished this with unprecedented speed and enthusiasm. In fact, the *Emergency Banking Act* was introduced, passed, and signed into law the very first day of the session. The *Economy Act* (March 20), the *Beer-Wine Revenue Act* (March 22), *the Civilian Conservation Corps Reforestation Relief Act* (March 31), the *Federal Emergency Relief Act* (May 12), the *Tennessee Valley Authority* (May 18), the *Federal Securities Act* (May 27), the *National Employment System Act* (June 6), the *Homeowners Refinancing Act* (June 13), the *Glass-Steagal Act*, the *Farm Credit Act*, the *Emergency Railroad Transportation Act*, and the *National Industrial Recovery Act* (all June 16) followed. Such a body of legislation has never been enacted before or since in such a short time or with so little opposition. True, the New Deal did not end the Depression—World War II did that—but it did stop the downward spiraling of the economy, saved the American banking system from ruin, and provided hope to an American people who had been quickly running out of that precious commodity.

View of London across the Thames, with "Big Ben" (right)

Political Ideas and Political System

SEPARATION OF POWERS

Although the federal Constitution contains no specific declaration concerning separation of powers, the principle is implicit in the organization of the first three articles: (1) "All legislative powers herein granted shall be vested in a Congress of the United States"; (2) "The executive power shall be vested in a President of the United States"; (3) "The judicial power shall be vested in one Supreme Court and in such inferior courts as the Congress shall . . . ordain and establish." From this separation is derived the doctrine that certain functions, due to their essential nature, may be properly exercised by only one particular branch of government; that such functions cannot be delegated to any other branch; and that one department may not interfere with another by usurping its powers or by supervising their exercise.

At the Constitutional Convention of 1787, separation of powers was unanimously endorsed. "No political truth," James Madison remarked at the time, "is of greater intrinsic value." In *Federalist Papers* 47, 48 and 51, Madison explored the principle. Inherited from Montesquieu, it is inspired by the conviction that "every man vested with power is apt to abuse it; and carry his authority as far as it will go." "Is it not strange," Montesquieu asked rhetorically, "that virtue itself has need of limits?"

The *Federalist Papers* were a series of essays written by Alexander Hamilton, James Madison, and John Jay to persuade voters to ratify the Constitution. These are still widely viewed as a masterly work of political philosophy and one of the most profound single treatises on the Constitution. The three collaborators—Hamilton, Jay, and Madison—were of different political leanings and were destined to play different roles later, yet their preferences on politics were submerged in their common assumptions about the art of government. They had read widely and deeply, had studied the new political science of their day, and were skillful in conscripting the beliefs and experience of antiquity to the purposes of the new venture in government. Yet, they were not closet students but men who focused on the idea-in-action. They had a sense of the potential perils of the social fabric and at the same time of the tenacity of social habits, yet even as conservatives, which all of them were in varying degrees, they had a bold capacity for political innovation.

The authors of the *Federalist Papers* displayed considerable strategic skill in meeting objections to the Constitution, and with that dexterity came a knack for blending two strains of the democratic idea. To the charge that the Constitution was a revolutionary *coup d'état*, their riposte was that the residual sovereignty in the people themselves allowed the alteration of inadequate governmental instruments. To those who feared a strong central government, their answers invariably alluded to the need for effective national power at the center in order to avert ineffectuality and chaos. By a masterful distinction, they argued that the new power would be federal in its extent, that is, divided between two political spheres and leaving an area of state power to balance the central power, yet essentially national in its functioning. The national government would have power to act in the sphere where the states could not act effectively. To those who felt that a mixed government with separated powers and a system of checks and balances was too timid an expedient in a revolutionary age, their answer was the classic one of the corruption and ambition of political leaders and the need for the rule of law to guard the people against their own worst impulses. Hence, the Founding Fathers sought not so much to guard the rights of the property owners alone, or to give unchecked rein to revolutionary impulse, but to find an equilibrium between the charged tensions of the democratic idea.

Stressing his lingering concern with abuse of power in the 1920s, Justice Louis Brandeis, who was the first Jewish judge on the country's highest court, wrote: "The doctrine of the separation of powers was adopted by the Convention of 1787, not to promote efficiency but to preclude the exercise of arbitrary power. The purpose was, not to avoid friction, but by means of the inevitable friction incident to the distribution of governmental powers among three departments, to save the people from autocracy. . ." The sharing of powers through checks and balances was, as Madison explained, a valuable additional restraint on government that complements the principle of the separation of powers. Not only does the partition of powers limit government itself, but it also provides instruments by which each department can defend its position in the constitutional system. The presidential veto, for example, protects the executive against legislative encroachments, and the President's power of appointment gives him influence against judicial assault. The Court has the power to assess legislation in an appeal and its judges are protected by life tenure. The House of Representatives can impeach, that is, formally charge, a president and members of the Court. The national lawmakers control the purse upon which both other departments depend. The Senate passes on judicial appointments and tries officials impeached by the lower house. The Congress as a whole controls the appellate jurisdiction of the Supreme Court.

Although the courts do not legislate in the strictest sense of the term, their decisions may be realistically regarded as a form of law making. The courts, within limits, may also exercise the executive power of appointment. Congress may confer on them the power to suspend a sentence, even though such power is cus-

The Constitutional Convention, 1787

United States

Weather

Today: Partly sunny, cold.
High 38. Low 24.
Sunday: Afternoon snow.
High 38. Low 30.

Details, Page B10.

The Washington Post

Inside: **Real Estate**
Today's Contents on Page A2

122ND YEAR No. 70 •   SATURDAY, FEBRUARY 13, 1999   M4   25¢

Prices may vary in areas outside
metropolitan Washington. (See box on Page A2)

Clinton Acquitted

2 Impeachment Articles Fail to Win Senate Majority

Alone, President Responds With Simple Apology

By John F. Harris
Washington Post Staff Writer

There was no forgiving spouse by his side, no loyal vice president rallying the partisan troops, no defiant smile as he strode to the microphone. This time, President Clinton was all alone.

Exactly two hours after winning the votes that secured his future in office, he walked slowly out of the Oval Office to face a throng of reporters, cameras and boom microphones clustered in the Rose Garden. On this day of victory, the president said nothing that sounded victorious, seeking instead to convey the humility that his unyielding critics doubt he genuinely feels.

The contrast was plain and purposeful. Two months ago, on the day of Clinton's House impeachment, he surrounded himself with people to send the message that he was undefeated, that he would never resign. Yesterday, Clinton's somber expression and his self-critical words projected a different sort of resignation: an acceptance of his role in bringing about the nation's 13-month Monica S. Lewinsky ordeal, and his obligation to devote the remaining 23 months of his tenure to repairing the damage.

"Now that the Senate has fulfilled its constitutional responsibility," Clinton said, "bringing this process to a conclusion, I want to say again to the American people how profoundly sorry I am for what I said and did to trigger these

Five Republicans Join Democrats In Voting Down Both Charges

By Peter Baker
and Helen Dewar
Washington Post Staff Writers

The United States Senate acquitted William Jefferson Clinton yesterday on charges that he committed perjury and obstruction of justice to hide sexual indiscretions with a one-time White House intern, permitting the 42nd president to complete the remaining 708 days of his term.

After a tumultuous year of scandal that tested the Constitution and tried the nation's patience, neither of the two articles of impeachment brought by the House garnered a simple majority, much less the two-thirds necessary to convict Clinton of high crimes and misdemeanors. Article I alleging perjury was defeated on a 45 to 55 vote at 12:21 p.m. Just 18 minutes later, Article II charging obstruction failed on a 50 to 50 tie. Five Republicans joined all 45 Democrats in supporting full acquittal.

"It is, therefore, ordered and adjudged that the said William Jefferson Clinton be, and he is hereby, acquitted of the charges in said articles," declared Chief Justice William H. Rehnquist, the presiding officer, marking the conclusion of the first impeachment trial of a president in 131 years.

Clinton emerged from the Oval Office two hours later to tell the nation that he was "profoundly sorry" for his actions and the "great burden they have imposed on the Congress

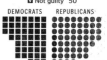

How They Voted

PERJURY
■ Guilty 45
☑ Not guilty 55

DEMOCRATS   REPUBLICANS

Republicans voting no: Chaffee, Collins, Jeffords, Gorton, Shelby, Snowe, Specter, Stevens, Thompson, Warner

OBSTRUCTION OF JUSTICE
■ Guilty 50
☑ Not guilty 50

DEMOCRATS   REPUBLICANS

Republicans voting no: Chaffee, Collins, Jeffords, Snowe, Specter

THE WASHINGTON POST

That distinction will almost certainly remain the only official sanction imposed by Congress. Soon after yesterday's acquittal votes, a bipartisan majority tried and failed to force

---

tomarily legislative in nature. The President's power over foreign relations is such that the function of advising about and consenting to treaties and of declaring war, entrusted by the Constitution to the legislature, have come largely under executive control. Executive officers and administrative bodies also exercise functions belonging to other departments. For example, independent regulatory commissions exercise both legislative and judicial powers.

In short, separation of powers is flexible in practice. Chief Justice John Marshall used it in 1803 to bolster his argument for judicial review in *Marbury v. Madison.* Separation of powers was President Richard

Nixon's primary reliance in his struggle to withhold incriminating tapes during the Watergate investigations. The Court ruled that though executive privilege is "fundamental to the operation of government and inextricably rooted in the separation of powers under the Constitution," it cannot "sustain an absolute, unqualified presidential privilege of immunity from judicial process under all circumstances." The political system designed by the constitutional framers was based largely on the assumption that a cardinal problem was to prevent government from becoming too powerful. The separation of powers and other constitutional checks and balances intended to make policymaking

difficult can be confusing and often mystifies foreigners. Indeed, many people at home and abroad wonder who really speaks for "Washington." Seldom do easy answers come.

CHECKS AND BALANCES

While the United States has three separate and distinct branches of national government, these are not completely independent of each other. Each branch has its own field of powers, but it is also subject to a series of constitutional restraints that either of the other two branches may exercise against it. The Constitution interlaces the three branches with several of these

Chief Justice John Marshall

checks. For example, the Congress has the power to make laws, but the President may veto an act of Congress, and Congress may pass legislation over a president's veto by a two-thirds vote in each house. Congress may refuse to approve appointments or treaties made by the President. The President has the power to appoint all federal judges. The courts have the authority to review the constitutionality of acts of Congress or actions of the President.

Head-on clashes between the branches seldom occur, but the check-and-balance system operates constantly, in almost routine fashion. The very existence of the system shapes much that happens in the national government. For example, in making an important appointment to a post in his administration, the president must always bear in mind that whomever he appoints must be acceptable to the Senate. In framing legislation, Congress must keep in mind the president's veto power and the Supreme Court's power to declare an act unconstitutional.

Of course, dramatic applications of the check-and-balance system do occur occasionally. The effectiveness with which President Eisenhower used the veto power provides an illustration. Congress was controlled by the Democrats for all but the first two of his eight years in office. Even so, it was not until he had been in office nearly seven years before one of his vetoes was overridden. Altogether, only two of his 181 vetoes were overridden by Congress during his eight years in office.

The Founding Fathers intended the check-and-balance system to prevent an "unjust combination of the majority." On the whole, the system has worked well. The people have learned, however, that

while mistakes or evil designs of one department may be checked by another, so also can well-planned, honest policies be checked for political reasons.

THE CHANGING CONSTITUTION

The Enduring Document

The Constitution has been in force for over 215 years-longer by far than the written constitution of any other nation in the world. How has the Constitution, written in 1787, managed to endure, to keep pace with the expansion of the country? The answer in part is that the Constitution today, at one and the same time, is and is not the document of 1787. True, many of the words are the same, and much of their meaning remains the same. Yet, some words have been changed, some have been eliminated, and some have been added. This process of constitutional change and growth has come about by formal and informal amendment.

The Founding Fathers were well aware that even the wisest of constitution drafters could not hope to develop a permanent document for all time. Hence, they included within the Constitution certain provisions for its amendment. Article V sets out the ways in which the Constitution may be amended. Two methods of proposal and two methods of ratification are specified. By combining one or the other method of proposal with one or the other method of ratification, four different means of amendment present themselves.

The Amendment Process

First, an amendment may be proposed by a two-thirds vote in each house of Congress and ratified by three-fourths of the state legislatures. Twenty-three of the twenty-four amendments have been adopted in this way. Second, an amendment may be proposed by a two-thirds vote in each house of Congress and ratified by conventions in three-fourths of the states. Only the 21st Amendment was adopted in this way. Under this method there is only one opportunity in each state for ratification. If a convention rejects an amendment, it is quite unlikely that another would be held. Under the first method, however, if a legislature refuses to ratify at one session, a later one might do so. The Supreme Court has held that even though a state has rejected an amendment, it may always reconsider that action. Once a state does ratify, it can never rescind that action. The 21st Amendment was ratified by the convention method because Congress felt that the people, who chose the delegates to the conventions, would be more favorable to it than the state legislators. Third, an amendment may be proposed by a national convention, called by Congress at the request of two-thirds of the state legislatures, and ratified by the

Congress in session

United States

legislatures of three-fourths of the states. To date, Congress has never had occasion to call a national convention for proposing an amendment. Fourth, an amendment may be proposed by a national convention, called by Congress at the request of two-thirds of the state legislatures, and ratified by conventions in three-fourths of the states. The Constitution itself was originally adopted in a manner quite similar to this.

The amendment process underscores the federal nature of the U.S. governmental system: proposal of amendments is a national function and ratification is a state matter. In theoretical terms, the adoption of an amendment represents the expression of the people's sovereign will. When Congress passes a joint resolution proposing an amendment, the resolution is not sent to the President for his signature or veto, despite the fact that the Constitution would seem to require it. In proposing an amendment the Congress is not legislating, and the vote required to propose an amendment is the same as the vote required to override a presidential veto.

The wording of Article V is quite specific. No state may require for itself additional steps in the ratification process. If it could, that state would, in effect, be amending the Constitution for its own purposes. Thus, in 1920 the Supreme Court held that Ohio, or any other state for that matter, could not require that a proposed amendment be approved by the people at a referendum before it could be ratified by the state legislature. A legislature could be influenced, but not bound, by an advisory vote of the people. Only one constitutional restriction is placed on the subjects with which a proposed amendment may deal. Article V provides that the amendment process cannot be used to deprive any state, "without its consent . . . Its equal suffrage in the Senate."

Important as they are, the formal amendments have not been primarily responsible for the Constitution's vitality. Rather, the informal amendments have been most responsible. As the Constitution has changed and grown through the years, the Constitution has kept pace through changes that have not involved additions or deletions in its actual wording. These changes have come through the day-to-day, year-to-year experiences of government under the Constitution.

To be sure, the constitutional framers did not intend to place future generations in a constitutional straitjacket. In this regard, Jefferson wrote:

I am certainly not an advocate for frequent and untried changes in laws and constitutions. I think moderate imperfections had better be born

with; because, when once known, we accommodate ourselves to them, and find practical means of correcting their ill effects.

But I know also, that laws and institutions must go hand in hand with the progress of the human mind. As that becomes more developed, more enlightened, as new discoveries are made, new truths disclosed, and manners and opinions change with the change of circumstances, institutions must advance also, and keep pace with the times. We might as well require a man to wear still the coat which fitted him when a boy, as civilized society to remain ever under the regimen of their barbarous ancestors.

To gain a true understanding of the nature of the U.S. constitutional system as it exists today, one must consider the five methods whereby the Constitution has changed and developed aside from formal amendment. Many portions of the Constitution are vague and skeletal. The constitutional framers purposely left it to Congress to fill in the details as circumstances required. In so doing, Congress has spelled out many of the Constitution's provisions. For example, the entire federal court system, except the Supreme Court itself, has been created by acts of Congress. So have all the numerous departments, agencies, and offices of the executive branch, except the offices of President and Vice-President.

Courtesy of Special Collections,
University of Virginia Library

Congress has also added to the Constitution by the manner in which it has exercised its various powers. For example, Congress is given the expressed power to regulate interstate commerce. In passing thousands of laws carrying out its commerce power, Congress has, in effect,

Proponents of the 19th Amendment: Suffragettes

150

Political Ideas and Political System

The Jefferson Memorial

become something of a rubber stamp for party action. The national convention system for selecting party candidates for the presidency is not provided for in the Constitution, and it was the parties that originally devised the procedure. Party caucuses often determine actions and policies of the House of Representatives and the President makes major federal appointments with an eye toward party politics.

Unwritten custom can at times be as strong as written law. For example, when the President dies in office, the Vice-President becomes President. Yet, this succession is not what the Constitution actually provides, specifying only that the powers and duties of the President shall devolve on the Vice-President. It is a well-established custom for the Senate to reject an appointment by the President if it is opposed by a senator of the majority party from the state where the appointee is to serve. This practice, known as senatorial courtesy, partially shifts the power to appoint many federal officers from the president to the senators.

The significance of unwritten custom is illustrated by the rare instance when one of them was nullified. From the time George Washington refused a third term as president in 1796, there had existed the so-called "no-third-term tradition" in American politics. In 1940, and again in 1944, Franklin D. Roosevelt broke with tradition, however, by seeking and winning a third, and later a fourth term.

helped to define the meaning of the constitutional provision, and thus has informally amended the document.

The manner in which the various presidents have exercised their powers has also contributed to the informal amendment process. Stronger presidents, in particular, George Washington, Thomas Jefferson, Andrew Jackson, Abraham Lincoln, Woodrow Wilson, and the two Roosevelts unflinchingly availed themselves of executive authority. Although only Congress may declare war, the President serves as commander-in-chief of the armed forces and presidents have used the armed forces for military action abroad on perhaps 200 occasions without a formal declaration of war. Among other examples, the device of "executive agreements" is typical. Recent presidents have made many such agreements instead of using the process of treaty-making outlined in the Constitution. Executive agreements are accords made personally between the President and heads of foreign states or their subordinates. Though executive agreements do not require Senate approval, the courts consider them legally binding.

Under the principle of judicial review, the courts have the power to interpret and apply the provisions of the Constitution. As the ultimate interpreter of the Constitution, the Supreme Court may be viewed in the fitting words of former Chief Justice Charles Evans Hughes as "a continuous constitutional convention." Hughes also remarked that "the Constitution means what the judges say it means." In expanding constitutional authority through judicial interpretation, the Court has been apt to lean heavily on the Necessary and Proper Clause, the Commerce Power, and the Taxing Power, all in Article I, Section 8.

Political parties have also contributed to the informal amendment process. It is somewhat ironic that parties themselves have grown up extra-constitutionally. The Constitution makes no mention of parties, and most of the Founding Fathers were opposed to their growth. In his Farewell Address in 1796, George Washington warned the people against "the baneful effects of the spirit of party." Yet, in many ways today, government in the United States is government by party. As an illustration, the electoral college system has

The Supreme Court

United States

Since then the 22nd Amendment has been added to the Constitution, making an unwritten custom part of the codified law of the land.

THE FEDERAL SYSTEM

Advantages of Federalism

In a federal system, a constitution divides the powers of government on a territorial basis, between a central government and several local governments. Each level exercises its own distinct field of powers, and neither, acting alone, can alter the division the Constitution creates between them. In the United States, the central government is the national government, and the constituent governments are the state governments.

The chief political benefit of a federal system is that it provides for local action in matters that are primarily of local concern and, at the same time, for national action in matters of wider concern. Local needs and desires vary from one section or state to another, and the federal system is designed to acknowledge this circumstance. While federalism permits local preferences in many matters, it also fosters the strength that derives from union. If natural disaster should strike a state or region, the resources of the rest of the nation are available to assist the stricken area.

Division of Powers

The Constitution outlines the basic scheme of the American federal system. It provides for a division of powers between the national government on the one hand and the states on the other. This division of powers is most clearly stated in the 10th Amendment: "The powers not delegated to the United States by the Constitution, nor prohibited by it to the states, are reserved to the states respectively, or to the people." The national government possesses only those powers that are delegated to it by the Constitution, and hence it is a government of *delegated powers*. The Constitution delegates three types of powers to the national government: expressed, implied, and inherent.

The expressed powers are stated in so many words in the Constitution. Most, but not all, are contained in Article I, Section 8. They include, among others, the power to

- Declare war and make peace
- Maintain armed forces
- Make treaties and otherwise conduct foreign relations
- Regulate foreign and interstate commerce
- Levy and collect taxes
- Establish post offices and post roads
- Issue money

- Fix uniform standards of weights and measures
- Borrow on credit of the United States
- Grant patents and copyrights
- Establish a federal court system
- Regulate bankruptcy
- Regulate naturalization
- Do those things "necessary and proper for carrying into execution" the various expressed powers

The implied powers are those that may be reasonably understood as accruing from the expressed powers—those necessary and proper to carry out explicit authority, for example, the regulation of labor-management relations, the construction of power dams, river and harbor improvements, flood control, and prosecution as a federal crime the transportation of stolen goods across a state line. These and many other powers are exercised by the national government because they may be reasonably implied from the expressed power to regulate interstate commerce.

The inherent powers belong to the federal government because it is the government of the nation. Although these are not specifically mentioned in the Constitution, they are powers that have customarily belonged to national governments. It logically follows that the constitutional framers, since they were creating the government of a nation, took for granted that these powers would be exercised by the

federal government. The inherent powers are few in number and include the authority to regulate immigration, deport aliens, extend diplomatic recognition, and protect the nation against rebellion. Actually, each of the inherent powers might also be categorized as an implied power. It is relatively easy to infer the power to regulate immigration from the expressed power to regulate foreign commerce, or the power of diplomatic recognition from the power to make treaties.

While the Constitution delegates authority to the national government, it also denies it certain powers. Some powers are withheld from the national government in so many words in the Constitution, for example, the powers to levy export duties, to grant titles of nobility, or to restrict freedom of speech, press, and religion. Some powers are denied to the national government because the Constitution does not mention them. The national government is one of delegated powers and has only those granted by the Constitution. Certain powers are simply not afforded to the national government, for instance, the authority to create a national school system, to enact a national marriage and divorce law, and to establish units of local government. Some powers are denied to the national government because of the very nature of the federal system. The national government is not permitted to do certain things because to do so would be to strike

British Prime Minister Margaret Thatcher receives delegation of U.S. Senators

152

Political Ideas and Political System

at the existence of the states. The national government, therefore, cannot tax the governmental functions of a state such as public education, road construction, and law enforcement.

The Constitution reserves to the states those powers not granted to the national government and are not at the same time denied to the states. A state may require police consent for the conduct of religious services in public parks or buildings, for example. It may forbid people under a certain age to marry or buy liquor, and it may prohibit the possession of certain types of firearms in its jurisdiction. It may charter or regulate corporations doing business in the state. It may also establish public school systems and units of local government and may set the conditions under which divorces may be granted.

The Constitution prohibits the states from undertaking several sorts of actions. For example, no state may enter into any treaty, alliance, or confederation; nor may it coin money, make any law impairing the obligations of a contract, grant titles of nobility, or deprive any person of life, liberty, or property without due process of law. Some powers are denied to the states because of the very nature of the federal system. Hence, the states are not permitted to tax the national government. Moreover, each state has its own constitution containing many prohibitions on the state. Some of the powers delegated to the national government are in turn denied to the states. The authority to coin money, make treaties, and levy import duties are expressly granted to the national government and explicitly denied to the states. These powers are among the exclusive powers of the federal government. Yet, some of the delegated powers are not denied to the states. While the federal government may lay or collect taxes, define and punish crimes, or condemn private property for public use, so may the states. These powers are among the concurrent powers; that is, they are the powers held by both the national government and the states.

The Supreme Law

The division of powers between the federal government and the states is a complex arrangement, producing what is widely known as a "dual system of government." In other words, the United States has two basic levels of government, and each of these has jurisdiction over the same territory and the same people at one and the same time. In such a situation, conflicts between national and state law invariably arise from time to time. Hence, the constitutional framers wrote the Supremacy Clause into the Constitution. Article VI, Section 2 specifies: "This

Constitution and the laws of the United States which shall be made in pursuance thereof, and all treaties made or which shall be made under the authority of the United States, shall be the Supreme law of the land. . ." The provision adds: ". . . and the judges in every state shall be bound thereby, anything in the Constitution or laws of any State to the contrary notwithstanding." This section, then, makes the Constitution and the acts and treaties of the United States the highest forms of law. The Constitution stands at the top, and immediately beneath it are the acts and treaties of the United States.

No form of state law may conflict with any form of national law. For instance, when Oregon entered the Union in 1859, its constitution prohibited voting by any person of Chinese descent. When the 15th Amendment was added to the U.S. Constitution in 1870 prohibiting any state to deny any person the right to vote on account of race, color, or previous condition of servitude, the provision of the Oregon constitution ceased to be effective. Other forms of state law—city charters, city ordinances, and other local laws—cannot conflict with federal law either. Many city ordinances forbidding the use of public meeting places by particular groups simply because local officials disapprove of them have been held unconstitutional. Such ordinances conflict with the 14th Amendment's guarantee of liberty. The final authority on questions of constitutionality is the Supreme Court of the United States.

The "Fourth Branch": The Media

Federal Obligations

The Constitution imposes several obligations on the federal government for the benefit of the states. Most of these are to be found in Article IV. The national government is to "guarantee to every state in this union a republican form of government." Although the phrase "republican form of government" has never been defined by the courts, it is generally understood to mean a representative democracy. President John Tyler acted under this constitutional guarantee when he moved to crush "Dorr's rebellion" in Rhode Island in 1841–42. The followers of Thomas Dorr attempted to force the conservative ruling group in the state to adopt a new constitution and ease the voting laws. They proclaimed a new constitution and named Dorr governor. When Dorr attempted to put his new government into operation, however, the legally elected governor appealed to President Tyler for help. When the federal government took measures to put down the rebellion, it collapsed.

In a case growing out of this incident, the Supreme Court held in 1849 that the question of whether or not a state has a republican form of government is a political and not a judicial one and is to be decided by the political branches of the government. The Court upheld this position in a 1912 ruling involving an Oregon corporation's refusal to pay a tax enacted by the voters of the state. The company claimed that the use of the initiative and referendum, "direct legislation" by which voters propose and enact laws at the polls, meant that Oregon lacked a representative government.

In addition to guaranteeing each state a republican form of government, the federal government is required to "protect each of them against invasion; and on application of the legislature, or of the executive (when the legislature cannot be convened), against domestic violence. Today, an invasion of one state would be considered an attack upon the United States as a whole. The President, as commander-in-chief of the armed forces, may use federal troops to quell domestic violence, such as riots and looting. Normally, the President would send troops only when requested to do so by the governor or legislature of the state involved. When a compelling issue of federalism arises, however, he need not wait for such an appeal. President Grover Cleveland sent federal troops to restore order in the Chicago rail-yards during the Pullman strike of 1894, acting over the express objections of the governor of Illinois. The Supreme Court upheld this action in 1896 because rioters had threatened federal property and impeded the mails and interstate commerce. Several presidents since have also acted without a

153

United States

Former U.S. presidents

state request, as President Eisenhower did at Little Rock in 1957, as well as President Kennedy at the University of Mississippi in 1962 and at the University of Alabama in 1963 to halt the unlawful obstruction of school integration orders issued by federal courts.

The federal government is further obligated to respect the geographic identity or integrity of each of the states. Thus, Congress may not create a new state from territory belonging to one or more of the existing states unless it first has the consent of the state legislatures involved. Nor may a state be denied its equal representation in the Senate without its own consent.

States and the federal government cooperate in many areas, of course. Perhaps the best-known example is the grant-in-aid program. The federal government gives the states tens of billions of dollars annually in grants. The money is given to the states for particular programs, such as highway construction, aid to dependent children, unemployment insurance, support for the aged, hospital construction, disease control, wildlife conservation, various educational programs, and forest-fire work. Usually, the states are required to match the federal funds, often on a dollar-for-dollar basis. The states must also meet certain conditions in order to use federal money. For example, they must meet rigid construction standards in order to receive federal grants-in-aid for highway construction.

The federal government aids the states in many other ways. For example, the Federal Bureau of Investigation (FBI) aids state and local police in criminal law enforcement. The Department of Agricul-

ture works with the state colleges of agriculture and state agriculture agencies to aid the farmers of each state. The Census Bureau makes its studies available to state school systems to help them plan for the future. The states assist the federal government also. National elections are conducted in each state by local officials acting largely under state laws, and federal prisoners are often lodged in state or local jails while awaiting trial.

Interstate Relations

Each state is legally separate from every other state in the Union. When states act within the sphere of their reserved powers, they essentially constitute independent entities. Expressed the other way around, each state has no jurisdiction outside its own boundaries. Interstate relations are covered by the Constitution in several important respects. Although states may not enter into any treaty, alliance or confederation, they may, with the consent of Congress, enter into compacts or agreements among themselves and even with foreign countries.

The negotiation of compacts between and among states is not infrequent. Many states have compacts relating to their borders and to the use of natural resources. New York and New Jersey created the Port of New York Authority to provide wharves, tunnels, bridges, street approaches, bus terminals, and airports, and to deal otherwise with common problems in the New York harbor area. Several states have joined with their neighbors to meet various common problems like combating forest fires and water pollution, sharing higher education facilities, and promot-

ing law enforcement. Every state has ratified the Parole and Probation Compact in which each agrees to supervise parolees and probationers from other states. Many states have "hot-pursuit" agreements with neighboring states. These states permit police officers from an adjoining state to pursue a lawbreaker across the state line. When fugitives are captured in such circumstances, they must be turned over to local authorities. In effect, the "hot-pursuit agreements" make a police officer of one state temporarily an officer of another state.

Many compacts deal one way or another with the common use of natural resources. The Colorado River (Hoover Dam) Compact of 1928, involving the states of the Colorado River Basin, was the first great attempt to bring several of the states together for the development, control, and management of a regional river. The Constitution requires each state to give "full faith and credit . . . to the public acts, records, and judicial proceedings of every other state." The words "public acts, records, and judicial proceedings" as employed here refer to state laws and local ordinances; records of births and marriages; deeds and contracts; judgments and decrees; licenses to drive and practice law, medicine, or dentistry.

The Full Faith and Credit Clause normally operates as a routine matter among the states with an important exception to the rule. The Clause applies only to civil matters and one state will not enforce another state's criminal law. The Constitution provides that "a person charged in any state with treason, felony, or other crime, who shall flee from justice, and be found in another State, shall, on demand of the executive authority of the State from which he fled, be delivered up, to be removed to the State having jurisdiction of the crime." (Article IV, Section 2) The return of a fugitive is customary. Occasionally, however, a governor will refuse to surrender a wanted person. Constitutional practice and Supreme Court decisions dating from 1961 have made the word "shall" actually read *may* in the Extradition Clause. The federal government cannot force a governor to act, and when one governor refuses the request of another, whatever the reasons may be, the matter ends there.

The Constitution provides that "the citizens of each state shall be entitled to all privileges and immunities of citizens in the several states." Essentially, this provision means that a resident of one state will not be discriminated against unreasonably by another state. Among the privileges and immunities of "interstate citizenship" are: the right to pass through or reside in any other state for the purpose of trade,

Capitol Hill

agriculture, or professional pursuits; to demand the writ of *habeas corpus*; to sue in court; to make contracts; to buy, sell, and hold property; to pay no higher taxes than the residents of the state; to marry.

A state is not required to grant public and political privileges to nonresidents. All states require that a person reside in the state for a certain period before being eligible to vote or hold public office. A state may require a period of residence within the state before it grants a person a license to practice medicine or dentistry, and it may restrict the practice of law to residents of the state. Wild fish and game are the common property of the people of a state, and therefore a nonresident may be compelled to pay a higher fee for a hunting or fishing license than a resident who pays taxes to maintain game and provide fish hatcheries. By the same token, state colleges and universities usually charge higher tuition to students from other states than to residents of the states in which the colleges and universities are located.

THE LEGISLATIVE BRANCH

Law-Making

U.S. legislatures include both federal and state lawmaking bodies. In addition to the federal and state levels, legislation also takes place at the local and city levels. Statutes, whether federal or state, often follow a similar process, from the proposal stage to approval by the executive. At the federal level, all laws begin as bills, and these become laws through several possible routes. Article I, Section 7 of the Constitution specifies that "all bills raising

Revenue shall originate in the House of Representatives; but the Senate may propose or concur with Amendments as on other Bills." As a rule, appropriation bills also originate in the House; all other bills may originate in either the House or the Senate. Representatives and senators introduce bills in their respective chambers. A bill goes through a process of consideration, sometimes never reaching a vote. Those bills that do come to a vote require the assent of the majority of at least a quorum of each chamber's members. The Constitution sets a quorum at a minimum of one-half of the members for each chamber. If a bill fails to reach the voting stage in either chamber, it dies. If it fails to get enough votes in either house, it also dies.

If a bill passes in both chambers, but the House and Senate versions of the bill are not identical, the members of a conference committee, made up of legislators from each chamber, must negotiate to make them so. If bargaining is successful, the new compromise bill goes back to each chamber for another vote. If the revised bill receives the necessary votes in both the House and the Senate, it goes to the President for his signature. If the House and the Senate versions of the bill are identical before a conference committee, which is an infrequent event for important bills, the original bill goes directly to the President.

The President then considers the bill and must decide whether or not to approve it. He can indicate approval in one of two ways: he can sign the bill, in which case it becomes law; or, he can fail to sign it, but if the Congress has not yet adjourned ten days after the President receives the bill

for consideration, it nonetheless becomes law. The President can also withhold approval in two ways. He can veto the bill outright, sending it back to the chamber in which it originated and stating the reasons for disapproval; or, he can fail to sign it, and if the Congress has adjourned within ten days of his receiving it for consideration, it does not become law. This latter method of withholding presidential approval is known as the pocket veto.

If the President vetoes the bill, the members of Congress have an opportunity to make it law anyway, although they succeed only about 5% of the time. The bill returns to the chamber in which it originated, and if two-thirds of a quorum of that chamber votes to pass it, then the bill goes to the other chamber, in which a similar process occurs. If two-thirds of a quorum of the second chamber passes the bill, then the House and Senate are said to have overridden the President's veto and the bill becomes law. Otherwise, it dies. The Constitution prescribes the process in Article I, Section 7.

Committee Work

Bills that come out of committee may be privileged or not privileged. Privileged bills go directly to the members of the House for consideration, while bills without privilege must go through the Rules Committee. Privileged bills fall into several classes. Private bills, which are submitted to aid particular persons, go on a private calendar. Limited bills without controversial substance might go on the consent calendar. Bills from the Appropriations Committee (those concerning rais-

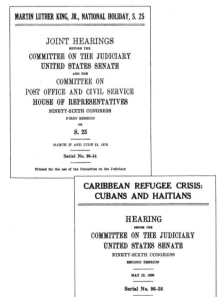

Congressional committee hearing reports

United States

A Senate hearing

ing federal revenues), the Public Works and Transportation Committee, and the Veterans Affairs Committee, and from the Rules Committee itself (for resolutions on how the consideration of a bill will be conducted), are similarly all privileged.

Bills without privilege must go to the Rules Committee. The members of this committee, the "traffic cop of the House," decide whether to report each bill they consider to the full House. If Rules Committee members so decide, a bill can die in their committee, unless a discharge petition on the bill's behalf gets enough signatures, at least 218, or unless a motion to suspend the rules succeeds on the floor of the House. Rules Committee members also set the terms of full House consideration for bills they send to the floor. Such bills are accompanied by one rule that specifies the time allowed for floor debate and another stating whether the bill can be amended on the floor of the House. Bills with an open rule can be amended; bills with a closed rule cannot. Finally, if a bill gets to the House floor through one of these many routes, it minimally requires a vote of over one-half of a quorum, at least 110 of 218 representatives, to pass.

While the Senate's lawmaking process resembles that of the House, it also has significant differences. First, while a presiding officer in the Senate refers bills to committees, as in the House, bills can also come to the floor of the Senate for consideration through other means. Senators may vote to suspend the rules, but they can also offer rider amendments to bills already under consideration by the full

Senate. Unlike requirements in the House, Senate rider amendments need not be relevant to the original bill. A rider amendment to a bill already under consideration can put an entirely new bill before the Senate for debate, thus entirely avoiding the committee process. Senators may directly consider any bill that the House has passed, and, as in the House, they can use discharge petitions to dislodge bills from Senate committee consideration.

While the Senate has no Rules Committee, its majority and minority party leaders customarily act together to schedule debate. Senate committees are somewhat less important in lawmaking than are House committees, but they are more important in other matters, such as conducting hearings on presidential appointments and on treaties. In both instances, these are the first steps for the Senate to advise and consent to presidential decisions. The filibuster is a Senate device that can stall legislation as effectively as can the members of the House committee. Senate floor debate is almost unlimited. Senators literally can continue to talk about a bill, or anything else that comes to mind for that matter, until the desire to get on with other business leads the bill's supporters or Senate leadership to drop its consideration. A vote on cloture to end a filibuster requires an affirmative vote from 60% of all senators. Before 1975, cloture required a two-thirds vote of the senators present and voting.

Three committees in the House—Appropriations, Ways and Means, and Rules—and two in the Senate—Appro-

priations and Finance—are preeminent in legislative matters. The members of most of the other committees, most of the time, concern themselves with particular substantive public policy subject matters. In the House, the members of two of the chief committees, Appropriations and Ways and Means, must decide whether to fund the program the members of the other committees are successful in passing through the lawmaking process. The members of the Rules Committee usually must decide whether those programs will indeed get through that process in the first place. Most public policies involving money must proceed through the money committees, the members of which enjoy the "power of the purse." The Rules Committee members, for their part, must decide whether to report the authorization bill or not and, if requested, must decide again on the appropriations and revenue bills. Rules Committee members also set the terms for floor debates and the permissibility of floor amendments on any bills they report.

House and Senate members' fortunes are closely tied to the committee assignments they receive. Generally, legislators prefer seats on one of the principal subcommittees, but all serve on several committees and subcommittees. Secondarily they may also seek appointments to committees whose substantive concerns are related to their respective constituents' interests. The importance of committee assignments to House and Senate members should not be underestimated, and even those assigned to committees of little apparent substantive connection with their constituents' interests often use their positions to advantage. Members usually request specific committee assignments, but because they are competing for the scarce resources that assignments represent, conflicting preferences and demands for committee positions constantly arise. As a result, the members of each party in the Congress have developed elaborate committee assignment procedures to reduce the otherwise inevitable conflict over committee positions. The committee system in both the House and Senate accords with ordinary principles of a division of labor. Moreover, it is useful in competing with the executive branch for influence in public policymaking. Members of committees who are personally knowledgeable about a particular subject will customarily collect useful information and direct their respective staffs to take appropriate action. Members can also focus public attention on specific problems to balance the president's publicity advantage. Such was surely the case with the Senate Foreign Relations Committee's Vietnam War hearings of 1973–74.

Political Ideas and Political System

A Most Deliberative Body

Members of Congress engage in other activities besides making laws, and most of these also have some effect on public policy. These include Senate advice and consent on treaties and presidential appointments, congressional oversight and investigation, and impeachment. The Constitution specifies in Article II, Section 2, that the President "shall nominate, and by and with the Advice and Consent of the Senate, shall appoint Ambassadors, and other public Ministers and Consuls, Judges of the Supreme Court, and all other Officers of the United States, whose Appointments are not herein otherwise provided for, and which shall be established by law; but the Congress may by Law vest the Appointment of such inferior Officers, as they may think proper, in the President alone, in the Courts of Law, or in the Heads of Departments."

The appointment process bears a crucial relationship to public policy because many of the people presidents nominate and senators confirm fill positions that allow them to make or implement policy. Members of the independent regulatory agencies, such as the National Highway Traffic Safety Administration, the Food and Drug Administration, and the Environmental Protection Agency, are supposed to implement and execute acts of Congress. Supreme Court justices and members of the lower courts are themselves often in the business of lawmaking and regulating; they can declare acts of Congress unconstitutional and can prescribe what public policy will be. Examples are to be found in the judicial activism in the realm of civil rights and civil liberties.

Senators, for their part, consider presidential nominations in much the same way they consider bills. A nomination goes to the most relevant substantive committee. For instance, the nomination of an attorney general or of a Supreme Court justice goes to the Senate Judiciary Committee, while the nomination of a secretary of state goes to the Senate Foreign Relations Committee. The committee members conduct hearings, interviewing the nominee and others who have an interest in the matter. They afterward report to the full Senate on the nomination, either favorably or unfavorably. The senators then vote on the nomination. Senators apply political and ideological standards in their confirmation decisions. Interest-group leaders often pay close attention to the nominee's record both in and out of government. Senators try to respect the opinions of those leaders in confirmation hearings. Frequently, if the objections to a nomination are over public policy, opposing senators will go even further than usual into the nominee's background in search of other grounds for rejection.

Article II, Section 2 of the Constitution specifies that the President "shall have Power, by and with the Advice and Consent of the Senate, to make Treaties, provided two-thirds of the senators present concur." Treaties with other nations proceed through the Foreign Relations Committee, and are important not only because they affect international relations but also because they influence domestic matters and are the law of the land. Yet, modern presidents have come to use executive agreements more often than treaties. These resemble treaties, but they do not require the advice and consent of the Senate. Presidents tend to favor executive agreements since these do not require congressional action. Often, though, executive agreements receive congressional approval as with other bills and resolutions. Congress frequently provides consent following the agreement's conclusion.

Some observers regard the use of executive agreements as diminishing congressional control of foreign affairs. Be that as it may, presidents almost always try to bring Foreign Relations Committee senators into the treaty formulation process. Otherwise, senators are delivered a *fait accompli* to ratify, which many strongly resent. For example, following the First World War, President Woodrow Wilson failed to get Senate approval for U.S. membership in the League of Nations because he excluded senators from treaty deliberations. President Jimmy Carter's protracted problems over Senate ratification of the Strategic Arms Limitation Treaty with the Soviet Union, SALT II, stemmed partially from the same difficulty.

The role of Congress in foreign policy should not be underestimated. Who exercises authority in foreign policy often depends on what issues are involved. The public tends to support the President on majoritarian matters abroad and accepts the general direction of foreign policy. Yet, when client and interest group politics are involved, Congress tends to assume an assertive role. For instance, Congress will be substantially engaged in decisions pertaining to foreign economic issues, support for certain key allies, and the building of new weapon systems. Domestic industries still claim to be hurt by "cheap foreign labor" and "cheap foreign goods," although the principal and more plausible reasons are innovation and higher productivity. American ethnic politics have long featured the "three I's"—Italy, Ireland and Israel—which have considerable effect upon foreign policy. Since the establishment of Israel over a half-century ago, the pro-Israeli lobby has been an influential force in U.S. politics. Moreover, by thwarting international accords such as the one on the establishment of the International Criminal Court (ICC) or the Comprehensive Test Ban Treaty (CTBT) dealing with nuclear weapons, Congress can be a major player on the world stage. "Who speaks for Washington?" is frequently a relevant question.

Through committee hearings, House and Senate members can examine the workings of the laws and agencies they create. Such scrutinizing is the practice of congressional oversight. Similarly, mem-

The Kennedys (Edward, Jackie, John, Robert), a family of legislators

Courtesy of Special Collections, University of Virginia Library

United States

bers can study problems before, during, and after the consideration of bills, which is called congressional investigation. While the Constitution does not expressly authorize these practices, nevertheless they are inherent powers because they provide clear and useful resources for lawmaking.

THE EXECUTIVE BRANCH

Executive Clout

The executive branch of government is responsible for enforcing the laws made by the legislative branch. The executive branch consists of the President, presidential appointees, and all administrative agencies. At the state level, it includes the Governor, the Governor's appointees, and all administrative agencies. Administrative agencies include boards, commissions, and offices, or departments established to implement the laws that generally originate with the legislative branch of government.

The authority of the President and the executive branch is granted by the Constitution of the United States, and it is likewise limited by the Constitution. For example, although the President has the authority to appoint several representatives of the United States such as ambassadors, federal judges, and the heads of several administrative agencies, such as the Federal Bureau of Investigation and the General Services Administration (GSA), many of those appointments must be approved by the legislative branch of government through an affirmative vote of at least two-thirds of the Senate. State constitutions place similar limitations on the executive branch of state governments. The executive branch of the federal government is divided into more than a dozen main departments whose heads are appointed by the president. Most of the heads (or "secretaries") of these departments are members of the President's cabinet.

Addressing himself to the executive in *Federalist* No. 70, Alexander Hamilton wrote:

There is an idea, which is not without its advocates, that a vigorous executive is inconsistent with the genius of republican government. The enlightened well-wishers to this species of government must at least hope that the supposition is destitute of foundation. Energy in the Executive is a leading character in the definition of good government. It is essential to the protection of the community against foreign attacks; it is not less essential to the steady administration of the laws; to the protection of prop-

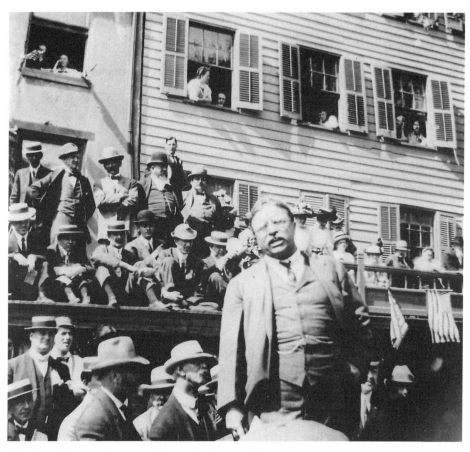

Theodore Roosevelt campaigning for the presidency

Courtesy of Special Collections, University of Virginia Library

erty against those irregular and high-handed combinations which sometimes interrupt the ordinary course of justice; to the security of liberty against the enterprises and assaults of ambition, of faction, and of anarchy.

A feeble executive implies a feeble execution of the government. A feeble execution is but another phrase for a bad execution; and a government is ill executed, whatever it may be in theory, must be, in practice, a bad government.

The ingredients which constitute energy in the Executive are, first, unity; secondly, duration; thirdly, an adequate provision for its support; fourthly, competent powers . . . The ingredients which constitute safety in the republican sense are, first, a due dependence on the people, secondly, a due responsibility.

Like most modern governments, the United States has displayed a tendency toward concentration of power in the hands of the executive in the last half-century. The President is the political head of the country in extraconstitutional affairs; he exercises the power of pardon, the veto

power, and extensive war powers, and he has almost complete control over foreign affairs. Under certain limitations, Congress may grant the executive sweeping powers when swift and coordinated action is required. Moreover, the conduct of government, increasingly in the multiple hands of administrative authority, has given rise to the expressions "government by commission" and "government by executive order," both indicative of aggrandizement as the characteristic mark of presidential power.

The members of the Convention of 1787 who feared that presidential authority would succumb to an all-powerful legislature were proved wrong. Although the Supreme Court has from the time of John Marshall, its third Chief Justice, asserted and maintained a role of considerable significance, it is the presidential office that has expanded most in power and shown the greatest increase in both number and variety of its activities. This swelling of executive power is not unique with America. The hey-day of the legislature has passed when the dominance of the concept of limited government permitted long debate preceding any change in governmental policy, and the dearth of gov-

158

Prime Minister Margaret Thatcher and President George H. W. Bush at the Prime Minister's residence in London, Number 10 Downing Street

ernmental programs facilitated extensive legislative surveillance of administration. War, economic crises, and the complexity of problems confronting modern societies have thrust power and responsibility upon the executive not contemplated in an earlier age.

Three divergent theories bring to mind the nature and scope of presidential power: the constitutional theory, the stewardship theory, and the prerogative theory. The constitutional theory holds that Article II contains an enumeration of executive powers and that the President must be prepared to justify all his actions on the basis of either enumerated or implied power. The best statement of the constitutional theory appears in former President William Howard Taft's book, *Our Chief Magistrate and His Powers* (1916). In opposition to Taft, Theodore Roosevelt contended that the President is a "steward of the people," and is therefore under the duty to do "anything that the needs of the nation demanded unless such action was forbidden by the Constitution and the laws." Taft denounced Roosevelt's theory as calculated to render the presidency a "universal Providence." As Chief Justice of the Supreme Court, however, he indicated greater sympathy for it. In this *Autobiography*, Roosevelt wrote:

I declined to adopt the view that what was imperatively necessary for the Nation could not be done by the President unless he could find some specific authorization to do it. My belief was that it was not only his right but his duty to do anything that the needs of the Nation demanded un-

less such action was forbidden by the Constitution or by the laws. Under this interpretation of executive power I did and caused to be done many things not previously done by the President and heads of the departments. I did not usurp power, but I did greatly broaden the use of executive power. In other words, I acted for the public welfare, I acted for the common well-being of all our people, whenever and in whatever manner was necessary, unless prevented by direct constitutional or legislative prohibition. I did not care a rap for the mere form and show of power; I cared immensely for the use that could be made of the substance.

Going beyond Theodore Roosevelt's stewardship theory, Franklin D. Roosevelt's concept of his duties conforms essentially to John Locke's description of "prerogative"—the power to act according to discretion for the public good, without the prescription of the law and sometimes even against it. During his long incumbency, Roosevelt often sacrificed constitutional and legal restrictions on the altar of "emergency" and an overriding public interest.

Separated Powers

It is notable that some observers of the American presidency bemoan the constitutionally created inability to overcome congressional opposition of executive programs. In this view, the U.S. President often cannot command House and Senate support for his programs. The President has no dependable way, as the British

Prime Minister does, to command the legislature's support. The likelihood is that a President who seeks important, and therefore controversial social and economic legislation, will face stiff opposition from legislative leaders even of his own party. Checks and balances, along with a particular president's legislative and party weaknesses, affect other functions as well. Even where his authority is greatest, say the critics, in foreign affairs and as commander-in-chief, the President depends on congressional support. President Gerald Ford, barely able to conceal his frustration as chief executive, argued the case for presidential supremacy in military and foreign affairs in his last State of the Union address in January 1977:

I express the hope that this new Congress will re-examine its constitutional roles in international affairs. The exclusive right to declare war, the duty to advise and consent on the part of the Senate, and the power of the purse on the part of the House, are ample authority for the legislative branch and should be jealously guarded.

But because we may have been too careless of these powers in the past does not justify congressional intrusion into, or obstruction of, the proper exercise of Presidential responsibilities now or in the future. There can be only one Commander-in-Chief. In these times crises cannot be managed and wars cannot be waged by committee. Nor can peace be pursued by parliamentary debate. To the ears of the world, the President speaks for the Nation. While he is, of course, ultimately accountable to the Congress, the courts and the people, he and his emissaries must not be handicapped in advance in their relations with foreign governments as has sometimes happened in the past.

The President has the duty under Article IV, Section 4, to furnish military assistance to repress domestic violence upon call of a state legislature or governor. From the Whiskey Rebellion in 1794 to the present, presidents have been called upon for aid, either because of insurrection against the lawful state government or because of disorders arising from economic or social disputes. The action of the President in sending or even agreeing to commit troops to the aid of one of the contending factions in a state dispute entails recognition that there is a lawful government in that state. If the disorder results in the violation of federal laws, the President may then act in accordance with his duty to "take care that the laws be faithfully executed." In the actual dispatching of troops, he acts in his capacity as commander-in-chief. With or

United States

without approval of a state governor, the President may use military force or any other means deemed necessary to fulfill his obligation faithfully to execute the laws of the United States. His power to protect the peace of the United States and execute the laws has no effective judicial limits. Martial law may be authorized whenever a state governor or the President considers it necessary for the restoration of order.

As protector of the peace, the President is called upon to respond to emergencies and disasters. The authority does not derive directly from the Constitution, but over the years, Congress has increasingly granted to the President the right to take unilateral action in the face of emergencies and disasters. After storms and earthquakes and during strikes, riots, financial crises, or military attacks, the President enjoys the congressionally granted right to act on his own.

The President's scope as protector of the civic peace usually seems innocuous enough. He may send family or cabinet members to inspect disaster areas and then make the appropriate declarations, activate the necessary personnel, and provide emergency relief supplies and low-interest government loans for rebuilding damaged areas. That said, the President's activities as protector of the peace may also be hotly disputed, especially if these invoke presidential prerogatives more closely associated with constitutional provisions. For example, the President may act the part of a dedicated statesman by calling labor and management representatives together to settle a violent or economically damaging strike. People sometimes demand presidential intervention, but the situation is frequently no-win for the chief executive. If the White House negotiations fail, the President will receive much of the blame. If the President tries to prod the negotiations along by exerting pressure on one of the bargainers, he might lose that bargainer as a political ally. Sometimes presidents are forced into these situations, and whether they succeed or fail, the popular expectation that they should be protectors of the peace can be as costly for them to fulfill as not.

As discussed above, the power of the federal government over the armed forces of the nation is divided between the President and Congress. The legislature has the power to raise armies and provide a navy (Article I, Section 8). The President, as commander-in-chief of the armed forces (Article II, Section 2), may issue regulations of his own and may take charge of all military operations in time of peace and war. As commander-in-chief, the President exercises control over many subsidiary aspects of public policy. The stockpiling and international trading of

Weather
Today: *Partly sunny, mild.*
High 50. Low 36.
Thursday: *Mostly cloudy.*
High 54. Low 41.
Details, **B8**

The Washington Post

DISTRICT & MARYLAND EDITION
35¢
179TH YEAR No. 58 · R · DC MD · · · WEDNESDAY, FEBRUARY 1, 2006

In 1968, Coretta Scott King created the Martin Luther King Jr. Center for Social Change in Atlanta to continue his work.

Coretta Scott King, 1927–2006

A Full Partner in The Dream

Widow Quickly Found Own Voice for Change

By YVONNE SHINHOSTER LAMB
Washington Post Staff Writer

Coretta Scott King, who with grace and determination kept her husband's legacy alive and emerged as one of America's most influential voices for social change and human rights, died yesterday at an alternative medical clinic in Mexico. She was 78.

Mrs. King, who suffered a debilitating stroke and heart attack in August, went to Hospital Santa Monica in Rosarito Beach, a few miles south of San Diego in Baja California, Mexico, within the past two weeks for observation and treatment of ovarian cancer.

Widowed by an assassin's bullet on April 4, 1968, Mrs. King did not grieve publicly. Instead, she immediately filled the void of leadership and continued to preach the Rev. Martin Luther King Jr.'s philosophy of nonviolence, making it her own. To ensure that his dream of racial equality and justice remained etched in the collective consciousness of the nation and the world, Mrs. King founded the Martin Luther King Jr. Center for Nonviolent Social Change in his home town of Atlanta. She also overcame persis-

THE STATE OF THE UNION

President Bush greets Reps. Sherwood L. Boehlert (R-N.Y.), left, and Jesse L. Jackson Jr. (D-Ill.) before his address.

Bush Says U.S. Must Remain a World Leader

New Supreme Court Justice Samuel A. Alito Jr., at right, listens to President Bush's State of the Union address.

President Calls for Oil Alternatives, Affordable Care

By PETER BAKER
and MICHAEL A. FLETCHER
Washington Post Staff Writers

President Bush last night defended his vision for a robust U.S. role in world affairs and outlined a litany of domestic initiatives to make the nation more competitive abroad in a State of the Union address designed to rejuvenate his troubled presidency at the start of a midterm election year.

Bush, a onetime Texas oil industry executive, declared that "America is addicted to oil" and vowed to push for al-

Alito Is Sworn In On High Court

Senators Confirm Conservative Judge Largely on Party Lines

By CHARLES BABINGTON
Washington Post Staff Writer

Samuel A. Alito Jr. was sworn in as the nation's 110th Supreme Court justice yesterday, marking a major victory for conservatives in their decades-old drive to move the court rightward, and alarming liberals who fear that long-standing rights might be in jeopardy.

By the narrowest margin since Clarence Thomas's 1991 nomination, the Senate voted 58 to 42, largely along party lines, to confirm Alito to succeed the retiring Sandra Day O'Connor, who often was the pivotal vote on a closely divided court. Alito, 55, was quickly sworn in by Chief Justice John G. Roberts Jr., the other conservative whom President Bush named to the nine-member court after 11 years without a vacancy.

Four Democratic senators voted for Alito, and one Republican — Lincoln D. Chafee, who faces a tough reelection battle this year in Democratic-leaning Rhode Island — voted against him. Roberts was confirmed 78 to 22 last fall, backed by every Republican and 22 Democrats.

Breaking ranks yesterday by backing Alito were Democrats from four states that Bush carried easily, and three of them face reelection this fall: Robert C. Byrd (W.Va.), Kent Conrad (N.D.) and Ben Nelson (Neb.). The fourth, Tim Johnson (S.D.), is up for election in 2008. All other Democrats and one independent voted against Alito's confirmation, and 54 Republicans voted aye. Incumbents hope the cerebral and

See **ALITO**, A11, Col. 1

INSIDE

THE WORLD
Nuclear Diplomacy, Iranian-Style
In its bid to proceed with a program opposed by the West, Iran reaches out to Fidel Castro, Hugo Chavez and the leaders of other defiant, nonaligned nations. A18

Executive-Judicial Interaction

strategic materials, such as uranium, petroleum, and chromium, come under his control. High-tech equipment, such as computers, often cannot be sold abroad without presidential approval. During World War I, President Woodrow Wilson nationalized the railroads. Yet, the justices of the Supreme Court rejected President Harry Truman's contention that the authority vested by the Constitution and laws of the United States allowed him to nationalize the steel industry in April 1952 to avoid the economic and military damage he argued would come from a strike.

War does not necessarily suspend constitutional guarantees. Justice Oliver Wendell Holmes remarked in a 1919 court case: "We do not lose our right to condemn either measures or men because the country is at war." Yet, practice does not always coincide with principle, and reality is often complex. Under President Abraham Lincoln, Congress was largely ignored or asked to ratify executive actions already carried out or under way. In both world wars, Congress passed a vast number of general statutes of wide scope, delegating to the President, or to persons desig-

nated by him, vast discretionary powers. The widest of these delegations was upheld in a 1944 court case allowing, among other things, the relocation of American citizens. When statutory authority is thus added to the President's already expansive powers as commander-in-chief, constitutional limitations are significantly impacted, as seen in the Japanese-American relocation cases during the Second World War. Even without the support of statutes, presidential power in wartime is subject to few limitations. The chief executive can control the movement of the armed forces, and prescribe rules for the administration of occupied territory. He may order the seizure of former enemy officers and officials after the conclusion of hostilities, as was recently done in 2001 in the wake of military operations in Afghanistan, and set up military commissions to try such individuals in proceedings not limited by the Constitution, a politically charged and emotion-laden issue.

All the President's Men

The President's immediate staff began with a few aides to President George

Washington and now numbers several thousand people. The members of various executive departments, such as Treasury, State, and Defense, exclusive of uniformed military and postal workers, number over a million. Millions more work for the federal government, and most of these are ultimately responsible to the President in some way.

The Constitution contemplated the existence of executive departments, whose heads must respond to the President's demand for counsel and opinions, and who are chosen by the President with the advice and consent of the Senate. It is notable, though, that the Constitution did not anticipate a presidential cabinet. This organization consists of the President, the Vice-President, the heads of departments, and other persons as the chief executive might choose. The Executive Office of the President includes his immediate aides and assistants as well as leaders of several councils and public policy groups. By convention, the Central Intelligence Agency is also included. The Executive Office includes the following principal offices, organizations, councils and groups

- The White House Office
- The Executive Residence
- Office of Management and Budget (OMB)
- Council of Economic Advisors
- Council on Environmental Quality
- Domestic Policy Staff
- Economic Policy Group
- National Security Council (NSC)
- Office of Science and Technology Policy
- Office of the U.S. Trade Representative
- Office of the Vice-President

Unlike the cabinet, whose members often represent special interests, the members of the Executive Office are entirely the President's subordinates and are expected to have interests and incentives paralleling his own.

The composition of the executive branch represents the accumulation of two centuries of growth and custom, some of it purposive, and some of it not. The theory behind the Executive Office of the President is that a large number of people can operate as the President's eyes and ears, screening information and problems, separating what is significant from what is not. The ultimate goal of the process is to enable the President to accomplish all that statute law, the Constitution, and the members of the electorate require.

Here again, reality is complex. Aides and department heads must often speak for the President. The result can be confusion about what the President actually wants, since each aide might offer a slightly different interpretation of the

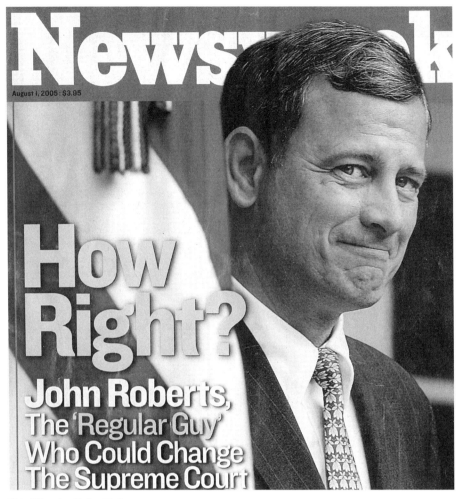

Chief Justice John Roberts

President's position. In domestic policy, the ambiguity generated can hamper the success of the President's legislative program. On the other hand, ambiguity is often an important election strategy. But in foreign and military policy, ambiguity fostered by contradictory statements of different presidential aides can lead to dangerous confrontations. Ambiguity on an international scale can defeat purpose and policy. In short, the executive branch is a complicated organization of sometimes fractious individuals holding diverse preferences and with all the difficulties attendant to any such organization. It seldom works with a single will in the service of the President, although the latter must theoretically manage and direct the members of an organization who propose and execute the laws.

THE JUDICIAL BRANCH

Humanity, Reason and Justice

The judicial branch is charged with the administration of justice. The courts administer justice by acting as the conduit for dispute resolution. The courts are where civil and criminal disputes are resolved if the parties cannot reach a resolution themselves. Often people think of the courts as enforcers of the law. Although true in a sense, this is wide of the mark, in that the judicial branch does not work with the executive branch to achieve criminal convictions. It is the duty of the courts to remain neutral and apply the laws in a fair and impartial manner. The U.S. Constitution established a judiciary system shielded from interference from the other two branches. For example, the Constitution prohibits Congress from reducing the pay of federal judges after they are appointed. This provision prevents congress from coercing the court into action under threat of no pay. The Constitution also provides for lifetime appointment of federal judges, thereby keeping the judicial branch from being influenced by political concerns, which may cause judges to ignore the law and make decisions based on what is best for their political careers. Judicial independence permits courts to make decisions that are disadvantageous

Weather
Today: *Cloudy, sleet later.*
High 34. Low 30.
Thursday: *Morning rain,*
cloudy. High 42. Low 32.
Details, Page **B8**

The Washington Post

Inside: Food, Classified
Today's Contents on Page A2

124TH YEAR No. 8   R   DM   VA   WEDNESDAY, DECEMBER 13, 2000

25¢
Prices may vary in areas outside metropolitan
Washington. (See box on Page A4)

Court Overturns Recounts, Giving Bush the Presidency

Long Day's Wait for the Decision

By MIKE ALLEN
and DAVID MONTGOMERY
Washington Post Staff Writers

On Capitol Hill, a rumor spread that a poinsettia had been moved from the table where copies of Supreme Court opinions are piled upon release.

In the cramped Supreme Court press room, a network legal analyst played the computer game Tetris.

In Austin, George W. Bush, Supreme Court petitioner and presidential candidate, skipped his beloved noon workout and stayed holed up in the Texas governor's mansion.

After waiting 34 days and 34 nights for a president-elect, Americans had expected a final answer. Once again, that hope seemed just a tease.

The nine justices had halted the recounting of Florida ballots on Saturday, set Sunday as the deadline for legal papers and heard oral arguments on Monday. In a FedEx culture, why not a ruling Tuesday?

Instead, the day passed, no word came and the political earth stood still. The 24-hour news channels began lingering lovingly over seating charts of the justices. Correspondents started larding their updates with "I would assume" and "I would imagine." On MSNBC, former Supreme Court clerks were reduced to analyzing the influ-

Workmen building an inaugural viewing stand in front of the White House are silhouetted against a cold winter sky.

BY JAMES A. PARCELL — THE WASHINGTON POST

Divided Justices Cite Concerns With Timeframe

By DAN BALZ *and* CHARLES LANE
Washington Post Staff Writers

A deeply divided U.S. Supreme Court last night overturned the Florida Supreme Court decision allowing continued manual recounts across the state and said there was no time to create a new standard for counting. The decision effectively ended the historic dispute over the presidential election and left Texas Gov. George W. Bush the winner over Vice President Gore.

"Upon due consideration of the difficulties identified to this point, it is obvious that the count cannot be conducted in compliance with the requirement of equal protection and due process without substantial additional work," the court said.

In an unsigned decision, the justices said the recounting process ordered by the Florida court was constitutionally flawed because it lacked uniform standards for counting the ballots.

A majority of seven justices agreed that there are constitutional problems, but the justices were far more fractured on the issue of whether there was any way to fashion a remedy that would allow more counting under a uniform standard before the electoral college meets next Monday to cast their votes.

The justices said that because the Florida Legislature had indicated its desire to take advantage of the provision of federal law that insulates state's electors from challenge so long as they are selected by Dec. 12, it would be unconstitutional for the court to now prolong the process.

"Because it is evident that any recount seeking to meet the Dec. 12 date will be unconstitutional . . . we reverse the judgment of the Supreme Court of Florida ordering the recount to proceed," the court said.

---

to the government, yet required by law, without fear of retribution from the other two branches. Alexander Hamilton wrote of the importance of an independent judiciary in the *Federalist Papers*: "Permanency in office frees the judges from political pressures and prevents invasions on judicial power by the president and Congress."

In an effort to resolve disputes, courts must apply the laws of the land. To enact the law, judges must interpret legislation and the constitutions of the nation. To *interpret* here means to read the law in an attempt to grasp its meaning. All courts, whether local, state, or federal, are bound by the United States Constitution, and

hence all courts have a duty to apply federal constitutional law.

The nation's courts have the final word in declaring the meaning of written law. If a court interprets a statute's meaning contrary to the intent of a legislature, then the latter may later rewrite the statute to make its intent more clear, which has the effect of reversing the judicial interpretation of the statute. The process can be more difficult if a legislature desires to change a judicial interpretation of a constitution. At the national level, the federal Constitution has been amended 26 times. The amendment process, found in Article V of the Constitution, requires not only initiative by the Congress but also action

by the states, resulting in an intricate process indeed. To amend a constitution is a far more cumbersome and time-consuming endeavor than amending legislation.

Constitutional Guardians

Only the Constitution is fundamental law, for the Constitution establishes the principles and structure of the government. To argue that the Constitution is not superior to the laws suggests that the representatives of the people are somehow superior to the people themselves, and that the constitution is inferior to the government established. Such reasoning, of course, makes no sense in a democracy. The courts are the arbiters between the

162

Third, federal courts can strike down laws only on appeal. They are not empowered to routinely review statutes and declare them unconstitutional.

The duties of the judicial branch of government focus on the court systems. Different court systems are established for each of the states as well as for the federal government. Furthermore, each court system contains many different courts. Although these court systems differ from one another in many ways, they nonetheless have some characteristics in common. All court systems have trial courts and courts of appeal or review. Many court systems have two levels of review courts, intermediate courts of appeal and highest courts of appeal or courts of last resort, sometimes referred to as supreme courts. Functions of trial courts are quite similar, as are the tasks of courts of appeal and courts of last resort.

Judicial observers have suggested that the Supreme Court has been a major policymaker for decades in at least five areas: desegregation, reapportionment, criminal justice procedures, freedom of speech and abortion. Some suggest the Court has frequently overextended its authority, and observations of court proceedings are part of an ongoing debate concerning judicial activism and judicial restraint. These two terms invariably assume different meanings depending upon use and context, and they can also refer to the way the Court arrives at decisions. If its opinions proceed slowly from one case to the next, deciding disputes on narrow grounds of

Thank you for helping us secure a Democratic presidential victory in November, and a better future for America.
Most Sincerely,

Presidential candidate John F. Kerry and his running mate, Senator John Edwards, opponents in the primaries and partners in the 2004 general election.

Abortion remains an emotion-laden issue.

legislative branch and the people, and the courts must place the Constitution higher than the laws passed by Congress. In the landmark case dealing with judicial review, *Marbury v. Madison*, Marshall determined that, although the Constitution does not contain explicit language providing for the power of judicial review, Article III of the Constitution indirectly endows the power in the judiciary. It is now a well-established principle of American justice that the courts possess the authority to review the actions of the executive and legislative branches and to declare any law void if it is deemed to violate the Constitution. Such power is vested in both state and federal courts. Any state law that violates the U.S.

Constitution may be struck down by either federal or state courts. State laws that violate state constitutions may be stricken for the same reason.

The power to invalidate statutes is employed sparingly for three reasons. First, members of the judiciary are aware how sweeping their authority can be, and are inclined to use it prudently. Second, many rules of statutory construction exist, which have the effect of preserving legislation. For example, if two interpretations of a statute are feasible, one violating the Constitution and one not in violation, a basic rule of statutory construction requires that the statute be constructed as to be consistent with the Constitution.

United States

technicalities rather than on broader principles, while at the same time appealing to the weight of precedent, then the Court is said to be exercising judicial restraint. On the other hand, if the Court leaps into new territory by enunciating the widest decision possible in a particular case, even though the case could be decided on narrower grounds, then it is often said to be engaging in judicial activism.

The "activist" school, championed in the second half of the 20th century primarily by Justice Hugo Black and Justice William O. Douglas, was derived largely from Justice Louis Brandeis and holds that the Supreme Court has a positive role to play not only in guarding civil liberties but in setting a legal framework for the quest of a greater measure of economic and social democracy. This approach was strengthened by the New Deal and the appointments that President Franklin Roosevelt made to the Court. At base it represents an instrumental approach to the judicial process. It distinguishes between the protection of individual freedom and the progress of economic and social advance. In the latter case, it is willing to go along with legislative majorities and administrative action on the theory that these broad issues have been hammered out under long public debate and represent the response to the needs of the time. In the case of civil liberties, where freedoms of long standing may be threatened by emotional new doctrines expressed through hasty majorities, it holds that the role of the Court is that of acting to protect old freedoms against new dangers.

Judicial activism and judicial restraint also apply to the Court's interaction with other branches of the federal government. If the Supreme Court refuses to accept a case it regards as "political," or if it customarily defers to the other branches of government, asserting that a petitioner either has not exhausted all remedies or must work through the legislative process, then the approach might be one of judicial restraint. On the other hand, if the Court becomes a sort of legislator in the governing process, and if its decisions state that it is suited to assume this role, critics will charge the Court with judicial activism. The controversy tends to be politically charged. The sweeping orders designed to correct the problems associated with overcrowded prisons are an example. The 2000 decision to halt the recounting of votes in Florida for the presidential election and thus effectively to hand the presidency to George W. Bush is a notable and, above all, controversial and emotion-laden recent instance.

Positions concerning judicial restraint and judicial activism innately entail value judgments regarding the scope of judicial activity in general. People employ different definitions of the rule of law and the use of legal procedures, while attitudes toward judicial activism and restraint depend on the actual decisions of the Court at a particular time. During Chief Justice Earl Warren's tenure on the Court from 1953–1969, for example, many observers were appalled by what they regarded as the Court's commitment to social engineering. Some expressed their disagreement with the Court not merely in terms of the specific decisions involved, but also in terms of insistence that the Court exercise judicial restraint. When Chief Justice Warren Burger was appointed to the Court in 1969 and three other more conservative justices were selected in the 1980s, the shoe was on the other foot, and many prior advocates of judicial restraint became proponents of judicial activism who urged the Court to overturn the decisions they found unacceptable. By the same notion, many who tended to favor judicial activism in the era of the Warren Court suddenly found considerable merit in judicial restraint, given the sort of relatively conservative decisions the Burger Court was inclined to make. Beyond such ongoing controversies, though, and the differing interpretations of judicial activism and judicial restraint, a salient question lingers about the appropriateness of members of the federal judiciary acting or refusing to act as lawmakers rather than mere interpreters of the law. Whether courts should be bold or timid is ultimately a highly political issue.

And the shoe can truly be on the other foot. Theodore Roosevelt appointed Oliver Wendell Holmes to the Supreme Court in 1902, only later to quip in consternation, "I could carve out of a banana a judge with more backbone than that." Holmes, a thrice-wounded Civil War veteran, was nobody's idea of a coward, however. He was known frequently to have remarked that he simply did not care what Roosevelt thought and he saddened Roosevelt hugely by voting against his administration's antitrust policies. President Richard Nixon, an ardent opponent of court-ordered school busing, appointed Warren Burger to be chief justice in 1969. Burger reciprocated by promptly writing the majority opinion upholding school busing. Another Nixon appointee, Harry Blackmun wrote the majority opinion declaring the right to abortion to be constitutionally protected in *Roe v. Wade* in 1973, also against Nixon's wishes. Supreme Court justices are renowned for going their own way after being carefully selected for political reasons. Justices recurrently disappoint their presidential benefactors. More recently, Senator John Kerry of Massachusetts and a 2004 presidential contender expressed his opposition to "litmus tests" for the Supreme Court. He claimed not to be one of the "intolerant" sort who demand that nominees to the Court pledge their opposition to abortion rights. Yet, Kerry also announced that his prospective nominees to the Court should pledge their support for *Roe v. Wade*. Such a position does not involve a "litmus test," Kerry explained, because *Roe v. Wade* is "settled law." "I think people who go to the Supreme Court ought to interpret the Constitution as it is interpreted," he stated somewhat tautologically. Here is the rub, of course. Kerry's position, if strictly interpreted, suggests that no Supreme Court decision, however wrong-headed, should ever be reversed. Senator Kerry is unlikely to believe that himself. On the one hand, pundits and officials wax eloquent about the "living Constitution," the interpretation of which must change with the times. On the other hand, some issues are sacrosanct, with juridical decisions apparently fixed and immutable. Much depends, of course, on whose ox is being gored.

There has been considerable recent discussion about the Supreme Court as a democratic instrument of government. The stronger view would seem that it is democratic in its response to the larger fluctuations of public opinion, and its accessibility to changing presidential regimes. One should add, however, that for long stretches, especially from the 1880s to the 1930s, it lagged behind the best legal and judicial opinion. In essence what this means is that the Court is part of the changes and chances of its time, and also part of the power structure in the society as a whole. It was this quality, of being part of the power structure, that has made social thinkers periodically to attack it as "undemocratic." On balance one may say that the court is part of American democracy, but that it serves as a tempering influence both upon social and economic advance and also upon attacks on the freedom of the person. There can be no single formula for the judicial process, and judges cannot escape the difficult task of weighing their intellectual caution and skepticism against social boldness and moral faith in human possibility. One of the best instances of how the Court acted properly was the unanimous decision in the school segregation cases, written by Chief Justice Warren. It represented a break from the turn-of-the-century segregation decisions, and it broke with them sharply and boldly, without any apparatus of protective citation and without the hypocrisy of trying to distinguish so that an actual judicial change would seem to be no change at all. In this sense it was a political decision, yet not in the narrow spirit of being a partisan one. North and

South alike, Republicans and Democrats on the Court, joined in it because it aimed to sum up the conscience and progress of the nation in the area of civil rights, and because it boldly completed a long line of decisions that had been moving in the same direction. It went outside traditional legal categories by taking notice of studies by psychologists and sociologists which showed that separate and segregated schools could not be "equal" because the fact of their separateness was the fact that left a scar on the minds of the schoolchildren, black and white alike. Yet it was a decision reached not in haste but only after long deliberation; and it directed that the states and local school districts carry it out "with all deliberate speed."

In this sense the Court had an important role as national educator, trying to set standards of social control taken from the best levels of thought and asking the nation as a whole to measure itself by those standards. It cannot place itself in the vanguard of social thought, since its job is to distill what has already been thought and one and translate it into legal norms. But neither does it have to wait forever, until the bold has been frustrated and destroyed or until the novel has become archaic. Its task is a creative one in the sense that it must recognize when the action and thinking of popular majorities is valid for the long term, and when it is dangerous, must seize upon the thinking of the creative minority to hold it up as a standard for the majority to follow.

The National Court System

The lack of a national judiciary was one of the most serious weaknesses in the Articles of Confederation. The Founding Fathers corrected this shortcoming in Article III of the Constitution, establishing the Supreme Court and giving Congress the authority to create whatever lower courts are needed. Constitutional and special courts are the two types of federal courts that have subsequently been created. The constitutional courts are the District Courts, the Court of Appeals, the Supreme Court, the Court of Claims, the Customs Court, and the Court of Customs and Patent Appeals. The special courts are the territorial courts, the courts of the District of Columbia, and the Court of Military Appeals.

The constitutional courts have jurisdiction over a case either because of the subject matter or the parties involved. Some cases are within the exclusive jurisdiction of the federal courts while in others concurrent jurisdiction exists with state courts. Cases first heard in a court are within its original jurisdiction. Those heard on appeal are within its appellate jurisdiction. The 89 District Courts hear

most federal cases. The 11 Courts of Appeals hear appeals from the constitutional and special courts and the independent regulatory commissions. The Supreme Court generally chooses the cases it will hear from the lower federal courts and the highest state courts. It has original jurisdiction over cases against ambassadors and other public ministers and over cases involving one state against another state. The Court of Claims hears cases involving claims against the United States. The Customs Court hears appeals taken from the disputed decisions of customs officers. The Court of Customs and Patent Appeals hears appeals from decisions of the Customs Court, patent and trademark decisions of the Patent Office, and certain findings of the Tariff Commission.

The special courts are those Congress has created to exercise jurisdiction only in certain cases—cases involving subjects within the expressed powers of Congress. These courts have no jurisdiction under Article III of the Constitution. Acting under its authority to provide for the governing of the territories, Congress created local courts for the Panama Canal Zone, the Virgin Islands, Puerto Rico, and Guam. These territorial courts function in much the same manner as the local courts in the 50 states.

Acting under its power to exercise exclusive sovereignty over the District of Columbia, Congress has provided a judicial system for the nation's capital. The District Court and the Court of Appeals in the District hear many local cases as well as the cases they hear as constitutional courts. Congress has also created four local courts in the District: a Court of General Sessions, a Court of Appeals, a Juvenile Court, and a Tax Court.

Under its authority to make rules for the armed forces, Congress created the Court of Military Appeals in 1950, consisting of a chief judge and two associate judges appointed by the President, with Senate confirmation, to serve 15-year terms. It is independent of the executive and legislative branches, as are all United States courts, but is attached to the Defense Department for administrative purposes. Sometimes called the "GI Supreme Court," the Court of Military Appeals reviews the more serious court-martial decisions, that is, decisions in trials of members of the armed forces under an act of Congress, the Uniform Code of Military Justice.

The Tax Court is not a part of the national judiciary. Rather, it is an independent agency within the executive branch. It was first created as the Board of Tax Appeals in 1924, and it became the Tax Court in 1942. The court is composed of 16 judges appointed by the President, with Senate confirmation, for 12-year

Associate Justice Samuel A. Alito, Jr.
Courtesy of Judicial Watch

terms. Every second year the judges select one of their number to serve a term as chief judge. The court hears appeals from decisions of tax officers within the Treasury Department. Although their offices are in Washington, the judges hear cases throughout the country.

Sources of Law

American law is a collection of laws stemming from many sources, including common law; administrative law; court rules; statutory law, that is, laws made by legislatures; and constitutional law, deriving from written constitutions. The oldest of these is common law, which developed in England in the Middle Ages and was brought to the new world by English colonists. In the United States, common law is largely judge-made law, originating in both England and America. The legal concepts of precedent and *stare decisis* are crucial aspects of common law and essential to comprehending its essence. Whenever a court renders a legal decision, the latter becomes binding on the court and on inferior courts when the same issue again presents itself. The decision of the court is known as precedent, and the principle that inferior courts will comply with that decision when the issue is raised in the future is the doctrine of *stare decisis*. This term derives from the Latin phrase *stare decisis et non queta overa*, loosely translated as "stand by precedents and do not disturb settled points." The reasoning behind the doctrine is the legal necessity of promoting certainty, stability, and predictability.

Common law is somewhat fluid, transforming itself as societal norms and values change. As aptly stated by a court

United States

many years ago, "The common law of the land is based upon human experience in the unceasing effort of an enlightened people to ascertain what is right and just between men." Perhaps more important, common law must keep pace with technological advances. For example, with the coming of air and motor transport, a completely new assemblage of the common law became necessary. In *MacPherson v. Buick Motor Co.* (1916), a new common law right was accorded to a purchaser against the manufacturer for injuries sustained by allegedly inherent defects in merchandise purchased at retail.

The 13 original American colonies embraced the common law of the mother country long prior to achieving independence. Today, only Louisiana, with extensive French influence and whose legal system is based largely on French civil law, has not adopted the common law in some form. All other states have implemented common law, at least in part, but the actual application of the law varies considerably from state to state. Most states of the Union have expressly accepted common law by statute or by constitutional authority. Fewer that half the states still recognize common-law crimes, although civil common law and portions of the criminal common law remain in force.

Alteration and nullification of the common law are effected in myriad ways. In some instances, the courts have decided that the common law must be modified to accord with contemporary conditions. On occasion, aspects of the common law have been abolished. Because legislatures are tasked with the duty of making laws, they must make the final decisions about the status of common laws, unless the state constitution has special provisions in this regard. Some legislatures have explicitly afforded their judiciaries the authority to modify, partially eliminate, or even abolish the common law so long as the state constitution and the U.S. Constitution are not violated by so doing. Common law is customarily inferior to legislation, so if a legislature acts in an area previously dealt with by common law, the new statute will usually be controlling.

By definition, legislatures are responsible for the formation of law. Although legislative authority is substantial throughout America, it is constrained in a number of significant ways. The federal Constitution, as well as the constitutions of the respective states, restrains legislative power, as, for example, the Bill of Rights places limits upon national and state legislatures. For instance, the First Amendment to the U.S. Constitution prohibits governments from punishing people for exercising a choice of religion or speaking out on a controversial subject. If a legislature does enact a law vi-

olating a constitutional provision, it is the right, indeed, the duty of a federal court to declare the law null and void.

The constitutional framers appreciated the validity and significance of international law (or the "law of nations"), for they incorporated in the founding document the explicit directive that treaties form part of the supreme law of the land. In the *Paquete Habana* case (1900), the Supreme Court, reiterating a fundamental principle of U.S. law, wrote: "International law is part of our law, and must be ascertained and administered by the courts of justice of appropriate jurisdiction, as often as questions of right depending upon it are duly presented for their determination." The Court went on to say:

> Where there is no treaty, and no controlling executive or legislative act or judicial decision, resort must be had to the customs and usages of civilized nations; and, as evidence of these, to the works of jurists and commentators, who by years of labor, research, and experience, have made themselves peculiarly well acquainted with the subjects of which they treat. Such works are resorted to by judicial tribunals, not for the speculations of their authors concerning what the law ought to be, but for trustworthy evidence of what the law really is.

Some observers suggest that the United States has recently been moving away from its prior commitment to constructing an international order around multilateral institutions, rule-based agreements, and alliance partnerships. In the last years, it has displayed a marked, even assertive unilateralism in its rejection of pending international accords and treaties, including the Rome Statute of the International Criminal Court (ICC), the Kyoto Protocol on Climate Change, the Germ Weapons Convention, and the Programme of Action on Illicit Trade in Small and Light Arms. Defying many allies and the U.N. Security Council in 2003, the United States in cooperation with a "coalition of the willing" launched a preventive war against Iraq. President Bush captured the spirit of American unilateralism in stating that year, "When it comes to our security, we really don't need anybody's permission."

Written laws of municipalities are generally known as ordinances, which are passed by city councils and normally regulate zoning, building, construction, and other related matters. Many cities have criminal ordinances mirroring state statutes, but these apply only to those acts occurring within the city jurisdiction. Ordinances must not conflict with state or federal law, and any that are deemed in-

consistent with higher law will be invalidated by a court. States limit the authority of cities to punish for ordinance violations, and most city court trials are before a judge, not a jury.

Administrative agencies are federal, state, and local governmental entities, administering the affairs of the government. Although the distinction is often blurred, agencies generally fall into two categories, administrative and regulatory. The former put into effect government programs. For example, state departments of public welfare administer the distribution of public money to those deemed in need of assistance. By contrast, state medical licensing boards are regulatory, since their duty is to oversee and regulate the practice of medicine in the various states. Both regulatory and administrative agencies receive their powers from the legislative branch. Because legislatures seldom have the time or expertise to draft specific statutes, they often enact a very general statute granting administrative agencies the authority to make more precise laws, known as regulations.

THE STATES

State Constitutions

When the 13 colonies threw off the yoke of British rule in 1776 and declared their independence, each one faced the problem of establishing its own government. The Continental Congress advised each of the new states to adopt "such governments as shall, in the opinion of the representatives of the people, best conduce to the happiness and safety of their constituents in particular, and America in general." Even with their faults, most of the colonial charters served as models for the new state constitutions. Indeed, in Connecticut and Rhode Island the old charters seemed so well adapted to the needs of the day that they were carried over as constitutions almost without change. Connecticut did not adopt a new fundamental law until 1818, and Rhode Island not until 1842.

The adoption of the first state constitutions came about in a variety of ways. The people were given scant opportunity to approve or reject them. In Connecticut and Rhode Island the legislature made the minor changes in the old charters, and no special action by the people was involved in either state. In 1776 the Revolutionary legislatures in six states (Maryland, New Jersey, North Carolina, Pennsylvania, South Carolina, and Virginia) drew up new constitutions and proclaimed them to be in force. These new constitutions were not submitted to the voters for ratification. In Delaware (1776), New Hampshire (1776), Georgia (1777), and New York (1777) the constitutions were drafted by conventions called by the legislature, but none of these was submitted to the voters. In 1780 a popularly elected convention drafted the Massachusetts constitution, which was then submitted to the voters for ratification. Thus, Massachusetts set the pattern of popular participation that has been followed since.

As new states came into the Union and as constitutions of the older states were revised, popular participation became the rule. All of the state constitutions in existence were drafted by assemblies representing the people, and most of them have been approved by the people. Contents of the first state constitutions varied greatly in detail. They also had many general features in common. The people were recognized as the sole source for governmental authority, and the power of the new state governments were strictly limited. Some of the documents began with a lengthy bill of rights, and all of them made clear that the sovereign people had inalienable rights that must always be respected. For their time, the first state constitutions were quite democratic. Each, however, contained several provisions (and some important omissions) which today would be considered legally and politically dubious. For example, none of them provided for complete religious freedom, each set rigid qualifications for voting and office holding, and all gave property owners a highly preferred status.

As discussed above, the U.S. Constitution has been changed over the years by the formal and informal amending process. The state constitutions have been subjected to both processes also. But the informal amendment process has not been nearly so significant at the state level as it has been nationally. For one thing, the state constitutions have been and are less flexible than the national document. The structure, powers, and procedures of state government are usually treated at some length in state constitutions. The state courts have often proved a block to the wide use of the informal amendment process. Unlike the federal courts, they have been generally quite strict in their roles as constitutional interpreters. The states have had to rely mostly on formal amendments as the chief method of constitutional change. When many changes are to be made, a convention is usually called to revise the existing constitution or to frame a new one. For one or a few changes, the simpler device of partial amendment is commonly used.

The legislature in every state may call a constitutional convention. Regularly, the legislature's call for a convention must be submitted to the people for their approval or rejection. In ten states the constitution requires that the question of calling a con-

vention must be submitted to the voters at regular intervals. Three elections are commonly held in connection with the work of a convention: (1) the vote at which the people authorize the calling of a convention, (2) the popular election of delegates, and (3) the admission of the convention's product to the people. On occasion, one or more of these votes may be dispensed with. Louisiana's constitution provides an example. The legislature's call for a convention was approved at the regular election in November 1920. The next month the voters elected delegates who then met in convention from March 1 to June 18, 1921. Then the convention itself, acting as "the people of the State of Louisiana in Constitutional Convention assembled," adopted the new constitution for the State.

The most recently adopted of the 50 state constitutions were each written by conventions: Alaska's and Hawaii's became effective when the two newest states entered the Union in 1959, and Michigan's new constitution took effect on January 1, 1964. The partial amendment procedure involves two formal steps: proposal and ratification. In each of the 50 states the legislatures may propose amendments to the constitution. And in 13 of the states the people themselves may also do so through the initiative. Beginning with Oregon in 1902, 13 states provide for the proposal of constitutional amendments by the people themselves. This procedure is known as the initiative because the amendments are initiated by the voters. Any individual or group may draft a proposal and then circulate initiative petitions in an attempt to secure the signatures of a specified number of voters.

State Legislatures

The size of the legislature, the details of its organization and its procedures, and the frequency and the length of its sessions, and even the official name given to it vary among the states. But the basic reason for its existence is everywhere the same: the legislature is the lawmaking branch of state government. It is charged with the high duty of translating the will of the people into the public policy of the state. The legislature has often been described as "the powerhouse of state government." Through the exercise of its lawmaking powers it creates the energy necessary to keep the government machinery of the state and its local units operating.

With the exception of Nebraska, all the state legislatures are bicameral. Nebraska's voters approved the creation of a unicameral legislature in 1934, and the first session of that body met in 1937. Over the years, many have supported bicameralism at the state level because they

advocated a "little federal plan" for their own state's legislature. That is, they favored two houses, with one based upon area and the other upon population. Otherwise, they argued, the more populous cities would so dominate the legislature that rural interests would be virtually unrepresented. The U.S. Supreme Court ruled this view unconstitutional in 1964 by holding that the 14th Amendment's Equal Protection Clause requires that both houses of a state's legislature be based upon population.

On what particular basis should the seats in the legislature be distributed (apportioned) within the state? Should they be distributed among legislative districts of substantially equal population? Or should the apportionment be on the basis of area, with districts drawn along economic and geographic lines? Or should some combination of both population and area be the basis of apportionment?

These are crucial questions. The answers determine which groups and regions in a state control the legislative machinery and shape its public policies. Each state's constitution makes some provision for apportionment. Although there are wide variations among them, most follow the principle of "one person, one vote" and provide for population as either the only or the major basis for apportionment. Most state constitutions assign the task of reapportionment to the legislature itself. That is, they direct the legislature to make periodic adjustments in the distribution of its seats to account for increases, decreases, and shifts of population within the state.

Each state has trained assistants who put into proper form the ideas that members wish to enact into law; they are usually connected with a legislative reference bureau or the attorney general's office. Many states now maintain a special bureau, which is either a division of the state library or has a library of its own to assist members. Specialists collect reference materials such as court decisions, newspaper clippings, magazine articles, and books on government and its problems, official reports, party platforms, governors' messages, information on other states, and any other material that might be valuable to legislators. Its experts prepare reports, draft bills, and generally assist the members with legislative problems. Bills are often prepared by state executive agencies, lobbyists, and private persons and handed to a member to introduce. Just as in Congress, hundreds of "by-request" bills turn up in every session.

Members of either house may introduce as many bills as they choose. Important bills, however, are commonly prepared by a committee and introduced by its

United States

GENERAL NOVEMBER ELECTION
County of Ingham, Tuesday, Nov. 5, 1968

PARTISAN BALLOT
A

Presidential election, 1968

ten enjoy greater freedom of action at the state level. Then, too, many legislators are not as experienced as most members of Congress, nor are they provided with the kind of office staffs, committee assistants, and other help available to Congresspersons. Often state legislators find that they must rely on lobbyists for information on particular bills and even about the legislature itself.

State Governors

The governor in each of the 50 states occupies an office which is the direct descendant of the earliest executive office in America. The history of the post dates back to the first colonial governorship, established in Virginia in 1607. Much of the resentment that finally brought on the Revolutionary War was directed at the royal governors and, when the first state constitutions were written, most powers granted to the original state governments were given to the legislature. The governor for the most part had rather meager authority. In every state except Massachusetts and New York he was chosen by the legislature. Only in Massachusetts and South Carolina did the governor have the veto power.

The governor is chosen by popular vote in every state. In all but three, a candidate must have only a plurality (more votes than any other candidate) in order to be elected. In Georgia, Mississippi, and Vermont, a candidate must receive a majority of all the votes cast. The powers of a state governor can be classified under three major headings: (1) the executive powers, (2) the legislative powers, (3) the judicial powers. The governor also performs a great many miscellaneous jobs. In taking "care that the laws be faithfully executed," the governor must direct the day-to-day work of the several state administrative agencies. The governor's ability to supervise state administration depends in large part on just how much the constitution and the legislature allow the executive to control the agencies within the executive branch. The governor's ability to supervise the agencies also depends upon the extent of the power to appoint and remove principal subordinates. When governors have little formal power to control state administrations, they are still able to do so because of the position as party leader and as representative of all of the people of the state.

As part of the executive duties, the governor is responsible for general law enforcement in the state. In its broadest sense, the job of law enforcing is done by all of the state's administrative agencies. For example, the State Board of Medical Examiners is enforcing the law when it examines and licenses doctors who wish to

chairman. To introduce bills, the members merely file them with the clerk. Some legislatures prohibit the introduction of bills after the legislature has been in session a certain number of days; others require that bills of a local or private character must be announced in the locality to be affected; and still others require that local bills receive a two-thirds vote of each house instead of simply a bare majority, which is sufficient for public bills.

As is the case in Congress, lobbyists and special interest groups seek to influence state legislatures. Many organized interests in a state are represented by one or more lobbyists at the state capitol. Lobbyists are usually more influential and effective in the states than they are in Washington. One reason for this is that the work of the legislature seldom receives as much publicity and public attention as does that of Congress. Thus, lobbyists of-practice in the state. In its particular sense, the governor's overall responsibility for law enforcement involves the enforcing of criminal law. Once again the governor does not usually have the authority to match the responsibility. The chief legal officer, the attorney general, is popularly elected in most states. Most local law enforcement officers, such as the sheriff, constable, coroner, and district attorney, are also elective.

Each state's constitution makes the governor commander-in-chief of the state militia. Although defense is a function of the national government, each state has a militia to maintain peace within that state. In 1916 Congress provided that each state's militia should consist of able-bodied men between 17 and 45 years of age. The National Guard is the formal, organized part of the militia. It is trained by the regular Army and Air Force and supported by federal grants-in-aid. In cases of national emergency, the president may call it into federal service.

When the state's National Guard units are not in federal service, they are commanded by the governor, who is assisted by an adjutant-general. Many governors have used (called out) the National Guard to deal with emergencies such as prison riots and strike disturbances, to aid in evacuation and relief work, to prevent looting during and after floods, violent storms, and other natural disasters, and to augment the state police in campaigns to reduce holiday traffic mishaps.

As chief executive officers, state governors have legislative powers consisting of (1) message power to the state legislature, (2) special session authority, (3) the veto power. The value of the governor's power to send messages—that is, to recommend legislation to the legislature—depends largely upon the governor's personality, popularity, and party position. A strong governor is often able to accomplish a great deal by sending messages and addressing the legislature in person. Governors will use informal pressures to advance their programs also. Every state affords the governor the power to call the legislature into special session. In several states the constitution forbids the legislature to consider any subjects at a special session except those for which the governor called it into session. Governors have often found this power an important weapon in their dealings with the legislature. For example, governors have often forced a reluctant legislature to pass a measure by threatening to call a special session if the regular session adjourns without having done so. Governors have the power to veto bills passed by the legislature. This power, including the threat to use it, is often the most po-

tent weapon governors have for influencing the legislature.

ELECTIONS IN THE UNITED STATES

The two major systems for choosing legislators in representative democracies are the proportional representation (PR) system and the single-member district (SMD) system. The use of one system or the other leads to important differences in election outcomes, although the actual effects on public policy are perennially debated. PR accords each party a legislative seat proportion roughly equal to its vote proportion. PR elections differ substantially from SMD elections, which tend to under-represent minor parties and over-represent major ones. The resulting fractionalization of parties under the PR system usually means that no party has enough seats to govern alone and hence

necessitates the formation of "coalition governments." The lack of a majority in turn reinforces the importance of minor parties. Compared to those in SMD systems, politicians in PR systems have a reduced incentive to belong to a major party instead of a minor one, and hence minor parties are easier to form.

Single-Member Districts

With SMD systems, a country or state is divided into a number of election districts, although it should be pointed out that countries using PR can also be districted, with party slates running in each district. Each district's voters usually elect only one representative, and as the name of the system connotes, each district sends a single member to the legislature. Elections in the United States House of Representatives clearly exhibit the enhancement of the majority party's legislative strength and the subsequent decline of the minor-

United States

ity party's vigor. Elections to the House are largely two-party contests between a Republican and a Democrat, and it seldom pays to run on a third-party ticket in SMD elections. Fielding as a candidate from a smaller party is certainly more likely to be profitable in PR systems. There are 435 districts from which American citizens elect members of the House of Representatives. Theoretically, if Democratic candidates in a particular congressional election received 51% of the vote nationally, and if they also won 51% of the vote in each district, then they would win all 435 votes in the House. Of course, the reason why Republicans will win a certain number of seats with 49% of the national vote is that Republican voters are concentrated more heavily in some districts than in others. The following example demonstrates the comparative tendencies of the two systems. Elections to the city council of New York City in 1935 were from SMDs. The results were: Democrats, 63; Republicans, 2. In 1937, the voters of New York, having reduced the number of members, decided to try a system of proportional representation. The results of a characteristic election (1945) were: Democrats, 14; Republicans, 3; American Labor Party, 2; Communist, 2; Liberals, 2. The two Communists being unwelcome to New York's staid citizens, the city beat a retreat back to SMD. Results in the next election in 1949: Democrats 24; Republicans, 1. In a word, SMD can be rough for second parties, but fatal for third parties.

Two other potential distorting features of SMD exist as well and have been fairly common over the years in American politics. These are the gerrymander and malapportionment. The SMD system requires that someone draw district boundaries. For the House of Representatives and for the state legislatures, this is the legal prerogative of state governments. Article I, Section 4 of the Constitution specifies that

"the Times, Places and Manner of holding Elections for Senators and Representatives shall be prescribed in each State by the Legislature thereof; but the Congress may at any time by Law make or alter such Regulations, except as to the Places of choosing Senators." Hence, within the strictures of Supreme Court and congressional action, state legislatures draw up congressional, as well as their own, district boundaries. City council members, for their part, usually draw district lines for city elections.

It should come as no surprise that legislators try to draw district lines in a manner favorable to themselves, so the party members controlling the legislature often contrive district boundaries to maximize the number of congressional or legislative districts their party can win. For example, if the citizens of a state are entitled to send five representatives to the House, a "fair" districting would divide the state like a pie into five wedges, all of which have an equal number of voters as well as an equal number of Democratic and Republican voters. With this kind of districting, party members can expect each congressional election to be a toss-up. If the Republicans control the state legislature, though, they are likely to enact a districting plan providing more weight to the rural areas, where the voters, by stereotype, are faithful Republicans. But if Democrats are in charge, they are inclined to give more influence to urban areas, whose voters also by stereotype are loyal Democrats. Redistricting, as with the apportionment of House seats among states, occurs every ten years if population changes require it.

Observers call this practice of districting for political advantage "gerrymandering" after an early governor of Massachusetts, Elbridge Gerry. The governor's name lives on in infamy in political history after he helped redistrict the Massachusetts state legislature in 1811–12 to the unabashed

benefit of his party. One district with a distinctly reptilian shape inspired a perceptive journalist to coin the name from Gerry and salamander. The reptilian form resulted because people do not neatly and conveniently distribute themselves over landmasses by party affiliation. Political persuasions of populations are many and varied, so districts with little rhyme or reason emerge, and shapes of apparent meaninglessness or outright grotesqueness are not unknown.

The gerrymander is ultimately an intractable problem of a district system, since few court cases exist for guidance, and people frequently disagree about districting standards. Some states require districts to be contiguous and compact, while others consider additional topological properties. On occasion, legislators turn over the districting task to nonpartisan commissions, and computer programs now assist in districting. But who then is to guard the guardians? If legislators employ impartial consultants, how do they instruct them? Should districts produce representatives who reflect a state's party, racial, ethnic, or economic divisions? Any standard is likely to help one party at the expense of the other, so if political districting is left to political persons, these are sure to act in their own interest.

Another problem arising in SMD systems is legislative apportionment. If a state has, say, one million residents and a legislature of 100 representatives elected from single-member districts, and the same number of persons (10,000) lived in each district, then the state would have perfect apportionment, and the districting would accord with the principle of "one person, one vote." Malapportionment would occur in the event of grossly disparate numbers of persons in different districts. Until the 1960s, malapportionment was widespread in the United States. By 1960, the largest congressional district in each state with more than one district was twice as populous as its smallest district. The Connecticut state legislature's largest district was 242 times as large as its smallest district. The figures for the Nevada senate were over 200 to one; for the Rhode Island Senate, 141 to one; for the Georgia Senate, nine to one. The malapportionment stemmed largely from migration from the farms to urban areas. Rural legislators refused to reapportion themselves out of a job. Until 1962, the most recent legislative reapportionment in Alabama, Delaware, Indiana, and Vermont had been carried through in 1920.

Congressional Elections

Article I, Section 2 of the Constitution describes the rules for electing representa-

Electoral College votes in first decade of 21st century

tives. The Constitution requires, first, that voters choose representatives every two years in popular elections. Second, representatives must be twenty-five years old upon taking office and must have been citizens of the United States for at least seven years. They need not be residents of the districts that elect them, but they must be residents of the district's state. Third, the governor must call an election to fill a vacancy in any state's congressional delegation. Finally, Article I, Section 4 affords state legislators control over "The Times, Places, and Manner of holding elections for Senators and Representatives," yet "the Congress may at any time by Law make or alter such Regulations, except as to the Places of choosing Senators." By Article I, Section 5, furthermore, "Each House shall be the Judge of the Elections, Returns, and Qualifications of its own members. . ." Hence, state governments are a first level of authority for congressional elections, and the members of each house are the final authority.

Presidential Elections

Procedures for electing presidents and vice presidents are more intricate than those for the House and Senate. The original constitutional provisions are listed in Article II, Section 1 and specify that state legislatures should determine how representatives to a national electoral college should be chosen. The Founding Fathers created the electoral college as yet another check on the concentration or abuse of power, providing that the states would select presidential electors in whatever manner they wished. In fact, the framers assumed the process would induce most state electors to vote for their respective state's favorite son. They envisioned the frequent occurrence that no candidate would win a majority of the popular vote. The House of Representatives would then make the choice, with each state delegation casting one vote. This procedure would be a means of counterbalancing the influence of the most populous states. The plan seemed to offer something to everybody, since large states would wield their influence, yet small states would have a minimum of three votes regardless of population, since every state would have two senate votes and one for every representative. The small states would together exercise considerable clout in the event of an election going to the House. What the constitutional framers apparently did not foresee was the rise of national political parties that would support a list of candidates. The electoral college reflects the effort to strengthen the federal system and provide representation to all sections of the country but also manifests a certain distrust of the "masses" who, the framers

"Bush or Kerry—America votes today." All eyes are on American presidential elections. Article on right: America is Everywhere.

feared, might be swayed by regional demagogues. Some of the framers feared the people could become "dupes of pretended patriots" and most harbored reservations about the direct election of a president.

Accordingly, Article II mandates the following procedure. First, each state legislature controls the process of appointing electors, and each state would have a number of electors equal to its number of senators (two) plus its number of representatives, and thus at least three. Second, if one candidate has a majority of votes based on the number of electors, and no other candidate has an equal number of votes, then the majority candidate becomes president; if two candidates have an equal number of votes, then state delegations in the House of Representatives, each delegation casting one vote, would choose one of these candidates to become president. Third, in the event no candidate has a majority vote, then the House of Representatives, voting again as state delegations, would choose the President from among the two candidates with the greatest number of votes. Finally, whoever had the second most electoral votes would be chosen Vice-President, unless a tie occurred for Vice-President, in which case the Senate would choose the Vice-President from between the tied candidates.

This arrangement functioned reasonably well in the first years of the republic.

In the elections of 1788 and 1792, George Washington received a vote from every elector, since these voted more than once, and there was sufficient division among all other candidates for Washington to receive the clear majority. In the election of 1796, John Adams received a majority and Thomas Jefferson placed second. They became president and vice president, respectively. By 1800, however, two political parties emerged, and their leaders attempted to exploit presidential election rules to their advantage. Party members successfully sought to commit electors prior to the election. Federalist party electors were to vote for Adams and Thomas Pinckney, while Democratic-Republican electors, who were in a majority, were to vote for Jefferson and Aaron Burr. The Federalists intended to elect Adams president, and Thomas Pinckney vice president. The Democratic-Republicans intended to elect Jefferson president, and Burr vice president. Nearly every elector followed this pattern, but presidential votes were indistinguishable from vice-presidential votes. Both Jefferson and Burr received a majority and an equal number of votes, throwing the election into the House of Representatives. There, Federalist party members tried to reverse Democratic-Republican objectives by electing Burr president, and Jefferson vice president. Although the ploy failed and Jeffer-

United States

son was elected president after all, the attendant intrigue and confusion prompted the adoption of the Twelfth Amendment to the Constitution in 1804.

This amendment required distinct balloting in presidential and vice-presidential voting. According to the amendment, the presidential candidate who has the greatest number of votes will be president "if such number be a majority of the whole number of electors appointed." In the absence of a majority, the House of Representatives, voting as state delegations with one vote for each delegation, chooses the president from among the three candidates with the most electoral votes. If the House fails to choose a president by January 20, then the vice president becomes the acting president. Moreover, a vice-presidential candidate with a majority of the whole number of electors appointed assumes that office. In the event of no majority candidate for vice president, then the Senate chooses a vice president from the two candidates with the greatest number of electoral votes.

The electoral college is a source of continuing controversy in American politics, especially after the 2000 election, when the Republican candidate, George W. Bush, who became president by virtue of his narrow win in the electoral college, won fewer popular votes than did his opponent, Democratic contender Al Gore. The electoral college is comprised of presidential electors, chosen by elections held in each state. The number of presidential electors in each state is equal to the number of representatives and senators from each state except in the District of Columbia, which has three votes for a total of 538 electors. The electors meet following the general election and cast their ballots for president. They then cast a separate ballot for vice president. All states, except for Maine, operate under a unit rule, which means the candidate who gets the most popular votes (plurality) receives all the electoral votes (unanimity) from that state. The chief rationale of the unit rule is to enhance the importance of each state. Because every candidate has a separate slate of electors, voters, in effect, vote for the slate of candidates pledged to the candidate when they go to the polls. Yet, not all states require the electors to vote for their party's candidate, producing occasional "unfaithful" electors, as happened in 1968, 1976, and 1980. If no candidate receives an absolute majority of the electoral vote (270), then the election would be decided by the House of Representatives, using a rule giving each state one vote, but this has not happened since 1804.

The principal source of controversy about the electoral college is its ability to produce presidents not only who have less than a majority of the popular vote, when three or more candidates are campaigning, but who also have fewer popular votes than their major opponent. This anomaly occurred twice prior to the contested election of 2000. In the election of 1876, Rutherford B. Hayes received 48% of the popular vote and a majority of the electoral vote, even though his major opponent, John Tilden, received 51% of the popular vote. In the election of 1888, Benjamin Harrison received 48% of the popular vote and a majority in the electoral college, even though his opponent, Grover Cleveland, received 48.66% of the popular vote. Other presidents elected with a plurality but less than a majority of the popular vote include James Polk (1844), Zachary Taylor (1848), James Buchanan (1856), Abraham Lincoln (1860), James Garfield (1880), Grover Cleveland (1884 and 1892), Woodrow Wilson (1912 and 1916), Harry Truman (1948), John Kennedy (1960), Richard Nixon (1968), and William Clinton (1992). These unusual results occur primarily because of the unit rule or "winner take all" method whereby the plurality winner in a state receives all the state's electoral votes. Secondarily, small states have an advantage in the two extra votes they receive beyond what population alone would permit.

Primaries

All states now use primaries to select at least some candidates for public office. A primary is essentially a polling held before a general election for the purpose of nominating a party's candidate for office. In order to make the parties more "democratic" and to reduce the influence of party organizations, reformers have advocated a direct primary where the voters choose the candidates rather than the party caucus. The method most widely employed, however, is the closed primary where only registered party members can vote. Of course, this method excludes a sizeable segment of the electorate who are registered independents. Some states circumvent this problem by permitting independents to vote in party primaries. These are open primaries allowing voters regardless of their registration to select in which party's primary they wish to participate. In blanket primaries, used in a few states, voters get only one ballot listing all the candidates by party affiliation for each office. People can vote in only one party primary per office, but they can switch from one party to the other as they move down the ballot. Several states also have a nonpartisan primary, open to all voters. Some states use conventions to name a candidate or candidates to run in the primaries, and anyone whom the convention fails to nominate but who nonetheless wished to get on the primary ballot must collect petitions. This is known as the challenge primary.

Primaries are not without supporters and detractors. Supporters assert that the primary system better represents the voting public, affording a larger number of people the opportunity to participate in the nominating procedure than does the caucus process in which only party leaders participate. The primary system may also allow a greater diversity of candidates to run for office. Moreover, because the media are so crucial in projecting the qualities (or lack thereof) of the candidates to the public, proponents of the system argue that primary appearances are a useful means of judging the character of candidates.

Detractors of the primary system argue that the quality of voter participation often suffers in primaries. As they would have it, voters are more inclined to pay attention to personalities than to issues, and their knowledge of the issues is often distorted through media coverage. Critics also assert that primaries are often poorly scheduled and the entire process is too long and tiresome, resulting in the unfortunate consequence of a lethargic electorate. In the eyes of many foreigners, the primary system, if not the electoral system more widely, enables unknown and largely inexperienced candidates to aspire and rise to high political office.

The 2008 Presidential Election

Senator Barack Obama of Illinois clinched the Democratic presidential nomination the first week of June 2008, an historic step toward his once-unlikely objective of becoming the nation's first black president. A defeated Hillary Rodham Clinton maneuvered for the vice presidential spot on the Democratic ticket, and eventually settled for secretary of state in the Obama administration.

Obama's primary victory led to a five-month political showdown with Republican Senator John McCain of Arizona, a race between a 46-year-old opponent of the Iraq War and a 71-year-old former Vietnam prisoner of war and staunch supporter of current U.S. military operations. McCain and Obama agreed that the presidential race would focus on change. "But the choice is between the right change and the wrong change, between going forward and going backward," McCain argued.

Obama sealed the party nomination based on primary elections, state Democratic caucuses and delegates' public declarations as well as support from over two dozen delegates and "superdelegates" who privately confirmed their intentions. Obama, a first-term senator who was virtually unknown on the national stage five years ago, defeated Clinton, the former first lady and one-time campaign frontrunner, in a 17-month marathon for the Democratic nomination.

The Illinois senator's success amounted to a victory of hope over experience, earned across an enervating 56 primaries and caucuses that sorely tested the political skills and human endurance of all involved. Obama stood for hope, and change. Clinton was the candidate of experience, immediately ready, she repeatedly pointed out, to serve in the Oval Office. Together, they drew record turnouts in primary after primary—more than 34 million voters in all, independents and Republicans as well as Democrats.

The contest between a black man and a white woman exposed deep racial and gender divisions within the party. Obama drew strength from blacks, and from the younger, more liberal and wealthier voters in many states. Older, less affluent voters, and women preferred Clinton.

Obama won an historic victory in November 2008, becoming the first black president of the United States. It is remarkable that when the president was born, in 1961, many states still enforced segregation, disallowed mixed-race marriages, and restricted voting rights. After the election, America could more credibly claim to be a truly multi-ethnic, color-blind society.

The presidential transition was one of the most challenging in history, quite possibly in a league with that of 1860. For the first time, a new president assumed control in the middle of war and recession. Moreover, the outgoing and incoming administrations had to oversee a massive rescue of the financial services sector. The president and president-elect moved quickly and efficiently, though; some Bush aides stayed on for a while; and Obama tapped many former Clinton officials for the new administration. With economic issues so pressing, Obama began planning early for his first 100 days in office. Fighting the recession and stimulating growth dominated Obama's first year in office. Following his election, Obama signaled moderation early on, telling business and labor leaders that he would go easy on divisive issues, above all, in the interest of battling the economic downturn. Obama governed largely from the center, as he has little choice in the matter. His historic victory was built on a broad coalition, one transcending young and minority voters. He won over 55% of moderates and independents, as well as nearly half of college-educated whites.

The size of government grew substantially in the first months of 2009. Congress passed a huge stimulus package exceeding $500 billion during the first 100 days of the new administration. The package includes over $100 billion for road and bridge

Presidential contenders 2008: Barack Obama, John McCain, Hillary Clinton

work, $15 billion a year in green technology investment, and multiple billions for school repairs, classroom computers, infrastructure to bring the Internet to rural areas, assistance for states to pay soaring Medicare costs, and a middle-class tax reduction. The package comes on top of the $700 billion debt rescue plan approved under the prior administration. Increased government spending resulted in a deficit exceeding $1.5 trillion by 2011, enough to push the national debt past $16 trillion.

The 2012 Presidential Election

President Obama won a decisive re-election victory in November 2012, overcoming the twin obstacles of the worst recession since the Great Depression and a country divided over his policies. Obama became the first president since Franklin D. Roosevelt to win re-election with unemployment higher than 7.2 percent, propped up by a stubbornly improving economy and voters' apparent confidence that he better understands their needs and, as he repeatedly intoned, that he required more time.

The Obama movement has won more time. Though the optimism that lifted Obama to an historic victory four years ago has been muted, and though the country remains rattled by a sluggish economy, a virtual electoral standoff cut the president's way, allowing him another term to realize the potential his supporters see in him. The United States is headed into a second presidential term much like the end of the first: a divided, gridlocked government facing monumental challenges and vexed questions about whether the country's leaders are big enough to tackle them. The country kept the status quo, with a Democratic president, a GOP-controlled House and a narrow Democratic majority in the Senate.

Pessimism over the economy ran high among voters, but half of all voters said former President George W. Bush was largely to blame for economic problems. Mitt Romney, the former Massachusetts governor, campaigned on his business credentials, insisting he was better equipped to turn around the economy, and the unpopularity of Obama's health care law. In the end, the law, which helped cost Democrats a lock on Congress in 2010, was low in voters' minds. The 2012 presidential election was the climactic conclusion to a campaign that burned for nearly two years, starting with the Republican primary, its colorful cast each taking a brief turn at the top, inducing Romney to take a harder line on issues, none more damaging than immigration.

Obama and his allies spent tens of millions of dollars on negative ads based on Romney's career at the private equity firm Bain Capital, painting him as a heartless corporate raider who squeezed jobs for profit. The race appeared to be over heading into the autumn, amid Romney's failure to connect with voters and self-inflicted political wounds, until the first debate in October. Romney dominated a lethargic opponent and was rewarded with a boost in the polls. Obama rebounded in the next two debates and the race slipped back into a dead heat as early voting began.

REVVED UP WITH SOMEWHERE TO GO

Candidates in U.S. elections use resources such as money, time, and paid volunteer labor that they must decide how to allocate efficiently and within a specified budget. Allocation strategies concern decisions such as how much time to spend campaigning in various areas of

United States

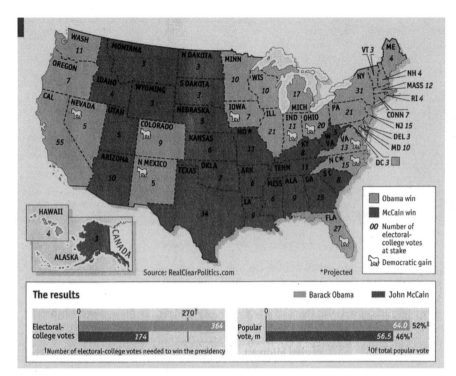

Source: RealClearPolitics.com   *Projected

The results   ■ Barack Obama ■ John McCain

	0	270†	
Electoral-college votes		364	
	174		

†Number of electoral-college votes needed to win the presidency

	0		
Popular vote, m		64.0	52%‡
	56.5		46%‡

‡Of total popular vote

Source: *The Economist*

a constituency, what part of limited funds to use for billboards, bumper stickers, and radio and television advertisements, and at what point in the campaign and at what rate to spend these resources.

Some allocation strategy dilemmas have intuitive solutions. For example, as a general rule presidential candidates should spend little time campaigning in states they are certain to win or lose. Allocation strategies figure prominently in primary elections and caucuses. "Momentum" waxes and wanes in importance as the candidates play out a set of dynamic games over a period of time. Here we will consider the allocation factors that can assist or injure the chances of candidates. Money tends to drive modern campaigns. Thirty-second television and radio ads, websites, pollsters, and plane tickets are all essential to the conduct of a congressional race. Ready cash allows the candidate to finance these considerable expenses. Of course, the need for campaign finances applies to incumbent and challenger alike. Why then does a sitting congressman, for example, hold a distinct advantage in this area?

First, incumbents have the length of their term to continue tapping donors who contributed during their campaign. Representatives thus have two years from the time of their elections to raise money for the next contest, while senators can build their war chests over a six-year period. Former Senator Bill Bradley of New Jersey estimated that he needed to raise $20,000 per week throughout his term

in order to have sufficient funds for the following election. By contrast, challengers are rarely identified years in advance. Thus, the challenger must raise significant amounts of money on a much more compressed schedule as the primaries approach.

A second fundraising advantage of incumbency is the primary, or lack thereof, prior to the general election. An incumbent is far less likely to face an opponent in his party's primary than a challenger. The challenger must deplete some, or even most, of his funds just to win his party's nomination. Therefore, the challenger must compete in, and spend money on, two elections, held just months apart. The sitting legislator, with an uncontested party nomination, is free throughout primary season to raise money and focus his expenditures on the fall general election.

Third, incumbents are usually proven fundraisers and nothing quite substitutes for experience. Incumbents previously learned which individuals, constituencies, and organizations are both enthusiastic about their candidacy, and also able monetarily to contribute to its success. Sitting legislators can focus their advertisements and fundraising events, and "hunt where the ducks are." As one example, Senator John McCain received $100,000 for three consecutive campaigns from influential businessman Charles Keating. The challenger, by contrast, must use much more trial and error in order to find his own financial supporters. Special interest groups make fundraising even easier for the in-

cumbent, as they often seek out the legislator. These groups often donate to both candidates, in order to ensure access following the election. Nonetheless, they support incumbents by a ratio of seven to one. Thus, a large and often decisive financial advantage lies with the incumbent.

Another area that favors incumbents is political pork. "Citizens Against Government Waste," a watchdog group, qualifies domestic spending as "pork" when it meets some or all of the following criteria:

- Requested by only one chamber of Congress;
- Not specifically authorized;
- Not competitively awarded;
- Not requested by the President;
- Greatly exceeds the President's budget request or the previous year's funding;
- Not the subject of congressional hearings; and
- Serves only a local or special interest.

As legislators serve for several consecutive terms, they rise in seniority and assume leadership positions in committees and subcommittees. These legislative groups determine where and how public dollars are spent. Self-interested chairmen reward their constituents and do much to ensure reelection by steering both essential and questionable projects towards their districts and states. The 2004 contest between former Senate Minority Leader Tom Daschle of South Dakota and his Republican challenger highlighted this incumbent advantage. The pithy rhetorical question posed by political writer Joseph Bottum encapsulates the matter: "If Daschle's positions on abortion and gun control differ from those of his constituents, if he lives a high-celebrity life in Washington while posing as a populist at home, what's that compared with a federal-pork power that John Thune will need ten to twenty years in the Senate to match?" Yet, in Daschle's 2004 reelection bid, other factors outweighed the incumbent advantage, not least that Daschle was targeted by a highly organized Republican Party.

Dan Rostenkowski, as chairman of the House Ways and Means Committee, delivered large amounts of pork to his constituents in the Illinois 5th District in the 1970s and 1980s. Two billion dollars for the Deep Tunnel project in Chicago and the annual $90 million tax assessed on O'Hare International Airport travelers are but two of the hundreds of projects proudly itemized in his fifteen page, "Accomplishments of Congressman Dan Rostenkowski on Behalf of the Chicago Metropolitan Area (Partial List)" brochure. The congressman's fiscal might did much to ensure his reelection for seventeen terms.

Some incumbents find themselves facing little or no competition in the general election. Five of Georgia's thirteen sitting congressmen faced no opponent in the November 2004 contests. Twenty-seven of New York's twenty-nine districts had two or more candidates seeking the congressional seat. Most of these races were not truly competitive, however, as the challenger raised little or no money to battle the incumbent. Only nine of the New York congressional races pitted two candidates who each raised $100,000 or more.

One reason that an incumbent faces no opposition is his popularity, whether for pork delivery, personal charisma, national stature, or other reasons. Another reason, far more prevalent, is that the congressman resides in a safe district. Demographics are often reliable indicators of voting patterns; urban blacks vote overwhelming Democratic, while married whites are a reliable Republican base, as two examples. State legislatures use gerrymandering, the carving of odd-shaped federal districts in order to concentrate or disburse certain demographic groups. The state's majority party seeks to maximize its number of safe districts, while necessarily conceding some districts to the opposing party. Those who win their party's nominations in safe districts are positioned for long careers in the House of Representatives. These incumbent advantages resulted in recent House and Senate reelection rates of greater than ninety percent.

General election challengers can avail themselves of certain opportunities, though. It is ironic that a lack of legislative experience may actually aid the challenger. Challengers can claim one or both of the coveted titles of "independent" and "outsider," hammering home the point on the campaign trail. They can use perfect hindsight to point out the poor decisions and ill-advised votes of their incumbent opponents. Since they have no voting records to pick apart, incumbents cannot respond in kind. Connecticut Senator Joseph Lieberman writes that many of his congressional peers believe, with good reason, that a single vote would come back to haunt them on television in the following election. Former Arkansas Senator Dale Bumpers recalled:

> The most politically volatile issue I faced in my twenty-four years in the Senate was the vote on the Panama Canal treaties. I voted for the treaties [to ultimately return control of the canal to the Panamanian government] knowing that should I have a fairly well-financed opponent in 1980, I would surely be defeated on that one vote. For three weeks prior to the vote, my office received three

Former Secretary of State Hillary Clinton   Courtesy of the Department of State

thousand calls and letters a day, ninety-nine percent of which were in opposition to the treaties. . . . My pollster said my vote cost me ten percent of the vote in my race in 1980, five percent in 1986, and three percent in 1992.

Because few challengers have had to compromise in order to pass legislation, they can issue rather lofty statements and ideals as their platforms. The incumbent must spend much of the campaign defending his own, often imperfect, record.

The next step is an actual strategy of ambiguity, employed far more frequently by challengers than incumbents. Inconsistency in elections can be profound. Candidates benefit by inconsistency by saying little about public policy issues. Instead, they salute the flag, sample ethnic food, and rail at their opponents' inadequacies. The strategy of ambiguity is far more difficult for incumbents to succeed with than challengers. Without a substan-

tial political record—"a paper trail"—the challenger has the luxury of being able to foster ambiguity. For example, as a presidential candidate, Jimmy Carter successfully issued vague and conflicting messages to the electorate in the 1976 campaign. President Ford, as the incumbent, was constantly on the defensive and could do little more than call attention to Carter's ambiguity.

By 1980, however, the shoe was on the other foot. Perhaps to conceal his administration's shortcomings, President Carter continued to employ the strategy of ambiguity. Providing few specifics about his plans for the country, he repeatedly rebuked Republican candidate Ronald Reagan and mocked his political ideas. The stratagem eventually backfired, above all, because the president came across to many voters as inept and mean-spirited.

Scandals sometimes provide openings for challengers. Whether political or personal, improprieties can taint a legislator who is otherwise likely to coast to reelec-

United States

Bob McDonnell
Attorney General

Paid for by McDonnell for Virginia. Authorized by Bob McDonnell

tween Republicans and Democrats, but foreigners often find it hard to tell them apart. They are understandably puzzled by a political system without profoundly differentiated parties, while most Americans take for granted that Republicans and Democrats differ enough. Americans easily pick out detailed differences among their familiar political trees, but fail to see the overall likeness of the forest.

Official Republican and Democratic organization charts can be misleading. Each seems to depict a hierarchical chain of command, with authority running down from top to bottom as in a business or military organization. But the actual power structure within American major parties is quite different. Decentralization of power is the most important single characteristic of the American major party. More than anything else this trait distinguishes it from all others.

This unique trait is manifested in the fact that national major party leaders cannot control local usage of the party label. It is as if local bottling forms could label any beverage Coca-Cola without authorization by the national Coca-Cola Company. Even the most popular presidents, Franklin D. Roosevelt for example, failed in efforts to withhold their party's nomination from programmatically unreliable legislators. In other nations, where nominations are passed on by central party committees, much stronger disciplinary sanctions restrain successful candidates from opposing their party on important issues. Both aspects of party decentralization—local rather than national power over party nominations and feeble national discipline over the party's elected officeholders—are distinctive elements of American politics. The informal distribution of power within both major parties closely parallels the formal constitutional power structure.

The states under the Federal Constitution supply 50 separate governmental bases for party organizations to develop. Each separate state party can wax powerful irrespective of national party defeats and independent of national party control. Consequently, the major American parties are often described as loose associations of largely autonomous state parties.

Money has become so important to campaigns that politicians are guided in their choice of candidates by the amount of support aspirants for office can win from organized labor, wealthy individuals, and businessmen. Cash often becomes the key to party nomination. Money must be in hand or nailed down by firm promises. A man who has served both as a big-city mayor and as governor of his state said he never accepted a nomination without knowing exactly where campaign money was coming from. "I want to see the cash on the barrel-head," he quipped.

Political scientists suggest that money has its greatest effect on political trades before the candidate is chosen. The hold of politicians on the nominating process is being weakened by the substitution of civil service for patronage in hiring employees at many levels of government. Patronage gives men with campaign money a more important voice in picking candidates in maneuvers behind the scenes. Only occasionally does a candidate come along with so much popular support that he can run as a free agent. Usually the back-room managers either get the candidate they want or block the people they do not want until a compromise is reached.

In a rough, off-the-cuff analysis, politicians say that power companies run four states. Labor unions have the loudest voice in six others. Three states are dominated by mining interests. A cattleman's association has the controlling interest in one state. Oil companies dictate the course of two, and drug and insurance companies can claim another.

Like most generalities, this is not entirely true. Nothing is ever that simple, especially in politics. It takes a combination of interests to win an election in any state, and the people who pull the strings are often quiet about it. The people who

In 1948 President Truman defeated the polls as well as Dewey.

Political Ideas and Political System

produce large amounts of money, either from their own or from others' pockets, gain easy access to the officeholders. In many cases, they get important jobs in the administrations of the people they have helped.

Frequently, the only means to document this patronage is by a backward glance at history. Current contributions are clouded by hazy records and by donations that are listed under the names of secretaries, relatives, and friends. Connections between contributions and rewards are not always visible. Only after people close to the event speak out in later years do the items fall into place.

In 1932, William Woodin, formerly a Republican, who had been president of the American Can and Foundry Company, gave early and often to the campaign of Franklin D. Roosevelt for president. Once he called at campaign headquarters in New York, and a pompous doorman would not admit him to the office of James A. Farley, the campaign manager. Woodin went to a pay telephone and called Farley to ask how a man with a $50,000 contribution could see the chairman. Woodin became secretary of the treasury for Roosevelt.

Among others in that group of contributors for the 1932 campaign were Henry Morgenthau, Sr., and Joseph P. Kennedy. Morgenthau's son, Henry, Jr., later became secretary of the treasury. Kennedy became first chairman of the Securities and Exchange Commission and later ambassador to London.

Activists in this and later Roosevelt campaigns were Robert Jackson of New Hampshire, W. Forbes Morgan of New York, and L. W. "Chip" Robert of Georgia. Jackson developed clients interested in legislation and removed himself from the Democratic National Committee. Morgan did likewise when various whiskey franchises came to him with the repeal of prohibition. During World War II, Robert collected too many war contracts to take an active hand in politics. Like Jackson and Morgan, he moved off the scene.

Every administration produces illustrations of this kind. Winthrop W. Aldrich, a New York banker, was heavily involved in raising and providing money for Dwight D. Eisenhower's 1952 campaign. The Republican finance committee headed by Aldrich was credited with producing $2,250,000 for the campaign. Less than a month after Eisenhower was elected it was announced that Aldrich would be the new ambassador to Great Britain. Aldrich was a man of wide experience and knew his way around the international jungle of finance and diplomacy. Such sophistication is not always characteristic of diplomatic appointments.

President Barack Obama

In 1956, the owner of a chain of dress shops gave $26,500 to Republicans. A few months later, he was appointed ambassador to Ceylon. During public hearings by a Senate committee, relating to confirmation by the Senate, he was unable, when questioned, to name the prime minister of India or Ceylon.

The influence of fund-raisers in any administration usually is broader than the simple appointment of a few men to jobs. A man with much experience at the White House suggested that the character of a president's administration is set by the people who raise large sums of money for the party. These men are always given a chance to express their views on subjects in which they are interested. They do not always get what they want, but they have a hearing, and they regard this as being of great importance.

Access to the decision maker applies all the way down the line from president to county board of commissioners. The chief collector for one party in a state said his work in producing money had given

him a voice in party nominations ranging from mayor to president. He also had a veto power over which demands of his big contributors would be sent to Washington, since they flowed through him.

A hearing at the top, access to the decision maker, a chance to be heard—these things are often more important to big contributors than are contracts.

A striking example of the power of big contributors was provided by the 1952 Democratic Convention in Chicago. Vice President Allen Barkley went to that convention with many assurances that he had substantial support from President Truman and from the upper levels of organized labor. During a long career in Congress, Barkley had supported labor causes.

Nonetheless, half a dozen labor politicians held a meeting and decided that Barkley, at 74, was too old to be a candidate for president. The labor leaders included Walther Reuther, president of the United Automobile Workers, and the directors of labor's political action groups.

United States

Barkley was shocked when he learned of their decision. He withdrew from the race with a statement saying:

> Since arriving in Chicago, I have learned that certain self-appointed labor leaders have taken upon themselves to announce their opposition to me as a Democratic nominee for president. They have admitted to me that weeks ago they committed themselves to a program and to candidates other than myself which would give them greater control of the machinery and politics of the Democratic Party.

The problem of raising campaign money is a constant worry to politicians. Thoughtful people are troubled by the forces that tug at government; some speak of the danger of an oligarchy. They resent and resist the pressure applied by people and groups that provide campaign money. Still, no one has been able to produce a better way of financing campaigns. Reliance on big donors continues. Most elective jobs at congressional and state levels cost far more to win than they pay in salaries. Politicians live in constant danger of losing the support either of the people who provide the money or of the voters who cast the ballots. Several facts of political life come into play here:

- Different interests of people who pay for political campaigns bring pressures on officeholders from various directions. Labor wants one thing. Industry wants another. Professional organizations make other demands. Community action groups have their own ideas. All industries do not want the same thing. Out of this mingling of forces comes a compromise that achieves a kind of balance. Politics becomes the art of the possible.
- Quite a few wealthy people in and out of the industrial community give time, thought, and money to politics and want little or nothing from officeholders. They spearhead drives to raise campaign funds for good candidates. Bernard Baruch of New York gave generously of time, advice, and money to politicians of both parties at the presidential and state levels. Robert W. Woodruff of Georgia, whose fortune came from soft drinks, railroads, and banks, worked for stable government in Georgia for years.
- There are times when independent or fusion candidates rise successfully to disrupt the established system, upsetting the major political parties. While organization and central backing count for much, the powers in the background cannot afford to ignore popular trends

and desires, as indicated by the voices of many groups, some small, some growing to formidable size, but not represented in the controlling power hierarchy. At times they, too, can disrupt well-established processes.
- Usually in places of political power there are honest people who keep watch over those who soften under pressure. A watchful press corps can provide publicity. Then there is that poll of "customer" opinion which has to be faced at various intervals. When aroused and angry, voters can act. Thus, while dollars are essential and often dominant in politics, there are other factors that can be determinant and help serve the public interest.

GLOSSARY OF POLITICAL TERMS

Activist A participant in politics who does more than simply vote, but less than run for office.

Administrative law The body of law controlling the procedures of various government bureaus, agencies, commissions, and administrations.

Advice and consent The constitutionally granted right of members of the Senate to approve or withhold approval of treaties and certain presidential appointments.

Amicus curiae A "friend of the court," i.e., a person or group that submits a statement in a case before the court, with the intention of helping the court reach a decision.

Appellate jurisdiction The authority of a court to hear cases on appeal from the decisions of other courts.

Bicameralism The constitutional provision for a legislature of two houses.

Bill of attainder A legislative act that names a particular person for punishment, or an act designed to punish specific persons.

Chief executive The president's constitutionally derived right to be head of the executive branch of government.

Chief legislator The president's constitutionally derived right to influence the legislative process by initiation of legislation, veto, and recommendation and through other means derived from those rights.

Civil law Civil law has two meanings. First, the term denotes law that is not criminal law. Second, the term refers to law that is not derived from the common law.

Closed primary One in which voters must indicate their party identification beforehand, and in which they can vote only in the primary election of their party.

Cloture A mechanism for ending a filibuster or for otherwise stopping a bill.

Constitutional law The body of law including the Constitution and all subsequent court opinions that interpret it or refer to it for authority in finding another law or action constitutional or unconstitutional.

Cross-filing The practice of candidates running in the primary elections of more than one party.

Electoral college An institution used to elect the president of the United States, whereby electors from the states (made up of its number of senators plus representatives) become members of the electoral college.

Executive department The departments of the federal government whose heads (secretaries) are members of the president's cabinet.

Ex post facto **law** Retroactive legislation: a law that imposes a penalty or increases a penalty for an action that was not illegal when undertaken.

Filibuster In the Senate, a mechanism for stalling a bill by carrying on a continual debate, until the need to turn to other business induces the bill's sponsor to drop its consideration.

Free-rider problem The difficulty of getting people to contribute to the supply of a collective good displaying a positive externality.

Gerrymander The practice of constructing election districts to maximize the number of districts the candidates of one party might win.

Injunction An order by a court that a party to a judicial process act or cease acting in a certain manner.

Interest group An organization whose members seek to influence electoral and governmental processes but who do not directly put forth candidates for nomination and election.

Issue salience The relative importance a citizen attaches to an issue.

Judicial activism The tendency of appellate courts to enter new territory by enunciating the broadest decisions in particular cases and by ignoring or overturning precedent, even though such cases could be decided on narrower grounds.

Judicial restraint The tendency of appellate courts to refuse cases involving overtly political questions and to defer to other branches of government, asserting that petitioners either have not exhausted their remedies or must go to the legislature for relief.

Judicial review The action of the Supreme Court in deciding on the constitutionality of acts of Congress or of other agencies of the federal government.

Political Ideas and Political System

Logrolling Vote trading by elected representatives in support of each other's bills.

Monopoly A public or private firm that alone produces a good or service for which there are no close substitutes.

Nomination by convention A system of selection for major elected offices, whereby delegates are chosen at the state and local level by various means.

Nomination by primary A popular election to choose a party's candidates in a general election.

Open primary A primary election in which voters do not have to declare their party identification and may vote for any candidate of the political party in whose primary contest they want to vote.

Opinion of the Court A single opinion issued by at least a majority of the justices of the Supreme Court. Such an opinion becomes the law of the land, and it is binding on all lower courts in subsequent cases.

Original jurisdiction The right of a court to hear a case before it has been heard by any other court.

Oversight Procedures whereby House and Senate members scrutinize the workings of the laws and agencies they have created.

Pluralist theory A view of the political process presupposing substantial societal diversity and resting on the assumption that interest group predominance in one area does not aid in dominating another.

Pocket veto The president exercises a pocket veto if he fails to sign a bill within ten days after he receives it for consideration from Congress provided that Congress has adjourned before ten days have elapsed.

Pork-barrel legislation Measures designed largely to benefit particular legislative districts.

Proportional representation system An election system in which voters choose from a slate of candidates and in which a party wins a proportion of the seats in the representative assembly according to the proportion of votes its slate wins in the election.

Rational choice The postulate that people efficiently pursue their goals by purposive choice.

Resource redistribution An increase in one person's wealth, income, or utility at the expense of another person's wealth, income, or utility.

Seniority The number of uninterrupted terms an elected official has been in office.

Single-member district system An election system in which the state, nation, or other political unit is divided into districts or jurisdictions, and a single district sends a member to the legislature.

Stare decisis The position of a court to stand by precedent and not to overturn settled points.

Systemic reforms Those reforms designed to change the entire environment or consequences of public policy decision making.

TANSTAAFL There ain't no such thing as a free lunch.

Unicameralism The constitutional provision for a legislative body of only one house.

Writ of *certiorari* In this procedure, a petitioner explains to the Supreme Court why it should be interested in a case and why the case falls within the Court's jurisdiction.

Writ of *habeas corpus* A writ issued by a judge requiring that a person be released from custody when the judge is convinced of the unlawfulness of detention.

Writ of *mandamus* A directive given by a court to a lower court or government official requiring the completion or cessation of a particular act.

Courtesy of the White House

Chapter Six
The U.S. Economy

The significance of global economic relations goes beyond the transition in the international position of the United States. Economic interdependence among virtually all states compels one to assess the implications of international economic transactions everywhere. The volume and speed with which economic resources can be transferred between countries creates wealth, but also tensions. Modern communications and management capabilities of international corporations and banks, which command assets greater than the Gross Domestic Product (GDP) of many countries, allow massive capital transfers in response to market conditions. The "information age" and the resulting global network have linked together individuals and businesses far beyond what governments can manage or control. Countries are more susceptible to outside influence, to the point that the "domestic versus foreign" dichotomy has lost much of its relevance. Whether as a young, struggling republic or as a world power, the United States has been economically involved with many other countries.

GOING COMMERCIAL

At the beginning of the 19th century, most U.S. business activity was handled through small businesses, that is, sole proprietorships and partnerships. The corporation played at best a secondary role. Yet, by the end of the century, the corporation was firmly established, and combinations of corporations, widely known as "trusts," became a hallmark of the time. In 1800, two-thirds of American productive labor was employed in agriculture. By 1900, agriculture accounted for only one-sixth of total employment. Hence, the United States had transformed itself from an underdeveloped, extractive economy to a complex industrial economic system. At the start of the 19th century, markets were still largely local in scope, and transportation and communications facilities were still primitive. By the end of the century, a system of canals, railroads, and highways had made national markets commonplace. The development process necessitated great quantities of invested capital, and the substantial fixed costs of the railroads and other major economic sectors required mass markets and large volume. As the 20th century opened, the country was attempting to live with a creaky monetary system with a bimetallic (gold and silver) base. At the dawn of the 20th century, the nation had adopted the largely internationalized gold standard. Yet, during the 19th century, the country proved unable to solve the problems associated with central banking. In fact, the United States did not permanently establish a functional central bank until 1913, with the creation of the Federal Reserve System.

Business Cycles

An essential element of continuity in U.S. commercial life for nearly two centuries has been the persistence of cyclical economic fluctuations. After America became a world economic power in the late 19th century, downturns and uptrends would have profound effects abroad. Entire regions of the world have come to look upon America as the engine of international economic growth. On the other hand, it is scarcely a simplification and more than merely a cliché to assert that a U.S. economic sneeze causes other countries to catch cold. In times of lengthy recession, some forecasters invariably announce the end of the business cycle and its displacement by conditions of long-run stagnation. By contrast, during periods of prolonged prosperity, more than a few optimists have similarly been ready to herald the dawn of a new day devoid of cycles, that is, a sort of plateau of continuing prosperity. In the roaring 1990s, with year after year of consistent economic growth and eye-popping stock market returns to match, many pundits spoke of an information technology-driven "new economy" with few downturns and steadily rising equity markets. Such theories, as intriguing as they may sound, should be catalogued among the best-laid plans of mice and men. Without the perspective historical analysis affords, we are likely to become preoccupied with temporary incidents of fleeting cyclical events, witness the deplorable forecasts oscillating between undeviating stagnation on the one side and everlasting prosperity on the other.

FLUCTUATIONS BEFORE 1860

Prior to 1815 and the end of the War of 1812, U.S. economic cycles were primar-

Currier & Ives

A MIDNIGHT RACE ON THE MISSISSIPPI

ily responses of an immature economy to international pressures. The intermittent periods of Anglo-French hostility cast a long shadow upon American economic production, for example. When the European powers found themselves in a shooting war, the American economy tended to prosper. When, as during the interim Peace of Amiens in 1802–1803, the British and French stopped fighting, the United States quickly slipped into recession because of the lost trade to both belligerent sides. The 20-year period prior to the War of 1812 was generally one of prosperity in America, although punctuated on occasion by shifts in the foreign situation. Profits in trade and shipbuilding were particularly high, and increased domestic demand put considerable upward pressure on prices. In this regard, it is noteworthy that Congress failed to renew the charter of the First Bank of the United States, essentially a central bank, in 1811. The bank had substantially dampened inflationary tendencies in the years prior, a circumstance that, somewhat paradoxically, largely explains its unpopularity. Inflation, a general rise in the price level, is usually, although not always, triggered by the increased demand for goods and services associated with rapid economic growth. When inflation is rapid, the holding of money becomes very costly because the real value of money falls as prices rise. It has been well said that the chief role of central bankers is to take away the proverbial punch bowl just as the party gets going. The bank had intentionally slowed economic growth to prevent what economists would now refer to as "overheating." The untimely demise of the First Bank of the United States brought a significant inflationary increase, especially with the spurt in public spending following the outbreak of hostilities in 1812, although the curtailment of many imports during the war appeared to have pushed much of the savings accumulated during the prior prosperous years into industrial development.

Banks of the United States

Both the First Bank of the United States, chartered from 1791 to 1811, and the Second Bank of the United States, in operation from 1816 to 1836, performed major central banking functions. In each case, the bank's 20-year charter was not renewed because of political opposition. Both had been owned partially by the federal government and partially by private individuals. The national government owned a minority of shares and had only a minority voice in the central bank's management. Both had branches in important cities and carried out commercial banking functions, accepting de-

The First Bank of the United States in Philadelphia, drawn and engraved in 1799

Courtesy of Independence National Historical Park

posits and making loans to individuals and business firms. Both handled federal government deposits. Because of their large size, both of these banks were able to regulate the lending and note issuing of the numerous state banks, an authority similar to the control the Federal Reserve banks have over the expansion of bank credit and deposits by the member banks today. If either the First or the Second Bank of the United States wished to restrain the state banks, it could reduce their "specie reserves," effectively cash deposits and holdings of precious metals, and force them to trim down the amount of their loans largely by presenting some of their outstanding notes to them for redemption. To ease monetary conditions, the banks of the United States would either retain outstanding state banks' notes or hand them out to their own customers. If the Banks of the United States reduced their own loans, the reserves of the state banks were usually affected because the loans would often be paid off with checks drawn on a state bank. On the other hand, if the central banking authority expanded its loans, the reserves of the state banks were usually increased.

In some countries, a central bank operated by the national government sets monetary policy in accordance with policy directives. The U.S. Constitution says nothing about banking, but in 1819 the Supreme Court in *McCulloch v. Maryland* upheld the constitutionality of a central bank as a proper and necessary means for the national government to create a uniform currency and to protect assets

of the United States. Following the closure of the United States Bank in 1836, state banks, heretofore restrained by the national bank, began issuing their own currency notes that were often unredeemable. Military exigencies forced reform of the system in 1863, during the American Civil War. To stabilize the war economy, Congress authorized the chartering of national banks. These were privately owned corporations, nothing like a central bank or the United States Bank. A subsequent 10% tax on state bank notes rapidly drove these out of existence.

Government operations during the Civil War were largely financed by means of the monetary printing press. Paper currency issued in the 1860s were popularly known as "greenbacks," since these had no real backing. When they were originally issued, these United States notes were not redeemable in gold or silver. The period of unredeemability lasted until 1879 when, with the Specie Resumption Act of 1875, Congress authorized the Treasury to redeem the greenbacks in gold. Once U.S. notes were made redeemable in gold, the United States was said to have shifted from a paper standard to a gold standard. Under the paper standard, the price of an ounce of gold in terms of greenbacks varied. Because gold was used as foreign exchange to purchase goods from other countries, the price of foreign exchange also varied. Prior to 1875, therefore, exchange rates were uncontrolled and flexible. After 1879 the price of an ounce of gold was fixed at $20.67 and the Treasury stood ready to convert U.S.

United States

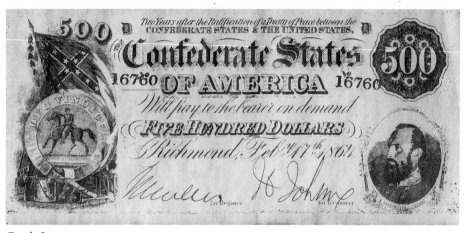

Confederate currency

notes or other types of currency into gold at that price, ending the period of flexible exchange rates. By the 1880s, America effectively had a single currency.

Western Expansion

Between 1816 and 1840, foreign influences continued to exert marked influence on the American economy, although domestic developments began to effect greater economic change. Internal manufacturing had been stimulated by the lack of foreign goods during the War of 1812, even though the loss of export markets hurt the agricultural sector. In the postwar period, foreign goods began to flow back into the economy, and a rise in unemployment prompted a westward movement of population. In 1817, a growing demand for American crops and raw materials developed in Great Britain and France. An

agricultural boom ensued, accompanied by widespread speculation and credit expansion. The period of prosperity was followed by a collapse in 1819, when farm prices fell nearly 50%, loans were called in, and mortgages foreclosed. Interest rates rose sharply, and credit dried up. The subsequent wave of unemployment fostered new westward migration.

The opening of the western lands was accompanied by heavy capital investment in the system of canals, including the Erie, the Hudson River-Lake Champlain, and the Erie-Ohio River Canal, among others. A wave of speculation in urban and rural western lands reached major proportions in the early thirties. Rapid growth caused economic dislocations, and widespread labor shortages ensued. The excesses of the speculative land boom peaked in the mid 1830s, and these became closely related to

the fate of the Second Bank of the United States. The typically restrictive policies of the bank became dicey political issues in the South and the emerging West, where easy money was the economic lodestar. President Andrew Jackson campaigned for reelection in 1832 promising to oppose renewal of the Bank charter. During Jackson's second term in office, the U.S. Treasury began to withdraw funds from the central bank and to redeposit these in state banks, where they became the base for wild credit expansion. Money was perceived to be cheap and easy, and the impact upon real estate, canal- and railroad-building ventures became quickly evident. Foreign funds flowed from overseas investors wishing to avail themselves of unusually high profits.

The Specie Circular in 1836, requiring payment for government lands to be made in specie, that is, precious metals, then precipitated a decline in land sales. A recession in large parts of Europe and growing concern over the soundness of the American market led to the withdrawal of much European investment, which in turn caused a general price deflation. The economic contraction that followed in 1837 is generally regarded as one of the most pronounced on record, and the subsequent depression is usually listed among the major economic downturns in U.S. history. Growth rates in America had exceeded sustainable levels and gave way to sharp cyclical adjustment.

In the period 1838–1860, economic fluctuations began to more closely resemble the modern variety. Over this span of years, economic oscillation was largely the product of variations in the rate of growth of private investment, the development of organized channels for the flow of savings and investment, and the emergence of manufacturing production methods. In the absence of a central bank, the large city banks assumed most of the functions ordinarily attributed to a central banking system. Large market and export centers developed in Boston, New York, New Orleans, and Philadelphia. Behind the major banks in these urban areas, there emerged a large number of private, diversely managed financial institutions providing an easy flow of credit for local development but highly vulnerable in economically troubled times.

By the end of the 1840s, a swelling wave of private domestic investment centered around the national railroad expansion. Some 1,500 miles of railroad were in operation in 1837. A decade later, the figure exceeded 5,500, and by 1860 it stood at more than 30,000 miles. The rapid expansion of water, rail, and highway transportation facilities had the further effect of widening markets and expanding areas from

Government spending during the Civil War

which raw materials could be dispatched to manufacturing centers. The interdependence of different sections of the country with one another became manifest.

Outside the United States, revolutions in Europe in the late 1840s precipitated a flight of funds to North America. The discovery of gold in California in 1848 was followed by a similar discovery in Australia in 1851, and the easy-money, go-go mood of the times was hence further fueled. By 1857, speculation and excessive debt had grown to major proportions. That year, the failure of one of the leading New York financial institutions, the Ohio Life Insurance and Trust Company, precipitated a general collapse of stock and bond prices, along with a cumulative spiral of economic fright. European investors withdrew funds to compensate for the credit tightening in their own markets, and financial panic subsequently occurred in European capitals. A noticeable upturn did not come until 1859.

Over the first six decades of the 19th century, the economy of the United States grew from an immature system whose ups and downs were largely the result of developments outside the country to a more complex one that was able to attract large amounts of foreign investments to blend with its own savings for the constructions of factories, canals, highways, and railroads. The absence of an adequate banking system magnified the tendency toward instability in the domestic economy, and recurrent periods of domestic financial crisis were common.

CALLED TO ACCOUNT

In many ways, the American economy came of age in the period 1860–1898. It consolidated and all but completed its railway network. The corporation came into its own as an instrument for directing and utilizing the flow of large quantities of capital. Manufacturing became widespread, and great waves of immigration furnished an energetic labor force for such enterprises. The war period, 1861–1865, displayed a characteristic cyclical war pattern, with large government expenditures and deficits, material and manpower shortages, and a basic disruption of economic life. These factors were greatly magnified in the Confederacy, which suffered economic ruination and lost 25% of its adult white male population during the war. The South did not really recover from the economic setback until after the Second World War.

Paper currency was first issued by the federal government during the Civil War. Though the constitutionality of greenbacks remained a matter of dispute for some years, in 1870 and 1874, the Su-

preme Court clarified the issue in several decisions and concluded that the federal government had the right to issue paper money and designate it legal tender. In the mid-1860s the federal government established the National Banking System in which national banks were authorized to issue paper money called national bank notes. From 1865 to 1913, the principal types of paper money in use were national bank notes, Civil War greenbacks, and silver certificates issued by the U.S. Treasury. During the latter half of the 19th century, demand deposits, for the most part checking accounts at banks, as a type of money gradually became more important than paper money. As the term suggests, demand deposits are bank holdings that may be immediately converted into types of money that are legal tender, that is, upon demand. Although money was still widely defined in terms of coins and specie, demand deposits must be regarded as money because they are used to buy goods and services. Demand deposits became money through common usage, and money in essence is generalized purchasing power.

Between 1871 and 1873, speculative activity increased markedly, spearheaded by numerous railway construction ventures and security speculation. Much of the latter was in fact "derivative," that is, repackaged. The barrenness of many of these ventures was perhaps best illustrated by the ignominious collapse of Jay Cook and Company in 1873. Corruption during the so-called "Gilded Age" abounded. The exposure of the notorious Tweed Ring in New York and the financial shenanigans associated with the Credit Mobilier, which had financed the Union Pacific Railroad construction, reached into the legislative and executive branches of the federal government. Unemployment skyrocketed in 1873, and the plunging stock market brought down

State and local currencies in the 19th century

banks, railroads, manufacturers, creditors and merchants in its wake. The subsequent depression of 1873–1879 was the longest continuous slump in American history.

In the late 1870s, better times returned. Record American agricultural output coincided with crop failures in Europe, and the combination fostered a sharp rise in exports and farm incomes. In the early 1880s, railroad investment again reached boom proportions and the effects were transmitted to all parts of the economy. Corporate organization began to assume major proportions outside the railway field for the first time and investment from abroad flowed back in as America prospered. In the 1880s, nearly 40,000 miles of railroad track were laid, and nearly two billion dollars were added to the capital stock of the railroad companies. The sig-

U.S. railroads in the 1880s

United States

Construction of the Brooklyn Bridge

nificance of the large investments was magnified by the fact that a large portion of the investments, especially foreign investments in America, were leveraged; that is, they were investments made with borrowed funds. The expansion opened up the last parts of the frontier with the final push for homesteading in the Dakotas, Nebraska and Colorado. The country began to realize that the continent was all but settled and the large supply of desirable, free land was rapidly becoming depleted. In this period, the country maintained a net import balance on goods and services and a net inflow of gold. The

rather favorable situation was facilitated by the large quantities of American securities sold to European investors who were heavily involved in the general speculation that carried them far from their domestic markets into both South and North America as well as Asia.

The year 1890 brought a new crisis. Revolution in Argentina fostered considerable uncertainty throughout the region, and prompted a financial shakedown among London banking houses that had heavily underwritten South American securities. In an effort to maintain solvency, London banks began to liquidate their foreign holdings. The consequent gold outflow from the United States assumed significant proportions, and bank reserves quickly dried up. Late that year, the great British banking house of Baring Brothers failed, and the ensuing liquidity crisis in Europe became acute. During the latter portion of the 19th century, the expansion of commercial farming and the factory system clearly illustrated the growing interdependence of the agricultural and industrial sectors of the economies of numerous countries, including that of the United States. Certain defects in the money and banking system continued to trouble the developing American economy. Moreover, fluctuations in the U.S. economy were beginning to produce unsettling effects abroad, especially in the European economies. On balance, the economic ups and downs and tos and fros of the U.S. economy were characteristic of underdeveloped economies. High profits, large risks, and violent swings in investment activity were all aspects of the business activity during the 19th century. At the dawn of the new century, though, the economy had the customary indications of one that was maturing.

ALL THE WORLD'S AN EXCHANGE

At the turn of the century, the U.S. economy exhibited one of its great expansions. Investment houses, which in earlier periods had been involved in railroad financial operations, turned to the field of corporate promotion and consolidation. They supplied the funds needed for rapid industrial expansion. The U.S. Steel Corporation, America's first billion-dollar company, was the product of consolidations begun in 1901. The tenor of the day is indicated in various economic figures, for example, those showing that the volume of shares traded on the New York Stock Exchange doubled in 1901.

Pig-iron production, an indicator of activity in the heavy goods sector, increased by more than 150% during the expansion in the first years of the century. Freight ton-miles increased more than 50%. The substantial expansion of 1904–1907 coincided with record crops that were sold worldwide at favorable prices. Wages continued to rise and the large numbers of emigrants from abroad, mostly from Southern and Eastern Europe were rapidly absorbed into the American labor force. By 1908, America was finally forced to conclude that its banking system needed a complete overhauling. The Senate Finance Committee accordingly sponsored a study group known as the Aldrich Monetary Commission whose multiyear work ultimately led to the creation of the Federal Reserve System, whose functioning will be discussed in some detail below.

Shocking Experiences

Few Americans today grasp how vulnerable the American economy was to external shocks and financial panic prior to the establishment of a permanent central bank and a commitment on the part of the Federal government to nearly full employment. Although the differences in America during the 19th century regarding tariffs were pronounced, especially between the Northern and Southern states, and these without doubt contributed to sectionalism and ultimately war, an equally bitter policy debate raged for decades about the establishment of a central bank. Some have argued that the absence of a competent central banking authority had an even greater long-term impact than did the enduring disagreements about external tariffs. In the early years of the republic, Alexander Hamilton and the Federalists favored a central bank, while Thomas Jefferson, James Madison, and most of the Democratic-Republicans opposed it. Following its establishment, the Bank of the United States was controversial, and an emotion-laden political backlash eventually engendered the revoking of its charter. For much of the 19th century, individual state banks issued their own currency and bank panics were a frequent occurrence. Banking regulation was sporadic until 1913, and it was not until the 1940s that the principle of Federal Reserve independence was universally accepted.

In 1912, poor harvests in Europe coincided with bumper crops in North America that provided a short-term stimulus to the U.S. economy. Yet, in that year, America began to come under the influence of the dark clouds appearing on the European horizon. The Balkan crises in Europe in 1912 and 1913 shook markets worldwide, and an economic downturn in the United States thereafter set in. Calamitously, and with virtually no advance warning, the European continent found itself plunged into war in August 1914. Indeed, few signs of increasing international tension ordinarily associated with such occurrences had presented themselves at the time. There was no attendant tightening of money supplies, little increase in the production of war materials, no substantial stockpiling of strategic materials. What followed the declarations of war was not so much financial and commercial panic, but rather international economic paralysis, a largely unprecedented condition, which, if anything, was all the more difficult for the American authorities to manage. The Western world plunged into the abyss.

The London Stock Exchange closed indefinitely, as did other continental bourses. The New York Stock Exchange, facing the likelihood of panic-selling and consequent liquidation, followed suit. For years, securities were valued for collateral and other purposes at July 1914 prices. In the autumn of 1914, the net outflow of

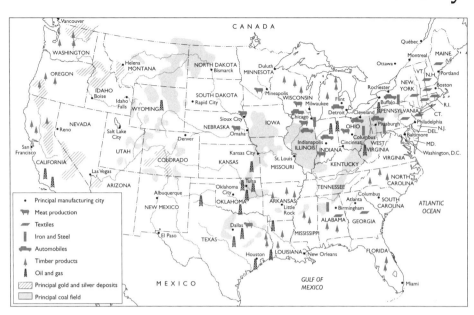

American resources and manufacturing by 1920

gold from the United States amounted to some $45 million.

WAR AND PEACE, 1914–1919

The outbreak of war in Europe induced an agonizing reappraisal of the economic situation in America. By 1914, more than 50% of the country's cotton crop and a fifth of its wheat were customarily sold abroad. Manufactured products such as copper, steel, and oil depended upon foreign sales for sizeable parts of their markets. With German shipping recalled and the threat that belligerent powers might sweep other commercial shipping from the international sea lanes, the ramifications for the United States were profound.

Although the United States was cast in the role of a neutral with Europe involved in war, a situation which past experience suggested would be favorable to economic expansion, the country could not initially avail itself of the commercial opportunities that beckoned. The country did not dash into war production, nor did it rush to build product inventories for potential export. On the contrary, economic downturn and ensuing pessimism characterized the economic climate of opinion in America. The steel industry was operating at around half-capacity through 1915. Cotton was at its lowest price for nearly two decades. Export sales were plummeting, and unemployment was relatively high.

Yet, toward the end of 1915, an abrupt turnaround came, and the American outlook suddenly and unexpectedly perked up. Britain seemed to have gained control of the sea lanes, the German submarine threat diminished, and overseas orders for North American agricultural products,

except from the Central Powers, Germany and Austria-Hungary, that were largely embargoed, began once more to roll in. The New York Stock Exchange reopened, and a net inflow of gold into the United States commenced. In 1915, the U.S. economy took in $25 billion in gold; in 1916, $530 million flowed in. U.S. exports continued to expand throughout the conflict, and the country provided more and more of the shipping tonnages and services formerly provided by the belligerent powers.

In the monetary sphere, the domestic effects of the substantial gold inflow were rapid. Demand deposits increased approximately 75% between 1914 and 1919, and the total money supply increased by more than 80%. Following U.S. entry into the war in April 1917, government deficits contributed hugely to the expansion of the money supply. During the years 1917–1919, government deficits ran to $1 billion, $9 billion, and then more than $13 billion. For the economy as a whole, the peak of wartime expansion is generally placed around August 1918. During the autumn and winter of 1918–1919, a moderate recession occurred as the economy began the conversion process back to a peacetime economy, commonly referred to as a "return to normalcy." Factory employment declined over 10% from the wartime peak. "Normalcy" depended to some extent upon perspective, of course, and hugely upon whether or not one had a job.

THE CREST OF THE WAVE

Foreign demand, although not at the record levels of wartime, remained fairly strong. Exports of agricultural goods climbed to all-time high levels in the post-

United States

Wall Street, 1929

That part of the 20th century coming to a close with the end of the First World War saw the growth of the U.S. economy to industrial maturity, with corporate organization firmly entrenched in industrial fields. Those years witnessed a largely inflexible and often destabilizing banking system yield to one guided by the Federal Reserve, a monetary organization that seemed finally to offer the promise of effectively handling severe economic downturns and financial panics. The period also brought substantial shifts in international economic relations. The United States, heretofore a net importer of capital, became the principal underwriter of the European economies. With its wild frontier tamed, domestic savings were available for a significant role in international investment. On the eve of what would become the Roaring Twenties, the United States was an industrial powerhouse with the world's largest economy.

war period as European agriculture was tardily put back into effective operation and Continental production remained sluggish. The American agricultural sector was soon to enjoy one of its record booms beginning around 1920. Farmland and rural realty speculation intensified accordingly, as can be expected in periods of bullish prices, with farm mortgage debt surging and many owners of farmsteads becoming overextended.

The immediate postwar period was the first opportunity the newly created Federal Reserve had to manage a potentially difficult economic adjustment. Nearly all parts of the economy had based their expansion during the war on an enlarged supply of easy money. Much of the country's export business had been fuelled by liberal loans made available to foreign purchasers. Production in the United States and abroad became geared to relatively high prices and costs, as worldwide conflict almost constantly pushed demand upward. In the 1920s, many came to believe in a new era of faster growth arising from new technology, an outlook that now elicits a sense of *déja vu*. To be sure, the parallels with the "Golden Twenties" and the "Roaring Nineties" are not to be missed. The cardinal difference was that in the "Golden Twenties" most of the economic excitement was generated by cars, aircraft, electrification and radios, rather than by computers, the internet, and telecoms. Convinced, as were many others, that the boom-bust cycle was a thing of the past, Irving Fisher, a Yale economist, made the remarkable observation on the eve of the 1929 equities crash that "stock prices have reached a permanent and high plateau." Another analogy is the case of Japan, which, in the late 1980s

had become economically so successful that many domestic and foreign observers, especially in the United States, persuaded themselves that the Japanese economic "model" was somehow vastly superior to those of other countries. Exhibiting the mentality of the herd, many investors made up their minds that strong growth, complemented by rising stock and property prices, could continue forever in one way or another. The supposition was yet another economic fool's errand. Japan's economy slipped into recession for most of the 1990s, and the leading Japanese stock market index, the Nikkei, which soared to over 30,000 in the late 1980s, plunged to under 8,000 in 2002. Then, as now, speculators chased fool's gold.

As vulnerable as the American economy was to a postwar downturn, the early 1920s brought neither financial panic nor bank failures. The principal reason for the relative stability is that the new Federal Reserve System took the lead in encouraging the extension of credit at the first whiff of a potential slump, rather than forcing a drastic contraction that could send the economy into a tailspin. Monetary authorities made a concerted effort to accommodate companies and financial institutions thought to be in only temporary difficulties. The Federal Reserve maintained adequate liquidity in the system and ensured adequate credit supplies in the face of looming economic doldrums. America's central bankers appeared able to keep a stiff upper lip. The early 1920s passed without the financial panic of the sort that had become associated with similar periods in the past, paving the way for the temporary prosperity in America beginning in the mid-1920s.

Global Connections

For the economy of the United States in the decade of the 1920s, no change was more profound and none more significant than its transformed relationship to the economies of other nations. The United States entered the First World War as a net debtor country, emerging just a few years later as far and away the world's leading creditor. As a debtor country, the United States had been able for decades to maintain a relative export balance. As a creditor, the ponderous new responsibilities in the world economy virtually necessitated substantial trade and monetary adjustments, fostering at least transitory import imbalances, among other adaptations. Americans, for their part, were not prepared to accept their new role in the world generally, though. In particular, most abhorred anything smacking of trade imbalances, although few had much notion of their deeper meaning. Indeed, the new role of the United States required a major reordering of economic affairs, both domestically and internationally, calling for a fresh vision only a small number of its leaders displayed, and which in any event outran by a wide margin the experience of the American people.

The unwillingness of the country to accept trade imbalances or an "adverse" balance was demonstrated by the continued pursuit of a high-tariff policy and the adoption of the policy of "dollar diplomacy." The latter was designed to expand the overseas markets for U.S. goods. By discouraging imports and stimulating the export sector, the United States was following an economic course contrary to that dictated by significantly changed circumstances. How were war-weakened trading partners expected to afford U.S.

products unless they themselves had vibrant export sectors? The world had no use for neo-mercantilism, which is generally defined as state assistance, regulation, and protection of specific industrial sectors in order to increase international competitiveness.

Such economic policies were in fact sustainable only as long as a great amount of both public and private credit from the United States to other countries was made available. As long as American loans were on hand to other countries, the latter were able to make payments on their imports from America and other trading partners. Hence, the flow of trade in the 1920s was largely underwritten by the flow of international loans out of the United States. The delicate situation endured as long as global expansion continued, but a sharp downturn would result in a slackening of international credit, which would invariably endanger the whole fragile structure. This crack-up was, of course, exactly what occurred in the fateful autumn of 1929, to the great misfortune of the entire world.

Closely related to the precariousness of the international economic structure was the vexed question of the international gold standard in the postwar order. During World War I, most countries had been compelled to suspend gold payments, and the international gold standard had consequently become inoperative. With the exception of the United States, no country was in a position to resume gold payments until around the middle of the 1920s, if at all. Britain, whose prewar pound had been tied to gold at $4.86, decided, largely for reasons of national prestige, to return to the gold standard in 1925 at the equivalent par value, that is, at the prewar exchange rate. The position proved unsustainable since the British cost-price structure over the prior decade had been altered by a considerable amount of inflation, while the U.S. dollar had appreciated substantially against the pound sterling. Economic circumstances required a downward adjustment of British prices and costs if British goods were to compete in world markets. Failure to make such a correction produced a widening gap between imports and exports, in turn bringing about a net outflow of gold. Hence, the resumption of the prewar par value caused deflation and economic contraction in Britain and all other countries following such a course. British adherence to the gold standard by the logic of the system invariably resulted in a loss of gold to finance unfavorable trade balances, the largest of which was with the United States. Britain's role as the world's leading economic and financial power was over, but the United States was not yet willing to discharge the global duties thrust upon it. The new responsibil-

ity that was America's largely by default overstrained the sophistication of its people. Throughout the 1920s, the shaky condition of the gold standard was the source of lingering volatility and would curtail various stabilization measures that might otherwise have been put in place with its termination.

From 1920–1924, the U.S. gold stock increased in value from around $2.5 billion to over $4 billion, providing an enlarged monetary base for credit expansion. The Dawes Plan, and later the Young Plan, furnished mostly public loans to Germany and were tracked by an additional outflow of private credit to Europe that afforded the crucial buttressing of the Continental economies. Yet, the years following Britain's return to the gold standard constituted a period of constant concern about the ability to maintain the standard. In Britain, deflation was producing unemployment and growing internal tension. To Federal Reserve officials, sluggish European economies discouraged any significant shift to tight-credit policies, lest diminished loans cause deep recessions abroad.

To a considerable degree, Federal Reserve policies in the 1920s reflected widespread apprehension in financial circles about the plight of the international gold standard. By maintaining an easy-money policy, the Fed made the flow of funds to other countries easier. The adoption of a tight-money policy would surely have put a damper on this stream of foreign investment, which, in turn, would have prompted an outflow of gold from other countries and to the United States. For its part, the U.S. economy continued to ex-

pand into 1929, with the peak of expansive growth posted during August 1929. Public awareness of the expansion's end and the beginning of decline in growth lagged considerably, as is usually the case in such circumstances, and it was not until the spectacular stock market crash in October 1929 that public attention began to focus on the possibility that something more significant than a minor recession might be on the horizon.

The Bubble Bursts

The chief features of the boom years of the "Golden Twenties" are conspicuous. Prices hardly fluctuated during the period, while retail sales remained comparatively steady. Industrial production moved robustly upward during the expansion. Durable goods production exceeded the average, and employment levels moved progressively to new record heights. Wage rates remained almost steady. As the patterns of economic expansion emerged, and the attendant factors interacted with one another, they produced one of the most spectacular booms in American history. Then, with the seeming inevitability of a Greek tragedy, they somehow gave rise to forces causing a major depression in a manner that even today is not completely understood. In the austere years after 1929, it was a popular pastime to dig up quotes from various individuals who in the halcyon years of affluence were expounding doctrines of permanent prosperity, the emergence of a new economy brightened by the dawn of a recession-proof era. In point of fact, a close examination of many aspects of the American economy in the 1920s, as well

The Great Crash

United States

Child labor, before the Fair Labor Standards Act of 1938 forbade the employment of children under sixteen.

as in the 1990s, might have justified a belief that the system was indeed operating on a solid new plateau. Above all, in neither of these milk-and-honey decades did much evidence of a significantly rising price level that customarily accompanies periods of rapidly rising prosperity present itself. At the peak of the boom in 1929, both wholesale and retail prices were at lower levels than had prevailed in 1921, a truly astonishing achievement. The Fed saw little reason to pursue tight-money policies, especially in light of the lingering weakness of European economies. The good times were rolling in the United States, and the Fed was hesitant to take away the punch bowl as the party simply drifted along, although by 1928 the monetary authorities were already harboring serious concerns about the domestic speculative boom.

High profits in the late 1920s from security speculation attracted foreign capital, and the return flow of investment into the United States brought a net inflow of gold and hence contributed to the subsequent decrease of the gold reserves of other countries. Domestic investors who had been putting their money overseas found the returns from the American speculative boom attractive in growing measure and were thus given considerable incentive to shift their assets. The combination of bullish investment returns and an attendant speculative frame of mind actually began setting into motion the drying up of American credit abroad toward the end of the decade. The stock market panic in October was a dramatic capstone to a number of preceding events, the enduring infirmity of Europe certainly among them. The lofty extremes to which the market climbed fostered distortions and strains throughout the economy, and these played a large part in the arduous

adjustment process later on. Although it is a popular thesis that the stock market bubble and the general speculative movement account largely for the enormity of the later decline, investment exuberance alone cannot be blamed for the widespread and enduring downturn.

EXIT PROSPERITY

Although the decade of the 1930s is properly regarded as a depressed period, it was nonetheless characterized by cyclical patterns, by modest crests and yawning troughs. Starting with the peak in August 1929, the economy moved into a stage of contraction that did not end until March of 1933. A period of slow, drawn-out recovery followed until the next downturn in May 1937. From the middle of 1938, the economy moved upward until the moderate expansion was engulfed by the productive effort of the war into which the United States was drawn in 1941.

The decline that began in August of 1929 was not the longest in the American experience; let us not forget that the depression of the 1870s has retained that dubious distinction. The initial stages of the 1929 downturn provided few surface indications that the economy was in for anything more than the sort of minor recession the country had become accustomed to. Although the stock market collapse of 1929 had been a spectacular and distressing incident, to be sure, stock prices actually strengthened by the end of the year. Industrial production, which had begun to decline in the summer of 1929, was off some 12% by the end of the year, but appeared to be stabilizing at those lower levels during the early part of 1930. Even durable goods production, which had dropped more than 20% from

its peak levels, was holding steady by the end of the year, and had actually begun to increase moderately in the early 1930s. Hence, President Herbert Hoover seemed justified in assuring the American people that "prosperity is just around the corner."

With certainty, no easy answer comes to the question why the seemingly moderate recession gave way to an accelerating downward movement after 1930, or why it was that this major depression gathered momentum as it progressed and finally gave way to widespread economic anxiety. The banking sector and the monetary system had a good deal to do with the eventual upheaval, but shortcomings in these areas comprise merely facets of far deeper problems. During the 1920s, the banking system underwent a substantial shift from demand to time deposits, or interest-bearing "near money." This financial swing, promoted by easier reserve requirements, that is, the amount banks are legally obligated to hold in their vaults, permitted banks to participate heavily in the underwriting of both real estate and security market speculation. Such credit expansion, conducive to sharp economic downswings under certain circumstances, doubtless prompted a slump in the early 1930s. Beyond this, the most egregious borrowing practice of the late "Roaring Twenties," the purchase of equities on the margin, involving the use of paper profits as loan collateral for further stock and bond market investment, had weighty effects. In boom times, such procedures of credit overextension tend to function as long as the markets continue to rise. When the good times end, though, markets will ratchet downward relentlessly in a tumult of irretrievable ruin for those drawn into the economic maelstrom. Large exposure to the markets constituted a monetary house of cards for many unfortunate individuals caught up in the frenzy of equity speculation.

Financial institutions were extending credit freely in the late 1920s, and borrowers who harbored illusions about a golden touch or, somewhat less pretentiously, anticipated the continuance of prosperity in America were content to incur debts. Heavy liabilities consequently hung over the economy, absorbing a sizeable portion of current income for payment of interest and principal. It also seems likely that the decline in automotive sales in 1929 reflected the broader problem of consumer saturation. Other types of consumer durables had been acquired in great quantities during the boom years, and, as it turned out, sales of many consumer products were relatively vulnerable to any sort of economic downturn.

The debt structure extended far beyond commonplace consumer debt. It involved

THE PLEASE-EVERYONE BUDGET | WALTER GRETZKY ON THE NHL

MACLEAN'S

CANADA'S WEEKLY NEWSMAGAZINE | www.macleans.ca

MARCH 7 2005

IS AMERICA GOING BROKE?

Record deficits. Colossal debt. If the U.S. sinks, Canada will go down with it.
BY STEVE MAICH

$4.95

PM 40070230 R 08973

7 78624 70001 8   10

The largest economy in the world always affects other countries.

heavy mortgage commitments on both urban and rural real estate, ran to overstretched margin positions in the securities markets, as well as to somewhat strained capital structures in businesses. These factors represented pressures that had built up slowly over time, whose potential impact went largely unnoticed until current income could no longer sustain the debt servicing, that is, people and businesses were not able to pay back what was owed. Then, the downward movement became cumulative and multiplied. Financial insolvency in one area affected positions in others. In the consumer realm, consequences often manifested themselves in property repossessions. In business, these took shape in bankruptcies, bank failures or mortgage foreclosures. In finance, these entailed diminished or worthless investment portfolios.

The international economic environment had been reconstructed painfully during the 1920s and remained fragile,

United States

pushed through a series of increased expenditure programs that were largely responsible for sustaining the sputtering economic recovery.

By the late 1930s, international developments began influencing the U.S. economy in a large way once again. The rise of the European dictators, above all, Adolf Hitler in Germany and Benito Mussolini in Italy, along with the general rise in political tension, did little to stimulate confidence in the export sector. That said, some industrialists anticipated extensive public investment in the military industrial sector as America increasingly acknowledged the need to strengthen defenses. Other aspects of international relations would directly affect domestic monetary policy as well. Political anxiety abroad prompted a considerable shifting of gold holdings to the United States. In five years, some $10 billion of bullion flowed into American vaults, and the consequent expansion of the gold monetary base swelled bank reserves significantly. In 1938, the Federal Reserve System, through new legislation enacted that year, was granted the authority to adjust member bank minimum reserve ratios, the amount of cash banks must keep on hand. New statutes allowed the Fed to use the old reserve requirements as a floor and to raise the ceiling for these to more than twice that level as circumstances dictated.

Government intervention in the economy in the 1930s was of necessity improvised and provisional since the public sector in America had hitherto been relatively small. The executive office had no permanent economic advisors, and about the only consistent economic counsel available to President Hoover was his own. President Calvin Coolidge still answered his own telephone in 1925, and the White House did not even have a telephone switchboard for most of the 1920s. Introductory government intervention was almost as disruptive of stability on occasion as it was beneficial at other times. Monetary and fiscal policies were not consistently coordinated, and the objectives of the latter were not always clear, above all, because of the absence of professional economic advisors. Furthermore, expansionary government spending programs sometimes coincided with tax policies that tended to offset the anticipated stimulatory effects. Some observers argue that economic confidence was frequently undermined by government programs since business executives were left in a state of uncertainty, something hardly conducive to the formulation of long-range investment plans. Others suggest the U.S. economy had reached a plateau of "maturity" in the late 1920s and that it would never again be capable of pro-

viding full employment without sizeable doses of public investment. Be that as it may, despair had become so pervasive by 1932 that governments had to be popularly perceived as "doing something." President Roosevelt struck a chord with the American people in the assertion that "all we have to fear is fear itself."

An example of the federal government "doing something" was the establishment of the Federal Deposit Insurance Corporation (FDIC) in 1934. Its principal purpose is to insure the deposits of commercial banks. The organization of deposit insurance is the most significant banking legislation since the creation of the Federal Reserve System.

All banks that are members of the Federal Reserve System are required to belong to the FDIC, which insures the deposit of each individual or firm in each bank up to $100,000. And the FDIC does more than protect depositors against possible losses. The psychological effect of insuring deposits diminishes the prospect of having runs on banks. Prior to the establishment of the FDIC, if people feared that a bank might fail, they withdrew their deposits. Because banks typically have only a small amount of cash reserve behind their deposits, such runs caused them extreme difficulty. In the century prior to the establishment of the FDIC, runs on banks contributed to the financial panics that accompanied most recessions. The removal of this incentive to withdraw deposits is an important contribution to financial stability.

WORLD WAR II

The U.S. economy in the half-decade after 1941 was geared for international conflict. Cumulative GDP growth in those years was approximately 140%, and industrial production rose some 170%. Unemployment dropped from around 15% of the labor force in 1940 to virtually zero in 1945. In fact, with over 12 million of the population in uniform during the peak years of war mobilization, the United States actually had a labor shortage, necessitating the extensive recruitment of women for industrial work.

War almost invariably creates inflationary pressures, as new demands for goods and services surge. The U.S. goods and services needed to fight the Second World War were paid for through increased public-sector spending, higher wages and profits, and expanded credit. As federal government spending began to make its effects felt, unemployed labor and industrial facilities were returned to active use, and the economy, for the first time since 1929, was at full employment levels toward the end of 1942. Government expenditure rose from less than ten

billion dollars annually in 1940 to over 90 billion in 1943, expanding beyond anyone's imagination. A country that had heatedly debated $12 billion annual budgets quickly had to come to grips with the notion of spending levels perhaps ten times that high. Public debt rose from around $43 billion to over $137 billion in the same timeframe. In the years 1940–46, public debt increased by nearly $227 billion. As government expenditure soared, so did employee compensation, business profits, farm income and other shares of the national product. At no time were tax planners in a large, decentralized country with a comparatively small public sector like the United States able to handle expenditure schedules that continuously grew. In consequence, the tax authorities failed to draw off most of the increased disposable income the government was bestowing upon the private economy by high expenditure levels. In short, many people made money hand over fist.

This is not to say, though, that the federal government neglected tax collection. Tax figures during the war years underscore the expanding role of the government in the economy. Receipts from personal income taxes jumped thirteen-fold during the war and from corporate income taxes, six-fold. Personal income tax exemption levels were reduced so that the federal tax, which had been collected from merely four million people before the war, was imposed upon over ten times that many during the conflict. Such a fiscal system operated in a country that had a federal income tax in effect for less than three decades, where few people actually paid income tax even during the boom years of the "Golden Twenties." Income tax rates were raised sharply, particularly at the low and high ends of the progression. Corporate income taxes were also boosted, and an "excess profit" tax was introduced on some companies deemed unusually well off. Other taxes were also inaugurated, and internal revenue levies grew. Wartime inflation did not reach unmanageable proportions mainly because various forms of direct controls were instituted, including price, rationing, rent, wage, and credit regulation.

Monetary and Fiscal Policy

Rightly or wrongly, lingering confidence on the part of some in the effectiveness of fiscal policy is rooted largely in U.S. experience during the war years. True, the large increases in the size of the deficit from 1940 to 1943 doubtless had a stimulating effect upon the economy. Be that as it may, significant portions of the wartime deficits were financed by money creation. The most liquid form of money, cash and demand deposits, in-

NEW YORK Herald Tribune

LATE CITY EDITION

THE WEATHER
Today: Cloudy and showers with strong winds

VOL. CIV No. 35,723 — TUESDAY, SEPTEMBER 5, 1944 — THREE CENTS in New York City

Antwerp, Brussels Fall; British in Holland; 100,000 Germans Trapped Along Channel; Finn-Red War Ends, Nazis Reported Leaving

Plane Output To Be Cut 40% Day Nazis Fall

Army's X Day Program Also Calls for Drop of 50% in Munition Work

W.P.B. Master Plan Likely by Week End

Production of B-29s and Air Transports to Go On for War With Japanese

By Tom Twitty

Hamilton Fish Armstrong to Aid Winant on European Council

Editor of 'Foreign Affairs' Will Leave for England With Rank of Minister

By Bert Andrews

Hamilton Fish Armstrong

12 Tokyo Ships Sunk or Blasted Off Mindanao

3-Day Allied Air-Sea Blow in Volcanos and Bonins Nets 13 Craft, 85 Planes

Reds Less Than 50 Miles From Yugoslav Line

Other Soviet Units Capture Brasov; Germans Report Russians Are in Bulgaria

Finn-Russian Guns Stilled By Armistice

Seven Nazi Divisions in North Reported To Be On Move Into Norway

Helsinki's Troops Retire to 1940 Line

Britain Joins Moscow in Criticizing Statement by the Finnish Premier

A Marne Bridge Destroyed by Retreating German Forces

Civilians cautiously pick their way across the Marne on a blasted span at Chalons

Paris Is Getting Sufficient Food To Bar Hunger

But City Is Asked to Scrimp So Allies May Use Trucks to Keep Armies Moving

By John O'Reilly

Eisenhower Calls on Holland To Strike at Foe as France Did

Broadcast Says Victory Is Assured, Tells Norway To Be Confident Its Day Is Coming, Too; Luxemburg Patriots Are Told to Rise

By Richard L. Tobin

Allies Sweeping Beyond Lyon in Pursuit of Nazis

Americans Enter Center of City as Patriots Battle Vichy Militia in France

By Homer Bigart

Dutch Report Allies 5 Miles Into Holland

Breda Won, Eisenhower Bids Rotterdam Patriots Seize City's Key Points

Two U. S. Armies May Be in Reich

Antwerp Fall Gives Allies Great Ocean Port, Splits Foe; Troops Enter Lille

Allies Accused of 'Abandoning' Warsaw Poles, Who Fight On

Nazis Call for Last-Ditch Fight; Some Leaders Reported in Spain

News on Inside Pages

Opportunities for Work

---

creased nearly threefold over the course of the war. In the early years of conflict, commercial banks were able to expand their total assets and liabilities by using excess reserves they had acquired in the latter part of the 1930s. As the war ground on, the Federal Reserve banks purchased enough securities in the open market and increased bank reserves sufficiently to enable the banks to create the money the U.S. Treasury needed to finance its deficits. In 1945, the federal government was still running a deficit of $45 billion, huge by the standards of the time, which swung to a modest surplus two years later. Some predicted at the time that this shift would result in a deep recession. Nothing of the sort happened, though, and the economy continued to grow while the money supply increased moderately.

THE BRETTON WOODS SYSTEM

In July 1944, the United Nations Monetary and Financial Conference laid the economic foundation of the coming peace at the Bretton Woods resort in the New Hampshire mountains. Some 1,300 specialists from 44 countries developed the trade and monetary systems deemed necessary for the postwar world. Above

United States

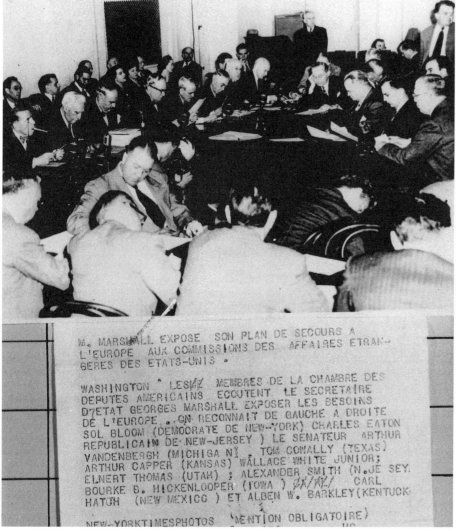

M. MARSHALL EXPOSE SON PLAN DE SECOURS A
L'EUROPE AUX COMMISSIONS DES AFFAIRES ETRAN-
GERES DES ETATS-UNIS.

WASHINGTON. LES MEMBRES DE LA CHAMBRE DES
DEPUTES AMERICAINS ECOUTENT LE SECRETAIRE
D'ETAT GEORGES MARSHALL EXPOSER LES BESOINS
DE L'EUROPE. ON RECONNAIT DE GAUCHE A DROITE
SOL BLOOM (DEMOCRATE DE NEW-YORK) CHARLES EATON
REPUBLICAIN DE NEW-JERSEY) LE SENATEUR ARTHUR
VANDENBERGH (MICHIGAN N) TOM CONALLY (TEXAS)
ARTHUR CAPPER (KANSAS) WALLACE WHITE JUNIOR;
ELNERT THOMAS (UTAH) ; ALEXANDER SMITH (N.JE SEY,
BOURKE B. HICKENLOOPER (IOWA) ZX/AY/ CARL
HATCH (NEW MEXICO) ET ALBEN W. BARKLEY(KENTUCK-

NEW-YORKTIMESPHOTOS MENTION OBLIGATOIRE)

Secretary of State George C. Marshall (right) discusses the Marshall Plan before the Senate and House Foreign Relations Committees.

Courtesy of George C. Marshall Research Library, Lexington, Virginia. GCMRL #162

all, the framers of the agreement endeavored to create an international order designed to prevent the excessive monetary and trade nationalism that destroyed the global economy in the 1930s. Thus, the Bretton Woods system that established the economic structure of the noncommunist world was intended first and foremost to prevent a recurrence of the 1930s. In setting the overriding goal of international economic openness, Bretton Woods reflected U.S. interests and served U.S. needs. The economic structure established by Bretton Woods rested on four pillars, described below.

The International Monetary Fund (IMF)

The IMF system is based upon the dual premise that international economic imbalances are two-sided between deficit and surplus countries, and, following this logic, that adjustment obligations are mutual. A country's foreign exchange rate (the value of its currency in relation to other currencies) was recognized as a matter of international concern, and the IMF was devised to increase national gold and currency reserves so that no country would be forced to meet short-term balance-of-payment deficits by suffering domestic inflation and unemployment. Member countries are accordingly granted "drawing rights" from several IMF accounts or "tranches." The IMF provides credits to member states to tide them over temporary balance-of-payments difficulties. Loans are intended to furnish an alternative to states imposing wrenching internal adjustment measures that could be socially disruptive. In the case of a country suffering a balance-of-payments disequilibrium due to structural difficulties, the IMF is authorized to make credits contingent upon certain domestic economic

reforms. The IMF may also take other measures to correct what it perceives as a disequilibrium, such as declaring that a currency suffers from a "general scarcity." If the "general scarcity" clause is directed toward a country running a perennial surplus in its balance of payments, for example, the IMF can encourage members temporarily to limit exchange of the scarce currency. A deficit country is expected to undertake remedial action to correct a fundamental disequilibrium in its balance of payments. Measures should go beyond the utilization of the secondary reserves of the Fund, but not entail manipulation of the exchange rate. Pending the adoption of measures to restore equilibrium in its balance of payments, a deficit country has recourse to the international pool of currencies held by the Fund. A member country's access to the Fund's resources is always contingent upon the willingness to undertake the necessary processes of adjustment.

International Bank for Reconstruction and Development (IBRD)

The IBRD, popularly known as the World Bank, was established for the purposes of rebuilding war-ravaged economies and financing the longer-term development of member countries. Because of the extent of war damage and the prewar default problem on international loans, most countries anticipated difficulties attracting capital and investment after the conflict. The World Bank was thus initially designed to address the problems associated with international investor confidence by guaranteeing private credits and providing funds for direct investment.

In the wake of the Second World War, most countries recognized the need to foster development. It was assumed that both industrialized and non-industrialized countries enjoy the same priority for reconstruction. Latin American countries in particular emphasized this point, and certain measures were provided through the Havana Charter, a sequel to Bretton Woods, to furnish development assistance in the form of below-interest credits and non-remunerative loans, essentially grants. The World Bank continues to extend long-term development credit at market interest rates as well as on concessional terms, that is, below market rates. Loans are geared to specific development projects, normally to build the infrastructure of developing countries as a prerequisite to industrialization, such as highways, railroads, power and port facilities. By tradition, the president of the World Bank is an American, and the president of the IMF a European. Members were assigned quotas, according to a formula intended to reflect each country's relative importance in the world economy, and were obligated to pay into the funds subscriptions of equal amounts.

Organization for European Economic Cooperation (OEEC)

Originally established to coordinate European use of Marshall Plan aid from the United States, the OEEC eventually evolved into the Organization for Economic Cooperation and Development, the association of developed countries, commonly known now as the "club of the rich." Although the latter designation is colloquial, it bespeaks the success of the Bretton Woods system, and indirectly of U.S. policies, in rebuilding a war-torn world and advancing international development. The OEEC initially undertook three major tasks: (1) programming the recovery effort of the cooperating nations, (2) allocating American aid among them, (3) promoting intra-European trade.

Now, the OECD is the international organization of prosperous nations and includes several Asian and Pacific countries that, along with Western Europe, achieved relative affluence in the decades after the Second World War. The OECD provides a forum for multinational management where financial specialists discuss policies, exchange information, and study the operation of monetary adjustment processes. The OECD is the main forum in which governments of well-heeled countries meet to discuss economic matters. Through its convention, they have agreed to pursue three uncontroversial aims: to achieve the highest rate of growth while maintaining financial stability; to promote free trade; and to support development in poorer, nonmember countries. The OECD is headquartered in the Chateau de la Muette in Paris. Its top policy-making body is the Council, which has the power to take decisions by agreement of all the members.

International Trade Organization (ITO)

Originally envisaged as the trade equivalent of the IMF, the ITO was conceived to promote the international exchange of goods and services by establishing a permanent institution with mechanisms for consultation and collaboration on trade matters. Its principal objective was to facilitate the expansion and balanced growth of international trade. The ITO was in fact part and parcel of a sweeping U.S. plan for a multilateral commercial convention focusing on all aspects of international trade, including preferences, tariffs, subsidies, competitive devaluation, quantitative restrictions and international commodity agreements. In short, the United States endeavored to use its preeminent international position to implement a new world trading order.

European coal mining

The ITO, however, was not to be, until it reemerged decades later in a similar form to the World Trade Organization (WTO). In the 1940s, Great Britain still demanded provisions for its Imperial Preference System, which gave trade preferences to the colonies and discriminated against many countries, including the United States, whose large, affluent domestic market was essential for global recovery. Some European countries advocated safeguards for balance-of-payments difficulties, and France, for its part, was intent on reestablishing its own system of imperial preference, which, to a certain extent, it did. Some underdeveloped countries wished to have internationally sanctioned provisions for development.

Finally, the U.S. Congress effectively killed the ITO. The American public was not yet prepared for such a comprehensive new international trading order. The traditional high tariff policy of the Republican Party was still a *leitmotif* for many. Opposition came from both sides of the political spectrum, with the advocates of protectionism insisting that the international accord went too far, and liberal internationalists suggesting it did not go far enough.

The General Agreement on Tariffs and Trade (GATT), a provisional arrangement establishing guiding principles of trade, replaced the ITO by default in 1947. The GATT would become the expression of a basic international consensus on trade in the noncommunist world for nearly half a century. In the preamble of the GATT, parties to the accord agreed to "reciprocal and mutually advantageous arrangements directed to the substantial reduction of tariffs and other barriers to trade and to elimination of discriminatory treatment in international commerce."

The fundamental tenet of the GATT was the so-called most-favored-nation (MFN) principle, which, although used widely and in other contexts, was somewhat of a misnomer. MFN was economic code for nondiscrimination in international trade provisions. Hence, the MFN provision of the GATT stipulated that "any advantage, favour, privilege or immunity granted by any contracting party to any product originating in or destined for any country shall be accorded immediately and unconditionally to the like product originating in or destined for the territories of all other contracting parties." The GATT

United States

also put in place a general international commercial code regulating such issues as subsidies and trade dumping. It strove to eliminate the use of quantitative restrictions upon trade, such as quotas, although countries over the years have found ways around the accord's provisions in this area.

In the years following its promulgation as a provisional arrangement for global trade, the GATT evolved into an international commercial code and developed a small international organization designed to oversee the functioning of the West's trade regime. This organization would provide an institutional forum in which trade discussions took place in growing measure and where the provisions of the follow-on agreement, the WTO, would largely be negotiated. The GATT would eventually monitor 90% of world merchandise trade and encourage industrialized countries to reduce their tariffs on average from 40% to 5% at the time of the WTO's founding in 1995. The GATT eventually played a major role in lowering the average tariff on manufactured goods among major countries from about 50% in the 1930s to roughly 5% in the 1980s.

GATT rules applied primarily to manufactured goods, and the arguments that supported free trade did not apply for various reasons to services. Yet, liberalization of trade in services invariably promotes free trade in goods, since the two are closely linked. Neither was agriculture ever brought under normal GATT discipline. Many countries, particularly developed ones, pursued farm policies that were inconsistent, to put it mildly, with liberalized trade in order to achieve other goals, above all, the income maintenance of farmers. Restrictive agricultural polices imposed, and still impose, substantial costs on consumers and taxpayers. These costs consistently far exceeded the gains to farmers, and yet, they have continued for decades. By some estimates, world GNP might have increased by $40 billion annually in the 1980s and 1990s had the major industrial countries liberalized their agricultural sectors.

PATTERNS OF INTERNATIONAL ECONOMIC COOPERATION

The end of global conflict in 1945 meant for most of the belligerents, victor or vanquished, a struggle for sheer existence. So immense had been the destruction of human and material resources that many nations were on the verge of economic and social collapse, and some faced actual starvation.

An unparalleled global recovery effort was launched to meet the emergency. The United States, by far the least damaged by the war along with Canada, was necessarily the chief provider of funds and supplies. Mutual assistance for the devastated war victims and basic support from other countries set an auspicious pattern of collective international action. A new era of world economic collaboration was introduced as countries made a virtue of necessity. As countries came to confront a litany of long-term problems, including stabilization, development, and economic integration, they built sets of institutions and programs that incorporated the essential methods of combined action improvised during the struggle for postwar recovery.

The Marshall Plan

When U.S. Secretary of State George Marshall announced in June 1947 at Harvard University that the United States was prepared to take a fresh look at Europe's economic plight, he astutely turned the initiative back to the Europeans, inviting them to get together and furnish an analysis of their needs and proposals for meeting these. During the months of planning and negotiation that followed, a new pattern of international negotiation emerged. Sixteen Western European states pledged themselves to work jointly for recovery. They agreed to set common targets for development of their production, mobilize full use of their productive capacity and manpower to meet those targets, modernize equipment and transportation, maintain financial stability, reduce trade barriers, remove obstacles to free movement of persons across their boundaries, and work together in developing common resources. Hence, they dramatically broke with a sad three-decade tradition of economic nationalism, at least among themselves. The Soviet Union forbade its satellites from participating in the Marshall Plan.

The second aspect of the partnership was the American commitment to make up the deficits of the operation over a four-year period, a bill originally estimated at between $17 and $19 billion, on condition that the European countries would put forth their maximum effort to help themselves and that, moreover, they would do this jointly. The United States insisted on this "partnership within a partnership" arrangement, since it at last recognized the pressing need for an enduring relationship with the whole of Europe, not merely with some of its constituent parts. In effect, America served an economic ultimatum to Europe: "Unite or Perish." In addition to this general condition, the United States set up an intricate system of controls ensuring that both basic policies and day-to-day operations would conform to standards meeting the criteria of acceptability specified by the moneyed partner. The Marshall Plan entailed neither altruistic international charity nor did it enact a cunning form of imperialism, but represented a sound business arrangement based on a broad calculated risk and with firm management to satisfy both sides of the partnership that their mutual interests were being effectively served.

In the decades after World War II, the United States bolstered the economic and financial system it was instrumental in establishing by supporting trade liberalization and assisting Europe and Japan to revamp their production. In the second decade of the 1940s, the European Recovery Program (ERP) was a cardinal instrument of U.S. policies toward European countries. The ERP not only helped finance international trade and encouraged longer-term commercial competitiveness, but it also fostered regional trade liberalization on the Continent. By making economic assistance contingent upon European cooperation, the United States nurtured the development of large European regions and thereby ultimately endorsed the emergence of the European Economic Community (EEC) toward the end of the 1950s.

Shock therapy, as economists often describe the transformation method, worked in this case. Through the painful decision process, the OEEC established itself as an effective instrument of collaboration capable of economic planning as well as disciplined cross-border management. "We feared it would wreck the Organization," recalled Baron Charles J. Snoy of Belgium, Second Chairman of the OEEC Council. "Yet it was possible. We had to learn cooperation. No one could take responsibility for jeopardizing the whole plan, even if dissatisfied with any particular decision." Four experts (widely known as the "Four Wise Men") were assigned the task of reconciling the estimates of need with the aid actually available. They examined and trimmed each country's program, generally keeping consumption of food and other consumer goods at the low 1947 level, trying to find ways of cutting back planned dollar imports, and substituting supplies that could be secured without dollars.

Economic Cooperation

In the grand design of European recovery, the United States planned to furnish "friendly aid in the drafting of a European program and the later support of such a program," in the words used by Secretary Marshall in 1947. The program took concrete form in the various U.S. foreign assistance acts from 1948 to 1951 and in the functioning of the Economic Cooperation Administration (ECA) set up to administer American participation. Around $12 billion of American assistance was provided outright, and about $1 billion more lent. In physical terms, this became food, feed and fertilizer; fuel; machinery and vehicles; raw material and semi-finished products; and other commodities. While most of this was American produced, about 20% was purchased outside the United States. Almost half the aid went to the United Kingdom and France. Italy, Western Germany, and the Netherlands each received around a billion dollars each. The remaining two billion went to the other eight countries.

The United States advised the European countries in the preparation of their recovery programs and ultimately approved them. The OEEC framed the proposals, in accordance with the basic Marshall Plan concept of European initiative, but these had to pass ECA examination and conform to American-legislated policy before qualifying for American support. The ECA also applied to the European recovery programs certain "yardsticks" of strictly American interest. For example, ECA determined whether specific proposals for American assistance would have an adverse effect on the American economy, and if so, what alternatives presented themselves. Requests for steel and some foodstuffs in the early period exceeded what was regarded to be the amount that could be supplied out of American production without risking serious domestic shortages and inflationary prices. Non-American sources of supply were provided in some cases, but where these were also insufficient, demands were trimmed. The spirit of the ECA was to get on with a vital and urgent job, and to find agreement with the European governments as quickly as possible on the scope and character of the recovery efforts and the American assistance to be provided.

THE YELLOW BRICK ROAD

By the closing days of the Second World War, the U.S. executive branch was largely influenced by a liberal economic vision of the world. American elites were willing to use the predominant position of the United States to found a postwar commercial order based on open markets and free trade. Indeed, American policy makers had gleaned an important lesson from the interwar period. Faltering U.S. leadership and substantial withdrawal from international affairs after the First World War had been major factors contributing to the collapse of the global economic system and subsequently of world peace. Many Americans came to accept that the country could isolate itself from international affairs no longer. America's

Present at the creation of post-World War II U.S. foreign policy: Secretary of State Dean Acheson (right) and Secretary of Defense (earlier Secretary of State) George Marshall.

liberal economic vision was perhaps best articulated in the Havana Charter, but a clear statement of purpose was discernible some years earlier when President Roosevelt urged Congress to adopt the proposed Bretton Woods system:

It is time for the United States to take the lead in establishing the principle of economic cooperation as the foundation for expanded world trade. We propose to do this, not by setting up a super-government, but by international negotiation and agreement, directed to the improvement of the monetary institutions of the world and of the laws that govern trade. The United Nations Monetary Conference at Bretton Woods has taken a long step forward on a matter of great practical importance to us all. The Conference submitted a plan to create an International Monetary Fund which will put an end to monetary chaos. The Fund is a financial institution to preserve stability and order in the exchange rates between different moneys . . . Changes in the value of foreign currencies will be made only after careful consideration by the Fund of the factors involved. Furthermore, and equally important, the Fund Agreement establishes a code of agreed principles for the conduct of exchange and currency affairs.

Cash and Carry

The operation of the IMF and the role of the U.S. dollar as the principal international or "kingpin" currency provided the

international monetary system its shape for nearly three decades of the postwar period. The essential feature of this system was the gold-exchange standard or quasi-gold standard that represented an effort to reestablish the international commodity standard largely in place prior to the First World War, but that had collapsed following the outbreak of hostilities and could not be effectively reconstituted. The most important facets of the gold-exchange standard were its system of pegged, but adjustable, rates and its provisions for providing funding and liquidity internationally. According to Article IV of the IMF's Articles of Agreement: "The par value of the currency of each member shall be expressed in terms of gold as a common denominator or in terms of the United States dollar of the weight and fineness in effect on July 1, 1944."

The United States set the value of its currency at $35 per ounce and made the dollar interconvertible with gold through transactions with official monetary authorities. As European currencies became convertible in the 1950s, when economic recovery reached the take-off stage, these were in turn pegged to the dollar and to gold. Other countries maintained the value of their respective currencies by using the dollar as the intervention currency, entering foreign exchange markets to buy or sell dollars as needed to maintain their currencies within certain value parameters.

Gold constituted an official reserve asset and was a means of ultimate settlement in the balance of payments. Values of local currencies were expressed in terms of gold or the dollar, and the dol-

United States

lar was expressed in terms of gold so that par values (the currency exchange rates) connected with gold. Gold was effectively demonetized under the IMF, that is, it was used only as an expression of value and a monetary base. It was retired from the central position it had occupied under the "classical" gold standard. Reserve assets consisted of official gold holdings, the unconditional drawing rights at the IMF in a reserve account (tranche), the special drawing rights (SDRs or "paper gold") allocated to member countries of the IMF, and official holdings of convertible foreign currencies. Under the gold-exchange standard, official monetary authorities could sell gold to the U.S. Treasury for dollars, and could convert their holdings of dollars to gold at the U.S. Treasury.

The international economy, like domestic economies, requires a common monetary standard to function smoothly. Domestically and internationally, money serves three basic purposes: a medium of exchange, a unit of account, and a store of value. In international trade and payments, a variety of common measures are conceivable, and in practice, the two unadulterated cases are the commodity standard and the international currency standard. The gold-exchange standard established at Bretton Woods was a clever hybrid, arguably combining the best features of both. Unencumbered by the rigidities of the traditional commodity standard, it was contingent only upon the retention of the dollar as the kingpin or vehicle currency and American willingness to follow the international economic rules of the road. As long as the United States was willing to maintain the integrity of the IMF gold-exchange standard, the dollar was not only as good as gold, it was in fact better than gold.

Many in the country realized in the years immediately after the war that direct government controls had been a temporary, thin line holding back inflation. Consumer prices, which had risen some 30% during four years of war, increased another 25% in the years thereafter. The lack of available goods during the war, coupled with an expansion in employment and the money supply, resulted in huge accumulated savings that burst forth in a propensity to consume. On top of all this came the deferred investment spending of business firms that had been involved in the war effort in some capacity. Hence, for the first time in its history, the U.S. economy faced a potentially long-term wage-price spiral.

Jobs, Jobs, Jobs

Without doubt, the Depression of the 1930s was one of the great traumatic events in U.S. history. It cast a heavy shadow over nearly every American, especially those who, in the latter stages of the Second World War, thought about the potential problems of the postwar period. As the war wound down, prevailing opinion focused upon the major effort that would be required to avoid settling back to the economic doldrums of the 1930s. The principal concern was, of course, about unemployment. Hence, an inflationary bias was inherent in stabilization policies of the late 1940s, as the federal government became committed to reflate the economy during a significant downswing. The propensity would linger on, and some have identified it as a legacy of the Depression. The Employment Act of 1946 assigned to the federal government responsibility for directing the economy to avoid major depression. In the introduction to his first *Economic Report*, submitted under the terms of the Employment Act, President Harry Truman wrote:

The job at hand is to see to it that America is not ravaged by recurring depressions and long periods of unemployment, but that instead we build an economy so fruitful, so dynamic, so progressive that each citizen can count upon opportunity and security for himself and his family. Nor is prosperity in the United States important to the American people alone. It is the foundation of world prosperity and world peace. And the world is looking to us. I believe that the American people have the wisdom and the will to use our abundant resources so all may prosper. I reject and I know the American people reject, the notion that we must have another depression . . . This need not happen again, and must not happen again.

The Act itself declared:

It is the continuing policy and responsibility of the federal government to use all practicable means consistent with its needs and obligations and other considerations of national policy, with the assistance and cooperation of industry, agriculture, labor, and state and local governments, to coordinate and utilize all its plans, functions, and resources for the purpose of creating and maintaining, in a manner calculated to foster and promote free competitive enterprise and the general welfare, conditions under which there will be afforded useful employment, for those able, willing, and seeking to work, and to promote maximum employment, production, and purchasing power.

The bill reflected a patchwork and mixture of political compromise and rhetoric, but in its essence, it made the federal government responsible for full employment. To this end, it established several important policy-making instruments that remain prominent in economic policy.

The Council of Economic Advisors (CEA). This group is appointed by the president with the consent of the Senate. It analyzes and forecasts economic trends, assesses the contributions of federal programs to national employment, and advises the president about "national economic policies to foster and promote free competition, to avoid the economic fluctuations or to diminish the effects thereof, and to maintain employment, production, and purchasing power."

The Economic Report of the President. Early in the calendar year, the president submits to Congress an economic report based on the data and forecasts of the CEA. The report includes recommendations putting the provisions of the act into effect. It may also include suggestions for legislation.

Joint Economic Committee (JEC). This congressional committee composed of senators and representatives reports its findings and provides recommendations in response to the annual executive report. In addition to publishing several reports annually, the JEC endeavors to furnish the Congress with an overview of the economy.

It has become widely assumed that the many institutional changes made since 1929 have made a repeat of the Great Depression unlikely if not impossible. Such reasoning identifies deposit insurance, social security, the various types of housing legislation and home insurance, and the automatic stabilizers of the tax system as anti-recession measures. Surely, the possibility of another great liquidity crisis like that of the early 1930s seems highly remote. Deposit insurance prevents runs on banks, and unemployment insurance mitigates the precipitous declines in consumer purchasing power that many countries experienced in the 1930s. The "automatic stabilizers" built into the tax system serve similar functions. These prevent after-tax incomes from falling as far as they would if the tax structure were not progressive, that is, if the tax rate did not increase with income. Federal Housing Administration (FHA) and Veterans' Administration (VA) housing insurance programs assist in maintaining the stability of financial institutions, although these by themselves make only modest contributions to bolstering the housing industry.

In short, high-level employment was a goal permanently consigned to the federal government after the Second World War. But, with hindsight, economists know that widespread concern about the maintenance of full employment was unnecessary in the postwar years. It is paradoxical that a chief facet of the problem of maintaining full employment in the half-decade after World War II was a product of the Great Depression. High levels of unemployment and steadily declining incomes in those years fostered relatively low birth rates in America. The country's principal economic difficulty, as it turned out, was not a labor surplus, but a labor shortage. War casualties, of course, played some role as well. For nearly a decade after the war, labor was a scarce factor of production, an economic bottleneck that was alleviated by the large spike in the birthrate in the 1950s, the so-called "baby boom." The limits on economic growth were not therefore on the demand side, as was largely the case during the 1930s, but on the supply side, and the critically tight factor was manpower.

Until the 1930s, mercantilist thought retained considerable prominence in the realm of political economy in the United States. As a rule, mercantilists see politics as determining economics. Economic relations are to be understood in terms of competition for the distribution of wealth and power among states, as distinct from the individual and worldwide welfare maximization advocated by liberal economists. Only after the rigorous debates about the causes and effects of the Great Depression and the restructuring of global trade and finance after the Second World War did a basic consensus about the principles of a liberal economy emerge in the United States. American public figures then took the lead worldwide in putting these principles into effect. Although the United States had been a leading industrial power for over six decades, it was not until the end of the Second World War that the country developed a coherent set of workable ideas about its involvement in the global economy. Above all, U.S. interests were generally perceived as being served in an open global trading and financial system. America's new economic conception was a crucial aspect of the novel role in the world that the country was assuming.

America's Role

The post-World War II economic consensus in America coalesced around three essential elements: first, prudent bank regulation and an active monetary policy directed by an independent Federal Reserve system; second, countercyclical fiscal policies with an overall aim of

Several countries call their currencies "dollars." On these notes Sir Edmund Hillary and Queen Elizabeth II are depicted.

maintaining full employment; third, the opening of world markets and the stimulation of international economic growth. Bretton Woods was designed to overcome the mercantilist behavior worldwide that was by and large acknowledged as having deepened and prolonged the Great Depression.

The federal budget showed a substantial surplus in the years 1947–1948, the first for some time. Expenditures tumbled from over $100 billion during the height of war mobilization to just over $41 billion in 1949 and only $43 billion in 1950, notwithstanding the outbreak of war in Korea in June of that year. Federal and corporate income taxes were reduced somewhat in the postwar years, and the "excess-profits" tax was eliminated, only to be occasionally reintroduced in the future as circumstances were deemed necessary.

The pattern of economic cycles in the 1940s was clearly an abnormal one, completely dominated by World War II and its aftermath. Inflationary pressures existed during the entire period and owed their persistence largely to wartime

expenditure. A short, eight-month recession in 1945 was precipitated by reduced government spending. Yet, as far as most of the private sector was concerned, the postwar years were marked by rising consumer spending and sharply increasing private investment. As price controls were lifted in 1946, consumer prices shot up as a result of pent-up demand. Wholesale prices rose even more rapidly. The large increase in the money supply ensured relatively easy credit. In effect, Americans were expending their money on deferred plant and equipment, housing and consumer durables. Surging expenditure must be seen against the backdrop of the depressed economy of the 1930s. By 1949, the rapid rate of postwar expenditure was slackening, inventories were largely replenished, and the initial plant and equipment boom was completed.

Immediately following World War II, the United States had a surplus in its balance of payments. Exports of food, machinery, and capital equipment were large and expanding. Marshall Plan aid and public grants made it possible for foreign coun-

United States

tries to purchase goods and services from the United States, and tended to reduce the deficits in their balance of payments and also U.S. surpluses. Yet, in 1950 the surplus in the U.S. balance of payments shifted to a deficit, and since then the United States has frequently run a deficit in its balance of payments. This swing to deficits surprised many observers of international trade, since most accepted, in the late 1940s, that certain structural changes had occurred in the international economy that would cause the United States to have a nearly continuous surplus in its balance of payments. The United States, it was thought, would import little because the country was superbly stocked with goods and well-endowed with resources. The country also maintained relatively high tariff barriers. U.S. exports were expected to be large since Europe needed the primary commodities produced in the United States and because of the rapid increase in U.S. exports of manufactured goods. These conditions were expected to create a "dollar shortage" because U.S. imports, which supply trading partners with dollars, would be less than U.S. exports, which require dollars in payment and result in a net dollar inflow.

Economic growth in 1949–1950 received a stimulus from Korean War expenditures. National defense spending, which in 1949 had amounted to 7.5% of GNP, took more than 14% in 1952 and 1953. Public debt, most of it accumulated during the Second World War, rose from around $257 billion in 1950 to $275 billion in 1953. The end of the Korean War coincided with a recession, likely caused in part by cutbacks in government spending and a modified fiscal policy that could not kick in quickly enough. In the 1950s, the American economy experienced several booms followed by minor recessions. Modest, albeit lingering, inflation and high-level employment generally characterized the economic situation in America during the 1950s. By the end of the 1950s, as the economy grew fairly rapidly, inflationary pressures appeared to have subsided and did not reassert themselves again until the second half of the 1960s. Monetary and fiscal policy became primary and frequently employed instruments of stabilization in the 1950s. The government's role in the economy and the size of the public sector became subjects of debate that would intensify in the following decade when the federal government introduced extensive new social programs under the rubric of the "Great Society."

The United States was joined by numerous countries with similar technologies, productivity and standards of living, a multipolar economic arrangement not dissimilar from the one that existed prior to 1914. The period after World War II witnessed an unparalleled growth of the world economy due largely to the opening of markets and the expansion of international commerce. America's global engagement was instrumental to such developments and this was one of history's prime examples of power used wisely.

THE "SOARING SIXTIES"

President John F. Kennedy was the first U.S. president to have formally studied modern macroeconomics, and his Council of Economic Advisors assisted with his continuing education. Presidential references to such matters as budgetary balancing over the years of the economic cycle indicated the role the administration envisaged for the federal government in economic affairs. Within the administration, a more innovative position certainly took shape. Among other things, it reflected a view going beyond traditional fiscal policy and embracing the position that budget deficits would always be necessary as long as the economy failed to operate at near capacity.

After 1962, the economy set off on an upward climb that established new records for peace and longevity. It began to grow at annual rates twice the long-term average, and unemployment fell from a fairly high level in the late 1950s to rates below the magic 4% target and doing so even with a rapidly expanding labor force. Moreover, it seemed for a time that this buoyant economy was hardly subjected to inflationary pressures. But as the expansion continued and increased spending on the widening Vietnam War was added to other expenditures, public and private, the economy went into the condition of overfull employment. The American economy began to overheat and inflation subsequently began to manifest itself.

Good Times, Bad Times

Let us consider briefly what is means for an economy to overheat and the implications of this condition. Strange as this may seem to some, it is indeed possible for an economy to be "too prosperous." To be sure, joblessness, lost purchasing power, and breadlines are hallmarks of the proverbial economic nightmare. Yet, inflationary periods like the ones the United States experienced on occasion in the second half of the 20th century are in a sense the other side of the coin. An excess of purchasing power, experienced under conditions of overfull employment with attendant labor shortages, represents a partial breakdown of a smoothly functioning economic system. Such an overheating economy is usually marked by creeping inflation and the ensuing diminution of purchasing power. Those on fixed incomes are hit hardest, as their money buys less. Across the economy, excessive purchasing power quickly bids up the price of scarce resources. Prices of raw materials rise, and price-cost relationships can become distorted. Demands for higher wages are made, further ratcheting up the price level. Higher wage demands that are met by employers are passed on to the consumer in the form of higher prices. The U.S. economy experienced this problem of excess purchasing power in the late 1960s and into the 1970s, until the 1973 oil shock threw most of the industrial economies into outright recession.

In fact, severe international economic problems began to appear in the late 1960s. Notwithstanding the increasing interdependence of Western countries, the U.S. economy, as the largest player, could in a number of ways remain sheltered from global economic and financial forces. Capital flows had less effect on the huge American economy than they did upon those of the European countries and Japan. Public and private U.S. debts were denominated in the country's own currency and could be readily serviced by increasing the number of dollars in circulation without jeopardizing the currency's value. As long as other countries could absorb large dollar outflows, the United States was spared taking domestic measures to balance international accounts. The amount of "Eurodollars," that is, dollars in the form of bank deposits held and traded abroad, became sizeable in the 1960s. No one has ever been able to determine the amount of Eurodollars permanently in circulation abroad, but the figure is huge, certainly in the trillions of dollars. The Eurocurrency market, which in fact has expanded far beyond Europe in the last decades, is an enormous international capital market, and because it consists largely of short-term funds, it is characterized by considerable mobility and volatility. One must think in terms of a domestic U.S. money supply over which the Fed has considerable control and the international dollar supply that is beyond the supervision of U.S. monetary authorities and is indeterminate.

Hence, certain advantages and disadvantages accrued to the United States under Bretton Woods, and to a considerable extent this continues to be the case insofar as the system has retained its basic features. Because foreigners are as a rule willing to accumulate dollars, the United States is able to sustain a larger balance-of-payments deficit than would otherwise be financially possible. Instead of losing gold in the decades of the gold-exchange standard, America financed its deficits through voluntary accumulations of dollar liabilities abroad. As long as confidence is maintained in the dollar, the United States could sustain relatively large cumulative deficits over time. By running deficits in its balance of payments, the United States has the luxury of creating internationally held dollars in a relatively inexpensive fashion, while currently increasing national expenditure. On the other hand, the cost of being the leading economic player can be substantial in the policy-making sphere. Monetary authorities have little control of dollar-denominated funds held abroad, nor can they check the rapid flow of such funds. Under the fixed exchange rate system, the very size of dollar liabilities at times prevented U.S. policy makers from undertaking the expansionary monetary and fiscal policies they might have been inclined to, lest foreigners' confidence in American willingness or ability to maintain the dollar's value, and thus the integrity of the system, be undermined.

Dollar Deluge

The leading factor shaping international finance in the several decades following the Second World War was the evolution from "dollar shortage" until around 1960 to the "dollar glut" thereafter. The dollar was commonly regarded as undervalued internationally until the mid-1950s, although from then on most economists considered it becoming increasingly overvalued. The dollar came under mounting pressure in the 1960s, above all, because of the significant expansion of public spending in the United States and the attendant budget deficits contributing to inflationary pressures. Moreover, the golden age of the OECD in the 1960s, marking economic recovery in Europe and the growing internationalization of production, fostered a partial supplanting of the dollar by other currencies, especially rock-ribbed German marks and Swiss franks. The first OECD ministerial meeting set a target of 50% growth for the decade, but real GNP actually grew 70%, while inflation rarely rose above 3%. OECD economists would gladly confront such forecasting errors now. But they probably won't have to: the OECD countries as a whole have never since duplicated such economic performance. Under the Bretton Woods system, the dollar was the primary reserve currency, and in the initial years, the only reserve currency, insofar as the dollar was the instrument for store-of-value purposes in reserve assets, public and private. Convertible currencies under the IMF Agreement were always convertible into dollars, but to some extent other currencies began to assume a reserve role.

The Alliance for Progress

In the early 1960s, the United States set the pace for the most ambitious regional

President Jimmy Carter joins other Group-of-Seven leaders in Tokyo, 1979.

development program since the Marshall Plan, the Alliance for Progress, a "partnership" akin to the earlier European arrangement in which the United States and the Latin American countries (without Cuba) agreed to collaborate and support one another in a "vast effort to bring a better life to all the peoples of the Continent." Among the goals expressed in the "Charter of Punta del Este," which launched the program in 1961, were: per capita growth in income of at least 2.5% annually; more equitable distribution of income; more balanced diversification of the economies; programs of agrarian reform; elimination of adult illiteracy and six years of primary education for all children; an increase in life expectancy of at least five years; low cost housing; price stability; and regional economic integration leading to an extension of trade. A price tag of $20 billion for ten years was set for the operation, including what public funds the Latin countries would themselves raise and approximately $11 billion pledged by the United States, mainly in the form of long-term, low-interest loans.

Following an enlivening send-off under President Kennedy's impetus, the program bogged down. Economically, it proved difficult to integrate the goals of countries that differed greatly in the nature of their economies and their economic philosophies. Nothing like the common, tightly coordinated plans of the ERP emerged, although a group of nine "Wise Men" labored to emulate the Marshall Plan in this respect. The sweeping multilateral cooperative arrangement envisioned in the Charter of Punta del Este never came off. Each country went on much as before, in fact, meeting each critical policy decision

on its own and negotiating directly with the United States for aid. The nine "Wise Men" ruefully observed that "the great concepts of permanence, of continuity, of long-term tasks, of self-help, are apparently being subordinated to the immediate difficulties of balance-of-payments disequilibria, to budget deficits, to the tendency to develop certain isolated projects that have a social impact and to the ups and downs of world tension, i.e., to circumstantial conditions that can obscure the real philosophy of the Alliance."

Political instability also plagued the Alliance. One government after another of those that had undertaken the original commitments was overturned. Most were replaced by military regimes that hardly shared the broadly democratic and internationalist perspectives in which the Alliance had been conceived, though some proved dedicated to both economic development and social reform on a nationalist or authoritarian basis. Meanwhile, violent social unrest swept the Americas, and this took a strong anti-American turn with substantial impact upon the Alliance. The latter was widely accused of being an extension of U.S. intervention even while the detractors castigated the northern capitalists for not fulfilling their share of the partnership. Uncle Sam, it seemed, could not win. The mood in South America became especially ugly after Richard Nixon became president, and Governor Nelson Rockefeller returned from a grim mission in 1968 on the President's behalf with the recommendation to terminate U.S. participation in the Alliance.

Yet, the Alliance did not exactly die. Certain measures were even taken to revitalize it as a multilateral partnership.

United States

The American heads of state gathered in 1967 symbolically at Punta del Este, the birthplace of the Alliance, and solemnly pledged "to give vigorous impetus to the Alliance for Progress and to emphasize its multilateral character, with a view to encouraging balanced development of the region at a pace substantially faster than attained thus far." The United States, for its part, put some muscle behind the call for greater multilateral action by limiting its loans to programs that were approved by the inter-American committee for the Alliance, a rather weak coordinating mechanism reluctantly accepted by some of the larger Latin American countries who preferred to pursue their interests independently. In 1969, the United States exceeded its basic commitment of $1 billion of official aid per year. This amount contributed to strengthening the combined resources of the Inter-American Development Bank, so it was able to up its annual lending to around $600 million as part of the total Alliance effort.

TRADE WITH THE EAST BLOC

During the first two decades of the cold war, East-West economic policy in the United States was uncontroversial. It was seen mainly as an instrument in the East-West conflict geared to deny communist countries the benefits of access to Western goods and capital. Export control was the key, meaning in essence tight restrictions upon trade. East-West trade policy was an instrument for containment and was for the most part subordinate to security interests. Some characterized U.S. embargo policies, with considerable justification, as constituting economic warfare. To be sure, relations with communist countries deviated from the U.S. tradition as a trading nation that explicitly granted its business community the right to realize profits from foreign trade. Communist countries, especially the Soviet Union, were refused

commercial benefits, while the U.S. economy was denied the opportunity to profit from such trade. The latter was no real matter for complaint as long as Western Europe also held back from trade with the East. When, in the early 1960s, though, Western European countries reestablished their traditional trade relations with the East and continued to expand them, the United States was confronted with a conflict between political and security considerations favoring continued controls, and business interests favoring liberalization. Under the Kennedy administration came the first attempts to loosen export controls, that is, to adapt to the West European level of controls.

The dilemma was an enduring one, but it came to a head beginning in the 1970s when President Richard Nixon and his National Security Advisor Henry Kissinger pushed through certain liberalization policies. Under pressure for a reduction in control in favor of increased trade from the business community and also from some in Congress, the administration pursued a determined liberalization policy. True, at no time was the administration, with the possible exception of some voices in the Department of Commerce, prepared to allow a policy of free trade toward communist countries solely geared to business interests. Kissinger, for his part, regarded East-West trade policy as an aspect of his diplomatic linkage concept, and liberalization was perceived as a concession to the East designed to foster reciprocal political concessions. East-West trade policy was to satisfy American interests by forming one part of the network of relations that was to moderate the Soviet Union by increasing its economic dependency.

The Nixon-Kissinger policy of détente, encompassing East-West trade policy, provided for a hitherto unknown degree of cooperation with the Soviet Union and came under pressure from opponents of

the entire foreign-political approach beginning in 1972. Under the leadership of Senator Henry (Scoop) Jackson, these succeeded in forming a large congressional coalition of conservatives and liberals advocating greater emphasis upon human rights in Western policies. Because if its broad political base, this group often obstructed Kissinger's policy of linkage, but not the expansion of trade relations for which East-West traders in the business community continued to lobby.

During the 1970s, U.S. agriculture became the chief beneficiary of trade with the East. Chronic overproduction, the result of increased efficiency and continued subsidization, furnished producers and exporters of grain a powerful incentive to deliver to the huge Soviet market. The year 1972 brought a tenfold increase in U.S. agricultural exports to the Soviet Union, and 1973 saw a further doubling. The U.S. agricultural lobby not only availed itself of the opportunity to export, but also pressed for ongoing expansion. The major farm lobbies, such as the American Farm Bureau Federation, the National Farmer's Union, and the National Association of Wheat Growers, demanded unrestricted export of agricultural products to the East Bloc. Their conservatism on most domestic issues notwithstanding, these lobbies became leading proponents of détente with the Soviet Union.

Neither the executive branch nor the Congress challenged the farm lobby's interest in exporting to the East until 1980, when President Jimmy Carter's grain embargo, in response to the Soviet Union's invasion of Afghanistan, undermined any commercial "right" to export to the Soviet Union, which had been consolidated during the prior decade. The Carter administration embargo provoked the entire agricultural lobby, including the farming community and the multinational grain trading companies, which endeavored to undercut the embargo at every opportunity. Under the Reagan administration (1981–1989), the farm lobby succeeded in having the grain embargo lifted as Reagan had promised during the election campaign. During that period, the farm community managed to preserve its special role by consolidating domestic acceptance of agricultural exports to the Soviet Union. It is notable that agriculture was excluded from all economic sanctions against the Soviet Union and Poland in the 1980s, and the Soviet grain agreement was extended in 1981 and 1982, at the height of the Polish "crackdown," and renewed in 1983.

The second significant group of East-West traders, the transnational manufacturing sector, proved overly optimistic in its assessment of the growth in East-West

The U.S. Economy

trade in the 1970s. Buoyant prospects for trade were based on the generally low level of exports to the East Bloc and the East's exorbitant demands for Western technology. Since America led its Japanese and Western European competitors in many high technology areas, it was a reasonable assumption that U.S. industry could avail itself of the opportunity to increase exports at the expense of established competition in Eastern markets.

The interest in East-West trade in U.S. industry was demonstrated by the establishment of new lobbying organizations and various joint cooperation councils, as well as growing public support for liberalization. In 1972, the East-West Trade Council was founded in Washington, and by 1974 it had 150 members including 100 companies engaged in business with the East. In 1973, with administration encouragement, the US-USSR Trade and Economic Council was established, which functioned as an effective Soviet-American Chamber of Commerce. By the following year, this had a membership of 168 U.S. companies. Many U.S. corporations, banks and trade organizations thereafter insisted upon most-favored-nation treatment for East Bloc countries and Export-Import Bank credits for trade with the East.

As the euphoria of détente faded in the late 1970s, the U.S. business community also became more circumspect in its demands. In sharp contrast to the opposition of agricultural lobbies, the Carter administration's sanctions in 1980 fostered no significant resistance from the major producers of oil, gas equipment and computers. The U.S. business community also seemed resigned to the increased restrictions on East-West industrial trade that were imposed during the first year of the Reagan administration. Yet, the embargo of the Soviet-West European gas pipeline deal in 1982 and the associated sanctions against West European companies imposed by the United States in an effort to thwart the arrangements incensed many business groups. They perceived the pipeline embargo as undermining the U.S. reputation as a reliable source of supply, which would jeopardize the participation of U.S. companies in future international industrial cooperation. Nonetheless, until the collapse of communism, U.S. industrial lobbies were more reluctant to press for the liberalization of East-West trade than were the agricultural groups. Two principal reasons for this suggest themselves. First, exports to the East remained a minor factor for U.S. business, accounting for less than 5% of total exports of finished products. Second, a large share of business with the East was conducted through West European subsidiaries of

Britain's Prime Minister Thatcher, "the Iron Lady," goes shopping to show voters she is aware of rising food costs.

U.S.-based multinational corporations anyway. Such transactions provided an alternative means of trading without concerns about lobbying or restrictions.

SHOCKS TO THE SYSTEM

New difficulties stemming largely from monetary interdependence, above all, from huge international capital flows beyond the control of any country's monetary authorities, overburdened the fixed exchange rate system and increasingly complicated national economic management. In the years 1968–1971, international monetary administration effectively broke down. The Europeans and the Japanese groused about expanding U.S. deficits and the strains these were placing upon the exchange rate system. Some countries began to reduce their dollar holdings, and the Germans and Japanese appeared increasingly less interested in addressing the problems stemming from their sizeable and growing surpluses. Few countries were willing to maintain the dollar's pivotal role by revaluing their own currencies as U.S. policy makers

recommended. The huge foreign dollar buildup continued, and the U.S. government continued its own expansionary domestic policies, seemingly oblivious to the international consequences and the potential for rampant inflation. By mid-1971, the U.S. gold stock had diminished by tens of billions of dollars worth of the commodity, and the U.S. economy was clearly exporting inflation. Of all the postwar currency crises, the dollar crisis of the summer of 1971 had the most far-reaching implications, forcing some sort of reform of the international monetary system.

In light of the special role of the dollar, U.S. international monetary policy differed substantially from that of other countries. Until August 1971, the United States maintained its exchange rate within the IMF parity band by freely buying and selling gold against dollars offered by foreign monetary authorities at the fixed price of $35 per ounce. In maintaining the place of the kingpin currency internationally, the United States was the only country committed to selling gold at a fixed price. Because other countries used the dollar as a unit of account and

United States

for many commercial transactions as well, U.S. monetary authorities were unable to change the relationship between the dollar and other convertible currencies. Foreign currencies had to be devalued or revalued, or else maintained within the set parameters of parity vis-à-vis the dollar. Other countries had to change the price at which they bought and sold dollars to alter exchange rates.

Floating Exchange

On August 15, 1971, President Richard Nixon cut the monetary Gordian knot, announcing that the dollar would no longer be convertible into gold. Without consulting the other principal actors in the international monetary system, and indeed without taking the matter up with his own State Department, Nixon jerked gold out from under the dollar and moreover imposed a 10% surcharge on dutiable imports into the United States. August 1971 thus marked the end of the quasi-gold standard and the initiation of floating exchange rates. Efforts in the following years have been made to reimpose order on the system with only limited and sporadic success. A new exchange rate system has not come into being and is unlikely to, although the establishment of the Economic and Monetary Union (EMU) in the late 1990s in Europe obviated the need for such an arrangement in those countries using the euro as their currency. After 1971, some currencies floated jointly, some floated independently, and some were pegged to other currencies or the SDR. Currencies are said to float when monetary authorities in national economies largely allow market forces to determine exchange rates. Yet, the dollar has retained its pivotal international role largely by default. The sheer size of the U.S. economy with its highly developed financial markets virtually guarantees the currency an international position. Moreover, no other leading players with strong currencies, such as Germany or Japan, were willing to allow their currencies to expand their international roles. Over time, though, the euro may begin supplanting the dollar at least in certain areas.

The oil shock of 1973, resulting in a rapid quadrupling of energy prices within a brief space of time, caused galloping inflation and so exacerbated the difficulties associated with unstable monetary arrangements that the world economy slid into a deep recession whose impact was felt for most of the decade. For the better part of two years, the Western countries focused upon the dual problems of inflation and recession. It was then that the term "stagflation" entered the economic vocabulary, depicting the horror scenario of plummeting production and skyrocketing prices.

Indeed, much changed in the world economy in the 1970s, mostly for the worse. The first oil crisis, sparked by a local war in the Middle East, shook the economies of the Atlantic Community like a battering ram. The harsh reality of the economic situation confounded all optimistic predictions. The second oil crisis, in 1979–1980, revealed the true nature of matters to the public at large. This latter crisis put many national economies back into recession just as they were on the road to recovery, rendering any serious combating of inflation difficult in the extreme. Export-oriented growth in Europe and America was hampered by competition from low-cost countries eager to sell abroad and to open themselves to the world. U.S. direct investment in Europe plummeted to less than $4 billion a year in the early 1980s after reaching levels of over three times more than a decade prior. Moreover, European countries' export difficulties were aggravated by the high-interest rates in the United States in the early 1980s as the Fed endeavored to fight double-digit inflation. Few countries even then, and certainly no Western countries, were economic islands, and the best-laid plans to strengthen one's own economy had substantial effects elsewhere in the world. In this case, drastic monetary measures in America helped to throw the economies of several friendly countries into recession.

Inflation

The American economy entered the 1980s in relatively bad shape. Inflation rose to a postwar high of nearly 20%, and the dollar exchange rate hit its all-time low. The effects of economic turmoil reached into people's daily lives, and the international economic climate became nearly unrecognizable. People in the United States and in Europe began to notice that an increasing number of everyday items came from distant countries. Meanwhile, factories were closing down and unemployment was rising. Industrial activity was declining sharply. Industries that had previously been symbols of industrial might fell on hard times, and the very structure of some began to dissolve under the effects of aggravated economic crisis. Entire economic sectors were labeled for the first time as "declining," and America's industrial fabric in some areas, especially heavy industry, began to fritter away. By the early 1980s, most countries realized how closely poor productivity gains, excessive pay raises, and low corporate profits are interrelated. Inflation, for its part, could be properly regarded as both a cause and an effect. Exchange rates fluctuated wildly at times, with the dollar hitting all-time lows against many other

currencies in the late 1970s, then soaring in the 1980s as U.S. interest rates skyrocketed. In 1980, the dollar was worth only 45% of its 1973 value in relation to the German mark, whereas in 1984, the dollar had a higher value against the mark than it did in 1973. In 1985, by nearly every measure of competitiveness, the currency was egregiously overvalued. In September 1985, a sustained, joint currency intervention by the United States, Japan, Great Britain, West Germany and France succeeded in producing a controlled devaluation of the dollar, which plummeted over 12% against the trade-weighted (market-oriented) average of the ten leading currencies by March 1986. During this time, the Japanese yen appreciated from 242 to the dollar to 165.

In the ideally functioning flexible exchange rate system, all states pursue their preferred domestic economic policy goals, and the exchange rates of their currencies internationally are allowed to find their own level in financial markets according to global supply and demand for different currencies. That is, currency values are completely market-determined. The reality is more complex, of course. Serious international problems emerge when a country's currency is either substantially undervalued or overvalued. An undervalued currency improves a country's international competitiveness by rendering its exports of goods and services less expensive, raising the price of imports, and attracting direct foreign investments. At the same time, an undervalued currency typically increases inflation by inhibiting the import competition that imposes price restraint on domestic producers. An overvalued currency tends to have the opposite effect. It is harmful to the international competitiveness of national producers. A country's trade and payments balances deteriorate accordingly, and unemployment rises. On the other hand, an overvalued currency can reduce inflation by permitting stiff competition from foreign producers.

Another problem under floating exchange rates, as it turned out, is that the world's goods markets are not as well integrated as some have assumed. The prices of goods converted into a common currency under the floating exchange rate regime, in fact, vary widely even between countries that trade freely with one another. Excess supply in one market does not always move smoothly at the going world-market price to another. Moreover, when a deficit country tightens its monetary or fiscal policy, and thus reduces demand in its home market, the result will be excess supply of its products. To clear the market, either production must be cut, causing unemployment, or prices must fall, relative to those abroad.

Weather

Today: *Partly sunny, warm.*
High 75. Low 65.
Monday: *Thunderstorm.*
High 83. Low 69.

Details, Page **C14**

127TH YEAR NO. 184   R   DC MD VA

The Washington Post

SUNDAY, JUNE 6, 2004

Inside: **Book World, TV Week,**
The Post Magazine, Comics
Today's Contents on Page A2

$1.50

Prices may vary in areas outside metropolitan
Washington. (See box on Page A21)

V₃

Ronald Reagan Dies

40th President Reshaped American Politics

1911-2004

Actor, Governor, President, Icon

By LOU CANNON
Washington Post Staff Writer

A movie actor who became one of the most popular presidents of the 20th century, Ronald Wilson Reagan redefined the nation's political agenda and dramatically reshaped U.S.-Soviet relations while serving as president from 1981 to 1989.

After leaving office, Reagan suffered in his final years from the mind-destroying illness of Alzheimer's disease. He announced his condition Nov. 5, 1994, in a poignant letter to the American people in which he thanked them "for giving me the great honor of allowing me to serve as your president."

Often called the Great Communicator, the Republican president was an icon to American conservatives, whom he led out of the political wilderness. But his legacy eluded easy ideological classification. Former Senate Republican leader Howard H. Baker Jr. (Tenn.), who served as White House chief of staff during a key period in the Reagan presidency, observed that Reagan, despite a proclaimed constancy of values, also displayed "a capacity to surprise."

This capacity was especially evident in Reagan's dealings with Soviet leader Mikhail Gorbachev. Although Reagan was an outspoken anti-communist who described the Soviet Union as an "evil empire," he forged a constructive relationship with the reform-minded Gorbachev, who ascended to power midway through the Reagan presidency.

The two leaders held five summits, beginning with a 1985 meeting in Geneva. At a 1987 summit in Washington, they signed the Intermediate-Range Nuclear Forces (INF) Treaty, the first pact to reduce

See REAGAN, *A28, Col. 3*

President Ronald Reagan, shown in 1991, announced his Alzheimer's disease to the nation in 1994.

BY WILLIAM COUPON—CORBIS

By DAVID VON DREHLE
Washington Post Staff Writer

Ronald Wilson Reagan, 40th president of the United States, who transformed the Republican Party and substantially defined the terms of contemporary political debate during two momentous terms in office, died yesterday afternoon. He was 93.

Ten years after he announced his Alzheimer's disease in an open letter to the American people, Reagan's long twilight reached its end at his home in Bel Air, Calif., in the company of his wife and their children.

"My family and I would like the world to know that President Ronald Reagan has passed away," former first lady Nancy Reagan said in a written statement. "We appreciate everyone's prayers."

President Bush received the news shortly after 4 p.m. Eastern time; he was in Paris and had just left a dinner with French President Jacques Chirac. In Washington and California, plans were quickly implemented for the capital's first presidential funeral in more than 30 years.

Initial plans call for Reagan's body to travel by Air Force One to Washington, where he will lie in state in the Capitol Rotunda. Around midweek there will be a funeral procession with horse-drawn caisson from the Capitol to a spot near the White House. From there, a hearse will carry the casket to Washington National Cathedral for a funeral officiated by the newly nominated ambassador to the United Nations, John C. Danforth, an Episcopalian minister and a former Republican senator from Missouri.

The body will then be flown back to California to be buried at the Ronald W. Reagan Presidential Library and Museum.

Official plans will be announced this morning, a library spokesman said.

"This is a sad hour in the life of America," Bush said after speaking with Nancy Reagan by telephone. "A great American life has come to an end. Ronald Reagan won America's respect with his greatness and won its love with his goodness. He had the confidence that comes with conviction, the strength that comes with character, the grace that comes with humility and the humor that comes with wisdom."

Blinking back tears, Bush added: "He always told

See REAGAN, *A32, Col. 2*

Global Legacy

Key Role in Ending the Cold War

By DAVID E. HOFFMAN
Washington Post Staff Writer

Former president Ronald Reagan left as his greatest legacy to the world a role in helping accelerate the end of the Cold War. The global competition between the United States and the Soviet Union, which consumed both nations for 46 years, cost hundreds of billions of dollars and led to building of the most destructive weapons ever known, reached a peak during Reagan's White House days and then expired only a few years after he left office.

The reasons for this extraordinary turn of events are larger than Reagan and span events far beyond his presidency. The roots can be found in the stagnation of the Soviet system in the late 1970s and early 1980s and perhaps most importantly in the ascension of Soviet

leader Mikhail Gorbachev, who opened the floodgates of change.

Yet the denouement might not have happened but for outside pressures, and this is where Reagan's legacy lies.

The United States, in the years before and during the Reagan presidency, underwent a revolution in high technology that the Soviets could not match. The Soviet system was under pressure from Reagan's defense buildup and deployment of medium-range missiles in Europe, the CIA-backed mujaheddin fighting Soviet forces in Afghanistan and Reagan's proposed missile defense system, the Strategic Defense Initiative. Reagan also launched a challenge to Soviet regional power in several conflicts from Nicaragua to Angola and lent

See GLOBAL, *A31, Col. 1*

The Reagan Style

As an actor, Reagan brought bright-eyed earnestness to the movies; as president, he brought glamour to the White House; as a husband, he brought steadfast love to his marriage.
STYLE, Page D1

A Life, a Legacy

The impact of Ronald Reagan's right-leaning economic policies, nicknamed Reaganomics, is still being felt 20 years later in California as word spread of the former president's death.
Special Section,
Pages A27-34

Political Legacy

Sagging GOP Rebuilt in His Image

By DAN BALZ *and* MIKE ALLEN
Washington Post Staff Writers

Ronald Reagan leaves behind many legacies, but among his most significant is a profound impact on American politics. Through the force of his convictions, his genial personality and his buoyant optimism, Reagan reshaped the Republican Party in his conservative image and with it transformed the politics of his country.

When he first appeared on the national political stage, Reagan was a speechmaker for Barry Goldwater in the closing weeks of the 1964 presidential campaign, an election that brought the worst drubbing for the GOP in the postwar era but also marked the birth of the modern Republican Party.

At the time of Reagan's Oct. 27, 1964,

speech, the Republicans were in the minority and in the throes of a brutal battle pitting the long-dominant moderate eastern wing of the party against an emerging, conservative, grass-roots army of activists in the Sun Belt. By the time of Reagan's death, the two parties were at rough parity in support but Republicans held the presidency, controlled both houses of Congress, and held a majority of governorships and roughly half the state legislative seats in the country.

Beyond that, Reagan indelibly stamped his conservative image on economic policy, devoted to cutting taxes and reining in the domestic side of the federal government. He left a party dominated by the South and the West, its moderate wing nearly a distant memory and the

See POLITICS, *A33, Col. 1*

United States

Oil production in Texas

International Tensions

The system of floating exchange rates had significant political-economic implications for the United States, far greater in fact than many had anticipated. Shifts in the exchange rate of the dollar fostered a relatively close link between America's international payments position and the performance of its domestic economy prior to 1971. Under fixed exchange rates, international monetary policies could largely be subordinated to domestic economic policies. Under the floating regime, the United States often finds it necessary to subordinate domestic economic policy to developments in its international economic relations. For example, the timing of the U.S. decision to increase interest rates in late 1978, which occasioned higher unemployment in an economy on the verge of recession, was prompted by the precipitous decline in the value of the dollar. Later, in the 1980s, America's economic growth and burgeoning budget deficits were financed in the main by substantial inflows of foreign capital whose withdrawal would surely have caused a financial crisis and a sharp fall in the dollar's value. Since then, many observers

have harbored concerns that the United States would be compelled to ratchet up domestic interest rates to sustain the flows of capital from abroad upon which the economy was considerably relying. U. S. trade deficits and the overvalued dollar in the 1980s stimulated political pressure for protection across a wide array of manufacturing industries of substantial export importance to less developed countries, in particular, textiles, shoes and steel. Restrictive trade policies in the industrialized countries to deal with trade imbalances inhibit underdeveloped countries' industrialization efforts and their capacity to service foreign debt through export earnings.

The Reagan Administration came into office in 1981 determined to effect dramatic change in macroeconomic management. Providing substantial tax breaks for individuals and corporations, it operated on the assumption that lower taxes would not only stimulate the economy but would, in the medium and longer term, result in greater public revenue as economic growth returned. The Fed, for its part, tightened monetary policy to wring inflation out of the system. It was

fortuitous that the widening budget deficit precipitated by the combination of tax cuts and increased defense spending was financed to a considerable extent by the influx of foreign capital attracted by high U.S. interest rates. As President Reagan, the inveterate optimist, trumpeted his belief in "morning in America," good times indeed seemed to return. By the end of Reagan's first term in office, the United States was enjoying a veritable economic boom, marked by a two-digit GDP increase during 1983–1984. The good times were rolling, to be sure, and Reagan was reelected in the largest electoral college landslide ever. Yet, rapid growth undoubtedly had its downside in the form of considerable structural imbalances. The overvalued dollar helped precipitate a record trade account deficit of nearly $140 billion by the middle of the 1980s. The combination of loose fiscal policy and across-the-board tax reductions engendered an annual federal deficit of over $220 billion by 1985.

Economists continue to debate the interaction of budget deficits and trade deficits, but it suffices for our purposes here to point out that budget deficits became a large problem for the U.S. economy in the 1980s and are likely to become so again in future years. Much of the Reagan Administration's economic policies reflected a preoccupation with supply-side economics, while more traditional economic policies tend to focus on stimulating or depressing demand as appropriate. There is something to be said about both approaches, because such is the magic of the marketplace that unsatisfied human wants do not long go unfilled. So what of budget deficits? For the first 150 years of its history, America was remarkably frugal. From 1789 to 1849, the U.S. government ran a net surplus of $70 million. From 1850 through 1900—including the Civil War, the Spanish-American War and the depression of the 1890s—the cumulative deficit was just under $1 billion. The country began piling up substantial debt during the Great Depression and World War II. The national debt held by the public rose from 16% of GDP in 1930 to 109% in 1946. It decreased somewhat for the next 35 years. Then came the only peacetime period during which the national debt grew significantly. It rose from 25.8% of GDP in 1981 to 48.2% in 1992. The 1998 budget surplus was the first since 1969.

Budget deficits in the United States began ballooning again in 2001. The deficit reached $400 billion in 2003, more than double its level the previous year. Many economists assert that the actual amount of the deficit is far less important than its size relative to the economy. In 2003, it represented less than 2.5% of GDP. It was as high as 5% of GDP in the early 1990s.

The deficit increases when the government spends money without augmenting revenue. Tax cuts usually result in larger deficits unless the government reduces spending. Substantial tax cuts in the years 2001–2003 contributed hugely to increases in the deficit. In the longer term, the Bush administration hoped the tax cuts would reduce the deficit by encouraging consumers to spend more on goods and services. Businesses in turn will achieve higher profits, pay more taxes and hire more employees who also pay taxes. Some observers are concerned that high deficits will increase the risk of recession. If the government is forced to issue large amounts of bonds to investors, the resultant new debt levels could drive up interest rates in the private sector. High rates would make it more expensive to finance large-ticket items and credit card purchases.

Supply Side

Economists have focused increasingly upon the supply side of economics in the last two decades, with some explicitly advocating the stimulation of production through cutting taxes and reducing government regulation. One of the more colorful and controversial of these economists is Arthur Laffer, who theorized in the 1980s that large tax cuts would "spur economic growth, increase tax revenues and curb inflation—all without a painful slash on government spending." According to Laffer, the government would collect "less per person in each bracket, but there would be more people in the higher brackets because of increased economic activity." Critics of the supply-siders in the 1980s argued that tax cutting would be highly inflationary, since the increasing amounts of money in people's pockets produced by tax reductions would increase already top-heavy consumer demand and encourage an inflationary psychology whereby consumers come to expect continuously rising price levels. Time has proven the critics largely mistaken on this score, but it is undisputed that the Reagan Administration's supply-side approach, commonly known as "Reaganomics," created burgeoning federal deficits.

Economic imbalances in America helped to promote a slowdown in domestic growth rates after 1985 that was widely perceived to have global impact. As protectionist sentiments in America intensified and international partners expressed growing concern about the state of world economy, the U.S. administration increasingly had to correct economic difficulties. A September 1985 agreement ac-

Karl Marx

celerated the depreciation of the dollar in the anticipation that a significantly lower dollar would narrow, if not eliminate, the yawning deficit on the trade account. Yet, the administration made little progress in reducing the budget deficit, and continuing high consumer demand in America pushed the trade deficit even higher, to levels approaching $200 billion by the late 1980s. Lingering imbalances played a huge part in the October 1987 stock market crash, when the Dow Jones Industrial Average of share prices fell by nearly 23% on "Black Monday," October 19, 1987.

MEDDLING AND MUDDLING

In Europe, the expanding role of the public sector had far-reaching consequences. The conjunction of an enlarged welfare state, growing public spending and declining growth discouraged investment. Economic slowdown contributed to the expansion of the "submerged economy," that moonlighting sector that escapes the eyes of the tax authorities. In some European countries, the submerged economy would even create its own class of small businesses, in, for example, the housing and transport sectors. In some countries, estimates of the moonlighting component's size of the overall economy ranges up to 20% of GDP.

The EMS

A number of European countries attempted to correct the vicissitudes of floating exchange rates with the formation in 1972 of the European Monetary System (EMS) within the EEC. The EMS was designed to maintain all EEC currencies within plus or minus 2.25% of a cen-

tral rate between each pair, and originally, each within plus or minus 2.25% of a rate against the dollar, the so-called "snake in the tunnel." The chief objectives of the EMS were to reduce currency instability among the EEC countries and to create a community exchange-rate regime that would provide a "zone of monetary stability" in Europe. Inflation, the oil crises, and an erratically fluctuating dollar complicated the functioning of the "snake," and plans for an eventual European Monetary Union had to be abandoned, although these would be revived two decades later. Many in Europe were stronger advocates of stabilizing exchange rates than were most Americans. The chief proponents of the EMS, many of them German and Dutch, argued that variable exchange rates could function internationally as unpredictable adjustable customs barriers. If one agreed, they suggested, that customs barriers are detrimental to trade, then one should take the next logical step and acknowledge that erratic exchange rates are also.

The EMS was arguably an early test of the readiness of major European countries to return to fixed exchange rates, and more broadly, it was the first significant move toward a currency union. By the mid-1970s, the EEC introduced a European currency unit, the ecu, that would be employed for the exchange-rate mechanism, above all, to calculate financial operations under both the intervention and credit mechanisms and for the transactions of the European Monetary Cooperation Fund (EMCF). At the outset, the value of the ecu consisted of a basket of the nine currencies of EEC members, and the weights were reexamined periodically. Greater exchange rate stability was widely perceived in Europe as contributing to higher growth in several ways.

Exchange rate stability would allow a higher level of both foreign and domestic demand to develop, the proponents asserted, since monetary instability has invariably been a drag upon national economies. In countries with strong currencies, appreciation contributed to deflationary pressures by reducing profits in export industries. A rise in the value of the currency relative to others was the principal cause for the periodic downward revisions of growth in West Germany, for instance. Countries whose currencies depreciated in relation to other currencies have experienced inflationary pressures through increased import prices, and in the case of Italy, wage indexation, which involves the automatic adjustment of wages for inflation. The latter has adversely affected economic growth over time. Governments have been leery about permitting their economies to grow faster, lest expansion

United States

contribute to further currency depreciation and generate yet more inflation.

Hence, monetary stability should have significant multiplier effects in light of the openness of Western European economies and the high proportion of intra-European trade in relation to total trade. For example, trade with European partners represents over three-quarters of total Belgian trade, and around half of the trade of France, Germany, Denmark and Italy. Greater monetary stability also encourages business confidence and investment. European business executives complained for decades about their inability to furnish their companies a full European dimension because of the exchange-rate and inflation risks. To be sure, it has often been difficult to forecast correctly the cost in national currency of inputs from abroad or the amount of revenue generated by exports. Such uncertainties have contributed to the difficulties businesses have encountered in harvesting the potential benefits of a market the size of Europe. Moreover, economic infirmity and unpredictability tend to reinforce protectionist pressures and paralyze investment.

Eurocurrencies and Petrodollars

In addition to increases in official holdings of international reserves, private bank lending to governments during the 1970s and 1980s underwent explosive growth, primarily through the expansion of the Eurocurrency market, where European currencies were traded. Advanced industrial states, a number of East Bloc countries, and less developed countries borrowed exten-sively in Eurocurrency markets to finance staggering current account deficits caused largely by oil price hikes and soaring inflation during the 1970s and 1980s. Throughout the 1980s, approximately 80% of Euro-currencies were still Eurodollars. Increases in oil prices in the 1970s transferred huge sums, an estimated $70 billion in 1974 alone, from the oil-consuming countries to the oil-producing ones. Wealth transfers had tremendous international monetary impact, creating substantial new recycling dilemmas. Had the surpluses of the oil-producing states not been so large, the extra earnings of these states would have been channeled back to the oil-consuming countries in the form of revenue from the import of goods and services from the oil consumers. The ensuing sums could be absorbed only with great difficulty, and the international monetary system could scarcely cope with the enormous wealth transfers. According to estimates, the 1979–1980 oil price spike resulted in perhaps $120 billion of earnings surpluses. Banks played an instrumental role in recycling "petrodollars" from the states belonging to the Organization of Petroleum Exporting Countries (OPEC) to oil-importing countries, both affluent and less affluent, with payments deficits. Many oil-consuming countries were unable to reduce their petroleum consumption sufficiently or to increase their exports adequately to correct their payment imbalances. In consequence, they had to borrow to finance their deficits, and the only source internationally of such funds was the surplus from petroleum export earnings.

The initial recycling problem became a debt crisis in the less developed countries within a decade. Private banks accepted the deposits of the oil-exporting countries and proceeded to lend these funds to oil-importing countries. Financial institutions accumulated huge Eurocurrency deposits as well as international loan portfolios. To a lesser extent, petroleum-generated revenues were recycled through government securities and investments by the oil-producing states. Yet, no consensus on international monetary relations emerged, much less on measures to deal with the political-economic implications of the explosive growth of international financial institutions. By the 1980s, international capital flows exceeded the value of world trade by between 10 and 15 times, and the amounts have continued to grow since then. Most economists agree that the opening of financial markets is an effective means of moving funds to where these will be used most efficiently. Yet, many countries have found swift flows of international "hot money" to be difficult to handle, and small capital markets can be engulfed by linkages to the huge and highly liquid capital markets of New York, London, and Tokyo. The East Asian financial contagion of the late 1990s brought in its wake heightened skepticism about the openness and integration of financial markets.

Interconnected

At the same time, the expansion of world trade in goods and services has underscored growing interdependence. Trade grew at an annual average of 4.7% in the 1980s and skyrocketed to a yearly annual growth rate of 6.1% in the 1990s. Trade in goods and services across national borders in 1970 amounted to about 15% of world output; by 1995, this number had grown to nearly 30%. Despite the volatility in some years of the 1990s, expanded world trade fostered annual average growth rates in the developing countries of over 4% in the 1980s and 5.4% in the 1990s. Relatively high growth rates in the United States in the last two decades suggest that it has been among the leading beneficiaries of expanding global markets. To be sure, being located in the largest single market has permitted American firms to set many standards in fast-growing economic sectors such as biotechnology, software and microprocessors. American firms often have a significant edge because of the openness and the sheer size of the domestic economy. In the years since the end of the cold war, the U.S. economy has grown faster than those of Japan or the European Union. Besides maintaining its share of world output, the United States has increased its lead in the infor-

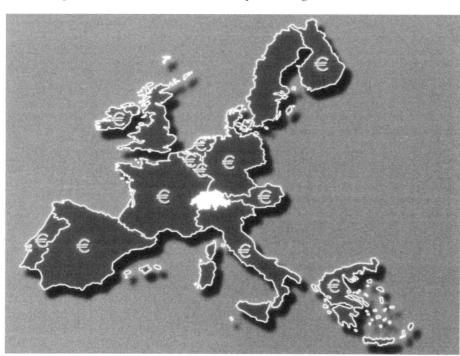

Countries using the euro

mation industries, including in the crucial software sector, giving it a commanding position in the technologies central to future economic growth.

In recent decades, advances in technology and finance have caused many of the world's nations to become more integrated. Since 1970, the volume of world exports has increased over tenfold, while the volume of world output has grown over fivefold. Dramatic increases in international financial flows have accompanied this expansion of trade. The daily volume of exchange rate transactions began to exceed $1 trillion per day in the 1990s. As with technology, production and manufacturing spill over national borders, and hence "American" automobiles customarily have components from Brazil, Japan, Mexico, France, Germany, Singapore and Australia.

Insofar as economists are able to agree about anything, it is that an open international economic system accelerates economic growth. Open markets facilitate economies of scale and allow countries to specialize in fields in which they have the greatest relative advantage. The arguments arise not only from theoretical economics but also from practical experience. Trade across borders and prosperity within borders are inextricably linked. The postwar successes of the United States, Canada, Western Europe and Japan have not been lost on the rest of the world. Western European economies were largely free to expand, while the initiative and talents of the people of Eastern Europe and the former Soviet Union were smothered in the Marx-in-wonderland nonsense of central planning. Japan, for instance, demonstrated remarkable postwar performance, especially in exports. Japan's growth in export volume averaged over 10% annually for a quarter of a century, and growth in GDP averaged over 5% in real terms in the 1980s, roughly twice the rate of growth of the rest of the OECD countries. At one point in the 1980s, Japan's per capita GDP was nominally higher than that of the United States, although it has slipped substantially since then. Two-way trade between the United States and Japan has exceeded $100 billion annually, more than the GDP of most countries, for over a quarter of a century now. Total direct investment in each other's economies has exceeded $25 billion for decades. Japan's net long-term capital outflow in the 1980s averaged over $100 billion a year.

The most dramatic examples of the success of market-based, open economies are the spectacular growth performances of the newly industrialized economies of Asia—Taiwan, South Korea, Hong Kong and Singapore, often called the "Asian Tigers."

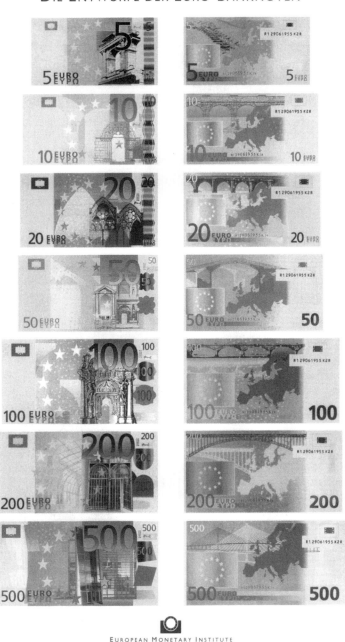

THE EURO BANKNOTE DESIGNS
LES MAQUETTES DES BILLETS EN EURO
DIE ENTWÜRFE DER EURO-BANKNOTEN

EUROPEAN MONETARY INSTITUTE

Courtesy of Central Audiovisual Library, European Commission

United States

Former Fed head: Board of Governors Chairman Alan Greenspan

Although their current growth has slowed, for nearly a quarter of a century, this group had economic growth rates exceeding 10% per annum in real terms. Despite the considerable differences in civic culture and political structure, each of these economies shares two common traits. First, the governments avoided the temptation to set prices, thus permitting market-based allocation of their resources according to decentralized price signals. Second, they have maintained outward-looking development strategies based on the global marketplace. Together these four economies are one of the top half-dozen trading partners of the United States.

The story of economic summitry began with the breakdown of the Bretton Woods system in the early 1970s and the first OPEC oil price and supply shocks in 1973. The curtain then went up on a new form of economic consultation, one involving the highest elected officials of the world's foremost industrial countries, which became the conferences of the G-7. International policy coordination made considerable progress thereafter. As major trading nations experienced the effects resulting from the decisions of other trading partners, the usefulness of consultation and policy coordination became more and more clear. In an increasingly integrated international economy, most countries more or less accept that it is in everyone's interest that decision makers be aware of the impact of their economic policies on other nations. Recognizing this, officials of leading economic powers have encouraged the evolution of mechanisms for economic policy coordination, with the participation of the IMF and the OECD.

To be sure, being an economic powerhouse is never without burdens and costs. In the case of United States, trade-driven growth brings about frictions and potential dilemmas on occasion. The foremost concern of many observers is the soar-

ing deficit on current account, the latter a broad measure of international transactions comprising goods and services plus net transfers. In the 1980s, some economists argued that deficits did not represent significant long-term difficulties primarily because the United States is the world's leading exporter of services, from architectural design to financial management. The deficit in traded goods, it was widely thought, would be counterbalanced by surpluses on services. In the 1990s, however, with continued high economic growth rates in the United States, imports surged, while massive payments to foreign lenders and investors resulted in large trade and current account deficits. The U.S. current account deficit rose from just over $4 billion in 1991 to a staggering $300 billion in 2000, when the U.S. equity markets spiked at almost unimagined levels. As long as overseas holders of U.S. dollars prefer the greenback to other currencies, the U.S. economy can probably sustain high deficits on current account. Should many holders of U.S. dollars decide to sell the hundreds of billions of dollars held overseas, however, then the currency will plummet in value, the price of imports will rise, and average U.S. citizens will experience a decline in their standard of living. Few believe the United States can continue to absorb increasing amounts of tradable goods and investments from abroad, and any deep and protracted recession in the United States, with the ensuing prolonged fall-off in consumer demand, could have profound economic and social repercussions overseas.

Former Treasury Secretary Timothy Geithner
Courtesy of the Federal Reserve Bank of New York

On the other hand, many economists emphasize that deficits indicate little about the technological strength or competitiveness of U.S. industry. Deficits do not mean the United States has lost or is losing its competitiveness. On the contrary: deficits in particular contexts and circumstances are a sign of economic strength rather than of economic weakness because these result primarily from the attractiveness of the economy for investment, especially foreign investment. Total production in the United States and output per capita tend to be high when the United States runs large trade deficits, which has been often. And the United States remains the world's largest exporter.

THE NAVIGATOR

Over 130 U.S. government agencies have some input into economic policy. These regulate business, provide subsidies, and offer concessional (low-interest) loans, among other administrative functions. Humorists would, of course, say that these are the creators of infamous bureaucratic "red tape." As foreign trade becomes more important to the United States, economically and politically, the State and Commerce Departments invariably acquire greater interest in economic policy. The most important of the federal agencies, apart from the Congress itself, and the one largely responsible for controlling inflation and providing economic stimulation in the last two decades is the Federal Reserve System, commonly know as the "Fed." In any overview of the U.S. economy, this organization warrants some consideration. The Fed's principal function is to regulate the lending and deposit-creating activities of the commercial banks. These activities significantly affect the level of output and prices.

The Federal Reserve System
"How can the Federal Reserve System most effectively use its powers to regulate the commercial banks so as to achieve its broad economic objectives?" is likely one of the most perplexing basic questions in the study of contemporary economic policy. Initially, one must recall that U.S. money not only serves as legal tender within the country, but it has become part of the money used by foreign countries for international trade and investment. Foreign countries hold international money for a variety of reasons, among them to settle temporary differences between expenditures in international transactions and receipts. The study of U.S. money and banking must include the international as well as the domestic monetary system.

According to law, the Federal Reserve System is an independent agency chartered by the federal government. As an independent agency, it is not under the direction of the executive branch. Because of its close working relationship with the Treasury Department, one might expect a chain of command from the secretary of the Treasury to the board of governors. In fact, no such chain of command exists, and anything smacking of executive interference in the operations of the Fed is highly improper.

Legally, the Federal Reserve System is an agent of the Congress. As such, it submits an annual report to Congress and regularly publishes several other reports requested by the legislative branch. Among the reasons given for limiting the influence of the Treasury over the Federal Reserve System is to prevent political manipulation of the monetary system. Actually, the secretary of the Treasury and the Comptroller of the Currency, head of the Office of the Comptroller of the Currency (OCC), were, for two decades, *ex officio* members of the board of governors, but the Banking Act of 1935 ended this arrangement. Congress has, over the years, set some limits on the amount of debt sold by the Treasury directly to the Federal Reserve. Yet, this type of limited control has little effect because the Federal Reserve can usually invest in securities that the Treasury has first sold to others.

Another important means of avoiding political control is the maintenance of an independent budget. No budgetary appropriation from Congress is necessary since the Federal Reserve banks are supported primarily by interest on their investments in U.S. government securities. The board is supported in turn by the Federal Reserve banks. To avoid both political control and abrupt changes in policies, the terms in office of members of the board of governors are long and do not coincide with the term of the president. Board members are appointed by the executive branch.

Despite the firm basis for Fed independence, most economists and policy makers agree that its policies ought to reinforce other federal government policies aimed at stabilizing the economy and promoting full employment. Regular weekly meetings of the Fed chairman, the secretary of the Treasury, and the chairman of the Council of Economic Advisors are held at which these officials discuss overall economic conditions and the appropriate economic policies of the federal government. Although most observers value Fed independence and advocate the strict safeguarding of this, some remain critical whenever discrepancies are observed between the economic goals of the executive and Fed policies. In December 1965, the board of governors approved a rise

World leaders at the 1995 G7 Summit, Halifax, Canada

in the discount rate despite the disapproval of President Lyndon Johnson and his team of economic advisors. The Joint Economic Committee subsequently arranged for hearings at which Fed officials and several prominent economists were asked to appear. Professor John Kenneth Galbraith of Harvard told the committee that "Men who prefer shadow to substance still speak of the independence of the Federal Reserve System. It hasn't existed for years." Another witness stated, "I have never had much sympathy with the theory of independence. The Government certainly should not move in one direction and the monetary authority in another." Economists are, of course, famous for their heated discussions, and in the esoteric, indeed often mysterious, world of monetary policy, easy answers seldom if ever come.

The significance of the Fed's independence ought not to be exaggerated, and it is rarely in the interests of the officials involved, or that of their organizations, to be in conflict with top officials in the executive branch of government. Occasional disputes at the highest levels nonetheless occur. During the 1980 presidential election, Fed policies helped keep interest rates high, a circumstance hardly improving the reelection bid of the politically embattled President Jimmy Carter. This was the same President Carter who two years prior sought to influence the policy decisions of Fed Chairman Arthur F. Burns, a Nixon appointee. When Carter unabashedly offered Burns reappointment only if he would comply with executive branch wishes, Burns balked and was replaced by G. William Miller, widely regarded as weak-kneed, without a will of his own.

That the Fed has grown in influence and independence under the chairmanship of Paul Volcker and Alan Greenspan is beyond doubt. Both chairmen made a strong

case that a major source of inflation in the last decades has been government overspending in response to demands from the electorate. Basic consensus now exists both inside and outside the government that monetary policy is a crucial instrument in combating recession, controlling inflation, promoting full employment, and stimulating economic growth. As soon as the economy begins a downturn, people clamor for the Fed to "do something." In theory, the Fed has the means either to counterbalance or assist efforts by the executive or the Congress to provide economic stimulation. Whether the United States can retain a system in which the Fed might tell powerful branches of government to "go fly a kite" remains somewhat of an open question. Much depends on the personalities of the respective members of the board of governors, but the last two chairmen of the board have not been renowned for modesty.

On the Fed board are seven full-time members appointed by the President with the approval of the Senate. To ensure adequate geographical representation, no two governors can come from the same Federal Reserve district. The country is divided into twelve Federal Reserve districts each of which has a Federal Reserve bank. Each Federal Reserve bank is owned by member banks. All national banks must join the system, and state banks that meet standards are permitted to do so as well.

Each appointee to the Fed board may serve only one full 14-year term and cannot be reappointed for another. One term expires every two years and unexpired terms are filled for the remaining time as need arises. Members of the board of governors are the only politically appointed officials in the Fed System. They in turn choose three of the directors, including

United States

Second United States Bank in Philadelphia, Lithograph 1838
Courtesy of Independence National Historical Park

the chairman, of each of the Federal Reserve banks and must approve the selection of the president of each bank. The ability of the executive branch to influence the board by appointing people of its choice is limited because of the long 14-year term of appointment and, barring resignations or deaths, the possibility of only two appointments in each four-year presidential term.

The board of governors has a chairman and a vice chairman. These are appointed by the president, and each holds office for a period of four years. The offices of the board are located in Washington, D.C. and the board has approximately 900 employees. Leading members of the Fed staff are mostly professional economists and a few are lawyers. Departments of the Fed engage in research on domestic and international financial trends—information needed by the board members in assessing prevailing economic and credit conditions. These departments publish the results of their research and furnish up-to-date statistics on money and credit in the monthly *Federal Reserve Bulletin*.

Fed Tools

The board meets in Washington, D.C., at least four times a year and determines general monetary and credit polices. It has four instruments to influence the activities of the nation's banks and ultimately the U.S. economy.

- It can increase or decrease within certain limits the reserves member banks' need to maintain against their deposits in the Federal Reserve banks.
- It can raise or lower the discount rate charged by the Federal Reserve banks to member banks. The discount rate is

the interest rate member banks must pay to obtain funds from the Federal Reserve banks for commercial notes the banks hold.
- Through the Federal Open Market Committee (FOMC), it can sell or buy government securities, certain other bills of exchange and bank acceptances.
- It can exercise direct control over the credit that may be extended in order to purchase securities (called margin requirements).

Only one of these instruments used to conduct monetary policy—changes in the legal reserve requirements of member banks—is the sole responsibility of the board. Policies concerning open market operations, the most important item in the toolbox of monetary policy instruments, are determined by the Federal Open Market Committee, on which members of the board sit. Changes in the discount rate are initiated by the individual Reserve banks, but must be approved by the board.

The FOMC was formally established in 1935, although a committee to coordinate open market purchases was set up by the Federal Reserve banks in the early 1920s. The FOMC is directly responsible for determining policy with respect to the purchase and sale of U.S. government securities. In recent years, transactions have included the purchase and sale of foreign currencies. Since 1962, the Fed has bought and sold foreign currencies in addition to U.S. government securities. The objective of these transactions is related to the balance of payments as well as to the general objectives of monetary policy. By holding foreign currencies, the Fed is in a position to purchase dollars in the foreign exchange market if it deems such action

necessary to temporarily raise or lower the dollar's value. At FOMC meetings, conditions of the economy are discussed and decisions must be made concerning the appropriate monetary policy in view of the overall economic situation. Staff economists of the board and the Federal Reserve banks are called upon to provide information. The policies determined by the FOMC are issued as directives to the manager of the System Open Market Account (SOMA), a vice president of the Federal Reserve Bank of New York. The actual purchase and sale of securities are performed by the Federal Reserve Bank of New York and are made through private securities dealers, most of whom have their offices in New York, where the principal equity markets are located.

Fed Banks

The Federal Reserve banks are the operating units of the system. Each of the 12 banks performs routine services for its respective region. Each issues and supplies Federal Reserve notes (greenbacks), clears checks on commercial banks, processes Treasury checks, stores coins, handles government debt issues, and examines and supervises the state-chartered member banks in its area. In addition, it links the financial institutions in the area to the national policy makers in Washington. Five Federal Reserve bank presidents are on the FOMC. Each bank is a federally chartered corporation with stockholders, directors, and a president. The stockholders of the Federal Reserve banks are the member banks in its district, and these select six of its nine directors.

The diffuse organization of the Federal Reserve System is somewhat misleading in practice. The formation of monetary policy and the operation of the instruments of control of the system are in fact quite unified. The bulk of the Fed's actions are defensive, designed not so much to effect a change in monetary circumstances, but to prevent other factors from causing changes that are not considered desirable. Through defensive open market operations, the Fed can counterbalance the effect on monetary reserves of other factors. Another important type of defensive operation is to offset the weekly variations in float and in the deposits of the U.S. Treasury. Both of these factors may change considerably from one week to the next. Such fluctuations can have disturbing short-run effects on bank reserves, and the Fed may attempt to neutralize their effects through appropriate open market operations. Above all, the organization of the system preserves the effectual representation of borrowers, lenders, and the public in different geographical regions. Although the Federal Reserve System has developed into a centrally controlled monetary system, it has retained a high degree of participation by those its policies affect.

GO-GO GLOBAL

"Globalization" generally refers to the establishment of international markets on the input side for labor, capital, and technology, and on the output side for final products and services. Globalization has several key features in trade and finance. International trade has increased more rapidly than global economic output. Trade in services has grown along with merchandise trade. The substantial decrease in transportation costs has resulted in more and more goods being tradable. The vast expansion of world trade has heightened international competition. In many ways, therefore, the United States is traveling the open globalization road back to the future. The American economy was actually *more* international before 1914 than it was even in the decades following the Second World War. Some observers have therefore been inclined to quip that one of the major economic accomplishments of the post-World War II era has been to restore the level of international economic integration that existed prior to the First World War. Far too few Americans now seem to understand that globalization represents a sort of homecoming for the American economy, rather than a new tendency or international development. Between 1890 and 1914, America was the world's largest trading economy after Great Britain, yet even this depiction is somewhat deceptive since so much of Britain's trade was with its colonies at the time. With adequate adjustment for colonial trade, one could make the case that the United States had become the world's leading trader by the dawn of the 20th century. A significant proportion of the economy consisted of imports or exports in 1900, and by then U.S. trade amounted to nearly 15% of total world commerce.

Massive direct foreign investments at the time dwarf those flowing into America now as a percentage of GDP. Analysts estimate that nearly 25% of American GDP in 1914 accrued from foreign investment. American railroad companies were quoted on the London stock exchange beginning in 1838. British investors acquired the Pillsbury flour company, then America's largest miller, in 1899, and it was repurchased in 1989 by a British company after it had reverted back to American ownership several decades prior. It is only by comparison with the years after 1945 that foreign investment appears to be an anomaly. Foreigners have been eagerly buying American property, assets,

British Prime Minister Margaret Thatcher "sweeps out" all remnants of Keynesian economics in the 1980s.

and technology for nearly 200 years. In the 19th century, most of the funds came from Great Britain, although money increasingly flowed in from other European countries until the outbreak of war in 1914 put an abrupt end to the investments.

President Hoover epitomized the international public figure of the early 20th century. From the time he graduated from Stanford University until becoming commerce secretary, Hoover resided outside the United States continuously. Although he officially had an office in San Francisco, his headquarters were in London, with branch offices in St. Petersburg and Shanghai and several other places. He enjoyed substantial international respect and was even offered a cabinet ministry in Great Britain during the First World War. He assisted Polish schoolchildren in the days after the armistice and was instrumental in the rebuilding of Belgium. He organized famine relief in the Ukraine in the 1920s and assumed a key role in European reconstruction. No American public figure, indeed, few Americans at all, in an age in which the economy is supposedly globalizing and the world is said to be shrinking, has had anything like this amount of international experience. It is remarkable that such a cosmopolitan person was not at a political disadvantage in the America of the 1920s, as he doubtless would be now.

Trade and cross-border investment boomed in the period 1870–1913, and the world's economy approached integration at an even faster pace than in the last decade of the 20th century and the early years of the 21st. Investment from relatively slow-growing Europe rushed

to the newly industrializing countries of the time, mainly, the United States, Canada, Argentina and Australia. Most of the world took part in the quasi-monetary union, the international gold standard, which began emerging around the middle of the 19th century. World trade grew more than 25-fold in the century before 1913. Huge numbers of people migrated from Europe to North America, and in consequence, the labor market in this vast internal market rapidly integrated. This globalization process ended by the sets of non-tariff "barriers" and regulatory "obstacles" commonly called the First World War, followed by the genuine tariff barriers and "beggar-thy-neighbor" policies of the 1920s and 1930s.

In fact, the thrust of much domestic and international economic policy after the First World War, and even after the Second World War when countries simply should have known better, was away from interdependence. Many nations in the 20th century placed a higher priority on domestic stability and full employment than on the maintenance of international links. Some sought extensive national control over their monetary and other economic policies. To a considerable extent, such control is what the Keynesian "revolution" and its emphasis on the domestic economy were about. The British economist John Maynard Keynes postulated that the state through "macroeconomic," that is, fiscal and monetary, policies could harness the economy to its own political and social ends and thus improve upon the autonomous markets of 19th-century laissez faire. Some have characterized such a change as the "commerce of nations"

United States

displacing the 19th-century international economy. The same desire for greater control in domestic policy underlies the movement toward regional trade blocks. Indeed, many economists now warn that economic regionalism, evidenced by efforts to conclude new bilateral or regional free trade agreements, threatens to damage the foreign and trade policies of some countries, including those of the United States. It is preferable, they argue, to work to strengthen the WTO and the single world trade system it represents.

Be that as it may, two facets of 21st century globalization, which arguably have an impact upon all countries in some form, make it substantially different from the early period of commercial internationalization. The first and primary one is the swiftness with which orders for trade, capital, and technology are carried out. The rapidity of transfer and the sheer size of the amounts of "hot money," that is, capital, moving about the world, render it much more difficult for governments to respond when a crisis develops. Financial contagion has become a fact of life. The world teetered on the brink of a financial sector implosion in 1997–1998, for example, when the East Asian financial meltdown spread to Russia and Brazil, and as highly leveraged hedge funds (ones with large amounts of short-term debt) went belly-up. Flows of capital investment have grown hugely since the 1980s and these have become more concentrated in the richest parts of the world. Some developing countries have become cut off from international capital markets because of debt problems and/or restrictions on for-

eign portfolio investments. This impasse precipitated the Mexican economic crisis in 1994, which ultimately necessitated a large U.S. bail out. The fundamental problem in Mexico was ultimately the small volume of sustained net capital inflow. Mexico encountered genuine difficulties when its rate of investment continuously exceeded its savings rate, and its leaders blithely assumed that other countries would bankroll the difference. As the current account deficit rose above 6% of GDP annually in the early 1990s, the deficit became untenable largely because global capital markets are far less integrated than the domestic funds markets of many developing countries. In short, Mexico was headed straight down. In North America, the EU and Japan, barriers to the free flow of capital have been falling. With the establishment of the EMU, capital controls within Europe have been dismantled for the most part. Financial market regulations in Japan, Britain and the United States have been significantly relaxed. The United States in particular maintains an enormous appetite for foreign capital.

Second, the pervasiveness of outside political and cultural influences threatens the autonomy of non-Western cultures. The undermining of indigenous cultures and the insecurity borne of global economic forces engender considerable backlash in many areas to modernization. Countries with little industry, less competitive production and rudimentary capital markets are invariably those most threatened by an open, globalized economy. Even in the United States, significant segments of society have suffered dislocation because

of global interdependence. Unemployment in the steel, automobile, textile and shoe industries in the last two decades has reached what some regard as unacceptable levels. Adjustment difficulties in other countries have been more severe. In such an open world, disruptions and dislocations are unavoidable, relatively rapid conversions are inevitable. The overall challenge is to ease transitions and to render adjustment smooth and efficient. Yet, as is frequently the case in human affairs, the devil lies in the details.

Data indicate that international firms are also becoming more "global." For instance, in 1970, of the some 7,000 multinational corporations identified by the UN, more than half were headquartered in the United States and Great Britain. Now, fewer than half of the approximately 35,000 multinational firms are from four developed countries: the United States, Japan, Germany and Switzerland. Britain is not even in the first half dozen. Corporate America has over 20,000 majority- and minority-owned affiliates strategically positioned around the world, with a combined gross output of over one-half trillion dollars annually. Currency transfers, capital surpluses, and accelerated growth rates have assisted multinational corporations from other countries to involve themselves in global business operations. Although many of these firms are relatively small, an increasing amount of foreign investment by firms from the third world and the "Asian Tigers" is taking place. Moreover, foreign direct investment has developed a more pronounced regional flavor. For most of the 1990s, the countries of the European Union plus Scandinavia and Switzerland were the world's leading foreign investors. To be sure, they invested sizably in North America. Yet, they invested even more heavily closer to home, especially after new and lucrative commercial opportunities in East-Central Europe began to present themselves. Although the Japanese still invested substantially in North America, in the 1990s, they have concentrated their investment efforts even more upon Southeast Asia, South Korea and China. U.S. firms, for their part, have invested principally in Canada, Mexico and Latin America. More than half of these world flows of foreign direct investments were in industries classified as services. A sizeable chunk of that investment came from the financing affiliates of multinational manufacturers or traders, such as General Motors, IBM, Matsushita or Mitsubishi.

Globalization and Its Discontents

For its supporters, globalization promotes a coalescing of people, ideas, and economies. Globalization will assist in al-

Circuit board manufacturing machinery

John Kenneth Galbraith

Milton Friedman

Economic Thinkers

John Maynard Keynes

Arthur B. Laffer

leviating poverty and hardship by creating jobs and expertise. Globalization will help people around the world become sensitive to other cultures and render nations more interdependent, thereby strengthening political ties and reducing the chances of conflict.

For its detractors, globalization is undesirable at best and malevolent at worst. Globalization undermines individual cultures by exporting callous "Americanization" that upsets established social orders. Globalization contributes to environmental degradation by allowing multinational corporations to set up shop in developing countries with loose environmental controls. The development process strips nation-states of their sovereignty, as they become subject to decisions of the International Monetary Fund, World Bank, World Trade Organization and multinational corporations. Globalization accelerates a "race to the bottom" in which a small minority becomes increasingly wealthy and influential while growing numbers of people face misery and economic despair.

In fact, the process of globalization is neither a panacea nor an evil. To grasp the benefits and problems of globalization, one must consider the basic economics driving globalization. The process, which involves the freer movement of goods, services, labor, and capital across borders has three fundamental and contemporary aspects: deregulation, liberalization, and privatization.

Deregulation, or the free flow of capital, is perhaps the chief point of contention with the more sophisticated critics of globalization. It has been condemned as both eroding national sovereignty due to lack of government control over capital inflows/outflows from a nation, and

as leading to unstable national economic conditions triggering financial meltdowns that in turn can affect the world at large. Yet, large international capital flows are routine in modern economies, and only rarely do these beget financial crises.

Capital flows are properly divided into several categories. Foreign aid is one type of capital flow, although it is controversial for reasons that have little to do with globalization. The two more significant types of capital flow that are closely associated with globalization are short-term investment, or "hot money," and long-term investment, known as Foreign Direct Investment (FDI). Short-term investment can under certain circumstances be harmful to a national economy, while FDI is generally beneficial. When critics of globalization berate the lack of capital controls, they are usually referring to short-term investment, but actual distinctions often become blurred. The major problem with short-term investment is that it is in actuality short-term credit. One or more countries or financial institutions are essentially lending money to another country. The lending countries see an opportunity to make a profit, as the country receiving the money will eventually pay back the loan with interest. The borrowing country also sees an opportunity to make money.

Credit allows a borrowing country to invest in an endeavor it would otherwise not have the resources for, such as real estate development, or the improvement of energy sector infrastructure. The recipient country eventually has to repay the loans, but thereafter all profits made from the endeavor accrue to the borrowing country. Much like individuals who end up in massive credit card debt, countries have a tendency to live beyond their means.

Returning to the example of Mexico, the country suffered a string of financial crises starting in the mid-1970s. Because of its plentiful oil reserves, short-term investment has over the years poured into the country from lenders who were confident of repayment from oil revenues. Unfortunately, Mexico has spent borrowed money lavishly, only to confront the hard reality that world prices of natural resources fluctuate substantially. With periodic declines in oil prices, Mexico has found itself in dire financial straits. On several occasions, Mexico faced a structural inability to service its debts, a predicament commonly known as a "balance of payment crisis." Subsequent financial crunches have had severe consequences in Mexico, as well as in countries that loaned money to Mexico.

The devaluation of the peso has periodically rocked the U.S. financial market, as tens of millions of dollars lent to Mexico by American banks became unserviceable loans. Moreover, Mexico's ability to purchase imported items diminished, since a less valuable currency raises import prices. Countries that exported to Mexico found their profits plummeting. Mexico has been bailed out by massive loans from the United States several times, yet the difficulties appear to linger.

Profligate governmental spending habits tend to prompt financial crises. Financial crises can also be triggered by lending countries. Known as "liquidity crises" these exigencies are largely caused by the flight of capital from a borrowing country. For whatever reason, investors come to believe that the borrowing country will not be able to repay its debts. Afraid of losing money, investors pull their money out of the borrowing country. The withdrawal of funds usually leads to a self-fulfilling

United States

Containers at docks

prophecy. A country without capital cannot afford to invest in any sort of capital-producing endeavor, which means it has diminished earning power, and therefore could default on its loans. In modern economies, the potential consequences of a financial crisis are harsh, as evidenced by the Asian financial crisis of 1997–1998. The crisis began as a devaluation of the Thai baht. Thai banks borrowed money from various foreign banks throughout the 1990s, and in turn lent the borrowed money to Thai investors. In 1997, the Thai real estate bubble burst, and many of the Thai investors could not afford to pay back Thai banks, which in turn could no longer service foreign loans. Foreign investors with money in Thailand converted Thai baht into U.S. dollars and pulled the money out of Thailand. Thailand did not have a floating exchange rate, as the baht was "pegged" to the U.S. dollar.

Pegging currency means that a country prints only as much of its currency as it has equal to dollar reserves. When a country runs out of dollar reserves, its currency suddenly plummets in value. Rapid devaluation is what Thailand faced in the autumn of 1997. Currency speculation exacerbated the crisis. Essentially gambling upon the decline in a national currency's value, speculators borrow large sums of national currency and convert it into dollars. When the value of the national currency falls, the speculators pay back the cheaper loans, earning a tidy profit. The conversion of large sums of baht to dollars wiped out the Thai dollar reserve, forcing the Thai government to drop the dollar peg, and therefore guaranteeing a devaluation of the Thai baht.

The Asian financial crisis did not stop at Thailand. In a process known as "contagion," Thailand's financial crisis spread to Malaysia, Indonesia, the Philippines, and South Korea. Investors in these countries, convinced the economic conditions in Thailand were similar to those of the other four nations, repeated the same cycle of currency conversion and capital flight, accompanied by speculative attacks on each of these countries' currencies. As the economies of these nations spiraled downward, their misfortune spread to other countries far from Asia. Russia, for example, suffered its own financial crisis in 1998, partly due to the decrease in its oil revenues. The countries affected by the Asian financial crisis could no longer afford to purchase large quantities of oil from Russia. Eventually, the crisis even affected Argentina, which suffered financial meltdown in 2001. Although Argentina had few direct economic ties with the countries involved in the Asian financial crisis, its economic situation in 2001 was similar to that of Thailand's in 1997. That circumstance alone contributed substantially to a massive flight of capital from Argentina.

Globalization critics argue that the entire Asian financial crisis could have been averted had Asian governments imposed capital controls. In the early 1990s the nations affected by the crisis had largely deregulated their financial markets. The governments of these countries had little control over who their banks borrowed from, how much they borrowed, or whom they lent money to. The IMF has often advocated deregulation as a way to increase foreign investment and capital flow. Indeed, the impressive economic performance of many Asian nations in the early 1990s suggests that deregulation played a crucial role in providing capital for Asian economic endeavors. Nonetheless, in a capital control-free environment, money that is easily invested is just as easily removed. This flow of "hot money," can contribute to financial crises that have global ramifications.

Shipping yard

As opposed to short-term investment, FDI is often a boon to a country's economy. FDI involves the purchase of tangible assets, such as factories and machinery. Since FDI is in effect tied down, it is not subject to speculative attacks and liquidity crises. The host country is also not subject to interest payments, since FDI is not a monetary loan. FDI tends to provide long-term improvement in a country's economy by boosting wages to local workers and by providing technological innovation to the host country. China, which is now one of the largest recipients of FDI in the world, has had burgeoning economic growth over the last decade. It has largely ignored advice to deregulate its financial markets, and has not been subject to the same liquidity crises that have struck its Asian neighbors in part since it has largely maintained capital controls. Singapore, a stable country that also receives large amounts of FDI maintains strict capital controls.

Globalization's supporters view increased trade as being perhaps the most positive aspect of globalization. Increased trade provides a greater worldwide market for a country's goods, leading to increased production and economic profits. On the other hand, critics of trade liberalization generally fall into two camps. The first camp charges that trade liberalization is applied unequally. Rich industrialized nations are taking advantage of poorer developing countries by forcing them to lower trade barriers, but not acting in a reciprocal manner, they allege. Such unfair practices result in the rich countries getting richer from export wealth, and the poor countries remaining mired in poverty since they cannot compete in world markets. The second camp charges that trade liberalization damages developed countries by exporting jobs to developing countries where wages and production costs are lower.

Populism and Nationalism

No country in the world truly practices free trade. While trade liberalization is widely accepted as conducive to successful economic growth, in reality most countries carry out some form of trade restriction. Certain sectors of the economy, often those with substantial political clout, are protected domestically and thus not subject to the same market competition as others. Protectionism in the United States extends primarily to agriculture, steel and textiles. For example, the U.S. government has periodically imposed import tariffs on foreign steel. Trade barriers raise the price of imported steel, so American companies will tend to purchase American-made steel since the prices are lower. While this arrangement is beneficial to the U.S. steel

industry, it is detrimental to its foreign competitors and to American consumers. In the absence of steel tariffs, U.S. manufacturers would have to lower prices to compete with foreign imports. Domestic prices would fall, and foreign competitors would likely make a greater profit from steel sales. Agricultural products and textiles are major export items from developing countries, and trade restrictions in these areas can be ruinous. The agricultural sectors of developing countries also fall victim to the pernicious practice of farm subsidization in affluent countries. The U.S. government, for instance, encourages U.S. farmers to boost production by providing price supports, or to curb production by paying them to leave fields fallow. Subsidization tends to keep prices of agricultural products in the United States fairly constant, but at the same time prevents the entry of less expensive imports. Far worse, overproduced agricultural products from developed nations, mostly from Europe and the United States, get dumped onto the world market, driving down prices of products worldwide and jeopardizing entire product sectors in developing countries.

Developing nations have little choice but to begin their journey to economic prosperity by producing commodities, and only relatively advanced economies produce computers, electronic equipment and automobiles. As some globalization critics and advocates agree, developing countries will continue to suffer economic hardships as long as affluent nations continue to practice trade protectionism instead of trade liberalization. Another camp of trade liberalization critics claims developed nations suffer economic hardships due to job flight to developing nations. While multinational corporations have subsidiaries in developing countries, many mature industries, such as steel manufacturing, have contracted sharply over the last several decades, resulting in substantial job losses. The former has not been the primary cause of the latter, though. The difficulty for much heavy industry in the developed world is not trade liberalization. Rather, it is technological advancement. Sectors such as agriculture, steel, and automobile manufacturing have shed massive numbers of employees over the last two decades, but such reductions are hardly because these industries have suddenly started outsourcing all their job positions to the developing world. Instead, these industries have become far more efficient, able to produce the same amount of product with far fewer personnel. For example, Bethlehem Steel, one of the primary U.S. steel companies, needed 30,000 employees to produce four million tons of steel in the 1960s. Today, it needs

fewer than 3,500 employees to produce the same amount. U.S. farmers are in a similar situation. Family farms have nearly disappeared in America, having been replaced by large agricultural operations requiring a modest number of personnel with modern farm equipment.

The percentage of GDP in developed countries produced by commodities and manufacturing is decreasing, while the service sector grows by leaps and bounds. Developed countries compete less with developing nations in service sectors largely because these require greater numbers of skilled workers. Agriculture and basic manufacturing in developing countries need far fewer skilled workers. Therefore, the competition between developed and developing nations is for the most part between unskilled and semi-skilled workers in these countries, not all workers.

Critics insist that this competition puts unskilled workers in developing countries at an advantage. True, corporations often move to developing countries because they can pay workers lower wages and thereby increase profitability. Nonetheless, lower wages are not the only criterion of acceptability for corporations establishing foreign subsidiaries. Corporations shun countries wracked by violence. They avoid investing in countries with corrupt governments. They want their employees to have at least basic skill sets, so they can keep on-site training costs low. Corporations will generally incur higher costs to ensure their subsidiaries are successful. If all corporations cared about were lower wages, sub-Saharan Africa would be getting far more than 2% of worldwide FDI. Instead, developed and advanced developing countries continue to be the largest recipients of FDI. The United States draws in large amounts of FDI every year.

In principle, few but the hard-core critics doubt that trade liberalization is one of globalization's greatest benefits. Greater economic openness benefits both producers and consumers. Producers receive more profits to invest in further capital-producing endeavors, and consumers save money, which can in turn be spent in other sectors of their national economies. Critics of trade liberalization tend to focus on wealth and income inequalities, not on the practice itself.

Virtue of Necessity

Privatization involves the shift from public, or state-owned industry, to privately owned production. Privatization in the last decades has covered a variety of economic sectors, including banks, airlines, telecommunications, transportation, and some energy production. Supporters of globalization note that privatization is

United States

beneficial because it encourages competition. Competition in turn results in lower prices and better quality products. Critics, for their part, assert that privatization is disadvantageous for developing nations. Acquisitive corporations charge prices developing nations cannot afford to pay for some goods and services benefiting everyone, such as health care. Privatization allows a few individuals to become wealthy at the expense of the many, they allege.

Privatization doubtless promotes competition. Countries with open markets enjoy the beneficial effects of competition. State-run industries are notoriously inefficient and can charge whatever prices they want for products and services. The consumer's choice is either to pay the price or do without. Additionally, lack of competition creates no incentive to provide high quality merchandise. The consumer must make do with inferior products and services if these are available at all. Privatization induces companies to either improve products and services or go out of business. A recent example is British Telecom, which for years was the only telecommunications provider in the United Kingdom. Complaints about government-owned British Telecom's service were proverbial, but consumers had no alternative. When the British telecommunications market was opened to competition, British Telecom nearly went out of business as other service providers, both foreign and domestic, moved in. British Telecom, now privately owned, has since improved its service and managed to stay in business.

In addition to promoting beneficial competition, privatization represents another opportunity for developing countries to receive FDI. When countries privatize, global corporations have an incentive to invest. Privatization of parts of the energy sector has provided one of the few sources of FDI for poverty-stricken Africa. Privatization can have serious repercussions, above all, for the lower income citizens of developing as well as developed nations. For example, partial privatization of health care has resulted in that sector becoming one of considerable political strife.

Most European countries have national health care. The United States, on the other hand, does not. In the United States, health insurance is not universal, and is usually provided by employers. Benefits vary widely from employer to employer and region to region, and people without jobs find themselves with no health insurance. The cost of health care in the United States without insurance is simply more than many can afford. Critics of privatizing health care point out that if the poor in the United States cannot afford private health care, then the poor in the developing world will be even less likely to.

Critics of privatization often single out pharmaceutical companies and drug patents for severe criticism. Pharmaceutical companies in developed nations are nearly all private. Patenting drugs results in at least partial monopolization of product, which tends to raise prices. Drug prices in developed countries are high enough, and often unaffordable for people in developing countries. Privatization critics express dismay that poor countries with the highest infection rates of deadly diseases, such as HIV/AIDS, are unable to afford life-saving medication simply because prices are out of reach. Moreover, private drug companies sometimes adamantly oppose the release of generic versions of the patented drugs, which are far more affordable, because they fear that citizens of rich countries will refuse to pay for the more expensive name-brand product if cheaper alternatives are available. Drug companies insist they must maintain their profits in order to continue to fund research and development for new medications. Such a line of argument is of little comfort to those dying of treatable diseases.

International development need not exacerbate social and economic problems, despite what globalization's discontents assert. Globalization is more a process than an end state. In fact, parts of the world have been more globalized in the past than they are at present, and globalization is not irreversible. Countries have considerable choices about globalization, and the fact remains that globalization correlates tightly with economic development. Open economies tend to be the most prosperous. Impoverishment is the invariable consequence of economic autarky. One needs only to look at a country like North Korea to see the alternative to economic openness.

The chief issue that critics of globalization must resolve for themselves is that globalization is essentially the spread of worldwide capitalism. What globalization's discontents should grasp is that the alternatives to market capitalism have been tried and have failed miserably. Given the opportunity, people strive to improve their situation in life. Critics bemoan the spread of commercialism and "Americanization," but ideas and methods would not spread if they were not popular. Capitalism has succeeded for a reason.

Yet, unregulated capitalism via globalization can lead to gross wealth and income inequalities that are unsustainable in the longer term. In a relatively open world economy, a financial crisis anywhere affects economies everywhere. Domestic legislation and international trade agreements can control monopolies, ensure competition, prevent unfair trade

Mercedes-Benz production in Germany

practices, regulate equity markets, and ensure corporations obey local environmental and labor laws. Globalization is ultimately what people make of it.

HOME TO ROOST

In the 1990s, economic interests generally received greater priority in U.S. foreign policy, reflecting the relative waning of security concerns in the wake of the demise of the Soviet Union, but returning with a vengeance after the terrorist attacks on the United States in September 2001, and the general dissatisfaction on the part of the American public about the supposed decline in the country's economic performance. Some observers identify the renewed questioning whether further benefits of trade liberalization and interdependence are worth the accompanying costs in some industrialized countries, including the United States, as an aspect of a popular groundswell. With certainty, interdependence can accentuate domestic economic problems as instabilities in one economy spill over into others. Globalization causes labor dislocations, augments inequalities of income distribution at least in the short run, renders national planning more difficult, and increases society's vulnerability to external political pressures. In the view of some Americans, the erosion of national self-sufficiency has gone too far, and the world has surpassed the limits of beneficial interdependence. To them, the woes associated with interdependence run the gamut from social upheaval to virulent financial contagion.

Among the important developments in the data is the change in the actual posi-

The U.S. Economy

A farmer graphically protests price support level.

tion of the United States in the world economy in the past decades. True, the United States remains the world's largest national economy, with a gross national product amounting to nearly half that of the OECD countries combined. From the 1970s through the early 1990s, U.S. productivity grew slowly, but in the 1990s, it began rising and has continued to rise despite a somewhat sluggish economy in the early years of the new millennium. Productivity even rose during the 2001 recession, and in 2002 it jumped 4.8%, as rapid as any increase since the Second World War. Nonetheless, the U.S. share of world GDP has fallen by nearly half since 1950: from 39% in that year to just over 20% at present. In certain industrial sectors, the U.S. portion of world production dropped even more sharply in the last four decades. U.S. world motor vehicle production plummeted from 76% in 1950 to under 20% in the 1990s. The share of world steel production declined from 46% in 1950 to under 10% in the 1990s. Some industrial sectors, such as shoes and basic textiles, have nearly ceased to exist in North America.

Yet, the U.S. share of world exports has remained fairly steady at around 15% in the last decades and at least two important areas represent important exceptions to the pattern of declining world share of production: agriculture and computer software. In the case of the latter, the United States is the undisputed world leader. With respect to the former, the U.S. economy is a more significant agricultural exporter than ever before. Even Japan, with its hugely subsidized agricultural sector, is the largest customer for U.S. agricultural exports. America's farmers, who are far more efficient than many competitors abroad, could provide substantially greater amounts of food to consumers worldwide at much lower prices than many currently pay. American agricultural producers are often prevented

from exporting what they could by quotas and high tariffs, state trading, and other restrictive practices. It is simply uneconomical for Japan stringently to restrict imports of products in which its trading partners benefit from a comparative advantage, especially since those partners welcome products in which Japan enjoys a comparative advantage, such as electronics, robotics, and automobiles. If Japan and other countries deem it necessary to subsidize their agricultural sectors for political and social reasons, economists agree they should do so in ways that limit trade distortions. The large amounts of farm income consisting of social welfare payments could be transferred in ways not involving agricultural production. Moreover, freer Japanese markets in service sectors such as insurance and financial services would bring about greater efficiencies and much lower user costs.

In the view of some, to stress the declining share of the United States in the world economy is to put an unwarranted negative emphasis on a phenomenon that is in large part a result of rapid recovery and subsequent healthy growth of the economies of other industrialized countries since the Second World War. It would be better to discuss the growing portion of the rest of the world in the global economy, especially the republics of the former Soviet Bloc, newly developing, and it is hoped, newly democratizing. Moreover, a mere glance at the American export record in the last century indicates that the economy has maintained a quite steady 12%–13% share of world exports. At the beginning of the 20th century, commodities and agricultural products comprised the lion's share of American exports, while Europe as a whole, including its sprawling empires, still dominated global trade. The U.S. component of world commerce spiked only for brief periods following the two world wars when trade competitors were ruined by devastating

conflict and America enjoyed an artificial monopoly in some areas. It is notable that in the years 1900, 1913, 1997 and 1998, otherwise poles apart politically and socially, U.S. export figures were strikingly similar at around 12.5%.

Another significant yet widely disregarded feature of the American economy's export sector is the evenness of its global distribution. More than a third of America's exports focus upon the geographic neighbors, Canada and Mexico. Half are spread nearly equally between Europe and Asia. Hence, the preponderance of U.S. exports goes fairly uniformly to the world's main economic regions, East Asia, the EU and North America. No other leading export nation can make such a claim, since the vast majority of exports, even in a globalized age, go to nearby markets. The export sectors of the EU countries have the least broad horizons, since over two-thirds of Europe's trade is within the region. Patterns of East Asian trade are similar. So the United States has arguably been the chief catalyst for greater openness in the world economy, and its huge domestic market has continued to absorb many of the world's exports. The general affluence of America, the versatility of its financial markets, and the stunning rate of technological innovation have prompted many foreign producers in the last two decades to orient themselves to the American market.

Economists differ about the broader implications of international commercial allocation, and on occasion even about the trade statistics themselves. For example, some economists add America's imports and exports, which is the equivalent of over 20% of GNP, to better portray overall trade effects. To be sure, America's global economic involvement entails a great deal more than trade, and few serious observers suggest that the extent of economic interconnectivity in the modern world is accurately reflected in export and import figures. Imports, which are on a par with around 11% of American GNP, equal nearly half of national manufacturing output, and by some estimates, the impact of trade is felt by at least half the U.S. economy when all the linkages are considered. A good deal can be said for these arguments. U.S. imports of goods and services total just over $1 trillion annually, but foreign-owned affiliates of international corporations operating in the United States have nearly $2 trillion in sales. These affiliates number nearly 10,000 and contribute over $400 billion in output. This latter number exceeds the GDP of most countries, including affluent ones such as Sweden and Denmark. The U.S. automobile industry is not a particularly large exporter, and vehicle imports

United States

account for less than 20% of the U.S. market. Yet, the prices and quality of those imports largely determine the retail prices U.S. manufacturers can charge, the wages of U.S. automobile plant workers and the incomes of those who service the U.S. automobile industry.

There can be no question, though, that the shift in the relative importance in the tradable goods side of the global economy has affected the nature of the interactions between the United States and the rest of the world. The change has been particularly significant because it has been accompanied by an increase in the openness of the U.S. economy and therefore in its sensitivity to influences from abroad. Partly as a result of these developments, some in America are currently having second thoughts about interdependence if not expressing their outright opposition to it. Labor leaders as well as two recent presidential candidates, Ralph Nader and Patrick Buchanan, have vehemently opposed globalization.

During the heyday of Bretton Woods, Americans had an easier time perceiving the rapid growth of international trade and investment in "classical" terms: as a development enhancing specialization and efficiency, raising output, income, and standards of living in the participating countries. More recently, however, other aspects of this growth of interdependence have come to the fore and been duly exploited by the tub-thumpers, in particular, the increasing sensitivity of national economies to events and policies originating outside their borders and therefore beyond their control.

The equity markets are a salient example. Markets tend now to move in lockstep with one another, and events anywhere in the world can cause jitters in U.S. stock markets where a substantial majority of Americans now have investments and where most of Americans' retirement funds are to be found. Wall Street has in a sense become main street in 21st-century America. In just a few weeks of declining markets, tens of billions of dollars of the public's savings can be eliminated. In the recent prolonged bear market in 2000–2003, the Dow Jones average declined by nearly 40%, and the broader market indicator, the Standard and Poor's 500 index declined by over a third. In one of the greatest equity market slides in history, the technology-heavy Nasdaq, which reached stratospheric levels in the spring of 2000 of over 5,000 points, plunged to under 1,100 in the autumn of 2002, as the swelling tide of the market tech-wreck obliterated paper fortunes. Officially, the U.S. economy slipped into a recession in March 2001 that lasted for the rest of the year. Corporate profits continued to

decline into 2002, and although the economy began to turn around by the start of the year, the recovery in 2002–2003 was a "jobless" one, with unemployment remaining high, at least by U.S. standards. Nearly two years after the 2001 recession ended, private-sector employment continued to decrease. In the first few years of the 21st century, the American economy shed over three million jobs, and a decline in employment during two years of growth, however modest, is most unusual. By way of comparison, two years after the deep recession in 1981–82, the economy had added more than three million jobs to the employment level when the recession began. These numbers should be seen in the context of the 1990s, when, in the last five years of that decade, the apparently indomitable American job-creating machine was adding some two million positions a year.

The bursting of the stock market bubble beginning in the spring of 2000 contributed to the most severe economic deceleration in America and many of its commercial associates since the 1973 oil price shock. In October 2002, the Dow Jones average fell to a five-year low. America's main trading partners, Canada, Mexico, Japan, the United Kingdom and Germany, were all adversely affected. World growth slowed to just over 2% in 2001, the worst year for OECD economic performance since 1982, and remained anemic in 2002. The economies of developing countries were subsequently hard hit by the downturn in OECD countries.

Consumer spending, by far the largest component of America's economy and accounting for nearly 70% of total GDP, was disrupted by the terrorist attacks upon the country on September 11, 2001, a downturn that deepened the economic slump already in train. Later that autumn, the Federal Open Market Committee depicted the American economy bleakly, stating unequivocally that "heightened uncertainty and concerns about a deterioration in business conditions both here and abroad are damping economic activity." U.S. spending data thereafter reflected customary economic woes, including stagnant incomes, increasing joblessness and plunging equity markets. Business investment, already in the doldrums prior to the September 2001 attacks, continued to fall throughout 2002 and showed little sign of significant upturn in 2003. Corporate pretax profits fell for five consecutive quarters beginning in late 2000, and according to a survey of nearly 1,500 companies in the U.S. component of the Dow Jones Global Market Index, total corporate net income was 72% lower toward the end of 2001 than a year prior. Manufacturing failed to recover significantly by 2003,

largely the result of the overcapacity that developed in technology areas during the boom years of the 1990s.

In response, the Fed cut interest rates by over 500 basis points (5%), beginning in early 2001 when the first indications of severe economic downturn presented themselves. Three interest rate reductions of 50 basis points (.5%) transpired following the September 2001 terrorist attacks. By the middle of 2003, the Fed funds rate was at around 1%, a four-decade low. With the consumer price index hovering around 2%, real interest rates in 2003 were effectively negative. When the Fed reduced short-term interest rates in June 2003 to a 45-year low, the move was aimed at spurring the economy and staving off deflation. Low interest rates did not help in some sectors, and many companies still felt pressure on profit margins, above all, because of rising costs.

WHAT IS PAST IS PROLOGUE

It is surely paradoxical that as the weight of historical evidence has won the intellectual battle for open markets, policies geared to greater internationalization have come under attack in some of the world's most developed industrial countries. Large trade imbalances have fueled rising concern about, and frustration with, the world trading system in the United States. Protectionist measures have gained wider support as a misguided remedy. Policy makers in the Western democracies face conflicts between the generalized benefits that accompany global economic integration and the interests of particular domestic constituencies. It is ironic that by one measure, world trade, integration actually slowed considerably in the 1980s. Although trade grew rapidly in 1950–1975, as successive GATT rounds lowered tariffs, and fixed exchange rates helped businesses plan ahead, its growth slackened measurably after 1975, as currencies became more volatile and, in the 1980s, as non-tariff barriers rose to restrict trade in goods and services among the industrial countries. The integration of the world economy over the past 40 years has markedly increased the intensity of competition and forced structural changes some individuals have difficulty handling. Policies that soothe powerful domestic interests by promoting isolationism and claiming to advance self-interest have a superficial albeit wrong-headed attractiveness.

Protectionist Sentiments
Economic policy is closely intertwined with politics. Policy makers are especially sensitive to the opinions of the public because dissatisfaction with the economy is often translated into votes. Unemploy-

ment and inflation have a powerful influence on officials and other policy makers. The state of the economy can affect the outcome of elections. The defeat of Herbert Hoover in the 1932 presidential election is one of the best-known historical examples.

Few Americans think it feasible or desirable to seclude the United States from the rest of the world. Yet, many, including some decision makers, think it possible that America can be integrated on its own terms. The short-sightedness of such an approach should be apparent. American policies toward trade and foreign investment are more influential than any other factor upon the international business climate. An America leaning toward protectionism, one that shuns its economic competitors in Japan and the EU or scorns exports from Latin America, is likely to dissuade other countries from opening their borders to trade and investment flows. An America that seeks to restrict foreign multinationals' acquisition of high-technology companies and even to pressure their existing subsidiaries in an attempt to open other countries' markets to trade and investment is likely to be the forerunner of the retreat from global economic integration. Needless to say, American politicians are in denial about such inclinations on their part. Few speak of protectionism or border closing. Rather, intentions and measures are cloaked behind such vague concepts as "industrial policy" or taking the "long-term view" of the U.S. economy. A Republican administration supposedly committed to free trade substantially augmented agricultural subsidies in 2002 and imposed surcharges on steel imports, by way of example. "This nation has got to eat," President George W. Bush said in a February 2002 speech supporting the $170 billion farm subsidy bill. He went on to say that U.S. "farmers and ranchers are the most efficient producers in the world . . . We're really good at it." Does the federal government really need to subsidize such an efficient industry? Does America need farming subsidies for its people to eat? True, economic nationalism is not especially popular with U.S. voters, yet politicians full of sound and fury can nonetheless strike a popular chord. Notwithstanding widespread acceptance that trade barriers and subsidies entail costs and impose sacrifices on consumers at home, "sacrifice" is a word passing officials' lips easily, especially after the autumn of 2001. Indeed, American protectionist policies triggering retaliation around the world could represent one of the greatest potential threats in the relations among nations.

Americans should be concerned about the changing position of the United States in global affairs, including the economic situation. Portraying economic difficulties as evidence of decline is grossly misleading, though. Such arguments direct attention away from the real issues, which involve long-term global changes, and advocate remedies that would weaken rather than strengthen American standing. Any sort of withdrawal from international commitments would reduce U.S. influence without strengthening the domestic economy. Yet, national decline is an episodic subject of popular discussion, and it is a common theme for pundits, politicians and academics. The following is a typical depiction of the country's waning: "America is sauntering through her resources, and through the mazes of her politics with an easy nonchalance; but presently there will come a time when she will be surprised to find herself grown old—a country, crowded, strained, perplexed—when she will be obliged to pull herself together, husband her resources, concentrate her strength, steady her methods, sober her views, restrict her vagaries, trust her best, not her average, members. That will be the time of change."

One could hardly find a more succinct and eloquent statement of the Declinist case than this, which in fact poses a genuine problem for modern Declinist theorists. These words were written by none other than Woodrow Wilson in 1889. American concerns about meeting national challenges are nothing new. They are as old as the republic. The tradition of handling national challenges is time-honored as well.

Perceived economic weakness in America strengthens protectionist sentiment, while generating popular feelings of national decline. Even though a large majority of Americans favor an active role for their country in the world, around half the U.S. public favor tariffs or other forms of economic protectionism, along with perhaps a third of the country's political leaders. Many Americans appear unable to grasp that any market closure furnishes other countries with an excuse to close theirs. This will not be the first time that a failure to understand changing international circumstances has led to the consideration of policies that are contrary to America's interests.

In the 21st century, it will be increasingly difficult to separate domestic economic performance from international economic relations. Trade balances and trade policies have substantial impact on inflation and employment in the domestic economy of even the largest countries, including the United States. Two examples spring to mind. Imports play an important role in reducing inflation by increasing the supply of goods in the economy and providing price discipline on domestic manufacturers. On the other hand, high trade deficits result in the loss of American jobs. The U.S. trade deficit during the 1980s was widely acknowledged as a leading cause of unemployment and a restraint on higher levels of domestic economic growth. Some economists estimate that as many as 20,000 American jobs are lost for each billion of dollars in the U.S. trade deficit. This interrelationship suggests that a $100 billion trade deficit will ultimately result in the loss of two million jobs.

On the other hand, a fair number of perceptive economists suggest that trade deficits are a dangerous popular obsession. As they would have it, trade is no longer a valid measure of global competitiveness, especially among developed countries. In the 21st century, firms will compete in growing measure through foreign-affiliate sales instead of exports. By the late 1990s, exports of U.S. affiliates totaled well over $600 billion, matching the total value of U.S. goods exports and surpassing the export levels of Germany and Japan. Europe absorbed more than half of these sales. U.S. exports to Canada in 1998 totaled $157 billion, while U.S. foreign-affiliate sales in that year were over $209 billion. U.S. exports to Japan in 1998 were around $58 billion, yet U.S. foreign-affiliate sales were over $77 billion. U.S. exports to Brazil were just $15 billion, but foreign-affiliate sales amounted to a whopping $53 billion. The United Kingdom accounted for some $224 billion in affiliate sales in 1998, six times the official export figure. Using official export figures, Italy, Spain and Switzerland would not appear to have much commercial association with America, and yet, foreign affiliate sales with these countries is relatively high, amounting to tens of billions of dollars annually. The relationship cuts both ways in many cases. Although U.S. imports from Britain totaled less than $40 billion annually in the late 1990s, which is only half the value of annual imports from China, affiliate sales of British firms operating in America approach $200 billion annually, far exceeding the sales of Chinese companies.

Wall Street Wickedness

Americans had no shortage of bad economic news in the first years of the 21st century. Corporate and financial scandals shook America in the autumn of 2002, a sensitive time when the country was emerging from a recession and tens of millions of people endured substantial equity market losses. The most prominent of these, the collapse of Enron, one of the world's largest energy and commodity traders and the seventh largest company

223

United States

in the Fortune "Top 500," undermined public confidence in corporate America when assurance was most needed. Houston-based Enron availed itself of the deregulation of energy markets to make the transition from a basic fuel pipeline operator to an innovative trader of energy as well as a slew of other commodities and services. In fact, Enron had become so diversified that company executives themselves were hard-pressed to explain all the corporate pursuits. Since a great deal of its business was conducted over the Internet, Enron embodied the "new economy" for many. How much greater therefore the popular disillusionment when the huge "off budget" sheet losses surfaced and the company's accounting methods displayed momentous improprieties. As the Enron share price plummeted from over $90 to less than $1 in a matter of months, and stockholders and employees faced heartbreaking losses, Enron attempted to avoid bankruptcy by consenting to a corporate takeover by Dynergy. When the deal fell through, Enron simply went belly-up. Enron's collapse and the associated scandals surfacing in the wake of bankruptcy had wide ramifications, raising all sorts of doubts about auditing and accounting procedures, disclosure of company information, regulation of online operations and corporate leadership behavior in general. Enron's astonishing insolvency not only affected other businesses as far removed as Europe, but raised such a hue and cry about corporate accounting methods and potential "book cooking" that

the actual amounts of corporate earnings across the board during the roaring 1990s were called into question. When the earnings statements of other firms were shown to be dubious, even though no company had ever quite cooked its books as Enron had, equity markets in America and Europe plunged as investors large and small lost faith in corporate America, whose image worldwide had become severely tarnished. One of the world's leading accounting firms, Arthur Andersen, which had audited some of the usual corporate suspects, went under. Others were disgraced.

One cannot help but recall the old yarn about the American accounting profession. In a congressional hearing in the early 1930s, during the depths of the Depression, Representative Alben Barkley of Kentucky queried the head of one of America's largest accounting firms about how scrupulously his accountants examined the operations of their respective clients. "And who audits you?" Barkley then inquired, apparently not altogether satisfied with the answers he was receiving. "Our conscience," came the terse reply. The point is prosaic, the implications profound. "Who is to guard the guardians?" is one of the oldest dilemmas of social organization.

The litany of scandals is now all too familiar. Around the world, Enron and WorldCom are infamous household names. In America, there are also Adelphia, HealthSouth, ImClone, Global Crossing, Xerox, Qwest, the hundreds

Peter Drucker early in life
Courtesy of Claremont Graduate University

of public companies that restated their accounts in recent years, as well as the Wall Street investment banks accused of conflicts of interest and shady practices. In Europe, the false accounts of Royal Ahold, a large Dutch food distributor and retailer, surfaced; the controversial payments to the German executives of Mannesmann upon the acceptance of Vodafone's takeover bid in 2000; the travails of telecom giants Vivendi in France and Marconi in Great Britain; as well as the bribery and other legal charges surrounding Italy's wealthiest businessman, Silvio Berlusconi, who became the country's prime minister and president of the European Union's Council of Ministers, the latter appointed on a rotational basis. Since the beginning of the economic downturn in Japan, corporate and banking scandals involving debt mountains, cover-ups and sheer incompetence have continued to present themselves.

In a more open world economy, corrupt business and banking practices, shoddy accounting, and basic unsatisfactory economic policymaking will invariably have adverse effects upon societies far removed. Even though the United States, with its huge internal market, is less globalized than most other developed economies, millions of American jobs and tens of billions of dollars are linked to economic developments elsewhere. Hence, the quality of corporate earnings and the prospects for profit growth remain matters of considerable concern. The spate of commercial outrages at home and abroad in 2001–2002 was damaging to the U.S. economy, above all, because business scandals rep-

Peter and Doris Drucker work together at their home in Claremont.
Courtesy of Claremont Graduate University

funds they considered surplus to future liabilities. Lower investment returns have caused many pension accounts to be severely underfunded, and some companies are being forced to top up pension funds when they are financially pinched. According to some studies, pension plans offered by over 300 of the companies in the S&P 500 index are underfunded by several billion dollars. Accounting rules some corporations have utilized exacerbate the difficulties, as, for example, when companies estimate their pension funds' average annual return over a certain period of time and automatically identify the amounts as profits, even when losses have accrued. Several dozen of the largest U.S. companies classified some $50 billion of pension fund gains as profits in 2001, when in fact the funds suffered losses of perhaps $30 billion dollars. General Motors had to make up for deficits in its pension fund to the tune of $2.2 billion in 2002, and IBM committed itself to topping up its pension fund by $1.5 billion annually beginning in 2002. Unfortunately for the automobile giant, Standard and Poor's downgraded GM's credit rating largely because of the company's underfunded pension liabilities. Pension fund deficits could have a broad impact upon the economy, since these are already compelling companies to reduce capital spending and lower dividend payments.

This cash crunch is transpiring in Western societies where older people are becoming the dominant force. The fastest growing population segment of many post-industrial societies, including America, is over age 50. For the first time in American history, people of advanced years are expected to displace those under age 14. Not since the last years of the Roman Empire have societies experienced such a shrinking young population. Retirees' pensions will inevitably be lower to prevent the burden on the working population from becoming insupportable.

For over 40 years, demographers have been studying the baby boom generation—a demographic bulge of more than 75 million people born from 1946 through 1964 and now ranging in age from 40 to 58. Just as boomers have altered America's economic and social landscapes—from classroom shortages in the 1950s to the housing boom of recent years—their impact on the nation's stock and bond markets, retirement system, and economy could be huge. Government projections show that as boomers begin collecting Social Security and Medicare benefits, federal budget deficits will balloon. Beyond purely financial matters, experts predict significant changes in the nature of retirement itself.

resent a breach of trust upon which democratic capitalism depends. Yet, one of the virtues of the system is its constant ability to reform and renew itself. The creation of the Securities and Exchange Commission in the early 1930s, for instance, came in the aftermath of scandal and economic depression. Current reforms, particularly those affording independence to the company's board of directors, thus assuring investors of the existence of a functioning system of checks and balances in corporate governance, are largely for the better. Some of the changes will have to be modified or scrapped, but time and experience are needed to make determinations. A genuine danger, many suggest, would be if courts and regulators do not distinguish between fraud and legitimate business risks that do not work out. Honest business mistakes, such as new products that flop in the marketplace should not be subject to criminal or civil penalties. Risktaking, they would point out, is an essential element of free enterprise.

The rash of credit downgrades in 2002, combined with investors' continued suspicions about company balance sheets, put a damper on the investment that was needed for a robust recovery in the following years. The year 2002 brought frequent disclosures of investigations by regulators dissatisfied with business practices and of earnings restatements by companies alleging to have discovered accounting irregularities. In each case, the company's future earnings will be affected, if for no other reason than that the accounting practices inflating past earnings can no longer be used. A related issue involves the controversy over how companies should account for stock options. If all companies were required to include these options in the calculation of earnings, the impact could be large indeed. Some observers have determined that the reported earnings of companies in the Standard and Poor's (S&P) 500 index would have been reduced by some 20% in 2001 if stock options had been handled as an expense.

It's the People, Stupid

The conjunction of plunging equity markets and the spate of corporate scandals scarcely inspired much confidence about the financial soundness of many pension funds, something affecting tens of millions of Americans. The long bull market produced such high returns that many companies reduced their contributions to pension funds or halted these altogether. In fact, some began to withdraw

United States

Oil field

Current practices of thrusting older people out of the workforce will, by necessity, terminate. In two decades time, the normal retirement age in developed countries is likely to be in the mid-70s. The most influential and widely read thinker and writer on modern organizations, the late Peter Drucker, predicted that the future will bring two distinct U.S. workforces, those under 50 working full-time in fairly permanent positions, and those over 50 combining traditional jobs and leisure in whatever proportion suits them.

Initially weighing heavily on the performance of global markets, the successful military action in Iraq in the spring of 2003 led to increased investor confidence and a resurgence in equity markets. Once the Iraq war was ended, despite the insurgency that followed, economic growth rapidly improved. With the fog of war lifted, people picked up their pace of spending, with a notable acceleration in both automobile and non-automobile retail sales. Housing and mortgage refinancing activity surged to record levels, fueled by low interest rates. Furthermore, the long-tepid capital goods sector improved. Likewise, although the onset of Severe Acute Respiratory Syndrome (SARS) in Asia taxed an already stressed global marketplace during the early months of 2003, the subsequent containment and apparent suppression of the viral illness provided Asia with an economic boost through the middle of the year. In the succeeding months, the overall economic picture seemed to brighten. The unemployment rate declined and manufacturing began to pick up.

Yet, the shadow of a potentially devastating influenza pandemic continues to loom over the world today. Some predictions of how quickly the disease might spread, and how many people it could kill have been grim. The H5N1 highly pathogenic avian influenza (HPAI) that currently worries the health community has caused the deaths by illness or culling of many millions of birds worldwide, and while it has killed relatively few people, its average mortality rate of approximately 63% is alarming. History provides three examples of influenza pandemics in the last century, the most devastating of which occurred in 1918. The disease first appeared in the highly crowded conditions of U.S. military training camps, probably beginning at Camp Funston, Kansas. It proved to be extraordinarily infectious, and due largely to troop movements it was quickly transmitted around the world. Records of the pandemic show that in 1918 over 121,000 U.S. service personnel were admitted to medical facilities. The medical system was so overwhelmed that treatment was often nonexistent. The pandemic decimated militaries and civilian populations alike, killing over 50 million people globally.

Years of Plenty

As 2004 progressed, several positive developments in various regions translated into increased global earnings expectations. Markets worldwide climbed on the basis of this news with nearly every industry in most regions experiencing broad gains. Companies were cutting costs and reining in debt. Interest rates remained low in major countries, contributing to the control of inflation. Global concerns about inflation saw many central banks keep rates at historic lows. The U.S. economy continued to grow at an annual rate of over 4%. The continued weakness of the U.S. dollar tended to aid the unhedged U.S. investor as the euro, British pound and the yen all gained relative to the U.S. currency. In Asia, the emergence of China as a secondary growth engine to the global economic recovery came at an appropriate time. In general, as the global economic situation improved, growth provided a backdrop for quality performance by the equity markets, more than offsetting any sell-off experienced in the year's opening months.

In 2005, business investment spending continued to benefit from improved profits, less uncertainty, and an expanding economy. Increased business capital spending was an essential component of better growth in 2006. The expected capital spending improvement was driven by three factors: the need to replace aging equipment and software; rising corporate cash flows; and the cost-effectiveness of substituting capital for labor. Following the capital spending boom of the late 1990s, firms curtailed capital expenditures, largely due to a weak economy and poor profitability. With the economy improving and profits picking up, firms began to spend again on capital equipment and software, in part to replenish their aging (and rapidly depreciating) capital base.

Foreign growth continued in 2005-2006, due in part to a pickup in U.S. demand and the impact of additional monetary and fiscal stimulus overseas. With U.S. and Asian demand increasing, growth improved even in Japan, where anemic conditions and deflation prevailed for some time. China continued to play a key role in sustaining Asian growth, with an economy that grew at a robust 8% percent clip.

The U.S. economy moved ahead at a healthy pace during 2005-2006. GDP expanded at an annualized rate of nearly 3.5% as job growth helped buoy consumer spending and rising profits boosted business spending. Employment data were solid. The economy added an average of 185,000 new jobs each month and the employment rate dipped to a four-year low of 4.9%.

Nonetheless, record-high energy prices began to weigh on economic growth as the period wore on. Signs of slower growth appeared in retail spending and industrial activity. Consumer confidence readings fell sharply in the weeks after Hurricane Katrina, which occurred in late August 2005. The decline was the largest

in 25 years, according to the University of Michigan's monthly survey. Yet, the economy dealt with the challenge of the storm-inflicted losses relatively well the next year. After a period of the lowest short-term interest rates in recent history, the Fed began raising the federal funds rate, a key short-term rate during 2005 and early 2006.

The economy continued to perform well into early 2007. Growth in real GDP averaged 2.75%; the unemployment rate fell to 4.5%, while inflation remained low. A strong stock market rally during the second half of 2006 more than compensated for a market downturn in early 2006. Economic performance was all the more noteworthy for a period in which oil prices fluctuated, geopolitical tensions remained high, and the housing market displayed serious difficulties.

Following 17 consecutive interest-rate increases beginning in June 2004, the FOMC announced in August 2006 that it would hold the federal funds rate at 5.25%. It kept the rate steady at four subsequent meetings with the direction and timing uncertain. While evidence of a sluggish housing market in 2007 indicated some risk to future economic growth, the Fed governors appeared to be more con-

cerned that declining productivity, low unemployment, and high energy prices could increase the inflation rate beyond the target level. The Fed decided to hold interest rates steady for most of 2007, which helped to keep mortgage lending rates relatively low. Nonetheless, a number of mortgage companies found themselves in serious financial trouble after years of aggressive lending and imaginative package loans. Healthy labor markets, growth in household incomes, and gains in net worth stemming from the strength of stock prices sustained household spending in 2007.

An economic tipping point came toward the middle of 2008. The long boom in housing was fueled in part by adjustable-rate mortgages usually offered to the least credit-worthy purchasers in what is generally known as the "subprime" market. As the rates on these mortgages were adjusted upward, increasing numbers of property owners were unable to meet their payments and the numbers of defaults nearly tripled within a year.

The failure of so many mortgages created turbulence in the markets, and before long in the broader economy. The subprime mortgages are held by financial institutions, including banks, brokerage firms, and various investment funds, around the world. As the insolvency rate of many mortgages skyrocketed, companies far and wide were forced to revalue their assets downward, resulting in large write-offs and plummeting earnings. Hence, the prices of their shares dropped sharply, causing stock markets to plunge.

Lending institutions subsequently stiffened the terms under which they loaned money, resulting in a credit crunch, which slowed economies and caused consumers to reduce spending. The run on a British bank made many investors worldwide somewhat nervous. The crisis in autumn 2007 at Northern Rock, a large mortgage lender in Britain, was linked to concerns about its exposure to subprime loans. Several times in 2008, the FOMC lowered interest rates in an effort to offset the tightening of credit and give the economy a lift.

CRY HAVOC

Muddle, Fuddle, Toil and Trouble

Until 2007, a massive property boom helped boost economic growth in America and Europe. Large numbers of people were able to take equity out of their homes to support spending. Many Americans already carry too much debt and are now unlikely to receive new loans from banks, which are reluctant to lend on collateral that is declining in value. It will take several years to work through the current

From a manufacturing to a service economy

United States

oversupply of unsold homes, keeping downward pressure on housing prices for the foreseeable future.

Volatility across the financial markets rose to record highs in 2008. Dislocations that had first surfaced in the subprime mortgage market after years of credit excesses and lax lending standards spread across the financial system. This contagion resulted in a vicious circle of declining asset values that escalated the credit crunch into a global financial crisis.

Delinquencies and foreclosures in the housing market continued to accelerate, further boosting housing inventory levels and depressing home prices. Mounting loan losses among lenders and a decline in the value of mortgage-backed securities (MBS) tied to those loans hurt the capital ratios of overleveraged institutions that held the securities. As the market for lower-quality securities dried up, financial institutions and other investors were forced to sell their most-liquid securities to maintain liquidity, required capital ratios, and, in some cases, their solvency. Such stress and strain caused further deterioration in the value of these and other securities, which in turn caused further deterioration in the asset bases of financial institutions that held the securities.

The financial landscape toward the end of 2008 was in the midst of its most consequential changes since the 1930s. Fear reached extreme levels during September and October in one of the most tumultuous two-month spans that the financial markets have ever experienced. Government takeover or outright failure of several of the nation's most well-known financial institutions led to a crisis of confidence that resulted in the global financial system becoming nearly frozen, with large financial institutions too fearful even to lend to one another. Credit conditions deteriorated rapidly, prompting the Fed to intervene with substantial interest rate cuts and newly designed methods for injecting capital into the financial systems. The economy slowed to a crawl in the first half of 2008, and the United States began facing greater economic uncertainty than it has experienced in some time.

The Fed orchestrated a buyout of the insolvent investment bank Bear Stearns to prevent systemic consequences for the broader financial markets. The situation in the credit markets went from bad to worse when investment bank Lehman Brothers filed Chapter 11 bankruptcy. True, the erosion of confidence in the financial system had been building up over time, but the realization that the U.S. Treasury would allow a major financial institution to fail accelerated industry-wide consolidation, and a series of arranged takeovers and fire sales ensued. Merrill Lynch was hastily sold to Bank of America, and the government effectively took over the large insurance company, American International Group (AIG). Investment banks Goldman Sachs and Morgan Stanley converted into bank holding companies, and JP Morgan Chase bought Washington Mutual. In October, Wells Fargo announced that it would acquire Wachovia, and in the following month, Citigroup received a government bailout.

In September 2008 came the consummation of the U.S. government's pledge to stand behind the two great mortgage giants, the Federal National Mortgage Association and the Federal Home Loan Mortgage Corporation, whose slang names are Fannie Mae and Freddie Mac, respectively. The two government-sponsored mortgage enterprises were seized by the federal government. These two agencies sell their own securities to obtain funds to lend to savings institutions, and to purchase mortgages and certain types of loans originally arranged by other institutions. The objective is not to make profits, but to promote or subsidize existing private institutions. The federal government originally held a portion of the stock of these agencies, but eventual ownership by their borrowers was specified as an objective. Fannie Mae and Freddie Mac completed this shift, and for some time no longer obtained subsidies from the government in the form of interest-free capital.

Hank Paulson, the Treasury secretary in the outgoing Bush administration, hoped that the July 2008 announcement to "stand by" Fannie Mae and Freddie Mac would calm nerves sufficiently that he would not have to take out his "bazooka." The opposite in fact happened. The firms' shares collapsed amid fears that investors would be wiped out in a government rescue. This severely curtailed their ability to issue much-needed capital, also infecting their mortgage-backed securities and the $1.6 trillion of debt they had issued to buy mortgages for themselves. It was only a matter of time before the government was forced to launch its largest-ever financial rescue.

The move to place both companies, which own or back $5.3 trillion in mortgages, into a government-run "conservatorship" grew out of deep concern among foreign investors that the companies' debt might not be repaid. Falling home prices, which were expected to lead to more defaults among the mortgages held or guaranteed by Fannie and Freddie, contributed to the urgency. Though some wanted to see the agencies fully nationalized, obstacles stood in the way—not least that this would have required an act of Congress.

The Treasury had to display some imagination, and the ensuing refurbishment plan had four facets. First, Fannie and Freddie would be taken into conservatorship, a watered-down form of receivership, by their revamped regulator, the Federal Housing Finance Agency, until they were again "sound and solvent." Second, they would have access to a loan facility, secured against their assets, until the end of 2009. Allowing them to tap the credit line was seen by many as a shrewd precautionary measure. The third involved Treasury purchase of preferred shares in the wake of the companies' substantial decline in net worth, designed primarily to protect taxpayers and avoid "moral hazard." To bolster mortgage markets, the fourth facet of the plan anticipated the Treasury becoming a buyer of last resort for bonds packaged by the agencies, purchasing them in the open market if demand decelerated. The chief risk with the plan was that the Treasury could have ended up burdened with piles of toxic debt. Moreover, the eventual cost to the public purse is still unknown and potentially huge. The Treasury indicates it bought over $150 billion of preferred stock in each of the two firms.

Long gone are the times in America when a buyer financed a home purchase with a mortgage from a neighborhood savings and loan and simply repaid it. Two decades ago, the savings and loan industry collapsed, and commercial banks began repackaging mortgages as bonds and selling them to investors. These bundles were then subdivided and categorized according to potential risk. The tranches then became another investment opportunity, a pattern replicated for financing mergers and acquisitions, creating an alphabet soup of investments that involved trillions of dollars. Who imposed any discipline on this free-for-all? Regulators have been in retreat for decades. Banks point to rating agencies, which assumed the fundamentals would be checked by investment banks, who, in turn, assumed global investors would exercise their own due diligence. Over a year into the effort to untangle the regulatory system, former Treasury Secretary James Baker could still say, "No one knows who owes what with which and to whom." There is plenty of blame to go around.

The Fed remained focused in 2008-2009 on lubricating the flywheels of the credit system, which is needed for the rest of the economic machinery to work. U.S. policy was committed to keeping interest rates low and access to liquid capital high. Challenges still lie ahead, and it is uncertain how long the sluggish job market will obtain. The stimulus packages amounting to nearly a trillion dollars the Obama administration implemented must now be financed.

Stock information board

In October 2008, Congress passed the Emergency Economic Stabilization Act of 2008, which authorized the Treasury to establish the $700 billion Troubled Asset Relief Program (TARP) to purchase distressed mortgage securities and other assets from financial institutions. This later morphed into a program for providing capital directly to banks and the automotive industry. In late November, two more programs were implemented: a $600 billion program to buy the debt and mortgage-backed securities of Fannie Mae, Freddie Mac, and other agencies and a $200 billion Term Asset-Backed Securities Loan Facility (TALK) to support the consumer credit and small business segments of the economy.

Economic growth continued to weaken in the middle of 2008, leading the National Bureau of Economic Research to declare that a U.S. recession had begun months earlier. GDP contracted 6.2% in the fourth quarter of 2008, after declining 0.5% in the third quarter. The unemployment rate rose to 7.6% in January 2009, and consumer spending dropped more than 3% in two consecutive quarters for the first time in recorded history. The Institute for Supply Management released figures that showed a substantially contracting level of manufacturing in the United States.

The 12 months to February 2009 were among the worst ever one-year spans for stocks. The broad U.S. stock market returned a negative 39%, while international stocks were off 45%. The trouble stemmed from the financial sector, where some of the world's largest institutions imploded, largely because of their exposure to low-quality mortgages in the United States. The effects of the credit crisis were wide and deep, with virtually no country or industry sector spared. As economic uncertainty and market volatility grew more pronounced in the second half of the year, investors sought the relative safety of short-term government issues. Such redirection drove prices for Treasury bonds and bills higher, and their yields lower. In some cases, investors were willing to accept very low—or even slightly negative—yields for the short-term safekeeping of their assets.

Second quarter GDP in 2009 dropped more than 2%, following a 4% plummet in the final quarter of 2008. This was the largest contraction since the early 1980s, when the United States weathered drops of 4.9% at the end of 1981 and 6.4% at the beginning of 1982. Joblessness and inflation were far higher then, but credit markets were not iced up as they were in 2008, and most consumers were carrying a lot less debt. At least two million jobs disappeared in 2009.

That Falling Feeling

The broad global recession made the U.S. recovery considerably more difficult. Worldwide growth dipped to zero in 2009, the worst overall economic performance since 1975 and far below the 2.5% accepted as a global recession. Trade shrank over 2% in 2009, and U.S. exports contracted by 0.5%, the first overall decline since the recession of 1982. Until 2009, trade was the strongest factor keeping the U.S. economy in positive growth territory. Weaker U.S. exports hurt most sectors, especially capital goods. Machine tools, chemicals, plastics, mining gear, and turbines were hardest hit. Service exports experienced a decline as well. Demand for U.S. financial services by foreign firms fell, as did sales of travel, hospitality, and leisure services. Imports are often

United States

a scapegoat in harsh economic times, and countries are still tempted to raise trade barriers to the legal limit under the World Trade Organization, rolling back recent gains.

Exacerbating U.S. economic difficulties was the arrival of tough times in China. Growth there slowed to around 6% in 2009, enviable by world standards, but far below the 9–10% China had become accustomed to. U.S. exporters were hit hard, especially firms selling semiconductors and the equipment needed to manufacture these, plus plastics, machinery, construction equipment, IT products, specialty steel, chemicals, and aluminum. The effects upon U.S. trade were large. China is America's third largest foreign market, absorbing over 6% of U.S. exports, worth nearly $70 billion. The sharp decline in sales by U.S. affiliates in China added to the financial woes of U.S. firms. Moreover, China's other main trading partners did not fare well either. Japan, South Korea, Taiwan, Singapore, Brazil, and Australia take some 16% of goods exported from the U.S. In 2009 China reduced its purchases of U.S. bonds, a development likely to put upward pressure on interest rates. As America buys less from China, the latter will have less to invest in America and its Asian neighbors.

The U.S. economy swung from recession to recovery in the second half of 2009. Growth in GDP was in the 1% to 2% range moving into 2010. The Fed and its central bank counterparts around the world responded with aggressive monetary stimulus efforts in 2008–2009, while governments opened the fiscal taps. Inflation remained low, despite the soft dollar and record gold prices. The beleaguered housing market continued to lose ground as prices fell and inventories rose. Foreclosures added to the inventory of homes for sale almost as fast as sales were reducing that inventory.

Go Figure

By mid-2012, financial markets were performing so strongly that it was almost difficult to remember that the global financial system stood on the brink of collapse in 2008. Markets pulled back from the abyss. Although unemployment remained at generational highs, and the prospects of a robust recovery seemed dim, the global economy began to grind into gear. The U.S. labor market shed more than six million jobs between 2008 and 2009, raising the unemployment rate to a lingering 9% and virtually wiping out all the jobs gained since the last recession. The Fed kept interest rates low and monitored indicators of economic growth and inflation. Seeking to support a stronger economic recovery, the Fed acknowledged the need

for further policy accommodation and consequently announced a fresh round of quantitative easing. This monetary injection consisted at one point of $40 billion of monthly purchases of mortgage-backed securities. The Fed also continued buying long-term Treasury bonds and selling short-term Treasury bills and notes in an effort to put downward pressure on long-term interest rates.

Parts of Europe, including Great Britain, slipped back into recession in 2012. Greece's economy has contracted every year for the past eight. Troubles in the Eurozone caused jitters in global equity markets, which experienced significant volatility. Markets reacted to reports regarding various European government proposals to address the Eurozone financial crisis, as well as leadership changes in Greece, Italy and the European Central Bank (ECB). By the end of May 2012, fears were renewed that Greece would not be able to honor the terms of the most recent restructuring, generating renewed speculation that it would abandon the euro. Many economists anticipate that the Eurozone will remain a trouble spot. ECB President Mario Draghi has tried to calm markets by stating the ECB would do "whatever it takes" to ensure the euro will survive. The most likely scenario is that the Eurozone will muddle through for several years, with occasional spikes in market volatility, as fiscal tightening continues in the face of weak economic growth.

In the United States, the prospect of extended monetary support from the Fed assuaged fears of a double-dip recession. Recent economic statistics indicate that the job market is improving, and consumer wealth is continuing to increase as home prices and other assets tend higher. As a first step toward normalizing U.S. monetary policy, the Fed announced its intent to terminate its quantitative easing program in 2014. This action reflects the Fed's assessment that the economy is continuing to make progress, but has further to go to reach "normal" conditions.

The U.S. economy is in its seventh year of economic recovery from the deep 2008-2009 recession and financial crisis. Inflation has often been a problem at this point in prior economic cycles. Nonetheless, this economic recovery has been slower than many others, helping keep inflation in check, despite aggressive monetary stimulus from the Fed. Some observers have been expecting inflation to increase because the Fed and other central banks have been pumping a large amount of liquidity into the financial system. But extra liquidity has not created inflation because consumers and businesses are not spending that money. Instead, they are using the extra liquidity to increase savings and

pay down debts. As a result, household and business finances are in better shape, especially since low inflation allows consumers to stretch their incomes further and companies to boost their profits.

In the emerging markets, slowing growth in China and efforts to stall inflation worried global markets, as China has been a major engine of worldwide growth. Former high-flying economies such as India, Brazil and Australia encountered meaningful deceleration in economic growth. Adding to market volatility and economic uncertainty were wild swings in the currency markets, including significant devaluations of some high-yield emerging market (EM) currencies, including the Brazilian real and South African rand against the U.S. dollar. Growing tensions in the Middle East emanating primarily from the Syrian civil war and continued posturing by political leadership in Iran resulted in volatility in oil prices. The year 2013 closed on a positive note for the markets, including developing market equities. Continued efforts by European policymakers to stabilize the situation in the region appeared to soothe market jitters somewhat in the final months of the year. Most observers now believe the global recovery that began in the second half of 2009 is developing into an economic expansion that will continue into 2016. The primary engine for this expansion is the EM economies, which achieved growth on average of 3% in 2014. Developed market (DM) economies managed gains of around 1%.

This two-speed expansion has created interesting crosscurrents. The Fed is still focused on preventing deflation as it aims to promote growth and lower unemployment. In contrast, the People's Bank of China is trying to dampen inflation as China embarks on a new five-year plan intended to increase domestic demand through higher incomes. The developing economies will persist as the most significant engine of global growth in a growth-challenged world. Economic expansion in the developed world will remain constrained. The twin problems of financial deleveraging and challenging demographics, particularly in continental Europe and Japan, are massive headwinds. Hence, the external climate for emerging markets that export to developed-market economies, especially the larger export-oriented economies of Asia, is not auspicious.

U.S. equity markets remained volatile in 2015. After a significant selloff in August and September, the S&P 500 rebounded during the fourth quarter to finish the year up just over 1%. Global oil prices declined 35% during the year, which aided U.S. household purchasing power and hindered the profitability of oil

The U.S. Economy

and gas companies. Traders and investors who dreaded oil prices could "go lower for longer" have seen their fears materialize. In fact, oil prices have been falling in a historical collapse. Oil prices are now down nearly 80% from the 20-year high of $145 notched in July 2008.

In the United States, economic activity expanded at a moderate pace: household spending and business investment increased, and the housing market strengthened. Labor market conditions continued to improve, with solid job gains and reduced unemployment. Growth was tempered by the stronger U.S. dollar and weaker demand for U.S. exports. In December, the Fed raised the federal funds rate for the first time in nine years. The 0.25 percentage point increase ended a historic seven-year period with the federal funds rate close to 0%, aimed at stimulating the economy. Fed Chair Janet Yellen reiterated the Fed's intent to normalize monetary policy gradually; the timing and size of future adjustments will be based on economic conditions in relation to the Fed's goals of maximum employment and 2% inflation. Global growth expectations declined and emerging markets faced significant macroeconomic challenges during the year. China's slowing economic growth contributed to depressed commodity prices and weighed on the global economy. The stronger U.S. dollar and prospects for higher U.S. interest rates negatively affected economies in need of external financing, such as Brazil.

To attempt to forecast the course of the world economy would be foolhardy. Yet the record of the years since the end of World War II provides some grounds for optimism. Compared to what occurred in the 1930s, when efforts at international collaborative solutions to economic problems proved fruitless and states sought to solve their economic problems through autarkic techniques, the record of the years since World War II has been one of remarkable achievements. A wide variety of international institutions has been created, and national officials have learned to use these institutions to forge cooperative solutions that benefited all states by making possible considerable increases in the gross world product. There is general awareness of global economic interdependence. This record of more than 60 years of successful collaboration provides a basis for believing that this collaboration will be continued. National and international officials seem to have learned how to surmount the obstacles that had plagued earlier efforts.

Another ground for optimism is the significant progress that has been made in understanding the operation of the world economy. Plausible and useful models of

the world economy have been developed. Because of their existence, it has become possible to analyze the consequences of the continued pursuit of existing policies as well as the probable consequences of different policy choices. The intellectual tools for managing the global economy are at hand. States trade for several purposes, the most fundamental of which is to obtain raw materials, food, and other resources not found within their own borders. With the growth and spread of industrialization, a more prevalent motive has been to obtain goods that can be produced more efficiently and therefore more cheaply abroad than at home. International trade permits international specialization and, through this, a greater total product. Countries can concentrate on those goods that they produce most efficiently or for which in technical terms they have a comparative advantage. Comparative advantages might be derived from such factors as natural resource endowments or special skills of labor forces. Through specialization in certain products and engaging in international trade to obtain others, countries can have larger production runs and reduce production costs by taking advantage of economies of scale.

REINDUSTRIALIZATION

America's resurgent manufacturing strength should have silenced the myth of "deindustrialization," but it still seems to live on in public discourse. Several significant developments present themselves here: the changing composition of U.S. manufactured goods, the greater productivity in manufacturing, and America's rapid movement toward energy self-sufficiency.

Nationwide, manufacturers large and small are creating new high-tech products on a regular basis—in biotech, telecommunications, scientific instruments, microelectronics and many other fields. The value added from these new kinds of goods more than offsets the declining income from older-style products such as apparel, shoes and small appliances. Hence, the case can be made that the U.S. is reindustrializing rather deindustrializing.

Increased oil production, combined with effective policies to improve energy efficiency, means—according to the International Energy Agency (IEA)—that the U.S. will become all but energy self-sufficient in terms of energy needs in roughly 20 years. A recent IEA report indicates that the U.S. will overtake Saudi Arabia as the world's leading oil producer by about 2017 and will become a net oil exporter by 2030. The IEA report predicts that the U.S. will overtake Russia as the world's leading producer of natural gas as

early as 2015. Moreover, since the United States is at the cutting edge of this energy technology wave, it is becoming easier to expand production as other energy producers see their output begin to decline. The United States is riding the wave of a fossil-fuel boom that is making it the foremost energy producer in the world, virtually guaranteeing its place as one of the world's leading manufacturing sites for decades to come.

The revival of hydrocarbon production in the U.S. comes in large part from the introduction of new methods for extracting oil and gas from shale rock. Techniques like hydraulic fracturing and horizontal drilling have allowed American producers to tap previously inaccessible reserves, sending the price of natural gas, for example, plummeting. The IEA estimates that U.S. electricity prices may fall to only half of those in Europe, primarily because of an increase in the number of power plants fueled by relatively inexpensive—and difficult to transport—natural gas.

Suddenly, and somewhat unexpectedly, the cards in the "great game" of global geo-politics are being reshuffled. Science and technology undergird international specialization in production and thus international trade. It is the application of science-based technology to production that has enabled the world to move forward economically. The development of science and the practical application of scientific findings through technology provide a powerful stimulus for states to seek resources outside their borders and made possible production on a large enough scale to call for international specialization.

GLOSSARY OF ECONOMIC TERMS

Aggregate demand The relationship between the aggregate quantity of real GDP demanded and the price level.

Aggregate production function The relationship between the quantity of real GDP supplied and the quantities of labor and capital and the state of technology.

Appreciation A term used in foreign exchange markets when one currency rises in value relative to another currency.

Automatic fiscal policy A change in fiscal policy triggered by the state of the economy.

Automatic stabilizers Mechanisms that stabilize real GDP without explicit action by the government.

Balanced budget A government budget in which tax revenues and expenditures are equal.

Balance of payments accounts A country's record of international trading, borrowing and lending.

231

United States

Balance of trade   The value of exports minus the value of imports.

Black markets   Markets that trade forbidden items, or legal items at forbidden prices. Many soft currency countries have black markets in currency, where exchanges are made at rates different from the official exchange rate.

Blocs   Groups of nation-states that are united or associated for some purpose. Examples of blocs are defense blocs, such as NATO, and trade blocs such as the European Union and NAFTA.

Budget deficit   A government's budget balance that is negative—expenditures exceed tax revenues.

Budget surplus   A government's budget balance that is positive—tax revenues exceed expenditures.

Business cycle   The periodic up and down movement in production.

Capital   The plant, equipment, buildings, and inventories of raw materials and semifinished goods and services that are used to produce other goods and services.

Capital account   The part of the balance of payments that records international borrowing, lending, and investment. If a nation has a capital account surplus, this means that it is a net debtor during a particular period.

Capital controls   Capital controls are government rules and regulations seeking to limit or control inflows and outflows of international investment funds. The goal of capital controls is to maintain orderly international capital movements and prevent financial and foreign exchange instability.

Capital mobility   The ability of investment funds to move from one nation to another. The degree of capital mobility depends on the domestic financial regulations of the nations involved, which can either encourage, permit, or restrict international investment flows, and on market forces seeking to profit from differences in returns between countries.

Capital stock   The total quantity of plant, equipment, buildings, and inventories.

Cartel   A group of firms or nations that form a bloc to restrict supply of and increase profits from a particular product. OPEC is an example of an oil cartel.

Central bank   A bank's bank and a public authority charged with regulating and controlling a country's monetary policy and financial institutions and markets.

Change in demand   A change in buyers' plans that occurs when some influence on those plans other than the price of the good changes. It is illustrated by a shift of the demand curve.

Change in supply   A change in sellers' plans that occurs when some influence on those plans other than the price of the good changes. It is illustrated by a shift of the supply curve.

Change in quantity demanded   A change in buyers' plans that occurs when the price of a good changes but all other influences on buyers' plans remains unchanged. It is illustrated by a movement along the demand curve.

Change in quantity supplied   A change in sellers' plans that occurs when the price of a good changes but all other influences on sellers' plans remain unchanged. It is illustrated by a movement along the supply curve.

Collective good   A tangible or intangible good that, once created, is available to all members of a group. The issue of collective goods raises questions about payment for these goods when they are to be provided to the entire group.

Common Agricultural Policy (CAP)   The system of agricultural subsidies employed by the European Union.

Comparative advantage   A person or country has a comparative advantage in an activity if that person or country can perform the activity at a lower opportunity cost than anyone else or any other country.

Consumer Price Index   An index that measures the average level of prices of goods and services that a typical urban family buys.

Corporatism   A system of political economy built upon collective organizations within society such as labor and business organizations.

Cost-push inflation   An inflation that results from an initial increase in costs.

Council of Economic Advisors   The President's council whose main work is to monitor the economy and keep the President and the public well informed about the current state of the economy and the best available forecasts of where it is heading.

Crowding-out effect   The tendency for a government budget deficit to cause a decrease in investment.

Currency board   Government institutions that regulate a nation's domestic money supply and its foreign exchange rate. The goal of a currency board is to use the commitment to a fixed foreign exchange rate as a tool to stabilize the domestic economy.

Currency devaluation (or depreciation)   By devaluing one's currency, exports become cheaper to other countries, while imports from abroad become more expensive. Currency depreciation tends to achieve the effects, temporarily at least, of both a tariff (raising import prices) and an export subsidy (lowering the costs of exports).

Customs union   A group of nations that agree to eliminate trade barriers among themselves and adopt a unified system of external trade barriers.

Cyclical surplus or deficit   The actual surplus or deficit minus the structural surplus or deficit.

Cyclical unemployment   The fluctuations in unemployment over the business cycle.

Deflation   A process in which the price level falls—a "negative" inflation. Deflation is commonly associated with falling incomes, as during a depression.

Demand for labor   The relationship between the quantity of labor demanded and the real wage rate when all other influences on a firm's hiring plans remain the same.

Demand-pull inflation   An inflation that results from an initial increase in aggregate demand.

Depreciation   The decrease in the capital stock resulting from wear and tear and obsolescence.

Direct foreign investment (DFI)   Investments made by a company in production, distribution, or sales facilities in another country. The term *direct* implies a measure of control exercised by the parent company on resources in the host nation.

Discount rate   The interest rate at which the Fed stands ready to lend reserves to commercial banks.

Dual economy   The theory of the dual economy is a liberal theory of economic development that views the world as having two sectors: a modern progressive sector and a traditional sector. Economic development and structural change take place as the progressive, market-driven sector interacts with and transforms the tradition-based less developed sector.

Dumping   The practice of selling an item for less than at home. Dumping is an "unfair" trade practice when it is used to drive out competitors from an export market with the goal of creating monopoly power.

Economic growth   The expansion of production possibilities resulting from capital accumulation and technological change.

Economic growth rate   The percentage change in the quantity of goods and services produced from one year to the next.

Elastic demand   Demand for a product is said to be elastic if a given change in price produces a relatively larger proportionate change in the quantity demanded. If a 10 percent price cut results in an increase in the quantity demanded of more than 10 percent, then the demand is elastic.

The U.S. Economy

Entrepreneurship The resource that organizes the other three factors of production: land, labor, and capital. Entrepreneurs develop new ideas about what, how, when, and where to produce.

Equilibrium price The price at which the quantity demanded equals the quantity supplied.

Exchange rate The ratio of exchange between the currencies of different countries. Changes in the exchange rate affect the prices of goods in international trade and have important internal effects in nations.

Exports The goods and services that one country sells to people in other countries.

Export-oriented growth A strategy for economic growth focusing on exports and integration into global markets.

Export quotas These international agreements limit the quantity of an item that a nation can export. The effect is to limit the number of goods imported into a country. Examples include Orderly Marketing Arrangements (OMAs), and Voluntary Export Restraints (VERs). The Multifibre Agreement established a system of export quotas for less developed countries.

Export subsidies Any measure that effectively reduces the price of an exported product, making it more attractive to potential foreign buyers.

Federal budget A statement of the federal government's financial plan, itemizing programs and their costs, tax revenues, and the proposed deficit or surplus.

Federal Open Market Committee The main policy-making organ of the Federal Reserve System.

Federal Reserve System The central bank of the United States.

Financial intermediary A firm that takes deposits from households and firms and makes loans to other households and firms.

Fiscal policy The government's attempt to influence the economy by setting and changing taxes, its purchases of goods and services, and transfer payments to achieve macroeconomic objectives.

Fixed (pegged) exchange rates Exchange rates that are determined principally by state actions, not market forces.

Flexible (floating) exchange rates Exchange rates that are determined principally by market forces, not state actions.

Foreign exchange market The market in which the currency of one country is exchanged for the currency of another.

Free trade area A group of nations that agrees to eliminate tariff barriers for trade among themselves, but which retains the right of individual nations to set their own tariffs for trade with non-member nations.

Full employment A situation in which the quantity of labor demanded equals the quantity supplied.

Gold standard A monetary system of fixed exchange rates where currency values are defined in terms of a fixed quantity of gold.

Gross investment The total amount spent on adding to the capital stock and on replacing depreciated capital.

Hard currency A currency of known value that can readily be exchanged on foreign exchange markets and is therefore generally accepted in international transactions.

Hot money Highly interest-sensitive short-term international capital movements.

Human capital The skill and knowledge of people, arising from their education and on-the-job training.

Imports The goods and services one country buys from people in other countries.

Import quotas A limit on the quantity of an item that can be imported into a nation. By limiting the quantity of imports, the quota tends to drive up the price of a good, while at the same time restricting competition.

Inelastic demand The demand for a product is said to be inelastic if a given change in price produces a relatively smaller proportionate change in the quantity demanded. If a 10 percent price cut results in an increase in the quantity demanded of less than 10 percent, then the demand is inelastic.

Infant-industry argument The proposition that protection is necessary to enable an infant industry to grow into a mature industry that can compete in world markets.

Inflation A process in which the price level is rising and money is losing value.

Inflation rate The percentage change in the price level from one year to the next.

Intellectual property rights Patents, copyrights, and other rights to ownership or control of ideas, innovation, and creations.

Investment demand The relationship between investment and the real interest rate, other influences on investment remaining the same.

Lender of last resort An institution that pledges to provide liquidity to financial markets during a panic in order to prevent the collapse of a financial bubble.

Liquidity The property of being convertible into a means of payment with little loss in value.

Market Any arrangement that enables buyers and sellers to obtain information and to do business with each other.

Market failure A situation in which the market does not use resources efficiently.

Mercantilism An ideology putting accumulation of national treasure as the main goal of society. Today, it is an economic philosophy and practice of government regulation of a nation's economic life to increase state power and security. Policies of import restriction and export promotion follow from this goal.

Microeconomics The study of the decisions of people and businesses, the interaction of those decisions in markets, and the effects of government regulation and taxes on the prices and quantities of goods and services.

Monetary base The sum of the Federal Reserve notes, coins, and banks' deposits at the Fed.

Monetary policy The Federal Reserve's attempt to keep inflation in check, maintain full employment, moderate the business cycle, and achieve long-term growth by adjusting the quantity of money in circulation and interest rates.

Most Favored Nation (MFN) Trade status granting imports from a nation the same degree of preference as those from the most preferred nations.

Multiplier The amount by which a change in autonomous expenditure is magnified or multiplied to determine the change in equilibrium expenditure and real GDP.

National saving Saving by households and businesses plus government saving.

Neomercantilism A version of mercantilism that evolved in the post-World War II period. Neomercantilism is basically mercantilist policy enacted with a liberal system of international trade.

Nominal GDP The value of the current period's production in current period prices.

Nontariff barrier An action other than a tariff that restricts international trade.

Open market operations The purchase or sale of government securities by the Federal Reserve System in the open market.

Opportunity cost The opportunity cost of an action is the highest-valued alternative forgone.

Price level The average level of prices as measured by a price index.

Productivity Production per unit of resource used in the production of goods and services.

Purchasing power parity (PPP) The equal value of different currencies.

Quantity demanded The amount of good or service that consumers plan to buy during a given time period at a particular price.

233

United States

Quantity supplied The amount of a good or service that producers plan to sell during a given time period at a particular price.

Quota A quantitative restriction on the import of a particular good specifying the maximum amount that can be imported in a given timeframe.

Rational choice theory A theory of political economy focusing on the incentives facing individuals and states and how those incentives affect their behavior. The structure of incentives of the international system is seen as an important determinant of state behavior by rational choice theorists.

Real interest rate The nominal interest rate adjusted for inflation; the nominal interest rate minus the inflation rate.

Recession A business cycle phase in which real GDP decreases for at least two successive quarters.

Reciprocity A principal of the international trade system whereby trading partners simultaneously reduce trade barriers, providing each greater access to foreign markets.

Relative price The ration of the price of one good or service to the price of another good or service. Relative price is an opportunity cost.

Reserve ratio The fraction of a bank's total deposits that are held in reserve.

Saving The amount of income remaining after meeting consumption expenditures.

Scarcity The state in which resources are insufficient to satisfy people's wants.

Soft currency Currencies of uncertain value that are not generally accepted in international transactions. Soft currencies can usually be spent only within the nation that issues it, whereas a hard currency can be exchanged and spent in most nations.

Stagflation The combination of a rise in the price level and a decrease in real GDP.

Structural unemployment The unemployment that arises when changes in technology or international competition change the skills needed to perform jobs or change the location of jobs.

Subsidy Government payment to encourage some activity or benefit some group.

Substitute A good that can be used in place of another good.

Supply curve A curve showing the relationship between the quantity supplied and the price of a good when all other influences on producers' planned sales remain the same.

Tariff A tax that is imposed by the importing country when an imported good crosses its international boundary.

Terms of trade The quantity of goods and services that a country exports to pay for its imports of goods and services.

Tradeoff A constraint involving giving up one thing to get something else.

U.S. interest rate differential The interest rate on a U.S. dollar asset minus the interest rate on a foreign currency asset.

Value added The value of a firm's output minus the value of the intermediate goods that the firm buys from other firms.

Voluntary export restraint A self-imposed restriction by an exporting country on the volume of its exports of a particular good.

Zero-sum game An activity where gains by one party create equal losses for others.

234

Chapter Seven
A Nation of Nations

IMMIGRATION

The United States is a nation of immigrants. Except for Native Americans, themselves the descendants of ancient immigrants, all Americans came to the country from abroad or are descended from those who did. The United States was founded in part as a sanctuary for the oppressed. One of the complaints listed in the Declaration of Independence against the British king was that "he has endeavored to prevent the population of these States; for that purpose obstructing the Laws of Naturalization of Foreigners; refusing to pass others to encourage their migration hither . . ." Fewer than four million persons lived in the 13 colonies when independence was declared in 1776. In the years since, the population has increased nearly one hundred fold and continues to rise. The tremendous growth has come from immigration as well as the natural increase in the population. Since 1820, when most national statistics began to be recorded, over 50 million immigrants have entered the United States.

The United States made little attempt to discourage or regulate immigration for more than a century after independence. Indeed, Congress did not enact its first resettlement statute until 1819, when it provided for the collection of immigration data and for the regulation of the transport of ship passengers. So long as land was plentiful and expanding industries maintained the demand for labor, immigration was encouraged.

By 1900, however, the open and unsettled frontier had become a thing of the past, and labor was no longer in critically short supply. At about the same time, the major geographical areas of emigration changed. Until the 1880s, most immigrants to America came from the countries of Northern and Western Europe, whereas the immigration after 1880 came chiefly from Southern and Eastern Europe. Each of these factors—the closing of the frontier, a more abundant labor supply, and the shift in the major source of newcomers—combined to modify and ultimately reverse the traditional policy of promoting immigration.

Congress placed the first substantial restriction on immigration with the passage of the Chinese Exclusion Act in 1882. The latter also barred the entry of "convicts, lunatics, paupers," and "others" likely to become public problems. Over the next several years, a substantial list of "undesirables" emerged. For example, contract laborers were banned in 1885, "immoral"

persons and "anarchists" in 1903, and illiterates in 1917. Congress originally provided in 1897 for the exclusion of those who could neither read nor write, but President Grover Cleveland vetoed the bill, insisting that literacy was more a measure of one's opportunities than of intelligence or other worthy qualifications. President William Taft vetoed a similar bill in 1913 on the same basis, and the 1917 law was passed over the veto of President Woodrow Wilson. By 1920, more than 30 groups were listed as ineligible for admission on grounds of personal characteristics.

Despite the growing restrictions, the tide of immigration mounted. In the ten years from 1905 through 1914, an average of more than a million people a year came to the United States. World War I stemmed the tide, but with the termination of hostilities after 1918, it rose rapidly again. By 1921, with immigration nearing the million-a-year level once more, many U.S. leaders became convinced that

broader restrictions were necessary. The major immigration facilities in New York were swamped, and thousands of potential entrants were forced to wait there for months while the administrative machinery determined their admissibility. Patriotic societies and labor unions expressed alarm, and nationalistic tub-thumpers were having a field day.

The 1921 immigration statute placed a quantitative restriction on immigration, adding a numerical limitation to the exclusion policies based on race and personal characteristics. The quota to be admitted from each European country was fixed at 3% of the natives of that country residing in the United States in 1910. Immigration from Europe was thus fixed at around 355,000 annually.

The 1921 law was intended as a stopgap measure, replaced by a more comprehensive and restrictive law, the Johnson Act of 1924. Under the new statute, the quota admissible from each European

The beacon of the oppressed. The Statue of Liberty: a gift from France.

235

United States

Immigration in the early 1900s

country was reduced to 2% of those in the United States in 1890. By pushing the base date back to the 1890 census, immigration from Northern and Western Europe was purposefully favored over that from Southern and Eastern Europe. The latter were considered less desirable. The National Origins Act of 1929 slightly amended the 1924 law, setting the basic pattern for the system of U.S. immigration control until 1965. It established an overall quota of 150,000 and changed the base for quota calculation to the 1920 census.

FREEDOM AND CIVIL LIBERTIES

One of the most elusive words in the political vocabulary, "freedom" is also one of the most important in the American consciousness. It is often the first image Americans invoke when they count the blessings of their state. In few civilizations has freedom flourished as it has in America. There are arguably three principal explanations for this—the environmental, the political, and the economic. Geographers emphasize the isolation of America, cut off by oceans for centuries from the wars and embroilments of Europe and Asia, kept it from standing armies and internal crises, and therefore free. They say also that the continuing availability of frontier land gave an outlet to energies that might otherwise have clashed in civil conflicts. The economic explanation holds that the core of American freedom is the free enterprise economy, on the theory that free markets make free people, that political and social freedoms could not have been preserved without freedom of investment and the job. The political explanation stresses the separation of powers, the limited state, and the *laissez-faire* tradition.

The geographic theories, though, fail to note that geography is only part of a larger social environment, that the span of distance America had from the European centers was less important than American institutions and their distance from European feudalism. Similarly, the economic approach must be seen as part of the economic expansionism of American life. During one phase of American history *laissez faire* played an important role, but later experience showed that a mixed economy was a better base for freedom, since one of the great threats to it is economic breakdown. Finally there is the political argument about the separation of powers. Yet, there are other forms of it more crucial than the traditional splitting of the three political areas of power: the separation of economic from political power, the separation of church from state power, the separation of military from civilian power, and the separation of majority passions from the power of the law.

American freedom is protected by the fact that the people who run the economy do not always run the country—and also the other way around. It is also protected by the fact the religious people, who organize and shape the beliefs of Americans, cannot use the power of the government to make their creed exclusive—and also the other way around, in the fact that the government cannot interfere with freedom of worship. Further, it is protected by the fact that those who can send people into harm's way in war are themselves held to account by civilian authority—and in the fact that the political leaders cannot make themselves military heroes and go off on adventures of glory. It is strengthened by the fact that there is an independent judiciary which need not, although it sometimes does, respond to temporary waves of popular resentment toward particular groups. A tradition of judicial nonparticipation in the tensions of political life also obtains.

Freedom should be seen partly as a function of the way power is distributed, separated, and diffused in a society. Americans tend to think of the government as a foe of freedom, and see the history of freedom in America as the story of a struggle between individualists and government. But government power is only one form of social power. Wherever power is concentrated, whether in a government bureaucracy, a

Naturalized Americans

236

corporate combine, a large trade union, a military staff, a media organization, or a church authority, those who care about freedom must find ways of isolating that power, keeping it from combining with other power clusters, and holding it to account and responsibility.

Yet, this effort to hold power accountable, which may sometimes involve attempts to break it up, may itself endanger freedom by rousing social hostilities. With its energies, American life has always had a considerable violence potential, which has flared into actual violence when a challenge has been offered to the continuance of some power structure. For concentrated power, it is never so dangerous as when it feels itself in danger. A number of the movements chipping away at the civil liberties tradition have come from power groups that felt their status to be in jeopardy. This was true of the Federalists who passed the Alien and Sedition Acts; of the white supremacy movement in the postwar South; of the Oriental Exclusion Acts, supported both by the landowners and the trade unionists of the West Coast; of the vigilantist violence used against labor organizers in communities where the police are tied in with the holders of economic power.

Despite much confusion on the question of freedom and security, there was a persistent belief that freedom is an unbroken web whose strands are interdependent, and that if it is arbitrarily broken at any point it becomes more breakable at all the others. Benjamin Franklin summed it up with this usual pungency: "those who would give up essential liberty to purchase a little temporary safety, deserve neither liberty nor safety." The real aim of the hunters of dangerous thoughts was less to protect national safety than to secure general conformity. In pursuit of that aim they were willing to endanger public freedom and veto the individual life. But the stakes of the civil-liberties crisis did not end in minority rights. Even more important was the process of genuine majority rule. The basis of the whole theory of the democratic will is that the people will have alternative courses of action between which they can make a choice. This is what Justice Holmes meant in his famous dissent in the Abrams case in 1919 when he spoke of "the power of the thought to get itself accepted in the competition of the market." Unless alternative policies can be freely presented, the majority will become truncated.

The force that has broken periodic assaults on freedom from within American life has been the civil-liberties tradition—the historical commitment of Americans to the public protection of the freedom of the individual person. Its roots go deep

New Citizens practice Pledge of Allegiance in 1940

into the history of American thoughts and attitudes. One can start with the generally Protestant emphasis on the importance of the individual conscience. Beyond that there was the teaching, from the religious tradition, of the intensity of sacrifice for individual conscience and for the ideal of justice and equality. Broadening out still further, there was the emphasis on the individual personality and its sanctity, resting on the tradition of natural rights, the religious belief that each person has a soul, and the premise of potential individual creativeness. Add to this the property complex which has put a premium on the value of individual effort and its relation to reward, and the success complex which has linked freedom with the sense of competitive worth and the impulse for self-improvement.

One might round this off with the two basic American attitudes toward freedom as ingredients in the social process. One is the pragmatic attitude expressed in Holmes' phrase about the competition of ideas. It says in effect that the idea which survives may not be necessarily the truth, but what better way does a society have for choosing the ideas it will live by? The second is the belief that the individual personality is more productive if it functions in freedom than if it must obey someone else's authoritarian behest. In

the convergence of intellectual, emotional, and institutional factors lies the strength of American freedom.

As originally written, the Constitution contained no definition of citizenship, making mention of both "citizens of the United States" and "citizens of the State." Until the 1860s it was generally agreed that national citizenship followed that of the States, whereby any person acknowledged as a citizen of one of the States was recognized as a citizen of the United States as well.

The question had little pertinence prior to the 1880s. Much of the population was the product of recent immigration, and little distinction existed between citizens and aliens. The Civil War and the subsequent adoption of the 13th Amendment abolishing slavery and involuntary servitude created a pressing need for a constitutional definition. Section I of the 14th Amendment, adopted in 1868, laid down the basic statement of national citizenship. The provision states: "All persons born or naturalized in the United States, and subject to the jurisdiction thereof, are citizens of the United States and of the State wherein they reside." In effect, the 14th Amendment specifies that one may acquire citizenship either by birth or by naturalization.

The two basic rules since applied for determining citizenship by birth are *jus*

United States

The promised land

soli, the law of the soil or "where born," and *jus sanguinus*, the law of the blood, or "to whom born." According to the 14th Amendment, any person born in the United States and subject to its jurisdiction automatically becomes an American citizen at birth. Any person born in any of the 50 states, the District of Columbia, or the organized territories is a citizen at birth. So, too, is any person born in a U.S. embassy or legation or on an American public vessel anywhere in the world.

The breadth of the 14th Amendment's statement of *jus soli* is conspicuous in a leading legal case regarding citizenship, *United States v. Wong Kim Ark*, 1898. Wong had been born in the United States

to parents who were citizens of China. After an extended visit to China, Wong was refused entry to the United States by immigration officials. They claimed the 14th Amendment should not be applied so literally as to afford Wong citizenship, insisting that the Chinese Exclusion Act of 1882 prohibited entry. The Supreme Court, however, ruled that under the clear words of the 14th Amendment Wong was, indeed, a native-born citizen and that the Act could not be applied to him.

A child born abroad to parents, at least one of whom is an American citizen and who has resided in the United States, also becomes an American citizen at birth. Although the 14th Amendment does not

specifically provide for *jus sanguinus*, Congress has recognized it by law ever since 1855, and the constitutionality of the arrangement has never been challenged. When a child is born abroad to an American parent or parents, the birth is usually registered with the nearest American consulate. If one of the parents is an alien, then the child must later live in the United States for at least five continuous years between the ages of 14 and 28 in order to retain citizenship.

Naturalization is the legal process by which a person acquires a new citizenship at some time after birth. Congress has the exclusive power to provide for naturalization, and no state may do so. The process of naturalization is usually applied to individuals, but it may also be collective. At various times, it has been advantageous for Congress to grant naturalization *en masse* to a number of persons. Collective naturalization has usually occurred when the United States acquired new territory. The residents of the area involved were naturalized by the terms of the treaties, acts, or joint resolutions. For example, all noncitizen American Indians were collectively naturalized by law in 1924.

THE "MELTING POT"

America is a myriad of stocks, each with some identity maintained from the earliest to the latest migration. The mingling of ethnic strains contributes substantially to America's biological richness, and what gives America its cultural vibrancy is the blend of traditions and temperaments. Unless people brought identities of their own to the new homeland, it would be meaningless to talk of cultural mingling. Unless those identities were altered in the process, shaped and reshaped, caught in the ever-flowing stream of communal life, talk about America would be largely meaningless.

For centuries, the strength and richness of America were augmented by the great tides of immigration from Europe, with ethnic origins shifting from the British Isles to Western Europe and the Scandinavian countries, to the Mediterranean area, to the Slavic countries. In 1790, approximately 80% of America's white population was of British origin. For the next 40 years, until around 1830, immigrants trickled in. Then, the Atlantic migration quickened, first with Irish peasants in the wake of the potato famine, then with German farmers and artisans largely as a result of political oppression, and thereafter with land-hungry Scandinavians. In the early 1880s came a greater wave of new immigration. It was "new" in the double sense that the immigrants were no longer from Western and Northern Europe, and that they were more likely to settle in the large cities and work in the mines, mills and factories than on the land.

The relevant figures tell a dramatic story. From 1800 to 1914, some 50 million people left Europe, of whom over 35 million came to the United States. In the century and a half from 1800 to 1950, some 40 million newcomers settled in the United States, 85% of them from Europe, 11% from other countries in the American hemisphere, 3% from Asian countries, and 2% from the rest of the world. In the single peak decade of 1904–1914, ten million came, and in the zenith year of 1907 more than a million and a quarter arrived.

As convulsions of tyranny, war, and famine shook many regions of the world, and as opportunities continued to present themselves in America, millions of people migrated. Companies sent out agents who often depicted the wealth and grandeur of the new star of the West to potential immigrants. Many Americans recall their grandparents reiterating the chatter in the old country about America's streets being paved with gold. Upon arrival, their forebears discovered the streets not to be paved at all and that *they* were expected to do the paving. Recruiting was aided by the declining cost of travel, but even without these stimuli, mass migration would doubtless have taken place. "America as magnet" continued to exercise a substantial force strong enough to draw millions to the shores of promise.

It was peasant farmers for the most part who came from Ireland, the Scandinavian countries, Italy, Russia and Poland, and the Balkans. Some came from the German cities—artisans without jobs, ruined shopkeepers, political dissidents, disheartened intellectuals. Most of the families had lived in rural areas, on land that had been unable to sustain them. Plots were too small, landowners often highhanded, and the village communities too callous to accept new agricultural techniques. Debt was a humiliating master, poverty a bleak companion. Exasperated by the weight of feudal and clerical tradition, with little hope left and no promise for one's children, nothing seemed more logical than to yield to the image of a country where land was available and one could keep moving in search of opportunity. For years, often for the rest of their lives, many of the immigrants remained alienated from the culture they left as well as from the new one that had not wholly welcomed them. Anti-immigrant groups persecuted them on occasion. The alien ways of bustling American cities and burgeoning farm communities were often bewildering.

Indeed, the immigrant experience could be somber. Yet, millions overcame the ordeals, became people of influence in their communities, and lived to see the realization of the American promise in their own lives, doubly fulfilled in the lives of their children. Much in the ordeal of a changed life enriched the immigrants and their new country. The experience of the immigrants recapitulated the early American pioneer hardships, in many ways on harder terms, since the difficulties they encountered were those of a survival game, whether in a rural or urban wilderness. Even in their most dreadful circumstances, though, immigrant experiences recreated the overall American experience year after year.

Most immigrants eventually found their place in the American economy, each new tier from below pushing up the earlier arrivals to the next level. The economy also felt the impact of the immigrants that provided the labor force for rapidly expanding industrialism. Whatever one may say of the importance of American natural resources, the greatest asset was what is now commonly known as "people power." Without the immigrants America would not have had the labor to build the railroads, mine the coal, man the blast furnaces, and run the precision machines. While many of the immigrants took unskilled, backbreaking jobs, a fair number of them were trained and practiced. They brought with them techniques from European industrialism that had made an earlier start, so that the migrations were not only ones of people, but of talents, skills, production techniques and cultural traditions. The increase of immigration also meant more consumers as well as more producers. New machines cut production costs and prices, yet the steadily mounting numbers of consumers kept profits flowing back into industry. Since many immigrants started with so little, their living standards kept steadily improving, and the home market grew by leaps and bounds.

The British Isles

The English, Scottish, and Welsh settlers to the United States came from the principal island of what is now Great Britain. Although Great Britain and Ireland together comprise the British Isles, the Irish have a separate ethnic label. The migration of British people to America began in earnest around 1630. Although some immigrants ultimately returned to Europe, the combination of high birth rates and continuing immigration for the next 140 years resulted in the settlement of nearly two million people of British ancestry by 1790. These constituted half the total population of North America and around 60% of the white population of the new United States of America. Contemporary demographic analysis suggests that these early descendants of Americans

British students celebrate their links to the U.S.

account for just under half the country's population today. Around a quarter of the country's population traces its ancestral line back to the pre-1790 British settlers.

In the 1770s, Americans began to move west of the Appalachian Mountains in substantial numbers. In the early 19th century, migrants were traveling down the Ohio River, settling the edges of the Great Lakes, and pushing westward from the Carolinas and Georgia. Indians considered to be threats to migration, which meant the vast majority, suffered brutality and expulsion. Initially, largely British-ancestry populations spread to interior areas. Thereafter, in most areas north and west of the Ohio River, settlers of more diverse ethnic backgrounds reduced the proportion of Americans with British ancestry.

By contrast, fertile land in the Southeastern states had been claimed, for the most part, prior to the arrival of 19th-century immigrants. The absence of an industrial base, along with an ample supply of labor, much of it held in slavery, discouraged immigration. Hence, communities there were mostly of British origin and Southerners have consistently reported British ancestry in large numbers.

The large percentage of British ancestry south of the Pennsylvania-Maryland border (the Mason-Dixon Line) is indicative of the late 18th-century developments in ethnic settlement. The British from Maryland moved westward along the Potomac River and its tributaries, whereas Germans became predominant in Pennsyl-

United States

vania. German immigrants who arrived at the port of Baltimore after 1800 found the land in Western Maryland already occupied and were apt to head west of the Appalachians.

Thereafter, and to the present day, the lowest percentages of people of British ancestry were to be found in rural areas where another ethnic group is prevalent. British ancestry is significantly underrepresented in large areas of Wisconsin and Minnesota, for instance, especially in those counties where Norwegian, German, or Russian-German ancestry is extensive. The Hawaiian Islands, Indian regions of the Dakotas, and the heavily Mexican-American areas of Texas are also prominent examples. New York City is unusually low in its proportion of British ancestry.

Most observers draw a clear distinction between Highlanders and Lowlanders in 18th-century Scotland. Highlanders lived in more isolated areas to the north and the west, were for the most part poor farmers, often spoke Gaelic, and tended to follow a feudal tradition emphasizing the authority of clan chiefs. The Lowlanders formed an essentially different society, living in the southern and eastern parts of the country, where acculturation and English influence were prevalent. Highlanders immigrated to America more frequently than Lowlanders, at least until the mid-19th century.

The Scotch-Irish constituted a distinct albeit related ethnic group. People arriving in America from the island of Ireland in the 18th century were predominantly Protestant, often strongly Presbyterian, whose ancestors had migrated from Scotland to Northeastern Ireland (Ulster). During the 17th century, about 200,000 Presbyterian Lowlanders settled in Ulster as part of an English effort to subdue the defiant Irish. Their descendants were commonly known in Britain as the Ulster Scots, and in America as the Scotch-Irish.

Many Ulster Scots who settled in the United States in fact first migrated to Canada. Numerous Scottish-born people and their offspring left Scottish communities in New Brunswick, moving across the border into Maine. In addition, Vermont, New York, Montana, and other border states became the homes of many Scots from Canada. Scots and other Canadians often worked in the logging areas of Washington, Idaho, Oregon and coastal northern California. Scots emigrated from Britain in larger numbers than the English or the Welsh after the mid-18th century, and they usually came as individuals or in small family groups, a circumstance that eased entry into a new society.

Well over a million Scotch-Irish ultimately migrated to North America, the majority in the 1700s, and by 1790, they represented perhaps 10% of the U.S. white population. Later, when substantial numbers of Catholic Irish arrived in American cities beginning in the 1840s, the description "Scotch-Irish" came into common usage to distinguish those of Protestant Irish background from the growing Catholic population. The single label "Irish," referring to people of Protestant Scotch-Irish ancestry, is generally used in America only in areas where few Irish Catholics have settled.

The chief reason both New York and Boston became focal points of Irish-ancestry population is to be found in the sea routes and ports of entry to America in the mid-19th century. Immigrants tended to cluster in those cities because of their proximity to Canadian ports and the numerous ships sailing from Liverpool, the main point of Irish embarkation. In the 1840s, at least two-thirds of all recorded ship arrivals in America were at New York City. Vessels transported both Irish and Germans in large numbers to New York, and Irish immigrants not landing in New York almost always arrived in Boston, whereas Baltimore and New Orleans were the alternative ports for Central European immigrants. Irish immigrants differed from others because they were typically destitute, yearned only for escape from their homeland and British rule, and had little choice about a destination in America. By contrast, immigrants from elsewhere usually had sufficient funds to be able to get away from the coastal cities and to settle somewhere in the Midwest.

Possessing few skills, Irish men filled local demand for manual labor. In Boston they built the docks, the warehouses, the mills, and the freight yards. The ready supply of cheap labor in that city during the 1840s assured lower wage levels than in New York. Reduced costs prompted the investment that made Boston into a manufacturing center. The city was transformed from a predominantly commercial and trade hub to a more mechanized, industrial area, one of the largest in America by 1880.

Irish men customarily took the most difficult and dangerous jobs in mills and factories, while Irish women, who typically immigrated as individuals in search of any sort of work in the wake of the Irish potato famine in the 1840s, eagerly took jobs many other women shunned. They often became seamstresses and household servants, and by the 1870s many were machine operators in the textile mills of Southern New England. After the 1870s, newly arrived immigrants from Southern and Eastern Europe took such jobs in growing numbers, and many Irish were able to move into better positions.

Carl Schurz

German immigrant Carl Schurz, Union General and Secretary of the Interior.

German-Speaking Areas

Germans constituted the most significant white ethnic group other than the British in the American colonies in the period before the American Revolution, accounting for around 9% of the population in 1790. Their descendants, combined with those of the 19th- and 20th-century immigrant groups, have since made the total population with German ancestry almost equal in size to the British.

Although substantial German immigration to Pennsylvania occurred during the colonial period, the 1820s saw the first phase of a much greater immigration, which peaked between 1850 and 1880 and set the pattern of German ethnic composition in the Midwest. Because religion tended to divide Germans into separate social worlds, their ethnicity was seldom cohesive. About one-third of the 19th-century German immigrants were Roman Catholics, with various Lutheran, Reformed, and Evangelical groups comprising most of the Protestants. For many Germans religion was as significant a facet of ethnic identity as language, and immigrants of the same religious denomination usually settled together. In rural areas, religious cohesion resulted in the congregating of German farmers in certain counties and the establishment of settlements according to religious affiliation.

Prior to the War of Independence, Southern Pennsylvania was the focal point of German settlement and culture, and by 1790, Pennsylvania's populace was around 40% German. Pennsylvania Germans and other Central Europeans in the area have customarily and mistakenly been known as "Pennsylvania Dutch." The term is a variant of Pennsylvania *Deutsch* or German, not "Dutch" from the Netherlands. Beginning in the 1730s,

Pennsylvania Germans in quest of more land moved into the Shenandoah Valley of Virginia and into the gently sloping Piedmont area of North Carolina. Parts of the northern Shenandoah Valley became solidly German in the late 1700s.

Upon debarkation at New York, Baltimore or New Orleans, Germans habitually followed the canals or the Ohio and Mississippi rivers, and many subsequently settled on the shores of the Great Lakes. Later, the railroads brought immigrants to the new lands and budding cities of the Midwest. Most German immigrants became farmers, occupying the fertile lands from Ohio westward through the Great Plains. Wisconsin was especially appealing, not only due to the availability of land at low prices, but also because many state officials were ethnic Germans, and Wisconsin's liberal constitution represented a welcome change for those fleeing authoritarian rule.

It is notable that a significant number of German-speaking immigrants arriving in America prior to 1900 hailed not from Germany proper but from other lands in Eastern Europe. Most were people whose ancestors had migrated in a prior century to eastern areas, some as far as the Volga River of the Russian Empire. Germans from Russia tended to comprise distinct and cohesive groups after immigrating to America. German farmers, whose ancestors had migrated to Southern Russia in the 1700s, became disappointed in growing measure with empty Russian promises of religious and cultural freedom. Accordingly, between 1870 and the First World War, many made a fresh start on the Great Plains of America. The majority of these German-speakers were Evangelical Protestants, and fewer than 20% of them Catholic. Depending on their region of origin, these "Russian-Germans" became commonly known in America as Black Sea Germans or Volga Germans. By 1930, a large percentage of agricultural production in Nebraska and Colorado were in the hands of Volga Germans. Russian-Germans comprised a substantial portion of the industrial labor force in Western cities and developed distinctive ethnic settlements in Chicago, Denver, Lincoln and Topeka. Black Sea Germans from the vast steppes north of the Black Sea led the cultivation of American wheat in the rough-and-tumble lands of the Dakotas. Their settlements were sizeable by any standards, the largest being situated in the central Dakotas and encompassing several counties in each state.

The Netherlands

Dutch seafarers explored considerable portions of America's Atlantic coast in the early 1600s, and soon thereafter settlers founded a colony called New Netherland along the shoreline of the Hudson River and lower Delaware River. Dutch control of the area waned with the triumph of British arms in 1664 although some Dutch people remained in communities along the Hudson River. In northeastern New Jersey, the Dutch comprised the principal ethnic group in the diverse population of the farming settlements during the colonial period.

In the mid-19th century, new Dutch immigrants settled in urban areas of the eastern seaboard, usually in communities with a high percentage of Dutch ancestry. From there, some would take the water and rail routes west, eventually settling in Midwestern cities and establishing major Dutch ethnic concentrations there. Dutch settlements on the outskirts of Chicago, for example, developed into centers of dairy farming and market gardening, and later into neighborhoods for urban industrial workers.

France

The North American population of French ancestry includes several distinct groups, the largest of which are of French Canadian origin, followed by those directly emigrating from France. Groups came from different social classes, with the result that the settlement patterns of the groups varied. Despite a basic similarity in religion and culture, French ethnic groups displayed diverse interests and contrasting attitudes in the new world.

The French, mostly from Canada, were the first white settlers in large parts of what later became the central United States. In the 1600s, French soldiers, fur traders, and priests followed the water routes of the Great Lakes, the Mississippi River, and its headwaters in their quest for wealth, pelts, and heathen souls to convert. In the 1750s, thousands of Acadian French people were forcibly deported from Canada by the British and are the ancestors of the "Cajuns" in Louisiana today. By 1760, the largest French settlements in America were in New Orleans and upstream on the shoreline of the Mississippi River to Natchez.

New Orleans constituted a small territorial capital, linked directly to Paris and to Saint Dominique, the French Creole colony in the Caribbean that would become Haiti. Upriver were also the small French communities located at the confluence of the Missouri and the Mississippi Rivers, in the Saint Louis and Sainte Genevieve areas. Another significant French

Manhattan Island, 1627, named at the time "New Amsterdam," a Dutch possession

United States

Confederate President Jefferson Davis and Union General Ulysses S. Grant, both descendents of Dutch settlers

lowing the earlier routes of the trappers. Some settled with fellow Canadians in the Detroit area, which was still largely agricultural, while others pushed the logging and farming frontiers northward. In Northwestern Minnesota, French Canadians settled the expanses of grassland, while additional immigrants from Quebec arrived following completion of the railroads in the 1880s, which provided for transportation connections with boats on the Great Lakes. Most farmers would later diversify, with cheese production becoming an especially successful enterprise.

Scandinavia

Norwegians, Swedes, and Danes are closely related in religious heritage, language and culture, and thus they have often been labeled simply "Scandinavians" in America. Rapid population growth in Northern Europe was the principal reason for the economic and psychological tensions that prompted emigration in the 19th century, but eagerness for adventure and escape from traditional and conservative societies were motivations also. Periodic economic depressions invariably triggered greater emigration. Some farm families emigrated in the wake of crop failures, although in Sweden departure rates were much less from areas afflicted by famine than from those where emigration had become customary.

Typical earlier immigrants were farm families and the young from towns or cities. Rural laborers saw little prospect of ever becoming independent farmers in their own country and thus set out for a new life abroad. Many would at least have a chance to own more land than would ever be possible in Europe. A distinctive and notable feature of the Scandinavian exodus was the group of Mormon converts, over 30,000 strong, who established new rural religious communities in the vast expanse of Utah.

Norwegian farm families began immigrating to America in the 1820s. What became generally known as "chain migrations" connected Norwegian communities and regions with particular settlements in America. Friends and extended family members followed earlier settlers to America. Strangers to America, especially those who spoke no English, were much more likely to migrate to a place where they knew people who could get them started. Many jobs went to people who knew someone already in the same line of work. Those relatively few pioneering individuals who either led group migrations or began chain migrations were the primary agents in the establishment of most settlements.

In later years the destinations expanded, but in most cases the immigrants'

General David Petraeus, also of Dutch origin   Courtesy of the Department of Defense

local Norwegian identities determined the composition of the farm communities established in America. As good farmland was rapidly occupied, those seeking available land moved westward, and in the 1850s, major Norwegian communities developed in Southwestern Wisconsin. The substantial concentrations of Norwegians in southeastern Minnesota began developing in the 1850s, the outcome for the most part of migration from southeastern Wisconsin. Land in these original Minnesota settlements was rapidly taken, inducing many Norwegians to move on to establish new settlements in the Minnesota River Valley.

Norwegians with prior experience in sailing and fishing often worked as seafarers on tugboats and merchant ships, as well as on ocean-going fishing vessels. Brooklyn became the major Norwegian focal point for commerce on America's East Coast, particularly after trade with Scandinavia increased in the late 19th century. On the West Coast, Norwegian commercial seamen operated out of San Francisco, Tacoma, or Seattle although fishing and coastal trade dispersed Scandinavians from Alaska to Los Angeles.

Immigration from Denmark took place for the most part in the latter half of the 19th century. Danish emigration to America was less a function of population pressures at home, as was the case in Norway or Sweden, than it was of group migrations following religious conversion. A sizeable number of Danes converted to the Mormon faith, and a somewhat smaller group became Baptists. Danes became

settlement, Detroit, was situated just above Lake Erie. By 1800, French settlement in Louisiana had been substantially strengthened by the arrival of thousands of Creole refugees.

The 19th century brought a second large exodus from Quebec, with people heading west via the Great Lakes and fol-

the second largest single ethnic group in the Church of Jesus Christ of Latter Day Saints after the British. Mormons of Danish heritage spread throughout Utah and Southern Idaho. Danes of other religious faiths settled mostly in California. San Francisco had distinct Danish neighborhoods as early as the 1870s, and a Danish community founded the Sun Maid raisin producers' cooperative toward the end of the century. Danish shipping and fishing communities emerged in the Pacific Northwest in the last quarter of the 19th century.

Beginning in the 1840s, Swedish farmers and craftsmen by the thousands began to arrive in America with their families. Most Swedes who emigrated came to find cheaper land than was available in Northern Europe. They headed for the Midwest where bountiful fertile land was still available for settlement.

Since Swedes tended toward chain migration, over the course of a few decades most members of the extended families of settlers to America themselves immigrated to the Midwest. Small Nordic communities were sometimes transported more or less intact to America, and the clustering of settlers according to region and parish in Sweden was largely due to the mindful selection of farmland near relatives or acquaintances. Later, destinations in the Northeast and Midwest were determined primarily on the basis of occupational skills at home. For example, Swedish workers from iron-mining parishes often chose to settle in Northern Michigan's mining communities, while those specializing in metal manufacturing often went to eastern Massachusetts for similar employment.

Following the Civil War, Chicago became the primary American center for channeling new Norwegian and Swedish immigrants to the burgeoning jobs on the railroads. Chicago labor agencies sent Scandinavian railway laborers to jobs on Southern railroads during the winter and as far west as Colorado during the warmer seasons. These migratory work experiences eventually spread Norwegians and Swedes throughout much of America. When the railway reached the Canadian border in the lower Red River Valley of Northwestern Minnesota in the late 1870s, the government opened a land-sale office and Swedes emigrated in record numbers. Plentiful jobs in growing manufacturing cities brought waves of Swedish immigration in the 1880s and 1890s. The Twin Cities, Minneapolis and Saint Paul, received almost half the new arrivals from Sweden in those years. In urban areas, they typically formed new ethnic settlements, blending with Norwegians in Scandinavian neighborhoods. Swedes who left Midwestern farms were apt to move to

the Pacific Northwest. Beginning in the 1880s, chain immigration brought loggers and fishermen from Sweden to satisfy the attendant demand for labor.

After the First World War, Swedish speakers comprised over 21% of emigrants from Finland, where Swedish is still an official language. These people immigrated for the most part to areas of Massachusetts, Minnesota, Michigan, Washington, and Wisconsin with prominent Swedish heritage. Finns usually worked as longshoremen, shipbuilders and carpenters, or quarrymen and miners, with the heaviest ethnic concentrations in the northern parts of Michigan, Wisconsin, and Minnesota. In the 1870s, many dockhands or railroad laborers at the western terminus of shipping on the Great Lakes were of Finnish origin. The iron mines that were established in the Vermilion and Mesabi ranges in the 1880s drew many Finnish immigrants to northern Minnesota. Farther west, the Finns dug coal in Red Lodge and copper in Butte, Montana. Finnish loggers felled trees in Northern California and Washington for lumber to be worked by Scandinavian carpenters in Southern California.

Despite cultural similarities, differences about religion sometimes resulted in tensions between subgroups within Northern European ethnic populations. Basic values divided Finnish communities, for example, into more socially and politically conservative people, called the "Church Finns" and the more secular, left-wing trade unionists and radical socialists, who comprised an unusually large minority of Finnish immigrants compared to other immigrant groups. Most "Church Finns" were devout Lutherans, not renowned for tolerance.

Belgium
Belgians are divided into two principal ethnic groups, the Flemish, who are Dutch-speakers, and the Walloons, whose language is French. Moreover, Belgium also has a sizeable community of approximately 40,000 German-speakers. Flemish and Walloons are essentially separate social groups in Belgium, and following this pattern they customarily settled in different places in America. In 1920, 72% of the people of Belgian heritage in America were Flemish, while 21% were of Walloon origin, and another 7% were of German ancestry.

Before 1890, the vast majority of Belgian immigrants were peasants from rural areas. They sought opportunities in farming and logging that were unavailable at home, establishing distinct Belgian communities in Midwestern small towns. Both the Flemish and Walloons are Catholic, and they typically joined Catholic parish communities in America. Although

Flemish people and immigrants from the Netherlands spoke the same language, the fierce anti-Catholicism of the Dutch made the Flemish settlers unwelcome in Midwestern towns, above all in Michigan, with its substantial and staid Dutch communities. Detroit and the surrounding towns, settled by Catholics of French origin, became large Flemish centers, and to this day that region has more people of Belgian ancestry than any other American metropolitan area.

Eastern European Peoples
Substantial numbers of Americans trace their origins to East-Central Europe. Many of their ancestors spoke languages such as Polish, Russian, Czech, Serbian, Croatian, which are all Slavic languages. A large number of Americans are of Hungarian, Romanian, Albanian, Lithuanian and Latvian stock, whose languages are not Slavic. The actual ethnicity of groups from this part of Europe has traditionally caused some confusion and has often been difficult to distinguish by census questions. For example, some people identified with a country of origin at the time of immigration, while some identified with an ethnic group. The inevitable result has been that the data for Austrian, Hungarian, Russian, and Romanian ancestors include many people who are not members of those ethnic groups. Descendants of Croatian and Polish immigrants from the early 20th century often specified their ancestry as Austrian, while some people whose ancestors spoke Slovak as their first language listed their region of origin as either Hungary or Czechoslovakia.

The most serious data problems of this sort are associated with the confusion surrounding Christians and Jews from the same country of origin. Jews constitute a distinct ethnic group, and people of Eastern European ancestries who are not Jewish seldom include Jews in their own ethnic group. Yet, little reliable data distinguishing Jews from Gentiles exist in America. In 1920, although most Jews from Eastern Europe customarily reported their mother tongue as Yiddish, Russian immigrant groups also contained a considerable proportion of Jews, and most Romanian-speakers in New York City after the First World War were also Jews. In all likelihood, the situation was similar with respect to other Eastern European languages in that many multilingual Jews specified Polish or Hungarian as their mother tongue.

People from Eastern Europe generally immigrated to America later than those from Western and Northern Europe, largely because advances in communication and transportation were far slower in the distant reaches of Prussia, Austria-Hungary, and Russia. In the early and

United States

The American dream

mid-19th century, some intellectuals, military officers, and members of a discontented middle class departed in the wake of failed revolutions against imperial tyranny. The first emigrants from small towns and villages of East-Central Europe were often Jewish traders and craftsmen who ventured to America as early as the 1850s. Some of these eventually returned, proclaiming America's opportunities to Christian acquaintances in rural areas. The chief motivation to leave was evident and widespread: in underdeveloped areas with a rapidly growing population and most good land still owned by the nobility, common people had few prospects. Work with comparatively high wages was plentiful in America, and avoidance of compulsory military service, especially in Russia, was itself a powerful incentive for many young men to emigrate.

Jews had additional grounds to immigrate, of course. Anti-Jewish restrictions were pervasive, particularly regarding land ownership and professional occupation. Russia conducted sporadic pogroms, vicious semiofficial operations involving brutality, thuggery, murder and torching, that began in the last quarter of the 19th century. As a rule, Jews emigrated as entire families, often as extended families, and departure was invariably permanent, especially after the cruel pogroms in Russia in the early 20th century.

Following the imposition of official quotas on immigration in the 1920s, fewer Eastern Europeans, Christian or Jewish, were allowed to enter the United States. Yet, between 1930 and 1941 nearly 150,000 middle-class Jewish merchants and professionals, including many scientists, fled

Nazi persecution and settled in America. These included some of the world's greatest minds, resulting in the prevalent recognition of this wave of immigration as Hitler's great and lasting gift to America.

U.S. census and immigration data for Austria-Hungary are nearly worthless for the identification of ethnic populations since people were typically classified in terms of habitation in the polyglot empire, instead of a particular ethnic group. The raw numbers included Poles, Slovenians, Jews, as well as German-speakers. In the early 20th century, the latter group comprised only about 10% of the immigration from the Austrian and Hungarian areas, but after World War I the proportion of German speakers was higher because the empire had fragmented and Austria was effectually reduced to a rump state. For over a century after 1800, many people who did not even speak German identified themselves as Austrians because they lived within the multiethnic empire.

To further confuse the issue, German speakers from the area of present-day Austria have often claimed German ancestry. For example, in eastern Austria is the German-speaking region of Burgenland, which was officially Hungarian territory before 1921. Immigrants from this area were not ethnically Hungarian, but many who settled in North Dakota were referred to locally as Hungarians. Yet, these people considered themselves *Volksdeutsche* or ethnic Germans. In the 20th century, the place of origin for most immigrants from present-day Austria proper was Burgenland, an area with a particularly large surplus of unskilled farm laborers. The only other notewor-

thy immigrations of German speakers from Austria to North America were in the 1730s, involving Protestants seeking religious freedom in rural Georgia, and a smattering of 19th-century migrations to certain farming areas in Illinois and Iowa.

Czech ethnicity is based predominantly on the ancestral or present use of the Czech language. Many immigrants from Bohemia and Morovia, in the western and central parts of the Czech Republic, spoke that language, yet ethnic Germans who emigrated from the same area would not be considered Czechs. Although Czechoslovakia no longer exists, many people of Slovak ancestry, who speak a language virtually indistinguishable from Czech, are counted in the Czechoslovakian data. In Pennsylvania, for example, the population of Slovak origin are 15 times larger than that of Czech origin although all are identified as Czechoslovakian.

With a few exceptions, Czech immigrants arrived after 1850, typically in families and with little intention of return migration. They were unusual among European immigrant groups in that a majority discarded formal religious viewpoints and adherence in the new country. Prior to emigration, most Czechs had been nominally Roman Catholic, and some retained this heritage, with a few even settling near German communities whose language they understood and religion they shared, despite past political oppression. Nonetheless, Czechs were apt to be a free-thinking lot, with a proud heritage of rationality that prompted doubts about organized religion. Immigration to America led some to abandon Catholicism and join Protestant denominations, and many urban families abandoned religious practice altogether. The result was that Czech communities in America were often bitterly divided into several groups, including converts, "free thinkers" and traditional Catholics. In rural areas many Protestant neighbors could not quite fathom how the hardworking and even enterprising Czechs could dance, guzzle beer, and enjoy themselves, especially on Sundays.

Census data have periodically and substantially underestimated the people of Slovak ancestry because the census has included all persons identifying themselves as Czechoslovakian in the Czech ancestry category. It is fair to assume that ethnic Slovaks usually reported their ancestry in terms of either the more modern country of Czechoslovakia, or Austria-Hungary, the old country of origin. Groups with Slovak ancestry, in contrast to the Czech-ancestry population, were doubtless somewhat larger than the totals reported. Both ethnic groups originated in what was once Czechoslovakia although until 1918 the region had been incorporated in the multi-ethnic empire. In 1920, following the major immigrations to America, the settler groups with Czech and Slovak heritage were probably about the same size.

In all likelihood, Slovaks were the largest foreign-born ethnic group in the nation's iron and steel industry in 1910. The mills of Johnstown, Pennsylvania, and Youngstown, Ohio, employed Slovak immigrants by the hundreds. The large industrial area in Indiana's Lake County, along the Lake Michigan shore just east of Chicago, relied heavily upon Slovak workers. At some oil refineries in the early 20th century they comprised the largest foreign-born ethnic group in the workforce. In 1909, when the first steel surged forth from the massive Gary works of U.S. Steel in Indiana, most workers there were immigrants. Only the Poles outnumbered Slovak steel workers.

Probably most immigrants who have identified their ancestry as Hungarian over the years either spoke that language as their mother tongue or had ancestors who did. Such people are true ethnic Hungarians, in contrast to those whose ancestral origins were in historical Hungary but whose first language was not Hungarian. Although the term "Magyar" (pronounced Ma-Jar) is the proper term for the culture and language and was once used to distinguish ethnic Hungarians from non-Magyars who came from Hungarian regions, that term is infrequently used today.

During the time of major emigration from Hungary, in the decades prior to World War I, that country's area was much larger, and the 1910 U.S. census indicated that only 46% of immigrants from Hungary spoke Hungarian as their first language. Of the group, 22% were Slovaks and 15% ethnic Germans. Thus, mother tongue has been a much better indicator of ethnic Hungarian population than country of origin.

The substantial migrations of Hungarians began only in the 1880s, when numerous people departed to take jobs in expanding American industries. Prior to World War I, as a rule around half the emigrants designated as coming from Hungary were ethnic Hungarians. In the 1920s, immigration dropped abruptly because of American restrictions, so that the next mass exodus comprised about 24,000 refugees from World War II and the subsequent Communist takeover of the country. In the wake of the failed 1956 revolution, about 200,000 Hungarians fled the country. Of these, the United States admitted about 35,000.

Immigrants from Hungary for the most part arrived too late to become farmers and most found work in heavy industry, often in iron and steel-making or steel product manufacture. Ethnic settlements were customarily close to the major industrial plants and usually merged with those of other Eastern Europeans working in the same facility. Most of the counties with the highest percentage of Hungarian ancestry in the United States were those in which extensive manufacturing operations were located.

Only a small number of Romanians immigrated to America prior to 1870, and until about 1895 most emigrants from that country were Jews. By the turn of the century, immigrants were likely to be ethnic Romanian Christian peasants. Upon their arrival, little good farmland remained, although job opportunities in the cities were growing. In the Midwest, Romanian men often worked in the iron and steel industry and later in automobile manufacturing. Detroit was the largest Romanian settlement in the Midwest in the 1920s, a hardly surprising number considering that by 1916, over 1,700 Romanians were employed at the Ford Highland Park plant alone. Shipbuilding and the car body plant brought Romanian job-seekers to Cleveland, which later became the intellectual hub of Romanian life in America. Churches, usually Orthodox, but sometimes Greek Catholic, were often integral parts of the Romanian communities, as, for example, in Cleveland and Detroit.

Although Ottoman power had been waning in the decades prior to the First World War, the empire still exercised some authority in what remained of Turkey in Europe until the eve of the great conflict. Furthermore, substantial parts of the Balkans were under the control of Austria-Hungary. Upon the defeat of these two ancient empires in the war, Serbia, Croatia, and certain other Balkan areas became the independent country of Yugoslavia. The long history of rule and misrule by outsiders, combined with the divergent regions and ethnic divisions within the newly formed Yugoslavia, resulted in an assortment of ancestry designations for immigrants and their offspring. Immigrants arriving before the First World War, when Croatia and Slovenia were still part of the Hapsburg Empire, usually considered their ancestry to be Austrian.

The actual sizes of the major Yugoslav ethnic groups in America will never be known. Accurate data have not been consistently accumulated, although the 1920 U.S. census indicates almost equal numbers of Slovene, Serbian and Croatian stock. People of Croatian ancestry in fact began appearing earlier than other ethnic groups from Eastern Europe, immigrating from the coastal and the north central parts of what was once the country of Yugoslavia and is now independent Croatia.

As early as the 1770s, people from Dalmatia on the Adriatic coast were settling in New Orleans and other towns along the Mississippi River or near the Gulf of Mexico. By 1860, at least 3,000 Croatians lived in the American South, a fair number of whom served in the Confederate army. Around the turn of the century, more immigrants from Dalmatia arrived, settling in New Orleans and upstream on the Mississippi River, where many mixed with the Cajuns, descendants of Acadians from what is now Canada. The immigrants were mostly seafaring people, and after World War II, hundreds more came, including refugees from the heavy fighting in the Balkans.

Upon the discovery of gold in California in 1848, Croatian immigrants generally headed for the West Coast, and in the 1860s many prospected for silver in Nevada. In later decades, Croatian communities were to be found in San Francisco and the agricultural areas of northern California. Croatians living in the Northeast were typically laborers, stevedores or construction workers. Some worked on ships, and by the 1930s as many as half the tugboats in New York Harbor had entirely Croatian crews. After 1880, immigrants from the area came less frequently from the Dalmatian coast and more frequently from the interior of Croatia, and their occupations and destinations changed markedly. Like so many other immigrants from Eastern Europe in the period between 1880 and World War I, these people found jobs chiefly in mining areas and industrial cities.

Serbian immigrants before the 1880s were largely from the coastal area of Dalmatia. A few accompanied Croatians to Louisiana and the large Gulf towns in the 1830s. During the gold rush, some Serbians left for California mining towns. San Francisco later became a significant area of settlement, and it was there that

Albanian immigrant

245

United States

Former Lithuanian President Valdas Adamkus lived most of his life in the U.S. but returned to Lithuania after the end of communism.

the Serbian Orthodox Church in America was founded in the 1860s. A much larger number of Serbian men landed in America after about 1880, especially during the 1903–1909 immigration period. They, like most other Eastern Europeans, moved to available unskilled laboring jobs, most of which were in heavy industry. After 1910, Serbs were particularly concentrated in the iron and steel industry.

Most Slovenians who settled in America also came before World War I. Like many other ethnic groups from the Austro-Hungarian Empire, Slovenians were inclined to identify themselves as Austrian. Slovenian settlements in the Great Lakes area were usually associated with mining and manufacturing. In substantial part because of chain migration, many Slovenian immigrants took jobs as miners and lumbermen on Michigan's Upper Peninsula. In Northeastern Minnesota, many Slovenians found work as miners in the Vermilion Range after 1885. The blast furnaces and rail, rod, and wire mills of Illinois during the late 1880s provided employment for newly arrived Slovenians. Prior to World War I in Colorado, the Slovenians were the largest foreign-born group in the smelting and refining industry, representing 18% of all the state's workers in that industry and 11% of all the hard-rock miners.

The Boston area has been the focal point of Albanian settlement in America. During the early 20th century, Albanians found employment mostly in factories or in hotels and restaurants. In Boston, Greek em-

ployers often hired Albanians, since most people from both ethnic groups were Orthodox Christian and many Greeks spoke Albanian. A fair number of immigrants who began as fruit peddlers were operating grocery stores in Boston within two decades. Shoe factories in several outlying cities also attracted many Albanian laborers.

It is somewhat ironic that Polish immigrants, who came to America in growing numbers in the second half of the 19th century, often settled in areas with high concentrations of ethnic Germans. Many Poles came from German-controlled areas and took offense at German attempts to undercut Polish culture and national identity. Yet, many Poles spoke German, and German contacts in America were useful to Polish immigrants seeking opportunity in the new country. Information about life and prospects in America filtered back to Austrian and Russian rural areas with high concentrations of Poles, and later immigration originated mostly from there, but the networks with ethnic Germans that evolved earlier continued to function. The vast majority of Poles embarked from the Northern European ports of Bremen and Hamburg, and the German connections to the new world largely account for the eventual development of Polish communities in cities with substantial German settlements such as Milwaukee, Chicago, Cleveland, and Buffalo.

Most Polish immigrants took unskilled jobs demanding hard physical labor. Of the nearly 50,000 male Polish workers

surveyed in the first decade of the 20th century, 18% were in the cotton goods industry, 16% in iron and steel, 15% in coal mining, and 14% in meatpacking. Over half of the employed Polish women surveyed at the same time were working in the cotton-goods industry. Few Polish immigrants settled in the South since economic backwardness in the region offered few opportunities and resulted in a large surplus of unskilled labor.

In the meatpacking industry, Irish and German immigrants established themselves as skillful butchers in the 1900s, but by the early 20th century, Poles and other Slavic laborers increasingly took jobs in the slaughterhouses. When Chicago came to have the largest Polish population in America at the dawn of the 20th century, the city already had five large ethnic neighborhoods, one located near the Union Stockyards and others near major industrial plants. The downtown settlement and the neighborhoods in the vicinity of South Chicago's steel mills were strongly Polish in character, yet Poles sometimes clustered in areas of mixed ethnicity. Polish identity was closely linked to Catholicism, and ethnic neighborhoods grew around parishes and parochial schools.

Detroit's sizeable Polish community was associated with employment in the automobile industry and the ethnic culture of nearby Polish working-class neighborhoods. As elsewhere, Catholic parishes and schools were the hubs of communal establishment. The opening of new automobile plants in the enclave cities of

A Nation of Nations

Currier & Ives

THE FARMER'S HOME-HARVEST

Lithuanians hailed from impoverished rural areas and had few skills to offer the employers of an industrializing America. For the most part, they took unskilled jobs, especially in mining and manufacturing. Earlier immigrants usually joined Polish communities in America, since most had some knowledge of Polish, and Lithuanian national identity was also intimately associated with Roman Catholicism. Lithuanians initially joined Polish parishes but later tended to establish their own.

In the aftermath of World War II, a fresh wave of Lithuanian immigration came to America. Some 35,000 displaced persons (DPs) from Lithuania arrived without means after more than three years in refugee camps in Germany. Many were literate and even intellectual, and most were intensely nationalistic. The new immigrants rejuvenated Lithuanian ethnic life, providing innovation and direction in the ethnic communities. Yet, their diversity, cosmopolitanism, and eventual success in America became the source of some resentment, especially among established blue-collar groups. It would not be the first time nor the last that distinct social differences emerged between recent and established immigrants.

Significant Lithuanian-Polish settlements appeared in Eastern Pennsylvania in the 1870s, where unskilled Eastern European laborers began to take jobs in the anthracite coalmines. Substantial Lithuanian communities emerged in Massachusetts and Connecticut, and in those states ethnic populations grew in the 20th century as the industrial cities that originally drew the immigrants expanded and the suburbs spread. Larger communities developed their own ethnic business sections, such as in South Boston with Lithuanian restaurants, taverns, real-estate offices, and stores lining many streets.

Reflecting the pattern of Lithuanian settlement in established Polish areas, Chicago developed the largest Lithuanian community in America. The garment industry, slaughterhouses, and metalworking factories offered numerous employment opportunities, especially to the semi- and unskilled. Lithuanians were second only to the Poles as the largest ethnic group in the meatpacking industry by 1910, surpassing the Irish and Germans. Beyond the stockyards were the heavy industries, extending from South Chicago into Indiana, where many East European laborers found employment.

Like immigrants from the other Baltic countries, Latvians in America have comprised two basic groups. The first group was composed largely of sailors, artisans, and peasants, and after the Russian Revolution of 1905, some educated

Wayne County brought a fresh influx of Polish labor, drawing people from other urban areas and contributing to an expansion of the Polish section of Detroit. At the Ford plant in Highland Park, the 7,500 Polish employees were by far the largest ethnic group of laborers, yet, characteristically, Poles continued to live in their own neighborhoods rather than the "Anglo" commune of Highland Park.

Polish immigrants who preferred land ownership and farming settled almost exclusively in northern Michigan, Wisconsin, and Minnesota. Those not able to purchase choice land in the Midwest often settled in the more northern Cutover region of Wisconsin and Minnesota, where farm income could be supplemented by part-time employment in the forests and sawmills. Cutover land was inexpensive but required arduous work. Nonetheless, it offered settlers the opportunity to become independent farmers they would not have had otherwise.

Polish settlers to Wisconsin arrived in Milwaukee long after the establishment of the German community there. When in the late 1850s, Germans began to move to Marathon County in the center of the

state, some Poles followed. A substantial Polish rural community emerged shortly thereafter in Portage County, just to the south. In the following decades, many ethnic Poles joined this community as farmers, railroad employees, paper-mill workers, craftsmen and traders. Stevens Point would later become the major urban center, and Portage County eventually emerged as the second largest Polish population center in the entire country.

In addition to tracts in the Cutover region, land owned by railroads was another possibility for Polish immigrants to acquire Midwestern land inexpensively. In Southern Illinois, Poles from urban areas procured expanses of marketable land from the Illinois Central Railroad in the 1870s. Those choosing to settle in Northwestern Indiana even found some industrial employment in the farm communities. Poles purchased most of the railroad land in central Nebraska, and given the lack of later settlement, the Polish legacy has endured.

Some Lithuanian immigrants came to America in the late 1860s, but most arrived in the three decades after 1880. As with many other Eastern Europeans, most

United States

individuals. The second group consisted of some 40,000 refugees from World War II and Soviet rule, many of whom immigrated to America as displaced persons. As with other peoples from the inner or outer Soviet empire, Latvians retained a strong sense of ethnic and national identity. Many in the second wave worked in some way for their homeland's independence after 1950.

Some Latvians settled in America during the last half of the 19th century, but most immigrants arrived in the early 20th century, taking unskilled labor jobs in the steel mills, packing houses, foundries, and textile factories. Many were hardworking and enterprising people who acquired job skills or established small businesses. The displaced persons settled mostly in larger metropolitan areas, such as Milwaukee, Cleveland, and Southwestern Michigan. Recent and established immigrant groups have tended to remain apart.

People of Russian Origin

Immigrant populations of Russian ancestry are in all likelihood more ethnically diverse than any other group. Several different immigrant peoples consider themselves to a large extent Russian, even though their origins vary considerably. Of the immigrants arriving in America from Russia in the early 20th century, fewer than 20% were actually ethnic Russians or Great Russians. The remainder included Jews, Belorussians, Ruthenians, Ukrainians, and such people as Cossacks from the Central Asian expanses of the empire. Estimates of the percentage of Jews among immigrants from Russia have ranged

Jewish contributions to America: sports

from 58% of the pre-1930 immigrants to 84% of the 1899–1924 immigrants and 95% of those coming between 1880 and 1899.

In the 1920s over 95,000 people in America specified Ruthenian as their first language, yet this group did not include the substantial but unknown numbers of ethnic Ruthenians who were Russian-speakers. The Russian Orthodox Church remained a focal point for many of these assorted ethnic groups. The Roman Catholic Church maintained authority over the Eastern Rite Catholic organization in America, but many of the same frictions between the religions that existed in Eastern Europe, for example, over the marriage of priests, presented themselves in the Eastern Catholic communities of America as well. Many Eastern Catholics were disposed to join the Orthodox Church in America, thus maintaining a close link to the broader immigrant Russian community. Eastern Rite refers generally to the Christian churches originating in the church of the Eastern Roman Empire and comprising various Eastern Orthodox, Uniate, Monophysite and Nestorian churches.

According to Russian Orthodox sources, over 40% of the Russian Orthodox population in America was of Rusyn or Ukrainian origin on the eve of the First World War. In some Russian Orthodox congregations, Rusyns represented over three-quarters of the flock. Grouping Rusyns with Russians generally added substantial numbers to the population described as having Russian ancestry. Rusyns and Ruthenians came from both sides of the Carpathian Mountains in what was before 1919 Austria-Hungary and today is roughly the area of the westernmost part of the Ukraine. They spoke a version of Ukrainian, but often identified themselves as Austrian.

Some descendants of German-Russian immigrants have periodically identified themselves as Russian, despite their disgruntlement with their adopted homeland. Distinctly German but having lived in the Russian Empire for several generations, ethnic designations of the group have shifted. Labels tended to vary with American attitudes toward Germany and Russia. During the Russo-Japanese War in the early 20th century and the Cold War, American hostility toward Russia caused most German-Russians to identify themselves as German. During the world wars, above all because of Nazi atrocities, most understandably preferred to describe their ethnicity as Russian. Recently, the label German-Russian has been commonly used.

The Russian-ancestry population of America probably has a larger percentage of political refugees and their offspring than any other ethnic group. Some two

million Russians fled to Western Europe in the wake of the 1917 revolution, and of those at least 30,000 immigrated to America in the 1920s. As the Nazi specter haunted Europe, many Russians in France, Germany or other countries left for the United States. Opposition to communism first prompted most of these refugees to leave their homeland. None relished the notion of living under a Nazi regime and quite a few were Jewish, for whom the "new order" of Europe was beyond the pale. Generally, these were middle- and upper-class people, not inclined to settle in the areas where earlier Russian immigrants lived. Like many refugees, they had to take fairly menial jobs in their first years in a foreign country. The faithful among them reorganized the Orthodox Church in America. After World War II, thousands of Russian refugees settled in America after spending several years in temporary European refugee camps.

Most people specifying Russian ancestry in Alaska had their origins in Russia prior to the pre-1867 period of Russian colonization, when Alaska was a Russian outpost and a chief hub of the fur trade. Colonial administration had been handled principally by people of combined Russian and native ancestry, who had become culturally Russian and no longer belonged to the native societies. At the turn of the century, this group numbered over 2,000 in a string of settlements along the coast.

Ruthenian and Ukrainian Ancestry

From 1880 to 1914, when the principal Ukrainian settlements were created in America, most immigrants came from rural western parts of the Ukraine. The vast majority of those early immigrants who spoke some variety of Ukrainian were ethnically Rusyn or Ruthenian from areas that were part of Austria-Hungary and are now mostly in an independent Ukraine.

Prior to the 1920s, immigrants seldom thought of themselves as Ukrainian. As a rule, they identified themselves as Rusyn or Ruthenian, although some referred to themselves as Austrian or Hungarian because the multiethnic empire was their actual country of origin. The Rusyn sense of identity was weakened by efforts of the Russian government to bring people into the Orthodox Church and to russianize them in other ways. Census data from the 1930s indicated that preservation of a Rusyn or Ruthenian identity was far greater among those from the south side of the Carpathians, because of their affiliation with Hungary and the absence of contact with either Galicia or the Ukraine.

In the late 19th century, Ukrainians frequently mined coal and were dispersed throughout Pennsylvania, West Virginia, and Southeastern Ohio. Some pushed west to Oklahoma and Texas, and as more attractive employment became available to them elsewhere or as mines became more mechanized, many moved on. Most settled in the larger industrial cities of the East and Midwest. In upstate New York, a substantial Ukrainian community emerged in the Buffalo area, and Ukrainian neighborhoods grew in many of the cities located along the canal and rail-road lines across the state. In the bituminous coal mining and industrial areas of Pennsylvania and eastern Ohio, sizeable Ukrainian communities evolved. Allentown, Chester, and Philadelphia had the most substantial neighborhoods in the 1920s. The iron and steel cities of Johnstown, Pittsburgh, and Ambridge in Pennsylvania, and Youngstown and Cleveland in Ohio developed major Ukrainian communities. New York City, the chief port of arrival and a sprawling manufacturing center, retained many Ukrainian immigrants, and a large ethnic neighborhood on the Lower East Side became one of the largest in the country.

Jewish Population

Jewish people constitute a significant ethnic group in America, but because Judaism is also a religion, no formal census data about them exist. Jews customarily listed their national origin in censuses and were therefore included in the statistics for these national groups. Many Jewish immigrants came from Germany, Hungary, and Poland. Later, everyone in America specifying Israeli ancestry would be acknowledged as Jewish. It is notable, though, that by the 1920s, over 60% of American Jews had their origins in Russia. Hence the Jewish population corresponds fairly closely to the Russian-ancestry data. The proportion of Jews of Russian origin increased after 1966, when new Soviet emigration policies allowed substantial numbers of Jews to leave, most of whom settled in the United States.

Hence, differentiating Jewish people from the chiefly Christian populations of European countries for statistical purposes has been a perennial problem. Jewish organizations have been the principal source of the sketchy data. Jews began settling in the British colonies in North America around the middle of the 17th century, establishing communities in what would become New York City and later one in Newport, Rhode Island. Over the next century a modest number of immigrants followed, and Jewish quarters developed in Philadelphia, Charleston, and Savannah. Most of the earlier Jewish immigrants were Sephardic Jews, a term usually referring to people from the Mediterranean region. The founders of the first Jewish

New York state certificate of incorporation for a Jewish congregation

congregations in America had been expelled from the Iberian Peninsula in the 1500s. These Spanish and Portuguese Jews initially moved to Brazil or the Dutch possessions in the Caribbean prior to arriving in the American colonies. Enterprising and cosmopolitan, these early immigrants to America rapidly took advantage of the colonies' commercial opportunities. By the mid 1700s, many had become affluent, even by the standards of regions boasting some of the highest per capita incomes in the world.

By the 1770s, the Ashkenazic Jews, whose origins were in Germany or Poland, had become the majority in the American Jewish community. The Ashkenazim differed from Sephardic Jews in language and traditions, but intermarriage within the Jewish communities ensured the fading of clear distinctions between Sephardic and Ashkenazic populations over time. A fresh wave of Sephardic Jews did not arrive in America until the early 20th century, most of whom hailed from eastern Mediterranean regions or North Africa. In

United States

Hebrew text (in decorative lettering):
זיי געבענטשט דוא פרייע לאנד

Long Live the Land of the Free

WORDS BY
S. SMULOWITZ
MUSIC BY
J.M. RUMSHISKY

Piano 50¢
Violin 30¢

HEBREW PUBLISHING CO.
83-87 CANAL ST.   NEW YORK
COPYRIGHT   1911

Jewish culture in America

part because their speech and customs set them apart from the majority of East Central European Jews, they would encounter considerable integration difficulties.

The Ashkenazic Jews in America were themselves subdivided into two principal ethnic groups: German Jews, many from the Prussian territories of Poland, who dominated immigration until the 1880s, and Eastern European Jews who flowed into New York in the decades thereafter. Until the late 19th century, German Jews were customarily regarded as ethnic Germans, with religious affiliation having only a minor role in the public eye. As was often the case with established Jews, though, ethnic identity gained popular attention when the Ashkenazim acquired substantial wealth and spent it lavishly. Subsequent resentment fueled anti-Semitism. On the other hand, the influx of destitute Eastern European or Russian Jews prompted expressions of public concern about the potential consequences of mass migration. Even in the new world, Jews, it seemed, both rich and poor, were singled out for public criticism.

Jews from Germany arrived in significant numbers beginning in the 1830s, and comprised a large part of the broader 19th-century migration from Central Europe to the New World. Unlike Christians, most of whom became farmers or industrial workers, Jewish immigrants frequently worked as peddlers, bringing a host of textiles and other manufactured goods to rural and small-town America. After years of peripatetic and arduous work, many accumulated sufficient capital to establish themselves as small merchants. Roving sales work and the hunt for better prospects in life resulted in a wide dispersion of Jewish people throughout the country. Jewish merchants and entrepreneurs could be found in the remote mining settlements of California, Nevada, and Montana as well as in the Midwestern farm communities. Those settling in isolated areas of the South, where no established Jewish communities existed, were usually absorbed into the surrounding society and subsequently lost much sense of Jewish identity.

In Russia, where the vast majority of people lived in rural villages, Jews were forced into towns and cities where they were effectively ghettoized. Yet, Jews in Russia conducted much of the merchandise trade in large areas and many had acquired craft and manufacturing skills. Upon their arrival in America, they had at their disposal far more skills as watchmakers, hatters, furriers, tailors, bookbinders, tinsmiths, tanners, glaziers, bakers and carpenters than other immigrant groups. Employment in America's rapidly expanding textile manufacturing sector offered good opportunities and attractive compensation in comparison to other industries. With only modest capital needed to establish a small factory, many Jews founded their own small businesses soon after their arrival in the adopted country.

Occupational differences contributed significantly to the emergence of a distinctive Jewish culture in America. Jews seldom needed to labor in unskilled jobs in the mines and steel mills where so many other immigrants found employment. Instead, Jews tended to avail themselves of the ample opportunities for trading, craftsmanship, and entrepreneurship in major urban areas. Thriving Jewish communities provided support networks and offered sufficient markets for sales and services. While other Eastern European groups established their largest communities in cities associated with heavy industry, many Jews settled in New York City, regarding it as the essential core of opportunity and culture.

Despite suburbanization and the outflow of people from the metropolitan area, the effects of which have somewhat diminished the large numbers of Jewish residents of New York City, the "Big Apple" has preserved its ascendancy for the American Jewish community. Jews comprise some 15% of the city's population, and Jewish residents of New York City represent over 20% of the national Jewish population, which is approximately five million. Fully half of the Soviet/Russian Jewish refugees arriving in the United States since the 1960s reside in New York. Nearly two million Jews, some 40% of the national total live in the New York metropolitan area, when the suburban counties in New York and New Jersey are included. In recent decades, New York City has been the focal point in the lives of proportionately fewer American Jews and has not had the impact upon quite so many as it once did.

Southern European Ancestry

Substantial out-migrations from the impoverished and more isolated Southern Italian and Greek areas began in the 1880s. As with the Eastern Europeans migrations, the influx of people peaked in the years between about 1890 and 1914. The First World War rendered transatlantic travel hazardous, and moreover, U.S. immigration restrictions in the 1920s lowered quotas for Southern Europeans.

Migration to America was typically a function of the shortage of land and employment in Southern Europe that was in turn a consequence of rapid population growth and inadequate industrialization. The transatlantic voyage by steamship took less than two weeks by the 1870s and greater competition among the assortment of shipping companies reduced passage prices. Oddly few immigrants, though, regarded their sojourn to the new world as permanent. Prior to the 1880s, most emigrants from Italy went to Brazil or Argentina, and in later decades it was not uncommon for Italians to cross the Atlantic several times or even to labor in Italy or Latin America during the North American winters and then to return to the United States in the spring.

Most Spanish immigrants headed for countries in Latin America in the 19th century although some moved either to the New York area or the former Spanish colonies of Louisiana and California. Later, Florida would hold some appeal for Spanish immigrants, above all, because of job opportunities in tobacco production and the cigar factories. After 1910, some Spaniards joined the massive immigration from Southern Europe to America's industrial cities and mining towns in New Jersey, West Virginia and Pennsylvania. Spanish foreign stock statistics typically include Basques from the Iberian Peninsula, and most people of Spanish origin who settled in Idaho are Basques, as are many of those in Nevada and Arizona.

The Spanish Civil War (1936–39) and World War II (1939–45) caused a considerable outflow of refugees to the Western Hemisphere, and after the 1960s the removal of the previous low immigration quota resulted in more Spanish people settling in the United States. Those of Spanish ancestry are customarily included in the broad ethnic category "Hispanic" and are greatly outnumbered by the much larger group of Latin American origin, now usually called "Latinos."

The Basque area of Europe has been divided since the 16th century between France and Spain, and hence some people of Basque ancestry identify themselves as French. The difference between French and Spanish Basques has given rise to the emergence of two basically separate Basque communities in the United States. Basque immigration has been closely associated with American sheep farming. In the 19th century, Basque emigrants typically settled in South America, either in Argentina or Uruguay, which have the largest concentrations of Basques in the Western Hemisphere. In South America, most Basque

A first-generation American aviator in World War II

settlers were engaged in sheep ranching, and around the middle of the 19th century, some migrated to California.

Early Basque immigrants to the United States brought with them the large-scale sheep-farming skills they learned in South America, adapting these to the Western states. The California gold rush of the late 1840s brought a fair number of Basques to the West Coast, but within a decade these settlers had established themselves as cattlemen in Southern California. When California proved unsuitable for the cattle industry, Basques returned to their specialty of raising sheep, which tended to thrive in the semiarid environment of much of California. In the 1860s, Basque immigrants took their economic specialty into the Central Valley of California, and thereafter, new herders began to arrive directly from both the Spanish and French Basque homelands in Europe, as sheep ranching opportunities in the western part of the United States became commonly known. Bakersfield and Fresno became major French Basque settlements, and the sheep business operated by people of Spanish Basque origin became extensive around the Kern County area. From California's Central Valley, Basque-led sheep production expanded into other Western states, with Basques becoming predominant in herding, ranching and wool marketing.

Portuguese people first began coming to the United States in connection with the developing whaling industry in the early 19th century. With New England as the chief base of operations, the whaling industry typically sought foreign crew members willing to work for lower wages than Yankee seamen expected. The Portuguese, with a seafaring tradition and no job prospects at home, welcomed the opportunity to spend a year or two at sea with relatively good compensation. Young men from the Azores, Portuguese islands far out in the Atlantic Ocean, in particular welcomed the prospect of joining American whaling ships to escape the dullness of island life and to avoid military conscription, which often meant service in colonial areas. Some Portuguese men stayed on in the whaling fleets, while others accepted an essentially free passage to America.

The expanding cotton textile mills of Massachusetts began furnishing employment to the Portuguese and especially the Azoreans around the middle of the 19th century. Fall River in Massachusetts, which would become widely known as "Spindle City," developed a sizeable Portuguese community, and this group, together with Polish immigrants, furnished the bulk of the labor force needed to operate the new mills. After the turn of the

United States

Armenian immigrant

century, new immigrants arriving in the established Portuguese ethnic areas of Southern Massachusetts soon determined that employment prospects were better in other parts of the state such as Somerville and Lowell. The whaling port of New London, Connecticut, developed a substantial Portuguese community in the first half of the 19th century when the whaling business was at its height. Toward the end of the century, many people of Portuguese ancestry moved to the industrial cities of Hartford, New Haven, and Bridgeport. The early 20th century brought a fresh wave of immigrants from the Portuguese homeland, with most taking factory work in Connecticut and Massachusetts.

On the West Coast, farming became the favored occupation of the Portuguese in the 19th century, with most settlements developing in the San Francisco Bay area. By 1880 Azoreans were engaged in dairy farming in Marin County, and Azoreans comprised a fifth of the population of Sausalito around the same time. The largest ethnic Portuguese settlement was in San Leandro, where by the first decade of the 20th century, the Portuguese constituted two-thirds of the town's residents. Portuguese settlers would later establish fruit, vegetable, and dairy farms in San Joaquin Valley. The Portuguese agricultural tradition has spanned more than a century, as indicated by the numerous Portuguese and Azorean surnames among dairy farmers in many counties of Northern California.

Prior to 1880, Italian immigrants to America were mostly from the northern part of the country, the most prosperous region of a land that had become unified only in 1870. These émigrés, many of whom were professionals and skilled craftsmen such as stonecutters and masons, founded distinct ethnic communities in a number of American cities. In New Jersey and New York, for example, specialty garment manufacturers recruited skilled weavers and dyers from Lombardy and Piedmont in the 1870s. In most American urban areas, though, the nature of the early ethnic communities changed following the influx, after about 1880, of substantial numbers of illiterate and destitute peasants from Southern Italy and Sicily. Because regional identities in the homeland were prominent, chain migration tended to connect Italian regions and even individual villages with particular American communities. Italian neighborhoods in American cities frequently acquired the distinct characteristics of the region whence the immigrants came.

Because Italian immigration coincided quite closely with the waves of Eastern European migration, competition between ethnic groups for unskilled laboring jobs was fierce in many areas. Italian domination of the unskilled labor market often meant the exclusion of other ethnic groups such as the Hungarians, the Polish and other Slavic immigrants. It should come as no surprise that discrimination cut both ways. Industrial areas would typically have a high percentage of either Italian or Polish laborers, but not both.

The Italian workforce in America usually relied upon a labor contracting arrangement widely known as the padrone system, involving a boss who acted as service provider and mediator between workers and employers. Following the conclusion of the contract, the padrone moved with the immigrant workers to the worksite, arranged basic living accommodations, handled financial matters, and served as the supervisor. Labor contracts negotiated through padrone coordination were often well suited to furnishing short-term and itinerant groups of laborers required for the construction of railroads and public works such as streets, docks, and sewage systems.

The padrone system was instrumental in the diffusion of Italians throughout much of the United States, and by the 1890s, Italian workers supplanted the Irish as the principal source of labor for railway construction. Italians comprised half the railroad construction laborers dispatched from Chicago in the early 20th century and nearly all the sector crews performing track maintenance. Italian railway workers established most of the ethnic communities along the railroad lines in the Mississippi Valley in the last decade of the 19th century. Later, some railroad companies hired Italians directly, and permanent Italian settlements emerged near railroad hubs in Western and Midwestern cities such as Cheyenne, Omaha, and Fort Wayne.

Nearly all Italian immigrants after 1880 landed in New York, where those without set employment elsewhere could readily take on construction work arranged through a labor agency. Many immigrants simply remained in the New York area, which in the early years of the new century acquired the largest concentration of Italians in the country. Another area with a high percentage of ethnic Italians was in Western Pennsylvania, north of Pittsburgh. Beginning in the early 20th cen-

Algerian immigrant, Zoubir Ouarti, with his American wife

tury, Italian immigrants in that area comprised most of the labor force on farms and railroads, in quarries and cement plants, and on most construction sites. Italians worked in the tin-plated steel plant in New Castle, the largest in the country, and other specialty steel mills. Around two-thirds of the workforce of the Standard Steel Car Works outside of Pittsburgh were of Italian origin as well.

Substantial numbers of both Italians and Eastern Europeans settled in Chicago. The city's range of manufacturing and its location as the transportation and labor market center of the Midwest attracted many ethnic groups, including Italians. Although renowned for its meatpacking, steel production, and rail transport, on the eve of the First World War, Chicago was a national leader in the manufacture of men's clothing. Most Italian neighborhoods were adjacent to the factories and industrial plants on the banks of the Chicago River. Because the stockyards and steel mills of South Chicago were manned largely by workers of Slavic origin, few Italians lived nearby.

After about 1890, Italian workers frequently comprised the largest single ethnic group in bituminous coal-mining operations, which often involved strip mining. Italians made up over 12% of miners in Pennsylvania and West Virginia prior to the First World War. Italians from the northern home provinces were much more common in Western U.S. coal mining, whereas southern Italians were preponderant in the mining regions of Pennsylvania and West Virginia. Southern Italian immigrants mined iron ore in upper Michigan and northern Wisconsin, precious metals in the Colorado Rockies west of Denver, and copper in Butte. In the Butte area, Italians comprised the largest single ethnic group in the mixed force of workers drawn from previous mining jobs in the Midwest.

California's fertile valleys were the setting for the largest Italian farm communities in the Western United States. Early immigrants bought land in the San Francisco Bay area and grew produce for the local market, while others began the state's wine industry. The best-known producer over the years has probably been Italian-Swiss Colony, which Italian settlers established in the early 1880s in Sonoma County. Later, people of Italian ancestry established numerous vineyards and wineries in the Napa, Santa Clara, and San Joaquin Valleys, and a number of California wine production operations bear Italian names.

Initial Greek settlement in America began in Florida in the 1760s although descendants of these immigrants lost most awareness of Greek ancestry. Hundreds

of Greeks who consented to be indentured laborers for several years founded the New Smyrna community, south of Saint Augustine, later in the 18th century. Although the original settlement was abandoned, and the descendants of the immigrants disappeared, the city of New Smyrna exists today and has maintained a certain ethnic ambience. Floridians of Greek ancestry are for the most part descendants of unskilled immigrants who settled in the deep South between the 1880s and 1914. In Florida, Greek immigrants established their own version of the padrone system that provided railway workers and farm laborers. Large Greek-owned businesses sometimes arranged for chain migration, offering job opportunities for new arrivals, who became, in effect, indentured servants for set periods.

In Massachusetts and Southern New Hampshire, textile and shoe manufacturing areas began recruiting Greek immigrants in the 1890s, and expanding job opportunities in the mills of New England brought over thousands within a few years. Greek immigrants supplanted French Canadians in some areas as a major ethnic group in the workforce as textile mills shifted labor force recruitment from farm girls to Irish and French Canadians to workers of eastern Mediterranean origin.

Ethnic Greeks comprised the last wave of immigrants to America from Southern Europe. Many settled in Midwestern industrial cities, where they were frequently the last unskilled laborers of European origin to arrive. Greek immigrants to Wisconsin worked in steel mills and in the city's specialty industries, such as leather production. When Michigan's Ford plants began to pay five dollars per day in 1912, the word spread rapidly among workers in many areas. A fair number of Greeks gave up railway construction work in the Middle West and Far West to labor in Detroit's automobile factories.

Middle Eastern Origin

If we characterize the Middle East to include Southwest Asia and North Africa, stretching from Iran and Turkey through the Arabian Peninsula and the eastern shore of the Mediterranean Sea, then in the late 19th and early 20th centuries, patterns of immigration to the United States from this area resembled in crucial ways those from Southern and Eastern Europe. Most immigrants came from increasingly crowded rural areas and planned to migrate only temporarily. Few had job skills to offer employers in an industrializing country. The principal incentive to migrate was invariably economic, although avoidance of service in the Ottoman army was an additional consideration, and

some Jews and Christians left to escape religious persecution. Immigration from the Middle East to America reached its zenith between 1890 and World War I. Many of the Middle Eastern immigrants arriving at that time were Christians from the Ottoman province of Syria, though émigrés hailed from several areas of the Middle East. Most Syrian immigrants were from the Mount Lebanon region, the most prosperous area of a largely impoverished province. Most of these were of the Maronite religious tradition and many were Francophile in orientation. Other Christian groups included Antiochian Orthodox Christians and Syrian Orthodox. Less than 10% of the pre-1914 Syrian émigrés were Moslems. Today, approximately three-quarters of Arab-Americans are Christian.

The diversity of America's Arab population reflects the many-sided cultures of the Middle East and North Africa. Arabs generally identify with particular countries, regions, and religious groups as well as with the Arab heritage. The most conspicuous separation has traditionally been between Christianity and Islam, yet broad religious affiliation has been subdivided into a range of sects and groups. As Arab countries achieved their independence after World War II, most Americans of Arab ancestry associated in some way with the country that includes their area of origin.

Armenians came from the Ottoman Empire as well as from across the mountains in Russian territories. The two groups retained their individuality, usually settling in separate areas of the country. Moreover, Armenians differed from most other immigrants in that a large minority emigrated from towns and possessed skills as artisans or merchants. Although most Armenians came from the countryside, some had become prosperous tradesmen in towns along the long-established Middle Eastern caravan routes. With their knowledge and skills, a number of Armenians eventually achieved some affluence in America although most had to take unskilled laboring jobs at least temporarily.

In Massachusetts prior to the First World War, Armenians usually labored in the steel mills, the shoe factories and the textile plants. In Rhode Island, they comprised a large percentage of the workforce in silk and textile production. The pattern continued in New Jersey where the Armenians were a major component of the silk industry workforce.

Some Armenians later established a market niche in America's oriental carpet business. In New England and New York especially, Armenians came to dominate the retailing and cleaning of expensive rugs. In their homeland, many Armenians had been rug merchants prior to emigrat-

United States

ing and some maintained overseas supply connections. Armenian tradesmen profited hugely from the fashionableness among the affluent of oriental carpets in America beginning in the second half of the 19th century.

Later Armenian migration, domestic and foreign, to California eventually resulted in over half of the Armenians in America residing in that state by the end of the 20th century. Many Americans of Armenian lineage headed for the Los Angeles or San Francisco Bay areas during the Great Depression. More recent immigrants from Iran, the Levantine Arab countries, and the former Soviet Union contributed substantially to the expansion of California's Armenian community. In the two decades prior to its collapse, the Soviet Union allowed thousands of Armenians to immigrate, and most ultimately settled in California.

When new U.S. immigration laws in the late 1940s largely eliminated restrictions on the basis of national origin, migration from the Middle East to America began again. Many émigrés joined relatives in America, but substantial numbers of middle-class professionals and skilled people entered as well. Palestinian immigration surged in the wake of the 1967 war, and in contrast to the prior overwhelmingly Christian immigration, nearly two-thirds of the post-1948 émigrés have been Moslems. More recent immigrants have tended to have a stronger sense of Arab nationalism, which has sometimes influenced the self-identity of Americans of Syrian or Lebanese descent.

Immigrants who arrived in the second half of the 20th century typically settled in large metropolitan areas, where relatives lived and opportunities beckoned. Chain migration to older Arab communities has been frequent, and family businesses have sometimes offered employment to the new arrivals. Many Arabs came to the United States as students, and eventually changed their status to permanent resident. Jordanian professionals in particular have typically entered the United States on student visas, and later acquired "green cards" or U.S. citizenship.

Egyptian immigrants, virtually all of whom arrived after 1950, are clustered in the greater New York area, and over three-quarters of them are of Coptic Christian origin. Most left their homeland in the wake of deteriorating social and economic conditions there. The largest Jordanian and Palestinian communities are in the Chicago metropolitan areas, followed by Detroit and New York, where a substantial number of affluent people of Jordanian origin reside. Yemenis are the prominent exception to the essentially urban and often professional character of

Arab-American communities. Immigrants of Yemeni origin have for the most part been farm laborers in California, especially in the Central Valley.

The United States had few immigrants of Iranian origin until well after the Second World War. In the 1970s, opposition to the dictatorship of the Shah of Iran prompted some people to leave. Although many Iranians had a mind to reform and democracy, a substantial number, especially the religious minorities, dreaded the prospect of revolution. As the country slipped into turmoil in the late 1970s, Iranians headed for America by the thousands, and most Iranians studying or working in America remained there. The revolutionary theocratic regime that came to power in 1979 terminated Iran's westernizing path. In 1979–1980 alone, over 19,000 Iranians entered the United States as immigrants. At the same time, tens of thousands of Iranian Jews fled the country for either Israel or the United States. Eventually, Iran's entire Jewish community of over 70,000 emigrated. People of Iranian origin in the United States typically reside in metropolitan areas, especially in Washington, D.C. and the California cities. Usually skilled and educated, most have done well for themselves in their adopted homeland.

Only a small percentage of the pre-World War I immigrants from the Ottoman Empire were ethnic Turks. Of this group, all were Moslem and the better educated among them eventually returned to Turkey, leaving a small, unskilled Turkish population in America. These immigrants comprised minute enclaves in urban industrial areas, where nearly all labored in

factories. Isolated, poor, and often illiterate, they maintained their Turkish culture and identity for decades. These ethnic Turks are now widely dispersed and no longer have distinct communities. The modest numbers of more recent immigrants have settled in metropolitan areas, in particular New York City, which still has a few small albeit distinctive Turkish neighborhoods.

African Ancestry

Beginning in 1619, when a ship containing 20 African laborers landed in the harbor of Jamestown, Virginia, slaves began arriving in the American colonies. Substantial amounts of labor were needed for the cultivation of tobacco, rice, sugar, and cotton crops, all of which had considerable profit potential in the new world. Prosperous farmers could afford to purchase slaves as domestic servants and for labor in the fields. In 1698, the Royal African Company lost its royally conferred monopoly on transporting slaves to the American colonies. Upwardly mobile colonists, especially New England seafarers, took advantage of the lucrative opportunities, and the number of Africans transported to America soared. More than 10,000 Africans were brought to American shores in the first decade of the 18th century alone. Tens of thousands arrived in the next 50 years. Blacks accounted for nearly half the population of Virginia by the middle of the century, and by then, blacks outnumbered whites in South Carolina by two to one. For more than 150 years in the 17th and 18th centuries, Africans were herded into vessels bound for the Western Hemi-

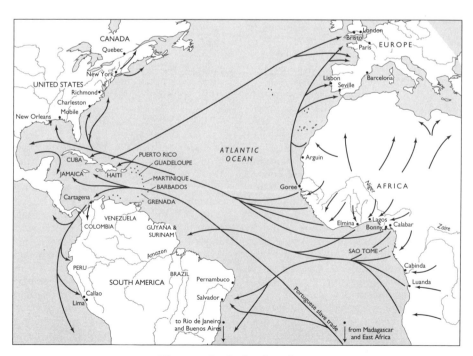

Slave routes to the Americas

254

sphere. By 1790, black people comprised over 19% of the U.S. population, the vast majority held in bondage and concentrated in the Southern states.

Most of the blacks transported to America were from the West Coast of Africa. Usually they were captured by coastal tribes and sold to European and American flesh merchants. Often branded and bound, the slaves were packed into slave vessels traveling the infamous "middle passage," on which death rates to the new world ran as high as 20%. They were then jostled onto auction blocks in colonial slave-handling ports such as Newport and Charleston, the latter maintaining a large and flourishing slave market for over a century.

Although the importation of slaves to the United States became illegal in 1808, smuggling was fairly common, and slave breeding and trading in the Southern states provided needed workforce numbers. Although escape to the North or the purchase of freedom were potential avenues of release from bondage, most African immigrants remained slaves until the last year of the U.S. Civil War. Emancipation was proclaimed in 1863 and realized in 1865 with the triumph of federal arms, but blacks still had a long march thereafter to freedom.

After the Civil War, most blacks remained in the largely impoverished South, where they typically became sharecroppers or tenants on white-owned farms. They were relegated to second-class citizenship by the "Jim Crow" society. Large-scale migration to Northern industrial areas began in the 1920s and accelerated in the 1930s as the economy went into a tailspin and farms were increasingly subjected to federal acreage restrictions. The demand for labor, especially in armament industries during World War II, along with the subsequent economic growth of Northern and Western cities promoted the further exodus of African-Americans from the South. Also, the mechanization of agriculture spurred by farm programs largely eliminated the need for cheap manual labor in rural areas by the end of the 1950s.

The second half of the 20th century brought sweeping economic change to the South. In agricultural areas, cotton has been replaced to a considerable extent by meat and specialty vegetable production, the harvesting of wood, and the mass poultry industry. Many small towns and cities expanded, as manufacturing in the South grew because of lower production costs and wage rates as well as less powerful labor unions.

During the 1970s, the migration went into reverse and black Americans have contributed significantly to the shift of the U.S. population to the Sunbelt. In con-

Statue of Martin Luther King on Westminster Cathedral, London

trast to the first half of the 20th century, blacks ceased migrating from the South to northern urban areas, and those settling in the South have doubled in recent decades. Black migrants from the Northern to the Southern states typically have relatively high levels of education and work experience, and many have prospered in the new South. The highest percentages of African-Americans still reside between Virginia's Tidewater and east Texas, the region that has been central to the black experience in America and represents the core of black American culture.

Considerable residential segregation between blacks and whites characterized American metropolitan areas in the 20th century. In 17 cities and metropolitan areas with the largest black populations, the metropolitan areas of Chicago, Cleveland, Detroit and Saint Louis were more segregated than the others. The general pattern has been one of greater segregation of blacks than of other ethnic groups, including Asians, people of Hispanic origin,

or people of various Southern and Eastern European ancestries.

Central and South American Origin

Work on the railroads brought the first sizeable entries of Mexicans to the United States, which occurred around 1910. Accommodation was typically primitive, in improvised camps, crude barracks, or even old boxcars. Railway employment was usually seasonal and low-paying, and workers were itinerant. The turbulence of the First World War and the subsequent immigrant restrictions of the 1920s choked off the ready supply of labor from Southern and Eastern Europe. The attendant shortfall opened new job opportunities for Mexicans, but also for African-Americans in the steel mills and slaughterhouses. Although many disheartened Mexicans left America during the Great Depression, labor recruitment for the U.S. workforce recommenced during World War II. Many Mexicans would remain in the postwar boom, yet these immigrants have not

United States

consistently been able to avail themselves of the opportunities on offer in America. Most continue to work in low-skill and low-paying industrial or agricultural jobs.

Demand for Mexican migrant workers skyrocketed in the large valleys and plains of the Southwest when irrigation for agriculture began in those areas in the early 20th century. California's reliance upon migrant farm labor has since become proverbial. Absence of immigration restrictions prior to 1917 allowed Mexicans freely to enter California, and the very expanse of the frontier area, along with unsystematic controls, has resulted in a porous border.

The Haitian Revolution, in the late 18th century, prompted over 50,000 Haitians, including white planters and farmers, free blacks, and slaves of African origin to flee to the United States. The island has had a troubled history, and continued turmoil brought eventual U.S. military intervention and subsequent occupation in the 20th century. Many Haitians who harbored resentments about their homeland effectively becoming a U.S. dominion somewhat disingenuously left for the United States. Most settled in New York, in which they established several neighborhoods where Creole, a French dialect of the Caribbean, is widely spoken. After World War II, more Haitian refugees joined these communities.

The Duvalier dictatorships in Haiti, which began in the late 1950s, resulted in record numbers of immigrants, and the Haitian communities in the United States expanded apace. People from all walks of life, including the rural poor, politicians, and professionals, came to America in the 1960s and 1970s to escape authoritarian oppression. Extended families often joined those who had already settled in America. Boatloads of refugees arrived in south Florida in 1972, as desperate people with little to lose risked the hazardous voyage north. U.S. border officials were hard-pressed to control the flow, and the foreign influx swelled again in 1977, as people in the Bahamas and the Dominican Republic, destinations of previous Haitian migrations, began harassing and banishing Haitians. As the situation in Haiti continued to deteriorate, the United States and Canada faced a veritable refugee crisis. The number of Haitians who have settled in the United States as illegal aliens is impossible to determine, but it is surely in the tens of thousands.

Within the Western Hemisphere current migration is generally the result of economic conditions, rather than security and safety issues as was the case two decades ago. The baneful combination of dreadful governance and the rapid rise in population invariably resulted in sluggish

A sad chapter in U.S. history

economic growth, low incomes, and high unemployment. Rampant poverty and inadequate property laws are frequently cited as reasons to emigrate, and the general perception that opportunities beckon in America induces many people to head north. A complicating factor is the sheer volume of remittances from legal and illegal migrants. Billions of dollars flow to the Central American states annually, sent by "economic refugees" in the United States. Although the amount of remittances to the Caribbean states is smaller, the percentage of GDP is higher, given the size of the area's economy. Hence, migration has assumed a crucial economic dimension. Every year, several hundred thousand undocumented immigrants join the mass of illegal aliens in America, estimated already to exceed six million. States most affected are California, Texas, New York, Florida, Illinois, New Jersey and Arizona. Some 80% of the immigrants to the United States come from within the hemisphere. Accessibility and relatively low transportation costs enable even the impoverished from Central America to enter the United States.

Since the 1959 revolution in Cuba, hundreds of thousands of refugees headed to the United States, and political turmoil thereafter in some Central American countries brought tens of thousands more. Central America's proximity to the United States has encouraged substantial numbers of people to migrate without authorization or documentation. Once undocumented immigrants arrive in America, they are usually able to remain.

The West Indies have also been a prominent immigration source to America. During the second half of the 20th century, inner-Caribbean migration for employment purposes was common, and immigration to America became merely an extension of such labor mobility. During the 1970s, Caribbean immigration to America surged, resulting in the islands of the West Indies sending the largest proportion of their population to the United States than any other single area.

Asian Origin

Immigrants from major Asian countries began to arrive in Hawaii and on the American West Coast in the 19th century. There they typically found employment as agricultural workers, miners, or construction laborers. The California gold rush of the late 1840s brought Chinese immigrants by the thousands to what was popularly known as Golden Mountain although most were fleeing the social turmoil and poverty associated with the dissolution of an empire.

Chinese who were supplanted by white settlers in gold-mining operations thereafter had to take unskilled jobs in the western areas of the United States. Beginning in the 1890s, as Japanese, Koreans, and some Asian Indians immigrated to the Western United States, these would fill similar positions. Sources of inexpensive Asian labor shifted periodically, in part the result of limitations imposed on specific ethnic groups, but also because some immigrants succeeded, especially the Japanese, in bettering themselves and moving out of unskilled labor jobs. By the 1920s Filipinos were substantially replacing other Asian groups as agricultural laborers in California. Next to Mexicans, people of Philippine origin became the chief source of California farm labor after the Second World War.

White settlement of Hawaii did not begin until the late 18th century. The prior inhabitants of the islands were largely Polynesian, and the new settlers rapidly established control over substantial portions of Hawaii, above all, through the development of plantations for sugar and fruit production. The ensuing high demand for agricultural labor prompted the immigration of a variety of ethnic groups. Most farm workers were initially Chinese and Japanese, but after 1900, Koreans, Portuguese, Puerto Ricans, Filipinos, and even some Spanish began to arrive.

Throughout the West, Chinese labor remained in high demand because the Chinese had a well-deserved reputation for working hard at low wages. The Chinese who resided in the various Chinatowns often labored in the local laundries and small factories, many of which had Chinese proprietors. Outside the ethnic communities, mining, construction, farming and manufacturing jobs dispersed Chinese men across the Western states. Chinese laborers built railroads in Central California and dug water conduits in Nevada. Over 10,000 Chinese workers constructed the Central Pacific section of the transcontinental railway from California to Utah in the late 1860s. In the following decade, Chinese labor contributed to the completion of the Northern Pacific route through Montana and the Southern Pacific line across Southern Arizona and Texas.

Unfortunately, the Chinese received precious little gratitude from a society for whom many had labored so diligently. Whites came to accuse the Chinese of unduly lowering wage levels by their general willingness to toil for low pay. Gangs and goons harassed and maltreated Chinese immigrants whose only offense was to work hard, and subsequent discriminatory official rules and regulations singled out Asian immigrants. In 1882, federal legislation brought Chinese immigration to a standstill, and tight restrictions remained in effect until the Second World War created a new demand for foreign labor.

Exact statistics about Chinese migration from various countries in the second half of the 20th century are unavailable because immigration numbers have often included Taiwan, Hong Kong, the People's Republic of China, as well as some overseas Chinese. Although ethnic Chinese from Southeast Asia tend to identify with their country of origin, a cer-

SP 3-228S (8-2004)

POLICÍA ESTADO DE PENNSYLVANIA

Honor, Servicio, Integridad, Respeto, Confianza, Valor, Deber

PROCEDIMIENTOS PARA ELOGIAR / QUEJARSE

NUESTRO PROPÓSITO

Para asegurar la justicia, preservar la paz y mejorar la calidad de vida para todos.

¿Cómo Estamos Haciendo?

Los elogios en cuanto al servicio de la policía estatal de Pennsylvania o su personal se pueden denunciar en cualquier comisaría de la policía estatal, 24 horas al día, siete días a la semana, en persona, por teléfono o escrito. Por favor, dirija su correspondencia a la atención del jefe de la comisaría.

Las quejas en cuanto a los miembros del departamento también se pueden informar en cualquier comisaría de la policía estatal, 24 horas por día, siete días por semana, en persona, por teléfono o escrito. Se puede obtener un formulario para verificar la queja en el sitio de internet (www.state.pa.us). La carta de queja debe ser en original (no se permite una copia) y contener la firma original. Cada queja sobre mal comportamiento de un miembro del departamento será evaluada por la Oficina de Integridad y Estándares Profesionales.

También, las quejas se pueden denunciar directamente con la Oficina de Integridad y Estándares Profesionales, División de Asuntos Internos, marcando gratis 866-426-9164. Un representante está disponible durante las horas normales del trabajo, de lunes a viernes, entre las 8 de la mañana hasta las 3:30 de la tarde.

A bilingual America?

tain number specify Chinese ethnicity. In any event, the Chinese population of the United States increased at least tenfold in the 20th century, and perhaps half of the Chinese in America in the last quarter of the century were born abroad. Furthermore, half the Chinese in America now live in just three metropolitan areas, the San Francisco Bay region, which has the largest concentration, followed by New York City and neighboring Nassau and Suffolk counties, and Los Angeles and Orange counties.

Japanese immigration to America actually began in Hawaii, where, beginning in the 1880s, thousands of Japanese were hired to labor on Hawaii's sugar plantations, whose demand for farm workers

increased continuously. The majority of Japanese laborers remained on the islands, and within several decades the Japanese became Hawaii's largest ethnic group. People of Japanese ancestry constitute over one-quarter of Hawaii's population. Although the sugar plantations strove to prevent Japanese agricultural laborers from migrating to the mainland, resettlement to the Western United States without immigration formalities was possible once Hawaii became a U.S. territory in 1900. Businesses on the West Coast needing labor and unable to draw upon Chinese sources because of immigration restrictions, recruited Japanese workers and often provided economic incentives in the bargain. In fact, so many Japanese

United States

Senator Barack Obama, the 2008 presidential nominee of the Democratic Party . . .

men migrated to California in following years that Hawaii's population became disproportionately female.

People of Japanese origin who migrated from Hawaii to California as well as émigrés from Japan proper initially took most of the unskilled work previously done by the Chinese. Japanese laborers in the West typically did farm, construction, and railway work. They contributed to the building of many railroad lines, such as the Denver and Rio Grande's route across the Colorado Rockies, and formed many of the track maintenance crews on all the lines.

Some Japanese settlers in urban areas of the West Coast remained domestic servants and kitchen helpers, but a substantial number were able to found their own small enterprises such as shoe repair, laundries, and barbershops shortly after their migration. Many also went into the grocery and restaurant business. These establishments were usually to be found in Japanese communities, serving a Japanese clientele. In urban areas with substantial ethnic Japanese populations, such as Los Angeles and Seattle, locally owned and operated commercial enterprises supported a communal economic base.

During World War II, in one of the saddest chapters in American history, some of Hawaii's Japanese, along with most of the Japanese in California, were deported

to internment camps in isolated areas of the Western and Middle Western states. Most of these returned after the war and many prospered once again. Following the attack on Pearl Harbor, Americans displayed unfounded anxiety bordering on collective hysteria about the loyalty of ethnic Japanese, including those who were U.S. citizens. The federal government ordered the relocation of all ethnic Japanese from the western parts of California, Oregon, and Washington, as well as from Alaska and Southern Arizona. In some cases, white associates and friends shielded assets and property until the deportees were permitted to return, but most people of Japanese origin were forced to abandon homes, shops, and property or to sell these at a substantial loss. These Japanese people, nearly two-thirds of whom were U.S. natives and hence citizens, were moved to an assortment of relocation camps in mostly desert areas of the Western states. There they were placed under guard and often behind barbed wire for up to three years.

Some internees were freed from the relocation camps in 1943, under the condition that they not return to the West Coast. Of those, most settled in Midwestern urban areas. Upon the release of all the deportees in 1945, the preponderance of the Japanese returned to the West

Coast for a fresh start, and the proportion of ethnic Japanese residing there returned to prewar levels in less than a decade. Nonetheless, some chose to shun the West Coast where they perceived racial bias to be manifest. By far the largest number moving eastward following internment settled in Chicago, which developed the largest Japanese community east of the Rocky Mountains.

The vast majority of Filipinos who settled in the United States did so after the latter seized the Philippine Islands from Spain in 1898. Hawaiian plantations recruited Filipino labor in the early 1900s, as Japanese migrated to California and Chinese were subject to immigration restrictions. In the 1950s and 1960s, Filipinos supplanted upwardly mobile people from other Asian countries as gardeners, truck drivers, and hospital workers.

In the continental United States, the Filipinos tended to take temporary and seasonal jobs wherever these were available, and few genuine communities emerged until later. As residents of a U.S. territory, Filipinos were regarded as nationals of the United States, and immigration was unrestricted until quotas were imposed during the Depression. In the Western states, Filipinos were often accorded the same deplorable treatment as other Asian immigrants. In the 1920s, bullying, attacks, and official chicanery drove many Filipinos in urban areas into the relative safety of the little Manilas or Chinatowns.

Since 1965, immigration from the Philippines to America has grown significantly. Tens of thousands have arrived every year for decades because quotas have been raised and close relatives of U.S. citizens are usually permitted entry. As many as 40,000 Filipinos are reported to have immigrated in some years, making the Philippines the leading source of recent immigration to the United States with the exception of Mexico. It is notable that many of these Filipinos are ethnic Chinese. The Filipino communities of metropolitan areas such as Chicago, Detroit, and New York City have expanded dramatically, and because most Filipinos speak English and are skilled, they tend to adapt rapidly and well to American society.

Vietnamese are the largest community in the United States with origins in Indochina. Other people from the region include Cambodians, Thais, and Loatians, the latter comprising both ethnic Loa and Hmong. Vietnamese are among the largest recent immigrant groups to arrive in the United States, since prior to the war in Southeast Asia, virtually no Vietnamese had settled in North America. During the war years of the 1960s, emigration was modest, but beginning around 1970, thousands of Vietnamese headed to America each year. Adaptation to a new society was difficult enough for many, and nearly all had lost property, home and family in Vietnam. With departure from Vietnam in the 1970s came drastic socioeconomic decline for those who had been managers, professionals or businessmen in their former homeland. Many had to take low-paying jobs as laborers in America, at least

temporarily. While some of the earlier immigrants and their families have done well for themselves, the more recent refugees, many of whom were "boat people," arrived destitute and lacking anything in the way of job skills.

DEMOGRAPHY AS DESTINY

Extraordinary demographic change is presently occurring in the United States. In contrast to most developed countries, America's fertility rate began rising sharply in the 1980s, while at the same time America admitted substantial numbers of immigrants. The combination of higher fertility rates and growing immigration has resulted in a soaring U.S. population. In the decade after 1992, America accepted over 11 million new immigrants, and this number does not include the estimated 8–9 million who entered the country illegally. If the upward population trend continues, demographers estimate that the U.S. population could reach 400 million within 25 years and even 550 million by 2050. The population increase will open a large gap between Europe and America that could have significant policy implications. By 2040 at the latest, the U.S. population will exceed that of the European Union. Moreover, the median age in America in 2050 will be around 36, just slightly above what it is now. Europe's median age will be around 53.

While Europe's population is ageing and will continue to gray, America's will in all likelihood remain much younger. A more youthful population will translate into a more vibrant economy with lower labor costs, a larger work force, greater diversity, and a more dynamic society in general. Hence, America's demography

Former Secretary of State Condoleeza Rice with German Chancellor Angela Merkel

could well be the basis for sustained, long-term economic growth. Long-term demographic tendencies are likely to entrench U.S. power.

True, a substantial population increase is not without its problems, including rising real estate costs, urban sprawl, and perhaps heightened social tensions. The main sources of U.S. immigration are Latin America and Southeast Asia. The fertility rate of non-Hispanic whites is currently 1.8, for blacks it is 2.1, and for Latinos it is nearly 3.0. America's population will not only grow, but could look increasingly different. Children already account for a large portion of the Hispanic population, and in some parts of America, half the Latino population is under 14.

The doubts some people in America harbor about the continuation of the melting pot effect revolve around the Latino population. Critics suggest that Latinos are not integrating quickly enough into the mainstream of American society, culturally, politically, or economically. The difficulties might reflect in part the sheer numbers; of nearly 35 million Latinos in the United States, more than half were born abroad.

Interest groups have profound effects upon U.S. policies, and group politics will continue to permeate governmental activity. Organizations of individuals partici-

. . . and President Barack Obama

Courtesy of the White House

United States

pate in the policy process at many points to try to achieve a set of goals. "In no country of the world has the principle of association been more successfully used, or more unsparingly applied to a multitude of different objects, than in America," remarked Alexis de Tocqueville. Interest groups are important in all democracies, but they are particularly diverse and powerful in the United States. An authoritative estimate found some 20,000 national associations plus an even greater number of locally organized groups. Not all are of political interest. Some are almost constantly involved with government, others almost never. Circumstances involve groups differently at different times. The American Medical Association (AMA), formed to promote professional standards and uniform licensing practices, became increasingly political in opposition to socialized medicine proposals.

The greatest number of politically concerned groups arises out of economic interests—James Madison's "most common and durable source of factions." Their extraordinary multiplicity or diversity is frequently obscured by an oversimplified division of economic groups into business, labor, and farm categories. Yet from the perspective of countries with more homogeneous economic classes, diversity is the salient feature of the American groups system. What surprises the European student of the American political process is the lack of concentration of effort by the important power blocs. Neither capital, nor labor, nor agriculture speaks politically with a single authoritative voice.

The complexity and fluidity of American politics are also increased by the multiplicity of places at which interest groups must exert pressure. The business community operates at a variety of levels of government, often as individual firms or industries, as well as through a number of organizations, for example. The same is true for all political groups. They tend to gravitate to every level where governmental power affects their interests.

The complexity of America—the large number of institutions and the diversity of the population—compels observers to seek methods of organizing their approaches to the study of the country.

Former secretaries of state Henry Kissinger and Madeleine Albright, both European-born Americans

Theories help them do this. Like natural scientists, social scientists use theories to organize and simplify what they study. Unlike natural scientists, however, social scientists are concerned with normative as well as empirical theories. Normative theories address the question of how politics and government ought to operate. Empirical theories describe how they operate and forecast how they *will* operate.

Both types of theories are important for understanding and evaluating American politics and society. Whatever theory is used, however, two standards can assist in evaluating it: democracy and effectiveness. Americans have traditionally employed these criteria to measure how well their government is doing. Applying the standard of democracy, they ask to what extent are policy makers selected and governments organized so as to ensure that policies represent the public's preferences. Applying the standard of effectiveness,

they ask to what extent does government (1) recognize important problems, (2) formulate likely solutions, (3) implement policies to bring about those solutions, and (4) solve problems.

Democracy and effectiveness are different and often conflicting standards. A government that is democratic may be ineffective and vice versa. By seeking to increase citizen information and citizen participation, a government may undermine its effectiveness. For example, the requirement that government adopt positions supported by the majority may prevent agreement on any specific policy. The criterion of equality may undermine policies that benefit some segment of the population more than another. If government becomes so immobilized that it cannot act, then it cannot represent or enact the will of the majority. Government would then fail to meet either standard, democracy or effectiveness.

The Future

SHORT TERM

After the momentous eight years in office that brought a bankrupt foreign-policy revolution, large tax cuts, attempted reform of American schools, an ill-considered transformation of the armed forces, two shooting wars, and much bluster internationally, President Bush left office as one of America's least popular presidents. Yet it is still too soon to say how history will judge the administration of George W. Bush. One lasting legacy will be in the establishment of a more conservative judiciary. More than a third of active judges were appointed by Bush. All have lifetime tenure and many are relatively young. President Obama has selected two Supreme Court justices, with the possibility of yet another appointment.

Bush receives some credit for uniting the country after the terrorist attacks of September 11, 2001, even if only briefly, but above all, for the absence of additional terrorist attacks on the territory of the United States. He will be remembered for moving rapidly to oust both the Taliban and al Qaeda from Afghanistan, although some observers blame him for easing up too soon, leading to further trouble. His Iraq legacy is still being written. The future of Iraq is indistinct, caught up in the wider geopolitics of Iranian nuclear proliferation and the fallout from the Arab spring—especially given the Obama administration's decision against retaining any U.S. bases in the country to monitor the situation on the ground. Bush will doubtless be linked by history with a sluggish economy, banking chaos, falling home and stock prices and surging budget deficits. Blame for the financial meltdown in 2008–2009 should be broadly shared, but presidents are inevitably held responsible for economic troubles, fairly or not.

After years of fighting, the war in Afghanistan is officially winding down. The Taliban and al Qaeda have been unable to defeat the NATO forces in conventional battle, but the coalition does not have sufficient manpower to put an end to frequent guerrilla attacks. Afghanistan's future remains uncertain. In Iraq, implementation of the "surge" operations to "clear, hold, and build" resulted in tenuous stability. By offering credible protection to the population, coalition forces undermined the militias. U.S. forces were pulled back from urban areas to remote bases in 2009, as Iraqi army and police forces stepped in. Although these are suitably equipped to fight the insurgents in Iraq, the risk of sectarian and ethnic conflict remains. Many Sunnis, feeling too pressured, have turned against the government. In December 2011, almost nine years after the first U.S. armored columns began massing on the Iraq border, the Pentagon declared an official end to its mission in Iraq, closing a sometimes bitter and often controversial conflict.

The second Obama administration faces crucial and complex foreign policy challenges including: international terrorism, weapons proliferation, weak and failing states, climate change, and global poverty. How the administration addresses salient international issues will have important implications for America and the world for years to come. Events in Europe, Russia, China and India will be at least as significant for the future of international relations as what occurs in the Middle East. For example, the 20-year military drawdown in Europe looks to be abruptly ending as the Russian invasion of Crimea fuels calls for reshaping the military mission there after decades of post-Cold War calm.

The Arab awakening that brought the weakening and toppling of regimes in early 2011 has resulted in a fluid situation in North Africa and beyond. Turmoil in Libya drew in the Western powers, and the United States joined the fight in which a determined rebel force eventually overthrew a tenacious dictator who vowed to drag the allies into a long and costly war. Fighting in the five-year crisis in Syria continues as Sunnis and Shiites from neighboring states stream into that benighted country to join both sides of the battle.

The re-elected president laid out a sweeping agenda covering gun control, immigration reform and climate change—issues that will fight for attention amid a continuing showdown with Republicans over the debt, a still-recovering economy and volatility overseas. The fast pace is out of necessity. Second-term power begins to steadily diminish within the first year to 18 months, when lawmakers turn attention to the midterm elections and jockeying begins over the next presidency.

Obama's historic three-day visit to Cuba was a tenet of what might be called the Obama Doctrine: that engaging with isolated authoritarian regimes can bring about greater prosperity, peace, democracy and human rights. It has been credited with initial success in Myanmar (also known as Burma), and met with controversy in Iran.

In the last seven years Americans have been subjected to almost continuous economic water torture—a maddening drip of bad news about the employment rate, deficits, declining home values, creeping inflation, the weak dollar, and jittery stock markets. In the months after September 2008, the U.S. economy faced the worst financial crisis since the Great Depression, then steadied itself as steps taken by a new administration began to show results in the autumn of 2009. GDP contracted by more than 6% in the second half of 2008. The lapse from growth resulted in the longest—and most severe—recession in nearly three decades. The chief source of America's economic problems began in the slumping housing market, where many borrowers with limited financial means obtained variable-rate mortgages. When interest rates began to rise, so did mortgage payments, and many holders of subprime mortgages defaulted on their loans. This sent tremors through financial markets worldwide, and the terms for lending money began to tighten. The housing markets are unlikely to return to normal until after 2015. Hundreds of banks failed in 2008–2010. The first ten years of the new millennium were largely lost, with little economic growth by a variety of measures. In real terms, GDP gained a mere 20% from 2000 to 2012. Total employment was essentially unchanged from the beginning of the decade to the end of it.

U.N. peacekeeping operations

The Future

Although America faced a miserable financial situation in these years, it was still not anywhere near as bad as the economic crisis of the 1930s. The Great Depression entailed global economic collapse on an immense scale. Arguably, this was preventable, and the lessons learned then substantially reduce the likelihood of a repeat of that time. Several quarters of declines in the low single digits, resulting in about a 2.5% drop from peak to trough is nothing like the sustained contraction of the 1930s. From 1929 to 1933, real national output dropped 30%. Neither did unemployment affect one in four workers, as it did in 1932, when most families depended on a single wage earner. In the 1930s, millions lost their life savings as over 9000 banks across the country failed. True, stock equity worth hundreds of billions has evaporated, and many more people own stocks now than in the 1930s, directly or in funds, in IRAs and 401(k)s. Yet, the market decline was nowhere near as drastic. Stock indexes were down somewhat more than in the prior recession of 2000–2002 and 1973–1975, but less than the 89% plunge of 1929–1932.

The longer term economic outlook is somewhat unfavorable, at least based upon the 10-year budget projections by the nonpartisan Congressional Budget Office (CBO). In fact, the CBO warned that the future is "worrisome." Projecting beyond 2025, the CBO asserts that "high and rising debt, relative to the size of the economy" could bring "the risk of fiscal crisis." Federal debt held by the public is currently nearly 75% of nominal GDP, "more than twice what it was at the end of 2007," the CBO observes, "and higher than in any year since 1950." Moreover, "beyond the coming decade," the CBO notes, "the fiscal outlook is significantly more worrisome," given the aging of the population, the growth in per capita spending on health care, and the ongoing expansion of federal subsidies for health insurance." A high debt-GDP ratio in the coming decades, a CBO report argues "could trigger a crisis in which government would lose its ability to borrow at affordable rates," accompanied by private-sector interest rates high enough to trigger a severe economic downturn.

LONG TERM

Since 1945, the United States helped rebuild Europe from the ashes of World War II, formed strong alliances with democratic countries through NATO, promoted development and economic reform in Third World countries through various bilateral and multilateral aid programs, contributed to the growth of world order through support of the United Nations and international law, furthered the cause of human rights around the world, and undertook

efforts to prevent the proliferation of nuclear weapons capability. World peace, prosperity, and the future of democratic institutions depend greatly on the continued involvement of the United States with the world.

This brief futuristic overview presents four hypothetical but conceivable scenarios of the longer-term global environment in which the United States might find itself. The forecast seeks to identify potential international developments and challenges in the 21st century. While some combination of all four is indeed possible, they are ranked in the order of likelihood.

Scenario One: America as World Peacekeeper

In this scenario, a competitive world emerges where certain undercurrents of external threats, both economic and military, to U.S. interests are mounting. Worldwide, large U.S. peacekeeping forces support an array of American assistance agreements. Continued economic development and the consolidation of representative government in many areas increase U.S. international influence, promote U.S. investments, and encourage the continuance of a substantial U.S. military presence overseas. American firms, with their advanced technology and facilities, maintain their global position.

Scenario Two: Subdued Multipolarity

This scenario presupposes a productive economic world where the United States focuses more on social investment at home and abroad than on defense. American leaders perceive threats to the country's interests as similar to those of the mid 1990s, that is, more economic than military and with unremitting demands for America to demonstrate peaceful global leadership.

Closely integrated and motivated by the need for expanding global markets, the European Union enjoys considerable economic growth while improving its competitive position, especially in the Asian-Pacific Rim. American economic and political influence intensifies worldwide as many countries concentrate on economic growth and actively seek U.S. trade and investment.

Scenario Three: Global Neonationalism

The rise of nationalism significantly diminishes American political, economic, and military influence and results in the removal of U.S. overseas military forces. A highly competitive world emerges where economic trade wars, embargoes, and restrictions abound. The United States and Europe drift apart. Transatlantic relations suffer severe damage as an inward-looking Europe remains preoccupied with its own continent and America is left overextended, trying to cope with global threats.

The EU experiences substantial pressures of economic nationalism domestically and internationally. The EU tends to dismiss threats to itself, its interests, or to the rest of Europe. With the exception of France, Poland, and the United Kingdom, EU countries largely demilitarize. NATO becomes a shadow of its former self. The EU and NATO are unable to organize peacekeeping forces effectively or to subdue ethnic conflicts in weakened states.

Iraq Study Group

262

Most U.S. forces leave Europe except for skeleton caretaker units.

Scenario Four: U.S. Isolationism

This scenario depicts a relatively unstable world whose troubles America seeks to avoid. U.S. military forces are substantially reduced in the new international environment. American political leadership becomes largely seclusionist, while the country's business infrastructure turns inward. Revivalist nationalism in many countries, including those with prior accords with the United States, shrinks U.S. international influence and eliminates American military presence overseas.

WEB SITES

Useful Web Sites on the United States:
www.aei.org (American Enterprise Institute for Public Policy Research)
www.army.mil/cmh-pg/ (Army Center of Military History)
www.usaid.gov (Agency for International Development)
www.ausa.org (Association of the United States Army)
www.ceip.org (Carnegie Endowment for International Peace)
www.cato.org (CATO Institute)
www.cdi.org (Center for Defense Information)
www.cdt.org (Center for Defense Technology)
www.puaf.umd.edu/pissm (Center for International and Security Studies)
www.ciponline.org (Center for International Policy)
www.cna.com (Center for Naval Analyses)
www.csis.org (Center for Strategic and International Studies)
www.coha.org (Council on Hemispheric Affairs)
www.marshall.org (George C. Marshall Institute)
www.stimson.org (Henry L. Stimson Center)
www.hudson.org (Hudson Institute)
www.ida.org (Institute for Defense Analyses)
www.ifpa.org (Institute for Foreign Policy Analysis)
www.mediaresearch.org (Media Research Center)
www.metc.org (Middle East Policy Council)
www.merip.org (Middle East Research and Information Project)
www.nara.gov (Presidential Libraries)
www.nationalcenter.org (National Center for Public Policy Research)
www.ndi.org (National Democratic Institute for International Affairs)

www.nci.org (Nuclear Control Institute)
www.rand.org (Rand Corporation)
www.sri.com (Stanford Research Institute)
www.ucsusa.org (Union of Concerned Scientists)
www.usip.org (United States Institute of Peace)
www.washingtoninstitute.org (Washington Institute for Near East Policy)
www.worldbank.org (World Bank)
www.worldwatch.org (World Watch Institute)
www.chicagotribune.com (Respected U.S. newspaper. Named best overall U.S. newspaper online service for newspapers with circulation over 100,000)
www.csmonitor.com (Respected U.S. newspaper, *Christian Science Monitor*. Named best overall U.S. newspaper online service for newspapers with circulation under 100,000)
www.nytimes.com (Respected U.S. newspaper, *The New York Times*)
www.washingtonpost.com (Respected U.S. newspaper)
www.cnn.com (24-hour video news channel)
www.odci.gov/cia/ciahome.html (To gain connection to other CIA sites and resources, such as the *CIA Factbook*, which provides extensive statistical and political information about every country in the world)
www.usia.gov/usis.html (U.S. Information Agency)

Useful Web Sites on European and U.S. Foreign Policy:
www.brookings.edu The Brookings Institution—U.S. foreign policy institute with broad range of policy briefs and articles, particularly related to US and European security issues
www.cer.org.uk Centre for European Reform—UK-based think tank headed by former defense editor of *The Economist*. Wide range of articles on EU foreign policy and other aspects of integration
www.ceps.be Centre for European Policy Studies—wide variety of research articles and working papers
www.clingendael.nl Clingendael Institute—Netherlands Institute of International Relations: good collection of articles on European security and international relations in general
http://ue.eu.int/pesc/default.asp?lang= en Council of the European Union—The Council's CFSP web site with official texts/conclusions as well as speeches and policy outlines
www.foreignpolicy.com *Foreign Policy*—respected American journal available on-line

www.gcsp.ch/ Geneva Centre for Security Policy—working papers and comprehensive links section (available in English and French)
www.ifri.org Institut francais des relations internationales—on-line papers and commentary
www.dgap.org/english/tip.htm *Internationale Politik* (Transatlantic Edition)—German periodical with a selection of articles available on-line in English.
www.isn.ethz.ch International Relations and Security Network (Centre for Security Studies and Conflict Research, ETH Zurich)—an international relations search engine and document database
www.riia.org The Royal Institute of International Affairs—a selection of articles and papers as well as international relations links and information on research projects

Web Sites on the UN, EU, OECD, NATO and other:
www.un.org (Web site for United Nations, many links)
www.unsystem.or (Official UN web site)
www.europa.eu.int (EU server site)
www.ue.eu.int (The Council of European Union site)
www.europa.eu.int/comm (European Commission site)
www.euobserver.com (EU news)
www.euractiv.com (European news)
www.EU-Values.org (Site maintained by students and staff of the College of Europe, Bruges)
www.europarl.eu.int (European Parliament)
www.european-convention.EU.int/ (Site for EU constitutional convention)
www.euractiv.com (Diverse news on EU and Europe)
www.aktion-euro.de (Site for the euro currency)
www.europeanaccess.co.uk (Links to various subjects)
www.eurunion.org (EU delegation of the European Commission to the U.S.)
www.europeanvalues.nl/ (site for European values)
www.knoweurope.net (search engine for all documents published by EU institutions—by subscription)
www.oecd.org/daf/cmis/fdi/statist.htm (OECD site)
www.osce.org (Site of OSCE)
www.nato.int/structur/nids/nids.htm (NATO documentation, NATO Review)
www.nato.int and www.NATO.int (Web sites for NATO. many links.)
www.wto.org (World Trade Organization site)
www.worldbank.org/html/Welcome.html (World Bank news, publications with links to other financial institutions)

Web Sites

www.ceip.org (Carnegie Endowment for International Peace, using a fully integrated Web-database system)

www.cia.gov/index.html (Central Intelligence Agency)

www.odci.gov/cia (Includes useful CIA publications, such as The World Factbook and maps)

www.state.gov/www/ind.html (U.S. Department of State, including country reports)

www.loc.gov (Library of Congress with coverage of over 100 countries)

www.xe.com/ucc/ (Site with most up-to-date foreign currency values)

Newspapers, Journals and Television:

www.economist.com (British weekly news magazine)

www.nytimes.com (Respected U.S. newspaper, *The New York Times*)

www.washingtonpost.com (Respected U.S. newspaper)

www.IHT.com (*International Herald Tribune*, published and distributed in Europe)

www.Europeanvoice.com (Weekly newspaper with EU and European news)

www.timeeurope.com (European edition of *Time*)

www.foreignaffairs.org (One of best-known international affairs journal)

www.cnn.com (Latest news with external links)

www.news.BBC.co.uk (British Broadcasting Corporation site)

www.c-span.org (Includes C-SPAN International)

www.libertaddigital.es (Spain's first online newspaper)

Other Web Sites:

www.africapolicy.org (African Policy Information Center)

www.embassy.org (This web site contains links to all embassies in Washington)

www.britain-info.org (British press reports with links)

www.fco.gov.UK (British Foreign and Commonwealth Office site)

www.pm.gov.uk (Prime minister site)

www.number-10.gov.uk (Prime minister site)

www.parliament.gov.uk (Parliament site)

www.mod.uk (British Ministry of Defense site)

www.european-defence.co.uk (UK-EU defense)

www.margaretthatcher.org (Margaret Thatcher's site)

www.irlgov.ie/frmain.htm (Irish government cite)

www.info-france-usa.org (French culture and government)

www.NBT.nl (Netherlands, with links to many subjects)

www.parlement.nl (Dutch parliamentary site)

www.expatica.com (Dutch news)

www.Belgium.fgov.be (Site of Belgian government)

www.vlaanderen.be (Flemish Community in Belgium)

www.cfwb.be (French Community in Belgium)

www.wallonie.org (Walloon Region in Belgium)

www.europeonline.com/bel/index_gb.htm (Belgian site)

www.restena.lu/luxembourg/ (various topics with links)

www.admin.ch (Swiss site)

www.firstlink.li (Liechtenstein site)

www.news.li (news of Liechtenstein)

www.tourismus.li (Liechtenstein tourism)

www.governo.it/ (Italian government)

www.esteri.it/eng/index.htm (Italian Ministry of Foreign Affairs)

www.mi.cnr.it/WOI/ (Italian history and cities)

www.cca.imediata.pt (American Chamber of Commerce in Portugal)

www.vatican.va/ (Vatican site)

www.searchmalta.com (Malta)

www.magnet.mt (Malta's government web site)

www.timesofmalta.com

www.independent.com.mt (Maltese newspaper in English)

www.inthenet.sm/rsm/intro.htm (San Marino)

www.greekembassy.org (Greek embassy)

www.mfa.gr (Greek Foreign Ministry)

www.greece.flash.gr (Greek news)

www.embassy.org/embassies (Site with links to all embassy web sites in Washington, D.C.)

www.eurasianet.org (News for Eurasia)

www.centraleurope.com (Contains updated information and news)

www.ucis.pitt.edu/reesweb (Full index on Central Europe and former USSR)

www.php.indiana.edu/~amgrose/ceepg.html (Political science resources on the region)

www.fas.harvard.edu/~aaass/ (Provides links to Slavic resources)

www.cco.caltech.edu (Bosnia home page)

www.esiweb.org (Site of Berlin-Based European Stability Initiative working to restore stability to southeastern Europe)

www.osa.ceu.hu (Extensive site of Open Society Archives of Central European University)

www.zzz.ee/tbr/ (Comprehensive Baltic links provided by the Baltic Review)

www.balticsww.com/cityp/citypape.htm (Site of *City Paper* published in Tallinn, Estonia, but with coverage of all Baltic States)

www.baltinfo.org (Baltic information)

www.setimes.com/html2/english/default.htm (*South Eastern European Times*, political magazine)

Country Web Sites:

www.sweden.nw.dc.us/sweden/ (Swedish embassy)

www.swedentrade.com/(Swedish trade)

www.sweden.se (Swedish news site)

www.riksdagen.se (Swedish parliament site)

www.norway.org (Norwegian embassy)

www.Norwaypost.no (Norwegian newspaper in English)

www.denmarkemb.org (Danish embassy)

www.berlingske.dk (Respected Danish newspaper)

www.virtual.finland.fi (Government institutions, current events, culture)

www.epin.org (Finnish Institute of International Affairs site)

www.projectfinland.org (Colorful, interactive site introducing American children to their Finnish counterparts)

www.iceland.org (Icelandic site)

www.estemb.org (Estonian embassy Washington)

www.lichr.ee (Estonian legal information; Center for Human Rights)

www.riik.ee (Estonian government links)

www.mfa.gov.lv (Latvian Foreign Ministry)

www.lem.gov.lv (Latvian Economics Ministry)

www.mod.gov.lv (Latvian Ministry of Defense)

www.elta.lt (Lithuanian News Agency)

www.urm.lt (Lithuanian Ministry of Foreign Affairs)

www.std.lt (Lithuanian statistical data including census figures)

www.germany-info.org (German subjects of all kinds with copious links)

www.bundestag.de (German parliament online)

www.weltpolitik.net (Research Institute of the German Council on Foreign Relations site)

www.AICGS.org (Site of American Institute for Contemporary German Studies, Washington D.C.)

www.berlin.de/partner (News of Berlin)

www.sozialisten.de (German PDS site)

www.magazine-deutschland.de (Site of the monthly magazine, *Deutschland*, with general news)

www.g-s-a.org (Site for the German Studies Association in the United States)

www.statistik-bund.de/wahlen/index.htm (German election news site)

www.austria.org (Austrian embassy site)

www.austriantradeus.org (U.S.-Austrian trade site)

www.pnb.pl (Polish news bulletin)

www.prezydent.pl (Polish president)

www.kprm.gov.pl (Polish government)

www.sejm.gov.pl (Polish parliament)

www.senat.gov.pl (Polish senate)

www.mzn.gov.pol (Polish Ministry of Foreign Affairs)

www.wp.mil.pl (Polish Ministry of National Defense)

www.bbn.gov.pol (Polish National Security Committee)

www.pnb.com (Polish News Bulletin)

www.pkw.gov.pl (State Election Commission, official election results in Poland)

www.mzv.cz (Czech Ministry of Foreign Affairs)

www.praguepost.com (Prague English-language newspaper)

www.government.gov.sk (Slovakian government site with photo gallery)

www.nrsr.sk (Slovakia)

www.ekormanyzat.hu/english (General Hungarian site with excellent links)

www.hungaryemb.org (Hungarian embassy site)

www.budapestsun.com/dailynews/bpsundailynews71.htm (Hungarian-English language newspaper)

www.hungarytourism.com (Hungarian tourism)

www.mfa.gov.hu (Hungarian Ministry of Foreign Affairs)

www.serbia.sr.gov.yu (Serbian government site)

www.gov.yu (Serbia-Montenegro government site)

www.mfa.gov.yu (Serbia-Montenegro Foreign Ministry)

www.titoville.com/ (a site with all kinds of information about Tito)

www.b92.net (Serbian site in English with news, photos, analyses)

www.uvi.si/eng/slovenia/ (Central site for Slovenia)

www.uvi.si/eng/service (Slovenian Public Relations and Media Office)

www.gov.si (Slovenian government site)

www.uvi.si (Slovenian information office)

www.vlada.hr/english/about-government.html (Croatian government)

www.mvp.hr/mvprh-www-eng/index.html (Croatian Ministry of Foreign Affairs)

www.fbihvlada.gov.ba/engleski/index.html (Government of Bosnia and Herzegovina)

www.mvp.gov.ba/Index_eng.htm (Bosnian Ministry of Foreign Affairs)

www.vladars.net/en/ (Government of Serbian Republic in Bosnia)

www.ohr.int (Office of High Representative in Kosovo)

www.gov.mk/English/index.htm (Macedonian government site)

www.president.gov.mk/index_eng.htm (Macedonian president and cabinet)

www.macedonia.org (Many Macedonian sites)

www.directory.macedonia.org/ (Site with wide variety of links on Macedonia)

www.press.org.mk/ (Macedonian news agencies)

www.newbalkanpolitics.org.mk/ (Online political magazine on Macedonian affairs)

www.mchamber.org.mk (Macedonian economic, political, cultural, historical information)

www.vmacedonia.com/welcome.asp (Macedonian tourism)

www.AlbanianNews (English-language newspaper)

www.Albanian.com (General news and information)

www.Albania.co.uk (General news and information)

www.romania.org (news and culture in Romania)

www.rol.ro (Romania online, includes photos)

www.guv.ro (Romanian government site)

www.ministerulturismului.ro (Romanian tourism, including photos)

www.bulgaria.com/history/bulgaria/ (Bulgarian history)

www.novinite.com (Site for subscribing to English-language *Sofia Morning News*, Bulgaria)

Web Sites for Canada

www.canoe.ca and www.Yahoo.ca (Canadian search engines.)

www.canadianembassy.org (This site is a key source containing a search engine, an issues menu, many links, a virtual reference desk and a virtual tour of the Canadian embassy in Washington.)

www.ambassadeducanada.org (All of the above functions in French)

www.usembassycanada.org (Site for U.S. embassy in Ottawa with reports and information)

www.canada.gc.ca (General Web site for information on Canada from the Canadian government. See links.)

www.cbc.ca (Web site for the Canadian Broadcasting Corporation. This is an excellent current source for all aspects of Canadian news, with numerous links. See also www..cbc.ca/newsworld/)

www.ctv.ca (Broad Canadian reporting)

www.radio-canada.ca/nouvelles (French-language news)

www.elections.ca (Election results. Phone: 1-800-463-6868)

www.pm.gc.ca (Web site for Canadian prime minister's office. By substituting the first letters of other ministries, access to other ministries' web sites can be gained. See below.)

www.fin.gc.ca (Web site for Canadian Finance Ministry)

www.strategis.ic.gc.ca (Industry Canada)

www.dfait-maeci.gc.ca (Web site for Department of Foreign Affairs and International Trade)

www.cfp-pec.gc.ca (Web site of Canadian Centre for Foreign Policy Development. See many links. For peacekeeping, add: /peacekeeping/menu-e.asp. For additional links, add: /y2k. For magazine, add: /Canada-magazine)

www.cbsa.asfc.gc.ca (Canada Border Services Agency)

www.cic.gc.ca (Citizenship and Immigration Canada)

www.mapleleafweb.com/main.shtml (Central site for Canadian affairs)

www.canschool.org (Web site for many aspects of Canadians in the World)

www.citizens.ca (Site for information relating to who Canadians are; description of people)

www.gov.nu.ca (Site for Nunavut)

www.parkscanada.gc.ca (Parks Canada site)

www.travelcanada.ca

www.liberal.ca (Liberal Party site)

www.conservative.ca (Conservative Party site)

www.ndp.ca (National Democratic Party site)

www.bloc.ca (Bloc Québécois party site)

www.greenparty.ca (Green Party site)

www.un.org (Web site for United Nations. Many links.)

www.nato.org (Web site for NATO. Many links.)

www.chatelaine.com (Web site for *Chatelaine* weekly Canadian magazine. In English and French.)

www.macleans.ca (Web site for *Maclean's* weekly Canadian news magazine)

www.mh-education.com (*Maclean's* educational Web site. See links.)

www.globeandmail.ca (Respected Canadian national newspaper)

www.nationalpost.com (Respected Canadian national newspaper)

www.torontostar.com (Respected Canadian national newspaper)

www.ottawacitizen.com (Respected Canadian national newspaper)

www.montrealgazette.com (Respected Canadian national newspaper)

www.winnipegfreepress.com (Respected Canadian national newspaper)

www.vancouversun.com (Respected Canadian national newspaper)

www.ledevoir.com (Respected Quebec French-language newspaper)

www.cyberpress.com (Canadian news)

www.iam.ca (Humorous web site for Molson beer's Canadian nationalism commercial)

www.economist.com (Respected British news weekly with some coverage of Canadian affairs)

Recommended Reading

www.chicagotribune.com (Respected U.S. newspaper with some coverage of Canadian affairs. Named best overall U.S. newspaper online service for newspapers with circulation over 100,000.)

www.csmonitor.com (Respected U.S. newspaper, *Christian Science Monitor*, with some coverage of Canadian affairs. Named best overall U.S. newspaper online service for newspapers with circulation under 100,000.)

www.nytimes.com (Respected U.S. newspaper, *The New York Times*, with some coverage of Canadian affairs)

www.washingtonpost.com (Respected U.S. newspaper with some coverage of Canadian affairs)

www.washingtontimes.com (Respected U.S. newspaper with some coverage of Canadian affairs)

www.canada.plattsburgh.edu (The Center for the Study of Canada at the State University of New York Plattsburgh maintains the major Web site for Canadian Studies. E-mail address: CANADA-ACSUS@Plattsburgh.EDU. Search also for Association for Canadian Studies in the U.S.—ACSUS.)

RECOMMENDED READING

Political and Legal

Abadinsky, Howard. *Law and Justice: An Introduction to the American Legal System,* 2nd ed. Chicago: Nelson-Hall, 1991.

Ackerman, Bruce. *Before the Next Attack: Preserving Civil Liberties in an Age of Terrorism.* New Haven: Yale University Press, 2006.

Aldrich, John. *Why Parties? The Origin and Transformation of Political Parties in America.* Chicago: University of Chicago Press, 1995.

Almond, Gabriel A. and Sidney Verba, eds. *The Civic Culture Revisited.* Newbury Park, CA: Sage, 1989.

Alterman, Eric. *When Presidents Lie: A History of Official Deception and Its Consequences.* New York: Viking, 2004.

Baker, Wayne E. *America's Crisis of Values: Reality and Perception.* Princeton: Princeton University Press, 2006.

Bibby, John F. and L. Sandy Maisel. *Two Parties or More?* Boulder, CO: Westview, 1998.

Birkland, Thomas A. *Lessons of Disaster: Policy Change after Catastrophic Events.* Washington, DC: Georgetown University Press, 2006.

Black, Earl and Merle Black. *Politics and Society in the South.* Cambridge, MA: Harvard University Press, 1987.

Black, Earl and Merle Black. *Divided America: The Ferocious Power Struggles in American Politics.* New York: Simon and Schuster, 2007.

Bowden, Brett. *The Empire of Civilization: The Evolution of an Imperial Idea.* Chicago: University of Chicago Press, 2009.

Bremmer, Ian. *Every Nation for Itself: Winners and Losers in a G-Zero World.* New York: Portfolio, 2012.

Bumiller, Elisabeth. *Condoleeza Rice: An American Life.* New York: Random House, 2008.

Burns, James MacGregor. *The Power to Lead: The Crisis of the American Presidency.* New York: Simon and Schuster, 1984.

Cannon, Carl M. *The Pursuit of Happiness in Times of War.* Lanham, MD: Rowman and Littlefield, 2004.

Charvet, John and Elisa Kaczynska-Nay. *The Liberal Project and Human Rights: The Theory and Practice of a New World Order.* New York: Cambridge University Press, 2008.

Chayes, Sarah. *Thieves of State: Why Corruption Threatens Global Security.* New York: Norton, 2015.

Coker, Christopher. *The Improbable War: China, the United States, and the Logic of Great Power Conflict.* New York: Oxford University Press, 2015.

Cook, Rhodes. *The Presidential Nominating Process: A Place for Us?* Lanham, MD: Rowman and Littlefield, 2003.

Cox, Gary and Samuel Kernell, eds. *The Politics of Divided Government.* Boulder, CO: Westview, 1991.

Diamond, Larry and Marc F. Plattner. *Democracy in Decline?* Baltimore: Johns Hopkins University Press, 2015.

Dodson, Debra L. *The Impact of Women in Congress.* New York: Oxford University Press, 2006.

Dobson, William J. *The Dictator's Learning Curve.* New York: Doubleday, 2012.

Donahue, John D. and Joseph S. Nye, Jr., eds. *Governance amid Bigger, Better Markets.* Washington, DC: Brookings Institution Press, 2001.

Doyle, Michael W. *Liberal Peace: Selected Essays.* London: Routledge, 2011.

Duffy, Monica, Daniel Philpott, and Timothy Samuel Shah. *God's Century: Resurgent Religion and Global Politics.* New York: Norton, 2011.

Elazar, Daniel J. *American Federalism: A View from the States,* 3rd ed. New York: Harper and Row, 1984.

El-Gamal, Mahmoud A, and Amy Myers Jaffe. *Oil, Dollars, Debt, and Crisis: The Global Curse of Black Gold.* New York: Cambridge University Press, 2010.

Erie, Steven. *Rainbow's End: Irish-Americans and the Dilemmas of Urban Machine Politics, 1840–1985.* Berkeley: University of California Press, 1988.

Etzioni, Amitai. *The Limits of Privacy.* New York: Basic Books, 1999.

Faux, Jeff. *The Global Class War: How America's Bipartisan Elite Lost Our Future—and What It Will Take to Win It Back.* New York: John Wiley, 2006.

Feaver, Peter D. and Christopher Gelpi. *Choosing Your Battles: American Civil-Military Relations and the Use of Force.* Princeton: Princeton University Press, 2003.

Feldman, Noah. *Divided by God: America's Church-State Problem—and What We Should Do About It.* New York: Farrar, Straus & Giroux, 2005.

Ford, Richard Thompson. *Universal Rights Down to Earth.* New York: Norton, 2011.

Frank, Thomas. *What's the Matter With Kansas? How Conservatives Won the Heart of America.* New York: Knopf, 2004.

Frantzich, Stephen E. *Citizen Democracy: Political Activists in a Cynical Age,* 2nd ed. Lanham, MD: Rowman and Littlefield, 2004.

Fukuyama, Francis. *America at the Crossroads: Democracy, Power, and the Neoconservative Legacy.* New Haven: Yale University Press, 2006.

Fukuyama, Francis. *Political Order and Political Decay: From the Industrial Revolution to the Globalization of Democracy.* New York: Farrar, Straus & Giroux, 2014.

Galvin, Daniel J. *Presidential Party Building.* Princeton: Princeton University Press, 2010.

Gear, John G., ed. *Politicians and Party Politics.* Baltimore: Johns Hopkins University Press, 1998.

Gelman, Andrew. *Red State, Blue State, Rich State, Poor State.* Princeton: Princeton University Press, 2010.

Genovese, Michael A. *Presidential Prerogative: Imperial Power in an Age of Terrorism.* Stanford, CA: Stanford University Press, 2010.

Glaser, James. *Race, Campaign Politics and the Realignment in the South.* New Haven: Yale University Press, 1996.

Glennon, Michael J. *The Fog of Law: Pragmatism, Security, and International Law.* Stanford, CA: Stanford University Press, 2010.

Goldsmith, Jack. *Power and Constraint: The Accountable Presidency After 9/11.* New York: Norton, 2012.

Gregg, Donald P. *Pot Shards: Fragments of a Life Lived in CIA, the White House, and the Two Koreas.* Washington, DC: New Academia Publishing, 2014.

Halberstam, David. *The Powers That Be.* New York: Knopf, 1979.

Hedges, Chris. *American Fascists: The Christian Right and the War on America.* New York: Free Press, 2007.

Herd, Graeme P., ed. *Great Powers and Strategic Stability in the Twenty-first Century: Competing Visions of World Order.* London: Routledge, 2010.

Herman, Susan N. *Taking Liberties: The War on Terror and the Erosion of American*

Recommended Reading

Democracy. New York: Oxford University Press, 2011.

Hertzberg, Hendrik. *Politics: Observations and Arguments, 1966–2004.* New York: Penguin Press, 2004.

Hobson, Christopher. *The Rise of Democracy: Revolution, War, and Transformation in International Politics since 1776.* New York: Oxford University Press, 2015.

Horowitz, Michael C., Allan C. Stam and Cali M. Ellis. *Why Leaders Fight.* New York: Cambridge University Press, 2015.

Hunter, James Davison. *Culture Wars: The Struggle to Define America.* New York: Basic Books, 1991.

Huntington, Samuel P. *Who Are We? The Challenges to America's National Identity.* New York: Simon and Schuster, 2004.

Hyde, Susan D. *The Pseudo-Democrat's Dilemma: Why Election Monitoring Became an International Norm.* Ithaca and London: Cornell University Press, 2011.

Jewell, Malcolm E. and Marcia Lynn Whicker. *Legislative Leadership in the American States.* Ann Arbor: University of Michigan Press, 1998.

Johnson-Cartee, Karen S. and Gary Copeland. *Inside Political Campaigns: Theory and Practice.* Westport, CT: Praeger, 1997.

Jones, Bruce, Carlos Pascal and Stephen J. Stedman. *Power and Responsibility: Building International Order in an Era of Transnational Threats.* Washington, DC: Brookings Institution Press, 2008.

Jones, Lee. *Societies Under Siege: Exploring How International Economic Sanctions (Do Not) Work.* New York: Oxford University Press, 2015.

Joppke, Christian. *Immigration and the Nation-State.* New York: Oxford University Press, 1999.

Kaiser, Robert G. *So Damn Much Money: The Triumph of Lobbying and the Corrosion of American Government.* New York: Vintage, 2010.

Kearns, Doris. *Lyndon Johnson and the American Dream.* New York: Harper and Row, 1976.

Khanna, Parag. *How to Run the World: Charting a Course to the Next Renaissance.* New York: Random House, 2011.

Khanna, Parag. *Connectography: Mapping the Future of Global Civilizations.* New York: Random House, 2016.

Kier, Elizabeth and Ronald R. Krebs, eds. *In War's Wake: International Conflict and the Fate of Liberal Democracy.* New York: Cambridge University Press, 2010.

Kliman, Daniel. *Fateful Transitions: How Democracies Manage Rising Powers, From the Eve of World War I to China's Ascendance.* Philadelphia: University of Pennsylvania Press, 2014.

Kruse, Kevin. *One Nation Under God: How Corporate America Invented Christian America.* New York: Basic Books, 2015.

Ku, Julian and John Yoo. *Taming Globalization: International Law, the U.S. Constitution, and the New World Order.* New York: Oxford University Press, 2012.

Kupchan, Charles A. *No One's World: The West, the Rising Rest, and the Coming Global Turn.* New York: Oxford University Press, 2012.

Kurlantzick, Joshua. *State Capitalism: How the Return of Statism Is Transforming the World.* New York: Oxford University Press, 2016.

Ladd, Everett Carll, Jr. *The American Polity: The People and Their Government.* New York: Norton, 1991.

Lepore, Jill. *The Whites of Their Eyes: The Tea Party's Revolution and the Battle Over American History.* Princeton: Princeton University Press, 2010.

Lindquist, Stephanie and Frank Cross. *Measuring Judicial Activism.* New York: Oxford University Press, 2009.

Lipset, Seymour Martin and William Schneider. *The Confidence Gap.* New York: The Free Press, 1983.

MacDonald, Paul K. *Networks of Domination: The Social Foundations of Peripheral Conquest in International Politics.* New York: Oxford University Press, 2014.

Mahnken, Thomas G., ed. *Competitive Strategies for the Twenty-first Century.* Stanford, CA: Stanford University Press, 2012.

Maisel, L. Sandy and Kara Z. Buckley, eds. *Parties and Elections in America: The Electoral Process,* 4th ed. Lanham, MD: Rowman and Littlefield, 2004.

Maisel, L. Sandy and Darrell M. West. *Running on Empty? Political Discourse in Congressional Elections.* Lanham, MD: Rowman and Littlefield, 2004.

Malloch-Brown, Mark. *The Unfinished Revolution: The Pursuit of a New International Politics.* New York: Penguin Press, 2011.

Marshall, David, ed. *The International Rule of Law Movement: A Crisis of Legitimacy and the Way Forward.* Cambridge, MA: Harvard University Press, 2014.

Mathews, Charles and Christopher McKnight Nichols. *Prophesies of Godlessness: Predictions of America's Imminent Secularization from the Puritans to the Present Day.* New York: Oxford University Press, 2008.

McClain, Paula D. and Joseph Stewart Jr. *Can We All Get Along? Racial and Ethnic Minorities in American Politics,* 3rd ed. Boulder, CO: Westview, 2002.

Melillo, Edward Dallam. *Strangers on Familiar Soil: Rediscovering the Chile-California Connection.* New Haven: Yale University Press, 2015.

Menon, Rajan. *The Conceit of Humanitarian Intervention.* New York: Oxford University Press, 2016.

Micklethwait, John and Adrian Wooldridge. *The Right Nation: Conserva-*

tive Power in America. New York: Penguin Press, 2004.

Moyn, Samuel. *The Last Utopia: Human Rights in History.* Cambridge, MA: Belknap Press, 2010.

Murray, Charles. *Coming Apart: The State of White America 1960–2010.* Washington, DC: Crown Forum, 2012.

Murray, Charles. *By the People: Rebuilding Liberty Without Permission.* New York: Crown Publishers, 2015.

Nau, Henry R. and Deepa M. Ollapally, eds. *World Views of Aspiring Powers.* New York: Oxford University Press, 2012.

Nemec, Mark R. *Ivory Towers and Nationalist Minds: Universities, Leadership, and the Development of the American State.* Ann Arbor: University of Michigan Press, 2006.

Nye, Joseph S., Jr. *The Future of Power.* New York: PublicAffairs, 2011.

O'Mara, Shane. *Why Torture Doesn't Work.* Cambridge, MA: Harvard University Press, 2015.

Owen, John M., IV. *Liberal Peace, Liberal War: American Politics and International Security.* Ithaca and London: Cornell University Press, 1997.

Owen, John M., IV. *The Clash of Ideas in World Politics: Transnational Networks, States, and Regime Change.* Princeton: Princeton University Press, 2010.

Page, Benjamin I., with Marshall Bouton. *The Foreign Policy Disconnect: What Americans Want from Our Leaders but Don't Get.* Chicago: University of Chicago Press, 2006.

Patterson, Thomas E. *The Mass Media Election: How Americans Choose Their President.* New York: Praeger, 1980.

Pedersen, Susan. *The Guardians: The League of Nations and the Crisis of Europe.* New York: Oxford University Press, 2015.

Peterson, Peter G. *Running on Empty: How the Democratic and Republican Parties Are Bankrupting Our Future and What Americans Can Do About It.* New York: Farrar, Straus & Giroux, 2004.

Phillips, Kevin P. *Post-Conservative America.* New York: Random House, 1982.

Porter, Patrick. *The Global Village Myth: Distance, War, and the Limits of Power.* Washington, DC: Georgetown University Press, 2015.

Posen, Barry R. *Restraint: A New Foundation for U.S. Grand Strategy.* Ithaca and London: Cornell University Press, 2014.

Posner, Eric A. *The Perils of Global Legalism.* Chicago: University of Chicago Press, 2009.

Putnam, Robert D. *Bowling Alone: The Collapse and Revival of American Community.* New York: Simon and Schuster, 2000.

Putnam, Robert D. and David E. Campbell. *American Grace: How Religion Divides and Unites Us.* New York: Simon and Schuster, 2010.

Recommended Reading

Ramo, Joshua Cooper. *The Seventh Sense: Power, Fortune, and Survival in the Age of Networks*. Boston: Little, Brown, 2016.

Reichley, A. James. *Conservatives in an Age of Change: The Nixon and Ford Administrations*. Washington, DC: Brookings Institution Press, 1981.

Renshon, Stanley A. *The 50% American: Immigration and National Identity in an Age of Terror*. Washington DC: Georgetown University Press, 2006.

Risse, Thomas, ed. *Governance Without a State? Policies and Politics in Areas of Limited Statehood*. New York: Columbia University Press, 2012.

Rosenau, James N., David C. Earnest, Yale H. Ferguson, and Ole R. Holsti. *On the Cutting Edge of Civilization: An Inquiry Into American Elites*. Lanham, MD: Rowman and Littlefield, 2005.

Rosenthal, Alan. *Legislative Life*. New York: Harper and Row, 1981.

Rothkopf, David. *Power, Inc.: The Epic Rivalry Between Big Business and Government—and the Reckoning That Lies Ahead*. New York: Farrar, Straus & Giroux, 2012.

Sharlet, Jeff. *C Street: The Fundamentalist Threat to American Diplomacy*. Boston: Little, Brown, 2010.

Simmons, Beth A. *Mobilizing for Human Rights: International Law in Domestic Politics*. New York: Cambridge University Press, 2009.

Smith, Jean Edward. *FDR*. New York: Random House, 2008.

Smith, Hedrick. *Rethinking America*. New York: Random House, 1995.

Snyder, Sarah B. *Human Rights Activism and the End of the Cold War*. New York: Cambridge University Press, 2011.

Stewart, Charles. *Analyzing Congress*. New York: Norton, 2001.

Tarrow, Sidney. *War, States, and Contention: A Comparative Historical Study*. Ithaca and London: Cornell University Press, 2015.

Thakur, Ramesh and William Malley, eds. *Theorizing the Responsibility to Protect*. New York: Cambridge University Press, 2015.

Wattenberg, Martin P. *The Decline of American Political Parties, 1952–1994*. Cambridge, MA: Harvard University Press, 1996.

Wattenberg, Martin P. *Where Have All the Voters Gone?* Cambridge, MA: Harvard University Press, 2002.

Williams, Michael C. *The Realist Tradition and the Limits of International Relations*. Cambridge, UK: Cambridge University Press, 2005.

Wittkopf, Eugene R. and James M. McCormick. *The Domestic Sources of American Foreign Policy: Insights and Evidence*, 4th ed. Lanham, MD: Rowman and Littlefield, 2004.

Woodward, Bob and Scott Armstrong. *The Brethren: Inside the Supreme Court*. New York: Simon and Schuster, 1979.

Zukin, Cliff et al. *A New Engagement? Political Participation, Civic Life, and the Changing American Citizen*. New York: Oxford University Press, 2006.

Economics

Akerlof, George A. and Robert J. Shiller. *Phishing for Phools: The Economics of Manipulation and Deception*. Princeton: Princeton University Press, 2015.

Akula, Vikram. *A Fistful of Rice: My Unexpected Quest to End Poverty Through Profitability*. Cambridge, MA: Harvard Business Press, 2010.

Appadurai, Arjun. *Modernity at Large: Cultural Dimensions of Globalization*, 4th ed. Minneapolis: University of Minnesota Press, 1998.

Arana, Marion, Kevin P. Gallagher, Paolo Giordano, Ananbel González, Stephen Lande, Isabel Studer, and José Raúl Perales, eds. *A New Trade Policy for the United States: Lessons from Latin America*. Washington, DC: Woodrow Wilson Center for International Politics, 2010.

Bakker, Karen. *Privatizing Water: Governance Failure and the World's Urban Water Crisis*. Ithaca and London: Cornell University Press, 2010.

Barber, Benjamin R. *Jihad Versus McWorld*. New York: Times Books, 1996.

Barr, Nicholas and Peter Diamond. *Reforming Pensions: Principles and Policy Choices*. New York: Oxford University Press, 2008.

Baumann, Zygmunt. *Globalization: The Human Consequences*. New York: Columbia University Press, 1998.

Bayrasli, Elmira. *From the Other Side of the World: Extraordinary Entrepreneurs, Unlikely Places*. New York: PublicAffairs, 2015.

Bergsten, C. Fred. *Global Economic Leadership and the Group of Seven*. Washington, DC: Institute for International Economics, 1996.

Berger, Suzanne and Robert Dore, eds. *National Diversity and Global Capitalism*. Ithaca and London: Cornell University Press, 1996.

Bhagwati, Jagdish. *Protectionism*. Cambridge, MA: MIT Press, 1988.

Bhagwati, Jagdish. *In Defense of Globalization*. New York: Oxford University Press, 2007.

Bhagwati, Jagdish. *Termites in the Trading System: How Preferential Agreements Undermine Free Trade*. New York: Oxford University Press, 2008.

Bhagwati, Jagdish and Alan S. Blinder. *Offshoring of American Jobs: What Response from U.S. Economic Policy?* Cambridge, MA: MIT Press, 2009.

Bhagwati, Jagdish and Robert E. Hudec, eds. *Fair Trade and Harmonization: Prerequisites for Free Trade?* Cambridge, MA: MIT Press, 1996.

Blanchard, Jean-Marc F., ed. *Power and the Purse: Economic Statecraft, Interdependence, and National Security*. Portland, OR: Frank Cass, 2000.

Brynjolfsson, Erik and Andrew McAfee. *The Second Machine Age: Work, Progress, and Prosperity in a Time of Brilliant Technologies*. New York: Norton, 2014.

Cadbury, Deborah. *Chocolate Wars: The 150-Year Rivalry Between the World's Greatest Chocolate Makers*. New York: PublicAffairs, 2010.

Cassidy, John. *How Markets Fail: The Logic of Economic Calamities*. New York: Farrar, Straus & Giroux, 2009.

Clark, Ian. *Globalization and Fragmentation: International Relations in the Twentieth Century*. New York: Oxford University Press, 1997.

Clayton, Blake C. *Market Madness: A Century of Oil Panics, Crises, and Crashes*. New York: Oxford University Press, 2015.

Cline, William R. *Financial Globalization, Economic Growth, and the Crisis of 2007–09*. Washington, DC: Peterson Institute, 2010.

Cohan, William D. *House of Cards: A Tale of Hubris and Wretched Excess on Wall Street*. New York: Anchor, 2010.

Cohen, Benjamin J. *The Geography of Money*. Ithaca and London: Cornell University Press, 1998.

Cohen, Stephen D., Robert A. Blecker, and Peter D. Whitney. *Fundamentals of U.S. Foreign Trade Policy: Economics, Politics, Laws, and Issues*, 2nd ed. Boulder, CO: Westview, 2002.

Coleman, William D. and Geoffrey R.D. Underhill. *Regionalism and Global Economic Integration*. Cambridge, MA: Harvard University Press, 1995.

Crystal, Jonathan. *Unwanted Company: Foreign Investment in American Industries*. Ithaca and London: Cornell University Press, 2003.

Davies, Howard and David Green. *Banking on the Future: The Fall and Rise of Central Banking*. Princeton: Princeton University Press, 2010.

Davis, Gerald F. *Managed by the Markets: How Finance Has Re-Shaped America*. New York: Oxford University Press, 2009.

Destler, I.M. *American Trade Politics*, 3rd ed. Washington, DC: Institute for International Economics, 1995.

De Ville, Ferdi and Gabriel Siles-Brügge. *TTIP: The Truth about the Transatlantic Trade and Investment Partnership*. Cambridge, UK: Polity, 2015.

Dietsch, Peter. *Catching Capital: The Ethics of Tax Competition*. New York: Oxford University Press, 2015.

Recommended Reading

Drezner, Daniel W. *The System Worked: How the World Stopped Another Great Depression.* New York: Oxford University Press, 2014.

Dunning, J.H. and K.A. Hamdani, eds. *The New Globalism and Developing Countries.* New York: UN University Press, 1997.

Ebenstein, Lanny. *Milton Friedman: A Biography.* London: Palgrave Macmillan, 2007.

Echevarria, Antulio. *Reconsidering the American Way of War: U.S. Military Practice from the Revolution to Afghanistan.* Washington, DC: Georgetown University Press, 2014.

Ehrlichman, Howard J. *Conquest, Tribute, and Trade: The Quest for Precious Metals and the Birth of Globalization.* New York: Prometheus Books, 2010.

Eichengreen, Barry, ed. *The Gold Standard in Theory and Practice.* New York: Methuen, 1985.

Eichengreen, Barry. *Toward a New International Financial Architecture.* Washington, DC: Institute for International Economics, 1999.

Eichengreen, Barry. *Exorbitant Privilege: The Rise and Fall of the Dollar and the Future of the International Monetary System.* New York: Oxford University Press, 2011.

Federico, Giovanni. *Feeding the World: An Economic History of World Agriculture, 1800–2000.* Princeton: Princeton University Press, 2005.

Feketekuty, Geza and Bruce Stokes, eds. *Trade Strategies for a New Era: Ensuring U.S. Leadership in a Global Economy.* New York: Council on Foreign Relations and the Monterey Institute of International Studies, 1998.

Ferguson, Niall. *The Cash Nexus: Economics and Politics from the Age of Warfare through the Age of Welfare, 1700–2000.* New York: Basic Books, 2002.

Ferguson, Niall. *The Ascent of Money: A Financial History of the World.* New York: Penguin Press, 2008.

Fischer, Stanley. *IMF Essays from a Time of Crisis: The International Financial System, Stabilization, and Development.* Cambridge, MA: MIT Press, 2004.

Fishlow, Albert and Stephen Haggard. *The United States and the Regionalization of the World Economy.* Paris: Organization for Economic Cooperation and Development, Development Centre, 1992.

Foer, Franklin. *How Soccer Explains the World: An Unlikely Theory of Globalization.* New York: HarperCollins, 2004.

Frankel, Jeffrey A., ed. *The Internationalization of Equity Markets.* Chicago: University of Chicago Press, 1994.

Friedman, Thomas L. *The Lexus and the Olive Tree: Understanding Globalization.* New York: Farrar, Straus & Giroux, 1999.

Gallarotti, Guilio M. *The Anatomy of an International Monetary Regime.* New York: Oxford University Press, 1995.

Gilpin, Robert. *Global Political Economy: Understanding the International Economic Order.* Princeton: Princeton University Press, 2001.

Graham, Edward M. and J. David Richardson. *Competition Policies for the Global Economy.* Washington, DC: Institute for International Economics, 1997.

Greenspan, Alan. *The Map and the Territory: Risk, Human Nature, and the Future of Forecasting.* New York: Penguin Press, 2013.

Greenstein, Shane. *How the Internet Became Commercial: Innovation, Privatization, and the Birth of a New Network.* Princeton: Princeton University Press, 2015.

Grenier, Robert. *88 Days to Kandahar: A CIA Diary.* New York: Simon and Schuster, 2015.

Hafner-Burton, Emilie M. *Forced to be Good: Why Trade Agreements Boost Human Rights.* Ithaca and London: Cornell University Press, 2009.

Holden, Robert H. and Eric Zolov. *Latin America and the United States: A Documentary History.* New York: Oxford University Press, 2010.

Hoover, Kenneth R. *Economics as Ideology: Keynes, Laski, Hayek, and the Creation of Contemporary Politics.* Lanham, MD: Rowman and Littlefield, 2004.

Huerta, Ignacio Palcios, ed. *In 100 Years: Leading Economists Predict the Future.* Cambridge, MA: MIT Press, 2014.

Hufbauer, Gary Clyde and Jeffrey J. Schott. *NAFTA Revisited: Achievements and Challenges.* Washington, DC: Institute for International Economics, 2005.

Hufbauer, Gary Clyde and Kati Suominen. *Globalization at Risk: Challenges to Finance and Trade.* New Haven: Yale University Press, 2010.

Isaacson, Walter. *Steve Jobs.* New York: Simon and Schuster, 2011.

Jackson, John J. *The World Trading System,* 2nd ed. Cambridge, MA: MIT Press, 1999.

James, Harold. *International Monetary Cooperation Since Bretton Woods.* New York: Oxford University Press, 1996.

Janeway, William H. *Doing Capitalism in the Innovative Economy.* New York: Cambridge University Press, 2012.

Johnson, Simon and James Kwak. *13 Bankers: The Wall Street Takeover and the Next Financial Crisis.* New York: Pantheon, 2010.

Kaul, Inge, Isabelle Grunberg, and Marc A. Stern, eds. *Global Public Goods: International Cooperation in the 21st Century.* New York: Oxford University Press, 1999.

Kiewer, D. Roderick. *Macroeconomics and Micropolitics.* Chicago: University of Chicago Press, 1983.

Kindleberger, Charles P. *International Capital Movements.* New York: Cambridge University Press, 1987.

Krugman, Paul. *The Return of Depression Economics.* Cambridge, MA: MIT Press, 1999.

Krugman, Paul. *The Return of Depression Economics und the Crisis of 2008.* New York: Norton, 2008.

Lardy, Nicholas R. *Sustaining China's Economic Growth After the Global Financial Crisis.* Washington, DC: Peterson Institute for International Economics, 2012.

Lin, Justin Yifu. *Against the Consensus: Reflections on the Great Recession.* New York: Cambridge University Press, 2013.

Locke, Richard M. and Rachel L. Wellhausen, eds. *Production in the Innovative Economy.* Cambridge, MA: MIT Press, 2014.

Lomborg, Bjorn, ed. *Prioritizing the World: Cost-Benefit to Identify the Smartest Targets for the Next 15 Years.* Copenhagen: Copenhagen Consensus Center, 2014.

Lynch, David J. *When the Luck of the Irish Ran Out: The World's Most Resilient Country and Its Struggle to Rise Again.* New York: Palgrave Macmillan, 2010.

Lynn, Barry C. *End of the Line: The Rise and Coming Fall of the Global Corporation.* New York: Doubleday, 2005.

Mansfield, Edward D. and Brian M. Pollins, eds. *Economic Interdependence and International Conflict: New Perspectives on an Enduring Debate.* Ann Arbor: University of Michigan Press, 2003.

Martin, Philip, Manolo Abella, and Christiane Kuptsch. *Managing Labor Migration in the Twenty-first Century.* New Haven: Yale University Press, 2005.

Mass, Peter. *Crude World: The Violent Twilight of Oil.* New York: Knopf, 2010.

Mazzucato, Mariana, ed. *The Entrepreneurial State: Debunking Public vs. Private Sector Myths.* New York: PublicAffairs, 2015.

Milanovic, Branko. *Global Inequality: A New Approach for the Age of Globalization.* Cambridge, MA: Harvard University Press, 2016.

Moran, Theodore H. *Foreign Direct Investment and Development: Launching a Second Generation of Policy Research.* Washington, DC: Peterson Institute for International Economics, 2011.

Newman, Abraham L. *Protectors of Privacy: Regulating Personal Data in the Global Economy.* Ithaca and London: Cornell University Press, 2008.

Norberg, Johan. *Financial Fiasco: How America's Infatuation with Homeownership and Easy Money Created the Economic Crisis.* Washington, DC: CATO Institute, 2009.

Odell, John S. *Negotiating the World Economy.* Ithaca and London: Cornell University Press, 2000.

Recommended Reading

Ohmae, Kenichi. *The End of the Nation-State: The Rise of Regional Economies.* London: HarperCollins, 1995.

Petrie, Thomas A. *Following Oil: Four Decades of Cycle-Testing Experiences and What They Foretell About U.S. Energy Independence.* Norman, OK: University of Oklahoma Press, 2014.

Prestowitz, Clyde. *Three Billion Capitalists: The Great Shift of Wealth and Power to the East.* New York: Basic Books, 2006.

Raustiala, Kal and Christopher Sprigman. *The Knockoff Economy: How Imitation Sparks Innovation.* New York: Oxford University Press, 2012.

Reich, Robert B. *The Work of Nations.* New York: Knopf, 1991.

Rodrik, Dani. *Has Globalization Gone Too Far?* Washington, DC: Institute for International Economics, 1997.

Romm, Joseph. *Climate Change: What Everyone Needs to Know.* New York: Oxford University Press, 2015.

Rosecrance, Richard N. *The Rise of the Virtual State: Wealth and Power in the Coming Century.* New York: Basic Books, 1999.

Rosecrance, Richard N. and Steven E. Miller, eds. *The Next War? The Roots of World War I and the Risk of U.S.-China Conflict.* Cambridge, MA: MIT Press, 2014.

Roy, Ravi K., Arthur T. Denzau, and Thomas D. Willett, eds. *Neoliberalism: National and Regional Experiments with Global Ideas.* London: Routledge, 2007.

Rozman, Gilbert. *The Sino-Russian Challenge to the World Order: National Identities, Bilateral Relations, and East versus West in the 2010s.* Stanford, CA: Stanford University Press, 2014.

Ruggie, John Gerard, ed. *Embedding Global Markets: An Enduring Challenge.* Aldershot: Ashgate, 2008.

Scharman, J.C. *The Money Laundry: Regulating Criminal Finance in the Global Economy.* Ithaca and London: Cornell University Press, 2011.

Scherrer, Amandine. *G8 against Transnational Organized Crime.* Aldershot: Ashgate, 2009.

Schiller, Robert J. *The Subprime Solution: How Today's Global Financial Crisis Happened, and What to Do About It.* Princeton: Princeton University Press, 2008.

Schott, Jeffrey J., ed. *Launching New Global Trade Talks: An Action Agenda.* Washington, DC: Institute for International Economics, 1998.

Schultz, Paul H., ed. *Perspectives on Dodd-Frank and Finance.* Cambridge, MA: MIT Press, 2014.

Shiffman, Gary M. *Economic Instruments of Security Policy: Influencing Choices of Leaders.* Basingstoke, UK: Palgrave Macmillan, 2006.

Steger, Manfred B., ed. *Globalism: Market Ideology Meets Terrorism.* Lanham, MD: Rowman and Littlefield, 2004.

Steil, Benn and Robert E. Litan. *Financial Statecraft: The Role of Financial Markets in American Foreign Policy.* New Haven: Yale University Press, 2005.

Steil, Benn and Manuel Hinds. *Money, Markets, and Sovereignty.* New Haven: Yale University Press, 2009.

Sterling, Claire. *Thieves' World: The Threat of the New Global Network of Organized Crime.* New York: Simon and Schuster, 1994.

Stern, Nicholas. *The Global Deal: Climate Change and the Creation of a New Era of Progress and Prosperity.* New York: Public Affairs, 2009.

Stiglitz, Joseph E. and Andrew Charlton. *Fair Trade for All: How Trade Can Promote Development.* New York: Oxford University Press, 2006.

Stiglitz, Joseph E. and Linda J. Bilmes. *The Three Trillion Dollar War: The True Cost of the Iraq Conflict.* New York: Norton, 2007.

Strange, Susan. *Mad Money: When Markets Outgrow Governments.* Ann Arbor: University of Michigan Press, 1998.

Tarullo, Daniel K. *Banking on Basel: The Future of International Financial Regulation.* Washington, DC: Peterson Institute for International Economics, 2008.

Truman, Edwin M. *Sovereign Wealth Funds: Threat or Salvation?* Washington, DC: Peterson Institute for International Economics, 2010.

Veltmeyer, Henry, ed. *New Perspectives on Globalization and Antiglobalization.* Aldershot: Ashgate, 2008.

Wells, Wyatt. *American Capitalism, 1945–2000: Continuity and Change from Mass Production to the Information Society.* Lanham, MD: Rowman and Littlefield, 2004.

Whitman, Marina. *New World, New Rules: The Changing Role of the American Corporation.* Cambridge, MA: Harvard Business School, 1999.

Wolf, Martin. *The Shifts and the Shocks: What We've Learned—and Have Still to Learn—From the Financial Crisis.* New York: Penguin Press, 2014.

Woll, Cornelia. *The Power of Inaction: Bank Bailouts in Comparison.* Ithaca and London: Cornell University Press, 2014.

Yavlinsky, Grigory. *Realeconomik: The Hidden Cause of the Great Recession.* New Haven: Yale University Press, 2011.

Yergin, Daniel and Joseph Stanislaw. *The Commanding Heights.* New York: Simon and Schuster, 1998.

Zank, Wolfgang, ed. *Clash or Cooperation of Civilizations?* Aldershot: Ashgate, 2009.

Military and Technological

Adams, Peter Caddick. *Snow and Steel: The Battle of the Bulge, 1944–45.* New York: Oxford University Press, 2014.

Adamsky, Dima. *The Culture of Military Intervention: The Impact of Cultural Factors on the Revolution in Military Affairs in Russia, the US, and Israel.* Stanford, CA: Stanford University Press, 2010.

Alberts, David S., John Garstka, and Frederick Stein. *Network Centric Warfare.* Washington, DC: National Defense University Press, 1999.

Albrow, Martin. *The Global Age: State and Society Beyond Modernity.* Stanford, CA: Stanford University Press, 1997.

Allawi, Ali A. *The Occupation of Iraq: Winning the War, Losing the Peace.* New Haven: Yale University Press, 2007.

Allison, Graham T. *Nuclear Terrorism: The Ultimate Preventable Catastrophe.* New York: Times Books, 2003.

Allison, Graham T., Owen R. Cote, Jr., Richard A. Falkenrath, and Steven E. Miller. *Avoiding Nuclear Anarchy.* Cambridge, MA: MIT Press, 1996.

Anderson, David I., ed. *The Columbia History of the Vietnam War.* New York: Columbia University Press, 2011.

Arquilla, John and David Ronfeldt. *In Athena's Camp: Preparing for Conflict in the Information Age.* Santa Monica, CA: RAND, 1997.

Atkinson, Rick. *In the Company of Soldiers: A Chronicle of Combat.* New York: Simon and Schuster, 2004.

Atkinson, Rick. *The Guns at Last Light: The War in Western Europe, 1944-1945.* New York: Henry Holt, 2013.

Bacevich, Andrew. *The New American Militarism: How Americans Are Seduced by War.* New York: Oxford University Press, 2005.

Bachman, Gideon. *Zero-Sum Future: American Power in an Age of Anxiety.* New York: Simon and Schuster, 2011.

Barnett, Thomas P.M. *The Pentagon's New Map: War and Peace in the Twenty-First Century.* New York: Putnam, 2003.

Beevor, Anthony. *D-Day: The Battle for Normandy.* New York: Viking, 2009.

Bergen, Peter L. *The Longest War: Inside the Enduring Conflict Between America and Al-Qaeda Since 9/11.* New York: Free Press, 2011.

Bergen, Peter L. *United States of Jihad: Investigating America's Homegrown Terrorists.* New York: Crown Publishers, 2016.

Berman, Eli. *Radical, Religious, and Violent: The New Economics of Terrorism.* Cambridge, MA: MIT Press, 2009.

Biddle, Stephen. *Military Power: Explaining Victory and Defeat in Modern Battle.* Princeton: Princeton University Press, 2004.

Black, Jeremy. *The Age of Total War, 1860–1945.* Lanham, MD: Rowman and Littlefield, 2011.

Blight, James G., Janet M. Lang, and David A Welch. *Vietnam If Kennedy Had*

Recommended Reading

Lived: Virtual JFK. Lanham, MD: Rowman and Littlefield, 2009.

Boot, Max. *War Made New: Technology, Warfare, and the Course of History, 1500 to Today*. New York: Gotham Books, 2006.

Boot, Max. *Invisible Armies: An Epic History of Guerrilla Warfare from Ancient Times to the Present*. New York: Liveright, 2013.

Bracken, Paul. *The Second Nuclear Age: Strategy, Danger, and the New Power Politics*. New York: Times Books, 2012.

Broadwell, Paula with Vernon Loeb. *All In: The Education of General David Petraeus*. New York: Penguin Press, 2012.

Burk, James, ed. *How 9/11 Changed Our Ways of War*. Stanford, CA: Stanford University Press, 2013.

Byman, Daniel. *Al Qaeda, the Islamic State, and the Global Jihadist Movement: What Everyone Needs to Know*. New York: Oxford University Press, 2015.

Clunan, Anne L., Peter R. Lavoy, and Susan B. Martin, eds. *Terrorism, War, or Disease? Unraveling the Use of Biological Weapons*. Stanford, CA: Stanford University Press, 2008.

Collingham, Lizzie. *The Taste of War: World War II and the Battle for Food*. New York: Penguin Press, 2012.

Cordesman, Anthony H. *The Arab-Israeli Military Balance and the Art of Operations: An Analysis of Military Lessons and Trends and Implications for Future Conflicts*. Washington, DC: American Enterprise Institute for Public Policy Research, 1987.

Cordesman, Anthony H. *Perilous Prospects: The Peace Process and Arab Israeli Military Balance*. Boulder, CO: Westview, 1996.

Cordesman, Anthony H. *Arab-Israeli Military Forces in an Era of Asymmetric Wars*. Westport, CT: Praeger, 2006.

Cortright, David. *Peace: A History of Movements and Ideas*. New York: Cambridge University Press, 2008.

Crawford, Neta. *Accountability for Killing: Moral Responsibility for Collateral Damage in America's Post-9/11 Wars*. New York: Oxford University Press, 2013.

DeLong, Michael and Noah Lukeman. *Inside Centcom: The Unvarnished Truth about the Wars in Afghanistan and Iraq*. Washington, DC: Regnery, 2004.

Dempsey, Jason K. *Our Army: Soldiers, Politics, and American Civil-Military Relations*. Princeton: Princeton University Press, 2010.

Dorman, Andrew M. and Joyce P. Kaufman, eds. *Providing for National Security: A Comparative Analysis*. Stanford, CA: Stanford University Press, 2014.

Drell, Sidney D. and James E. Goodby. *The Gravest Danger: Nuclear Weapons*. Stanford, CA: Hoover Institution Press, 2003.

Duelfer, Charles. *Hide and Seek: The Search for Truth in Iraq*. New York: Public Affairs, 2009.

Duffield, John S. and Peter Dombrowski. *Balance Sheet: The Iraq War and U.S. National Security*. Stanford, CA: Stanford University Press, 2009.

Dunnigan, James F. and Austin Bay. *From Shield to Storm: High-Tech Weapons, Military Strategy, and Coalition Warfare in the Persian Gulf*. New York: Morrow, 1991.

Ekirch, Arthur, Jr. *The Civilian and the Military: A History of the American Antimilitarist Tradition*. Oakland, CA: Independent Institute, 2010.

English, Richard. *Terrorism: How to Respond*. New York: Oxford University Press, 2009.

Fair, C. Christine and Sumit Ganguly, eds. *Treading on Hallowed Ground: Counterinsurgency Operations in Sacred Spaces*. New York: Oxford University Press, 2008.

Fawn, Rick and Raymond Hinnebusche, eds. *The Iraq War: Causes and Consequences*. Boulder, CO: Lynne Rienner, 2006.

Feaver, Peter D. *Guarding the Guardians: Civilian Control of Nuclear Weapons in the United States*. Ithaca and London: Cornell University Press, 1992.

Fettweis, Christopher. *Dangerous Times? The International Politics of Great Power Peace*. Washington, DC: Georgetown University Press, 2010.

Fidler, David P. and Lawrence O. Gostin. *Biosecurity in the Global Age: Biological Weapons, Public Health, and the Rule of Law*. Stanford, CA: Stanford University Press, 2007.

Fitzgerald, David. *Learning to Forget: US Army Counterinsurgency Doctrine and Practice from Vietnam to Iraq*. Stanford, CA: Stanford University Press, 2013.

Freedman, Lawrence and Efraim Karsh. *The Gulf Conflict 1990–1991: Diplomacy and War in the New World Order*. Princeton: Princeton University Press, 1993.

Fukuyama, Francis. *The Origins of Political Order: From Prehuman Times to the French Revolution*. New York: Farrar, Straus & Giroux, 2011.

Gansler, Jacques S. *Defense Conversion: Transforming the Arsenal of Democracy*. Cambridge, MA: MIT Press, 1995.

Gelpi, Christopher, Peter D. Feaver, and Jason Reifler. *Paying the Human Costs of War: American Public Opinion and Casualties in Military Conflicts*. Princeton: Princeton University Press, 2009.

Gilpin, Robert. *War and Change in World Politics*. New York: Cambridge University Press, 1981.

Gordin, Michael D. *Red Cloud at Dawn: Truman, Stalin, and the End of the Atomic Monopoly*. New York: Farrar, Straus & Giroux, 2009.

Gordon, Michael R. and Bernard E. Trainor. *Cobra II: The Inside Story of the Invasion and Occupation of Iraq*. New York: Pantheon Books, 2006.

Gordon, Michael R. and Bernard E. Trainor. *The Endgame: The Inside Story of the Struggle for Iraq, From George W. Bush to Barack Obama*. New York: Pantheon Books, 2012.

Gresh, Geoffrey F. *Gulf Security and the U.S. Military: Regime Survival and the Politics of Basing*. Stanford, CA: Stanford University Press, 2015.

Halperin, Morton H. *Bureaucratic Politics and Foreign Policy*. Washington, DC: Brookings Institution Press, 1974.

Hartley, Keith. *The Political Economy of NATO: Past, Present and into the 21st Century*. New York: Cambridge University Press, 1999.

Hays, Peter L., Brenda J. Vallance, and Alan R. Van Tassel, eds. *American Defense Policy*, 7th ed. Baltimore: The Johns Hopkins University Press, 1997.

Hickey, James E. *Precision-guided Munitions and Human Suffering in War*. Aldershot: Ashgate, 2012.

Hoffmann, Stanley. *Gulliver Unbound: America's Imperial Temptation and the War in Iraq*. Lanham, MD: Rowman and Littlefield, 2004.

Horowitz, Michael C. *The Diffusions of Military Power: Causes and Consequences for International Politics*. Princeton: Princeton University Press, 2010.

Huchthausen, Peter. *America's Splendid Little Wars: A Short History of U.S. Military Engagements, 1975–2000*. New York: Viking, 2003.

Jones, Seth G. *Hunting in the Shadows: The Pursuit of al Qa'ida Since 9/11*. New York: Norton, 2012.

Kahn, David. *The Reader of Gentlemen's Mail: Herbert O. Yardley and the Birth of American Codebreaking*. New Haven: Yale University Press, 2004.

Kamienski, Lukasz. *Shooting Up: A Short History of Drugs and War*. New York: Oxford University Press, 2016

Kaplan, Robert D. *Imperial Grunts: The American Military on the Ground*. New York: Random House, 2005.

Keeney, L. Douglas. *15 Minutes: General Curtis LeMay and the Countdown to Nuclear Annihilation*. New York: St. Martin's Press, 2011.

Kennedy, Paul. *Engineers of Victory: The Problem Solvers Who Turned the Tide in the Second World War*. New York: Random House, 2013.

Kilcullen, David. *The Accidental Guerrilla: Fighting Small Wars in the Midst of a Big One*. New York: Oxford University Press, 2009.

Kilcullen, David. *Out of the Mountains: The Coming Age of the Urban Guerrilla*. New York: Oxford University Press, 2013.

Recommended Reading

Kilcullen, David. *Blood Year: The Unraveling of Western Counterterrorism*. New York: Oxford University, Press, 2016.

Kinsey, Christopher and Malcolm Hugh Patterson, eds. *Contractors and War: The Transformation of US Expeditionary Operations*. Stanford, CA: Stanford University Press, 2012.

Klein, Maury. *A Call to Arms: Mobilizing America for World War II*. New York: Bloomsbury, 2013.

Klotz, Lynn C. and Edward J. Sylvester. *Breeding Bio Insecurity: How the U.S. Biodefense Is Exporting Fear, Globalizing Risk, and Making Us all Less Secure*. Chicago: University of Chicago Pres, 2009.

Koblentz, Gregory. *Living Weapons: Biological Warfare and International Security*. Ithaca and London: Cornell University Press, 2009.

Krepinevich, Andrew and Barry Watts. *The Last Warrior: Andrew Marshall and the Shaping of Modern American Defense Strategy*. New York: Basic Books, 2015.

Krepon, Michael. *Better Safe Than Sorry: The Ironies of Living with the Bomb*. Stanford, CA: Stanford University Press, 2009.

Lambeth, Benjamin S. *Air Power Against Terror: America's Conduct of Operation Enduring Freedom*. Santa Monica, CA: RAND, 2005.

Lambeth, Benjamin S. *American Carrier Air Power at the Dawn of a New Century*. Santa Monica, CA: RAND, 2006.

Ledbetter, James. *Unwarranted Influence: Dwight D. Eisenhower and the Military Industrial Complex*. New Haven: Yale University Press, 2011.

Lesser, Ian O., Bruce Hoffman, John Arquilla, David Ronfeldt, and Michael Zanini, eds. *Countering the New Terrorism*. Santa Monica, CA: RAND, 1999.

Licklider, Roy, ed. *New Armies from Old: Merging competing Military Forces after Civil Wars*. Washington, DC: Georgetown University Press, 2014.

Lieber, Keir. *War and the Engineers: The Primacy of Politics over Technology*. Ithaca and London: Cornell University Press, 2008.

Lind, Michael. *The American Way of Strategy: U.S. Foreign Policy and the American Way of Life*. New York: Oxford University Press, 2006.

Litwak, Robert. *Regime Change: U.S. Strategy Through the Prism of 9/11*. Baltimore: The Johns Hopkins University Press, 2007.

MacKenzie, Megan. *Beyond the Band of Brothers: The U.S. Military and the Myth That Women Can't Fight*. New York: Cambridge University Press, 2015.

May, Ernest R., Richard N. Rosecrance, and Zara Steiner, eds. *History and Neorealism*. New York: Cambridge University Press, 2010.

Mazzetti, Mark. *The Way of the Knife: The CIA, a Secret Army, and a War at the End of the Earth*. New York: Penguin Press, 2013.

McFate, Sean. *The Modern Mercenary: Private Armies and What They Mean for World Order*. New York: Oxford University Press, 2014.

Miskel, James F. *Disaster Response and Homeland Security: What Works, What Doesn't*. Stanford, CA: Stanford University Press, 2008.

Nichols, Thomas M. *No Use: Nuclear Weapons and U.S. National Security*. Philadelphia: University of Pennsylvania Press, 2013.

O'Connell Aaron B. *Underdogs: The Making of the Modern Marine Corps*. Cambridge, MA: Harvard University Press, 2012.

O'Hanlon, Michael E. *Technological Change and the Future of Warfare*. Washington, DC: Brookings Institution Press, 1999.

O'Hanlon, Michael E. *The Wounded Giant: America's Armed Forces in an Age of Austerity*. New York: Penguin Press, 2011.

Paul, T.V. *The Tradition of Non-Use of Nuclear Weapons*. Stanford, CA: Stanford University Press, 2009.

Perito, Robert M. *Where Is the Lone Ranger When We Need Him? America's Search for a Post-Stability Force*. Washington, DC: U.S. Institute of Peace Press, 2004.

Peritz, Aki and Eric Rosenbach. *Find, Fix, Finish: Inside the Counterterrorism Campaigns That Killed bin Laden and Devastated al Qaeda*. New York: PublicAffairs, 2012.

Perry, William. *My Journey at the Nuclear Brink*. Stanford, CA: Stanford University Press, 2015.

Pettegrew, John. *Light It Up: The Marine Eye for Battle in the War for Iraq*. Baltimore: Johns Hopkins University Press, 2015.

Pike, Francis. *Hirohito's War: The Pacific War, 1941–1945*. New York: Bloomsbury, 2015.

Quinlan, Michael. *Thinking About Nuclear Weapons: Principles, Problems, Prospects*. New York: Oxford University Press, 2009.

Reveron, Derek S. *Exporting Security: International Engagement, Security Cooperation, and the Changing Face of the US Military*. Washington, DC: Georgetown University Press, 2010.

Roberts, Brad. *The Case for U.S. Nuclear Weapons in the 21st Century*. Stanford, CA: Stanford University Press, 2015.

Robinson, Linda. *Tell Me How This Ends: General David Patraeus and the Search for a Way Out of Iraq*. New York: PublicAffairs, 2007.

Rose, Gideon. *How Wars End: Why We Always Fight the Last Battle*. New York: Simon and Schuster, 2010.

Rosen, Stephen Peter. *Winning the Next War: Innovations and the Modern Military*. Ithaca and London: Cornell University Press, 1991.

Ryan, Michael W.S. *Decoding Al-Qaeda's Strategy: The Deep Battle Against America*. New York: Columbia University Press, 2013.

Sarkesian, Sam C., ed. *The Military-Industrial Complex: A Reassessment*. Beverly Hills, CA: Sage, 1972.

Serena, Chad C. *A Revolution in Military Adaptation: The US Army in the Iraq War*. Washington, DC: Georgetown University Press, 2011.

Shadid, Anthony. *Night Draws Near: Iraq's People in the Shadow of America's War*. New York: Henry Holt, 2005.

Sheehan, Neil. *A Fiery Peace in a Cold War: Bernard Schriever and the Ultimate Weapon*. New York: Random House, 2009.

Shore, Zachary. *A Sense of the Enemy: The High Stakes History of Reading Your Rival's Mind*. New York: Oxford University Press, 2014.

Singer, P.W. *Wired for War: The Robotics Revolution and Conflict in the Twenty-first Century*. New York: Penguin Press, 2009.

Slayton, Rebecca. *Arguments That Count: Physics, Computing, and Missile Defense, 1949-2012*. Cambridge, MA: MIT Press, 2013.

Snow, Donald M. *National Security*, 4th ed. New York: Bedford Books, 1997.

Sparrow, James T. *Warfare State: World War II Americans and the Age of Big Government*. New York: Oxford University Press, 2012.

Speed, Roger D. *Strategic Deterrence in the 1980s*. Stanford, CA: Hoover Institution Press, 1979.

Strachan, Hew. *The Direction of War: Contemporary Strategy in Historical Perspective*. New York: Cambridge University Press, 2014.

Teorell, Jan. *Determinants of Democratization: Explaining Regime Change in the World, 1972-2006*. New York: Cambridge University Press, 2010.

Trachtenberg, Marc, ed. *Between Empire and Alliance: America and Europe during the Cold War*. Lanham, MD: Rowman and Littlefield, 2004.

Treverton, Gregory F. *Intelligence for an Age of Terror*. New York: Cambridge University Press, 2009.

Toft, Monica Duffy. *Securing the Peace: The Durable Settlement of Civil Wars*. Princeton: Princeton University Press, 2010.

Ucko, David H. *The New Counterinsurgency Era: Transforming the US Military for Modern Wars*. Washington, DC: Georgetown University Press, 2009.

Van Creveld, Martin. *The Age of Airpower*. New York: PublicAffairs, 2011.

Recommended Reading

Walker, William. *A Perpetual Menace: Nuclear Weapons and International Order*. London: Routledge, 2011.

Weis, Michael and Hassan Hassan. *ISIS: Inside the Army of Terror*. New York: Regan Arts, 2015.

Westad, Odd Arne. *The Global War: Third World Interventions and the Making of Our Times*. New York: Cambridge University Press, 2005.

Whitman, James Q. *The Verdict of Battle: The Law of Victory and the Making of Modern War*. Cambridge, MA: Harvard University Press, 2012.

Wiest, Andrew and Michael J. Doidge, eds. *Triumph Revisited: Historians Battle for the Vietnam War*. London: Routledge, 2010.

Woods, Kevin M. *The Mother of All Battles: Saddam Hussein's Strategic Plan for the Persian Gulf War*. Annapolis: Naval Institute Press, 2008.

Woodward, Bob. *The Commanders*. New York: Simon and Schuster, 1991.

Woodward, Bob. *Bush at War*. New York: Simon and Schuster, 2002.

Woodward, Bob. *Plan of Attack*. New York: Simon and Schuster, 2004.

Woodward, Bob. *State of Denial: Bush at War, Part III*. New York: Simon and Schuster, 2006.

Woodward, Bob. *The War Within: A Secret White House History, 2006–2008*. New York: Simon and Schuster, 2008.

Woodward, Bob. *Obama's Wars*. New York: Simon and Schuster, 2010.

Zarate, Robert and Henry Sokolski. *Nuclear Heuristics: Selected Writings of Albert and Roberta Wohlstetter*. Carlisle, PA: Strategic Studies Institute, 2009.

Zelizer, Julian E. *Arsenal of Democracy: The Politics of National Security—From World War II to the War on Terrorism*. New York: Basic Books, 2009.

Foreign Policy

Aarts, Paul and Gerd Nonneman. *Saudi Arabia in the Balance: Political Economy, Society, Foreign Affairs*. New York: New York University Press, 2006.

Abdo, Geneive and Jonathan Lyons. *Answering Only to God: Faith and Freedom in Twenty-First Century Iran*. New York: Henry Holt, 2003.

Abrahamian, Ervand. *A History of Modern Iran*. New York: Cambridge University Press, 2008.

Agha, Hussein, Shai Feldman, Ahmad Khalidi, and Zeev Schiff. *Track-II Diplomacy: Lessons From the Middle East*. Cambridge: MIT Press, 2004.

Agresto, John. *Mugged by Reality: The Liberation of Iraq and the Failure of Good Intentions*. New York: Encounter Books, 2007.

Ajami, Fouad. *The Syrian Rebellion*. Stanford: Hoover Institution Press, 2011.

Alfonsi, Christian. *Circle in the Sand: Why We Went Back to Iraq*. New York: Doubleday, 2006.

Allison, Graham T. and Philip Zelikow. *Essence of Decision: Explaining the Cuban Missile Crisis*, 2nd ed. New York: Longman, 1999.

Amos, Deborah. *Lines in the Sand: Desert Storm and the Remaking of the Arab World*. New York: Simon and Schuster, 1992.

Amstutz, Mark R. *Evangelicals and American Foreign Policy*. New York: Oxford University Press, 2013.

Anonymous. *Imperial Hubris: Why the West Is Losing the War on Terrorism*. Washington, DC: Brassey's 2004.

Applebaum, Anne. *Iron Curtain: The Crushing of Eastern Europe, 1944-1956*. New York: Doubleday, 2012.

Art, Robert J. *A Grand Strategy for America*. Ithaca and London: Cornell University Press, 2003.

Bacevich, Andrew J. *The Limits of Power: The End of American Exceptionalism*. New York: Metropolitan, 2008.

Baer, Robert. *The Devil We Know: Dealing With the New Iranian Superpower*. New York: Random House, 2007.

Baker, Peter. *Days of Fire: Bush and Cheney in the White House*. New York: Doubleday, 2013.

Balis, Christina and Simon Serfaty, eds. *Visions of America and Europe: September 11, Iraq, and Transatlantic Relations*. Washington, DC: Center for Strategic and International Studies, 2004.

Ball, Desmond, ed. *The Transformation of Security in the Asia/Pacific Region*. Portland, OR: Frank Cass, 1995.

Ball, George W. and Douglas B. Ball. *The Passionate Attachment: America's Involvement with Israel*. New York: Norton, 1992.

Bamford, James. *A Pretext for War: 9/11, Iraq, and the Abuse of America's Intelligence Agencies*. New York: Doubleday, 2004.

Barthop, Michael. *Afghan Wars and the Northwest Frontier, 1839–1947*. New York: Cassell, 2002.

Baylis, John and Steve Smith, eds. *The Globalization of World Politics: An Introduction to International Relations*. New York: Oxford University Press, 1999.

Bergen, Peter I. *The Osama bin Laden I know: An Oral History of al Qaeda's Leader*. New York: Free Press, 2006.

Bernanke, Ben S. *The Federal Reserve and the Financial Crisis*. Princeton: Princeton University Press, 2013.

Bill, James E. *The Eagle and the Lion: The Tragedy of American-Iranian Relations*. New Haven: Yale University Press, 1988.

Boli, John and George M. Thomas. *Constructing World Culture: International Nongovernmental Organizations Since 1875*. Stanford, CA: Stanford University Press, 1999.

Boot, Max. *Savage Wars of Peace: Small Wars and the Rise of American Power*. New York: Basic Books, 2002.

Booth, Ken. *Statecraft and Security: The Cold War and Beyond*. New York: Cambridge University Press, 1998.

Borgwardt, Elizabeth. *A New Deal for the World: America's Vision for Human Rights*. Cambridge, MA: Harvard University Press, 2005.

Bowden, Mark. *Guests of the Ayatollah: The First Battle in America's War with Militant Islam*. New York: Atlantic Monthly, 2007.

Boyne, Walter J. *Operation Iraqi Freedom: What Went Right, What Went Wrong, and Why*. New York: Forge, 2003.

Brands, Hal. *What Good is Grand Strategy? Power and Purpose in American Statecraft from Harry S. Truman to George W. Bush*. Ithaca and London: Cornell University Press, 2014.

Bremer, L. Paul. *My Year in Iraq: The Struggle to Build a Future of Hope*. New York: Simon and Schuster, 2006.

Brown, Nathan J. *Palestinian Politics after the Oslo Accords: Resuming Arab Palestine*. Berkeley: University of California Press, 2003.

Brzezinski, Zbigniew. *Second Chance: Three Presidents and the Crisis of the American Superpower*. New York: Basic Books, 2007.

Brzezinski, Zbigniew et al. *America and the World: Conversations on the Future of American Foreign Policy*. New York: Basic Books, 2008.

Brzezinski, Zbigniew. *Strategic Vision: America and the Crisis of Global Power*. New York: Basic Books, 2012.

Buell, Frederick. *National Culture and the New Global System*. Baltimore: Johns Hopkins University Press, 1994.

Bugajski, Janusz. *The Eastern Dimension of America's New European Allies*. Carlisle, PA: Strategic Studies Institute, 2007.

Campbell, Kurt M., ed. *Climatic Cataclysm: The Foreign Policy and National Security Implications of Climate Change*. Washington, DC: Brookings Institution Press, 2008.

Campbell, Kurt M. and James B. Steinberg. *Difficult Transitions: Foreign Policy Troubles at the Outset of Presidential Power*. Washington, DC: Brookings Institution Press, 2008.

Carothers, Thomas. *Aiding Democracy Abroad: The Learning Curve*. Washington, DC: Carnegie Endowment for International Peace, 1999.

Carothers, Thomas and Marina Ottaway, eds. *Uncharted Journey: Promoting Democracy in the Middle East*. Washington, DC: Carnegie Endowment for International Peace. 2005.

Recommended Reading

Carpenter, Ted Galen. *Smart Power: Toward a Prudent Foreign Policy for America.* Washington, DC: Cato Institute, 2008.

Carter, Jimmy. *Palestine: Peace Not Apartheid.* New York: Simon and Schuster, 2007.

Catherwood, Christopher. *Churchill's Folly: How Winston Churchill Created Modern Iraq.* New York: Carroll and Graf Publishers, 2004.

Chandrasekaran, Rajiv. *Imperial Life in the Emerald City: Inside Iraq's Green Zone.* New York: Knopf, 2006.

Chase, Robert S., Emily B. Hill, and Paul Kennedy, eds. *The Pivotal States. A New Framework for U.S. Policy in the Developing World.* New York: Norton, 1999.

Cimbala, Stephen J., ed. *Clinton and Post-Cold War Defense.* Westport, CT: Praeger, 1996.

Cimbala, Stephen J. *Collective Insecurity: U.S. Defense Policy and the New World Disorder.* Westport, CT: Greenwood Press, 1995.

Clements, Frank A. *Conflict in Afghanistan: A Historical Encyclopedia.* Santa Barbara, CA: ABC-CLIO. 2003.

Cleveland, William L. *A History of the Modern Middle East,* 3rd ed. Boulder, CO: Westview, 2004.

Clarke, Richard A. *Against All Enemies: Inside America's War on Terror.* New York: Free Press, 2003.

Clunan, Anne L. *The Social Construction of Russia's Resurgence: Aspirations, Identity, and Security Interests.* Baltimore: Johns Hopkins University Press, 2009.

Cohen, Roger and Claudio Gatti. *In the Eye of the Storm: The Life of General H. Norman Schwarzkopf.* New York: Farrar, Straus & Giroux, 1991.

Cohen, Steven F. *Soviet Fates and Lost Alternatives: From Stalinism to the New Cold War.* New York: Columbia University Press, 2009.

Cole, Juan. *Engaging the Muslim World.* New York: Palgrave Macmillan, 2009.

Coleman, Katharina P. *International Organization and Peace Enforcement: The Politics of International Legitimacy.* Cambridge, UK: Cambridge University Press, 2007.

Cook, David. *Understanding Jihad.* Berkeley: University of California Press, 2005.

Cooper, John Milton. ed. *Reconsidering Woodrow Wilson: Progessivism, Internationalism, War, and Peace.* Baltimore: Johns Hopkins University Press, 2008.

Cox, Robert W. and Timothy J. Sinclair. *Approaches to World Order.* Cambridge, UK: Cambridge University Press, 1996.

Craige, Betty Jean. *American Patriotism in a Global Society.* Albany: State University of New York Press, 1996.

Crandall, Britta H. *Hemispheric Giants: The Misunderstood History of U.S. Brazilian Relations.* Lanham, MD: Rowman and Littlefield, 2011.

Cronin, James E. *Global Rules: America, Britain, and a Disordered World.* New Haven: Yale University Press, 2014.

Cull, Nicholas J. *The Cold War and the United States Information Agency: American Propaganda and Public Diplomacy, 1945–1989.* New York: Cambridge University Press, 2008.

Daalder, Ivo H. and James M. Lindsay. *America Unbound: The Bush Revolution in Foreign Policy.* Washington, DC: Brookings Institution Press, 2003.

Daalder, Ivo H., Nicole Gnesotto and Philip H. Gordon. *Crescent of Crisis: U.S.-European Strategy for the Greater Middle East.* Washington, DC: Brookings Institution Press, 2006.

Danzig, Richard. *The Big Three: Our Greatest Security Threats and How to Address Them.* Washington, DC: National Defense University Press, 1999.

David, Steven R. *Catastrophic Consequences: Civil Wars and American Interests.* Baltimore: Johns Hopkins University Press, 2008.

Del Castillo, Graciana. *Rebuilding War-Torn States: The Challenge of Post-Conflict Economic Reconstruction.* New York Oxford University Press, 2008.

Diamond, Larry. *Developing Democracy: Toward Consolidation.* Baltimore: Johns Hopkins University Press, 1999.

Diamond, Larry. *Squandered Victory: The American Occupation and the Bungled Effort to Bring Democracy to Iraq.* New York: Henry Holt, 2005.

Dobbins, James, John G. McGinn, Keith Crane *et al. America's Role in Nation-Building: From Germany to Iraq.* Santa Monica, CA: RAND, 2003.

Dobbins, James *et al. After the War: Nation-Building From FDR to George W. Bush.* Santa Monica, CA: RAND, 2008.

Doenecke, Justus D. and Mark A. Stoler. *Debating Franklin D. Roosevelt's Foreign Policies, 1933–1945.* Lanham, MD: Rowman and Littlefield, 2005.

Dominguez, Jorge I. and Michael Shifter. *Constructing Democratic Governance in Latin America.* Baltimore: Johns Hopkins University Press, 2008.

Doyle, Michael W. *Striking First: Preemption and Prevention in International Conflict.* Princeton: Princeton University Press, 2008.

Dreyfus, Robert. *Devil's Game: How the United States Helped Unleash Fundamentalist Islam.* New York: Metropolitan Books, 2005.

Drezner, Daniel W., ed. *Avoiding Trivia: The Role of Strategic Planning in American Foreign Policy.* Washington, DC: Brookings Institution Press, 2009.

Drogin, Bob. *Curveball: Spies, Lies, and the Con Man Who Caused a War.* New York: Random House, 2007.

Edwards, Brian T. *After the American Century: The Ends of U.S. Culture in the Middle East.* New York: Columbia University Press, 2015.

Etzioni, Amitai. *Security First: For a Muscular, Moral Foreign Policy.* New Haven: Yale University Press, 2007.

Feldman, Noah. *The Fall and Rise of the Islamic State.* Princeton: Princeton University Press, 2008.

Finnemore, Martha. *National Interests in International Society.* Ithaca and London: Cornell University Press, 1996.

Ferguson, Niall. *Colossus: The Price of America's Empire.* New York: Penguin Press, 2003.

Flanagan, Stephen J. and James A Shear, eds. *Strategic Challenges: America's Global Security Agenda.* Washington, DC: National Defense University Press, 2008.

Fleshler, Dan. *Transforming America's Israel Lobby: The Limits of Its Power and the Potential for Change.* Washington, DC: Potomac Books, 2009.

Forsberg, Tuomas and Graeme P. Herd. *Divided West: European Security and the Transatlantic Relationship.* Oxford: Blackwell Publishing, 2006.

Friedman, George. *America's Secret War: Inside the Hidden Worldwide Struggle Between America and Its Enemies.* New York: Doubleday, 2004.

Friedman, Thomas L. *From Beirut to Jerusalem.* New York: Anchor Books, Doubleday, 1995.

Fukuyama, Francis, ed. *Nation-Building Beyond Afghanistan and Iraq.* Baltimore: Johns Hopkins University Press, 2005

Fuller, Graham E. and Rend Rahim Francke. *The Arab Shi'a: The Forgotten Muslims.* New York: St. Martin's, 2000.

Furnish, Timothy R. *Holiest Wars: Islamic Mahdis, Their Jihads, and Osama Bin Laden.* Westport, CT: Greenwood, 2006.

Gaddis, John Lewis. *The Cold War: A New History.* New York: Penguin Press, 2005.

Galbraith, Peter. *The End of Iraq: How American Incompetence Created a War Without End.* New York: Simon & Schuster, 2006.

Gardels, Nathan and Mike Medavoy. *American Idol After Iraq: Competing for Hearts and Minds in the Global Media Age.* New York: Wiley, 2009.

Gasiorowski, *Mark J.* and Malcolm Byrne. *Mohammad Mossaddeq and the 1953 Coup in Iran.* Syracuse: Syracuse University Press, 2004.

Gellner, Ernest. *Nations and Nationalism.* Cambridge, UK: Cambridge University Press, 1995.

Gerges, Fawaz A. *America and Political Islam: Clash of Cultures or Clash of Interests?* New York: Cambridge University Press, 1999.

Gordon, Philip and Jeremy Shapiro. *Allies at War: America, Europe, and the Split*

Recommended Reading

Over Iraq. New York: McGraw-Hill, 2004.

Graham-Brown, Sarah. *Sanctioning Saddam: The Politics of Intervention in Iraq*. London: I.B. Tauris, 1999.

Green, Michael J. and Patrick Cronin, eds. *The U.S.-Japan Alliance: Past, Present, and Future*. New York: Council on Foreign Relations, 1999.

Greenberg, Karen. *The Least Worst Place: Guantanamo's First 100 Days*. New York: Oxford University Press, 2009.

Greene, Julie. *The Canal Builders: Making America's Empire at the Panama Canal*. New York: Penguin Press, 2009.

Gries, Peter Hays. *The Politics of American Foreign Policy: How Ideology Divides Liberals and Conservatives over Foreign Affairs*. Stanford, CA: Stanford University Press, 2014.

Grygiel, Jakub J. and A. Wess Mitchell. *The Unquiet Frontier: Rising Rivals, Vulnerable Allies, and the Crisis of American Power*. Princeton: Princeton University Press, 2016.

Gunaratna, Rohan. *Inside Al Qaeda: Global Network of Terror*. New York: Columbia University Press, 2002.

Gustafson, Thane. *Wheel of Fortune: The Battle for Oil and Power in Russia*. Cambridge, MA: Harvard University Press, 2012.

Haas, Richard N. *The Reluctant Sheriff: The United States After the Cold War*. New York: Council on Foreign Relations, 1997.

Haas, Richard N. *The Opportunity: America's Moment to Alter History's Course*. New York: PublicAffairs, 2004.

Haas, Richard and Martin Indyk, eds. *Restoring the Balance: A Middle East Strategy for the Next President*. Washington, DC: Brookings Institution Press, 2008.

Haas, Richard. *Foreign Policy Begins at Home: The Case for Putting America's House in Order*. New York: Basic Books, 2013.

Hadar, Leon T. *Quagmire: America in the Middle East*. Washington, DC: Cato Institute, 1992.

Hadar, Leon T. *Sandstorm: Policy Failure in the Middle East*. New York: Palgrave Macmillan, 2005.

Haddad, Bassam. *Business Networks in Syria: The Political Economy of Authoritarian Resilience*. Stanford, CA: Stanford University Press, 2011.

Haddick, Robert. *Fire on the Water: China, America, and the Future of the Pacific*. Annapolis: Naval Institute Press, 2014.

Halper, Stefan and Jonathan Clarke. *The Silence of the Rational Center: Why American Foreign Policy Is Failing*. New York: Basic Books, 2007.

Hamilton, Daniel S. *Transatlantic Transformations: Equipping NATO for the 21st Century*. Washington, DC: Center for Transatlantic Relations, 2004.

Held, David, Anthony G. McGrew, David Goldblatt, and Jonathan Perraton. *Global Transformations: Politics, Economics, and Culture*. Stanford, CA: Stanford University Press, 1999.

Henry L. Stimson Center. *Equipped for the Future: Managing U.S. Foreign Affairs in the 21st Century*. Washington, DC: Henry L. Stimson Center, 1998.

Herring, Eric and Glen Rangwala. *Iraq in Fragments: The Occupation and Its Legacy*. Ithaca and London: Cornell University Press, 2006.

Hilsman, Roger. *The Politics of Policymaking in Defense and Foreign Affairs*. Englewood Cliffs, NJ: Prentice-Hall, 1987.

Hoffmann, Stanley. *World Disorders: Troubled Peace in the Post-Cold War Era*. Lanham, MD: Rowman and Littlefield, 1999.

Hogan, Michael, ed. *The Ambiguous Legacy: U.S. Foreign Relations in the "American Century."* New York: Cambridge University Press, 1999.

Holsti, Ole. *Public Opinion and American Foreign Policy*. Ann Arbor: University of Michigan Press, 1996.

Hubbard, Glenn and Tim Kane. *Balance: The Economics of Great Powers from Ancient Rome to Modern America*. New York: Simon and Schuster, 2013.

Hunter, Shireen T. *The Future of Islam and the West: Clash of Civilizations or Peaceful Coexistence?* Westport, CT: Praeger, 1998.

Huntington, Samuel P. *The Clash of Civilizations and the Remaking of World Order*. New York: Touchstone/Simon and Schuster, 1997.

Hussain, Zahid. *Frontline Pakistan: The Struggle With Militant Islam*. New York: Columbia University Press, 2007.

Hutchings, Robert L., ed. *At the End of the American Century: America's Role in the Post-Cold War World*. Washington, DC: Woodrow Wilson Center Press, 1998.

Hyndman, Jennifer. *Managing Displacement: Refugees and the Politics of Displacement*. Minneapolis, MN: University of Minnesota Press, 2000.

Ignatieff, Michael, ed., *American Exceptionalism and Human Rights*. Princeton: Princeton University Press, 2005.

Ignatieff, Michael. *The Lesser Evil: Political Ethics in an Age of Terror*. Princeton: Princeton University Press, 2004.

Ikenberry, G. John. *After Victory: Institutions, Strategic Restraint, and the Building of Order after Major War*. Princeton: Princeton University Press, 2001.

Ikenberry, G. John. *America Unrivaled: The Future of the Balance of Power*. Ithaca and London: Cornell University Press, 2002.

Ikenberry, G. John, Thomas J. Knock, Anne-Marie Slaughter, and Tony Smith. *The Crisis of American Foreign Policy: Wilsonianism in the Twenty-first Century*.

Princeton: Princeton University Press, 2008.

Isikoff, Michael and David Corn. *Hubris: The Inside Story of Spin, Scandal, and the Selling of the Iraq War*. New York: Crown Publishers, 2006.

Joffe, Josef. *The Myth of America's Decline: Politics, Economics, and a Half Century of False Prophecies*. New York: Liveright, 2013.

Judah, Tim. *Kosovo: War and Revenge*. New Haven: Yale University Press, 2000.

Judt, Tony with Timothy Snyder. *Thinking the Twentieth Century*. New York: Penguin Press, 2012.

Kagan, Robert. *The World America Made*. New York: Knopf, 2012.

Kaplan, Fred. *Daydream Believers: How a Few Grand Ideas Wrecked American Power*. New York: Wiley, 2007.

Kapstein, Ethan B. and Nathan Converse. *The Fate of Young Democracies*. New York: Cambridge University Press, 2008.

Kapstein, Ethan B. and Michael Mastanduno, eds. *Unipolar Politics: Realism and State Strategies after the Cold War*. New York: Columbia University Press, 1999.

Katzenstein, Peter J. *A World of Regions: Asia and Europe in the American Imperium*. Ithaca and London: Cornell University Press, 2005.

Kaufman, Joyce P. *A Concise History of U.S. Foreign Policy*, 3rd ed. Lanham, MD: Rowman and Littlefield, 2014.

Kaufman, Joyce P. and Andrew M. Dorman, eds. *The Future of Transatlantic Relations: Perceptions, Policy and Practice*. Stanford, CA: Stanford University Press, 2010.

Keegan, John. *The Iraq War*. New York: Knopf, 2004.

Kegley, Charles W., Jr., and Gregory Raymond. *After Iraq: The Imperiled American Imperium*. New York: Oxford University Press, 2007.

Kelsay, John. *Arguing the Just War in Islam*. Cambridge: Harvard University Press, 2007.

Kennan, George F. *American Diplomacy*, expanded edition. Chicago: University of Chicago Press, 1984.

Kennedy, Paul. *Preparing for the Twenty-First Century*. New York: Vintage, 1994.

Keohane, Robert O. *International Institutions and State Power: Essays in International Relations Theory*. Boulder, CO: Westview, 1989.

Kepel, Gilles. *Beyond Terror and Martyrdom: The Future of the Middle East*. Cambridge, MA: Harvard University Press, 2008.

Khalilzad, Zalmay M., Abram N. Shulsky, and Daniel Byman. *The United States and a Rising China: Strategies and Military Implications*. Santa Monica, CA: RAND, 1999.

Recommended Reading

Kieser, Lukas. *Nearest East: American Millennialism and Mission to the Middle East.* Philadelphia: Temple University Press, 2010.

Kissinger, Henry A. *Diplomacy.* New York: Simon and Schuster, 1994.

Kohut, Andrew and Bruce Stokes. *America Against the World: How We Are Different and Why We Are Disliked.* New York: Times Books, 2006.

Korb, Lawrence J. *A New National Security Strategy in An Age of Terrorists, Tyrants, and Weapons of Mass Destruction.* New York: Council on Foreign Relations, 2003.

Krasner, Stephen D. *Sovereignty: Organized Hypocrisy.* Princeton: Princeton University Press, 1999.

Krause, Keith and Andy W. Knight, eds. *State, Society, and the UN System: Changing Perspectives on Multilateralism.* New York: UN University Press, 1995.

Kugler, Richard L. and Ellen L. Frost, eds. *The Global Century: Globalization and National Security,* two volumes. Washington, DC: National Defense University Press, 2001.

Kupchan, Charles. *The Vulnerability of Empire.* Ithaca and London: Cornell University Press, 1994.

Kurtzer, Daniel C., Scott B. Lasensky, William B. Quandt, Steven L Spiegel and Shibley Z. Telhami. *The Peace Puzzle: America's Quest for Arab-Israeli Peace, 1989-2011.* Ithaca and London: Cornell University Press, 2012.

Latell, Brian. *Castro's Secrets: The CIA and Cuba's Intelligence Machine.* London: Palgrave Macmillan, 2012.

Latham, Michael E. *The Right Kind of Revolution: Modernization, Development, and U.S. Foreign Policy from the Cold War to the Present.* Ithaca and London: Cornell University Press, 2011.

Leebaert, Derek. *Magic and Mayhem: The Delusions of American Foreign Policy.* New York: Simon and Schuster, 2010.

Lesch, David W. *The Middle East and the United States: A Historical and Political Reassessment.* New York: Perseus Books, 2006.

Lesch, David W. *Syria: The Fall of the House of Assad.* New Haven: Yale University Press, 2012.

Lieber, Robert J, ed. *Eagle Rules? Foreign Policy and American Primacy in the Twenty-First Century.* Upper Saddle River, NJ: Prentice Hall, 2002.

Lieven, Anatol. *Pakistan: A Hard Country.* New York: PublicAffairs, 2011.

Little, Douglas. *American Orientalism: The United States and the Middle East since 1945.* Chapel Hill: University of North Carolina Press, 2002.

Limbert, John W. *Negotiating With Iran: Wrestling the Ghosts of History.* Washington, DC: U.S. Institute of Peace, 2009.

Lowenthal, Abraham F. *Global California: Rising to the Cosmopolitan Challenge.* Stanford, CA: Stanford University Press, 2009.

Lowenthal, Mark M. *Intelligence: From Secrets to Policy.* Washington: CQ Press, 2000.

Lynch, Marc. *The Arab Uprising: The Unfinished Revolution of the New Middle East.* New York: PublicAffairs, 2012.

Lyons, Gene and Michael Mastanduno, eds. *Beyond Westphalia: State Sovereignty and International Intervention.* Baltimore: Johns Hopkins University Press, 1995.

Madden, Thomas F. *Empires of Trust: How Rome Built—and America Is Building—a New World.* New York: Dutton, 2008.

Mandlebaum, Michael. *The Case for Goliath: How America Acts as the World's Government in the Twenty-first Century.* New York: PublicAffairs, 2005.

Mandelbaum, Michael. *The Frugal Superpower: America's Global Leadership in a Cash-Strapped Era.* New York: PublicAffairs, 2010.

Mandelbaum, Michael. *Mission Failure: America and the World in the Post-Cold War Era.* New York: Oxford University Press, 2016.

Mankoff, Jeffrey. *Russian Foreign Policy: The Return of Great Power Politics.* Lanham, MD: Rowman and Littlefield, 2009.

Martin, Lisa L. and Beth A. Simmons. *International Institutions: An International Organization Reader.* Cambridge, MA: MIT Press, 2001.

Mayer, Jane. *The Dark Side: The Inside Story of How the War on Terror Turned Into a War on American Ideals.* New York: Doubleday, 2009.

Mead, Walter Russell. *Special Providence: American Foreign Policy and How It Changed the World.* New York: Knopf, 2001.

Mead, Walter Russell. *Power, Terror, Peace, and War: America's Grand Strategy in a World at Risk.* New York: Knopf, 2004.

Mearsheimer, John. *The Tragedy of Great Power Politics.* New York: Norton, 2001.

Mearsheimer, John and Stephen M. Walt. *The Israeli Lobby and U.S. Foreign Policy.* New York: Farrar, Straus & Giroux, 2007.

Merry, Robert W. *Sands of Empire: Missionary Zeal, American Foreign Policy, and the Hazards of Global Ambition.* New York: Simon and Schuster, 2005.

Metz, Steven. *Learning from Iraq: Counterinsurgency in American Strategy.* Carlisle, PA: Strategic Studies Institute, 2007.

Meyer, Karl E. and Shareen Blair Brysac. *Kingmakers: The Invention of the Middle East.* New York: Norton, 2008.

Mingst, Karen A. and Margaret P. Karns. *The United Nations in the 21st Century,* 3rd ed. Boulder, CO: Westview Press, 2006.

Mitchell, Lincoln A. *Uncertain Democracy: U.S. Foreign Policy and Georgia's Rose Revolution.* Philadelphia: University of Pennsylvania Press, 2009.

Mitchell, Lincoln A. *Color Revolutions.* Philadelphia: University of Pennsylvania Press, 2012.

Mylorie, Laurie. *Bush vs. The Beltway: How the CIA and the State Department Tried to Stop the War on Terror.* New York: Regan Books, 2003.

Naftali, Timothy. *Blind Spot: The Secret History of American Counterterrorism.* New York: Basic Books, 2004.

Nasr, Vali. *The Shia Revival: How Conflicts Within Islam Will Shape the Future.* New York: Norton, 2006.

Nasr, Vali. *The Dispensable Nation: American Foreign Policy in Retreat.* New York: Doubleday, 2013.

Nassar, Jamal R. *Globalization and Terror: The Migration of Dreams and Nightmares.* Lanham, MD: Rowman and Littlefield, 2004.

Nathan, James and James Oliver. *U.S. Foreign Policy and World Order,* 4th ed. New York: Longman, 1989.

Navias, Martin. *Tanker Wars: The Assault on Merchant Shipping during the Iran-Iraq Conflict, 1980–1988.* London: I.B. Tauris, 1996.

Nau, Henry R. *Conservative Internationalism: Armed Diplomacy Under Jefferson, Polk, Truman, and Reagan.* Princeton: Princeton University Press, 2013.

Nolan, Jane E., ed. *Global Engagement: Cooperation and Security in the 21st Century.* Washington, DC: Brookings Institution Press, 1994.

Nye, Joseph S., Jr. *Bound to Lead: The Changing Nature of American Power.* New York: Basic Books, 1990.

Nye, Joseph S., Jr. *The Paradox of American Power.* New York: Oxford University Press, 2002.

Nye, Joseph S., Jr. *Soft Power: The Means to Success in World Politics.* New York: PublicAffairs, 2004.

Nye, Joseph S., Jr. *Presidential Leadership and the Creation of the American Era.* Princeton: Princeton University Press, 2013.

O'Ballance, Edgar. *Afghan Wars: 1839 to the Present Day.* London: Brassey's, 2003.

O'Leary, Brendan, John McGarry and Khaled Salih. *The Future of Kurdistan in Iraq.* Philadelphia: University of Pennsylvania Press, 2005.

O'Neil, Shannon K. *Two Nations Indivisible: Mexico, the United States, and the Road Ahead.* New York: Oxford University Press, 2013.

Oren, Michael B. *Power, Faith, and Fantasy: America in the Middle East, 1776 to the Present.* New York: Norton, 2007.

Oushakine, Serguei Alex. *The Patriotism of Despair: Nation, War, and Loss in Russia.* Ithaca and London: Cornell University Press, 2009.

Packer, George. *The Assassins' Gate: America in Iraq.* New York: Farrar, Straus, & Giroux, 2006.

Parmar, Inderjeet. *Foundations of the American Century: The Ford, Carnegie, and Rockefeller Foundations and the Rise of American Power.* New York: Columbia University Press, 2012.

Parsi, Trita. *A Single Roll of the Dice: Obama's Diplomacy with Iran.* New Haven: Yale University Press, 2012.

Parsi, Vittorio Emanuele. *The Inevitable Alliance: Europe and the United States beyond Iraq.* Basingstoke, UK: Palgrave Macmillan, 2006.

Patrick, Stewart. *The Best Laid Plans: The Origins of American Multilateralism and the Dawn of the Cold War.* Lanham, MD: Rowman and Littlefield, 2008.

Pastor. Robert A. *Exiting the Whirlpool: U.S. Foreign Policy Toward Latin America and the Caribbean.* Boulder, CO: Westview Press, 2001.

Patten, Chris. *Cousins and Strangers: America, Britain, and Empire in a New Century.* New York: Times Books, 2006.

Perry, John Curtis. *Facing West: Americans and the Opening of the Pacific.* Westport, CT: Praeger, 1994.

Phillips, David L. *Losing Iraq: Inside the Postwar Reconstruction Fiasco.* Boulder, CO: Westview, 2005.

Pillsbury, Michael. *The Hundred-Year Marathon: China's Secret Strategy to Replace America as the Global Superpower.* New York: Henry Holt, 2015.

Pintak, Lawrence. *Reflections in a Bloodshot Lens: America, Islam, and the War of Ideas.* Ann Arbor: University of Michigan Press, 2006.

Pollack, Kenneth M. *Arabs at War: Military Effectiveness, 1948–1991.* Lincoln: University of Nebraska Press, 2002.

Pollack, Kenneth M. *A Path out of the Desert: A Grand Strategy for America in the Middle East.* New York: Random House, 2008.

Pollack, Kenneth M. *Unthinkable: Iran, the Bomb, and American Strategy.* New York: Simon and Schuster, 2013.

Porter, Bernard. *Empire and Superempire: Britain, America, and the World.* New Haven: Yale University Press, 2006.

Potter, Lawrence G. and Gary G. Sick. *Iran, Iraq, and the Legacies of War.* New York: Palgrave Macmillan, 2004.

Percival, Bronson. *The Dragon Looks South: China and Southeast Asia in the New Century.* Westport, CT: Praeger, 2007.

Quandt, William B. *The United States and Egypt.* Washington, DC: Brookings Institution Press, 1990.

Rabkin, Jeremy. *Why Sovereignty Matters.* Washington, DC: American Enterprise Institute, 1998.

Radosh, Ronald and Allis Radosh. *A Safe Haven: Harry S. Truman and the Founding of Israel.* New York: HarperCollins, 2009.

Ranelagh, John. *The Agency: The Rise and Decline of the CIA.* New York: Touchstone/ Simon and Schuster, 1987.

Rashid, Ahmed. *Taliban: Militant Islam, Oil and Fundamentalism in Central Asia.* New Haven: Yale University Press, 2000.

Rashid, Ahmed. *Pakistan on the Brink: The Future of America, Pakistan, and Afghanistan.* New York: Viking Adult, 2012.

Ray, James Lee. *Democracy and International Conflict: An Evaluation of the Democratic Peace.* Columbia: University of South Carolina Press, 1995.

Reich, Bernard. *The United States and Israel: Influence in the Special Relationship.* New York: Praeger, 1984.

Reid, Michael. *Forgotten Continent: The Battle for Latin America's Soul.* New Haven: Yale University Press, 2007.

Reid, T.R. *The United States of Europe: The New Superpower and the End of American Supremacy.* New York: Penguin Press, 2004.

Renshon, Stanley A. and Deborah Welch Larson, eds. *Good Judgment in Foreign Policy.* Lanham, MD: Rowman and Littlefield, 2003.

Riedel, Bruce. *Deadly Embrace: Pakistan, America, and the Future of the Global Jihad.* Washington, DC: Brookings Institution Press, 2011.

Riedel, Bruce. *Avoiding Armageddon: America, India, and Pakistan to the Brink and Back.* Washington, DC: Brookings Institution Press, 2013.

Risen, James. *State of War: The Secret History of the CIA and the Bush Administration.* New York: Free Press, 2005.

Risse-Kappen, Thomas. *Cooperation among Democracies: The European Influence on U.S. Foreign Policy.* Princeton: Princeton University Press, 1995.

Roberts, Brad, ed. *U.S. Security in an Uncertain Era.* Cambridge, MA: MIT Press, 1993.

Ross, Dennis and David Makovsky. *Myths, Illusions, and Peace: Finding a New Direction for America in the Middle East.* New York: Viking, 2009.

Ross, Dennis. *The Missing Peace: The Inside Story of the Fight for Middle East Peace.* New York: Farrar, Straus & Giroux, 2004.

Ross, George. *The European Union and Its Crises: Through the Eyes of the Brussels Elite.* London: Palgrave Macmillan, 2011.

Rostow, Eugene V. *Toward a Managed Peace: The National Security Interest of the United States.* New Haven: Yale University Press, 1995.

Rotberg, Robert I. *When States Fail: Causes and Consequences.* Princeton: Princeton University Press, 2003.

Rothkopf, David J. *Running the World: The Inside Story of the National Security Council and the Architects of American Power.* New York: PublicAffairs, 2004.

Rothkopf, David J. *National Insecurity: American Leadership in an Age of Fear.* New York: PublicAffairs, 2014.

Roy, Oliver. *The Politics of Chaos in the Middle East.* New York: Columbia University Press, 2008.

Rubin, Barry M. and Judith Colp Rubin. *Anti-American Terrorism and the Middle East: A Documentary Reader.* New York: Oxford University Press, 2002.

Ruggie, John G. *Winning the Peace: America and the World in the New Era.* New York: Columbia University Press, 1996.

Ruggie, John G. *Constructing the World Polity: Essays on International Institutionalization.* London: Routledge, 1998.

Russett, Bruce, ed. *The Once and Future Security Council.* New York: St. Martin's Press, 1997.

Sands, Philippe. *Lawless World: America and the Making and Breaking of Global Rules From FDR's Atlantic Charter to George W. Bush's Illegal War.* New York: Viking, 2005.

Sarotte, Mary Elise. *1989: The Struggle to Create Post-Cold War Europe.* Princeton: Princeton University Press, 2009.

Scheuer, Michael. *Marching Toward Hell: America and Islam After Iraq.* New York: Free Press, 2008.

Shapiro, Ian. *Containment: Rebuilding a Strategy Against Global Terror.* Princeton: Princeton University Press, 2007.

Simpson, John. *The Wars Against Saddam: Taking the Hard Road to Baghdad.* New York: Macmillan, 2003.

Slaughter, Anne-Marie. *A New World Order.* Princeton: Princeton University Press, 2004.

Smith, Derek D. *Deterring America: Rogue States and the Proliferation of Weapons of Mass Destruction.* Cambridge: Cambridge University Press, 2006.

Smith, Peter H. and Andrew Selee. *Mexico and the United States: The Politics of Partnership.* Boulder, CO: Lynne Rienner, 2013.

Smith, Tony. *America's Mission: The United States and the Worldwide Struggle for Democracy in the Twentieth Century.* Princeton: Princeton University Press, 1994.

Smith, Tony. *Foreign Attachments: The Power of Ethnic Groups in the Making of American Foreign Policy.* Cambridge, MA: Harvard University Press, 2000.

Snyder, Glenn. *Alliance Politics.* Ithaca and London: Cornell University Press, 1997.

Recommended Reading

Sokolski, Henry, ed. *Taming the Next Set of Strategic Weapons Threats.* Carlisle, PA: Strategic Studies Institute, 2006.

Spink, Peter K., Peter M. Ward and Robert H. Wilson. *Metropolitan Governance in the Federalist Americas: Strategies for Equitable and Integrated Development.* South Bend, IN: University of Notre Dame Press, 2012.

St. John, Robert Bruce. *Libya and the United States: Two Centuries of Strife.* Philadelphia: University of Pennsylvania Press, 2002.

Stanger, Allison. *One Nation Under Contract: The Outsourcing of American Power and the Future of Foreign Policy.* New Haven: Yale University Press, 2009.

Steil, Benn. *The Battle of Bretton Woods: John Maynard Keynes, Harry Dexter White, and the Making of a New World Order.* Princeton: Princeton University Press, 2013.

Steinberg, James and Michael R. O'Hanlon. *Strategic Reassurance and Resolve: U.S.-China Relations in the Twenty-first Century.* Princeton: Princeton University Press, 2014.

Stent, Angela E. *The Limits of Partnership: U.S.-Russian Relations in the Twenty-First Century.* Princeton: Princeton University Press, 2014.

Suskind, Ron. *The Way of the World: A Story of Truth and Hope in an Age of Extremism.* New York: HarperCollins, 2008.

Sutter, Robert G. *U.S.-Chinese Relations: Perilous Past, Pragmatic Present,* 2nd ed. Lanham, MD: Rowman and Littlefield, 2013.

Sweig, Julia E. *Friendly Fire: Losing Friends and Making Enemies in the Anti-American Century.* New York: PublicAffairs, 2006.

Takeyh, Ray. *Guardians of the Revolution: Iran and the World in the Age of the Ayatollahs.* New York: Oxford University Press, 2009.

Teixeira, Carlos Gustavo Poggio. *Brazil, the United States, and the South American Subsystem: Regional Politics and Absent Empire.* Lexington, MA: Lexington Books, 2012.

Telhami, Shibley. *The Stakes: America and the Middle East.* Boulder, CO: Westview, 2002.

Tsang, Steve, ed. *Intelligence and Human Rights in the Era of Global Terrorism.* Stanford, CA: Stanford University Press, 2008.

Tucker, Nancy Bernkopf, ed. *Dangerous Strait: The U.S.-Taiwan-China Crisis.* New York: Columbia University Press, 2005.

Tucker, Nancy Bernkopf. *Strait Talk: United States-Taiwan Relations and the Crisis with China.* Cambridge, MA: Harvard University Press, 2009.

Tucker, Robert and David Hendrickson. *The Imperial Temptation: The New World Order and America's Purpose.* New York: Council on Foreign Relations, 1992.

Ullman, Richard, ed. *The World and Yugoslavia's Wars.* New York: Council on Foreign Relations, 1996.

Vitalis, Robert. *White World Order, Black Power Politics: The Birth of American International Relations.* Ithaca and London: Cornell University Press, 2015.

Walldorf, William Jr. *Just Politics: Human Rights and the Foreign Policy of Great Powers.* Ithaca and London: Cornell University Press, 2008.

Walt, Stephen M. *The Origins of Alliances.* Ithaca and London: Cornell University Press, 1987.

Walt, Stephen M. *The Taming of American Power: The Global Response to U.S. Primacy.* New York: Norton, 2005.

Weart, Spencer R. *Never at War: Why Democracies Will Not Fight One Another.* New Haven: Yale University Press, 1998.

Weigel, George. *The Cube and the Cathedral: Europe, America, and Politics Without God.* New York: Basic Books, 2005.

Weiner, Myron. *The Global Migration Crisis.* Reading, MA: Addison-Wesley, 1995.

Weitzman, Hal. *Latin Lessons: How South America Stopped Listening to the United States and Started Prospering.* New York: Wiley, 2012.

Weiss, Thomas G., David P. Forsythe, and Roger A. Cote, 3rd ed. *The United Nations and Changing World Politics.* Boulder, CO: Westview, 2001.

West, Bing. *The Strongest Tribe: War, Politics, and the Endgame in Iraq.* New York: Random House, 2008.

White, Jenny. *Muslim Nationalism and the New Turks.* Princeton: Princeton University Press, 2012.

Wright, Lawrence. *The Looming Tower: Al-Qaeda and the Road to 9/11.* New York: Knopf, 2006.

Wright, Robin, ed. *The Iran Primer: Power, Politics, and U.S. Foreign Policy.* Washington, DC: U.S. Institute of Peace Press, 2010.

Yaqub, Salim. *Containing Arab Nationalism: The Eisenhower Doctrine and the Middle East.* Chapel Hill: University of North Carolina Press, 2004.

Yetiv, Steve. *Explaining Foreign Policy: U.S. Decision-making and the Persian Gulf War.* Baltimore: Johns Hopkins University Press, 2004.

Zakaria, Fareed. *From Wealth to Power.* Princeton: Princeton University Press, 1998.

Zakaria, Fareed. *The Future of Freedom: Illiberal Democracy at Home and Abroad.* New York: Norton, 2003.

Zakaria, Fareed. *The Post-American World.* New York: Norton, 2008.

Zenko, Micah. *Between Threats and War: U.S. Discrete Military Operations in the Post-Cold War World.* Stanford, CA: Stanford University Press, 2010.

History

Bailey, Thomas A. *A Diplomatic History of the American People,* 9th ed. Englewood Cliffs, NJ: Prentice-Hall, 1970.

Bailey, Thomas A. and David M. Kennedy. *The American Pageant,* 8th ed. Lexington, MA: D.C. Heath, 1987.

Barlow, Jeffrey G. *From Hot War to Cold: The U.S. Navy and National Security Affairs, 1945–1955.* Stanford, CA: Stanford University Press.

Barrass, Gordon S. *The Great Cold War: A Journey through the Hall of Mirrors.* Stanford, CA: Stanford University Press, 2009.

Bass, Jack and Marilyn W. Thompson. *Strom: The Complicated Personal and Political Life of Strom Thurmond.* New York: PublicAffairs, 2005.

Beisner, Robert L. *From the Old Diplomacy to the New 1865–1900.* New York: Thomas Y. Crowell, 1975.

Bernstein, R.B. *The Founding Fathers Reconsidered.* New York: Oxford University Press, 2009.

Blum, John M., William McFeely, Edmund Morgan, Arthur Schlesinger, Jr., Kenneth Stampp, and C. Vann Woodward. *The American Experience: A History of the United States,* 8th ed. New York: Harcourt, 1993.

Branch, Taylor. *At Canaan's Edge: America in the King Years, 1965–68.* New York: Simon and Schuster, 2006.

Brands, H. W. *Andrew Jackson: His Life and Times.* New York: Doubleday, 2005.

Brands, Hal and Jeremy Suri, eds. *The Power of the Past: History and Statecraft.* Washington, DC: Brookings Institution Press, 2015.

Bowman, Shearer Davis. *At the Precipice: Americans North and South During the Succession Crisis.* Chapel Hill: University of North Carolina Press, 2010.

Buel, Richard. *America on the Brink: How the Political Struggle Over the War of 1812 Almost Destroyed the Young Republic.* London: Palgrave Macmillan, 2005.

Bundy, Carol. *The Nature of Sacrifice: A Biography of Charles Russell Lowell, Jr.* New York: Farrar, Straus & Giroux, 2005.

Bushman, Richard Lyman. *Joseph Smith: Rough Stone Rolling.* New York: Knopf, 2005.

Butler, Susan. *Roosevelt and Stalin: Portrait of a Partnership.* New York: Knopf, 2015.

Cadbury, Deborah. *Space Race: The Epic Battle Between America and the Soviet Union for Dominion of Space.* New York: HarperCollins, 2006.

Campbell, Tracy. *Deliver the Vote: A History of Election Fraud, an American Political Tradition—1742–2004.* New York: Carroll & Graf, 2005.

Cannato, Vincent J. *American Passage: The History of Ellis Island.* New York: HarperCollins, 2009.

Recommended Reading

Chace, James and Caleb Carr. *America Invulnerable: The Quest for Absolute Security from 1912 to Star Wars*. New York: Summit Books, 1988.

Chernow, Ron. *Alexander Hamilton*. New York: Penguin Press, 2004.

Chernow, Ron. *Washington: A Life*. New York: Penguin Press, 2010.

Chernus, Ira. *Apocalypse Management: Eisenhower and the Discourse of National Insecurity*. Stanford, CA: Stanford University Press. 2008.

Coram, Robert. *Brute: The Life of Victor Krulak, U.S. Marine*. Boston: Little, Brown, 2010.

Crandall, Russell. *Gunboat Diplomacy: U.S. Interventions in the Dominican Republic, Grenada, and Panama*. Lanham, MD: Rowman and Littlefield, 2006.

Crosswell, D.K.R. *Beetle: The Life of General Walter Bedell Smith*. Lexington: University Press of Kentucky, 2010.

Cobb, James C. *The South and America Since World War II*. New York: Oxford University Press, 2010.

Daalder, Ivo H. and I. M. Destler. *In the Shadows of the Oval Office: Portraits of the National Security Advisers and the Presidents They Served—From JFK to George W. Bush*. New York: Simon and Schuster, 2009.

Daniel, Marcus. *Scandal and Civility: Journalism and the Birth of American Democracy*. New York: Oxford University Press, 2009.

DeYoung, Karen. *Soldier: The Life of Colin Powell*. New York: Knopf, 2006.

Dizard, Wilson P., Jr. *Inventing Public Diplomacy: The Story of the U.S. Information Agency*. Boulder, CO: Lynne Rienner, 2004.

Donald, David Herbert. *We Are Lincoln Men: Abraham Lincoln and His Friends*. New York: Simon and Schuster, 2003.

Donaldson, Gary A. *The Making of Modern America: The Nation from 1945 to the Present*, 2nd ed. Lanham, MD: Rowman and Littlefield, 2013.

Doyle, Don H. *The Cause of All Nations: An International History of the American Civil War*. New York: Basic Books, 2014.

Dueck, Colin. *Reluctant Crusaders: Power, Culture, and Change in American Grand Strategy*. Princeton: Princeton University Press, 2006.

Edel, Charles N. *Nation Builder: John Quincy Adams and the Grand Strategy of the Republic*. Cambridge, MA: Harvard University Press, 2014.

Eichengreen, Barry. *Globalizing Capital: A History of the International Monetary System*. Princeton: Princeton University Press, 1996.

Eltis, David and David Richardson. *Atlas of the Transatlantic Slave Trade*. New Haven: Yale University Press, 2010.

Ferguson, Niall. *The War of the World: Twentieth-Century Conflict and the Descent of the West*. New York: Penguin Press, 2006.

Flynn, Mathew J. and Stephen E. Griffin. *Washington and Napoleon: Leadership to the Age of Revolution*. Washington, DC: Potomac Books, 2011.

Friedman, George. *The Next 100 Years: A Forecast for the 21st Century*. New York: Anchor, 2010.

Fukuyama, Francis. *The End of History and the Last Man*. New York: Free Press, 1992.

Fullilove, Michael. *Rendezvous With Destiny: How Franklin D. Roosevelt and Five Extraordinary Men Took America Into the War and Into the World*. New York: Penguin Press, 2013.

Gaddis, John Lewis. *The United States and the End of the Cold War*. New York: Oxford University Press, 1992.

Gaddis, John Lewis. *Surprise, Security, and the American Experience*. Cambridge, MA: Harvard University Press, 2004.

Garthoff, Raymond L. *Détente and Confrontation: American-Soviet Relations from Nixon to Reagan*. Washington, DC: Brookings Institution Press, 1985.

Goldstein, Gordon M. *Lessons in Disaster: McGeorge Bundy and the Path to War in Vietnam*. New York: Times Books, 2009.

Goldstein, Lyle J. *Preventive Attack and Weapons of Mass Destruction: A Comparative Historical Analysis*. Stanford, CA: Stanford University Press, 2006.

Goodman, Michael S. *Spying on the Nuclear Bear: Anglo-American Intelligence and the Soviet Bomb*. Stanford, CA: Stanford University Press, 2007.

Goodwin, Crawford D. *Walter Lippman: Public Economist*. Cambridge, MA: Harvard University Press, 2014.

Goodwin, Doris Kearns. *Team of Rivals: The Political Genius of Abraham Lincoln*. New York: Simon and Schuster, 2006.

Gordon, John Steele. *An Empire of Wealth: The Epic History of American Economic Power*. New York: HarperCollins, 2004.

Gould, Lewis L. *Grand Old Party: A History of the Republicans*. New York: Random House, 2003.

Graebner, Norman, ed. *Ideas and Diplomacy: Readings in the Intellectual Tradition of American Foreign Policy*. New York: Oxford University Press, 1964.

Greene, Benjamin P. *Eisenhower, Science Advice, and the Nuclear Test-Ban Debate, 1945–1963*. Stanford, CA: Stanford University Press, 2007.

Hansen, Keith A. *The Comprehensive Nuclear Test Ban Treaty: An Insider's Perspective*. Stanford, CA: Stanford University Press, 2006.

Hansen, Marcus Lee. *The Atlantic Migration, 1607–1860: A History of the Continuing Settlement of the United States*. Cambridge, MA: Harvard University Press, 1941.

Harper, John Lamberton. *American Machiavelli: Alexander Hamilton and the Origins of U.S. Foreign Policy*. New York: Cambridge University Press, 2004.

Herring, George C. *From Colony to Superpower: U.S. Foreign Relations since 1776*. New York: Oxford University Press, 2008.

Hitchcock, William I. *The Bitter Road to Freedom: A New History of the Liberation of Europe*. New York: Free Press, 2008.

Hodgson, Godfrey. *Woodrow Wilson's Right Hand: The Life of Colonel Edward*

British and American leaders face off with French and German leaders over Iraq.

M. *House.* New Haven: Yale University Press, 2006.

Horn, Jonathan. *The Man Who Would Not Be Washington: Robert E. Lee's Civil War and His Decision That Changed American History.* New York: Scribner, 2015.

Howe, Daniel Walker. *What Hath God Wrought: The Transformation of America, 1815–1848.* New York: Oxford University Press, 2007.

Jaffa, Harry V. *A New Birth of Freedom: Abraham Lincoln and the Coming of the Civil War.* Lanham, MD: Rowman and Littlefield, 2004.

Johnson, Paul. *Eisenhower: A Life.* New York: Viking, 2014. agan, Robert. *Dangerous Nation.* New York: Knopf, 2006.

Kagan, Robert. *Dangerous Nation.* New York: Knopf, 2006.

Kagan, Robert. *The World America Made.* New York: Knopf, 2012.

Kalb, Marvin. *Imperial Gamble: Putin, Ukraine, and the New Cold War.* Washington, DC: Brookings Institution Press, 2015.

Kissinger, Henry. *World Order.* New York: Penguin Press, 2014.

Korda, Michael. *Ike: An American Hero.* New York: Harper, 2008.

Knock, Thomas J. *To End All Wars: Woodrow Wilson and the Quest for a New World Order.* New York: Oxford University Press, 1992.

Kupchan, Charles. *The End of the American Era.* New York: Random House, 2003.

Kupchan, Charles. *How Enemies Become Friends: The Sources of Stable Peace.* Princeton: Princeton University Press, 2010.

Lafeber, Walter. *The American Age.* New York: Norton, 1989.

Lake, David A. *Entangling Relations: American Foreign Policy in Its Century.* Princeton: Princeton University Press, 1999.

Layne, Christopher. *The Peace of Illusions: American Grand Strategy from 1940 to the Present.* Ithaca and London: Cornell University Press, 2006.

Leonard, Thomas C. *Illiberal Reformers: Race, Eugenics, and American Economics in the Progressive Era.* Princeton: Princeton University Press, 2016.

Lewis, Tom. *Washington: A History of Our National City.* New York: Basic Books, 2015.

Lind, Michael. *What Lincoln Believed: The Values and Convictions of America's Greatest President.* New York: Doubleday, 2005.

Lindaman, Dana and Kyle Ward. *History Lessons: How Textbooks From Around the World Portray American History.* New York: New Press, 2004.

Love, Robert W. *The History of the U.S. Navy, 1775–1941.* Harrisburg, PA: Stackpole Books, 1992.

MacMillan, Margaret. *Nixon and Mao: The Week that Changed the World.* New York: Random House, 2006.

May, Ernest R. *"Lessons" of the Past: The Use and Misuse of History in American Foreign Policy.* New York: Oxford University Press, 1973.

McDougall, Walter A. *Freedom Just Around the Corner: A New American History, 1585–1828.* New York: HarperCollins, 2004.

McFarland, Philip. *Mark Twain and the Colonel. Samuel L. Clemens, Theodore Roosevelt, and the Arrival of a New Century.* Lanham, MD: Rowman and Littlefield, 2012.

McGerr, Michael. *A Fierce Discontent: The Rise and Fall of The Progressive Movement in America, 1870–1920.* New York: Free Press, 2003.

McPherson, James M. *Tried by War: Abraham Lincoln as Commander in Chief.* New York: Penguin Press, 2008.

McPherson, James M. *The War That Forged a Nation: Why the Civil War Still Matters.* New York: Oxford University Press, 2015.

Miller, John J. and Mark Molesky. *Our Oldest Enemy: A History of America's Disastrous Relationship With France.* New York: Doubleday, 2004.

Oakes, James. *Freedom National: The Destruction of Slavery in the United States, 1861-1865.* New York: Norton, 2012.

Oakes, James. *The Scorpion's Sting: Anti-Slavery and the Coming of the Civil War.* New York: Norton, 2014.

Oren, Michael B. *Power, Faith, and Fantasy: America in the Middle East, 1776 to the Present.* New York: Norton, 2006.

Osgood, Robert E. *Ideals and Self-Interest in America's Foreign Relations.* Chicago: University of Chicago Press, 1964.

Peraino, Kevin. *Lincoln in the World: The Making of a Statesman and the Dawn of American Power.* New York: Crown, 2013.

Ricks, Thomas E. *Fiasco: The American Military Adventure in Iraq.* New York: Penguin Press, 2006.

Rochester, J. Martin. *US Foreign Policy in the 21st Century: Gulliver's Travails.* Boulder, CO: Westview, 2008.

Rodman, Peter W. *Presidential Command: Power, Leadership, and the Making of Foreign Policy from Richard Nixon to George W. Bush.* New York: Vintage, 2010.

Rubin, Anne Sarah. *A Shattered Nation: The Rise and Fall of the Confederacy, 1861–1868.* Chapel Hill: University of North Carolina Press, 2005.

Sarotte, Mary Elise. *The Collapse: The Accidental Opening of the Berlin Wall.* New York: Basic Books, 2014.

Scheuer, Michael. *Marching Toward Hell: America and Islam after Iraq.* New York: Free Press, 2008.

Schlesinger, Arthur M., Jr. *A Thousand Days: John F. Kennedy in the White House.* Boston: Houghton Mifflin, 1965.

Schlesinger, Arthur M., Jr. *War and the American Presidency.* New York: Norton, 2004.

Schoen, Douglas and Michael Rowan. *The Threat Closer to Home: Hugo Chavez and the War Against America.* New York: Free Press, 2009.

Schoenbaum, Thomas J. *Waging Peace and War: Dean Rusk in the Truman, Kennedy, and Johnson Years.* New York: Simon and Schuster, 1988.

Schrecker, Ellen. *Cold War Triumphalism: The Misuse of History After the Fall of Communism.* New York: New Press, 2004.

Showalter, Elaine. *The Civil Wars of Julia Ward Howe: A Biography.* New York: Simon and Schuster, 2016.

Snyder, Timothy. *Bloodlands: Europe Between Hitler and Stalin.* New York: Basic Books, 2010.

Starr, Kevin. *Golden Dreams: California in an Age of Abundance, 1950–1963.* New York: Oxford University Press, 2009.

Stein, Herbert. *Presidential Economics: The Making of Economic Policy from Hoover to Reagan and Beyond.* New York: Simon and Schuster, 1984.

Stern, Sheldon M. *The Week the World Stood Still: Inside the Cuban Missile Crisis.* Stanford, CA: Stanford University Press, 2005.

Stiles, T. J. *The First Tycoon: The Epic Life of Cornelius Vanderbilt.* New York: Knopf, 2009.

Straus, Michael J. *The Leasing of Guantanamo Bay.* Westport, CT: Praeger, 2009.

Sutherland, Daniel E. *A Savage Conflict: The Decisive Role of Guerrillas in the American Civil War.* Chapel Hill: University of North Carolina Press, 2009.

Thomas, Emory M. *The Dogs of War: 1861.* New York: Oxford University Press, 2011.

Tooze, Adam. *The Great War, America, and the Remaking of the Global Order, 1916–1931.* New York: Viking, 2014.

Weiner, Tim. *Legacy of Ashes: The History of the CIA.* New York: Doubleday, 2007.

Weisbrode, Kenneth. *The Year of Indecision, 1946: A Tour through the Crucible of Harry Truman's America.* New York: Viking, 2015.

Wells, Allen. *Tropical Zion: General Trujillo, FDR, and the Jews of Sosúa.* Durham: Duke University Press, 2009.

Wilentz, Sean. *The Rise of American Democracy: Jefferson to Lincoln.* New York: Norton, 2005.

Williams, William Appleman. *The Roots of Modern American Empire.* New York: Vintage Books, 1969.

Wills, Garry. *Henry Adams and the Making of America*. Boston: Houghton Mifflin, 2005.

Witcover, Jules. *Party of the People: A History of the Democrats*. New York: Random House, 2003.

Yergin, Daniel. *Shattered Peace: The Origins of the Cold War and the National Security State*. Boston: Houghton Mifflin, 1978.

Zahra, Tara. *The Great Departure: Mass Migration from Eastern Europe and the Making of the Free World*. New York: Norton, 2015.

Memoirs

Acheson, Dean. *Present at the Creation: My Years in the State Department*. New York: Norton, 1969.

Bush, George W. *Decision Points*. New York: Crown, 2010.

Clinton, Bill. *My Life*. New York: Knopf, 2004.

Clinton, Hillary Rodham. *Hard Choices*. New York: Simon and Schuster, 2014.

Franks, Tommy. *American Soldier*. New York: HarperCollins, 2004.

Galvin, John R. *Fighting the Cold War: A Soldier's Memoir*. Lexington: University Press of Kentucky, 2015.

Gates, Robert. *Duty: Memoirs of a Secretary at War*. New York: Knopf, 2014.

Helms, Jesse. *Here's Where I Stand: A Memoir*. New York: Random House, 2005.

Hill, Christopher. *Outpost: Life on the Frontlines of American Diplomacy*. New York: Simon and Schuster, 2014.

Kennan, George F. *From Prague After Munich*. Princeton: Princeton University Press, 1968.

Kennan, George F. *Memoirs 1925–1950*. Boston: Little, Brown, 1967.

Kissinger, Henry A. *White House Years*. Boston: Little, Brown, 1979.

Kissinger, Henry A. *Years of Upheaval*. Boston: Little, Brown, 1982.

Marton, Kati. *Enemies of the People: My Family's Journey to America*. New York: Simon and Schuster, 2009.

Nixon, Richard. *The Memoirs of Richard Nixon*. New York: Grosset and Dunlap, 1978.

Panetta, Leon. *Worthy Fights: A Memoir of Leadership in War and Peace*. New York: Penguin Press, 2014.

Reston, James. *Deadline: A Memoir*. New York: Random House, 1991.

Rice, Condoleeza. *No Higher Honor: A Memoir of My Years in Washington*. Washington, DC: Crown, 2011.

Shelton, Hugh, with Ronald Levinson and Malcolm McConnell. *Without Hesitation: The Odyssey of an American Warrior*. New York: St. Martin's, 2010.

Truman, Harry S. *Year of Decisions*. Garden City, NY: Doubleday, 1955.